CAMPING AND WOODCRAFT

COMBINED TWO VOLUMES IN ONE
THE EXPANDED 1921 VERSION

THE DELUXE TWO-BOOK MASTERPIECE ON
OUTDOORS LIVING AND WILDERNESS TRAVEL

BY **HORACE KEPHART**

LEGACY EDITION

THE LIBRARY OF AMERICAN OUTDOORS CLASSICS

FEATURING
REMASTERED CLASSIC WORKS OF THE HIGHEST QUALITY
FROM **THE TIMELESS MASTERS AND TEACHERS**
OF CAMPING, OUTDOORS SKILLS, WOODCRAFT,
AND TRADITIONAL HANDCRAFTS

Doublebit Press

New content, introduction, and annotations
Copyright © 2021 by Doublebit Press. All rights reserved.
www.doublebitpress.com | Cherry, IL, USA

First published in 1916-1917 by Horace Kephart. Two-volumes-in-one version first published in 1921.

A part of the Library of American Outdoors Classics.

Doublebit Press Legacy Edition ISBNs (Two Volumes in One Printing)
Hardcover: 978-1-64389-184-2
Paperback: 978-1-64389-185-9

WARNING: Some of the material in this book may be outdated by modern safety standards. This antique text may contain outdated and unsafe recreational activities, projects, or mechanical, electrical, chemical, or medical practices. Any use of this book for purposes other than historic study may result in unsafe and hazardous conditions and individuals act at their own risk and are responsible for their own safety. Doublebit Press, its authors, or its agents assume no liability for any injury, harm, or damages to persons or property arising either directly or indirectly from any content contained in this text or the activities performed by readers. Remember to be safe with any activity or work you do and use good judgement by following proper health and safety protocols. In addition, because this book was from a past time and is presented in an unabridged form, the contents may be culturally or racially insensitive. Such content does not represent the opinions or positions of the publisher and are presented for historical posterity and accuracy to the original text.

DISCLAIMER: Doublebit Press has not tested or analyzed the methods, materials, and practices appearing in this public domain text and provides no warranty to the accuracy and reliability of the content. This text is provided only as a reprinted facsimile from the unedited public domain original as first published and authored. This text is published for historical study and personal literary enrichment purposes only and should only be used for such. The publisher assumes no liability for any injury, harm, or damages to persons or property arising either directly or indirectly from any information contained in this public domain book or activities performed by readers.

First Doublebit Press Legacy Edition Printing, 2021

INTRODUCTION
To The Doublebit Press Legacy Edition

Horace Kephart can probably be called the Dean of outdoors writing at the turn of the 20th Century. Although Nessmuk (George W. Sears) is the original old camper and woodsman who penned about the skills of the outdoorser, it was Kephart who voraciously collected tidbits and tips about outdoors life and used this information as he prolifically wrote about the outdoors.

Kephart commonly published in outdoors and sportsmen's magazines of the day and was a household name among people who avidly visited the fresh air of the forests and rivers. One day, Kephart finally collected his writings and compiled the book you hold in your hands, which is really one of the original how-to manuals of the outdoors and camp life. This present version, however, is a significantly expanded work of his original *Book of Camping And Woodcraft*, which was published in 1906. In this version, Kephart added hundreds of pages of new insights and illustrations to guide the traveler of the wilderness and to help folks to make the most of the time outdoors.

Inside these pages are decades, if not centuries of knowledge of the camping tradition, cookery and kitchen tips, and as much backwoods and bushcraft knowledge of the woods and wilderness that Kephart could find in the day. Many of the tips included within have been long lost to time, as more modern camping equipment and conveniences have become popular. However, the information contained within these pages is timeless and more important today than ever! The master woodsfolk of the 21st Century digital age stand to benefit from learning the old ways of the woods masters and camping traditionalists!

Kephart's two-volume work *Camping and Woodcraft* served as the standard for outdoors adventure for many decades after it was published. A true outdoorsperson has both versions of Kephart's *Camping and Woodcraft* series represented on their cabin shelves, in their camping kit, or proudly displayed in their home collection for study. Each version has overlapping, but unique information. This later 1916-17 version of *Camping and Woodcraft* is this most common version of Kephart's work over the 20th Century, and was later bound into a single, large volume (1921).

A TIMELINE OF HORACE KEPHART'S CAMPING & WOODCRAFT BOOKS
1906 – *The Book of Camping and Woodcraft* (first work)
1916-17 – *Camping* (significantly expanded work, first volume)
1916-17 – *Woodcraft* (significantly expanded work, second volume)
1921 – *Camping and Woodcraft*
(two volumes in one, no revisions)

About the Library of American Outdoors Classics

The old experts of the woods and mountains taught timeless principles and skills for decades. Through their books, the old experts offered rich descriptions of the outdoor world and encouraged learning through personal experiences in nature. Over the last 125 years, camping, outdoors recreation, and woods activities have substantially changed. Many things have gotten simpler as gear has improved, and life outside or on the trail now brings with it many of the same comforts enjoyed in town. In addition, some activities of the olden days are now no longer in vogue, or are even outright considered inappropriate or illegal, such as high-impact camping practices like chopping down live trees. However, despite many of the positive changes in outdoors methods that have occurred over the years, *there are many other skills and much knowledge that have been forgotten* from the golden era of American outdoors recreation.

By publishing the Library of American Outdoors Classics, it is our goal at Doublebit Press to do what we can to preserve and share the works from forgotten teachers that form the cornerstone of the history of the American outdoors. Through remastered reprint editions of timeless classics of outdoor recreation, perhaps we can regain some of this lost knowledge for future generations.

Because there were fewer options for finding outdoors gear in the early 1900's, experts in *"woodcraft"* skills (not to be confused with today's use of the word to mean woodworking or making things of wood) had to have a deep knowledge of the basic building blocks of outdoor living. This involved not only surviving in the outdoors, but to also have a comfortable and enjoyable time. As Nessmuk puts it in his book *Woodcraft*, "We do not go to the woods to rough it; we go to smooth it — we get it rough enough in town. But let us live the simple, natural life in the woods, and leave all frills behind." Nessmuk did not advocate for folks to go outside and have a terrible time. That would be contrary to the whole point of getting outside. Instead, he advocated for a "simpler" life by leaving some of the creature comforts of the city behind, but also entering the outdoors in a smart and practiced way that made the experience a much more satisfying vacation from home. The goal is to be comfortable so you can focus on having a good time outside and take in everything exposure to nature can offer. However, to be comfortable, one has to know the ins and outs of camping and outdoors life. Despite all the advances in campcraft and outdoors recreation, the old masters of the woods would all likely argue that this will only come from practicing the basics.

Because there was no market yet for specialty outdoors recreational gear (and thus, few outfitters), most outdoors gear came from military surplus piles or was custom made. As such, the old masters of woodcraft often made their own gear suited to their tastes. Through much experience in the woods and field, the great outdoors experts had to know why things worked the way they did by understanding the great web of cause and effect in nature. They had to learn from experience why certain gear worked better in different conditions or know how to solve problems off-the-cuff when things got hairy. They used the basic blocks of camping and outdoors knowledge to fine-tune their gear. They gained experience whenever they could and tried things different ways so they could gain mastery over the fundamentals and see challenges from many angles.

Today, much of the outdoor experience has been greatly simplified by neatly arranged campsites at public campgrounds and gear that has been meticulously improved and tested in both the lab and the field. Many modern conveniences are only a brief trek away, with many parks, campgrounds, and even forests having easy-access roads, convenience stores, and even cell phone signal. In some ways, it is much easier to camp and go outdoors today, and that is a good thing! We should not be miserable when we go outside — lovers of the outdoors know the essential restorative capability that the woods can have on the body, mind, and soul. Although things have gotten easier on us in the 21st Century when it comes to the outdoors, it certainly does not mean that we should forget the foundations of outdoors lore, though. All modern camping skills, outdoors equipment, and cool gizmos that make our lives easier are all founded on principles of the outdoors that the old masters knew well and taught to those who would listen.

Every woods master had their own curriculum or thought some things were more important than others. This includes the present author — certain things appear in this book that other masters leave out of theirs. The old masters also taught common things in slightly different ways or did things differently than others. That's what makes each of the experts different and worth reading. There's no universal way of doing something, especially now. Learning to go about something differently helps with mastery or learn a new skill altogether. Again, to use the metaphor from the above paragraphs, outdoors skills mastery consists of learning the basic building blocks of outdoors living, woods and nature lore, and the art of packing properly for trips. Each master goes about describing these building blocks differently or shows a different aspect of them.

Therefore, we have decided to publish this Legacy Edition in our Library of American Outdoors Classics series. This book is an important contribution to the early American recreational outdoors literature and has important historical and collector value toward preserving the American outdoors tradition. The knowledge it holds is an invaluable reference for practicing skills and hand craft methods. Its chapters thoroughly discuss some of the essential building blocks of knowledge that are fundamental but may have been forgotten as equipment gets fancier and technology gets smarter. In short, this book was chosen for Legacy Edition printing because much of the basic skills and knowledge it contains has been forgotten or put to the wayside in trade for more modern conveniences and methods.

Although the editors at Doublebit Press are thrilled to have comfortable experiences in the woods and love our high-tech and light-weight equipment, we are also realizing that the basic skills taught by the old masters are more essential than ever as our culture becomes more and more hooked on digital stuff. We don't want to risk forgetting the important steps, skills, or building blocks involved with thriving in the outdoors. The Legacy Edition series represents the essential contributions to the American outdoors tradition by the great experts of outdoors life and traditional hand crafting.

With technology playing a major role in everyday life, sometimes we need to take a step back in time to find those basic building blocks used for gaining mastery – the things that we have luckily not completely lost and has been recorded in books over the last two centuries. These skills aren't forgotten, they've just been shelved. *It's time to unshelve them once again and reclaim the lost knowledge of self-sufficiency.*

Based on this commitment to preserving our outdoors and handcraft heritage, we have taken great pride in publishing this book as a complete original work. We hope it is worthy of both study and collection by outdoors folk in the modern era of outdoors and traditional skills life.

Unlike many other photocopy reproductions of classic books that are common on the market, this Legacy Edition does not simply place poor photography of old texts on our pages and use error-prone optical scanning or computer-generated text. We want our work to speak for itself, and reflect the quality demanded by our customers who spend their hard-earned money. With this in mind, each Legacy Edition book that has been chosen for publication is carefully remastered from original print books, *with the Doublebit Legacy Edition printed and laid out in the exact way that it was presented at its original publication.* We provide a beautiful, memorable experience that is as true to the original text as best as possible, but with the aid of modern technology to make as beautiful a reading experience as possible for books that are typically over a century old.

Because of its age and because it is presented in its original form, the book may contain misspellings, inking errors, and other print blemishes that were common for the age. However, these are exactly the things that we feel give the book its character, which we preserved in this Legacy Edition. During digitization, we ensured that each illustration in the text was clean and sharp with the least amount of loss from being copied and digitized as possible. Full-page plate illustrations are presented as they were found, often including the extra blank page that was often behind a plate. For the covers, we use the original cover design to give the book its original feel. We are sure you'll appreciate the fine touches and attention to detail that your Legacy Edition has to offer.

For outdoors enthusiasts who demand the best from their equipment, this Doublebit Press Legacy Edition reprint was made with you in mind. Both important and minor details have equally both been accounted for by our publishing staff, down to the cover, font, layout, and images. It is the goal of Doublebit Legacy Edition series to preserve outdoors heritage, but also be cherished as collectible pieces, worthy of collection in any outdoorsperson's library and that can be passed to future generations.

Every book selected to be in this series offers unique views and instruction on important skills, advice, tips, tidbits, anecdotes, stories, and experiences that will enrich the repertoire of any person who enjoys escaping the city and finding their way to the trails of the wilds. To learn the most basic building blocks of outdoors life leads to mastery of all its aspects.

Studying This Book

The pages within this book present an overwhelming amount of information, facts, and directions to memorize that are often outdated and at the least, out of practice by modern standards. That doesn't mean that these pages have nothing to teach! It's just going to likely be new stuff for many readers.

Our one suggestion is *don't try to memorize everything,* especially when you're thumbing through the book or even reading it cover-to-cover. Writings from the late 1800's to early 1900's can be dense and out of style for someone not used to reading these types of books. Instead, gain some basic familiarity with each topic by thumbing through the pages, looking at the illustrations, and seeing the section headers. Then, choose a few topics or skills for deeper study.

Before camping or other outdoors trips can even begin, some planning and reflection is useful, which may be best done in town before you go out to the field. First, it might be helpful to read through the book with plans in mind. The book can provide useful material for close study and reflection when in town before you head out to the field to practice.

Secondly, once you've come up with a practice plan, you will of course want to start doing tasks and skills in the field. Doublebit Legacy books and the Library of American Outdoors Classics represents many field skills to master that have long sense been out of practice, but hopefully not forgotten! These include making and trying different kinds of tents or shelters, cooking (including any fish and game caught by you in the field), making many types of fires, setting up camp to suit your personal needs, beating the bugs and elements, understanding the terrain and weather, making furniture, brushing up on your nature lore, emergency survival, and testing your personal outfit and tools.

Any of the old tutors of woodcraft will tell you in their classic books that you can only truly learn how to go camping and do woodcraft by *actually doing it*. Home study indeed does you well by using the many guidebooks that have been published over the previous 125 years. However, hundreds more lessons will become immediately available to you the moment you start with some of the old-style tasks. This old style of outdoorsing is indeed outdated in many ways, but the approach still has much to teach modern campers who have become accustomed to carved out campsites, cabin and RV camping, and high-tech equipment.

Before the days of outfitters, outdoors adventurers made their gear, which was tailored to their individual needs. Many experiments were done in the field to tweak their gear to get that ever-changing point of "perfect." Aside from experiencing wonderful lessons in history, getting outside and doing some of the activities this book will give you an appreciation for modern advances in outdoors and handcraft method and tools of the trade, as well as a deeper understanding of the foundations of outdoors and hand-craft life in the event that your gear fails you or you otherwise find yourself in situations where knowing the principles will get you unstuck fast.

If we were to tally up each of the individual tips in the Doublebit Library of American Outdoors Classics, they would easily number in the thousands. The old masters represent centuries of previous knowledge that have been all but lost to 21st Century, technology-driven folks. To this point, although experience and *actually doing stuff* are the best forms of learning, taking a mindful approach to study of these works also benefit your development as a competent outdoorsperson and handcrafter.

You may also find it invaluable to take these volumes with you on your camping or other outdoors trips. In addition to having reading material on a variety of topics in the field for down time, you'll also find a thousand things to try in these pages if you're bored. Although skills may be best studied when in the field through experience and reflection, you may also study woods skills at home as well. Gaining familiarity through reading, videos, and other media are a great start toward building your ability toward gaining mastery in the field.

So, without blabbering on further, we hope you enjoy your Doublebit Legacy Edition. May your trails be clear and your experiences be memorable!

- The Doublebit Press Editors

CAMPING
AND
WOODCRAFT

A HANDBOOK FOR VACATION CAMPERS
AND FOR
TRAVELERS IN THE WILDERNESS

BY
HORACE KEPHART
Author of "Our Southern Highlanders," "Sporting
Firearms," "Camp Cookery," etc.

VOL. I
CAMPING

NEW YORK
OUTING PUBLISHING COMPANY
1916

Copyright, 1916, by
OUTING PUBLISHING COMPANY

To
THE SHADE OF NESSMUK
IN THE
HAPPY HUNTING GROUND

PREFACE

The present work is based upon my *Book of Camping and Woodcraft,* which appeared in 1906. All of the original material here retained has been revised, and so much new matter has been added that this is virtually a new work, filling two volumes instead of one.

My first book was intended as a pocket manual for those who travel where there are no roads and who perforce must go light. I took little thought of the fast-growing multitude who go to more accessible places and camp out just for the pleasure and healthfulness of open-air life. It had seemed to me that outfitting a party for fixed camp within reach of wagons was so simple that nobody would want advice about it. But I have learned that such matters are not so easy to the multitude as I had assumed; and there are, to be sure, "wrinkles," plenty of them, in equipping and managing stationary camps that save trouble, annoyance, or expense. Consequently I am adding several chapters expressly for that class of campers, and I treat the matter of outfitting much more fully than before.

It is not to be supposed that experienced travelers will agree with me all around in matters of equipment. Every old camper has his own notions about such things, and all of us are apt to be a bit dogmatic. As Richard Harding Davis says, "The same article that one declares is the most essential to his comfort, health, and happiness is the very first thing that another will throw into the trail. A man's outfit is a matter which seems to touch his private honor. I have heard veterans sitting

PREFACE

around a camp-fire proclaim the superiority of their kits with a jealousy, loyalty, and enthusiasm they would not exhibit for the flesh of their flesh and the bone of their bone. On a campaign you may attack a man's courage, the flag he serves, the newspaper for which he works, his intelligence, or his camp manners, and he will ignore you; but if you criticise his patent water-bottle he will fall upon you with both fists."

Yet all of us who spend much time in the woods are keen to learn about the other fellow's " kinks." And field equipment is a most excellent hobby to amuse one during the shut-in season. I know nothing else that so restores the buoyant optimism of youth as overhauling one's kit and planning trips for the next vacation. Solomon himself knew the heart of man no better than that fine old sportsman who said to me " It isn't the fellow who's catching lots of fish and shooting plenty of game that's having the good time: it's the chap who's *getting ready to do it.*"

I must thank the public for the favor it showed my *Book of Camping and Woodcraft,* which passed, with slight revision, through seven editions in ten years. For a long time I have wished to expand the work and bring it up to date. As there is a well-defined boundary between the two subjects of camping and woodcraft, it has seemed best to devote a separate volume to each. The first of these is here offered, to be followed as soon as practicable by the other, which will deal chiefly with such shifts and expedients as are learned or practised in the wilderness itself, where we have nothing to choose from but the raw materials that lie around us.

Acknowledgments are due to the D. T. Abercrombie Co., New York, the Abercrombie & Fitch Co., New York, and the New York Sporting Goods Co., for permission to reproduce certain illustrations of tents and other equipment.

This book had its origin in a series of articles

PREFACE

under the same title that I contributed, in 1904-1906, to the magazine *Field and Stream*. Other sections have been published, in whole or in part, in *Sports Afield, Recreation, Forest and Stream,* and *Outing*. A great deal of the work here appears for the first time.

Many of these pages were written in the wilderness, where there were abundant facilities for testing the value of suggestions that were outside the range of my previous experience. In this connection I must acknowledge indebtedness to a scrapbook full of notes and clippings from sportsmen's journals which was one of the most valued tomes in the rather select "library" that graced half a soap-box in one corner of my cabin.

I owe much both to the spirit and the letter of that classic in the literature of outdoor life, the little book on *Woodcraft,* by the late George R. Sears, who is best known by his Indian-given title of "Nessmuk." To me, in a peculiar sense, it has been *remedium utriusque fortunæ;* and it is but fitting that I should dedicate to the memory of its author this pendant to his work.

HORACE KEPHART.

Bryson City, N. C.,
February, 1916.

CONTENTS

CHAPTER		PAGE
I	Vacation Time	17
II	Outfitting	23
III	Tents for Fixed Camps	29
IV	Furniture, Tools, and Utensils for Fixed Camps	53
V	Tents for Shifting Camps	68
VI	Types of Light Tents	76
VII	Light Camp Equipment	109
VIII	Camp Bedding	124
IX	Clothing	138
X	Personal Kits	164
XI	Provisions	178
XII	Camp Making	208
XIII	The Camp-fire	225
XIV	Pests of the Woods	241
XV	Dressing and Keeping Game and Fish	264
XVI	Camp Cookery — Meats	290
XVII	Camp Cookery — Game	305
XVIII	Camp Cookery — Fish and Shellfish	321
XIX	Camp Cookery — Cured Meats, etc. — Eggs	332
XX	Camp Cookery — Breadstuffs and Cereals	342
XXI	Camp Cookery — Vegetables — Soups	363
XXII	Beverages and Desserts	378
XXIII	Cook's Miscellany	386
	Index	395

ILLUSTRATIONS

	PAGE
Wall Tent, with Fly	29
Extension Fly	36
Tropical Tent	37
Bobbinet Window	39
Mosquito Curtain	39
Asbestos Pipe Guard	40
Locating Corner of the Tent	42
Tent Stake and Guy Rope	43
U. S. Army Wall Tent with Fly (Officers' Tent)	45
Storm Set	45
Wall Tent on Shears with Guy Frame	46
Lashing for Shear Legs	47
Shear Legs Spread	47
Magnus Hitch (not apt to slip along a pole)	47
Wall Tent with Side Bars	48
Trenching Tent	49
Tent Floor	50
Guys Weighted with Log	51
Guy Rope Fastened to Fagot to Be Buried in Ground	51
Narrow Cot	54
Compact Cot	54
Telescoping Cot	54
Cot with Mosquito Screen	54
Folding Chair	56
Folding Arm Chair	56
Roll-up Table	56
Roll-up Table Top	56
Table with Shelf	57
Compact Table	57
Folding Shelves	57
Wall Pocket	57
Small Camp Stove	61
Stove Packed	61

ILLUSTRATIONS

	PAGE
Stove for Large Wood	61
Field Range	62
Field Range (packed)	62
Dutch Oven	64
U. S. A. Conical Tent	78
Sibley Tent Stoves	79
Miner's Tent	82
Frazer Tent	83
Marquee	83
George Tent	84
Layout of George Tent	85
Royce Tent	87
Royce Tent	89
Royce Tent	90
Wedge Tent, Outside Ridge Rope	92
Pegging Bottom of Tent	93
Side Parrels	93
Whymper Alpine Tent	95
Hudson Bay Tent	95
Ross Alpine Tent	96
Separable Shelter Tent	96
Shelter half with Wall	97
Tarpaulin Tent	98
Baker Tent	99
Camp-fire Tent	100
Canoe Tent with Pole	102
Canoe Tent with Ridge	102
Compac Tent	104
Snow Tent	105
Explorer's Tent	106
Little Giant Scale	115
Cooking Pot	119
Pot Chain	119
Coffee Pot	119
Miner's Coffee Pot	119
Cup	120
Miller Frying Pan	120
Reflector (angular back)	121
Reflector (flat back)	121
Reflector (folded in case)	121

ILLUSTRATIONS

	PAGE
Sheet Steel Oven	122
D. T. Abercrombie Sleeping Bag	130
Fiala Sleeping Bag	131
U. S. A. Regulation Sleeping Bag	136
Shattuck Camp Roll	136
Comfort Sleeping Pocket	137
Combination Bed Roll, Stretcher Bed and Bed Tick	137
Combination as Stretcher Bed	137
Combination as Hammock	137
Combination as Bed Roll	137
Neckerchief Folded for Hood	143
Neckerchief Hood Adjusted	143
U. S. Army Canvas Legging	145
Canvas Strap Puttee	145
Woolen Spiral Puttee	145
True Bow Knot	151
Reef Knot Formed	151
Reef Knot Drawn Tight	151
U. S. Army Shoe	152
Sole of Army Shoe, Showing Proper Method of Placing Hobnails	152
Soled Moccasin (made over last)	159
Dunnage Bag	164
Kit or Provision Pack	164
Screw Hook Fastening for Box Lid	164
Hatchet	166
Sheath Knife	167
Compass with Course Arrow	169
Map Case	171
U. S. A. Dispatch Case	171
To Fold Triangular Bandage	175
Rare Natural Crotch	219
Common Crotch	219
To Make a Crutch	219
Spring Box	221
Latrine	223
Indian Deer Pack	268
The Place to Use Your Knife	270

CAMPING AND WOODCRAFT

CHAPTER I

VACATION TIME

"So priketh hem Nature in hir coráges,—
Thanne longen folk to goon on pilgrimages,
And palmeres for to seken straunge strondes."
— *Canterbury Tales.*

To many a city man there comes a time when the great town wearies him. He hates its sights and smells and clangor. Every duty is a task and every caller is a bore. There come visions of green fields and far-rolling hills, of tall forests and cool, swift-flowing streams. He yearns for the thrill of the chase, for the keen-eyed silent stalking; or, rod in hand, he would seek that mysterious pool where the father of all trout lurks for his lure.

To be free, unbeholden, irresponsible for the nonce! Free to go or come at one's own sweet will, to tarry where he lists, to do this, or do that, or do nothing, as the humor veers; and for the hours,

"It shall be what o'clock I say it is!"

Thus basking and sporting in the great clean out-of-doors, one could, for the blessed interval,

"Forget six counties overhung with smoke,
Forget the snorting steam and piston-stroke,
Forget the spreading of the hideous town."

18   CAMPING AND WOODCRAFT

This instinct for a free life in the open is as natural and wholesome as the gratification of hunger and thirst and love. It is Nature's recall to the simple mode of existence that she intended us for.

Our modern life in cities is an abrupt and violent change from what the race has been bred to these many thousands of years. We come from a line of forebears who, back to a far-distant past, were hunters in the forest, herdsmen on the plains, shepherds in the hills, tillers of the soil, or fishermen or sailors at sea; and however adaptive the human mind may be, these human bodies of ours still stubbornly insist on obeying the same laws that Father Adam's did.

There are soothsayers who forecast that, in the course of evolution, we shall conform to what are now abnormal and mischievous conditions; that man is the most adaptive of all creatures, accommodating himself to greater extremes of temperature and so forth than any other of the higher animals; that moreover he is constantly inventing machines and processes to better his condition, so that we may reasonably expect him to make even the crowded city a wholesome place of residence, though people dwell tier above tier, and our old-fashioned domestic life be quite out of the question.

It may be so. We can fix no bounds to Nature's conforming power. She has produced certain vertebrates, such as the mud-turtle and the hellbender, so eminently adaptive to circumstances that they are equally at home whether immersed in air, water, or mud. And there is the Chinaman, who, being of a breed that has been crowded and coerced for thousands of years, seems to have done away with nerves. "He will stand all day in one position without seeming in the least distressed; he thrives amidst the most unsanitary surroundings; overcrowding and bad air are nothing to him; he does not demand quiet when he would sleep, nor even when he is sick; he can starve to death with supreme complacency." A

VACATION TIME

missionary says: "It would be easy to raise in China an army of a million men — nay, of ten millions — tested by competitive examination as to their capacity to go to sleep across three wheelbarrows, with head downwards like a spider, mouth wide open, and a fly inside."

Some of our own people seem to get no satisfaction out of anything but chasing after dollars without let-up from year to year, save when they are asleep, or in church, or both. We recall a certain rich man who boasted that in the eighty-eight years of his career he had not once taken a vacation or wanted one. Naturally his way was the right way, and he proceeded to show it. "What right," asked he, " has a clerk to demand or expect pay for two weeks' time for which he renders no equivalent? Is it not absurd to suppose that a man who can work eleven and a half months cannot as well work the whole year? The doctors may recommend a change of air when he's sick; but why be sick? Sickness is an irreparable loss of time." I am not misquoting this very rich man: his signed pronouncement lies before me — the sorriest thing that ever I saw in print.

Seriously, is it good for men and women and children to swarm together in cities and stay there, keep staying there, till their instincts are so far perverted that they lose all taste for their natural element, the wide world out-of-doors? In any case, although evolution be a very great and good law, yet is it not a trifle slow? How about you and me? Can we wait a few thousand years for fulfilment of the wise men's prophecy? We are neither coolies, nor mud-turtles, nor those other things with the awful name.

Granting, then, that one deserves relief now and then from the hurry and worry that would age him before his prime, why not go in for a complete change while you are about it? Why not exorcise the devil of business and everything that suggests it? The best vacation an over-civilized man can have is to go where he can hunt, capture, and cook his own meat, erect his own shelter, do his own chores, and so, in some measure, pick up again those lost arts of wildcraft that were our heritage through ages past, but of which not one modern man in a hundred knows anything at all. In cities our tasks are so highly specialized, and so many things are done for us by other specialists, that we tend to become a one-handed and one-idead race. The self-dependent life of the wilderness nomad brings bodily habits and mental processes back to normal, by exercise of muscles and lobes that otherwise might atrophy from want of use.

If one would realize in its perfection his dream of peace and freedom from every worldly care, let him keep away from summer resorts and even from farms; let him camp out; and let it be the real thing. There are "camps" so-called that are not camps at all. A rustic cottage furnished with tables and chairs and beds brought from town, with rugs on the floor and pictures on the walls, with a stove in the kitchen and crockery in the pantry, an ice-house hard by, and daily delivery of groceries, farm products, and mails, may be a pleasant place in which to spend the summer with one's family and friends; but it is not a camp. Neither is a wilderness club-house, built on a game preserve, looked after by a caretaker, and supplied during the season with servants and the appurtenances of a good hotel.

A camp proper is a nomad's biding-place. He may occupy it for a season, or only for a single night, according as the site and its surroundings please or do not please the wanderer's whim. If the fish do not bite, or the game has moved away, or unpleasant neighbors should intrude, or if anything else goes wrong, it is but an hour's work for him to pull up stakes and be off, seeking that particularly good place which generally lies beyond the horizon's rim.

Your thoroughbred camper likes not the atten-

VACATION TIME

tions of a landlord, nor will he suffer himself to be rooted to the soil by cares of ownership or lease. It is not possession of the land, but of the landscape, that he enjoys; and as for that, all the wild parts of the earth are his, by a title that carries with it no obligation but that he shall not desecrate nor lay them waste.

Houses, to such a one, in summer, are little better than cages; fences and walls are his abomination; plowed fields are only so many patches of torn and tormented earth. The sleek comeliness of pastures is too prim and artificial, domestic cattle have a meek and ignoble bearing, fields of grain are monotonous to his eyes, which turn for relief to some abandoned old-field, overgrown with thicket, that still harbors some of the shy children of the wild. It is not the clearing but the unfenced wilderness that is the camper's real home. He is brother to that good old friend of mine who, in gentle satire of our formal gardens and close-cropped lawns, was wont to say, "I love the unimproved works of God." He likes to wander in the forest tasting the raw sweets and pungencies that uncloyed palates craved in the childhood of our race. To him

> "The shelter of a rock
> Is sweeter than the roofs of all the world."

The charm of nomadic life is its freedom from care, its unrestrained liberty of action, and the proud self-reliance of one who is absolutely his own master, free to follow his bent in his own way, and who cheerfully in turn, suffers the penalties that Nature visits upon him for every slip of mind or bungling of his hand. Carrying with him, as he does, in a few small bundles, all that he needs to provide food and shelter in any land, habited or uninhabited, the camper is lord of himself and of his surroundings.

CAMPING AND WOODCRAFT

"Free is the bird in the air,
  And the fish where the river flows;
Free is the deer in the wood,
  And the gipsy wherever he goes.
    Hurrah!
  And the gipsy wherever he goes."

There is a dash of the gipsy in every one of us who is worth his salt.

CHAPTER II

OUTFITTING

> "By St. Nicholas
> I have a sudden passion for the wild wood —
> We should be free as air in the wild wood —
> What say you? Shall we go? Your hands, your hands!"
> — *Robin Hood.*

In some of our large cities there are professional outfitters to whom one can go and say: "So many of us wish to spend such a month in such a region, hunting and fishing: equip us." The dealer will name a price; you pay it, and leave the rest to him. When the time comes he will have the outfit ready and packed. It will include everything needed for the trip, well selected and of the best materials. When your party reaches the jumping-off place it will be met by professional guides and packers, who will take you to the best hunting grounds and fishing waters, and will do all the hard work of paddling, packing over portages, making camp, chopping wood, cooking, and cleaning up, besides showing you where the game and fish are "using," and how to get them. In this way a party of city men who know nothing of woodcraft can spend a season in the woods very comfortably, though getting little practical knowledge of the wilderness. This is touring, not campaigning. It is expensive; but it may be worth the price to such as can afford it, and who like that sort of thing.

But, aside from the expense of this kind of camping, it seems to me that whoever takes to the woods and waters for recreation should learn how to shift for himself in an emergency. He may employ guides and a cook — all that; but the day of disaster may come, the outfit may be destroyed, or the city man may find himself some day alone, lost in the forest, and compelled to meet the forces of Nature in a struggle for his life. Then it may go hard with him indeed if he be not only master of himself, but of that woodcraft which holds the key to Nature's storehouse. A camper should know for himself how to outfit, how to select and make a camp, how to wield an axe and make proper fires, how to cook, wash, mend, how to travel without losing his course, or what to do when he has lost it; how to trail, hunt, shoot, fish, dress game, manage boat or canoe, and how to extemporize such makeshifts as may be needed in wilderness faring. And he should know these things as he does the way to his mouth. Then is he truly a woodsman, sure to do promptly the right thing at the right time, whatever befalls. Such a man has an honest pride in his own resourcefulness, a sense of reserve force, a doughty self-reliance that is good to feel. His is the confidence of the lone sailorman, who whistles as he puts his tiny bark out to sea.

And there are many of us who, through some miscue of the Fates, are not rich enough to give *carte blanche* orders over the counter. We would like silk tents, air mattresses, fiber packing cases, and all that sort of thing; but we would soon "go broke" if we started in at that rate. I am saying nothing about guns, rods, reels, and such-like, because they are the things that every well conducted sportsman goes broke on, anyway, as a matter of course. I am speaking only of such purchases as might be thought extravagant. And it is conceivable that some folks might call it extravagant to pay thirty-five dollars for a thing to sleep in when you lie out of doors on the ground from choice, or thirty dollars for pots and pans to cook with when you are "playing hobo," as the unregenerate call our sylvan sport. To

OUTFITTING

practise shrewd economies in such things helps out if you are caught slipping in through the back gate with a brand-new gun, when everybody knows that you already possess more guns than you can find legitimate use for.

If one begins, as he should, six months in advance, to plan and prepare for his next summer or fall vacation, he can, by gradual and surreptitious hoarding, get together a commendable camping equipment, and nobody will notice the outlay. The best way is to make many of the things yourself. This gives your pastime an air of thrift, and propitiates the Lares and Penates by keeping you home o' nights. And there is a world of solid comfort in having everything fixed just to suit you. The only way to have it so is to do the work yourself. One can wear ready-made clothing, he can exist in ready-furnished rooms, but a ready-made camping outfit is a delusion and a snare. It is sure to be loaded with gimcracks that you have no use for, and to lack something that you will be miserable without.

It is great fun, in the long winter evenings, to sort over your beloved duffel, to make and fit up the little boxes and hold-alls in which everything has its proper place, to contrive new wrinkles that nobody but yourself has the gigantic brain to conceive, to concoct mysterious dopes that fill the house with unsanctimonious smells, to fish around for materials, in odd corners where you have no business, and, generally, to set the female members of the household buzzing around in curiosity, disapproval, and sundry other states of mind.

To be sure, even though a man rigs up his own outfit, he never gets it quite to suit him. Every season sees the downfall of some cherished scheme, the failure of some fond contrivance. Every winter sees you again fussing over your kit, altering this, substituting that, and flogging your wits with the same old problem of how to save weight and bulk without sacrifice of utility. All thoroughbred campers do this as regularly as the birds come back in spring, and their kind has been doing it since the world began. It is good for us. If some misguided genius should invent a camping equipment that nobody could find fault with, half our pleasure in life would be swept away.

This is not saying that outfitters' catalogues should be ignored. Get them, by all means, and study them with care. Do this at home, comparing one catalogue with another, that you may know just what you want and what you don't want, before you go out to make purchases. Then you will not be such easy prey to the plausible clerk, and your selection will bear the stamp of your individuality.

The joys and sorrows of camp life, and the proportion of each to the other, depend very much upon how one chooses his companions — granting that he has any choice in the matter at all. It may be noticed that old-timers are apt to be a bit distant when a novice betrays any eagerness to share in their pilgrimages. There is no churlishness in this; rather it is commendable caution. Not every good fellow in town makes a pleasant comrade in the woods. So it is that experienced campers are chary of admitting new members to their lodges. To be one of them you must be of the right stuff, ready to endure trial and privation without a murmur, and — what is harder for most men — to put up with petty inconveniences without grumbling.

For there is a seamy side to camp life, as to everything else. Even in the best of camps things do happen sometimes that are enough to make a saint swear silently through his teeth. But no one is fit for such life who cannot turn ordinary ill-luck into a joke, and bear downright calamity like a gentleman.

Yet there are other qualities in a good camp-mate that are rarer than fortitude and endurance. Chief of these is a love of Nature for her own sake — not the " put on " kind that expresses itself in gushy

OUTFITTING

sentimentalism, but that pure, intense, though ordinarily mute affection which finds pleasure in her companionship and needs none other. As Olive Shreiner says: " It is not he who praises Nature, but he who lies continually on her breast *and is satisfied,* who is actually united to her." Donald G. Mitchell once remarked that nobody should go to the country with the expectation of deriving much pleasure from it, as country, who has not a keen eye for the things of the country, for scenery, or for trees, or flowers, or some kind of culture; to which a New York editor replied that " Of this not one city man in a thousand has a particle in his composition." No doubt a gross exaggeration; but the proportion of city men who do thoroughly enjoy the hardy sports and adventures of the wilderness is certainly much larger than those who could be entertained on a farm; yet the elect of these, the ones who can find plenty to interest them in the woods when fishing and hunting fail, are not to be found on every street corner.

If your party be made up of men inexperienced in the woods, hire a guide, and, if there be more than three of you, take along a cook as well. Treat your guide as one of yourselves. A good one deserves such consideration; a poor one is not worth having at all. But if you cannot afford this expense, then leave the real wilderness out of account for the present; go to some pleasant woodland, within hail of civilization, and start an experimental camp, spending a good part of your time in learning how to wield an axe, how to build proper fires, how to cook good meals out-of-doors, and so forth. Be sure to get the privilege beforehand of cutting what wood you will need. It is worth paying some wood-geld that you may learn how to fell and hew. Here, with fair fishing and some small game hunting, you can have a jolly good time, and will be fitted for something more ambitious the next season.

In any case, be sure to get together a company of

good-hearted, manly fellows, who will take things as they come, do their fair share of the camp chores, and agree to have no arguments before breakfast. There are plenty of such men, steel-true and blade-straight. Then will your trip be a lasting pleasure, to be lived over time and again in after years. There are no friendships like those that are made under canvas and in the open field.

In the following pages I treat the matter of outfitting in detail, not that elaborate outfits are usually desirable — for they are not — but because in town there is so much to pick and choose from. There are many patterns of this, that, and the other article of equipment, some good for one kind of camping, some for another. I try to explain their " points," that the reader may choose intelligently according to his needs.

CHAPTER III

TENTS FOR FIXED CAMPS

When camp is made in a certain locality with no intention of moving it until the party is ready to go home, it usually is called a "permanent camp." This is a misuse of terms; for a camp of any kind is only a temporary biding place. "The camp and not the soil," says Gibbon, "is the native country of the genuine Tartar." When speaking of a camp fixed in one place for a considerable time, I shall call it a fixed camp or stationary camp. It differs from a shifting camp, so far as outfitting is concerned, in permitting the use of heavy and bulky equipment and more of the comforts of home.

WALL TENTS.— For fixed camps, situated where there are wagon roads or other adequate ways of transportation, the best cloth shelter is a wall tent, rectangular or square, of strong and rather heavy material.

Fig. 1.— Wall Tent, with Fly

It is a trade custom to list tents according to an arbitrary scale of ground dimensions, in even feet, although the cloth seldom works out exactly so; for ground dimensions are governed by the number of widths of cloth used and the number of inches to the width, allowing for seams. To slit the cloth lengthwise would destroy its strongest part, the selvage, besides being a waste of material. Moreover, cloth stretches or shrinks in handling.

In the following table are given the trade sizes, actual ground dimensions (these may vary), standard heights of wall and center, and weights of unproofed tents (without flies, poles, or stakes) in sizes commonly used by campers. These sizes apply only to tents made of standard 29-inch duck. If 36-inch stuff, or some other width, is used, proportional allowances must be made.

STANDARD WALL TENTS.
29-INCH DUCK.

Trade sizes.	Actual width and length.	Height wall.	Height center
9 x 9 ft.	9⅓ x 9⅓ ft.	3 ft.	7½ ft.
9 x 12 ft.	9⅓ x 11½ ft.	3 ft.	7½ ft.
12 x 12 ft.	11½ x 11½ ft.	3½ ft.	8 ft.
12 x 14 ft.	11½ x 14½ ft.	3½ ft.	8 ft.
12 x 16 ft.	11½ x 16¼ ft.	3½ ft.	8 ft.
14 x 14 ft.	14 x 14 ft.	4 ft.	9 ft.
14 x 16 ft.	14 x 16¼ ft.	4 ft.	9 ft.

Trade sizes	Weights of tents.			Poles and Stakes.
	8 oz.	10 oz.	12 oz.	
9 x 9 ft.	24 lbs.	30 lbs.	36 lbs.	28 lbs.
9 x 12 ft.	29½ lbs.	35 lbs.	42 lbs.	30 lbs.
12 x 12 ft.	36 lbs.	41½ lbs.	50 lbs.	35 lbs.
12 x 14 ft.	40 lbs.	49 lbs.	59 lbs.	39 lbs.
12 x 16 ft.	44 lbs.	57½ lbs.	63 lbs.	40 lbs.
14 x 14 ft.	44½ lbs.	58 lbs.	68 lbs.	41 lbs.
14 x 16 ft.	51½ lbs.	63 lbs.	76 lbs.	45 lbs.

Weight of poles and stakes varies a good deal, according to size and density of wood.

Flies of same length as tent, and same kind of duck, weigh about half as much as the tent itself.

As a rule, not more than four persons should occupy one tent. Two in a tent will get along better; for camp life is very intimate in any case.

TENTS FOR FIXED CAMPS

A group of small tents around a common campfire is quite as sociable as if the party were all bunked together — except when sociability is *not* wanted, as when some wish to sleep and others want to play cards. Even a camper does not care to reduce his individuality to a least common multiple.

Two small tents need not be made of so heavy material as a large one of cubic capacity equal to both of them. They are easier to erect and manage. They are more adaptable to various camp sites. Their short poles are handier to transport (for that matter, jointed ones may be bought, up to a limit of twelve feet total length). And small tents are stancher in a gale than big ones.

Roominess is not to be estimated by ground dimensions alone. It depends much upon height of center and walls. If a tent is to be used right on the ground, not elevated over a floor with baseboards, it should be made higher in center and walls than the standard proportions given in the table. This is not expensive: the charge is only five per cent. of the cost of regular tent for each six inches of added height.

To my notion the best all-round size of wall tent for two people, if weight and bulk and cost are of any consequence, is the so-called 9 x 9 or a 9 x 12, built with 3½-foot walls, instead of 3-foot, and 8-foot center, instead of 7½-foot. For four persons a 12 x 14 is commonly used; but a 14 x 14 with 4-foot walls and 9-foot center has double the head-room of the standard 12 x 14, and 2½ feet more space between cots, if these are set lengthwise of the tent, two on a side.

Before selecting a tent, consider the number of people to occupy it, and their dunnage, and the furniture. Then draw diagrams of floor and end elevation, of various sizes, fitting in the cots, etc., according to scale; so you can get just what you want — no more, no less.

TENT MATERIALS.— The conventional tent is

made of plain cotton duck. A single roof of such material will shed rain, if the stuff is closely woven, but only so long as it is stretched at a proper angle, rather taut, and nothing touches it from the inside. If so much as a finger-tip should be rubbed against the under side of the roof, a leak would spring there, due to capillary action. It is of little use to draw the finger from the drip spot down to the tent wall, for, although this runs the water off for a time, fresh dripping will start on each side of the line.

Nor is it possible to avoid slackness in a roof of plain canvas during a wet spell of weather. Cloth that is not water-proofed will shrink a great deal as soon as it gets wet; hence the guy ropes must be let out, and the roof allowed to sag, before the rain comes; otherwise the shrinkage of the canvas will loosen your tent stakes, or even pull them all up together, when down goes your house about your ears!

For these reasons, a tent should either be water-proofed, or should have a supplementary roof called a fly. These matters will be considered later.

Cotton duck comes in three general grades, known as single filling, double filling, and army duck.

Single filling duck is made of coarse yarn, loosely woven, and of an inferior grade of cotton. It is suitable only for cheap tents that are not intended for continuous use, and generally is a bad "bargain" even then. It is weaker than the same weight of the other grades and is poor stuff to shed water.

Double filling duck is of closer texture, better fiber, and is equal to all but the hardest service. For average summer camping it is good enough.

Army duck is the best grade made, of selected cotton free from sizing, both warp and filling doubled and twisted, closely woven, and free from imperfections — if it comes up to army standard. It will outwear any other tent material of the same weight, except flax (which I have not seen used

TENTS FOR FIXED CAMPS   33

in this country), and sheds water much better than cheaper grades.

Khaki generally means simply duck or twill that has been colored to the familiar leaf brown of hunting togs. It may be had in almost any grade, the best, of course, being army tent khaki.

The strength and durability of duck depends largely upon its weight per square foot. Standard tent duck comes in weights of 8 ounces, 10 ounces, 12 ounces, and upwards, to the running yard of material 29 inches wide (army duck, 28½ inches). But other duck is made in 36-inch width, or wider. The 36-inch stuff is about one-fourth lighter per running yard than 29-inch duck; in other words, its "8-ounce" weight is really about 6-ounce, its "10-ounce" is 7½-ounce, its "12-ounce" is 9-ounce stuff, as compared with standard goods. *Bear this in mind* when comparing qualities and prices of tents by different makers. Some tent makers specify in their catalogues which width is used; others do not. In case of doubt, get samples of cloth before purchasing.

Since guys and beckets (loops for the pegs) generally are fitted only where there are seams, it follows that a tent made of wide duck is not so stanch as one of standard widths. All things considered, 8-ounce army duck (28½-inch) and 10-ounce double filling standard (29-inch) are superior to 12-ounce double filling of 36-inch width.

For fixed camps, nothing less than 10-ounce standard duck for tents, and 8-ounce for flies, should be used; 12-ounce for tents, and 10-ounce for flies, is preferable, unless the tent be quite small and portability is a factor to be considered.

TRICKS OF THE TRADE.— Not all of them, by any means; but a few tricks for the novice to look out for if he is not sure of his tent maker.

Prices fluctuate, of course, with the cotton market, at least in the better grades of duck. And yet, in the same season we may notice considerable difference in prices for what is ostensibly the same thing. There is a legitimate margin of variation in tent prices according to local cost of production; but when " bargains " are offered, keep your weather eye open. There are many different qualities of duck in grades that nominally are alike — all the way from honest clear cotton to weighted stuff that is almost shoddy.

A tent may be stunted in height to deceive the purchaser, since most buyers consider only the ground dimensions. A flattened roof and low walls mean less head-room and greater danger of leakage. Very cheap tents may have worthless jute ropes, instead of hemp or sisal, and their poles and stakes may be defective.

Low prices generally go with inferior workmanship. Look out for single seams, chain stitching, insufficient stay-pieces or reinforcements where the chief strains come, and machine-clamped brass grommets, that tear out easily, instead of galvanized iron rings sewed in by hand.

High prices, on the contrary, may mean refinements that ordinary campers do not need. Between the two extremes there is wide room for choice. For example, at the time of this writing, you can get a new 9 x 9 wall tent of single filling duck (29-inch), complete with fly, poles, stakes, and ropes, for as little as $11.50. For the best grade of U. S. Army 9 x 9 officers' tent you would pay $51.50. Of course, the army tent is of far better material than the cheap one, and it is higher at center and walls, but a good part of the difference in price is due to hand sewing and hand workmanship throughout, in the officers' model, even to finishing every becket and door-string with a Matthew Walker knot.

WATERPROOF TENTS.— A waterproof tent needs no fly to shed rain; but it should have eaves to carry drip free from the walls, if there are any. It costs less than a plain tent of equal quality with fly,

TENTS FOR FIXED CAMPS 35

weighs less, bulks less when packed, does not mildew, does not have to be dried out every time before moving, and is easier to set up and manage than one with a fly.

A prime advantage of the processed cloth is that it does not shrink when rained on. This means a lot of trouble saved. With a tent of ordinary canvas it is necessary to slacken guys before a rain, and at night before turning in, lest the stakes be pulled loose. Of course, if long guy ropes are used they will shrink, and must be eased before a rain, even though the tent itself be waterproof.

Waterproof materials, and home methods of waterproofing tents, are discussed in Chapter V. For heavy tents, such as we are now considering, my own preference is either "green waterproof" (Willesden) duck or a cravenetted khaki. Both of these are perfectly rainproof, in heavy and closely woven stuffs; they are soft, and are not affected by heat or cold.

Colored tents, either khaki or green, are restful to the eyes, blend pleasantly with their surroundings, and are not so likely as white ones to attract the attention of unwelcome visitors, from insects to tramps. They do not soil so easily as white canvas, and do not make shadow pictures of the inmates by lantern light. Khaki or green is cooler under the summer sun than white. It moderates the glare for those who would sleep late or take a siesta (some cannot sleep well in a white tent under a full moon), and it does not light up so brilliantly as white canvas when the lightning flashes.

TENT FLIES.—A fly is an auxiliary roof of canvas, to shed rain and to make the tent cooler.

Most tent flies are set tight on top of the regular ridge pole. A better plan, when the camp is not to be shifted for a good while, is to use two ridge poles, and so have a space between the fly and the ridge for air to circulate through. In small tents, it is handier to have a stout band on the ridge of the tent itself, with strings by which it can be suspended from an outside ridge pole that is cut in the woods, this pole being set up on shears at each end. This leaves the doorway unobstructed. Such a rig permits the use of any sized fly, with only one ridge pole (Fig. 11).

Many like to have the fly large enough to form a 7- or 8-foot canopy in front of the tent; but there are disadvantages in this rig: it cuts off side entrance, and it makes the fly a sport of the winds. A gust can get tremendous purchase under a pro-

Fig. 2.— Extension Fly

truding roof and is likely to send it sailing. Even in moderate winds there will be a great slatting and banging, just when one wants to drop off to sleep. Generally it is best to have a spare fly, as I have mentioned for the dining place, and erect a frame in front of the tent over which this cloth can be stretched for an awning (Fig. 2). In this case the awning can be rigged as high as one wishes, and will not be in the way of entering the tent from one side..

A fly large enough to project three or four feet for shelter over the doorway is not objectionable; in fact it is a good thing, especially if made long enough to come almost to the ground at the sides.

TENTS FOR FIXED CAMPS 37

Figure 3 shows one of Edgington's tropical tents with such a fly (similar ones are made in this country). Note the liberal air-space between fly and tent. The shelter outside the tent walls is useful

Fig. 3.— Tropical Tent

for baggage, dry wood, dogs, etc. Such a fly weighs and costs about as much as the tent itself. For security in a wind, the "storm set" should be used (Fig. 10).

SOD-CLOTH.— If a tent is not to be floored and fitted with a base-board, it should have a sod-cloth. This is a strip of 8-ounce canvas, about 9 inches wide, that is sewed all along the bottom edge of the tent walls, both sides and ends (Fig. 16). When the tent has been set up, this sod-cloth is turned in on the floor and weighted down with poles or stones. Its function is to keep out insects and draughts that otherwise would enter through the numerous gaps that are left between tent pegs. The bottom edge of a tent is the worst possible place to get ventilation from; one might as well seek to ventilate a house through cracks in the floor. Banking the tent inside with leaves and earth is a poor substitute for a sod-cloth. It will not stay tight for an hour, and the earth rots the canvas.

GROUND-SHEET.— In a small tent that often is shifted from place to place, a ground-sheet to cover the floor and lap over the sod-cloth is a good thing to keep the interior dry and secure against insects; but in a fixed camp such a carpet is a nuisance. It gets filthy, and it stays so. Bare earth is soon trodden down hard so that it is easy to sweep and keep clean. I have lived for months in an unfloored cabin, and my partner and I had no trouble to keep the earthen floor neat to the eye and more sanitary than any carpet. If you want a floor in a tent, build a real one of dressed boards brought along for the purpose.

VENTILATION.— " Nessmuk " used to rail at wall tents and wedge tents because they were so fusty and damp and cheerless. So they are when improperly built and carelessly managed. One's main reason for camping out should be to get plenty of fresh air and sunshine. It is not enough to have good air in daytime. One-third of our time is spent in bed. And yet it is common practice to close the tent tight at night, especially if there are any mosquitoes about. Consider. Who would spend summer nights at home with no window open? Well, a tent closed up is less permeable to air than the average house with windows down.

The notion that night air in the woods is malarial or otherwise unwholesome is idiotic. It is the best air there is. Still, you can't buy a wall tent in America that has proper means of ventilation, unless you have it built to order. Army tents have ventilators, so-called, that are nothing but a hole at each peak, four inches wide and eight inches long. A tent window, to be of any account, should be not less than 12 x 18 inches.

Our best tent makers will fit one or more windows in a tent wherever the owner wants them, at from $1.00 to $2.50 each. The opening is covered with fine-mesh bobbinet, taped around the edges and crosswise, with a canvas storm flap that can be raised or lowered from the inside (Fig. 4). A more elaborate kind, that may be detached and rolled up when the tent is folded, is made of copper mosquito

TENTS FOR FIXED CAMPS 39

bar, and has a celluloid window that can be slipped in when it rains.

In a tent of ordinary size, one such window at the rear, with the doorway left wide open in fair weather, will make the place a cheerful and wholesome abode instead of a fusty den.

MOSQUITO BAR.— The doorway may be screened by a sort of drop-curtain of bobbinet or cheesecloth; ordinary mosquito netting is too easily torn, and its mesh is too open to exclude the smaller mosquitoes and gnats. Bobbinet is expensive. The tent-

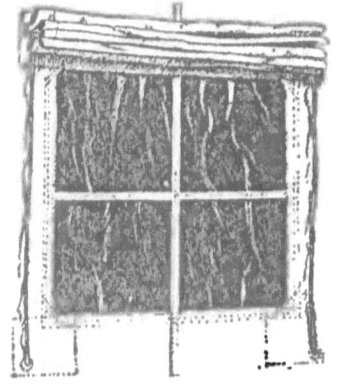 

Fig. 4.— Bobbinet Window   Fig. 5.— Mosquito Curtain

maker will attach a cheesecloth front to a tent 9 to 14 feet wide for about $2.85.

REAR DOOR.— For about the same price as a window, and serving as well for ventilation, the tent-maker will put an extra door in the rear end of the tent, with cheesecloth screen. This is a better arrangement for hot weather, and often convenient when there is a driving rain or a contrary wind; but it reduces the space for wall-pockets, shelves, etc.

DOOR WEIGHTS.— To do away with pegs at the entrance, that you are apt to stumble over, tie a short and rather heavy pole to the bottom of each flap. This holds the door open when desired, and closes it securely against dogs, "varmints," and the elements.

STOVE-PIPE HOLE.— A simple tin protector for this opening is an annoyance at night, for it scrapes and skreeks when the canvas slats in the wind. Tent-makers supply pipe shields of asbestos that are quite safe, noiseless, and roll up nicely with the tent when it is stored or *en route*. A flap covers the opening when no stove is in use (Fig. 6).

Fig. 6.— Asbestos Pipe Guard

TENT POLES AND PINS.— Poles should be of ash, white pine, or spruce, straight-grained and free from defects. At each end there should be a galvanized iron band to keep the pole from splitting.

A wall tent requires stakes (unless a frame is built for the guys) about two feet long, and becket pins about sixteen inches. Shorter ones will not hold in loose or sandy soil. Wooden ones do very well for stationary camps.

CARE OF TENTS.— Never except when unavoidable should a tent be rolled up when wet. Even if it be only damp from dew, an unprocessed tent will soon mildew if packed away in that state. The parts that require most drying are where the material is doubled, as at the seams and along the edges: the bottom edge especially, and the sod-cloth, are sure to rot if not thoroughly dried before stowing away.

To protect the tent in transport, it should be carried in a stout bag; otherwise it is likely to be punctured.

Tent pins are to be carried in a bag of their own, not only to save them from being lost, but also because their inevitable dampness when camp is struck would rot the tent if they were rolled up with it.

TO MEND A TEAR IN CANVAS.— Cross-stitch it flat, using a sail needle and twine, and taking a narrow hold on each side with one stitch, then a wider hold with the next one, and so on alternately.

TENTS FOR FIXED CAMPS 41

Then it will not tear again so easily as if narrow stitches were taken all along, nor will it be likely to ruck. Temporary repairs can be made with adhesive plaster.

SECOND-HAND TENTS.— Second-hand army tents that are in good, serviceable condition, having been condemned for stains or other trifling defects, may be bought cheaply from dealers who get them at government auctions. These army tents are always well designed and well made. Second-hand tents, however, should not be bought without inspection; they may be mildewed or otherwise unserviceable.

TENT RENTAL.— Some tent-makers and outfitters have tents for rent. From a list at hand I copy the following charges for wall tents: 10 x 12, $2.00 first week, and half this for each succeeding week; 12 x 14, $2.00 *do.*; 14 x 16, $3.00 *do.*; flies, half these prices. In some places a whole camp equipment can be rented.

PITCHING WALL TENTS.— A tent should stand squared and taut and trim. This not only that one's eyes may dwell with pride upon his camp, but because a tent that is wrinkled and set askew will not shed a downpour nor stand stanchly against a gale.

In erecting any square or rectangular tent, the first thing is to locate the corners, and from them to determine where the corner guy stakes are to be driven. Soldiers do this by measuring with the upright poles, but as the height of a common tent may not bear the right relation to its spread, for this purpose, a knotted string may be better.

Set up the tent in your yard at home and adjust poles and guys until the angles of the wall are true and the canvas is drawn smooth all around. To square the corners, observe that a triangle the sides of which are 3, 4 and 5 ft., or multiples of these, forms a right angle.

Then take a stout fish-line, fasten a small peg at one end, and drive this peg close into one corner of the tent (*A*, Fig. 7). Draw the line straight (gently, so as not to stretch it) to center of upright pole (*B*) (if there be one) in the doorway; tie a knot in it there, and then go on to the corner *C*, where it is knotted again. Drive a small peg at *C*, pass the string around it, and on to the corner *D*, where another knot is tied and peg driven. Then draw the line diagonally back to *A*, and knot it. Cut the line at the last knot, reel it up on its peg, and keep it stowed with the tent for future use.

When the camp ground is reached, it is but the work of a moment to peg out, with the knotted

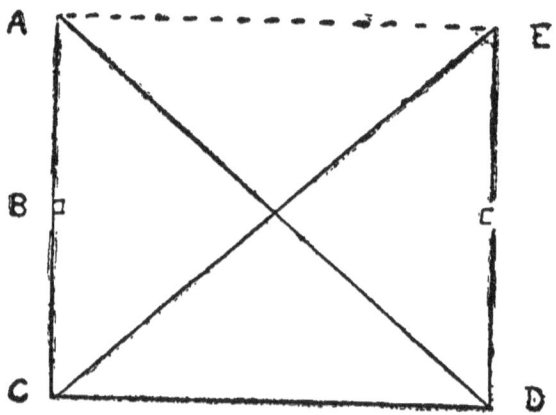

Fig. 7.— Locating Corners of the Tent

string, first the triangle *ACD* and then, reversing, *EDC*. You then have located exactly the positions of the four corners for your tent, and marked where the uprights shall be set, and the tent is sure to stand "square."

A wall tent is set up with inside or outside poles, and its wall and fly are guyed out either to stakes or to horizontal poles set up on posts. We will consider these methods in turn.

WALL TENT ON INSIDE POLES, STAKED.— This is the usual way of setting up a wall tent, with or without a fly; but it is not the best, except when it is necessary or expedient to carry shop-made poles and stakes with the outfit, as in the case of an army,

TENTS FOR FIXED CAMPS 43

or of a party traveling by wagon and frequently moving camp.

Having chosen the best frontage, lay out the corners and end centers with cord and small pegs, as described. Then drive the corner guy stakes diagonally outward from tent corners, slanting them as shown in Fig. 8. If fly guys are to be looped over them, as well as wall guys, the stakes should be long enough to project well and still take firm hold in the ground. (When striking a tent, do not work

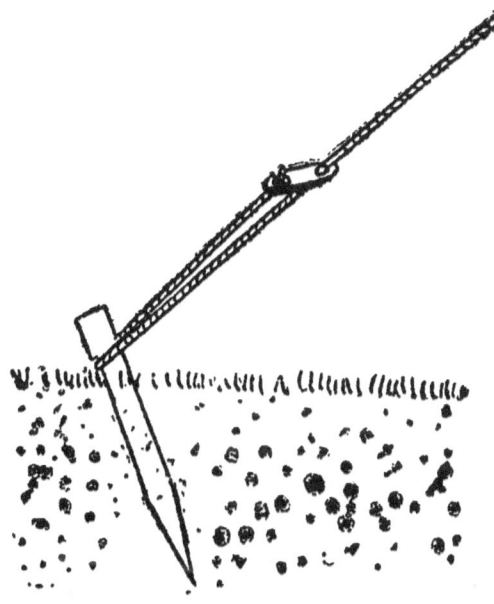

Fig. 8.— Tent Stake and Guy Rope

the stakes forward and backward to loosen them, but slip a looped rope over the notch and pull at angle that stake was driven.) Corner stakes are driven several feet away from tent, depending on slope of roof, and two or three feet outward, fore and aft, to make the guys draw diagonally.

Now unroll the tent and drag it away by the ridge until it is laid out flat over the ground selected.

Insert ridge pole (rounded side up) inside the tent, with its holes for the spindles (iron pins in end of uprights) meeting the grommets or large eyelets at ends of tent ridge. Place uprights at front and rear, at right angles to ridge, spindles inserted in ridge pole and passing out through peak grommets.

If a fly is to be used, lay it out flat over the tent, spindles passing through grommets as in the tent.

If end guys are to be run out fore and aft, or the storm set is used (Fig. 10), slip the loops of the long guys over the spindles.

A man at each end now takes hold of an upright, and the two raise tent and fly together. Then one or two men hold the tent in position while one or two others guy out the corners (beginning on the windward side) so that the tent will stand by itself. See that the uprights stand truly perpendicular.

Tie up the door and peg down the corners of the tent wall.

Guy out the sides to stakes, tightening or slackening the ropes alternately with their slides until the tent stands true and the guys draw evenly.

Stretch the fly similarly, making sure that it touches the tent nowhere except at the ridge. It should clear the eaves by at least 6 inches, preferably 9 or 10 inches. This requires an extra set of stakes driven outside the wall stakes, or a single set of long stakes with double notches (army tents). In the latter case there is not enough clearance for hot weather, unless the fly ropes are propped up on crotched sticks (see further under ACTION OF WIND ON TENTS). A better method, without any stakes, is described later.

Finish pegging down the tent wall; or, if there is a sod cloth, weight it down with flat rocks or poles, which is a better rig, not only to exclude draughts and insects, but also because then the tent wall can readily be clewed up to the eaves, in fine weather, to sun and air the interior.

The tent now stands square and taut all around (Fig. 9), secure against all but heavy end winds. To brace it against end strain you could run a pair of long guys out fore and aft; but such a rig is a

TENTS FOR FIXED CAMPS 45

never-ending source of wrath and objurgation. It is forever in the way, prevents having the camp-fire in front where you want it, and is sure to be run into or tripped over by anyone who goes out of the tent at night.

Fig. 9.— U. S. Army Wall Tent with Fly. (Officers' Tent)

STORM SET.— Better end braces are rigged with a pair of long guy ropes each of which has a loop in the middle to go over the upright spindle and a regulating lashing at each end. These may be made fast to corner stakes set diagonally outward from

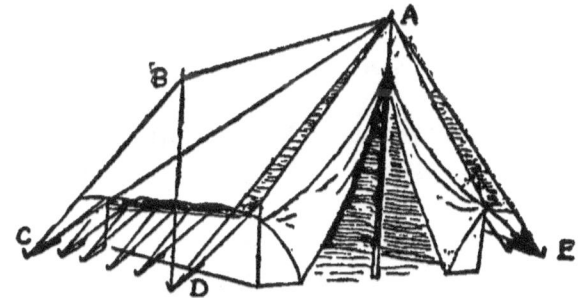

Fig. 10.— Storm Set

the tent corners, as with army hospital tents; but a better plan is what I call the storm set (Fig. 10), in which the ropes are carried backward to the opposite corners. The storm set leaves both ends of the tent free from obstruction, takes less room, does not tend to pull apart a jointed ridge pole, if such is used, keeps the fly from "ballooning" when wind gets under it, and is the most secure of all end braces because the strain each way is met by ropes pulling, over a triangle of wide base, directly back against the wind.

In the illustration, the loop at middle of one guy is slipped over the spindle A, one end is drawn back to C and the other to the stake opposite C. Similarly the other guy runs from B to D and E.

WALL TENT WITH GUY FRAMES.— Tent stakes are troublesome things at best. Generally when you go to driving them you find stones or roots in the way. They do not hold well except in favorable

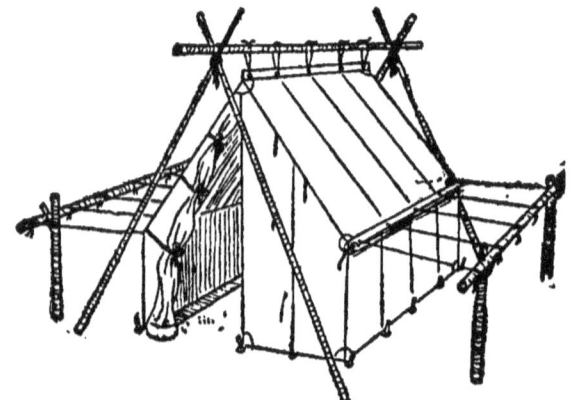

Fig. 11.— Wall Tent on Shears with Guy Frame

soil and in dry weather. When guy ropes get wet they shrink and engage in a tug of war that loosens the stakes.

If poles grow near the camp site it is more satisfactory to drive four heavy crotched corner stakes and lay a stiff pole across each pair of them at about the height of the tent wall and parallel to its sides, to which the guy ropes are made fast (see Fig. 11).

If a fly is used, lash a rather heavy pole to each edge and drop these poles over the guy rods. Their weight automatically keeps the fly taut at all times, wet or dry.

TENT ON SHEARS.— Tent poles are bothersome

TENTS FOR FIXED CAMPS 47

on the train and in a wagon, and impossible in a canoe or on a pack train unless they are jointed. Socketed poles become useless, or hard to refit, if a ferrule is stepped on or otherwise dented. An upright pole in the doorway must be dodged every time you go in or out. A pair of shear legs at each end of the tent, to support the ridge pole, is a stancher " set."

Cut four straight poles a couple of feet longer than the distance from peak to corner of tent, and a stiff stick for ridge pole about two feet longer than

Fig. 12.— Lashing for Shear Legs. (For Tent Shears it is not Necessary to Take so many Turns)

Fig. 14.— Magnus Hitch. (Not Apt to Slip Along a Pole)

Fig. 13.— Shear Legs Spread

the tent. To bind the shear poles, lay a pair of them side by side; with a small rope take several turns around both poles near their upper ends, not too tightly, then pass the ends of the rope one up and the other down, to form a cross-lashing, and tie them with a reef knot (Fig. 12). When the butts of the shear legs are drawn apart the crossing of the tips puts a strain on the knot and effectually secures them (Fig. 13).

Having spread out the tent and inserted the ridge pole (or tied it outside), raise tent with the shears, and spread their legs until the tent just touches the ground when ready to be pegged down (Fig. 11). One man can raise a rather heavy tent in this way by working first at one end and then at the other.

In the case of a wall tent with fly, erect side frames for the guys (Fig. 11); but if no fly is used, all that is needed is to lash side poles to the shears and tie the eaves fast to them: this is the best rig for a small waterproof tent that is to be moved often (Fig. 15).

Sometimes the rear end of the ridge pole can be lashed to a convenient sapling, or rested in the fork of a limb. Some campers plant a single crotched post at the rear, but usually it is easier to set up shears than to find a suitable crotch and plant it

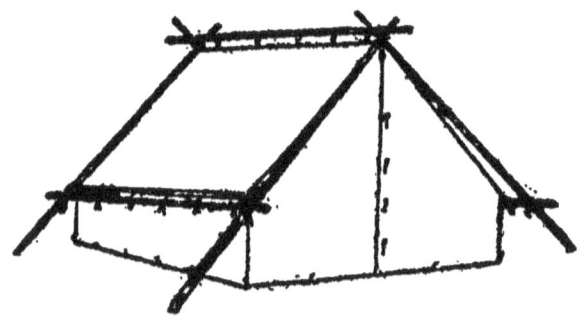

Fig. 15.—Wall Tent with Side Bars

firmly. It is one advantage of shear legs that they can be erected without difficulty anywhere, although the ground may be rocky or frozen.

This rig has several other merits. It leaves the doorway unobstructed. The legs do not sink so much in soft soil or sand as single uprights; if they should sink, they can be raised in a trice by drawing the butts closer together. Similarly, when the tent shrinks, from wetting, the strain can be eased by simply lifting one shear leg and pushing it a little farther outward. When the canvas sags, draw the legs closer to their mates, and you stretch the tent as taut as a drum-head.

An inside ridge pole is best for a large, heavy

TENTS FOR FIXED CAMPS 49

tent; but it must be straight and smooth, or it will wear the canvas and make it leak. Small or medium-size tents are best made with a strongly reinforced outer ridge with cords by which the tent is tied to an *outside* ridge pole (Fig. 11). In this case the pole need not be so straight nor so carefully trimmed.

An outside ridge pole is excellent to keep a tent fly clear all around from the tent roof, permitting a free circulation of air between the two, which keeps the tent cool in summer.

TRENCHING THE TENT.— This should always be done if camp is not to be moved frequently. Do not dig the ditch V-shaped, but cut straight down, just outside the tent pegs and slope the trench inward toward this dam (Fig. 16). Cast the dirt away; never bank it against the tent, for it would quickly rot the canvas. Give the ditch a uniform slope toward the lowest ground around the tent. In the shallowest places it need not be over three inches deep. A trench that does not drain well is worse than none.

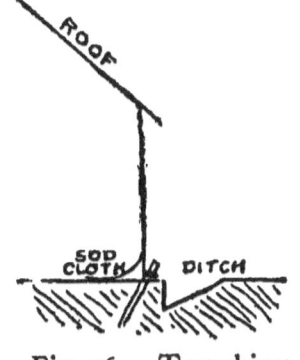

Fig. 16.— Trenching Tent

TENT FLOORS.— In fixed camp, especially if it is in a sandy place, the tent should have a board floor. Lay down the requisite number of 2" x 4" scantling as floor-joists, setting them on flat rocks or posts if necessary. (It is well to let the front and rear joists project far enough for a guy-rope frame to be nailed to them.) Plank them over with dressed lumber. The edges should be dressed to match; tongued and grooved flooring is best.

If you have enough lumber, run a base-board around the sides and rear. Inside the base-boards, at each corner, set up a 2" x 4" joist to height of tent wall, and connect these corner posts at top by narrow boards, on the outside, corresponding to the base-boards (Fig. 17).

Such a frame helps to hold the tent in shape. The upper boards are convenient for hanging up wall-pockets, guns, etc., where they are handy but out of the way.

Loop the tent-pin beckets over nails in the base-boards: then the walls can be clewed up in warm weather.

Before laying a floor the tent first should be set up without it and accurate measurements taken (or the measuring string previously mentioned may be used). If the floor is too small there will be en-

Fig. 17.—Tent Floor, with Wall Rail, Base-board, and End Joists Projecting that Corner Stakes May Be Nailed to Them

trance for draughts and insects; if it projects, the canvas will not fit over it, and rainwater will run in.

A portable tent floor may be made in sections that bolt together. The sections should not be too large to lie flat in a wagon box (for standard roads, wagon boxes are usually 42 inches wide; for narrow tracks, 38 inches; length of box usually 10½ ft.). Dimensions and number of sections will depend, of course, upon size of tent.

TENTS ON ROCKY OR SANDY GROUND.— If the ground is too rocky to drive stakes in it, or is hard frozen, erect the tent on shears and guy it out to rocks or growing bushes.

Tent stakes do not hold well in sand or in ground that has been soaked by rain. It is customary, in such cases, to attach the guys to a double row of

TENTS FOR FIXED CAMPS 51

stakes, one behind the other, or interlocking at right angles (one stake driven at a sharp angle toward the tent, the other outward so that its notch engages the head of the other stake, the two forming an inverted V, thus ⋀).

An easier and more secure way is to lay a heavy pole over the guy ropes close to the stakes (Fig. 18), and, if need be, weight it down with rocks, earth, or sand.

In a very sandy place, where no log is to be found, dig a small pit for each guy, tie the rope around a fagot or to a bag of sand (Fig. 19), bury this, and stamp the sand over it.

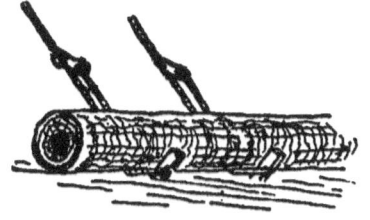 

Fig. 18.— Guys Weighted with Log

Fig. 19.— Guy Rope Fastened to Fagot to Be Buried in Ground.

ACTION OF WIND ON TENTS.— Unless one encamps in an open country the wind will seldom strike his tent steadily in a direction parallel with the ground. Rather it goes eddying and curling like driven smoke: hence the flapping and slatting of the fly-sheet.

During a squall a violent blow may fall straight down upon the roof as though bent on snapping the poles; then, rebounding, it will try to carry the tent away and aloft, as though your shelter were an open umbrella. This action is often marked in ravines and in a glade surrounded by tall trees, but it may occur anywhere. The stanchest tents for a very windy situation are those of conical or pyramidal form, set up on or under tripods.

A fly-sheet is a perfect wind trap, especially if it projects in the form of a porch, or is set well away from the ridge of the tent. This is one reason why I prefer a waterproofed tent without fly (except for hot climates). If a porch is wanted, rig a sheet of canvas over a separate frame in front of the tent; then, if it blows away, it will not wreck the tent too.

The flies of army tents, and of other patterns built for hard and varied service, are guyed to double-notched wall stakes, and so set rather close to the roof (see Fig. 9).

CHAPTER IV
FURNITURE, TOOLS, AND UTENSILS FOR FIXED CAMPS

When you go a-camping, make yourself as comfortable as you can. It is neither heroic nor sensible to put peas in your boots to mortify the flesh. There is no comfort in toting a lot of baggage over bad trails, but when there is a wagon to carry folding cots and camp chairs, take them along.

Pack your provisions, and some of the other things, in boxes that will serve for cupboards and cold-storage in camp. Put some ready-cut shelf boards in them, and leather for hinges. Make sure beforehand that you can get enough lumber at your destination to make a dining table and benches.

Straw beds on the ground soon get fusty, and they attract vermin. Fixed bunks in a tent harbor dirt and dampness.

COTS.— For a bed in fixed camp, or wherever transportation is adequate, choose a folding cot. It is easy to keep presentable. It makes a comfortable lounge or settee, as well as a good bed. It can be picked up bodily and carried out every morning to sun and air, leaving the tent floor free for sweeping.

Wire-bottomed cots are too cumbersome for general camping. Canvas stretcher-beds with frames that fold compactly are the right things. I have chosen four models for illustration.

Length.	Width.	Height.	Closed.	Weight.
78 in.	27 in.	14 in.	38 x 5 x 4 in.	17 lbs.
78 in.	27 in.	13 in.	29 x 8 x 4 in.	17 lbs.
78 in.	30 in.	20 in.	34 x 7 x 5 in.	15 lbs.
78 in.	36 in.	18 in.	38 x 6 x 6 in.	20 lbs.

Fig. 20.— Narrow Cot

Fig. 21.— Compact Cot

Fig. 22.— Telescoping Cot

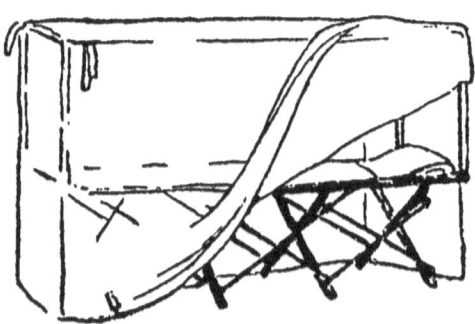

Fig. 23.— Cot with Mosquito Screen

FURNITURE FOR FIXED CAMPS 55

The first and fourth of these cots differ only in size and weight. The second folds so compactly that it can be stowed in a short chest or steamer trunk. The third opens like a lazy-tongs, can be set up in less than a minute, and is unusually high and roomy for its weight.

The wider the cot, the more comfortable it will be, especially in cold weather. On a very narrow cot the sleeper's body raises the covering free from the bed on both sides, leaving gaps through which cold air draws upward between mattress and blanket, chilling the sleeper, no matter how much covering he may pile on. Sleeping-bags obviate this.

The cotton pad mattresses made for camp cots are needlessly bulky and heavy, hard to lie on, and hard to keep dry in the moist forest air. Much better is a folded comforter stuffed with wool instead of cotton. It can be kept dry and sweet by hanging it out in the sun like a blanket. Wool stays fluffy and springy, but cotton batting mats down and gets lumpy, besides retaining moisture.

To be secure against insect pests is as essential to peace and comfort in camp as a dry roof overhead, if not more so.

If the tent itself is not thoroughly screened against flies and mosquitoes, then by all means get from the outfitter a cot frame and netting (Fig. 23), or, as a makeshift, rig for yourself a pyramidal head-screen of netting or cheesecloth, to be hung by a string above the bed, with the edges of three sides tucked under the mattress after you turn in.

CAMP CHAIRS.— Folding stools without backs are by no means comfortable. Far better is a chair in which you can recline and rest the whole body. The pattern shown in Fig. 24 folds as easily as an umbrella, to a size 3 ft. long by 3 in. square, and, when opened, adjusts itself perfectly to the body. It weighs 4½ pounds. A larger size, high enough to rest the head, weighs 6¼ pounds.

The armchair, Fig. 25, knocks down into six parts

which are carried in a bag, forming a package 29 x 6 in., that weighs 8 pounds. This is the Indian "Rhorkee" chair, a favorite with old campaigners the world over. With the addition of a foot-rest of

Fig. 24.— Folding Chair   Fig. 25.—
                           Folding Arm Chair

some sort it makes a fairly comfortable bed. Caspar Whitney and Richard Harding Davis consider it the best camp chair made. Several of our sporting goods houses carry it in stock.

CAMP TABLES.— A small table in the tent is an-

Fig. 26.— Roll-up Table   Fig. 27.—
                           Roll-up Table Top

other convenience that pays for its transportation. The model shown in Fig. 26, with roll top, comes in two sizes, 36 x 27 and 36 x 36 inches. It folds into a package about 6 inches in diameter, and weighs

FURNITURE FOR FIXED CAMPS 57

16 pounds. The top separately, weighing only 6 pounds, and costing but $1.25, can be set up on forked stakes, as illustrated in Fig. 27.

The table shown in Fig. 29 folds into a package only 27 inches long, and weighs 15 pounds.

Fig. 28.— Table with Shelf   Fig. 29.— Compact Table

A stronger and more rigid table than either of these has legs that cross in four directions (Fig. 28). It may be bought either plain (16 pounds) or with a folding shelf underneath (23 pounds). The top is 36 x 27 inches; size folded, 36 x 7 x 5 inches. By an interlocking device, two or more of these tables may be fastened together, for mess purposes.

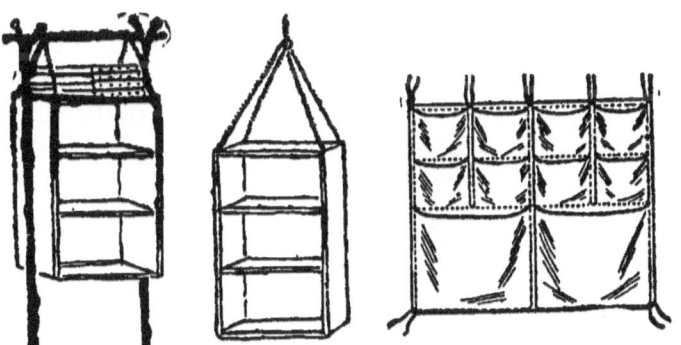

Fig. 30.— Folding Shelves   Fig. 31.— Wall Pocket

If boards are not procurable near the camp site, a portable dining table for a party of four to six is quickly rigged by setting up two roll table tops (Fig. 27) side by side.

SHELVES AND WALL POCKETS.— To keep a tent from being littered with small articles that are always in the way except when you want them and can't find them, shelves or wall pockets, or both, are well-nigh indispensable. These may be purchased ready-made.

The camp cupboard here illustrated (Fig. 30) has four shelves, each 10 x 30 inches, folds into a parcel 4 x 10 x 30 inches, and weighs 7 pounds. Other sizes are manufactured.

The wall pocket (Fig. 31) is 30 x 36 inches, and weighs 1½ pounds. Such things can easily be made at home to suit individual requirements.

CLOTHES HANGERS.— There are various kinds of tent-pole hooks for suspending clothing, a lantern, and accoutrements. Such a contrivance is to be clamped to the rear upright, or to the center pole, depending on the kind of tent. Some are made of leather or webbing so as to be adjustable to poles of any size.

In any tent with a ridge pole two screw-eyes should be put in at opposite ends from which to suspend by cords a straight stick to hang clothes on. This is especially handy for wet clothes on rainy days.

MEDICAL KIT.— About the best thing of this sort, for average campers who do not have to go very light, is the "Household (B)" first aid box fitted up by the American National Red Cross, Washington, D. C. The case is of heavy tin, 10 x 9½ x 3½ inches, white enameled inside and out, and contains the following articles:

1 2-oz. bottle Alcohol.
1 2-oz. bottle Aromatic Spirits of Ammonia.
1 2-oz. bottle Syrup of Ipecac.
1 2-oz. bottle Jamaica Ginger.
1 2-oz. bottle Liniment.
1 2-dram vial Olive Oil.

1 2-dram vial Oil of Cloves.
1 Bottle Soda Mint Tablets.
1 Bottle Cascara Sagrada Tablets.
2 Iodine Containers.
1 Package A. R. C. Finger Dressings (6).

FURNITURE FOR FIXED CAMPS 59

1 Package A. R. C. Small Dressings (3)
2 A. R. C. First Aid Outfits.
6 Assorted Bandages.
1 1-yard package Picric Acid Gauze.
1 Spool Adhesive Plaster.
1 Pair Scissors.
1 Paper Safety Pins.
6 Wooden Tongue Depressors.
1 Medicine Dropper.
1 Package Paper Cups.
1 Tourniquet.
1 Clinical Thermometer.
1 2-oz. Package Absorbent Cotton.

Brief directions telling how to use these are pasted inside the lid, but one should order at the same time a copy of the excellent little *American Red Cross Abridged Text-book on First Aid* (General Edition) by Major Charles Lynch, Medical Corps, U. S. A. For prices see the Red Cross catalogue, which is sent free on application to the address given above.

TOOLS.— An axe and a hatchet are indispensable (see Chapters VII and X). If much wood is to be cut, and there are poor axemen in the party, a crosscut saw is the tool for them. The long pattern for two men is much the easiest to cut with, but mean to transport; a one-man cross-cut with 3-ft. blade and auxiliary handle for the left hand will do very well.

A hand saw is necessary if you are to make a dining table, tent floor, and so on. Make the cook swear on his cook-book that he will not use that saw on meat bones (provide him with a cheap kitchen saw).

A spade or miner's shovel will be needed for trenching, and for excavating the refuse pit, latrine, and perhaps a cold-storage hole and a camp oven.

For small tools, see Chapter VII.

Take an assortment of nails and tacks, a spool of annealed wire, a ball of strong twine, and a bundle of braided cotton sash cord (for clothes line, emergency guys to tent, etc.).

If you have a dog, string some heavy wire between two trees as a "trolley," and chain him to it at night, so he can move back and forth.

Here is a good wrinkle that I found in a sportsmen's magazine: If there are children in camp, "put a small cow-bell in the lunch basket or berry pail of the youngsters before you let them go into strange woods. It will reassure both them and you, and may be the means of preventing a tragedy. Trust them to shake it up if they get lost!"

LANTERNS.— If a powerful light is wanted in camp, a gas lantern of the type advertised in sportsmen's journals is a good thing, or an acetylene lantern that is made so that the flame can be regulated. Ordinarily a common kerosene lantern will serve very well.

CAMP STOVES.— If there is a separate commissary tent, the cooking can be done on a common blue-flame oil or gasolene stove, set up on a perfectly level stand. Such a stove is useless out of doors unless fitted with a wind-shield. Do no cooking in the living tent: it attracts flies and vermin.

The best cooking stoves for campers are those specially designed for the purpose, and burning wood. There are many patterns, of varying merit. Do not buy a folding stove for ordinary camping: they are bothersome and flimsy.

I leave out of account stoves without ovens (I can see no good reason for a stove at all unless it has an oven). There are shown here three different types of sheet steel camp stoves, each good in its way.

The first one (Figs. 32, 33) is very compact, yet large enough to cook for four persons, or six in a pinch. When packed and locked in its metal crate, it measures $10\frac{1}{2} \times 18 \times 21\frac{1}{2}$ inches, and can be checked as baggage. Inside the fire-box ($8 \times 10 \times 17$ inches) are packed three sections of adjustable 4-inch pipe, and two automatic locking bars. Inside the oven ($7\frac{1}{2} \times 10\frac{1}{2} \times 17$ inches) there is stowed a 5-. gallon water reservoir, and with it a set of sheet iron and tin cooking utensils and table service for six persons. When the stove is in use, the reservoir hooks on to the left side of the stove, next to the fire box, and increases the stove top to 17×28 inches.

FURNITURE FOR FIXED CAMPS

This is a most useful addition, since plenty of hot water is needed for cooking and in washing up.

The fire box takes in 16-inch wood. The oven is large enough for a 9 x 15-inch bread pan and will roast a good-sized fowl.

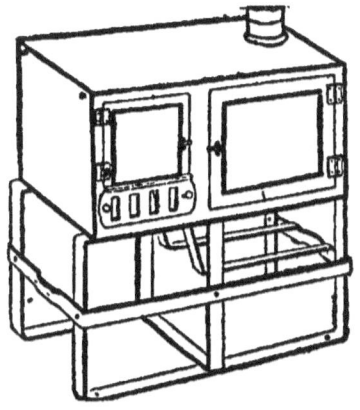
Fig. 32.— Small Camp Stove

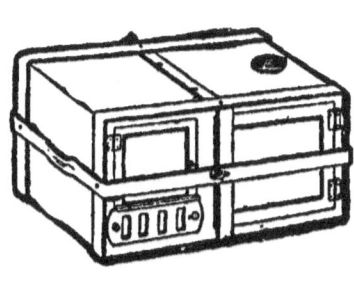
Fig. 33.— Stove Packed

When the stove is set up, it is mounted on its steel crate and the locking bars are attached under the oven to form a warming rack. It is not intended for tent heating.

This stove weighs 25 pounds, and the reservoir and utensils about 15 pounds more. To make the pots and pans nest in the oven, they are made square or rectangular. For fixed camps it is best to select your own utensils, and carry the larger ones in a separate box.

The second stove (Fig. 34) is made with fire box extending its entire length. It will take in a billet 28 inches long, which will keep a fire all night, and will be ready for cooking five minutes after the dampers are opened in the morning. When packed for transportation, the stove measures 30 x 14 x 12 inches, and weighs

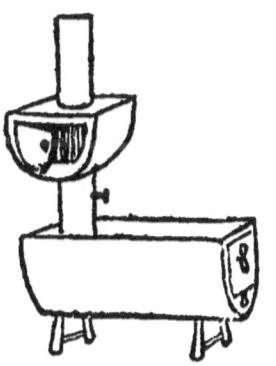
Fig. 34.— Stove for Large Wood

29 pounds (43½ pounds complete with grub box and utensils). When set up, the 14 x 30-inch top is free for utensils; the oven, above it, takes a 10 x 14-inch pan for baking or roasting. Oven, legs, and pipe stow inside the body of the stove, leaving space for a 12 x 13 x 9½-inch galvanized box that holds cooking utensils and is used in camp as a dish-pan or as a vermin-proof box for provisions.

A cook-stove with sheet-iron top needs no plates. If you get one with plates, be sure they are far

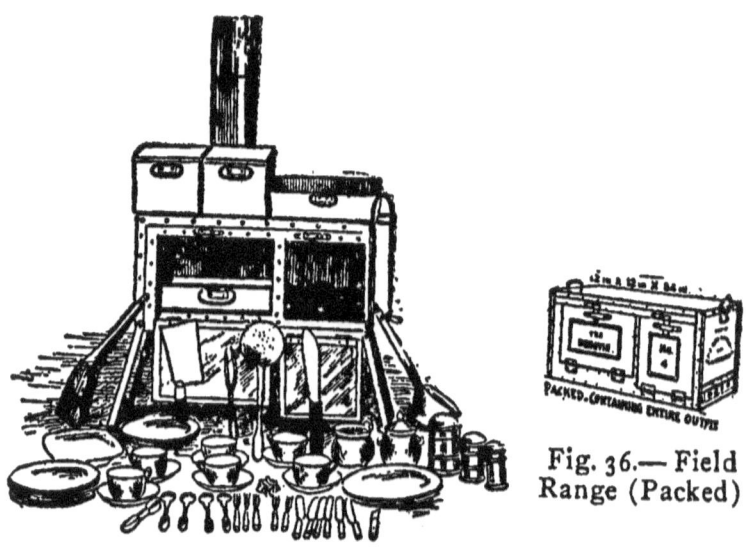

Fig. 36.— Field Range (Packed)

Fig. 35.— Field Range

enough apart so that the vessels do not interfere with each other.

The third type of stove (Figs. 35, 36) is one regularly used by our Geological Survey, Forestry Bureau, and is similar to the Army range, but smaller. The No. 4 size, to cook for 6 to 15 men, packs, with utensils, in a space 12 x 13 x 22 inches. The oven is 8 x 12 x 12 inches. The range weighs 52 pounds, the utensils 20 pounds, and a dining service for six persons, in enamel and white or plated metal, 13 pounds. For continuous field service this is a quite practical range.

FURNITURE FOR FIXED CAMPS 63

Personally, I never use a camp stove, preferring to cook in the open.

As for a heating stove in a tent, my experience tallies with that of Dr. Breck: "Either it bakes you with a temperature of ninety degrees, or it takes the first opportunity to go out directly you close your eyes, and you awake trembling with cold, the thermometer registering somewhere 'round zero." Someone else has called the tent stove "a portable hell." But there are those who like it, for cold-weather camping; and I admit that if the tent is not less than 10 x 14, and the stove's fire-box is big enough to take in a thick billet two feet long, so that it will keep a smouldering all-night fire without your everlastingly pottering around it, there are times and places where a stove in the tent may be a good thing.

If you do set up a stove, be sure to fix a spark-arrester over the top of the pipe. This need not be anything more costly than a piece of wire netting.

If the stove must be set rather close to the tent wall, take along a sheet of asbestos as a shield. One of the pads used for dining-tables will do very well. Such things can be bought at department stores, or of mail-order houses.

When starting a fire in an "air-tight," use little fuel at first, or you will smother the flame in its own smoke. If the stove has no legs, make a board frame like the sides of a low box, or a crib of notched logs, and fill in with gravel.

CAMP GRATES AND FIRE IRONS.— A stove is merely a convenience and an economizer of fuel. Quite as good meals can be cooked over an open fire. Even when it rains, a bonfire can be built to one side and hard coals shoveled from it to a spot sheltered by canvas where the cooking is done. But it pays to take along either a folding grate or a pair of fire irons to hold the frying-pan, etc., level and close over the coals. Then you will need no long stick attached to the frying-pan handle, nor must the cook give all his attention to that one utensil when frying or making pancakes.

Of folding grates there are many and ingenious patterns. I never use any of them; for they are likely to warp from heat or to rust in service, and become unmanageable. Simpler, cheaper, and quite as useful, are a pair of " fire-irons," which are simply two pieces of flat *steel* 24 x 1½ x ⅛ inches, weighing 2½ pounds to the pair, that any blacksmith will cut for you in a minute. Lay them across a couple of logs or flat rocks that are placed on either side of the fire. You can space them apart to suit vessels of different sizes. They will stand any amount of abuse; if they get bent, you can quickly hammer them back into shape.

OVENS.— When there is no stove in the outfit, you will need some kind of camp oven. For a fixed camp a good kind is the old-fashioned Dutch oven (Fig. 37). How to use it is explained in Chapter XX. For a party of four to six it should be of full 13-inch diameter, which will weigh about 17 pounds. Lighter ones, but much more expensive, are made of aluminum with iron tops. Aluminum will not stand the high heat necessary for the top, but does very well for the body of the vessel, if thick enough.

Fig. 37.—Dutch Oven

Such ovens are favorites in the South and the Far West. They are better than reflectors (see Chapter VII) for any baking or roasting that requires considerable time (inimitable for pot-roasts and baked beans), but rather unhandy for biscuits, though all right for biscuit-loaf.

OTHER UTENSILS.— For stationary camps, or for traveling by wagon, the most satisfactory material for pots and table service is enameled ware. It is easier to clean than any other metal, and it is not

FURNITURE FOR FIXED CAMPS 65

corroded, like tin, by fruits or vegetables steeped, cooked or left over in it. The tendency of enameled ware to chip and flake in cold weather can be tamed by warming gradually before exposing to fierce heat.

Pressed tinware of heavy gauge is good enough for most purposes, though hard to clean when greasy. It is unfit to cook tart fruit in, and it makes tea " taste." Thin soldered tinware is treacherous, dents and rusts easily, and lasts but a short time.

Aluminum is needlessly expensive for the class of camping we are now considering.

Where compactness need not be studied, frying-pans with stationary handles are more practical than the folding kind.

A complete cooking, washing, and table set, for six persons, is listed below. It is heavy (about 58 pounds, with oven and fire irons, or 38 pounds without them), but cheap (about $13.50 with, or $10.50 without oven and irons) and should last a long time.

UTENSILS FOR 6 PERSONS IN FIXED CAMP.

Dutch Oven, cast iron, $13\frac{1}{4}$ x 6 in. (omitted if there is a stove).
2 Fire Irons, flat steel, 24 x $1\frac{1}{2}$ x $\frac{1}{8}$ in. (omitted if there is a stove).
Dish Pan, enameled, 16 x 5 in.
Wash Basin, enameled, $13\frac{3}{4}$ in.
2 Milk Pans, enameled, $10\frac{1}{2}$ in. (for mixing and serving).
Water Pail, enameled, 10 qt.
3 Covered Pails, enameled, 3, $4\frac{1}{2}$ and 6 qt., nesting.
Double Boiler, enameled, $3\frac{1}{2}$ qt.
Coffee Pot, enameled, $3\frac{1}{4}$ qt.
Tea Pot, enameled, 2 qt.
Graduated Measure, enameled, 1 qt.
2 Frying-pans, steel, $10\frac{1}{8}$ in.
2 Pot Covers, tin, $10\frac{1}{2}$ in.
Broiler, wire, 9 x 14 in.
3 Pot Chains.
Tea Ball, aluminum.
Dipper, enameled, 1 qt.
Basting Spoon, enameled.
Skimmer, enameled.
Soup Ladle, enameled.

66 CAMPING AND WOODCRAFT

Cake Turner, steel.
Butcher Knife, steel.
Flesh Fork, steel.
Kitchen Saw, steel.
Spring Balance, 24 lb.
Pot Cleaner, wire.
Can Opener and Corkscrew.
Salt Shaker.
Pepper Shaker.
10 Dinner Plates, white enameled, 8½ in.
6 Cups, white enameled, 1 pint (handles cut to nest).
6 Cereal Bowls, white enameled.
6 Knives, steel.
6 Forks, white metal.
6 Teaspoons, white metal.
6 Dessert Spoons, white metal.
2 yds. Table Oilcloth.
2 yds. Turkish Toweling (dish towels and clouts).
100 Paper Napkins.
1 bar Sapolio.
1 bar Fels Naphtha Soap.

A milk-can should be added if the camp is near a farm-house.

FIRELESS COOKERS.— A great deal of the bother of cooking can be saved by using a fireless cooker, in which all of the slow processes are performed (roasting, baking, stewing, boiling, and making porridge). In this case only a few simple utensils are required, a wood stove is dispensed with, and there is no need of anyone staying in camp to watch the fire and the cooking. The soapstone radiators can be heated over an alcohol or blue-flame stove. Hot meals can be had at all hours, even when the party is traveling.

A rough-and-ready fireless cooker, which can also be used as a cold-storage box, was described some years ago in *Outing.*—

"When preparing your outfit this summer, pack some of your belongings in a soap or cracker box that has a fairly close-fitting lid. Take along an old white quilt or a blanket that can be folded into a pad to fit the box, or make a crude pad out of unbleached muslin with cotton batting, about one inch thick. Include in your outfit a granite cooking pail commensurate in capacity with the

FURNITURE FOR FIXED CAMPS 67

size of your party. In setting up camp, the soap box is to be lined with three or four thicknesses of newspaper (this can be done easily with the aid of a few tacks) and filled with clean hay or straw, packed firmly; and a close little nest hollowed out to fit the cooking pail.

This camp fireless cooker has been tested and has proved a pleasant luxury as well as a convenience in camp life. It makes possible cooked cereals, rice, evaporated fruits and slow-cooking vegetables, where otherwise they would be excluded from the menu. If there are children in the party, these things are particularly desirable. Keep the soap box in a sheltered place. Let the food in the cooking pail begin to boil briskly over the camp fire, then remove it, seeing that the cover is tightly closed (it should be a cover that shuts *in*), and place it in its hay nest. Tuck over it the cotton pad and three or four thicknesses of newspaper and shut down the lid of the box. Breakfast cereals may remain in the cooker over night. Meat, or slow-cooking foods should boil on the camp fire for fifteen minutes before being placed in the cooker.

This will also be found a heat-saving and labor-saving device for those housewives who remain at home — and it costs almost nothing.

It is not necessary to have ice for keeping milk cool and sweet in hot weather. The fireless-cooker, which conserves heat at the boiling point for many hours, will also conserve cold, or, more properly, keep heat out. A box lined with paper, packed with clean hay, straw or shavings and securely covered, is all that is needed. The bottle of milk, received ice-cold from the dairyman's wagon and placed directly in this device, will keep sweet as long as may be desired."

CHAPTER V
TENTS FOR SHIFTING CAMPS

Tents were devised long before the dawn of history, and they still are used as portable dwellings by men of all races and in all climes. Every year sees countless campers busy with new contrivances in canvas or other tent materials, seeking improvements — and still the prehistoric patterns hold their own. Wherever caravans or armies march, or people travel by wagon, or summer vacationists take to a gipsy life, we see wall tents of house shape, or conical ones, of heavy canvas.

But for a small party traveling in rough country, with pack animals, or in light water-craft, or perchance afoot, such cumbersome affairs are out of the question.

Wherever transportation is difficult it is imperative that the tent should be light, compact to carry, and, if you are to make camp and break camp every day or two, it must be so rigged that it can be set up easily and quickly by one or two men.

The tent should shed heavy rains and stand securely in a gale. It should keep out insects and cold draughts, yet let in plenty of pure air. If cold weather is to be encountered, either the tent should be fitted with a very portable stove, or it should be open in front and so shaped as to reflect the heat of a log fire down upon the occupants, yet not smother them with smoke. All of which is easily said, but harder to combine in fact. Hence the multitude of tent patterns.

In designing a light tent we begin by cutting

TENTS FOR SHIFTING CAMPS 69

down the size to what will "sleep" the occupants and their personal duffle. Since the party is to be out of doors all day, save in uncommonly bad weather, a small tent will suffice. Then we dispense with a fly, and make the tent of waterproof material, not only to shed rain but also because plain canvas is very heavy when wet. If the journey is through a well wooded country, no poles or stakes are carried: they are to be cut on the spot. If, however, saplings are scarce in the land, then the tent is made to set up with only one pole, and this pole may be jointed; no guy stakes are used, and the pegs are light things made of steel, as few as practicable.

Tents that are to be carried on pack animals need to be of strong, heavy duck, or else carried in stout bags; otherwise they will be ruined by the sawing of lash ropes and snagging or rubbing against trees and rocks. For such work the best of army duck is none too good.

MATERIALS FOR LIGHT TENTS.— Otherwise the most suitable material is very closely woven stuff made from Sea Island or Egyptian cotton, which has a long and strong fiber. A thin cloth of this kind is stout enough for most purposes, yet very light, and a tent made from it rolls up into a much smaller bundle than one of duck. It comes in various weights and fineness of texture. The standard grade of "balloon silk" runs about $3\frac{1}{2}$ oz. to the *square* yard in plain goods, and $5\frac{1}{2}$ oz. when waterproofed with paraffine. This trade name, by the way, is an absurdity: the stuff has no thread of silk in it, and the only ballooning it ever does is when a wind gets under it.

Cheaper goods, of coarser weave, and intermediate in weight between this and duck, do well enough for easy trips, if waterproofed.

WATERPROOF OR RAINPROOF CLOTHS.— These may be classed under two heads: (*A*) cloth filled with paraffine or other water-shedding substance; (*B*) cloth chemically treated so that each fiber or thread is itself repellant of water, but the interstices are left open.

In the first instance it is not practicable to treat the cloth before making it up; the whole tent should be soaked in a waterproofing mixture, or the "wax" ironed in, thus insuring that the seams are tight. Paraffine is used either plain (in which case it is liable to crack or flake in cold weather) or combined with some elastic substance. The "mineral wax" called ozocerite or cerasine (often used as a substitute for beeswax, and sold by dealers in crude drugs) is not so brittle as paraffine, adheres better, and, like paraffine, has no deleterious action on cloth, being chemically neutral. I have not known of it being used by tent-makers, but believe they should try it. Crude ozocerite is nearly black; when refined it is of a yellow color (cerasine) and resembles beeswax but is not so sticky. It makes a tough compound with rubber.

The plain wax process renders cloth quite waterproof, but adds considerable weight, makes the stuff rather stiff, and increases its liability to catch afire when exposed close to a stove or camp-fire.

Cloth of class *B* is subdivided in two groups:

(1) Cravenetted goods, like duxbak and gabardine, are processed in the yarn, or by chemical treatment applied to the raw strands themselves before they are twisted into thread. Such cloth is not so waterproof as waxed or oiled stuff, yet tents made of it can be depended upon to shed rain. It is as pliable as plain cloth, not perceptibly heavier, and is not affected by changes of temperature.

(2) Willesden canvas (or twill, etc., as the case may be), also known in England as "green rotproof," is cotton stuff soaked in an ammoniacal solution of copper that dissolves enough cellulose in the cloth to coat each fiber with a more or less impermeable "skin" of its own substance, and turns the material a light shade of green. It is not so waterproof as waxed cloth, yet sheds rain very well if the mate-

TENTS FOR SHIFTING CAMPS 71

rial is closely woven. What is known in this country as "green waterproof" has gone through the cupro-ammonium process and then is lightly waxed besides, making it quite waterproof but more pliable and slower burning than plain waxed stuff.

The mills produce many grades of light cloth suitable for tenting. Each tent-maker chooses for himself, and generally does his own waterproofing. In comparing samples, count the number of threads to the inch with a magnifying glass, then note weight per square yard, and strength.

Cloth proofed with linseed or other drying oil is not strong enough for tenting (for its weight); it is sticky in hot weather, stiff in cold, and dangerously inflammable.

FEATHERWEIGHT TENT MATERIALS.— Pedestrian and cycle campers sometimes go in for the utmost possible lightness and compactness of outfit that will serve their purposes. For tents they use the most finely woven cotton, linen, or silk, not waterproofed, but depending upon extreme closeness of texture to shed rain. The cloth may "spray" a little in the first heavy downpour, but it will not leak so long as nothing rubs it from within.

I have a sample of very close-woven silky cotton stuff from which a Puget Sound tent-maker turns out "A" tents complete of the following weights: $3\frac{1}{2}$ x 7 x 4 ft. high, 2 lbs.; $4\frac{1}{2}$ x $7\frac{1}{2}$ x 5 ft., $2\frac{3}{4}$ lbs.; $7\frac{1}{2}$ x $7\frac{1}{2}$ x 7 ft., 5 lbs.

Lightest of all rain-proof materials, strongest for its weight, and, of course, most expensive, is silk. It can be woven more closely than any other textile and so needs no waterproofing (oiled silk, such as surgeons use, weighs more than "balloon silk"). Genuine silk is the toughest of all fibers; but it does not stand much friction, hence should be reinforced at all friction surfaces, and rolled up when packed away, not folded in creases. It is unsuitable for any but special tents made for pedestrians. A London maker, T. H. Holding, sells a tentlette (if I may coin a term) of Japanese silk, in wedge shape, 6 x 5 x 4 ft. 6 in. high, that weighs under 12 ounces; and it is a practical little affair of its kind. Of one of these he reports: "It has stood some of the heaviest rains, in fact records for thirty hours at a stretch, without letting in wet, and I say this of an 11-oz. silk one."

WATERPROOFING CLOTH AT HOME.— If one has home facilities, there is no reason why he should not make a good job of waterproofing for himself.

PARAFFINE PROCESS.— The cheapest, simplest, and, in some respects, the most satisfactory way is to get a cake or two of paraffine or cerasine, lay the tent on a table, rub the outer side with the wax until it has a good coating evenly distributed, then iron the cloth with a medium-hot flatiron, which melts the wax and runs it into every pore of the cloth. The more closely woven the cloth, the less wax and less total weight.

Some prefer to treat the tent with a solution of paraffine. In this case, cut the wax into shavings so it will dissolve readily. Put 2 lbs. of the wax in 2 gallons of turpentine (for a 7 x 9 tent or thereabouts). Place the vessel in a tub of hot water until solution is completed. Meantime set up the tent true and taut. Then paint it with the hot solution, working rapidly, and using a stiff brush. Do this on a sunny morning and let tent stand until quite dry. The turpentine adds a certain elasticity to the wax; benzine does not.

For tents to be used in cold weather before an open fire, the following process is better:

ALUM AND SUGAR OF LEAD.— First soak the tent overnight in water to rid it of sizing, and hang up to dry. Then get enough *soft* water to make the solutions (rainwater is best; some city waters will do, others are too hard). Have two tubs or wash-boilers big enough for the purpose. In one, dissolve alum in hot soft water, in the proportion of ¼ lb. to the gallon. In the other, with the same amount of hot water, dissolve sugar of lead (lead acetate — *a poison*) in the same proportion. Let the solutions stand until clear; then add the sugar of lead solution to the alum liquor. Let stand about four hours, or until all the lead sulphate has precipitated. Then pour off the clear liquor from the dregs into the other tub, thoroughly work the tent in it with the hands

TENTS FOR SHIFTING CAMPS 73

until every part is quite penetrated, and let soak overnight. In the morning, rinse well, stretch, and hang up to dry.

A closely woven cloth should be used. This treatment fixes acetate of alumina in the fibers of the cloth. The final rinsing is to cleanse the fabric from the useless white powder of sulphate of lead that is deposited on it. Failures are usually due to using hard water, or a less proportion of alum than here recommended, or to not dissolving the chemicals separately and decanting off the clear liquor. When directions are followed, the cloth will be rain-proof and practically spark-proof, but not damp-proof if you use it as a ground-sheet to lie on, or if exposed to friction. After a good deal of use, the tent will need treating over again, as the mineral deposit gradually washes out.

Remember that cotton goods shrink considerably when first soaked.

ALUM AND SOAP.— Shave up about a pound of laundry soap and dissolve it in 2 gallons of hot water. Soak the cloth in it, dry out thoroughly, and then soak in an alum solution as above, and dry again.

I have had no success with the alum and lime method mentioned by "Nessmuk."

Good waterproofing compounds can be purchased ready-made from some tent-makers.

The following recipes, although not suitable for tents, are useful for other articles of equipment, and are included here while on the subject of waterproofing cloth:

OILED CLOTH.— For ground-sheets to use under bedding: get some of the best grade of *boiled* linseed oil of a reputable paint dealer. One quart will cover five or six square yards of heavy sheeting. Pour it into a pan big enough to dip your hand into. Lay out the cloth and rub the oil into it between your palms, using just enough oil at a time to soak the cloth through, filling the pores, but leaving no surplus. Then stretch it in a barn or garret, or other dry shady place, for one week. Finish drying by hanging in the sunlight three or four days, first one side up, then the other.

FLEXIBLE CELLULOID COATING.—A flexible enamel such as is used on fly lines for fishing is also useful for finishing seams in articles sewed up from waterproofed cloth.

Get some old photographic films, soak them in hot water, and scrub off the gelatine surface with a small stiff brush.

74 CAMPING AND WOODCRAFT

When they are dry, gradually add them to acetone until the solution is of the consistency of varnish. If a drop of it dries transparent and firm, it is fit. In this state it makes a strong cement or hard rod varnish that will not crack or peel. To make it flexible, proceed as follows:

Add common benzine to the amount of one-fourth the acetone. Shake well. Let the mixture stand and settle. Draw off the clear varnish from the water at the bottom, and test as before. If it does not dry clear and firm, add a little more benzine.

Now add castor oil to the amount of two-thirds the weight of the dry celluloid films that have been used, shake well, and give it time to thoroughly mix. Test: if not tough enough, add a little more oil. If too soft, add a little celluloid solution.

This does not evaporate so fast as a solution of celluloid in amyl acetate ("banana oil"). The castor oil gives it its flexibility.

DYEING CLOTH.— Use Diamond dye of a kind recommended by the makers for *cotton* goods. Follow directions on package. Dye the tent a deeper shade than what you want in service, for it will fade considerably in sun and rain. The dyeing must be done before waterproofing.

CONSTRUCTION OF LIGHT TENTS.— In a tent of thin material it is important that the widths be narrow, to keep the shelter taut when set up, and that the seams be reinforced with tape, to relieve the cloth itself from overstrain. Eaves, bottom, and corners should be strengthened with double cloth.

If there is a ridge, have it reinforced, with tapes attached whereby to suspend the tent from an *outside* ridge pole when desired.

There should be a sod-cloth all around, unless the tent has a sewed-in floor.

A tent that is to be used in "fly time" is certainly incomplete without a curtain of cheesecloth or bobbinet to exclude insects. This is best made to attach or detach at will, if the tent is also to be used late in the season with an all-night fire in front of it.

All tents that are made to close up at night or in

TENTS FOR SHIFTING CAMPS 75

bad weather should be fitted with screened windows for ventilation. The smaller the tent, the greater the need of this.

Guy-rope slides, if there are any, should be of galvanized wire. Grommets (galvanized iron rings worked in by hand) are much better than brass eyelets which are likely to pull out.

Ropes and beckets are to be small but strong; braided sash cord is best for a ridge rope.

Tent pins of steel are more durable and less cumbersome than wooden ones. In well forested countries none need be carried, but four steel corner pins help in setting up the tent quickly.

CHAPTER VI
TYPES OF LIGHT TENTS

Local conditions, means of transportation, and size of party, are to be considered in choosing among the many tent models that have been designed for campers who travel light. All depends on where you go, when you go, how you go, and what you want to do. The perfect all-round tent is a myth, like the perfect all-round gun. Of one thing, though, be sure: that whatever rig you choose shall be stanch against wind. The utmost pinnacle of comfort is reached when one lies at night under canvas, with a storm roaring toward him through the forest, and chortles over the certainty that no wind can blow *his* tent down. And it takes just one second of parting guys and ripping cloth to tumble him off his perch and cast him headlong into the very depths of woe.

LIGHT WALL TENTS.— A wall tent is the favorite cloth shelter of soldiers, engineers, explorers, naturalists, trappers, loggers, and other practical men who live away from civilization a great deal of the time. For one thing, it gives the most head-room for a given amount of material; and that counts, especially in continuous bad weather, or when one comes in wet all over and wants to hang up his clothes to dry. It is the best form of tent if a stove is carried; and that may be necessary in a thinly wooded country, late in the season. The vertical ends permit large ventilators or windows that may be kept open in almost any weather. There is no waste space, as in tents without walls.

Wall tents for flying camps should be much lighter, of course, than those mentioned in Chapter

III. In wooded country they are to be set up with shears, as previously described; or, if the ground favors, and a quick set is desired, run a ridge rope from tree to tree, or from a tree to a stake, stretch the guys, and do not bother to pin down the bottom but simply weight the sod-cloth.

Light waterproof wall tents may be had in great variety of sizes and materials, from which the following are selected as examples (width, depth, height, and wall, in order given):

BALLOON SILK (WHITE).

7⅓ x 7⅓ x 7 –2	10½ lbs.
8¾ x 8¾ x 7½–3	14¾ lbs.
10¼ x 10¼ x 8½–3½	20 lbs.

TANALITE (TAN), EMERALITE (GREEN).

7 x 7 x 7 –2	10 lbs.
8½ x 8½ x 7½–3	14 lbs.
10 x 10 x 8½–3½	19 lbs.

TANO (TAN), NILO (GREEN).

7½ x 7½ x 7–2	9 lbs.
7½ x 9 x 7–2½	11 lbs.
9 x 12 x 7–2½	13 lbs.

KIRO (OLIVE DRAB).

7 x 7 x 7–2½	12½ lbs.
9½ x 11¾ x 8–3	20¾ lbs.
11¾ x 14 x 9–3½	27 lbs.

EXTRA LIGHT GREEN.

6½ x 6½ x 6 –2	7 lbs.
8 x 8 x 7 –2½	10 lbs.
9½ x 9½ x 7½–3	13½ lbs.

GREEN EGYPTIAN.

7⅓ x 7⅓ x 7–2	9½ lbs.
9¾ x 9¾ x 8–3¼	16½ lbs.
9¾ x 12⅓ x 8–3¼	19 lbs.

GREEN STANDARD.

7⅙ x 7⅙ x 7 –2	12 lbs.
9½ x 9½ x 8 –3¼	19½ lbs.
11¾ x 11¾ x 9½–3½	27½ lbs.

All of the above-named tents have tape ridges that can be tied to outside poles, and are fitted with sodcloths.

Smaller, and larger, and intermediate sizes are made; but if a lighter shelter is wanted it is generally best to choose some other shape than a wall tent; and, if a larger one, then use heavier material that will stand up better and endure more strain.

Directions for setting up wall tents are given in Chapter III (see especially Figs. 11, 15).

CONICAL TENTS.— A tent may be "light" absolutely (so many pounds all told) or relatively (so

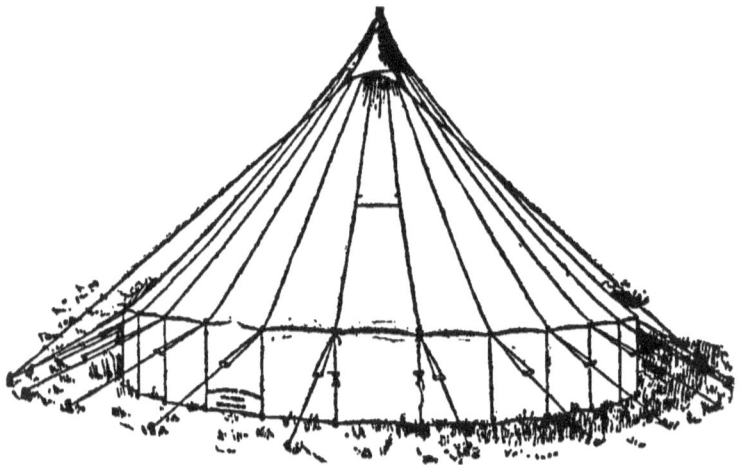

Fig. 38.— U. S. A. Conical Tent

many pounds per man sheltered). Conical tents of military pattern, such as the old Sibley, the present U. S. A., and the Bell tent of the British service, belong to the latter class.

The U. S. Army conical wall tent (Fig. 38) is 16 ft. 5 in. in diameter, 10 ft. high, and has a 3-ft. wall. It is erected by a single pole, the butt of which fits into a folding steel tripod, thus shortening the pole and giving it better bearing. At the top is an opening shielded by flaps. It is heated by a bottomless cone-shaped stove of 2-ft. diameter at the base (Fig. 39) with 5-in. pipe. This stove consumes little fuel. It is fed with sticks stood on end (dry "cow chips" will do), and the draught is regulated by banking earth around the bottom. Such a tent is roomy and comfortable for eight men in any weather. It will shelter a dozen or more at a pinch.

A conical tent is best for a party traveling on the plains, where violent windstorms or cloud-bursts or blizzards may suddenly be encountered, and where there is little or no timber. A cone sheds winds and rain better than any other shape, as it has a steep pitch and equal bracing in all directions. On the other hand, it is not fit for rough grounds; unless the site is smooth and level the tent bottom will gape in some places and sag in others. A conical tent cannot be set up properly without a full set of pegs, and it requires many of them.

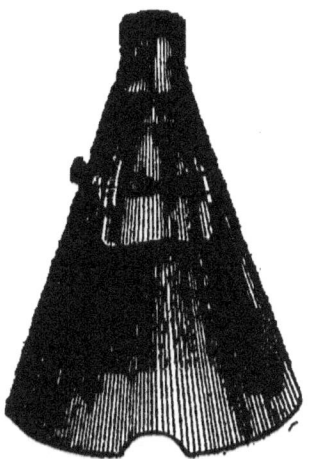

Fig. 39.—Sibley Tent Stove

Smaller and lighter conical tents are made for various tastes; but no tent of this shape should be of less diameter than 13 feet with wall, or 14 feet without one; for the occupants are supposed to lie like spokes of a wheel, and their feet must not come too near the center pole.

The army conical wall tent is usually pitched by eight men, of whom the director is designated as No. 8. They work as follows:

Upon the hood lines of the tent are placed three marks; the first about 8 feet 3 inches, the second about 11 feet 3 inches, the third about 14 feet 2 inches from the hood ring; the first marks the distance from the center to the wall pins, the second to the guy pins, and the distance between the second and third is the distance between guy pins. These distances vary slightly for different tents and should be verified by actual experiment before permanently marking the ropes. To locate the position of guy pins after the first, the hood ring being held on the center pin, with the left hand hold the outer mark on the pin last set, with the right hand grasp the rope at the center mark and move the hand to the right so as to have both sections of the rope taut; the center mark is then over the position desired; the inner mark is over the position of the corresponding wall pin.

To pitch the tent, No. 1 places the tent pole on the ground, socket end against the door pin, pole perpendicular to the company street. No. 2 drives the center pin at the other extremity of the pole. No. 3 drives a wall pin on each side of and 1 foot from the door pin. No. 4 places the open tripod flat on the ground with its center near the center pin. The whole detachment then places the tent, fully opened, on the ground it is to occupy, the center at the center pin, the door at the door pin.

No. 8 holds the hood ring on the center pin, and superintends from that position. No. 1 stretches the hood rope over the right (facing the tent) wall pin and No. 2 drives the first guy pin at the middle mark. No. 1 marks the position of the guy pins in succession and No. 2 drives a pin lightly in each position as soon as marked. At the same time No. 5 inserts small pins in succession through the wall loops and places the pins in position against the inner mark on the hood rope, where they are partly driven by No. 6. No. 4 distributes large pins ahead of Nos. 1 and 2; No. 7, small pins ahead of Nos. 5 and 6; No. 3 follows Nos. 1 and 2 and drives the guy pins home. No. 7, after distributing his pins, takes an ax and drives home the pins behind Nos. 5 and 6. No. 4, after distributing his pins, follows No. 3 and loops the guy ropes over the pins.

Nos. 1, 2, and 3, the pins being driven, slip under the tent and place the pin of the pole through the tent and hood rings while No. 8 places the hood in position. Nos. 1, 2, and 3 then raise the pole to a vertical position and insert the end in the socket of the tripod; they then raise the tripod to its proper height, keeping the center of the tripod over the center pin; while they hold the pole vertical. Nos. 4, 5, 6, and 7 adjust four guy ropes, one in each quadrant of the tent, to hold the pole in its vertical position, and then the remaining guy ropes. As soon as these are adjusted the men inside drive a pin at each foot of the tripod if necessary to hold it in place.

The tent may also be pitched by four men. No. 4 holds the hood ring and superintends. After the tent is in position on the ground it is to occupy, the pins are distributed by Nos. 2 and 3. Number 3 takes the place of

TYPES OF LIGHT TENTS 81

Nos. 5 and 6 in placing the wall loop pins. After all the pins are placed they are driven home, all assisting.

This takes a long time to describe, but the thing is done in a jiffy.

TEEPEES.— The teepee (pronounced *tee*-pee) of the plains Indians was an admirable shelter for the country they roamed over. Being of conical shape, and erected on a set of inside poles meeting at the top and with their butts radiating in every direction, it was proof against anything but a tornado. A very small fire in the center sufficed to keep it warm, and the smoke was wafted out of a hole at the top by an ingenious arrangement of flaps set according to the direction of the wind, in combination with an inner curtain around the bottom of the teepee, a little higher than a man's head, with its lower edge confined like a sod-cloth. The draught, entering freely through the gaps between tent pegs, emerged at top of curtain, and was drawn " a-fluking " upward by the warm current of air from the fire.* It has been said that no white man can manage a fire in a teepee without smoking the occupants out. This is an error: I have done it myself; but I had the best of dry wood in plenty, and I gave that fire more attention than it deserved.

The beauty of the teepee is that there is no center pole in the way. However, it needs at least nine lodge poles, and they should be slender, stiff, and straight. This rules it out of consideration by campers generally. Remember, too, that the real Indian teepee was made of skins, impermeable to wind and proof against sparks. Under modern conditions, if you must have a fire in your tent, use a stove.

PYRAMIDAL TENTS.— For a party of only two or three, traveling light, in a region where trees and saplings are scarce, as on the plains, or the coast, or in the mountains above timber-line, and where storms

* For details and illustrations see Edward Cave's *The Boy's Camp Book*, pp. 31–33.

may be violent, there is nothing better than a pyramidal or " miner's " tent (Fig. 40). It requires only one pole, and but few pegs. It has more available ground space than a conical tent of equal cubic capacity. It is economical of cloth. Next to the cone, it is the most stable form of tent, and it sheds rain and snow better than any other. One man, without assistance, can set it up in a trice. It sets well on uneven ground, and is easy to trench.

Pyramidal tents may be had with walls; but they are not nearly so easy to erect as one without a wall,

Fig. 40.— Miner's Tent

and many more pegs must be carried. This shape is at its best in the plain miner's form of a size suitable for two or three men: namely, a 7 x 7 x 7 or a 9½ x 9½ x 8½ ft., weighing, in different materials, from 5¼ to 14 lbs. A jointed pole of ash will weigh about 4½ lbs. in 7-ft., or 5 lbs. in 8½ ft. length, and a dozen 9-inch steel tent pins about 2 lbs.

Since the only head-room in such a tent is directly under the peak, a center pole is constantly in the way. If a little extra weight is not prohibited, it is better to carry a pair of jointed shear poles that set up inside the tent, one on either side, like two legs

TYPES OF LIGHT TENTS 83

of a tripod. Of course, if poles can be found near camp, the tent may be erected on outside shears or tripod. For this purpose, or for suspending from

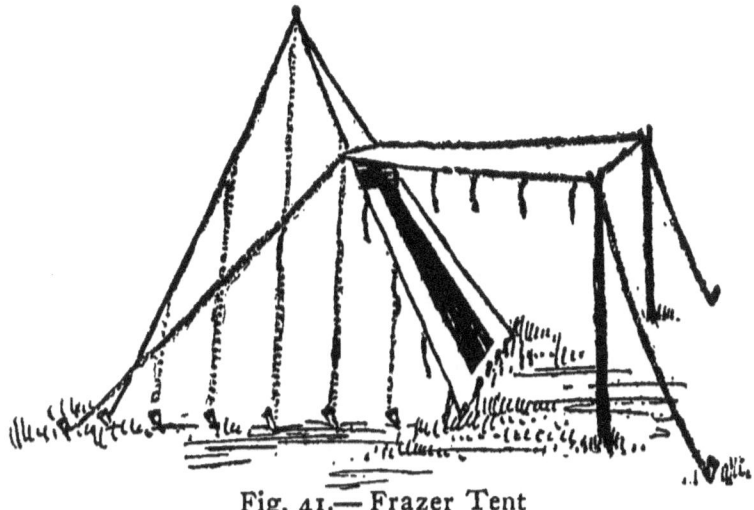

Fig. 41.—Frazer Tent

a limb, it should have a strong canvas loop sewed to the peak.

If the tent is to be used on a sandy coast or desert,

Fig. 42.—Marquee

or where insects are very bad, it is best made with a ground-cloth sewed fast to the bottom, or with a separate one that fits over a rather wide sod-cloth.

The Frazer tent (Fig. 41) has a small awning to shield the doorway, and a cloth "sill" that holds the bottom together. There is a window at the rear. Only a small screen is required at the doorway to keep out insects, yet the ventilation is good. It is not a cold-weather tent, as it cannot be thrown wide open, like a plain miner's tent, to receive the rays of a camp-fire.

Some canoeists in "civilized waters" prefer the marquee (Fig. 42), because it has more head-room than a pyramidal tent. It has spreaders attached to the center pole, like ribs of an umbrella, to extend the eaves, and guy ropes to stiffen them against wind; but in spite of these braces it is not very stable.

SEMI-PYRAMIDAL TENTS.— The lightest of enclosed tents that allow a man to stand upright under shelter is one shaped like a pyramid cut vertically in

Fig. 43.—George Tent

half. Since the pole, if one is used, stands in front, it is less in the way than the center pole of a pyramidal tent, but a guy or two must be run out for-

TYPES OF LIGHT TENTS 85

ward to brace it. A better rig, when poles can be cut on the spot, is an outside tripod (as an example see Fig. 66). If a small tree *happens* to stand conveniently on the camp site, the tent peak can be suspended from it.

A good example of this model is the George tent (Figs. 43, 44). For two men, its dimensions are 7 x 7 x 7 ft. In waterproofed "balloon silk" it weighs about 5¼ lbs., including pegs, and rolls up into a parcel 12 x 5 in., convenient for the knapsack. To pitch it: Peg down at 1 and 2 (Fig. 44),

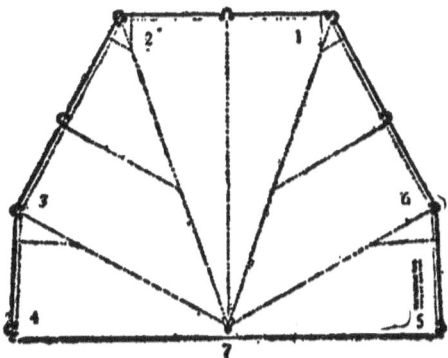

Fig. 44.—Layout of George Tent

carry 3 and 6 at right angles to 1 and 2, pull taut, peg down, insert pole, and raise; or suspend as above. This is done in one minute, if no poles have to be cut. A cheesecloth front is needed in fly time. In cold weather the front is left open, and the sloping back and sides reflect camp-fire heat down upon the sleepers.

Semi-pyramidal tents must be well guyed to stand up in a contrary wind. They are best suited to canoeists and forest cruisers.

MODIFIED PYRAMID TENT.—A shelter tent adaptable to varied conditions, and a very good model for "go light" trips, was recently described in *Outing* by its designer, R. S. Royce. His article is here reprinted in full, by permission of the publishers.

THE ROYCE TENT.

"Several seasons ago, desiring a very light tent for side trips, or, in fact, anywhere that a comfortable shelter was needed under conditions which would not permit of using a wall tent, one was designed which so well met all requirements and aroused so much interest among the outing brotherhood as to warrant presenting a detailed description of it.

Keeping away from the idea of a mere shelter to crawl under, and insisting on having something really comfortable in the event of several stormy days or nights, and with a spirit of comradeship that finds more fun in an outing shared by one or two friends, rather than alone, a tent was designed to afford room for two or three and high enough to sit, dress, or stand in.

This sounds like something too big for the ruck-sack, or a minor corner of a pack-basket, without crowding the other essentials of going light. However, it was accomplished at a weight of four pounds, making a package about 6 inches in diameter and 12 inches long for carrying; erected, it covers 56 square feet, as a closed half pyramid 7 feet 9 inches high and $7\frac{1}{2}$ feet square (Fig. 45). But this is not all, for it is extensible to a pyramid $7\frac{1}{2}$ x 13 feet, still 7 feet 9 inches high, but open at one end to the peak (Fig. 47); or it may be extended at the front of the half pyramid in a triangle the width of the tent, $7\frac{1}{2}$ x $2\frac{1}{2}$ feet, closing completely and increasing the length of the tent to 10 feet (Fig. 46). The objection is immediately presented that this is too large a tent for going even moderately light, but one may reasonably ask how much smaller package or lighter can you take, and get room for standing, sitting, and sleeping?

Considering this, first, as a half pyramid tent, $7\frac{1}{2}$ x $7\frac{1}{2}$ and $7\frac{3}{4}$ feet high; no form gives so much ground space with headroom from so little material as a pyramid; none sheds water better, nor resists wind so well, and none is simpler or quicker to erect.

The objections to a pyramid, of scant headroom and lost space on ground by rapidly sloping roofs; of presence of pole in the center, and of possible rain leak anywhere on the entrance side from peak to ground, are largely overcome by carrying the peak to $7\frac{3}{4}$ feet, giving more headroom and nearer perpendicular roofs; and by making the peak over the center of one side, instead of in the middle of the tent, giving a perpendicular entrance opening and no pole in the ground space. This gives better than a 45-degree pitch to the back roof and about 65-degree pitch to the side roofs; sheds rain well,

TYPES OF LIGHT TENTS 87

without necessary recourse to waterproofing, and allows of erection not only over a single upright pole, or suspension from overhanging branch, but also permits of setting up near any upright tree to which the peak-line may be extended diagonally upward in a general line with the slope of the back roof, thus generally eliminating the tent-pole problem.

Now, some of the arguments for this half pyramid be-

Fig. 45.— Front Upright   Fig. 46.— Wings Advanced
                                     2½ feet

 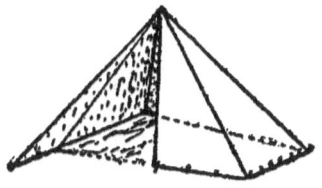

Fig. 47.— Wings Extended   Fig. 48.— One Wing Closed,
sheltering 7½ x 13 feet   One Open for Wind-break

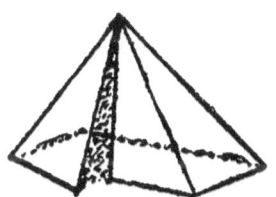

Fig. 49.— One Wing Partly
Extended

ROYCE TENT

ing given, another exists in the use of it with the front open (flaps turned away back on the side roofs), when it proves to be as truly a baker tent as the one usually described as such, and heats well with a fire in front.

The peculiar feature of this design is in the extra size and the form of the flaps, which make possible the triangular extension of the front for 2½ feet and still closing completely; and the further extension of the flaps, in plane with the side roofs, leaving an open-ended true pyramid 7½ x 13 feet, at an increase of only 2¹⁄₁₀₀ yards of material and not over one-quarter pound weight, over that required for the simple half pyramid 7½ feet square, barely closed.

This is worth while for most of us, for it permits of considerable extra room at practically no expense of weight or material, and allows of use in a variety of ways otherwise impossible: viz., the flaps extended completely, in plane with the side, leave an unroofed triangle, within which a fire may be built, allowing the camper to sit under either flap, and, protected, manipulate his frying pan, etc.; or one may be so extended and the other closed, affording a wind and rain protection with good ventilation, or one may be closed and the other extended 2½ feet (as for triangular front), leaving an open doorway without disclosing to view the interior, on account of the extra wide flaps (Fig. 48).

Another peculiarity is that in the event of finding only a short tent-pole and no tree to tie to, the tent may be set up with any height pole, under 7½ feet, and dress taut and trim, and, incidentally, cover a larger ground space, but, of course, at cost of less pitch to the roofs. The front being open clear to the peak, and all lines converging there, it is very easily cleared of insects by brush or smudge.

Of course, any pyramid tent, without perpendicular side walls, is free from the need of stakes, as only short pegs are necessary; when a quick shelter is needed, the peak-line over a branch or to a tree and pegs at the four corners will serve until it is convenient to place the intermediate pegs.

So many inquiries as to the details of this tent have been made, and so many requests for measurements and directions for making copies of it have occurred, that diagrams and measurements are here given.

Any tent-maker can reproduce it, for amateurs have, and it lends itself easily to those who enjoy making their own equipment.

The original is made of Lonsdale cambric and lightly waterproofed, and weighs only four pounds. It has had hard usage and has proved altogether satisfactory. Any thin material closely woven will serve, and that, too, without waterproofing, with roofs so steep.

Sheeting is practical, but would give a weight in excess of that quoted here.

DIRECTIONS FOR CUTTING AND SEWING

Material: Light, closely-woven cambric or other close material, 36 inches wide.

TYPES OF LIGHT TENTS 89

Dimensions: Seven feet 6 inches square on ground and 7 feet 9 inches high to peak.

Form: Half pyramid. Front "A," perpendicular; roof sloping three ways from pointed peak. Front flaps or wings are made to overlap considerably, and are longer than are necessary to reach the ground when closed perpendicularly.

LAYOUT FOR SIDE WALLS (FIG. 50)

Join two breadths 10′ 4″ long by edges, overlaid and double-stitched. Pin these out on floor smooth, and from point 1′ 9″ from end on one side to point same distance from other end of other side pin down a cord tight; close at either side of cord pin or baste a narrow tape, leaving

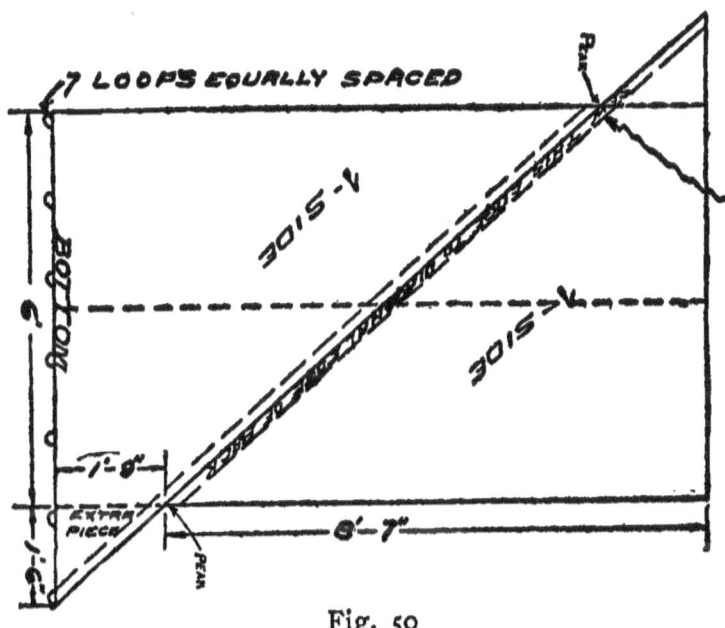

Fig. 50

tapes which cross the edges about two feet longer. Stitch these tapes down and divide goods in line between tapes. Sew to 1′ 9″ edge the selvage edge of a triangle 1′ 9″ by 1′ 6″ and sew tape to bias edge. These two triangles are the two side roofs.

LAYOUT OF MATERIAL FOR BACK (FIG. 51)

Pin out smooth one breadth 13′ long, and between points 2′ 2½″ from each end on opposite side edges draw line or pin tight cord and sew tapes either side of line, leaving tapes which cross the edges two feet longer. Against

90 CAMPING AND WOODCRAFT

these edges and to the tapes sew triangles 2' 2" by 9". Divide the goods between the tapes. These two triangles to be turned with selvage edges together and when joined form the back roof.

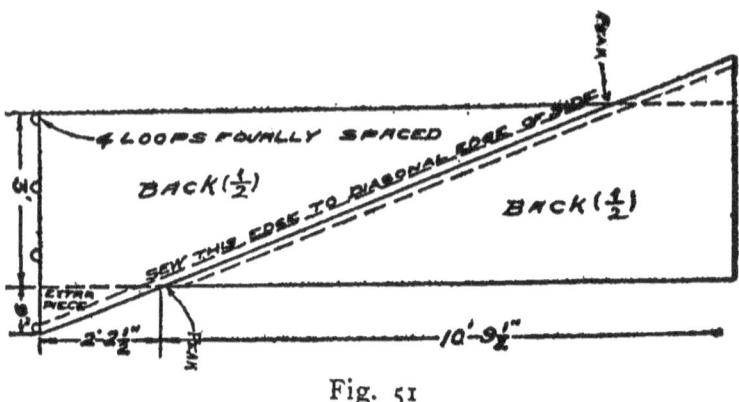

Fig. 51

This is to permit extending the front 2½ feet triangularly and still closing it tight; also allowing the wings to be extended 5 feet 6 inches in plane with the side roofs, producing a pyramid 13 feet by 7½ feet open at one end to the peak.

LAYOUT OF MATERIAL FOR WINGS (FIG. 52)

Pin out one breadth 8' 7½" long. From one corner to point on opposite side, and 3' 10½" from the opposite end,

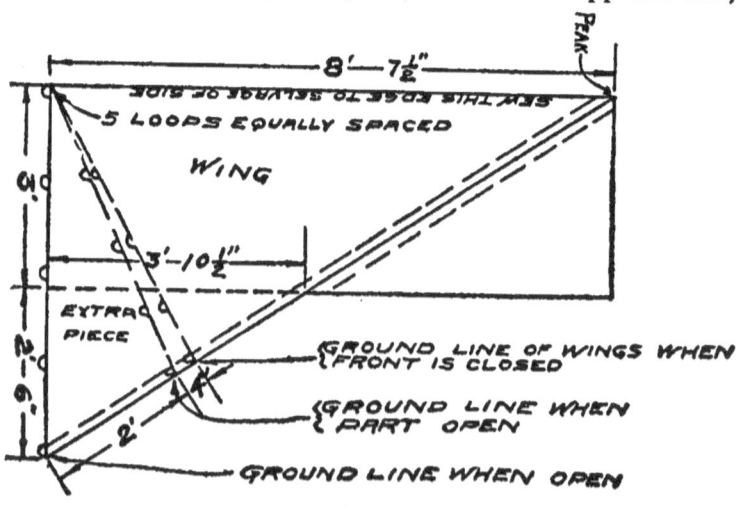

Fig. 52

draw line and sew tape on side of line toward larger piece, leaving tape about 4' 9" longer than reaching to the sel-

TYPES OF LIGHT TENTS   91

vage edge.. Against this 3′ 10½″ selvage edge sew triangle cut from other side of line, using right angled triangle 3′ 10½″ by 2′ 6″, binding bias edge with overhanging tape. This makes only one flap or wing. Duplicate.

HOW TO SET IT UP

Join to each diagonal edge of the back one of the diagonal edges of each sidepiece; and to the selvage edge of each side-piece a selvage edge of one of the wings.

Close the peak around a ¾-inch metal ring. Leave front wings open clear to peak. Turn in ground edge a little all around and attach strong tape loops for pegs at corners and five between on each side and back and four on bottom of each wing; also on a line from lower attached corner of each wing to a point 2 feet up from bottom of free edge of each wing put four loops on outside and again on a line from corner to a point 4 inches still higher four more loops. These loops are for pegging down wings in the three positions of extension in plane with sides, in partial extension, and when closed with perpendicular front.

If sod-cloth is desired, a breadth of cloth 7½ feet long split in three strips will make about a 10-inch sod cloth if attached to lower edge of sides and back before putting on a heavy tape which will finish the lower edge. No sod-cloth is needed at front as wings will turn in sufficient in all positions except when fully extended.

For light tent, flap-ties are best of tape and should be spaced along the free edges of each wing and also at line where edges fall when overlapped so as to make front bottom line of tent measure 7½ feet. Wings need hem or tape for free edges. A ⅛-inch braided cord 15 feet long is needed from peak where it can be attached to a metal ring just too large to pull through the peak ring. From this inside ring it is well to lead like cords down to the back corners of the tent and out through eyelet-holes through the sod-cloth just under the corner peg-loops. These two add to the trimness of tent, especially if of very light material, and can be run to front corners as well, if desired.

MATERIAL

36-inch wide stuff ....20½ yards.
½-inch tape ....75 feet.
¾-inch tape for bottom edge ....23 feet.
⅛ cord, peak 15 feet   }...................40 feet.
⅛ cord 2 back seams 25 ∫

92 CAMPING AND WOODCRAFT

WEDGE OR "A" TENTS.—The wedge tent is an "old stand-by" for those who go where portages must be made or camp shifted every day or two. It is light, cheap, easy to pitch with or without poles, and is well adapted to uneven ground.

In wooded country the camper often may find two trees or saplings from which to stretch a rope, above the level of his head, where it is out of the way. The tent is then pegged out and suspended by its ridge from the rope. This is a quick and satisfac-

Fig. 53.— Wedge Tent, Outside Ridge Rope

tory "set" in level forest. On rough ground it may be hard to find a place for the tent with trees growing just where you want them.

Common wedge tents are made with rope running through, under the ridge. The ridge then sags in what engineers call a catenary curve. This makes the sides sag inward, reducing the roominess all around, and the wind makes matters worse. A better plan is to have tapes on the outside of the ridge (Fig. 53), run the rope high and taut, then tie the

TYPES OF LIGHT TENTS 93

middle tapes closer to the rope than the outer ones.

The bottom of a wedge tent with rope ridge should be pegged in such way that the sides will be in arcs of a circle, instead of straight along the ground (Fig. 54): this takes up slack. The ground-cloth, if there

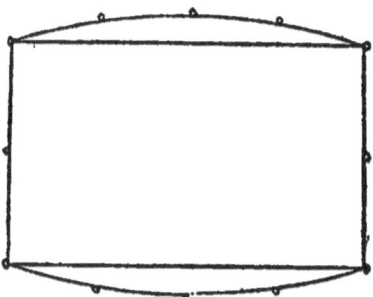

Fig. 54.— Pegging Bottom of Tent

is one, should be cut accordingly. The thinner the material, the more a tent will sag when erected without a ridge pole. Partially to obviate this, and to stiffen the tent in a gale, it is a good scheme to attach parrels (Figs. 55, 58) to ropes or strong seams in the sides. These pull outward and turn the

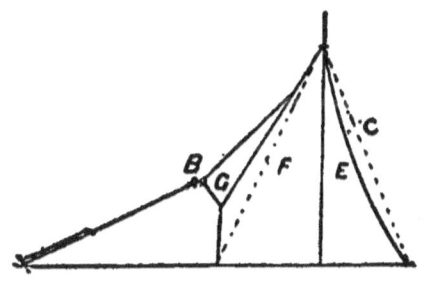

Fig. 55.— Side Parrels

wedge into a semi-wall tent. Referring to Fig 55, C shows the theoretically straight side of a wedge tent and E the actual inward sag from ridge droop and wind pressure. The dotted line F indicates the opposite side without parrels, and A is the same wall held out and made taut by the parrels BG. The illustration is adapted from one by T. H. Holding, of London.

Where no trees stand conveniently, a forked stake can be placed at each end of the tent, the rope run over the crotches and staked out as a guy fore and aft; but the front guy is much in the way. It is better to set up shears and a ridge pole, as in Fig. 11. Often a natural support can be found for one end of the pole.

When traveling where there are few or no trees, it will be necessary to carry jointed poles of wood, steel, or bamboo. There may as well be three of these, so that two can be straddled to leave the doorway free. A jointed ridge pole makes the tent stand trimmer; but, if all that weight can be carried, the party had better take a wall tent and be comfortable.

Wedge tents are not recommended in sizes larger than about 7 x 7 x 7 ft. Weights of a few examples are as follows:

TANALITE, EMERALITE
$4\frac{1}{3}$ x 7 x 5.   6 lbs.
7   x 7 x 7.   8 lbs.
Balloon silk a bit heavier.

EXTRA LIGHT GREEN
$4\frac{3}{4}$ x $6\frac{1}{2}$ x 5.   5   lbs.
$6\frac{1}{2}$ x $6\frac{1}{2}$ x 7. $6\frac{1}{2}$ lbs.

TANO, NILO
$4\frac{1}{2}$ x $7\frac{1}{2}$ x 5. $4\frac{1}{2}$ lbs.
$7\frac{1}{2}$ x $7\frac{1}{2}$ x 7. $7\frac{1}{4}$ lbs.

GREEN EGYPTIAN.
5   x $7\frac{1}{3}$ x 5. $6\frac{1}{2}$ lbs.
$7\frac{1}{3}$ x $7\frac{1}{3}$ x 7. $9\frac{1}{2}$ lbs.

The alpine tent shown in Fig. 58 was designed by Edward Whymper, and has been used by many other famous mountaineers, such as Sir Martin Conway, Douglas Freshfield, Dr. Hunter Workman, and the Duke of the Abruzzi, for exploration among the highest mountains of the globe. It is made of Willesden canvas or drill, with a sewed-in groundsheet, and a " sill " at the door, to cut out draughts and ground chill. Few pegs are required. When the floor is stretched taut, every peg finds its proper place. The poles form shears at each end, over

TYPES OF LIGHT TENTS 95

which the ridge rope is guyed out fore and aft. This is a very stanch "set." The standard size is 7 x 7 x 6½ ft.

Fig. 56.— Whymper Alpine Tent

MODIFIED WEDGE TENTS.— An angular lap or extension may be added to the lower edge of each door flap to serve as a wind shield for a cooking fire in bad weather. If the rear end of a wedge tent is made rounded instead of square, extra room for duffle is provided, with little additional weight.

The Hudson Bay tent (Fig 57) saves weight by

Fig. 57.— Hudson Bay Tent

having both ends rounded and the ridge short. It does not sag so much as a regular wedge tent, and is more stable in a wind, but affords less head-room.

96 CAMPING AND WOODCRAFT

To get more head-room in a tent without walls, the Ross alpine tent (Fig. 58) is fitted over a sectional bent frame. It has side parrels, and a door at each end. The dimensions are 7 x 7 x 6½ ft.

Fig. 58.— Ross Alpine Tent

SEPARABLE SHELTER TENTS.— When men travel in pairs, going light, it is a good plan for each to carry a "shelter-half," adequate to protect him if he should become separated from his companion, and so fitted with ridge flap and tapes that it can quickly be attached to its mate to form a low, broad wedge tent.

Fig. 59.— Separable Shelter Tent

The old-fashioned army shelter half was merely a rectangle of 7½- or 8-oz. duck, two of which, buttoned together, made an A-shaped roof open at both

TYPES OF LIGHT TENTS 97

ends. It was little protection against shifting winds. In the present military shelter tent, the halves, when joined, close at the rear end, which is lower than the front. A rifle stood up at the front is all the support needed, and it can instantly be recovered for emergency use by kicking the butt free.

For hikers, etc., a good separable tent consists of two lean-tos that close at both ends when joined (Fig. 59). Sometimes these halves are made with a 12 to 18-inch wall (Fig 60). Each half should be

Fig. 60.— Shelter Half with Wall

about 7 ft. long, 3½ or 3¾ ft. wide, and 4¼ ft. high, weighing about 3½ lbs.

SHELTER CLOTHS.— For side trips from camp, a simple rectangle of thin, closely woven waterproof cloth, with grommets and tapes, is all one needs in moderate weather. Set it up at an angle, facing the fire, and, if need be, thatch one or both sides with evergreen boughs or other windbreak. The cloth is useful as a "tarp" about camp and as a wrap for packs on the trail. One that I use, of Tanalite, 7 x 9 ft., weighs 2½ lbs. Set up with a 9-ft. slant, it stands 6 ft. high in front and shelters 7 x 5 ft. of ground. A small pyramidal mosquito bar should be taken along in summer.

TARPAULIN TENT.— A larger shelter cloth cut as in Fig. 61, the seams reinforced with tapes, beckets for tent pins added along three sides, and door tapes along the other, as indicated, has many uses. It serves, as one wishes, either for a simple lean-to shelter, a wedge tent open at both ends, a semi-pyramidal enclosed tent, a dining fly, a tarpaulin, a ground-sheet, a pack-cloth, or an emergency sail on a

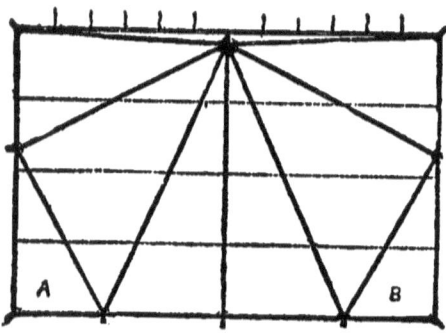

Fig. 61.— Tarpaulin Tent

boat. Referring to the diagram, it will be seen that when the triangular corners *A* and *B* are tucked under we have practically the George tent, and the cloth is erected in the same way.

These "tarp" tents are furnished by outfitters ready-made, in various materials, and in sizes from 7½ x 12 to 10 x 13 ft., making semi-pyramidal shelters from 4¾ x 9 x 6 to 7 x 7 x 6½ ft., waterproofed, weighing from 3½ to 6¾ lbs. Full directions for making one at home are given in *The Boy Scout's Hike Book* by Edward Cave.

BAKER TENT.— For a light tent in the hunting season, East or South, I prefer one with a shed-roof, rear wall, and a front that can be closed when one is away for the day, or when a contrary wind springs up with driving rain. Usually the front is left open, and in cold weather a good fire with back-logs of

TYPES OF LIGHT TENTS 99

green wood is kept going all night, about five feet in front of the tent. Of course, this takes a lot of wood, a good-sized hardwood tree being consumed in a single night, and the labor of chopping is rather severe to any one but a good axeman; but the work is well repaid by the exquisite comfort of lying before the blazing backlogs on a cold night, warm as toast, and breathing deeply the fresh air of the forest. Such a tent is never damp and cheerless, as closed tents are apt to be. The heat rays are reflected downward by the sloping roof, drying the ground and warming one's bed in a comparatively short time.

Fig. 62.—Baker Tent

A baker tent may be set up on shears (Fig. 62), or on stakes (Fig. 63), or on a pole nailed from one tree to another, or in various other ways suggested by the location. At the rear a stake is driven for each corner guy and a pole laid outside it, on the ground, to which the other guys are made fast; or a frame is made.

If the door is stretched straight forward as shown in these illustrations, it will prevent having a fire close in front where it should be. Ordinarily the flap is thrown backward over the roof when a camp-fire is going. A long pole on each side of the tent, run diagonally upward from rear to front, will lift the awning high enough to be out of the way. However, I prefer to have the door-flap separate, and so fitted with grommets or eyelets that it can be attached either to the top or to one side of the tent, as preferred. In warm weather, when no all-night fire is needed, it may be hung from the top as an awning, and the tent may be closed up by it when the occupants are away; but on nights when a fire is kept going the flap should be stretched forward vertically from the windward side of the tent front, so as to

Fig. 63.— Camp-fire Tent

check the draught from that direction, and the fire should be built close to the tent, the front of which is left wide open.

A fall of snow on the roof of an ordinary baker tent may cause trouble, unless an outside framework has been built and thatched with browse. The camp-fire tent (Fig. 63) has a steeper roof, which sheds rain and snow much better, and it affords more head-room without increased weight. This is the best pattern of baker tent. Sizes and weights of some examples are as follows, the dimensions being width, depth, height of front, center, and back, in turn:

TYPES OF LIGHT TENTS

EXTRA LIGHT GREEN
6½ x 6½ x 6 – 7   – 2.   8 lbs.
8   x 6½ x 6 – 7½ – 2½.   10 lbs.

GREEN EGYPTIAN
7⅓ x 7⅓ x 6 – 7½ – 2½.   11 lbs.
9¾ x 7⅓ x 6 – 7½ – 2½.   13 lbs.

GREEN WPF. STANDARD
7⅙ x 7⅙ x 6 – 7½ – 2½.   14   lbs.
9½ x 7⅙ x 6 – 7½ – 2½.   16½ lbs.

Weight in other materials may be judged from tables previously given of other patterns of tents.

One advantage of the baker or camp-fire type is that, in rainy weather, one has a dry, open space to move around in, and he can cook under shelter by building a *small* fire under the awning and feeding it a little at a time.

Such a tent is good for commissary quarters in fixed camp, as it is open and handy to work under. It is not recommended for parties that move frequently, nor for " bad fly-country."

But in a cool climate, where wood is plentiful and mosquitoes scarce, then for me the open lean-to or baker tent, before a hardwood fire, with the free breath of the forest filling my lungs! Let the sleet drive; let the mercury go where it listeth; my axe is my weapon against old Jack Frost. For me, a hunter's camp without a good log fire, burning all the night, is just no camp at all.

But understand: all my camping has been where I was free as an Indian to do with the forest whatever I pleased. I could cut down and burn any tree, any number of them — sweet birch, hickory, white ash, sugar maple, anything — heedless of what such timber might be worth if ever it got to market. I could burn choice wood when I did not need fire; burn just for the incense and comradry of it all.

Not so the average camper of to-day. He must cull old dead no-account stuff that he finds on the ground — peradventure he even be permitted to light a fire in the woods at all. Alas! the lean-to, and the hissing red logs that cheered us and kept us cosy through the long frosty nights under the hunter's moon.

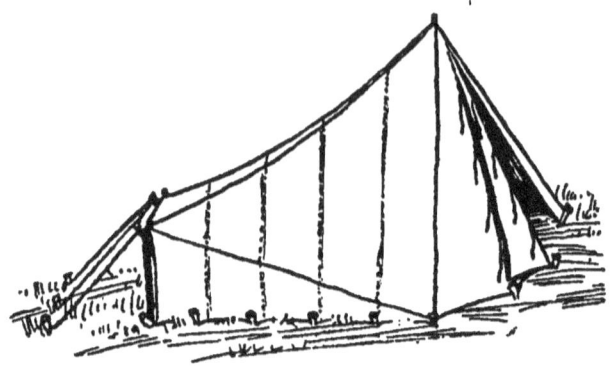

Fig. 64.— Canoe Tent with Pole

CANOE TENTS.— The old pattern canoe tent (Fig. 64) is erected with a single pole. The front is semi-circular, and the strain from it, pulling forward, does away with the need of a guy rope, unless

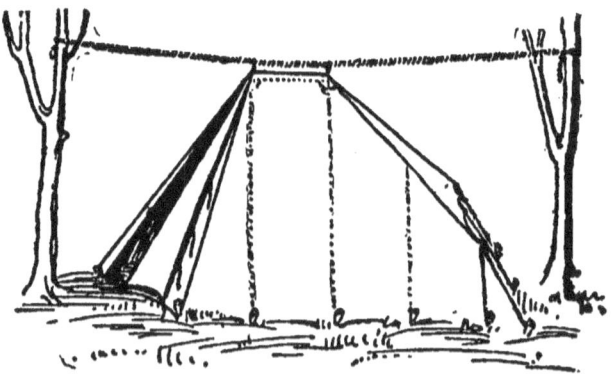

Fig. 65.— Canoe Tent with Ridge

the whole front is left open to the camp-fire, in which case two guys are run forward on either side of the fire.

A canoe tent with short ridge is shown in Fig. 65, suspended by a rope. When this pattern is used in

TYPES OF LIGHT TENTS 103

the open it is erected on a pair of shears, as in Fig. 68.

These models are advertised as "quick and easy to erect," but a glance at the cuts will show that they take too many pegs and stakes to really belong in that category. Still they are very popular, especially the one with ridge. Dimensions (not including the rounded front), and weights in various materials, are tabulated below. Other sizes and cloths are supplied by outfitters. The two patterns do not vary noticeably in weight.

TANALITE, EMERALITE

7 x 4½ x 6 − 1½ 7¼ lbs.
7⅓ x 7⅓ x 7 − 2. 10¼ lbs.
8¾ x 7⅓ x 7½ − 3. 12½ lbs.

TANO, NILO

7½ x 4½ x 6 − 1½. 5½ lbs.
7½ x 7½ x 7 − 2. 8½ lbs.
9 x 9 x 7½ − 2½. 11 lbs.

KIRO, DRIKI

7 x 4¾ x 7 − 2. 9¼ lbs.
7 x 7 x 7 − 2. 11¾ lbs.
9½ x 9½ x 8½ − 3. 17 lbs.

EXTRA LIGHT GREEN

6½ x 4¾ x 7 − 2. 6½ lbs.
6½ x 6½ x 7 − 2. 7¾ lbs.
8 x 6½ x 7½ − 3. 10 lbs.

GREEN EGYPTIAN

7⅓ x 4¾ x 7 − 2. 7½ lbs.
7⅓ x 7⅓ x 7 − 2. 10¼ lbs.
9¾ x 7⅓ x 7½ − 3. 13 lbs.

GREEN WPF. STANDARD

7⅙ x 4¾ x 7 − 2. 9½ lbs.
7⅙ x 7⅙ x 7 − 2. 13 lbs.
9½ x 7⅙ x 7½ − 3. 15¾ lbs.

"COMPAC" TENT.— This is a very light tent for pedestrians, canoeists, or others who want to get along with the least practicable outfit. For its size and weight, I have found it a good thing. It has a floor sewed to its walls; so, when the door flaps are snapped shut, nothing can get in. You can defy not only rain and wind, but bugs, flies, spiders, scorpions, snakes, skunks, wood rats, and all other vermin. Ventilation is provided by four little windows covered with bobbinet, with storm flaps that raise or lower from the inside. The cloth is very closely woven, and waterproofed. It may be had in tan, green, or the natural yellowish-white of unbleached cotton.

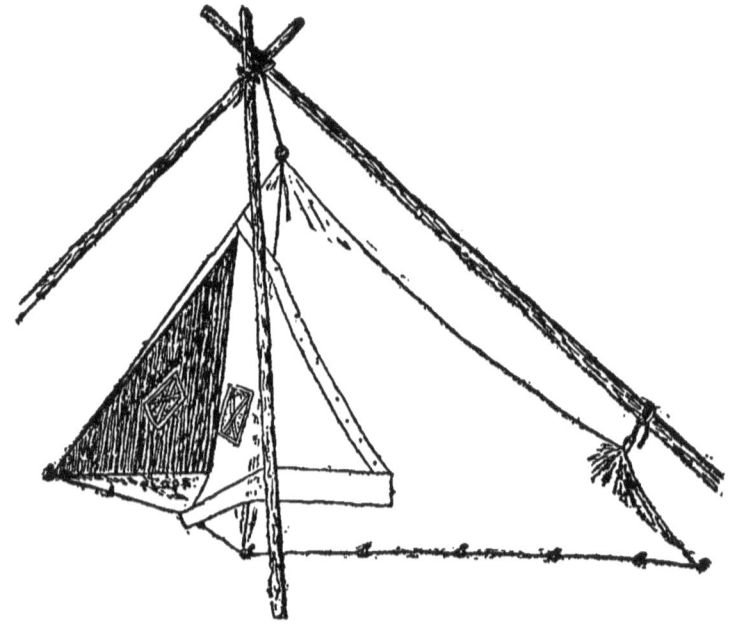

Fig. 66.— Compact Tent

This tent is easy to set up on any kind of ground. If a sapling happens to stand in the right place, peg out the corners of the floor and suspend the peak by its cord from a convenient limb. Otherwise, pitch with shears in front and a pole slanting backward from them, as shown in Fig. 66. Only a few pegs are required.

Being so low and so well braced, this pocket house will stand up against a gale that might overthrow wall tents and send their flies a-kiting. In cold

TYPES OF LIGHT TENTS 105

weather it can be warmed by radiation from a camp fire in front. It will accommodate two men and their duffle. Of course it is only high enough to sit up in, but that is all the room one needs on such trips, and it is best for a cloth floored tent anyhow, for it balks muddy feet. However, I do not like a sewed-in floor, for general camping. The reasons are given at the end of this chapter.

I have called this clever contrivance a "pocket-house." It deserves the name, being waterproof, wind-proof, bug-proof, ventilated, sheltering a space

Fig. 67.— Snow Tent

8 x 6 x 4–2 feet, and yet it rolls up into a 16 x 4-inch parcel, and weighs, with its rope, only 3¾ pounds.

SNOW TENT.— This pattern (Fig. 67) gets its name from the steepness of its slopes which makes it shed snow instead of holding it. With front flaps spread as shown, it can be warmed by a fire in front. The back has a low wall, and there is a short ridge; otherwise its qualities are those of a semi-pyramidal tent. It is made in sizes from 6½ x 6½ x 7½–2½ ft. to 9¾ x 9¾ x 7½–2½ ft., and the weights, in different materials, run from 7½ to 17 lbs.

106 CAMPING AND WOODCRAFT

The same model, with sewed-in floor, closed front, an oval door of bobbinet, and a ventilator, is known as the "explorer's" tent (Fig. 68). It is perfectly insect-proof. For the tropics a fly is added. A

Fig. 68.— Explorer's Tent

large number of these tents have been used by the Alaska Boundary Survey and by other scientific expeditions. The weights complete are only from $1\frac{1}{2}$ to 2 lbs. greater than for same size of the snow tent.

INSECT-PROOF TENTS.— I have spoken several times of the desirability of good ventilation in a tent (the smaller the tent, the stuffier it will be if tightly enclosed) and of the necessity of protection from insects in their season. The reader who has followed me thus far can readily understand the construction of an ideal tent, in these respects, for countries like Alaska, central Canada, the tropics, and other places where poisonous or germ-bearing insects abound. I quote from Emerson Hough:

"The most perfect mosquito tent I ever saw I ran across this summer for the first time. It was made in a western city after a design said to have been invented by a member of the Geological Survey in Alaska. If it will work in Alaska it will anywhere. The material was not of heavy duck, but a light Egyptian cotton sometimes called

TYPES OF LIGHT TENTS 107

'balloon silk.' In size 7 x 7, very high in the ridge and on the walls, the tent in its bag weighs only about 12 pounds. A light waterproof floor is sewn into it. Both ends are sewn into it. On each side there are two large netted windows, affording abundant ventilation. There are flaps arranged for these windows which can be buttoned down in case of rain.

In each end of this tent there is yet another large window for ventilation. The roof projects three or four inches all around over the walls, making eaves which keep the water out of the open windows in case of rain. The front door is not a door at all, but a hole, round, and not triangular. This hole is fitted with a sleeve, like the trap of a fyke-net, the sleeve, or funnel, itself being made of light material. You crawl through this hole and, so to speak, pull it in after you and tie a knot in it. At least there is a puckering string by which you can close the bag which makes the entrance of the tent. Once inside it, you have a large, roomy house in which you can stand up with comfort, lay down your beds in comfort, and do light housekeeping. No mosquito can get at you unless you brought it in on your clothes. In case you have done that you can put a wet sock into operation. At first you will think the tent a little close, but soon will see that the ventilation is perfect." (*Out of Doors*).

SEWED-IN FLOORS.— On the other hand, there are objections to a sewed-in floor. Muddy boots make it odious, and hob-nailed ones are its ruin. Every bit of snow that you track in will help make a puddle. A lantern is dangerous in such structures as the last two we have been considering, and one must be very careful about matches. In the case of the explorer's tent, which lacks the windows of the other, you can't cook inside, even on a vapor stove, without risk of disaster, and certainty of steam condensing where it cannot escape. Even the moisture of one's breath amounts to a good deal in the course of a night, and in cold weather it will keep the interior of such a tent constantly damp or coated with rime. As for the sewed-in floor serving as a mattress cover, to keep your bed of browse or leaves in place, if that bed is thick enough for comfort, the tent will not set well, and there will be too much strain on the pegs and seams.

So, anywhere but in extremely bad mosquito country, or on bleak and windy mountains, it is better to have a wide sod-cloth around the bottom of the tent, and a separate ground-sheet, overlapping, that you can roll aside when you want a bare spot, and can take out and wash when it needs it.

CHAPTER VII
LIGHT CAMP EQUIPMENT

The problem of what to take on a trip resolves itself chiefly into a question of transportation. If the party can travel by wagon, and intends to go into fixed camp, then almost anything can be carried along — trunks, chests, big wall tents and poles, cots, mattresses, pots and pans galore, camp stove, kerosene, mackintoshes and rubber boots, plentiful changes of clothing, books, folding bath-tubs — what you will. Such things are right and proper if you do not intend to move often from place to place. But in any case beware of impedimenta that will be forever in the way and seldom or never used.

It is quite another matter to fit out a man or a party for wilderness travel. First, and above all, be plain in the woods. In a far way you are emulating those grim heroes of the past who made the white man's trails across this continent. We seek the woods to escape civilization for a time, and all that suggests it. Let us sometimes broil our venison on a sharpened stick and serve it on a sheet of bark. It tastes better. It gets us closer to Nature, and closer to those good old times when every American was considered " a man for a' that " if he proved it in a manful way. And there is a pleasure in achieving creditable results by the simplest means. When you win your own way through the wilds with axe and rifle you win at the same time the imperturbability of a mind at ease with itself in any emergency by flood or field. Then you feel that you have red blood in your veins, and that it is good to be free and out of doors. It is one of the blessings of wilderness life that it shows us how few things we need in order to be perfectly happy.

Let me not be misunderstood as counseling anybody to "rough it" by sleeping on the bare ground and eating nothing but hardtack and bacon. Only a tenderfoot will parade a scorn of comfort and a taste for useless hardships. As "Nessmuk" says: "We do not go to the woods to rough it; we go to smooth it — we get it rough enough in town. But let us live the simple, natural life in the woods, and leave all frills behind."

An old campaigner is known by the simplicity and fitness of his equipment. He carries few "fixings," but every article has been well tested and it is the best that his purse can afford. He has learned by hard experience how steep are the mountain trails and how tangled the undergrowth and downwood in the primitive forest. He has learned, too, how to fashion on the spot many substitutes for "boughten" things that we consider necessary at home.

The art of going "light but right" is hard to learn. I never knew a camper who did not burden himself, at first, with a lot of kickshaws that he did not need in the woods; nor one who, if he learned anything, did not soon begin to weed them out; nor even a veteran who ever quite attained his own ideal of lightness and serviceability. Probably "Nessmuk" came as near to it as any one, after he got that famous ten-pound canoe. He said that his load, including canoe, knapsack, blanket-bag, extra clothing, hatchet, rod, and two days' rations, "never exceeded twenty-six pounds; and I went prepared to camp out any and every night." This, of course, was in summer.

In the days when game was plentiful and there were no closed seasons our frontiersmen thought nothing of making long expeditions into the unknown wilderness with no equipment but what they carried on their own persons, to wit: a blanket, rifle, ammu-

LIGHT CAMP EQUIPMENT

nition, flint and steel, tomahawk, knife, an awl, a spare pair of moccasins, perhaps, a small bag of jerked venison, and another of parched corn, ground to a coarse meal, which they called "rockahominy" or "coal flour." Their tutors in woodcraft often traveled lighter than this. An Indian runner would strip to his G-string and moccasins, roll up in his small blanket a pouch of rockahominy, and, armed only with a bow and arrows, he would perform journeys that no mammal but a wolf could equal. General Clark said that when he and Lewis, with their men, started afoot from the mouth of the Columbia River on their return trip across the continent, their total store of articles for barter with the Indians for horses and food could have been tied up in two handkerchiefs. But they were woodsmen, every inch of them.

Now it is not needful nor advisable for a camper in our time to suffer hardships from stinting his supplies. It is foolish to take insufficient bedding, or to rely upon a diet of pork, beans, and hardtack, in a country where game may be scarce. The knack is in striking a happy medium between too much luggage and too little. *Ideal outfitting is to have what we want, when we want it, and not to be bothered with anything else.* A pair of scales are good things to have at hand when one is making up his packs. Scales of another kind will then fall from his eyes. He will note how the little, unconsidered trifles mount up; how every bag or tin adds weight. Now let him imagine himself toiling uphill under an August sun, or forging through thickety woods, over rocks and roots and fallen trees, with all this stuff on his back. Again, let him think of a chill, wet night ahead, and of what he will really need to keep himself warm, dry, and well ballasted amidships. Balancing these two prospects one against the other, he cannot go far wrong in selecting his outfit.

In his charming book, *The Forest,* Stewart Edward White has spoken of that amusing foible, com-

CAMPING AND WOODCRAFT

mon to us all, which compels even an experienced woodsman to lug along some pet trifle that he does not need, but which he would be miserable without. The more absurd this trinket is, the more he loves it. One of my camp-mates for five seasons carried in his "packer" a big chunk of rosin. When asked what it was for, he confessed: "Oh, I'm going to get a fellow to make me a turkey-call, some day, and this is to make it 'turk.'" Jew's-harps, camp-stools, shaving-mugs, alarm-clocks, derringers that nobody could hit anything with, and other such trifles have been known to accompany very practical men who were otherwise in light marching order. If you have some such thing that you know you can't sleep well without, stow it religiously in your kit. It is your "medicine," your amulet against the spooks and bogies of the woods. It will dispel the koosy-oonek. (If you don't know what that means, ask an Eskimo. He may tell you that it means sorcery, witchcraft — and so, no doubt, it does to the children of nature; but to us children of guile it is the spell of that imp who hides our pipes, steals our last match, and brings rain on the just when they want to go fishing.)

No two men have the same "medicine." Mine is a porcelain teacup, minus the handle. It cost me much trouble to find one that would fit snugly inside the metal cup in which I brew my tea. Many's the time it has all but slipped from my fingers and dropped upon a rock; many's the gibe I have suffered for its dear sake. But I do love it. Hot indeed must be the sun, tangled the trail and weary the miles, before I forsake thee, O my frail, cool-lipped, but ardent teacup!

There is something to be said in favor of individual outfits, every man going completely equipped and quite independent of the others. It is one of the delights of single-handed canoeing, whether you go alone or cruise in squadron, that every man is fixed to suit himself. Then if any one carries too

LIGHT CAMP EQUIPMENT 113

much or too little, or cooks badly, or is too lazy to be neat, or lacks forethought in any way, he alone suffers the penalty; and this is but just. On the other hand, if one of the cruisers' outfits comes to grief, the others can help him out, since all the eggs are not in one basket. I like to have a complete camping outfit of my own, just big enough for two men, so that I can dispense a modest hospitality to a chance acquaintance, or take with me a comrade who, through no fault of his own, turns up at the last moment; but I want this outfit to be so light and compact that I can easily handle it myself when I am alone. Then I am always "fixed," and always independent, come good or ill, blow high or low.

Still, it is the general rule among campers to have "company stores." In so far as this means only those things that all use in common, such as tent, utensils, tools, and provisions, it is well enough; but it should be a point of honor with each and every man to carry for himself a complete kit of personal necessities, down to the least detail. As for company stores, everybody should bear a hand in collecting and packing them. To saddle this hard and thankless job on one man, merely because he is experienced and a willing worker, is selfish. Depend upon it, the fellow who " hasn't time " to do his share of the work before starting will be the very one to shirk in camp.

AXE.— A full-sized axe should be carried, in cold weather, if means of transportation permit. Its head need not weigh over 3 or 3½ pounds, but let the handle be of standard 36-inch length for a full-arm sweep. A single-bitt is best for campers, as the poll is useful for driving stakes, knocking off pine knots, to rive timber (striking with a mallet), and as an anvil (bitt stuck in a log or stump).

With this one tool a good axeman can build anything that is required in the wilderness, and he can quickly fell and log-up a tree large enough to keep a hot fire before his lean-to throughout the night.

If an axe is bought ready handled, see that the helve is of young growth hickory, straight grained, and free from knots. Sight along the back of the helve to see if it is straight in line with the eye of the axe, then turn it over and see if the edge of the axe ranges exactly in line with the center of the hilt (rear end of handle), as it should, and that the hilt is at right angles to the center of the eye. A good chopper is as critical about the heft and hang of his axe as a shooter is about the balance of his gun. If the handle is straight, score a $2\frac{1}{2}$-foot rule on it, in inches. Get the axe ground by a careful workman. The store edge is not thin enough or keen enough. One cannot be too careful in selecting this indispensable tool: some grades are of the best steel and hand-forged, but many others are just "bum."

Have a leather sheath for the axe-head, to prevent accidents when traveling. Some are made with strap attached for carrying on one's back, but this is needless: in the few cases that you carry an axe that way, tie it to outside of pack with a string.

An axe lying around camp has a fatal attraction for men who do not know how to use it. Not that they will do much chopping with it; but somebody will pick it up, make a few bungling whacks at a projecting root, or at a stick lying flat on the ground, drive the blade through into the earth and pebbles, and leave the edge nicked so that it will take an hour's hard work to put it in decent order again. And the fellow who does this is the one who could not sharpen an axe to save his life. It never seems to occur to him that an axe is of no use unless its edge is kept keen, or that the best way to ruin it is to strike it into the ground, or that a chopping block will prevent that. You may loan your last dollar to a friend; but never loan him your axe, unless you are certain that he knows how to use it.

LIGHT CAMP EQUIPMENT

If a full-grown axe cannot be carried, then take a hatchet with handle as long as practicable (see Chapter X).

OTHER TOOLS.— A small spade, or an army entrenching tool, is a handy implement about camp. One outfitter has produced a good thing in this line which he calls a trekking spade. The handle is detachable. In shoveling hot coals at the fire-place, work quickly, so as not to draw the temper of the steel.

A useful tool, when it can be carried, is one I found recently in the catalogue of a certain mail-order house: a nail-cutting compass saw (just like any compass saw except that it is tempered for nails, sheet metal, etc., as well as wood), with 12-inch blade and weighing only 5 ounces. It can be used, too, in butchering big game, saving your axe edge. A folding saw, sold by sporting-goods dealers, will do well enough in most outfits.

If you want to weigh the game you kill, carry what is called a Little Giant scale (Fig. 69). Although of pocket size and 12-oz. weight, it weighs by the small hook up to 40 lbs. by 2 lbs., and by the larger one up to 350 lbs. by 5 lbs. For fish, of course, a small spring balance is the thing.

A pair of side-cutting pliers, of the very best steel, is almost a necessity. I always carry a small one when fishing, to snip off the barb of an imbedded hook, which otherwise is a mighty mean thing to get rid of. The pliers are in daily use for other purposes.

Fig. 69.— Little Giant Scale

A 6 to 8-inch mill file, and a carborundum stone, will keep the axe and other cutlery in order. (A mill file is cut diagonally and parallel, instead of criss-cross like a common flat file.)

CAMPING AND WOODCRAFT

Select from the following list such articles as you *know* you will need, and make a light wooden box in which they will stow properly.

Folding Saw.
Mill File.
Triangular File.
Side-cutting Pliers.
Carborundum Stone.
Scales.
Gun Screw-driver.
Reel Screw-driver.
Small Hand Drill.
Tape Line.
Copper Wire (two sizes).
Nails, Brads, Tacks, Screws.
½ gill Le Page's Glue.
Marine Glue.
Solderene.
Winding Silk (or Dental Floss).
Rod Varnish.
Ferrule Cement.
Spare Tips and Guides.
Rubber Mending Tissue.

Gun or Rifle Cleaning Rod and Brush.
Gun Oil.
Gun Wipers.
Sandpaper.
Emery Cloth.
Shears.
Needles.
Thread.
Wax.
Spare Buttons.
Safety Pins.
Horse-blanket Pins.
Rubber Bands (large).
Spare Shoe Laces.
Lock-stitch Awl.
Shoe Nails.
Hob-nails.
Sail Needles.
Twine (in tobacco bag).
Split Rivets.
10 yds. 2-inch Adhesive Plaster.

Adhesive plaster (zinc oxide plaster) can be bought at any drug store. Besides its regular use to hold a dressing in place where bandaging is difficult (never apply it directly to a wound), and for protecting sore spots, such as a cut finger or a blistered foot, it is a lightning repairer for all sorts of things. When warmed it will stick to any dry surface, wood, metal, glass, cloth, leather, or skin. It can be peeled off and reapplied several times. As an instantaneous mender of rents and stopper of holes or cracks it has no equal. It is waterproof and airtight. With a broad strip you can seal a box or chest watertight, stop a leak in a canoe ("iron" it on with a hot spoon or stone) or mend a paddle, a gunstock, or even an axe-handle (first nailing it). A chest or cupboard can be extemporized from any

LIGHT CAMP EQUIPMENT 117

packing box, in a jiffy, by cleating the top and using surgeon's plaster for hinges.

One of the most bothersome things in shifting camp is to secure opened cans and bottles from spilling. Surgeon's plaster does the trick in a twinkling. Put a little square of it over each hole in the milk can that you opened for breakfast, and there will be no leakage. To hold a cork in a bottle, stick a narrow strip of the plaster over the cork and down opposite sides of the bottle's neck. To protect the bottle from breaking, run a strip around it at top and one at bottom. The caps of baking powder cans or similar tins can be secured to the bodies in the same way.

If your fishing rod sticks at the ferrules, wrap a bit of the plaster around each joint to give you a grip, then pull without twisting.

Rubber mending tissue (any dry-goods store) is good to patch a tent, a canoe, or rubber articles (waders, etc.). Cut canvas patch and tissue of same size, place the latter over rent and the patch on top, then press with a hot iron or rub with a hot, smooth stone.

Dental floss is fine for quick rod repairing, or to use as an emergency leader. It is very strong, ready waxed, waterproof, and durable.

The list of tools and supplies given above is, of course, only suggestive, and for trips where the going is fairly easy. To each according to his needs.

When traveling with horses, take along a hammer, a few spare horseshoes and their nails, leather mending kit, and the necessary ropes.

LANTERN.— Kerosene is a nuisance in carriage; if so much as a drop escapes anywhere near your provisions, it will taint them. Carbide is easy to carry, and, aside from its regular use in an acetylene lantern, makes it easy to start a fire when everything is wet. A folding pocket lantern of Stonebridge or Alpina type, for candles, is best for men in light marching order; but let it be of tin or brass; those made of aluminum are much too frail.

HORN.— When camping in a canebrake country have a huntsman's horn in the outfit. Leave it with the camp-keeper, who will blow it every evening about an hour before supper. The sound of a horn carries far, and its message is unmistakable. It is a dulcet note to one who is bewildered in a thick wood or brake.

SUNDRIES.— A length of small rope, such as braided sash cord, and a ball of strong twine, spare cloth and leather for mending, a few rawhide thongs, and some broad rubber bands, are likely to be needed.

A few yards of mosquito netting should be taken along to protect meat from blow-flies, and for various other purposes.

COOKING KIT.— In rough country, especially if camp is to be shifted frequently, a stove is out of the reckoning. If pack animals are taken, or the trip is by canoe, without long and difficult portages, it pays to take along either a folding grate or a pair of fire irons (see Chapter IV).

On light marching trips no support for the utensils will be carried. Rocks or logs will take their place. There may be a little more spilling and swearing, but less tired backs.

It is commonly agreed that four is the ideal number for a camping party, at least among hunters and fishermen. Certainly no larger number should attempt their own cooking. Utensils and table ware for such a party, going light, should include: a large frying-pan (more serviceable than two small ones); a pan to mix dough in and wash dishes (common milk pan); a stout, seamless, covered pot for boiling or stewing meat, baking beans, etc.; a medium pot or pail for hot water (always wanted, substitute for tea kettle); a smaller one for cereals, vegetables, fruit; and either a coffee pot low enough to nest in the latter, or a covered pail in its place.

LIGHT CAMP EQUIPMENT 119

There should be six plates (two for serving) and four each of cups, knives, forks, teaspoons, tablespoons. This is about as little as the party can well get along with.

It will be bothersome to bake bread for four in the frying-pan. Add a reflector or a sheet-steel oven, if practicable. A wire broiler, a tea percolator, and a corkscrew and can opener will nest with this set. If the cook wears no sheath knife a butcher knife is essential. Several dish towels (some to be divided into clouts) and a couple of yards of cheesecloth for straining and to hang meat in should be taken. Sapolio will be needed, or Bon Ami if the utensils are of aluminum.

The common utensils of the shops will not nest. They are all spouts and handles, bail ears and cover knobs. Still, a good deal can be done by substitution. Covered pails or pots (Fig. 70) do the work

Fig. 70.—Cooking Pot　　Fig. 71.—Pot Chain　　Fig. 72.—Coffee Pot　　Fig. 73.—Miner's Coffee Pot

of sauce pans and kettles, and are better all round, for they can either be set upon the coals or hung above the fire; besides, you can carry water in them, and their covers keep heat in and ashes out. All such vessels should be low and broad; then they will boil quickly and pack well. Good proportions are:

```
3 quarts....diameter 6¾ in. x 5¼ in. height.
4    "          "     7½ "  x 5¾ "    "
6    "          "     8½ "  x 6½ "    "
8    "          "     9¼ "  x 7½ "    "
```

Bail ears should project as little as possible. Lids should have fold-down rings instead of knobs, so they will nest well.

120   CAMPING AND WOODCRAFT

A set of pot-chains with hooks (Fig. 74) is worth taking. With one of these (weight 2 oz.) a kettle can be suspended at any desired height above the fire.

Ordinary coffee pots are not suitable for camping. A good pattern for the purpose is shown in Fig. 72. It has a bail, folding handles, and a solid spout that cannot melt off. A cheaper but very good article in tin (Fig. 73) is known as a "miner's coffee pot." When very compact nesting is sought, discard the coffee pot for a lidded pail: it has the merit that no aroma escapes through a spout. For tea, have an aluminum tea-ball; then you will not commit the cardinal sin of steeping the leaves too long.

Cups, to nest inside the coffee pot, have the lower part of the handle free (Fig. 74). In tin, the 1½-pint size is best (5 x 2⅛ in.). Small cups and small plates are impertinences to anybody with a woods appetite. Tin is not so bad for coffee, but aluminum blisters the unwary mouth. Enamel is best for cups and plates, no matter what the material of the rest of the kit may be. It is so much easier to clean than tin or aluminum. If the plates are deep and generous (9½-inch soup plates, nest-

Fig 74.— Cup   Fig. 75.— Miller Frying Pan

ing in the frying-pan) there will be no need of bowls for soup and porridge.

The frying-pan handle is a perennial problem. If detachable, it is likely to be lost. The best folding handled pan that I have used is the Miller pattern (Fig. 75). A common pan may be adapted by cutting off all but two inches of the handle and riveting a square socket to the top of the stub so that a stick may be fitted to it when you cook (if

LIGHT CAMP EQUIPMENT 121

the socket is round the stick will twist unless carefully fitted). I prefer the folding handle, because it saves time, and, on the very few occasions when one needs a long stick for handle, he can insert it in the rings of the Miller handle. Get a pan with hinge that won't work loose.

Some sort of baker is almost essential for comfortable life in the woods. The most portable form is the folding reflector sold by most outfitters. It is similar to those that our great-grandmothers used to bake biscuit in, before a hearth fire. The top slants like a shed roof, and the bottom like another shed roof turned upside down, the bread pan being in the middle. The slanting top and bottom reflect heat downward upon the top of the baking and upward against its bottom, so that bread, for instance, bakes evenly all around.

A prime advantage of this cunning utensil is that baking can proceed immediately when the fire is kindled, without waiting for the wood to burn down to coals, and without danger of burning the dough. Fish, flesh, and fowl can be roasted to a turn in this contrivance. It has several better points than an oven, chief of which is its portability, as it folds flat; but it is inferior for corn bread, army bread, etc., and impossible for pot-roasts or braising. How to use it is shown in Chapter XVI.

Fig. 76.—
Reflector
(Angular Back)

Fig. 77.—
Reflector
(Flat Back)

Fig. 78.—
Reflector
(Folded in Case)

There are two models of reflectors, one with a single joint at the rear (Fig. 76), the other with two (Fig. 77) and a flat back. The latter is more compact, but not so stiff as the other.

122   CAMPING AND WOODCRAFT

These ovens may be bought in tin or aluminum.

Tin	Aluminum	Aluminum
9 x 12 pan. 4 lbs.	8 x 12 pan. 2 lbs.	12 x 15 open. 2 lbs.
11 x 14 pan. 5½ lbs.	8 x 18 pan. 2¾ lbs.	15 x 18 open. 3 lbs.
	10 x 18 pan. 5 lbs.	15 x 24 open. 4 lbs.

An 8 x 12-in. pan holds just a dozen biscuits.

A canvas carrying case (Fig. 78) which is needed, for the baker is frail, adds another pound. A wire broiler packs inside the reflector; it is not necessary for broiling meat, but it is handy for the purpose, and especially for broiling fish.

A reflector must be kept bright to do good baking. The sheet steel oven shown in Fig. 79 is much cheaper than a reflector. It consists of two halves that nest, each 4 x 12 inches, and a perforated shelf on which a roast or a bake-pan may be placed. It is managed like a Dutch oven (see Chapter XX), but requires more attention, as the material is thin. A reflector is better for the amateur, as he can see at all times how the baking or roasting progresses.

Fig. 79.—
Sheet Steel Oven

Men who have neither time nor inclination to rummage the stores for "calamities" that will nest would do well to pay extra for outfits already kitted by camp outfitters. Using one outfitter's sets for illustration, we are offered:

Set for	Size, nested	In "Aluminol"	In "Amorsteel"
Two persons..	9½ x 8¾ in.	6¾ lbs. $4.00	6⅜ lbs. $9.85
Four persons..10	x 11¼ in. 12	lbs. 6.25	10⅞ lbs. 16.60
Six persons...11	x 12⅞ in. 17½ lbs.	8.50	17¼ lbs. 26.50
Eight persons.11	x 12⅞ in. 19¼ lbs.	9.40	18¾ lbs. 30.00

In the four-men and eight-men sets the coffee pots will be found rather stingy. An 8 x 18 folding aluminum reflector, broiler, canvas case, butcher knife, cooking spoon, percolator, and canvas water bucket, would add exactly 4½ pounds weight and $6.90 to the price.

LIGHT CAMP EQUIPMENT 123

Such sets as these are very nice for what I may call confirmed campers; but if the party is likely to split up after the first trip, and no one cares to buy a first-class outfit for future use, go to the department store and get, in tin or enameled ware, the articles I have listed. The reflector you must order from an outfitter, or make for yourself.

CHAPTER VIII
CAMP BEDDING

One's health and comfort in camp depend very much upon what kind of bed he has. In nothing does a tenderfoot show off more discreditably than in his disregard of the essentials of a good night's rest. He comes into camp after a hard day's tramp, sweating and tired, eats heartily, and then throws himself down in his blanket on the bare ground. For a time he rests in supreme ease, drowsily satisfied that this is the proper way to show that he can "rough it," and that no hardships of the field can daunt his spirit. Presently, as his eyes grow heavy and he cuddles up for the night, he discovers that a sharp stone is boring into his flesh. He shifts about, and rolls upon a sharper stub or projecting root. Cursing a little, he arises and clears the ground of his tormentors. Lying down again, he drops off peacefully and is soon snoring. An hour passes, and he rolls over on the other side; a half hour, and he rolls back again into his former position; ten minutes, and he rolls again; then he tosses, fidgets, groans, wakes up, and finds that his hips and shoulders ache from serving as piers for the arches of his back and sides.

He gets up, muttering, scoops out hollows to receive the projecting portions of his frame, and again lies down. An hour later he reawakens, this time with shivering flesh and teeth a-chatter. How cold the ground is! The blanket over him is sufficient cover, but the same thickness beneath, compacted by his weight and in contact with the cold earth, is not half enough to keep out the bone-searching chill that comes up from the damp ground. This will never do. Pneumonia or rheumatism may follow. He arises, this time for good, passes a wretched night before the fire, and dawn finds him a haggard, worn-out type of misery, disgusted with camp life and eager to hit the back trail for home.

The moral is plain. This sort of roughing it is bad enough when one is compelled to submit to it. It kills twice as many soldiers as bullets do. When it is endured merely to show off one's fancied toughness and hardihood it is rank folly. Even the dumb beasts know better, and they are particular about making their beds.

This matter of a good portable bed is the most serious problem in outfitting. A man can stand almost any hardship by day, and be none the worse for it, provided he gets a comfortable night's rest; but without sound sleep he will soon go to pieces, no matter how gritty he may be.

In selecting camp bedding we look for the most warmth with the least weight and bulk, for durability under hard usage, and for stuff that will not hold moisture long, but will dry out easily.

Warmth depends upon insulation. The best insulation is given by dry air confined in the interstices of the covering, this covering being thick enough to keep one's animal heat from escaping too readily.

Of course, materials vary in conductivity — cotton and other vegetable fibers being coldest, silk and wool warmer, fur and feathers warmest of all — but, irrespective of materials, the degree of insulation afforded by a covering depends upon its fluffiness, or looseness of texture, and its thickness of body. This means bulk; there is no way of getting around it; there must be room for confined air.

Innumerable expedients have been tried to keep down bulk by using impermeable insulators, such as paper, oiled cotton or silk, and rubber or rubberized fabric, but all such "skins to keep heat in" are total failures. The vapor from one's body must have an outlet or a man will chill, to say nothing of other unpleasant consequences.

The degree of insulation afforded by confined air may be judged roughly by a few comparisons. Here is a pack cloth of close-woven cotton duck; there is a cotton bed comforter of the same spread and weight, but thicker, of course. Size, weights, and materials are the same, yet what a difference in warmth! Well, it is just the enclosed air that makes the comforter "comfy," and lack of it that leaves the canvas cold as a covering. Similarly, a three-pound comforter filled with lamb's wool batting is as warm as a five-pound all-wool blanket, because it holds more dead air. Down filling is still warmer than wool, being fluffier, and its elasticity keeps it so — it does not mat from pressure.

After a cotton comforter has been used a long time, or kept tightly rolled up, its batting becomes matted down and then the cover is no warmer than a quilt of equal weight. Quilts — ugh! In the dank bedroom of a backwoods cabin, where the "kivvers" were heirlooms, but seldom had been aired, I have heaped those quilts on me till their very weight made my bones ache, and still shivered miserably through the long winter night.

Batting of any sort (but cotton the worst) will also mat from wet, and then its elasticity is gone. Water, moreover, is a good conductor of heat, and so a bed covering of any kind is cold when it is wet.

Note this, also, that the weight of one's body presses out a good deal of air from the bedding under him. Moreover, earth, being a good conductor, draws off one's animal heat faster than the air does. So, when sleeping on the ground, one needs more bedding underneath than over him — a cold, hard fact that some designers of sleeping bags have unaccountably overlooked. A bag with two thicknesses of blanket over the sleeper and only one under him is built upside-down. The man will have at least part of his back only half protected; and one's vertebral region is the very part of him that is most vulnerable to cold.

BLANKETS.— The warmest blanket for its weight is not a close-woven one but one that is loose-woven and fluffy. An army blanket is made for hard service, and so must be of firm weave, but a third of its weight is added for that purpose only, not for warmth. For use in a sleeping bag, where they are protected from wear, blankets of more open texture are better. Two three-pound blankets are warmer than a six-pound one of the same grade, owing to the thin stratum of air between them. Hence the best bags are made up of several layers of light, fluffy blanketing, instead of a thick, felted bag.

Camp blankets should be all-wool. A cotton or part-cotton one is much more prone to absorb moisture from the damp woods air and to hold that which exudes from the body of the sleeper, hence it is clammier and colder than wool. The difference may not be so noticeable in the dry air of a heated bedroom, but it will quickly make itself felt in the woods. Another bad quality of cotton is that fire will spread through it from an ember cast out by the camp-fire, whereas the coal would merely burn a hole in wool.

The warmest blankets for their weight are those made of camel's hair. They are expensive, but one of them is as much protection as two common woolen blankets. They are favorites among experienced travelers all over the world.

Hudson Bay blankets have a well-justified reputation, being much like the well-nigh everlasting products of the old hand-loom. Their size is distinguished by " points " (four points, three-and-a-half points, three points) and they are marked accordingly by black bars in one corner.

Blankets should be of dark or neutral color, so

as not to show dirt or attract insects. If used without a canvas cover they may well be waterproofed with lanolin, by the process that I will describe in the next chapter.

To roll up in a blanket in such a way that you will stay snugly wrapped, lie down and draw the blanket over you like a coverlet, lift the legs without bending at the knee, and tuck first one edge smoothly under your legs then the other. Lift your hips and do the same there. Fold the far end under your feet. Then wrap the free edges similarly around your shoulders one under the other. You will learn to do this without bunching, and will find yourself in a sort of cocoon.

Often it is convenient to use a blanket as a garment while drying out your clothes, or as a cape in cold weather. Wear it as a Mexican does his sérape. As a bed blanket is larger than a sérape, one end must first be folded, say about two feet, depending upon size and your own height. This fold being turned under, stand with your back toward the blanket and draw its right-hand corner snugly up under the right armpit so that the triangle hangs down in front of you, and hold it firmly there. With left hand then draw the blanket up over left shoulder from behind, tight against nape of neck, and down in front. That leaves the left corner trailing on the ground before you. With a quick flirt throw this corner up over right shoulder and let it hang down your back, where it will stay of its own weight. You are now wrapped up but with right arm free. The blanket can be cast off in an instant.

COMFORTERS.— Sometimes these are miscalled quilts, but they are knotted together instead of quilted, and have thicker, fluffier filling than quilts. Cotton comforters are wholly unsuitable for outdoor use. They are warm only when perfectly dry, and it is impossible to keep them so in the damp air of a forest. But a comforter filled with wool bat-

CAMP BEDDING

ting is very warm for its weight and does not take up moisture so readily. It is cheaper than a blanket, and makes a softer bed, but is bulkier. Comforters are much used by Western campers, along with a canvas " tarp." Whenever extreme compactness of outfit is not necessary, I recommend that each member of a party take with him a wool comforter, even if for no other use than as a mattress.

Warmest of all coverings of this sort are the so-called eiderdown quilts (really goose down). They are expensive, and must carefully be protected from the wet.

SLEEPING BAGS.— There is a good deal of waste material in blankets and comforters, especially at the foot end. Suppose we cut them into a sort of coffin shape, to conform to the outlines of the body, sew up a side and an end and the lower third of the other side, then attach buttons or laces or clasps to close the bag after one has got into it. A good deal of weight and bulk are saved.

The objections are that such an arrangement is hard to air and dry out, it is not readily adjustable to varying temperatures, and the occupant has a feeling of constraint when cooped up in the thing. Still, in some kinds of camping, it is essential that the bed be very warm, waterproof, windproof, and yet as portable as possible. Hence the sleeping bag.

It may be laid down as an axiom at the start that no sleeping bag is worthy of serious notice unless its blankets or other lining can be removed quickly and spread out on a line to dry. A lining sewed inside a waterproof cover is an abomination. So is a nest of blanket bags that can only be aired by propping each one open with a stick. Such things get musty and dirty. They are so bothersome to air that they will be neglected.

Of course, if the bag is of but a single thickness it may be sunned first on the outside and then turned inside out. But no single bag is practical, except for a polar climate, when one adopts a fur bag.

Bedding, to be comfortable and healthful, must be adaptable to variations of temperature. Remember that the night gets colder and colder till daylight. This is much more noticeable out-of-doors than indoors, and yet, even at home, when one goes to bed he generally has a spare cover handy to pull over him towards morning.

Now a tent is far less insulated than a house. So if one muffles himself up when he goes to bed in enough covering to meet the last few hours before dawn, he soon will be roasted out, whereas if he has only enough bedding for comfort through the first watches of the night, he will find the last one *his watch* in literal truth, for he won't sleep. The only sleeping bag worth talking about is one that

Fig. 80.— D. T. Abercrombie Sleeping Bag

has at least four layers of blanketing. Then one can turn in under one layer and the canvas; in the cold hours after midnight, he can emerge and crawl back under more cover (Fig. 80).

It is from lack of attention to these simple and obvious requirements that most designers of sleeping bags have failed. They have turned out contrivances that either were insufferably hot in the early part of the night or confoundedly cold before morning.

The explorer, Anthony Fiala, who has patented an extremely light and warm bag for use in high latitudes (Fig. 81), claims that not only the bag itself but its cover should be porous so as to throw off the bodily moisture which otherwise condenses

CAMP BEDDING

around the sleeper and chills him. So he uses plain khaki for a bag cover instead of waterproofed material. However, his type of sleeping bag is a snugger "fit" than the average, and so arranged with hood and closing flaps that it ventilates only through the cloth itself. The larger and heavier bags commonly used are roomy enough to provide considerable ventilation from the unconscious wriggling of the sleeper. Besides, the cover, though waterproof, is not impermeable to air, as rubber or oilskin would be.

If several layers of blanketing are used within a roomy cover of waterproofed canvas the outer layer will take up what little "sweating" occurs inside

Fig. 81.— Fiala Sleeping Bag

the canvas. Such a cover is desirable to protect the occupant from damp ground, from moist air, and from rain when he bivouacs away from camp. It also keeps the bedding dry while *en route,* as, for example, in a boat or canoe when water is shipped. If the bag is opened out and its lining sunned frequently, as should be done with any sort of bedding, no trouble from condensed moisture will be experienced in ordinary climates.

I have spoken of fur bags. They are much too hot for our climate, except in the high mountains where one must bivouac perhaps in wind and snow. The warmest of all coverings for its weight is a bag made of caribou or reindeer-skin. The hair of this animal is extraordinarily close and thick, and each hair is hollow, like a quill, and contains air (this is true of the whole deer family). Caribou pelts are in their prime when in the summer coat, in August and early September. After this the hair becomes too long and brittle. Skins of young animals should be used, being lighter than those of old ones, although almost as warm, and their hair is less liable to come out under conditions of dampness. They weigh about the same per square foot as raccoon or goat-skins (4½ to 5 ounces, as compared with 6½ for wolf and 7 for black bear, on the average). A bag made from such skins will weigh about twelve pounds, from the adult caribou about sixteen pounds. Sleeping bags made in Norway from skins of domesticated reindeer could be purchased, before the war, through the Army and Navy stores in London for about £5. Alaska reindeer skins can be bought from trading firms in Seattle.

In the old *Book of Camping and Woodcraft* I discoursed as follows *re* sleeping bags:

> It is snug, for a while, to be laced up in a bag, but not so snug when you roll over and find that some aperture at the top is letting a stream of cold air run down your spine, and that your weight and cooped-upness prevent you from readjusting the bag to your comfort. Likewise a sleeping bag may be an unpleasant trap to be in when a squall springs up suddenly at night, or the tent catches fire.
>
> I think that one is more likely to catch cold when emerging from a stuffy sleeping bag into the cold air than if he had slept between loose blankets. A waterproof cover without any opening except where your nose sticks out is no more wholesome to sleep in than a rubber boot is wholesome for one's foot. Nor is such a cover of much practical advantage, except underneath. The notion that it is any substitute for a roof overhead, on a rainy night, is a delusion.
>
> Blankets can be wrapped around one more snugly, they do not condense moisture inside, and they can be thrown open instantly in case of alarm. In blankets you can sleep double in cold weather. Taking it all in all, I choose the separate bed tick, pillow bag, poncho, and blanket, rather than the same bulk and weight of any kind of sleeping

CAMP BEDDING 133

bag that I have so far experimented with. There may be better bags that I have not tried.

In his excellent book on *The Way of the Woods,* Dr. Edward Breck replied:

"I have always looked up to Mr. Kephart as a woodsman *sans reproche,* but I am forced to believe that he has never made fair trial of a good sleeping bag; for, if there is one thing a bag does *not* do, it is letting in streams of cold air down your spine, and, to me at least it almost goes without saying that a man is wrapped up much more tightly in blankets than in a bag, and hence far more helpless to rearrange his bed without pulling things to pieces. It is just precisely the ability to turn over in comfort that makes me love a sleeping bag, and this springs from its general 'stay-puttedness.' As for the stuffiness of a bag I confess I have yet to discover it. A proper bag opens down the side and ventilates easily. It is a little more difficult to air out in the morning, but not much. The comparison with a rubber boot is most unjust, and, though harder to get into, it takes no longer to do so than to wrap oneself up properly in blankets. As to getting caught inside if a fire breaks out, I will engage to get outside of mine [a 'Comfort sleeping pocket'] in less than three seconds if necessary. The sleeping bag has come to stay. My Indians have made themselves a couple out of blankets and waterproof canvas. Mr. Kephart asserts that the waterproof cover is no substitute for a roof overhead on a rainy night; and yet I can assure him that I have slept out in mine without a tent many times in hard rain without getting wet in the *slightest degree,* except when rising. Imagine, if you please, the state I should have been in with blankets only. A lean-to of some kind would have been imperative, and even then misery would have been the result. Of course, spending the night without some kind of shelter is not to be recommended, but my experience shows what the bag is capable of."

As for the roof overhead, what I meant was that gun and duffel need protection, and so do you when you crawl out on a rainy morning. The weight of a sleeping-bag cover put into a little waterproof tent that you can carry in your pocket, and a ground sheet to go with it, will give you better protection from the elements at night and a sheltered place to dress and cook breakfast in. This for side trips from camp, or for long hikes.

Otherwise it is a matter of finding a *proper* sleeping bag, and I have tried here to make the essentials plain. Beyond this, one's personal taste must be the decisive factor. Let us hear from another old-timer, Emerson Hough:

> "As to your bed, let us have one more whack at the sleeping bag — that accursed invention of a misguided soul. Leave your sleeping bag at home, in the Adirondacks or in the Minnesota woods. Take a pair of good wool blankets which will weigh not less than ten pounds — more weight is better. Don't despise a good wool comforter or a 'Katy' which will fold double and make a nice mattress under you. And whatever you do, don't fail to have for your own use a good, big bed 'tarp' as it is known in the West. On the stock ranches we always used to have the tarpaulin of 20-oz. duck, about 7 x 14 ft., and sometimes it had harness hooks on it, sometimes not. It surely would turn rain. For the pack travel of today you will not need canvas of quite so much weight. But canvas and wool in abundance you surely should have for your bed. No hunting trip is a success when you don't sleep well and dry at night. Canvas and wool together are the correct dope for the mountains. Take an air mattress if you insist, or if your dealer does: don't blame me if you sleep cold."

When all is said, plain blankets are cheaper than sleeping bags, and they can be used at home: that settles the matter for most folks.

MATTRESSES AND PILLOWS.— It is folly to sleep on bare ground if one can help it. A bed of balsam browse is not excelled, if properly made and frequently renewed; but it takes fully an hour to make one right, and on many a camp ground there is no browse, not even spruce. As a substitute one may use pine needles, grass, ferns, the moss off old fallen trees, or even dead leaves. Such stuff, however, packs hard and spreads from under one unless confined in a bag. For years I carried a bag of common bed ticking for this purpose, 2½ feet wide by 6¼ feet long, and weighing only 1⅓ pounds. Such a bag made of tanalite is more practical than any kind of carryall or bed-sheet, for it serves just as well to protect the bedding *en route,* and then is easy to turn into a mattress when you make camp. A pillow bag, similarly stuffed, with spare clothing atop, was not the least important item in my very light kit. When one has room, it pays to carry a small feather pillow or a down cushion about 12 x 18 inches.

AIR MATTRESSES.— An air bed is luxurious in moderate weather, but too cold to use late in the season unless well insulated with blankets or a felt pad. The thinner the bed the less objectionable it is in this respect, as it does not then steal so much of one's animal heat.

There are sleeping bags combined with air mattresses, full-length or only "body size," that are good for canoe cruising, horseback journeys, or other trips when camp is changed every day or so and good sites are not always to be found. They save much work, and sometimes a good deal of anxiety. There is then no night wood to cut, no browse to gather, no tent to trench, and little bother about smoothing the ground. Wherever one may be, in damp forest or on sandy dune, on rocky ground or mucky ground, down goes the bundle, it is unrolled, and one inflates his "blow bed" with the bellows that nature gave him. In ten minutes he is assured of a dry, warm, elastic bed for the night, in spite of Jupiter Pluvius, or Boreas, or both of them allied. If water runs in on the floor, let it run. If the tent blows down, let it alone until you feel like getting up. Come morning there is no bed making to do, if you are too hurried to air things, except to deflate the mattress and roll the bag up. It straps into a waterproof pack that stows conveniently anywhere.

But such a bed is quite expensive. For ordinary service, blankets and a bed tick will do just as well. In any case, study your health and your ease at night. There is a veteran's wisdom in what Chauncey Thomas says: "I go camping to have a good time, and a third of that time is spent in bed."

136 CAMPING AND WOODCRAFT

BED ROLLS.— If one carries loose blankets he will need a waterproof canvas cover to protect them *en route* and to serve as a ground sheet between them and the damp earth when he sleeps on the ground. A bed roll made with flaps at sides and

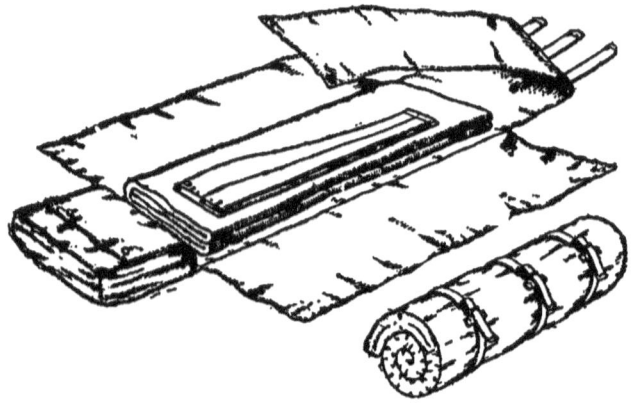

Fig. 82.— U. S. A. Regulation Bed Roll

end is best for this purpose. It is also a good thing when you sleep on a narrow cot, to keep cold air from coming up under the overhang of your blankets. The army regulation bed roll (Fig. 82) is

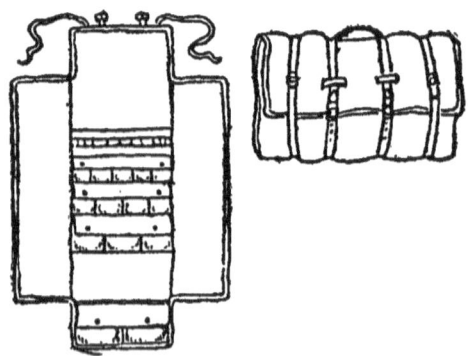

Fig. 83.— Shattuck Camp Roll

one type. There is a pocket for spare clothing that serves as pillow, and the blankets and a folding cot are rolled up in the main part of the sheet, covered by the flaps, and strapped up.

Another camp roll is shown in Fig. 83. It con-

CAMP BEDDING 137

tains a detachable wall pocket for small articles, which is to be hung up in the tent, and bellows pockets at the end.

There is a combination carryall and bed (Fig. 84) that I think a good deal of. In principle it is like the other bed rolls mentioned, but the bottom is double and open at both ends. A pair of stiff poles convert it into a stretcher bed (Fig. 86); cross poles

Fig. 84.—
Comfort Sleeping Pocket

Fig. 85.—
Combination Bed Roll, Stretcher Bed and Bed Tick

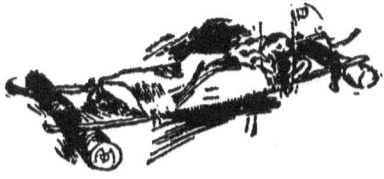

Fig. 86.—
Combination as Stretcher Bed

Fig. 87.—
Combination as Hammock

Fig. 88.—Combination as Bed Roll

added and lashed at the ends make a hammock frame (Fig. 87). The double bottom serves as a bed tick, to be filled with browse, grass, or whatever soft stuff the camp site affords. The ends can be closed with horse-blanket pins, after stuffing the bag. The roll is made of 12-oz. army duck, and weighs 7 or 8 pounds. It can be had with blanket lining, but this I do not recommend. Use separate blankets; then you can have as much thickness under as over you.

CHAPTER IX
CLOTHING

In a wild country one soon learns that the difference between comfort and misery, if not health and illness, may depend upon whether he is properly clad. Proper, in this case, does not mean modish, but suitable, serviceable, proven by the touchstone of experience to be best for the work or play that is in hand. When you seek a guide in the mountains he looks first in your eyes and then at your shoes. If both are right, you are right.

The chief uses of clothing are to help the body maintain its normal temperature, and to protect it from sun, frost, wind, rain and injuries. To *help*, mind you — the body must be allowed to do its share.

Perspiration is the heat-regulating mechanism of the body. Clothing should hinder its passage from the skin as little as possible. For this reason one's garments should be *permeable to air*. The body is cooled by rapid evaporation, on the familiar principle of a tropical water-bag that is porous enough to let some of the water exude. So the best summer clothing is that which permits free evaporation — and this means all over, from head to heel. In winter, just the same, there should be free passage for bodily moisture through the underclothes; but extra layers or thicknesses of outer clothing are needed to hold in the bodily heat and to protect one against wind; even so, all the garments should be permeable to air. If a man would freeze most horribly, let him, on a winter's night, crawl into a bag of India rubber and tie the opening tight about his neck.

CLOTHING 139

Cloth can be processed in such a way as to be rainproof and still self-ventilating (this will be considered later), but rubber garments and oilskins cannot safely be worn the day long, unless they are very roomy, and the wearer exercises but little. Rubber overshoes, boots, waders, are endurable only in cool weather or cold water, and then only if very thick oversocks are worn to hold air and absorb moisture.

All clothing worn by an outdoorman should be of such texture and fit as will allow free play to his muscles, so he may be active and agile, and should bind as little as possible, especially over vital organs. Garments that are too thick and stiff, or too loose at points of friction, will chafe the wearer.

These are general principles; now for particulars.

UNDERCLOTHING.— In discussing "togs" we usually begin on the wrong side — the outside. Now the outer garments will vary a great deal, according to climate, season, the terrain or waters, and according to the sport or work that one is to do; but the integument that comes next to one's skin should vary little for an outdoorman except in weight.

The material and quality of one's underwear are of more consequence than the shell he puts over it, for his comfort and health depend more on them. Whenever a man exercises heartily he is sure to perspire freely, no matter how cold the air may be. Arctic explorers all agree that their chief misery was from confined moisture freezing on them. How it is in the dog-days everybody knows — a glowing sun, humidity in the air, and sweat trickling from every pore because the atmosphere is not dry enough to take it up.

Permeability of cloth to air and moisture is largely a matter of *texture*. Consider the starched linen collar and the soft collar of an outing shirt; consider a leather sweat-band in the hat and a flannel one, or no sweat-band at all.

Underclothing, for any season, should be *loosely*

woven, so as to hold air and take up moisture from the body. The air confined in the interspaces is a non-conductor, and so helps to prevent sudden chilling on the one hand and over-heating on the other. A loose texture absorbs sweat but does not hold it — the moisture is free to pass on to and through the outer garments. In town we may endure close-woven underwear in summer, if thin enough, because we exercise little and can bathe and change frequently. In the woods we would have to change four times a day to keep near as dry.

WOOL VERSUS COTTON.— Permeability also depends upon material. Ordinary cotton and linen goods do not permit rapid evaporation. They absorb moisture from the skin, but hold it up to the limit of saturation. Then, when they can hold no more, they are clammy, and the sweat can only escape by running down one's skin.

After hard exertion in such garments, if you sit down to rest, or meet a sudden keen wind, as in topping a ridge, you are likely to get a chill — and the next thing is a " bad cold," or lumbago, rheumatism, or something worse.

Wool, on the contrary, is permeable. That is why (if of suitable weight and loose weave) it is both cooler in summer and warmer in winter than cloth made from vegetable fibre. " One wraps himself in a woolen blanket to keep warm — to keep the heat *in.* He wraps ice in a blanket to keep it from melting — to keep the heat *out.*" In other words, wool is the best material to maintain an equable, normal temperature.

However, the broad statement that one should wear nothing but wool at all seasons requires modification. It depends upon quality and weave. Some flannels are less absorptive and less permeable (especially after a few washings by the scrub-and-wring-out process) than open-texture cottons and linens.

And, speaking of washing, here comes another

CLOTHING

practical consideration. If woolen garments are washed like cotton ones — soap rubbed in, scrubbed on a washboard or the like, and wrung out — they will invariably shrink. The only way to prevent shrinkage is to soak them in lukewarm suds (preferably of fels-naphtha or a similar soap), then merely squeeze out the water by pulling through the hand, rinse, squeeze out again, stretch, and hang up to dry. This is easy, but it requires a large vessel, and such a vessel few campers have. The alternative is to buy your undershirts and overshirts a size too large, allowing for shrinkage. Drawers must not be oversize, or they will chafe. But one's legs perspire much less than his body, and need less protection; so, up to the time of frost, let the drawers be of ribbed cotton, which is permeable and dries out quickly. Cotton drawers have the further advantage that they do not shrink from the frequent wettings and constant rubbings that one's legs get in wilderness travel. Wool, however, is best for wading trout streams. For riding, the best drawers are of silk.

I conclude that for cold weather, for work in high altitudes where changes of temperature are sudden and severe, and for deep forests where the night air is chilly, woolen underclothes should be worn. In hot climates, and for summer wear in open country, a mixture of silk and wool is best, but open-texture linen or cotton does very well. Pajamas should be of flannel, at all seasons, if one sleeps in a tent or out-of-doors.

UNION SUITS are not practical in the wilds. If you wade a stream, or get your legs soaked from wet brush or snow, you can easily take off a pair of drawers to dry them, but if wearing a union suit you must strip from head to foot. Moreover, a union suit is hard to wash, and it is a perfect haven for fleas and ticks — you can't get rid of the brutes without stripping to the buff.

DRAWERS must fit snugly in the crotch, and be not too thick, or they will chafe the wearer. They should be loose in the leg, to permit free knee action. Full-length drawers are best because they protect the knees against dirt and bruises, and safety-pins can be used to hold up the socks (garters impede circulation).

Socks.— If trousers of full length are worn, then socks are preferable to stockings; they bulk less, weigh less, cost less, and are easier to wash. For forest travel, regardless of season, socks should be of soft wool, thick enough to cushion the feet and absorb moisture, and not closely knit but of rather open texture. But for open country, in hot sunny weather, cotton is better, because wool " draws " the feet at such times. On an all-day hike it pays to change to a fresh pair at noon.

The fit of socks is very important. If too loose, they wrinkle and chafe the feet; if too small, they are unendurable. To prevent woolen ones from shrinking is not difficult. Every night, or every time you come in with wet feet, remove your socks, put on fresh ones (having bathed the feet, of course), and put those you have worn to soak in a running stream; then draw them through the hand to squeeze out water, do not wring, but pull them gently into shape, and hang up to dry. On a long trip you will find means, now and then, to soak them in tepid suds, as they do not require a large vessel.

Take along enough socks so that when a pair gets "more holey than righteous" you can throw them away. Darned socks cause blisters, especially when a man does the darning.

Overshirts.— For summer wear the U. S. A. chambray shirt is as good as any. It is durable, does not fade, and shows dirt and perspiration stains less than khaki or common outing shirts. Army shirts have two roomy Stanley pockets with buttoned flaps. These are just right for pipe and tobacco, note-book and pencil, or whatever you want handy at all times without crowding the trousers pockets.

Later in the season, or for a cool climate, the

CLOTHING 143

standard infantry or officer's service shirt of olive-tan wool is excellent. It is always natty, and wears better than common flannel. The cloth is shrunk before making up, but will do some more shrinking from repeated wettings and washings, so get a size larger than what is worn at home. Gray is also a good color for overshirts.

NECKERCHIEFS.— A neckerchief worn with the peak in front is convenient to wipe perspiration from the face. Slewed around the other way, it shields the neck from sunburn. In a high wind, or in dense thickets, it can be used to hold the hat on by tying over the head; and it will protect one's ears when frost nips. It serves as a nightcap, or as a shield against insects, when folded and worn as shown in Figs. 89, 90.

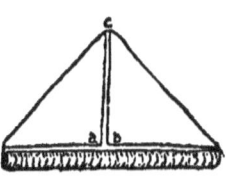

Fig. 89.—
Neckerchief
Folded for Hood

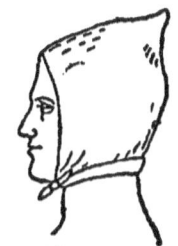

Fig. 90.—
Neckerchief
Hood Adjusted

Lay the kerchief out flat, fold over the upper corners a and b till they meet, roll the square lower edge toward the triangle thus formed, place kerchief over head with the slit ac in front, tie extremities of the roll under chin, and over ab, with a reef knot.

The neckerchief should be large (the army size, 27 x 27 in., or navy, 36 x 36 in.) and of silk. Silk neckerchiefs in any desired color can be bought of military outfitters. The army or navy size can be used as a doubled triangular bandage (or cut into two of them) in emergency. Tied around the abdomen it helps to keep a man warm when he is caught out at night, and it is a good thing in case of cramps.

TROUSERS.— Khaki, of standard army grade, is good for summer wear, as it is cool and can be washed. " Duxbak," or other closely woven cravanetted cotton, is better late in the season, since it sheds a good deal of wet and keeps out wind. Both of these materials dry readily. They are too noisy for still-hunting.

For cold weather the army trousers of olive-tan wool are good, unless one goes out for very rough travel. The woolen cloth called kersey is first choice in a cool, rainy climate, or wherever much wading is to be done. It is the favorite among those most practical of men, the log-drivers and lumberjacks generally.

Woolen trousers do not wear so well as firmly woven cotton ones. They "pick out" in brush, "snag," and collect burs. What has been said of cotton drawers applies also to trousers. Best of all trouser material, for rough service, is genuine English moleskin, which is a very strong, tough, twilled cotton cloth, with a fine pile or nap, the surface of which is "shaved" before dyeing. It wears like iron, is wind-proof, dries out quickly, and is comfortable in either warm or cold weather. Cheap moleskin is worthless.

Corduroy is easily torn, heavy, likely to chafe one, and it is notoriously hard to dry after a wetting. When wearing corduroy trousers there is a *swish-swash* at every stride that game can hear at a great distance.

Trousers should not be lined; it makes them stiff and hard to dry.

To wear with leggings the "foot breeches" of our infantry, which lace or button in front below the knee, fit better than trousers that must be lapped over; but for wilderness wear I prefer common trousers cut off about six inches below the knee: they are easier to put on and they dry out quicker.

Riding breeches are best for the saddle. They are cut too tight at the knee for foot travel, espe-

CLOTHING 145

cially for climbing. Knickerbockers are too baggy for the woods: they catch on snags and tear, or throw a man.

BELTS.— A belt drawn tight enough to hold up much weight is not only uncomfortable but dangerous. It checks circulation, interferes with digestion, and may cause rupture if one gets a fall. If common suspenders are objectionable, then wear the " invisible " kind that go under the overshirt. They prevent chafing, by holding the trousers snug up in the crotch. For ordinary service there is no need of a belt more than an inch wide. A cartridge belt should be worn sagging well down on the hips; or, if a heavy weight is to be carried on the belt (bad practice, anyway), by all means have shoulder-straps for it.

LEGGINGS.— Never buy leggings that strap under the instep. The strap collects mud, and it is soon cut to pieces on the rocks. Any legging that laces over hooks will catch in brush or high grass and soon the hooks bend outward or flatten. The present U. S. A. canvas legging (Fig. 91) has only one

Fig. 91.— U. S. Army Canvas Legging

Fig. 92.— Canvas Strap Puttee

Fig. 93.— Woolen Spiral Puttee

hook, in front; it is quickly adjusted. The strap puttee (Fig. 92) is better for a woodsman or mountaineer. Leather puttees are suitable only for horsemen; in walking and climbing they cut one in front and rear of the ankle joint. Genuine pigskin is the only leather that will stand hard service and frequent wettings.

For still-hunting I like spiral puttees (Fig. 93), not spat but plain, as here illustrated. They are strips of woolen cloth with selvage edges, specially woven and "formed," which wind round the leg like a surgeon's bandage and tie at the top. Do not wind too tightly. They are pliable, noiseless against brush, help to keep ticks and chiggers from crawling up one's legs, and, with the clothing underneath, are a sufficient defense against any snakes except the great diamond-back rattlers. "In experiments, only in rare instances has snake virus stained blotting-paper placed behind two thicknesses of heavy flannel."

German socks, instead of leggings, are good for still-hunting in severe cold weather.

Many dispense with leggings by wearing their trousers tucked inside boots or high-topped shoes. This will do when the woods are dry, but when all the bushes are wet from rain, or from heavy dew, the water runs down inside your shoes until they *slush-slush* as if you had been wading a creek.

COATS.— The conventional American hunting coat of tan-colored cotton is designed primarily for fishermen, bird-hunters, and others who can reach home or permanent camp every night. Being nearly "all pockets but the button-holes," its wearer needs no pouch or game-bag. A man can stuff all the pockets full (he generally does) and still cross fences and slip through thickets without anything catching or dangling in the way. A cravenetted coat of this sort turns rain and keeps out the wind. It is an excellent defence against burrs and briers. It is no heavier than a poncho, and more serviceable for everything but as a ground-sheet or shelter-cloth. These are good points.

On the other hand, the coat is too hot for summer (barring trout fishing), it impedes athletic movements, and, unless sleeveless, it is a poor thing to shoot in, as a gun butt is likely to slip from the shoulder. For summer hikes, canoeing, and big-

CLOTHING

game hunting (except when it is cold enough for Mackinaws) any coat is a downright nuisance.

Have the coat roomy enough to wear a sweater or thick vest under it. Never mind " fit "— the thing is hideous anyway. Of course, one can wear a modish and well-fitting shooting suit, or the like, in the fields near " civilization," but for wilderness travel it is as *outré* as a stag shirt and caulked boots would be on Fifth Avenue.

The coat should not be lined. Most linings are so tightly woven that they check ventilation of the skin, and they make a garment hard to dry out.

SWEATERS.— A sweater, or sweater jacket, is comfortable to wear around camp in the chill of the evening and early morning, and its elasticity makes it a good bed garment when there are not enough blankets. With nothing over it, a sweater is not serviceable in the woods, as it " picks out," " snags," and catches up burrs as a magnet does iron filings.

When you want such a garment at all, you need warmth a-plenty: so get a thick one of good quality, and don't kick at the price. It should have cuffs to draw down over the knuckles, and a wide collar to protect the neck and base of the head. The best colors are neutral gray and brown or tan. A sweater jacket that buttons up in front is more convenient than the kind that is drawn over one's head, but it is not so warm as the latter.

Personally, I usually discard the sweater in favor of a mackinaw shirt, worn hunting fashion with tail outside. It has all the good points of a sweater, except great elasticity, and has the advantages of shedding rain and snow, keeping out wind, wearing well under hard service, and not picking up so much trash.

LEATHER JACKETS.— In the cold dry air of the Far West a buckskin jacket or hunting shirt is often the best outer garment. It keeps out the keenest wind, is pliable as kid, noiseless, less bulky than a sweater or mackinaw, wears forever, and is proof against thorns and burrs. But when wet it is as cold and clammy as tripe.

Genuine buckskin shirts are still listed in the catalogues of certain dealers in the Northwest. Be sure the skins are "smoke-tanned," so that they will dry soft and not shrink so badly as those dressed by a commercial tanner. A fringed shirt dries better than a plain one, as the water tends to drip off the fringes.

Swedish dogskin jackets are rain-proof, but not so pliable as buckskin.

If one can get them (Hudson Bay posts) light caribou skins are better than buckskin. Caribou or reindeer hide has the singular property of not stretching when wet. When tanned with the hair on it is the warmest of all coverings.

VESTS.— A vest without coat may not be sightly, but it is mighty workmanlike. Suspenders can be worn under it without desecrating the landscape — and stout suspenders, say what you please, are a badge of good common sense on a woodsman.

But the vest worn in town is not fit for the wilderness. One's back is more vulnerable to cold than his chest; hence the thick cloth of a waistcoat should go all the way round. There should be four *roomy* pockets, the lower ones with buttoned flaps. Tabs fitted at the bottom will keep the vest from flapping when worn open.

WATERPROOFING WOOLENS.— Wet clothing is heavy and uncomfortable. It is much less permeable to air than dry clothing; consequently it interferes with evaporation of sweat; and it is chilly, because water, which is a good conductor of heat, has replaced the air, which is a non-conductor. Air passes through dry cloth more than twice as freely as through wet material.

The problem is to waterproof the outer garments and still leave them permeable to air. This is done with cotton goods by cravenetting the material, or,

CLOTHING 149

less effectively, by the alum and sugar-of-lead process which fixes acetate of alumina in the fibers.

It is easier to waterproof woolens than cotton clothing. Simply make a solution of anhydrous lanolin in benzine or gasoline, soak the garment in it about three minutes, wring out gently, stretch to shape, and hang up to dry, shifting position of garment frequently, until nearly dry, so that the lanolin will be evenly distributed. This process is very cheap, and old clothing can be treated by it as well as new, without injuring the buttons or anything else.

Cloth so treated permits the ready evaporation of sweat, and so may be worn without ill effects, no matter what the weather may be. In fact the perspiration escapes more freely than from plain woolen cloth, because moisture cannot penetrate the fibers and swell them — the interstices are left open for air to pass through. And yet woolens impregnated with lanolin shed rain better than cloth treated by any of the chemical processes. The goods are not changed in weight, color, or odor. Instead of being weakened, they are made stronger. The waterproofing is permanent.

Lanolin can be bought at any drug-store. It is simply purified wool fat. Wool, in its natural state, contains a grease known as suint. This suint is removed by alkalis before spinning the fiber into cloth. If it had been let alone, as in a Navajo blanket of the old type, the cloth would have shed water. But suint has an unpleasant odor, which is got rid of by purifying the fat into lanolin.

This lanolin, although it is a fat, has the singular property of taking up a great deal of water, and water is purposely added to it in preparing the common (hydrous) lanolin that is used as an ointment base and in cosmetics. In buying, specify that it be anhydrous (water-free). Cloth treated with lanolin absorbs little moisture because water cannot penetrate the fiber and is repelled from the interspaces.

The strength of solution to be used depends upon climate. For a hot, rainy climate, use four ounces of lanolin to a gallon of benzine; for average conditions in the temperate zone, three ounces to the gallon; for cold climate, or winter use exclusively, two ounces to the gallon, as cold has a tendency to stiffen cloth that has been steeped in a strong solution. The three-ounce formula is right for blankets.

If trouble is experienced in making a solution of lanolin, dissolve it first in a little chloroform, then pour into the benzine.

FOOTWEAR.— It is a truism that "a soldier is no better than his feet." Neither is anybody else who has much walking to do. Such shoes as we wear in town are wholly unfit for the field. They are too light, too short, and too narrow. We do little walking in town, and none that we do is over rough ground. We carry no burdens on our backs. So the "snug fit" is tolerated, and the thin socks.

On the trail it is different. One *must* have free play for his toes, or his feet will be cramped and blistered within a few hours — then misery! In marching with a pack, one's foot lengthens about half an inch every time his weight is thrown on it, and broadens nearly as much. And after hiking some distance the feet begin to swell.

The only way to insure a good fit is to put on thick socks, pick up a weight equal to the load you are to carry, slip a tape-measure under the sole, then throw your whole weight on that foot, and have someone do the measuring. Then the other foot similarly; for in many cases the two differ. Have the shoe made a half inch longer than the foot measurement, and wide enough to give a snug but easy fit over the ball when poised as above. Around the heel it should be snug enough to prevent slipping and chafing. These are the army rules, and they are right for anyone who marches and has equipment to carry.

When starting afield, lace the shoes rather tightly

CLOTHING 151

across the instep; then ease the lacing when your feet begin to swell. By the way, some people are always having their shoe laces come undone, because tied with a granny bow. A true bow knot (Fig. 94) is made like a reef knot (Figs. 95, 96) except that the ends are doubled back before tying.

Carry spare laces. They come handy for many purposes. Rawhide laces may be hardened at the ends by slightly roasting them.

SHOES.— It is not enough that the shoes be roomy. The lasts over which they are made should be anatomically correct. In 1911 a board of officers of our army was appointed to select a soldier's shoe. They tried many models, instituted thorough marching tests by thousands of men, and finally adopted a

Fig. 94.—
True Bow
Knot. Double the Ends
Back and
Tie as in a
Reef Knot

Fig. 95.—
Reef Knot Formed

Fig. 96.—
Reef Knot Drawn
Tight

shoe made over lasts designed by Surgeon-Major Munson, the well-known expert on military hygiene (Fig. 97). These lasts are straight on the inside, so that the big toe can point straight ahead, as Nature intended. The front is broad enough to give all the toes free play. There is no compression over the ball or arch of the foot. This is the perfect model, easy on one's feet from the word " go."

The army shoe has now been in use, by all arms of the service, long enough to have proved beyond question its merits. Lieutenant Whelan, so well known to us as a sportsman and military authority, says of it: " In the light of what the army now knows, sore feet are absolutely inexcusable. The presence of sore feet in an officer's command is a cause for investigation as to the efficiency of that officer."

To break in a new pair of shoes the soldier stands in about three inches of water for five minutes, then goes for a walk on level ground. When the shoes are not in use, care is taken that they shall not be packed away tightly or otherwise compressed out of the true shape that the breaking in gave them.

At night the shoes are dried by hanging them upside down on stakes before the fire — not too close, for wet leather "burns" easily. Or, fill a frying pan with clean pebbles, heat them (not too hot) over the fire, put them in the shoes, and shake them

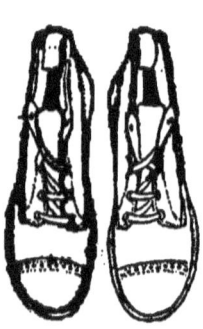

Fig. 97.—
U. S. Army Shoe

Fig. 98.—
Sole of Army Shoe, Showing Proper Method of Placing Hobnails

around after a while. Before the shoes are quite dry, rub just a little neatsfoot oil into them. The remaining dampness prevents the oil from striking clear through, but helps it to penetrate on the outside, as the oil follows the retreating water.

The army shoe has a single sole; so it is flexible — a prime desideratum for good walking. The heel is low, broad, and longer than usual, giving firm footing and having less tendency to "run down" than the common pattern of heel. The tongue is loose,

CLOTHING

making the shoe cool and easy to dry out. There are no hooks to catch in grass and bend out of shape. A pair of these shoes weighs only 2 to 2½ pounds, according to size. This is a proper weight for marching on ordinary roads, but is too light, of course, for rough service, such as a sportsman's shoes often are put to. For the hardscrabble of mountaineering, or going anywhere over sharp rocks or among thorns and saw-briers, the leather is too thin; when it gets wet it goes to pieces.

When buying shoes go to a maker who has made, and kept, a reputation for using none but good leather. There is no severer test of leather than hard usage during frequent wettings and dryings; so, when you find a firm of shoemakers that lumberjacks swear by, trust it to turn you out a good article.

WATERPROOFED SHOES.— The army board decided positively against using any waterproofing compound on shoe leather, because waterproofed shoes steam the feet in perspiration, congest them, and make them tender, if worn for any considerable time, especially in warm weather.

However, it is one thing to march on ordinary roads and another thing to follow wilderness trails or go where there are none at all. And sportsmen often are out in cold slush or wet snow. It is true that no harm comes from wet feet so long as one keeps moving; but if a man has much standing around to do with his feet cold and wet he will suffer discomfort and quite likely catch a cold. Besides, no matter how good the quality of leather may be, when it gets soggy it wears badly. Consequently, although the army shoe is just right for warm weather and marching on roads, it is neither strong enough nor dry enough for continuous wilderness use.

My advice is to get shoes made over the Munson last, of weight suitable for the service in view, and have them viscolized or otherwise waterproofed if you are to be out a good deal in the wet. Have a pair of the regulation army shoes for hot weather and easy going.

No leather is absolutely waterproof. The skin from which it is tanned is porous, and a waterproofing preparation only partially fills those pores, making the leather shed water so long as the filling remains intact, but not preventing air and moisture from gradually seeping through. This is as it should be. If the pores were completely and permanently stopped up, the shoe would be as uncomfortable and unhealthful to wear as if made of rubber. All we can reasonably ask is that the shoe shall shed water under marching conditions; not that we may wade or stand in water indefinitely and still keep dry feet.

There are several good waterproofing preparations on the market, to be bought of almost any dealer in sporting goods. If you prefer to make your own, either of the following recipes will do very well. Do not use a mineral oil on shoes: it "burns" leather; but vaseline and paraffine are harmless.

To WATERPROOF LEATHER.— A rather thick dubbing melted and rubbed into warmed leather is better than an oil, as it "stays put" and does not mix so much with water. Have the leather perfectly dry and apply the compound with a small brush, blowing it into the crack between the sole and upper, then rub well with the hand. Usually two coats, sometimes three, should be applied.

(1) Melt together one part paraffine and two parts yellow vaseline. Apply as above.

(2) Melt together equal parts paraffine or beeswax, tallow, and harness oil or neatsfoot oil.

(3) Boil together two parts pine tar and three parts cod-liver oil. Soak the leather in the hot mixture, rubbing in while hot. It will make boots waterproof, and will keep them soft for months, in spite of repeated wettings. This is a famous Norwegian recipe.

(4) Get a cake of cocoanut butter from a drug store and a small quantity of beeswax. Melt the cocoanut butter and add the beeswax in the proportion of about one

CLOTHING

part of beeswax to six of the cocoanut butter. Warm the shoe as thoroughly as possible to open the pores of the leather, and rub your melted waterproofing on while hot. Repeated warming of the shoe and application of the preparation will thoroughly fill the pores of the leather and also the stitching. The cocoanut butter when cold hardens somewhat like paraffine but not sufficiently to seal the stitching. The beeswax gets in its work there. A mixture of tallow or neatsfoot oil applied hot and with melted rubber mixed in, is also good. To melt the rubber, first chip it as small as possible. Rubber cuts easiest when wet. Apply to stitching with a stiff brush.— *Recreation,* April, 1911.

HOBNAILS.— If one is not traveling by canoe or on horseback, a few cone-headed Hungarian nails should be driven into the shoe soles in the pattern here shown (Fig. 98). The "natives" may stud their soles thickly, but that is only to save shoe leather. Too many nails hurt the feet, make the shoe stiff (whereas it can scarcely be too springy), cause the shoe to ball up in snow, and do not grip so well as a few nails well placed. I am not speaking here of mountaineering above snow-line, but of ordinary climbing, especially where leaves or pine needles may be thick, and of following the beds of trout streams. The nails under the instep are invaluable for crossing streams on fallen trees or poles.

The sharp points of cone-headed nails soon wear off, but edges are left that "bite" well. Broad hobnails with corrugated faces are good at first, but they quickly wear smooth, and then slip worse on the rocks than small ones. They also pull out sooner.

Many recommend short screw caulks. These, if sharp pointed, pick up trash at every step when you are in the woods; if blunt, they are treacherous on the "slick rocks," as they are made of hard steel.

Some prefer $\frac{3}{8}$-inch round head blued screws instead of hobnails or caulks. They claim that these "bite" better, and that they are easy to insert or remove.

Rubber heels save much jarring on a long hike,

but they do not grip on slippery roots, on footlogs, or on leaf-strewn mountain sides.

BOOTS.— By boots I mean any soled footgear with tops more than eight inches high. Engineers who do more standing around than walking may be all right in high-topped boots that lace up the legs, and have buckles besides, but there are mighty few places where a sportsman should be seen in such rig. The importance of going lightly shod when one has to do much tramping is not appreciated by a novice.

Let me show what it means. Suppose that a man in fair training can carry on his back a weight of forty pounds, on good roads, without excessive fatigue. Now shift that load from his back and fasten half of it on each foot — how far will he go? You see the difference between carrying on your back and lifting with your feet. Very well; a pair of single-soled low shoes weighs about two and a half pounds. A pair of boots with double soles and sixteen or seventeen-inch tops weighs about four and a half pounds. In ten miles there are 21,120 average paces. At one extra pound to the pace the boots make you lift, in a ten-mile tramp, over ten tons more footgear than if you wore the shoes.

Nor is that all. The boots afford no outlet for hot air and perspiration. They are stiff, clumsy, and very likely to blister your feet and ankles. When they are brand new, you can wade shallows in them and keep your feet dry; but soon the seams are bound to open and no dubbing will ever close them again. Anyhow, if you fall in fording, or step half an inch too deep, it will take five minutes to remove those boots, pour out the water, and put them on again. Then if they dry out overnight you are uncommonly lucky.

And how are the boots in warm, dry weather? They keep the feet and legs wet all the time with stagnant perspiration. No — take six-inch shoes and light leggings, with a pair of waterproofed "pacs" in reserve for wet going. If you hunt in a

CLOTHING

marsh, wear rubber boots, which are waterproof in something more than name.

There are times and places where an eight or ten-inch hunting shoe that started out to be waterproof is all right.

High-topped "cruisers" have all the faults of the boots except that they are lighter. They scald the feet on a warm day, and chill or freeze them on a cold one, from lack of ventilation and confinement of moisture.

PACS.— A "shoe-pac" or "larrigan" is a beef-hide moccasin with eight to ten-inch top, and with or without a light, flexible sole. It is practically waterproof so long as the seams (which are on top where they get less strain than those of a shoe) remain sound, and they are kept well greased. They are lighter and more pliable than shoes, and are first-rate "extras" to take along for wet days, dewy mornings, and swampy ground, or as the regular footwear for still-hunting. Get them big enough to accommodate heavy lumbermen's socks over your soft thinner ones. Otherwise your feet will generally be either too hot or too cold.

Pacs without soles are fine in a canoe. In trout fishing they can be worn with a pair of hemp sandals to prevent slipping. In extremely cold weather the oil-tanned leather freezes as stiff as horn, and gets dangerously "slick."

MOCCASINS.— In dry weather, on ground that is not too steep or stony, give me the velvety and pliant, pussy-footed moccasin, of real moose-hide, "smoke-tanned" so it will dry soft if I do get wet. I will see more that is worth seeing in the woods than anybody who wears shoes.

If your feet are too tender, at first, for moccasins, add insoles of good thick felt, or birch bark or the dried inner bark of red cedar. After a few days the feet will toughen, the tendons will learn to do their proper work without crutches, and you will be able to travel farther, faster, more noiselessly, and with less exertion, than in any kind of boots or shoes. This, too, in rough country. I have often gone tenderfooted from a year's office work and have traveled in moccasins for weeks, over flinty Ozark hills, through canebrakes, through cypress swamps where the sharp little immature " knees " are hidden under the needles, over unballasted railroad tracks at night, and in other rough places, and enjoyed nothing more than the lightness and ease of my footwear. After one's feet have become accustomed to this most rational of all covering they become almost like hands, feeling their way, and avoiding obstacles as though gifted with a special sense. They can bend freely. One can climb in moccasins as in nothing else. So long as they are dry, he can cross narrow logs like a cat, and pass in safety along treacherous slopes where thick-soled shoes might bring him swiftly to grief. Moccasined feet feel the dry sticks underneath, and glide softly over the telltales without cracking them. They do not stick fast in mud. One can swim with them as if he were barefoot. It is rarely indeed that one hears of a man spraining his ankle when wearing the Indian footgear.

Moccasins should be of moose-hide, or, better still, of caribou. Elk-hide is the next choice. Deerskin is too thin, hard on the feet for that reason, and soon wears out. The hide should be Indian-tanned, and " honest Injun " at that — that is to say, not tanned with bark or chemicals, in which case (unless of caribou-hide) they would shrink and dry hard after a wetting, but made of the raw hide, its fibers thoroughly broken up by a plentiful expenditure of elbow-grease, the skin softened by rubbing into it the brains of the animal, and then smoked, so that it will dry without shrinking and can be made as pliable as before by a little rubbing in the hands. Moccasins to be used in a prickly-pear or cactus country must be soled with rawhide.

Ordinary moccasins, tanned by the above process (which properly is not tanning at all), are only pleasant to wear in dry weather. But they are always a great comfort in a canoe or around camp, and are almost indispensable for still-hunting or snowshoeing. They weigh so little, take up so little room in the pack, and are so delightfully easy on the feet, that a pair should be in every camper's outfit. At night they are the best foot-warmers that one could wish, and they will be appreciated when one must get up and move about outside the tent.

In a mountainous region that is heavily timbered, moccasins are too slippery for use after the leaves fall.

Moccasins should be made over a regular shoe last (Fig. 99). Those commonly sold are too narrow at the toe. Remember that they will shrink some after getting wet, and that you must wear thick socks in them, or perhaps two pairs, so get them big enough.

Fig. 99.— Soled Moccasin (Made Over Last)

Heavy men, tender-footed from town, enjoy moccasins best in a hammock. In fact, most city men will get on better in soled moccasins, but these should be pliable and of not over 1½ pounds to the pair. Or canvas "sneakers" may be used. But beware the rubber soled variety. They are very hot, and will make your feet more tender than ever. Canvas with leather sole is cool and dries out quickly.

Either moccasins or sneakers are needed in camp to rest the feet, and to slip on at night if you stir out.

HEADWEAR.— For general use a soft felt hat, of good quality that will stand rain, is the best head covering. The rim should be just wide enough to shield the eyes from glare and the back of the neck from rain. I like a creased top, wearing it so until a hot sun beats down, then I push up the crown and have a good air space over my pate. The hat should have eyelets for ventilation. A strap or cord under one's "back hair," or chin if need be, holds the hat on in a wind.

A stiff rim is suitable only for mounted men; in the woods it is a plaything for brush and low branches.

A flannel sweat-band absorbs perspiration instead of holding it back like a leather one. (The Jaeger stores have them in stock.) It also helps to hold the hat on. In attaching, do not sew through the hat but through the narrow band under original sweat-band, otherwise the hat will leak.

A cap is of no account in the rain, and its crown is too low to protect one's head from the sun rays.

HEAD NETS.— A head net and gauntlets are the only adequate protection against insects when these are at their worst. The best net is of Brussels silk veiling of fine mesh, black, because that is the easiest color to see through. A net that tears easily is useless.

GLOVES.— Buckskin gloves are needed in mountain climbing and in a region where thorns and briers are common. Buy the regular army ones: they are real buck, and dry out soft. Cavalry gauntlets are better for horseback trips. By folding the hand of a gauntlet back against its cuff the latter serves as a drinking cup.

For "fly time" Dillon Wallace recommends "old loose kid gloves with the fingers cut off and farmer's satin elbow sleeves to fit under the wristbands of the outer shirt."

WATERPROOFS.— Rubber tears easily. Oilskins are superior, regular weight for the saddle and the duck blind, "feather-weight" for fishing and the like. A slicker should be quite roomy, to admit as much air as possible. Oilskin overalls are good things, at a fixed camp, to wear of a morning when dews are heavy and where the brush is thick.

On a hike there is no need of rubber or oilskins if you wear cravenetted or lanolined clothing; but one usually carries a light poncho as a ground-sheet

CLOTHING

at night, and on the march it will protect gun and pack, as well as the bearer, and let plenty of air circulate underneath it. A poncho makes a fair temporary shelter, a good wind-break, and is nice to sit on when the woods are damp. In a canoe it forms a waterproof cover for the pack. There are ponchos of "impervo" and similar oiled fabrics that outwear rubber ones two to one. A poncho is a nuisance on horseback; wear a pommel slicker.

Go over your oilskins each winter with an oil that the dealers sell for the purpose; then they will last for a long time.

RUBBER FOOTWEAR.— I never wear waders for summer trout fishing, but early spring fishing is a different matter. Wading stockings require special hobnailed shoes to go over them. I prefer a pair of light hip boots and separate wading sandals studded with nails. This combination costs less than the other, is more durable, and the boots by themselves are serviceable for general wet weather wear, marsh shooting, and the like. Light rubber boots of first-class quality will last as long as the common heavy ones, and have the advantage that the legs can be turned inside out clear to the ankle for drying. They need not weigh over 3 or 3½ pounds to the pair, and the sandals a pound more — together no more than the high-topped leather boots that I have been objurgating. Have them large enough for both socks and oversocks, then your feet are not likely to get "scalded." Carry a couple of "eezy-quick" menders, and have a rubber repair kit among your possibles in camp.

For hunting big game in wet snow and slush the best footwear is a pair of rubber shoes with ten-inch leather uppers, weighing a bit over two pounds. They should have heels, if you go into a hilly country, and rough corrugated soles. Dress the feet with soft woolen socks, and over these draw a pair of long, thick "German socks" that strap at the top. The latter are warmer than the loose felt boots worn by lumbermen, lighter, more flexible, fit better, and are easier to dry out. The rubbers should fit properly over the heavy socks, neither too tight nor too loose, but especially not too tight or you risk frostbite. Thus equipped, a still-hunter is "shod with silence." For cold weather the vital necessity is suppleness of the foot, and here you have it.

COLD WEATHER CLOTHING.— The main fault of most cold weather rigs is that, paradoxically, they are too hot. You go out into "twenty-some-odd" below zero, all muffled up in thick underwear, overshirt, heavy trousers, and a 32-ounce (to the yard) Mackinaw coat. Very nice, until you get your stride. In half an hour the sweat will be streaming from you enough to turn a mill. By and by you may have to stand still for quite a while. Then the moisture begins to freeze, and a buffalo robe wouldn't keep you warm.

Conditions vary; but for average winter work put on two suits of medium weight all-wool underwear, instead of one heavy one, moleskin trousers (heavy Mackinaws chafe), wool overshirt, Mackinaw shirt worn with tail outside, so it can easily be removed and worn behind you when not needed, the rubber "overs" and socks mentioned above, a Mackinaw cap with visor and ear laps, large, old kid gloves, and thick, woolen mittens held by a cord around the neck.

In buying Mackinaws get none but the best quality. Cheap Mackinaw is shoddy, or part cotton, and soaks up moisture like a sponge. A good grade sheds rain so long as the nap is not worn off; then it can be waterproofed by the lanolin process. It is noiseless, and stands rough usage. The natural gray color is best, except where the law requires you to wear red for protection against gun-bearing fools. (About this, saith our friend Crossman: "Yes, some fellow might take you for a deer if you wore an inconspicuous color in the woods, but what would you? He'd take you for a zebra if you wore

CLOTHING 163

green and yellow, or shoot you for a forest fire if you wore flaming crimson.")

CLOTHING FOR WOMEN.— So far as materials go, the same rules hold good for women in field and camp as for men.

The skirt, of course, should be short. For canoeing or forest travel it should come just below the knee. A Norfolk jacket, flannel waist or shirt, bloomers, cloth leggings, strong but light-weight and flexible shoes with broad, low heels, a soft felt hat, sweater jacket, and waterproofs — these suggest themselves. Ribbed cotton underwear may be worn on hot days, but fine woolen garments should be in reserve for the inevitable wet and chilly times.

Properly dressed for the woods, and not overburdened, the average woman can keep up anywhere with the average office man; but in a tight or draggy skirt she is simply hopeless. For real wilderness travel riding breeches, cut full at the knee, are far better than a skirt. A buttoned skirt that can be slipped on readily may be worn over them on occasion, as when approaching some village or camp where people are not yet civilized enough to approve common sense in a woman's costume. Alice Mac-Gowan was fairly driven out of a mountain county in Kentucky because she wore riding breeches, and yet many's the time I have seen a mountain woman riding astride a man's saddle in an undivided long skirt. O Modesty, what crimes have been committed in thy name!

CHAPTER X

PERSONAL KITS

When one is going into fixed camp, the best carrier for his personal belongings is a common steamer trunk — a light one, but long enough to take in the fishing rods. For canoe, pack train, or automobile, the kit will be much smaller, of course, and may be carried in one of the bed rolls already described, or in a knapsack, or a dunnage bag, according to circumstances.

DUNNAGE BAG.—A common sailor's bag or "war bag" (simple canvas sack closed by a puckering cord) has the merit of simplicity, but it is not

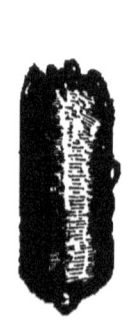 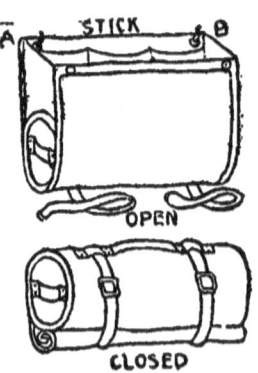 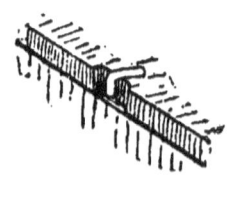

Fig. 100.—
Dunnage Bag

Fig. 101.—
Kit or Provision Pack

Fig. 102.—
Screw Hook Fastening for Box Lid

water-tight. If a bag is used for packing, get from a camp outfitter what he calls a duffel bag (Fig. 100), of waterproof canvas, made with an inside neck or throat-piece that is tied tightly before the

PERSONAL KITS 165

outside is closed. Then it will keep the contents dry even if your craft should fill or capsize. It should be about 3 feet long and 12 inches in diameter. Get a good quality, reasonably snag-proof, and with extra-strong seams and handles. If it is to be shipped as baggage, have it fasten with chain and padlock. I would not use a bag at all unless it was perfectly water-tight, for that is its only point of superiority; on the other hand, it is bothersome to pack, and when you want anything out of a bag you generally have to dump all the contents on the ground to find it.

The pack shown in Fig. 101 is almost as good protection against wet, and a deal handier. The top edge, AB, is stiffened by a stick, to hang it up by in camp, and there are pockets to keep things separated. To close it, fold in the sides, bringing front and back together, roll up, and strap.

DITTY BOXES, POUCHES.— Everyone will fit up these things to suit himself. When practicable to carry it, I prefer to put my small odds-and-ends in one or two low cigar boxes (the 50-size), with partitions, the lid being secured by a small screw-hook (Fig. 102). Otherwise little bags of cloth or soft leather answer the purpose.

As for pouches to carry on one's person, my reasons for not liking them will be given under the head of WALKING TRIPS, in Volume II.

HATCHET.— A woodsman should carry a hatchet, and he should be as critical in selecting it as in buying a gun. The notion that a heavy hunting knife can do the work of a hatchet is a delusion. When it comes to cleaving carcasses, chopping kindling, blazing thick-barked trees, driving tent pegs or trap stakes, and keeping up a bivouac fire, the knife never was made that will compare with a good tomahawk. The common hatchets of the hardware stores are unfit for a woodsman's use. They have broad blades with beveled edge, and they are generally made of poor, brittle stuff. A camper's hatchet should have the edge and temper of a good axe. It must be light enough to carry in or on one's knapsack, yet it should bite deep in timber. The best hatchet I have used (and it has been with me in the mountains for seven or eight years) is one shown in Fig. 103, except that the handle is a straight one, 17-inch, that I made myself. Its weight, with leather sheath, is 1 lb. 10 oz. With this keen little

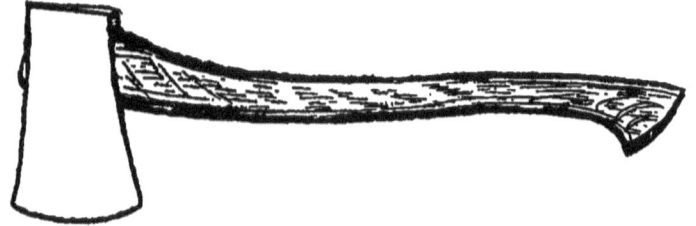

Fig. 103.— Hatchet

tool I have cut many a cord of the hardest woods — hickory, oak, dogwood, beech, etc.— up to young trees eight or more inches thick, often laying in a winter night's wood with it. (The way to learn chopping is to go slow, give all your attention to making every blow tell just where it is needed, and don't strike too hard.)

SHEATH KNIFE.— On the subject of hunting knives I am tempted to be diffuse. In my green and callow days I tried nearly everything in the knife line from a shoemaker's skiver to a machete, and I had knives made to order. The conventional hunting knife is, or was until recently, of the familiar dime-novel pattern invented by Colonel Bowie. It is too thick and clumsy to whittle with, much too thick for a good skinning knife, and too sharply pointed to cook and eat with. It is always tempered too hard. When put to the rough service for which it is supposed to be intended, as in cutting through the ossified false ribs of an old buck, it is an even bet that out will come a nick as big as a saw-tooth — and Sheridan forty miles from a grindstone! Such a knife is shaped expressly for stabbing, which

PERSONAL KITS 167

is about the very last thing that a woodsman ever has occasion to do, our lamented grandmothers to the contrary notwithstanding.

Many hunters do not carry sheath knives, saying (and it is quite true) that a common jackknife will skin anything from a squirrel to a bear. Still, I like a small, light sheath knife. It is always open and "get-at-able," ready not only for skinning game and cleaning fish, but for cutting sticks, slicing bread and bacon and peeling "spuds." It saves the pocket knife from wet and messy work, and preserves its edge for the fine jobs.

For years I used knives of my own design, because there was nothing on the market that met my notion of what a sensible, practical sheath knife should be; but we have it now in the knife here shown (Fig. 104). It is of the right size (4½-inch blade), the

Fig. 104.— Sheath Knife

right shape, and the proper thinness. I ground the front part of the back of mine to a blunt bevel edge for scaling fish and disarticulating joints. The sheath being flimsy, and the buttoned band a nuisance, I made one of good leather that binds well up on the handle and is fastened together with copper rivets besides the sewing.

Cutlery should be of the best steel obtainable. Knicks and dull edges are abominations, so use knives and hatchets for nothing but what they were made for, and whet them a little every day that they are in service.

POCKET KNIFE.— The jackknife has one stout blade equal to whittling seasoned hickory, and two small blades, of which one is ground thin for such surgery as you may have to perform (keep it clean). Beware of combination knives; they may be passable corkscrews and can openers, but that is about all.

COMPASS.— This instrument may not often be needed to guide one's course, but it is like the proverbial pistol in Texas. Besides, it is useful in reading a map, and indispensable for route sketching. If you get one of the common kind with both ends simply pointed and the north one blued or blackened scratch $B = N$ (Blue equals North) on the case. This seems like an absurd precaution, does it not? Well, it will not seem so if you get lost. The first time that a man loses his bearings in the wilderness his wits refuse to work. He cannot, to save his life, remember whether the black end of the needle is north or south. The first time I ever got lost in the big woods I was not frightened, and yet I did a perfectly idiotic thing: to hold my compass level and steady I set it on the thick muzzle of my rifle barrel! That made the needle swing away out of true. It was ten minutes before I thought of this, and tried again, with all iron carefully put aside. That shows what a dunderhead a fellow can be, even when he is fairly cool.

If dust accumulates inside the case of a compass it may interfere a little with its true pointing, and moisture will do so. But, so long as the needle moves freely, *do not quarrel with it,* no matter how sure you may think you are that it has been bewitched.

A compass with revolving dial (card compass) is somewhat easier to use than one with a needle, because the *N* on the dial always points north, no matter which way you turn; but it must be rather bulky, to traverse freely, is not so sensitive as a needle, and wears the pivot faster.

There are compasses with dials illuminated by a radio-active substance that are handy to use at night. The old-fashioned " luminous " compasses that have to be exposed to sunlight every day are not worth the extra cost, for you will forget to attend to them.

PERSONAL KITS

Anyway, a woodsman should carry a pocket electric flasher, and, with that along, a common compass serves very well.

My favorite compass is of a pattern known as the "Explorer's," as here shown (Fig. 105), except that it has a hinged cover. Twice I have crushed the glasses of open faced compasses and ruined the pivots. The moveable arrow is to be set toward one's objective, when the needle points north; it then indicates the general direction of the course. The dial is of 1¾ inches diameter, and is divided into spaces of two degrees, reading from left to right, which is better for an amateur than the contrary reading of a surveyor's compass.

Fig. 105.— Compass with Course Arrow

The use of the compass will be explained in Vol. II, under the head of ROUTE SKETCHING.

I wear the instrument in a small pocket sewed on my shirt for that purpose, so it fits, and attach it to a button-hole by a short, strong cord. A long cord would catch in brush. If the compass is carried in a large pocket it will flop out when you stoop over or fall down. Sometimes, when mapping, I have worn one in a leather bracelet, like a wristwatch; but a better way is to attach it, at such time, to the little board that your cross-section paper is tacked on.

WATCH.— Ordinarily a cheap watch is good enough for the woods. If you do carry a good one, and it is open-faced, there is a good way to protect it from wet that I read some years ago in a sportsman's journal. This also helps to keep it from falling out of a pocket. "To keep one's watch dry, even though you go overboard, take a piece of pure rubber dental dam 8 inches square, put the watch in the center, and bring the rubber together at the stem, tying the puckered up rubber with a bit of string. When you wish to see the face, simply stretch the rubber over the front and you can see the hands clearly through it."

If it is desired to make a sketch-map of some region for which you cannot obtain a government topographical sheet, and the country is too rough for pacing, it will help if one member of the party carries a stop-watch, with which to estimate distances by the sound of pistol shots, as described in Vol. II.

WHISTLE.— A party traveling in thick woods with only an old line of blazes to guide them may have to deploy to find the marks. It will save time, and perhaps a good deal of searching for each other, if they have shrill whistles and a prearranged code of signals. The army officer's whistle is a good one.

MAPS.— Write to The Director, U. S. Geological Survey, Washington, D. C., for an index map showing what topographical sheets have been published for the State that you are to travel in. These sheets are sold at ten cents each (no stamps). Their character is described as follows:

> The United States Geological Survey has been engaged since its organization in making a topographic survey and map of the United States. The unit of survey is a quadrangle 15', 30', or 1° in extent each way, covering an area of one-sixteenth, one-fourth, or one "square degree." The unit of publication is an atlas sheet 16½ by 20 inches, and each sheet is a topographic map of one of the above areas. As the atlas sheets are uniform in size, the greater the area covered the smaller the scale of the map. The scale of the full degree sheet is 1: 250,000, that of the 30' sheet is 1: 125,000, and that of the 15' sheet 1: 62,500. A sheet is designated by the name of some well-known place or feature appearing on it, and the names of adjoining published sheets are printed on the margins. The maps are engraved on copper and printed from stone. The cultural features, such as roads, railroads, cities, towns, etc., as well as all lettering, are in black; all water features are printed in blue; while the hill features are shown by brown contour lines. The contour interval varies with the scale of the map and the relief of the country.

These maps vary in merit. For some of the wilder and rougher regions they are only recon-

PERSONAL KITS

noissance maps and full of minor inaccuracies; but they are revised from time to time. A good part of the continental United States has already been surveyed.

Maps may be cut in sections and mounted on muslin in such way that they fold conveniently for the pocket, but there should be a cover to protect them from soiling and wet.

A better way is to use what the French call a *liseur de cartes*. There are many models and sizes, but all are alike in principle. The simplest form is a leather pocket to contain map sections, faced with

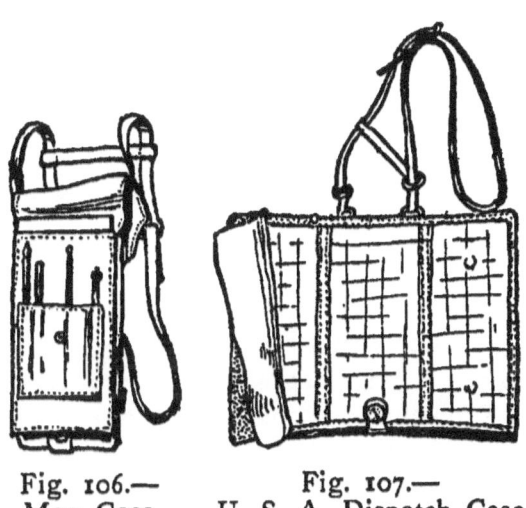

Fig. 106.—
Map Case

Fig. 107.—
U. S. A. Dispatch Case

transparent celluloid, ruled in squares, for the particular section in use at the time. Then there is no need of mounting the map on cloth (such a backing is likely to loosen in the humid air of the forest, and the edges will fray), nor is there risk of the map being soiled, torn, injured by rain, or blown away.

If one has much mapping, sketching, or writing to do, he may well carry a military dispatch case, of which one pattern is shown in Fig. 106, made of olive drab web, with celluloid windows divided into

1-inch squares, pockets for stationery, pencils, dividers, etc., and fitted with a military compass, or not, as one desires. The regulation U. S. Army dispatch case is of leather (Fig. 107).

For ordinary purposes a pocket case is more convenient. The London tackle makers, C. Farlow & Co., sell, at 5s. 6d. postpaid, a leather " fly and cast case," 5 x 4½ inches, with six transparent pockets of celluloid. A topographical sheet by the U. S. Geological Survey cuts into twelve sections that fit these pockets, two in each, back to back. Number the sections to show how they join. Small sheets of quadrille ruled paper for notes and route sketching go in the same case. The maps can readily be consulted without the bother of unfolding in a wind, and are protected.

STATIONERY.— Note-books and writing paper should be quadrille ruled, for convenience in mapping and drawing to scale. A loose-leaf memorandum book is best: then you can file your notes in a safe place every evening. Postal cards may suffice for correspondence. If envelopes are carried, let them be of linen, and take along a small stick of sealing-wax. Linen wears better than paper in the pocket of a native messenger. Gummed envelopes, in a moist climate, seal themselves before you want to use them. Sealing-wax thwarts the inquisitive rural postmaster and his family. On the route out from camp your mail may go through many hands: *à bon entendeur salut!* Carry stamps in books, not sheets.

A self-filling fountain pen, and a bottle of ink with screw top held tight by a spring, an indelible pencil for marking specimens or packages for shipment, and several large rubber bands, may be needed, according to circumstances.

Take along an almanac to regulate the watch, show the moon's changes (tides, if near the coast), and, by them, to determine the day of the month and week, which one is very apt to forget when he

PERSONAL KITS

is away from civilization. Have a time-table of the railroad that you expect to return by.

MATCHBOX.— Do not omit a *waterproof* matchbox, of such pattern as has a cover that cannot drop off. I prefer a flat one. It can be opened with one hand. The matches in this box are to be used only in emergency. Carry the daily supply loose where you can get at them. For this purpose I like a pigskin pocket with snap-button, worn on the belt. The matches I waterproof, before starting, by dipping them half-length in shellac varnish thinned with alcohol to the right consistency, which is found by experiment, and laying them out separately on a newspaper to dry. This is better than using paraffine or collodion, because shellac does not wear off, and it is itself inflammable, like sealing-wax. Matches so treated can be left a long time in water without spoiling.

A bit of candle is a handy thing to start fire with wet wood, besides its other obvious use in an emergency. Sick-room candles are less bulky than common ones, burn brighter, and last longer.

FLASHLIGHT.— To find things in the tent at night, or to find one's way if belated, a pocket electric flasher is so useful that a camper should always carry one. Get one with round edges that will not wear holes in the pocket. The kind shaped like a fountain pen is all right in some cases, but not on hunting or fishing trips: the less bright metal you expose, the better.

EYE GLASSES.— If you wear them, carry a spare pair; the woods are hard on such things.

The glare of the sun on water, or snow, or in deserts, is often very trying. The best sun glasses are what are called shooting glasses, of amber color, which excludes the ultra-violet rays. They are large enough to protect the eyes against wind, dust, and flying insects. They come handy when one is pursued for an hour by a swarm of " red pepper " gnats that are bent on suicide and on blinding somebody in doing it.

FIRST AID KITS.— There are many kinds of pocket medicine cases, and of first aid boxes fitted with both medical and surgical supplies. Most of them are too large and heavy to be carried constantly on the person when a man is afield: they will be left in camp — and camp is not the place where accidents are most likely to occur.

It is quite important that the little store of first aid appliances that one does keep always at hand should be contained in a case that is *air-tight and aseptic,* yet easy to open and close. I have not seen a ready fitted emergency case that is so, except the soldier's first aid packet, which is hermetically sealed in either tin or impermeable cloth. This package contains a triangular bandage, one or two compresses of sublimated gauze, two safety pins, and instructions.

A triangular bandage is made by dividing a piece of muslin a yard square into halves by a diagonal cut joining two opposite corners, and thoroughly sterilizing it. Cuts are printed on it showing how to bandage any major part of the body. Roller bandages are difficult for untrained people to handle, but anyone can see almost at a glance how to use the triangular one. A folded neckerchief, or any triangular piece of cloth, will do as a makeshift, if an aseptic dressing is first applied, in case of an open wound. How to fold the bandage before applying is shown in Fig. 108. A tourniquet to check bleeding is made by folding into a narrow cravat, as indicated, and then twisting into rope form.

The soldier's packet is intended for a first dressing of gunshot wounds, fractures (with the aid of improvised splints), and other serious injuries. One would not care to open it if he merely had cut his thumb, skinned his knuckle, or blistered his heel. Yet it is the lesser injuries that we are most apt to suffer, and they certainly should be treated anti-

PERSONAL KITS 175

septically on the spot, lest grave consequences follow.

So, get a small tin tobacco box, flat, with rounded corners; boil it in two waters, and dry thoroughly. Then pack it as follows: From the American National Red Cross, Washington, D. C., get a packet of dressings for small cuts, etc., and one of finger dressings. The former dressing is a gauze compress, 3 x 3 inches, sewed to a muslin bandage an inch wide and a yard long; the latter is similar but smaller. Get from them also a few ampules of 3½% tincture of iodine in wooden containers. All these are cheap, but very effective and easy to apply. Put one large dressing, a couple of smaller

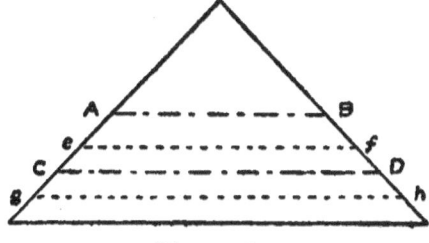

Fig. 108.—
To Fold Triangular Bandage. A B C D — Folds for Broad Cravat. AB, ef, gh — Folds for Narrow Cravat

ones, and an ampule, in your tin box, and the rest in the camp medical kit.

At the druggist's get some large capsules, and tablets of cascara, intestinal antiseptic, aspirin, potassium permanganate, and strychnine. Put a few tablets of each in capsule, label, and stow in box. Calomel and epsom salts may be added (one dose of the latter), or what you please. Fill whatever room is left with absorbent cotton. Then seal the box air-tight by running a narrow strip of the adhesive plaster around it. This is easy to open, and can be used over again many times.

In treating a wound, seize the end of the ampule that is encased in gauze and break off or crush the point of the glass, then hold the broken end down until the gauze is saturated with the iodine, clap directly to the surface of the wound, and apply either the larger or smaller dressing. A little emergency case of this sort is one of the most valuable pocket pieces that a man can carry on an outing.

Insect "dopes" are discussed in Chapter XIV.

POCKET REPAIR KIT.— Only a little of this and that, fitted into a quite small wallet. A pair of tiny, sharp-pointed scissors for trimming dressings, rigging tackle, and so on; pointed tweezers that can be used as dressing forceps, to remove splinters, and in manipulating gut for flies or leaders; some dental floss for emergency repairs on rods and the like; some 1-inch adhesive plaster; a needle or two, waxed linen thread on card, spare buttons, safety pins; one or two large rubber bands; a spare shoe lace; some strong twine; two feet of copper snare wire; a short rigged fishline, a few assorted hooks, minnow hooks with half the barb filed off, two or three split shot (tackle invaluable if you get lost); pipe cleaners (if you smoke): this exhausts the list of my own selection.

TOILET ARTICLES.— A small cake of soap in an oiled silk bag or a rubber tobacco pouch is convenient for light marching: compact, and does not rattle around. "Grandpa's" tar soap makes a good lather in any kind of water, hard or soft, warm or cold. Towels should be old (soft) and rather small (easy to wash and dry out). A pocket mirror is handy not only for toilet purposes but to examine mouth and throat or in removing a foreign substance from the eye. Other articles as required. On a hard trip cut out all but towel, soap, toothbrush, comb, and mirror.

CAMERA.— One cuts his coat according to his cloth, but if you can afford a camera with quick lens and high-speed shutter, it will pay well in good pictures. On wilderness trips it is the rule, not the exception, that you must "shoot" when the light is poor.

PERSONAL KITS

Again, you want a picture that *tells a story,* a true story, and, nine times out of ten, the only way to get it is by a snapshot taken unawares. When people pose for a camp scene or any other picture they are self-conscious, stiff, or showing off.

Your chance to get a story-picture always pops up unexpectedly. You must work quickly, or not at all. There is no chance to manœuvre for position, no time to wait on the sun. And if your camera is too large to carry in a pocket or on your belt, then, two to one, you haven't got it with you. So get a camera not over $3\frac{1}{4} \times 4\frac{1}{4}$, with special lens and shutter, if you can. At best you will spoil a good many exposures, and you can well afford to have the really good ones enlarged.

A handy way to carry a camera is to remove the sling, cut two slits in back of leather case, and wear it on your belt over the hip. Then it is out of the way, does not dangle when you stoop nor flop when you run, and yet is instantly at your service.

FIELD GLASSES.— The only satisfactory ones are those small enough to go with you everywhere, yet with good definition and wide field of view. This means prism binoculars of moderate power, say 6 diameters, or perhaps 8 for sheep or goat hunting.

Opera glasses do very well for bird study.

Some other articles of personal equipment, such as knapsacks and their substitutes, canteens, and individual cooking kits, will be discussed in Vol. II under the head of WALKING TRIPS.

CHAPTER XI
PROVISIONS

When a party camps where fresh meat and farm products can be procured as they are wanted, its provisioning is chiefly a matter of taste, and calls for no special comment here. But to have good meals in the wilderness is a different matter. A man will eat five or six pounds a day of fresh food. That is a heavy load on the trail. And fresh meat, dairy products, fruit, and vegetables, are generally too bulky, too perishable. So it is up to the woodsman to learn how to get the most nourishment out of the least weight and bulk, in materials that " keep " well.

Light outfitting, as regards food, is mainly a question of *how much water* we are willing to carry in our rations. For instance, canned peaches are 88 per cent. water. Can one afford to carry so much water from home when there is plenty of it at camp?

The following table is suggestive:

More than ¾ Water.
Fresh milk, fruit, vegetables (except potatoes).
Canned soups, tomatoes, peaches, pears, etc.

More than ½ Water.
Fresh beef, veal, mutton, poultry, eggs, potatoes.
Canned corn, baked beans, pineapple.
Evaported milk (unsweetened).

More than ⅓ Water.
Fresh bread, rolls, pork chops.
Potted chicken, etc.
Cheese.
Canned blackberries.

PROVISIONS

Less than ⅓ Water.

Dried apples, apricots, peaches, prunes.
Fruit jelly.

Less than ⅕ Water.

Salt pork. Bacon. Dried fish. Butter.
Desiccated eggs. Concentrated soups.
Powdered milk.
Wheat flour, corn meal, etc. Macaroni.
Rice, oatmeal, hominy, etc.
Dried beans, split peas.
Dehydrated vegetables.
Dried dates, figs, raisins.
Orange marmalade. Sugar. Chocolate.
Nuts. Nut butter.

Although this table is good in its way, it is not a fair measure of the relative value of foods. Even the solid part of some foodstuffs contains a good deal of refuse (fresh potatoes 20 per cent.), while others have none.

NUTRITIVE VALUES.— The nutritive elements of foodstuffs are protein, a little mineral matter, fats, and carbohydrates. Protein is the basis of muscle, bone, tendon, cartilage, skin, and the corpuscles of the blood. Fats and carbohydrates supply heat and muscular energy. In other words, the human body is an engine; protein keeps it in repair; fats and carbohydrates are the fuel to run it.

Familiar examples of proteids are lean meat and white of egg. The chief food fats are fat meat, butter, lard, oil, and cream. Carbohydrates are starchy foods (flour, cereals, etc.) and sugar (sweets of almost any kind).

Protein is the most important element of food, because nothing else can take its place in building up tissues and enriching the fluids of the body, whereas, in emergency, it can also supply power and heat, and thus run the human machine for a while without other fuel.

Men can live on foods deficient in protein, such as rice and potatoes, but they become anemic, weak, and subject to beriberi, pellagra, or other serious disease. Anyone can observe for himself the evil effects of a diet poor in protein but rich in heating power by traveling through our "hog and hominy belt." Fat pork contains hardly any protein; neither do the cabbage and potatoes that usually flank it on the negro's or poor-white's table. As for corn bread, when made as a plain hoecake or the like, it is in much the same class, and what protein it does contain is difficult to digest.

On the other hand, an undue proportion of lean meat, fish, dried beans, and other high-proteid foods, brings another train of ills. As Dr. Atwater says, "A dog can live on lean meat: he can convert its material into muscle and its energy into heat and muscular power. Man can do the same; but such a one-sided diet would not be best for the dog, and it would be still worse for the man."

The problem of a well-balanced ration consists in supplying daily the right proportion of nutritive elements in agreeable and digestible form. The problem of a campaign ration is the same, but cutting out most of the water and waste in which fresh foods abound. However, in getting rid of the water in fresh meats, fruits, and vegetables, we lose, unfortunately, much of the volatile essences that give these foods their good flavors. This loss — and it is a serious one — must be made up by the camp cook changing the menu as often as he can, by varying the ingredients and the processes of cooking.

VARIETY is quite as welcome at the camp board as anywhere else — in fact more so, for it is harder to get. Variety need not mean adding to the load. It means *substituting,* say, three 5-lb. parcels for one 15-lb. parcel, so as to have something "different" from day to day.

There is an old school of campers who affect to scorn such things. "We take nothing with us," they say, "but pork, flour, baking powder, salt, sugar, and coffee — our guns and rods furnish *us* variety." This sounds sturdy, but there is a deal of humbug in it. A spell of bad weather may defeat the best of hunters and fishermen. Even granting that luck is good, the kill is likely to be of one kind at a time. With only the six articles named, nobody can serve the same game in a variety of ways. Now, consider a moment: How would you like to sit down to nothing but fried chicken and biscuit, three times a day? Chicken everlastingly fried in pork grease — and, if you tire of that, well, eat fried "sow-belly," and sop your bread in the grease! It is just the same with trout or bass as it is with chicken; the same with pheasant or duck, rabbit or squirrel or bear. The only kind of wild meat that civilized man can relish for three consecutive meals, served in the same fashion, is venison of the deer family. Go, then, prepared to lend variety to your menu. Food that palls is bad food — worse in camp than anywhere else, for you can't escape to a restaurant.

FOOD AS A SOURCE OF ENERGY.— The energy developed by food is measured in calories. A calorie is the amount of heat required to raise one pound of water through four degrees Fahrenheit. A man at moderately active muscular work requires about 3,400 calories of food-fuel a day; one at hard muscular work, about 4,150; one at very hard work, about 5,500 calories (Atwater's figures).

According to the latest data supplied me by the U. S. Department of Agriculture (February, 1916) the fuel value of protein is about 1,815 calories per pound, that of carbohydrates is the same, and that of fats is about 4,080 calories per pound.

" A pound of wheat flour, which consists largely of starch, has an average fuel value of about 1,625 calories, and a pound of butter, which is mostly fat, about 3,410 calories. These are only about one-eighth water. Whole milk, which is seven-eighths water, has an average fuel value of 310 calories per pound; cream, which has more fat and less water, 865 calories, and skim milk, which is whole milk after the cream has been removed, 165 calories.

This high fuel value of fat explains the economy of nature in storing fat in the body for use in case of need. Fat is the most concentrated form of body fuel."

I have compiled the following table of food values, with special reference to the camp commissariat, from various reports of the U. S. Department of Agriculture. Some of the figures for fuel value, I am informed, were computed by using the factors given above; others were derived from actual determinations of the heat of combustion and the digestibility of the food materials.—

AVERAGE NUTRIENTS OF FOODS

REMAINING PERCENTAGES CONSIST OF WATER AND REFUSE

Food materials (as purchased)	Protein	Fat	Carbohydrates	Ash	Fuel value per pound
	Per ct.	Per ct.	Per ct.	Per ct.	Calories
ANIMAL FOOD					
Beef, fresh:					
Loin	16.1	17.5	—	0.9	1,025
Ribs	13.9	21.2	—	0.7	1,135
Round	19.0	12.8	—	1.0	890
Beef, cured:					
Corned	14.3	23.8	—	4.6	1,245
Dried	26.4	6.9	—	8.9	790
Salted (mess beef)	11.2	39.9	—	5.9	1,890
Tongue, pickled	11.9	19.2	—	4.3	1,010
Beef, canned:					
Boiled	25.5	22.5	—	1.3	1,425
Corned	26.3	18.7	—	4.0	1,280
Roast	25.9	14.8	—	1.3	1,105
Tongue, ground	19.5	23.2	—	4.0	1,340
Pork, cured:					
Bacon, smoked	9.1	62.2	—	4.1	2,715
Ham, smoked	14.2	33.4	—	4.2	1,635
Salt pork	1.9	86.2	—	3.9	3,555
Lard	—	100.0	—	—	4,080
Pork, canned:					
Ham, deviled	19.0	34.1	—	3.3	1,790
Sausage:					
Bologna	18.2	19.7	—	3.8	1,155
Summer	24.5	42.1	—	7.0	2,230
Sausage, canned:					
Frankfort	14.9	9.9	—	2.8	695
Oxford	9.9	58.5	0.6	2.1	2,665
Pork	14.5	21.6	—	1.8	1,180
Soups, canned (not dried):					
Beef	4.4	0.4	1.1	1.2	120
Chicken	2.9	3.3	5.1	1.6	300
Cream of celery	2.1	2.8	5.0	1.5	235
Tomato	1.8	1.1	5.6	1.5	185
Poultry, fresh:					
Chicken	14.4	12.6	—	0.7	910

Table continued.

Food materials (as purchased)	Protein	Fat	Carbohydrates	Ash	Fuel value per pound
	Per ct.	Per ct.	Per ct.	Per ct.	Calories
Duck	15.4	16.0	—	1.1	1,085
Goose	14.8	25.5	—	1.0	1,475
Pheasant	21.5	4.2	—	1.0	730
Quail	22.3	6.1	—	1.4	835
Turkey	19.0	16.2	—	1.0	1,185
Poultry, canned:					
Chicken, boned	27.7	12.8	—	2.2	1,245
Chicken, potted	19.4	20.3	—	2.5	1,390
Terrine de foie gras	13.6	38.2	4.3	2.6	2,075
Turkey, potted	17.2	22.0	—	3.0	1,390
Frogs' legs:	10.5	0.1	—	0.7	195
Fish, fresh, dressed:					
Bass, small-mouthed	11.7	1.3	—	0.7	263
Perch, white	8.8	1.8	—	0.5	231
Pickerel	12.0	0.2	—	0.7	227
Salmon	15.0	9.5	—	0.9	658
Trout, brook	11.9	1.3	—	0.7	268
Trout, lake	11.0	6.2	—	0.7	449
Fish, cured:					
Cod, salt	16.0	0.4	—	18.5	325
Halibut, smoked	19.3	14.0	—	1.9	916
Herring, smoked	20.5	8.8	—	7.4	755
Fish, canned:					
Salmon	19.5	7.5	—	2.0	658
Sardines	23.7	12.1	—	5.3	916
Shellfish, fresh:					
Clams, round	10.6	1.1	5.2	2.3	331
Oysters, "solids"	6.0	1.3	3.3	1.1	222
Eggs:					
Fresh hen's	13.1	9.3	—	0.9	635
Evaporated, whole	46.9	36.0	7.1	3.6	2,525
Evaporated, yolk	33.3	51.6	5.7	3.5	2,794
Milk:					
Fresh milk, whole	3.3	4.0	5.0	0.7	310
Cream	2.5	18.5	4.5	0.5	865
Condensed, sweetened	8.8	8.3	54.1	1.9	1,430
Evaporated, plain	7.4	8.5	11.1	1.7	683
Milk powder, from skimmed milk	34.0	3.1	51.9	8.0	1,785
Butter, Cheese:					
Butter	1.0	85.0	—	3.0	3,410
Cheese, full cream	25.9	33.7	2.4	3.8	1,885
VEGETABLE FOOD					
Flour, etc.:					
Corn meal	9.2	1.9	75.4	1.0	1,635
Corn, parched	11.5	8.4	72.3	2.6	1,915
Corn, popped	10.7	5.0	78.7	1.3	1,882
Hominy (grits)	8.6	0.6	79.6	0.3	1,671
Oats, rolled	16.1	7.4	66.5	1.8	1,759
Macaroni, etc.	13.4	0.9	74.1	1.3	1,645
Rice	6.9	0.3	80.0	0.5	1,546
Rye flour	6.8	0.9	78.7	0.7	1,620
Tapioca	0.4	0.1	88.0	0.1	1,650
Wheat breakfast food	12.1	1.8	75.2	1.3	1,680
Wheat flour, entire	13.8	1.9	71.9	1.0	1,650
Wheat flour, roller process	11.4	1.0	75.1	0.5	1,635

Food materials (as purchased)	Protein	Fat	Carbohydrates	Ash	Fuel value per pound
	Per ct.	Per ct.	Per ct.	Per ct.	Calories
Bread, etc.:					
Boston brown bread	6.3	2.1	45.8	1.9	1,110
Cake, sweet	6.3	9.0	63.3	1.5	1,630
Crackers, soda	9.8	9.1	73.1	2.1	1,875
Hoecake (plain corn bread)	4.0	0.6	40.2	2.4	885
Johnnycake	7.8	2.2	57.7	2.9	1,385
Rye bread	9.0	0.6	53.2	1.5	1,170
Wheat bread, white	9.2	1.3	53.1	1.1	1,200
Whole-wheat bread	9.7	0.9	49.7	1.3	1,130
Sweets:					
Candy, plain	—	—	96.0	—	1,680
Cane molasses	—	—	70.0	—	1,225
Cherry jelly	1.1	—	77.2	0.7	1,445
Honey	—	—	81.0	—	1,420
Maple sirup	—	—	71.4	—	1,250
Orange marmalade	0.6	—	84.5	0.3	1,585
Sugar, granulated	—	—	100.0	—	1,820
Vegetables, fresh:					
Onions	1.4	0.3	8.9	0.5	190
Potatoes	1.8	0.1	14.7	0.8	295
Vegetables, canned:					
Beans, baked	6.9	2.5	19.6	2.1	555
Corn, sweet	2.8	1.2	19.0	0.9	430
Peas	3.6	0.2	9.8	1.1	235
Tomatoes	1.2	0.2	4.0	0.6	95
Vegetables, dried:					
Beans, navy	22.5	1.8	59.6	3.5	1,520
Carrots, desiccated	7.7	0.6	80.3	4.9	1,790
Peas, split	24.6	1.0	62.0	2.9	1,565
Nuts:					
Almonds	21.4	54.4	16.8	2.5	2,895
Cocoanut, desiccated	6.3	57.4	31.5	1.3	3,125
Peanuts	29.8	43.5	17.1	2.2	2,610
Peanut butter	29.3	46.5	17.1	5.0	2,825
Pecans	12.1	70.7	12.2	1.6	3,300
Fruits, fresh:					
Apples	0.4	0.5	14.2	0.3	290
Bananas	1.3	0.6	22.0	0.8	460
Cranberries	0.4	0.6	9.9	0.2	215
Lemons	1.0	0.7	8.5	0.5	205
Oranges	0.8	0.2	11.6	0.5	240
Fruits, canned:					
Blackberries	0.8	2.1	56.4	0.7	1,150
Cherries	1.1	0.1	21.1	0.5	415
Olives, pickled	1.1	27.6	11.6	1.7	1,400
Peaches	0.7	0.1	10.8	0.3	220
Pineapples	0.4	0.7	36.4	0.7	715
Fruits, dried:					
Apples	1.6	2.2	68.1	2.0	1,350
Apricots	4.7	1.0	62.5	2.4	1,290
Dates, pitted	2.1	2.8	78.4	1.3	1,615
Figs	4.3	0.3	74.2	2.4	1,475
Prunes, pitted	2.1	—	73.3	2.3	1,400
Raisins	2.6	3.3	76.1	3.4	1,605
Miscellaneous:					
Chocolate	12.9	48.7	30.3	2.2	2,625
Cocoa	21.6	28.9	37.7	7.2	2,160
Olive Oil	—	100.0	—	—	4,080

PROVISIONS

Coffee, "cereal coffee," tea, condiments, and common beef extracts contain practically no nutriment, their function being to stimulate the nerves and digestive organs, to add agreeable flavor, or, in the case of salt, to furnish a necessary mineral ingredient.

DIGESTIBILITY.— In applying the above table we must bear in mind the adage that "we live not upon what we eat but upon what we digest." Some foods rich in protein, especially beans, peas, and oat meal, are not easily assimilated, unless cooked for a longer time than campers generally can spare. A considerable part of their protein is liable to putrefy in the alimentary canal, and so be worse than wasted. An excess of meat or fish will do the same thing. Other foods of very high theoretical value are constipating if used in large amounts, as cheese, nuts, chocolate.

The protein of animal food is more digestible than that of vegetable food by about 13 per cent. (average), and the protein of wheat is more easily assimilated than that of corn or oats. I quote the following from an article on army rations by Dr. Woods Hutchinson:

"Every imaginable grain, nut, root, pith or pulp that contains starch has been tried out as a substitute for it [wheat] because these are either cheaper in proportion to their starch content than wheat or can be grown in climates and latitudes where wheat will not flourish. Corn has been tried in the subtropics, rice in the tropics, oats, rye and barley in the north temperate zone, potatoes, sago from the palm, and tapioca from the manioc root.

"Only the net result can be given here, which is that no civilized nation that can raise the money or provide the transportation to get wheat will allow its army to live on any other yet discovered or invented grain or starch. Rice, corn meal, potatoes, sago and tapioca are, of course, ruled out at once, because they contain only starch and nothing to match in the slightest degree the twelve or fourteen per cent. of gluten, or vegetable meat, that gives wheat its supreme value.

"After our first food analyses a desperate attempt was made to substitute corn for wheat, because it contained from five to seven per cent. of protein — called zein — a perfectly good protein in the books and in the laboratories;

but it simply would not work in the field. Armies fed on it promptly showed signs of nitrogen starvation; and, about thirty years later, up came our physiologists with the belated explanation that, though zein was a right-enough protein in composition and chemical structure, only about a third of it could be utilized in the human body.

"Even the purely Oriental nations — the Japanese, Chinese and Hindus — born and brought up on rice, have formally abandoned it in their army ration and have endeavored to substitute wheat for it, though expense and the inborn prejudices of their soldiers have proved considerable obstacles. Troops or nations fed on rice are subject to beriberi and are cured by a diet rich in protein, either vegetable or animal, wheat or meat. Meat and wheat in the ration have wiped out four-fifths of the beriberi in the Japanese army and navy. Those fed on corn become subject to pellagra, which is ravaging our Southern States to-day.

"As for the northern grains, barley, rye and oats, which also contain some gluten, these are all inferior to wheat — rye and barley on account of their low protein content and considerable bulk of innutritious, gelatinous and gummy materials, which disturb the digestion; and oats on account of the irritating bitter extractives with which their high percentage of protein is combined. Nobody but a Scotchman can live on oatmeal as his sole breadstuff; and it has taken generations of training and gallons of whisky on the side to enable him to do it."

This is not saying that the grains here condemned are not good and proper food when used in the right combination with other nutrients; but it is saying that neither of them is fit for continuous use as the mainstay of one's rations.

FOOD COMPONENTS.— Let us now consider the material of field rations, item by item.—

Bacon.— Good old breakfast bacon worthily heads the list, for it is the campaigner's stand-by. It keeps well in any climate, and demands no special care in packing. It is easy to cook, combines well with almost anything, is handier than lard to fry things with, does just as well to shorten bread or biscuits, is very nutritious, and nearly everybody likes it. Take it with you from home, for you can seldom buy it away from railroad towns. Get the boneless, in 5 to 8-lb. flitches. Let canned bacon

PROVISIONS 187

alone: it lacks flavor, and costs more than it is worth. A little mould on the outside of a flitch does no harm, but reject bacon that is soft and watery, or with yellow fat, or with brownish or black spots in the lean.

Salt Pork (*alias* middlings, sides, bellies, Old Ned, *et al.*).— Commendable or accursed, according to how it is used. Nothing quite equals it in baking beans. Savory in some boiled dishes. When fried, as a *pièce de résistance*, it successfully resists most people's gastric juices, and is nauseous to many. Purchaseable at most frontier posts and at many backwoods farms.

Smoked Ham.— Small ones generally are tough and too salty. Hard to keep in warm or damp weather; moulds easily. Is attractive to blow-flies, which quickly fill it with "skippers," if they can get at it. If kept in a cheesecloth bag, and hung in a cool, airy place, a ham will last until eaten up, and will be relished. Ham will keep, even in warm weather, if packed in a stout paper bag so as to exclude flies. It will keep indefinitely if sliced, boiled, or fried, and put up in tins with melted lard poured over it to keep out air.

Dried Beef.— Cuts from large hams are best. Of limited use in pick-up meals. A notorious thirst-breeder. Not comparable to "jerked" beef, which, unfortunately, is not in the market. (For the process of jerking venison, see Chapter XV.)

Canned Meats and Poultry of all descriptions are quite unfit for steady diet. Devilled or potted ham, chicken, tongue, sausage, and the like, are endurable at picnics, and valuable in emergencies, as when a hard storm makes outdoor cooking impossible. Canned corned beef makes a passable hash.

There is a great difference in quality of canned meats. The cheaper brands found in every grocery store are, generally, abominations. Common canned "roast beef," for example (which has never been roasted at all, but boiled) is stringy, tasteless, and repugnant. Get catalogues from well-known grocers in the large cities who handle first-class goods.

Never eat meat that has been standing in an opened can: it soon undergoes putrefactive changes. A bulged can (unless frozen) indicates spoiled contents. If ever you have to treat a case of ptomaine poisoning you will not soon forget it.

Canned Soups.— These are wholesome enough, but the fluid kinds are very bulky for their meagre nutritive value. However, a few cans of consommé are fine for "stock" in camp soups or stews, and invaluable in case of sickness. Here, as with canned meat, avoid the country grocery kind.

Condensed Soups.— Soup powders are a great help in time of trouble — but don't rely on them for a full meal. There are some that are complete in themselves and require nothing but 15 to 20 minutes' cooking; others take longer, and demand (in small type on the label) the addition of ingredients that generally you haven't got. Try various brands at home, till you find what you like.

Cured Fish.— Shredded codfish, and smoked halibut, sprats, boneless herring, are portable and keep well. They will be relished for variety sake.

Canned Fish.— Not so objectionable as canned meat. Salmon and sardines are rich in protein. Canned codfish balls save a great deal of time in preparation, and are sometimes welcome when you have no potatoes for the real thing. But go light: these things are only for a change now and then, or for emergency use in bad weather.

Eggs.— To vary the camp bill of fare, eggs are simply invaluable, not only by themselves, but as ingredients in cooking. Look at the cook's time-table at the end of this volume and observe how many of the best dishes call for eggs in making them up.

When means of transportation permit, fresh eggs may be carried to advantage. A hand crate holding 12 dozen weighs about 24 pounds, filled.

Eggs can be packed along in winter without danger of breakage by carrying them frozen. Do not try to boil a frozen egg: peel it as you would a hard-boiled one, and then fry or poach.

To test an egg for freshness, drop it into cold water; if it sinks quickly it is fresh, if it stands on end it is doubtful, if it floats it is surely bad.

To preserve eggs, rub them all over with vaseline, being careful that no particle of shell is uncoated. They will keep good much longer than if treated with lime water, salt, paraffine, water-glass or any of the other common expedients.

On hard trips it is impracticable to carry eggs in the shell. Some campers break fresh eggs and pack them in friction-top cans. The yolks soon break, and they will keep but a short time. A *good* brand of desiccated eggs is the solution of this problem. It does away with all risk of breaking and spoiling, and reduces bulk and weight very much, as will be seen below.

Desiccated eggs vary a great deal in quality according to material and process employed. Condemned storage eggs have been used by unscrupulous manufacturers, and so, it is said, have the eggs of sea-fowl. I have tried some brands that were uneatable by themselves, nor did they improve any dish I combined them with. On the other hand, I have had five or six years' experience with evaporated eggs made by an Iowa firm which make excellent omelettes and scrambled eggs and are quite equal to fresh ones in bakestuffs and for various other culinary purposes. They are made from fresh hens' eggs (*whole,* but with sometimes more yolk added) by a strictly sanitary process. A 1-lb. can, equal to about 3 dozen fresh eggs, measures 6 x 3 x 3 inches and weighs 1 lb. 5 oz. gross. It costs little more than fresh eggs, and the powder will never spoil if kept dry. Of course, it cannot be used as fried, boiled, or poached eggs. For omelettes, etc., the powder must soak about an hour in cold or lukewarm water before using; it can be used dry in mixing dough. Thanks to this invention, the camp flapjack need no longer be a culinary horror.

Desiccated eggs made of the yolks only are merely useful as ingredients in cooking.

Milk.— Sweetened condensed milk (the "salve" of the lumberjacks) is distasteful to most people. Plain evaporated milk is the thing to carry — and don't leave it out if you can practicably tote it. The notion that this is a "baby food," to be scorned by real woodsmen, is nothing but a foolish conceit. Few things pay better for their transportation. It will be allowed that Admiral Peary knows something about food values. Here is what he says in *The North Pole*: "The essentials, and the only essentials, needed in a serious artic sledge journey, no matter what the season, the temperature, or the duration of the journey — whether one month or six — are four: pemmican, tea, ship's biscuit, condensed milk. . . . The standard daily ration for work on the final sledge journey toward the Pole on all expeditions has been as follows: 1 lb. pemmican, 1 lb. ship's biscuit, 4 oz. condensed milk, ½ oz. compressed tea."

Milk, either evaporated or powdered, is a very important ingredient in camp cookery. Look again at the cook's time-table previously mentioned.

Years ago I used to get an excellent powdered milk from a New York outfitter. It dissolved readily, was quite creamy rich, and had none of the scalded taste that one notices in most brands of evaporated milk. Then it went out of the market, and I have looked for it in vain. It was made of whole milk, retaining the butter fat. That was why it was rich, and that is why it was not a commercial success, for it would not keep well in storage — the fatty part would turn rancid, or at least grow stale.

I do not know of any but skim milk powders now on sale, excepting certain high-priced ones sold as food for infants or invalids, and none of these has the fresh milk flavor of the kind I got from the outfitter. However, skim milk powder is useful in cooking, and I would carry it where evaporated milk would be too heavy.

Butter.— This is another "soft" thing that pays its freight. Look up its nutritive value in the table already given.

There is a western firm that puts up very good butter hermetically sealed in 2-lb. cans. It will keep indefinitely.

For ordinary trips it suffices to pack butter firmly into pry-up tin cans which have been sterilized by thorough scalding and then cooled in a perfectly clean place. Keep it in a spring or in cold running water (hung in a net, or weighted with a rock) whenever you can. When traveling, wrap the cold can in a towel or other insulating material.

If I had to cut out either lard or butter, I would keep the butter. It serves all the purposes of lard in cooking, is wholesomer, and, beyond that, it is the most concentrated source of energy that one can use with impunity.

Cheese.— Cheese has nearly twice the fuel value of a porterhouse steak of equal weight, and it contains a fourth more protein. It is popularly supposed to be hard to digest, but in reality is not so, if used in moderation. The best kind for campers is potted cheese, or cream or "snappy" cheese put up in tin foil. If not so protected from air it soon dries out and grows stale. A tin of imported Camembert will be a pleasant surprise on some occasion.

Bread, Biscuits.— It is well to carry enough yeast bread for two or three days, until the game country is reached and camp routine is established. To keep it fresh, each loaf must be sealed up in waxed paper or parchment paper (the latter is best, because it is tough, waterproof, grease-proof). Bread freezes easily; for cold-weather luncheons carry toasted bread.

Hardtack (pilot bread, ship biscuit) can be recommended only for such trips or cruises as do not permit baking. It is a cracker prepared of plain flour and water, not even salted, and kiln-dried to a chip, so as to keep indefinitely, its only enemies being weevils. Get the coarsest grade. To make hardtack palatable, toast it until crisp, or soak in hot coffee and butter it, or at least salt it.

Swedish hardtack, made of whole rye flour, is good for a change.

Plasmon biscuit, imported from England, is the most nutritious breadstuff I have ever used. It is a round cracker, firm but not hard, of good flavor, containing a large percentage of the protein of milk, six of the small biscuits holding as much proteid as a quarter of a pound of beef. Plasmon will be discussed in Volume II, under EMERGENCY RATIONS.

Flour.— Graham and entire-wheat flours contain more protein than patent flour, but this is offset by the fact that it is not so digestible as the protein of standard flour. Practically there is little or no difference between them in the amount of protein assimilated. The same seems to be true of their mineral ingredients.

Many campers depend a good deal on self-raising flour because it saves a little trouble in mixing. But such flour is easily spoiled by dampness, it does not make as good biscuit or flapjacks as one can turn out in camp by doing his own mixing, and it will not do for thickening, dredging, etc.

Flour and meal should be sifted before starting on an expedition: there will be no sieve in camp.

Baking Powder.— Get the best, made with pure cream of tartar. It costs more than the alum powders, and does not go so far, bulk for bulk; but it is much kinder to the stomach. Baking soda will not be needed on short trips, but is required for longer ones, in making sour-dough, as a steady diet of baking-powder bread or biscuit will ruin the stomach, if persisted in for a considerable time. Soda also is useful medicinally.

Corn Meal.— Some like yellow, some prefer white. The flavor of freshly ground meal is best, but the ordinary granulated meal of commerce keeps better, because it has been kiln-dried. Corn meal should not be used as the leading breadstuff, for reasons already given, but johnnycake, corn pancakes, and mush, are a welcome change from hot wheat bread or biscuit, and the average novice at cooking may succeed better with them. The meal is useful to roll fish in, before frying.

Breakfast Cereals.— These according to taste, and for variety sake. Plain cereals, particularly oat meal, require long cooking, either in a double boiler or with constant stirring, to make them digestible; and then there is a messy pot to clean up. They do more harm than good to campers who hurry their cooking. So it is best to buy the partially cooked cereals that take only a few minutes to prepare. Otherwise the " patent breakfast foods " have no more nutritive quality than plain grain; some of them not so much. The notion that bran has remarkable food value is a delusion: it actually makes the protein of the grain less digestible. As for mineral matter, to " build up bone and teeth and brawn," there is enough of it in almost any mixed diet, without swallowing a lot of crude fiber.

Rice, although not very appetising by itself, combines so well in stews or the like, and goes so well in pudding, that it deserves a place in the commissariat.

Macaroni, etc.— The various *paste* (pas-tay), as the Italians call them, take the place of bread, may be cooked in many ways to lend variety, and are especially good in soups, which otherwise would have little nourishing power. Spaghetti, vermicelli, and noodles, all are good in their way. Break macaroni into inch pieces, and pack so that insects cannot get into it. It is more wholesome than flapjacks, and it " sticks to the ribs."

Sweets.— Sugar is stored-up energy, and is assimilated more quickly than any other food. Men in the open soon get to craving sweets.

The " substitute " variously known as saccharin,

saxin, crystallose, is no substitute at all, save in mere sweetening power (in this respect one ounce of it equals about eighteen pounds of sugar). This drug, which is derived from coal tar, has medicinal qualities and injures one's health if persistently taken. It has none of the nutritive value of sugar, and supplies no energy whatever. Its use in food products is forbidden under the Federal pure-food law.

Maple sugar is always welcome. Get the soft kind that can be spread on bread for luncheons. Sirup is easily made from it in camp by simply bringing it to a boil with the necessary amount of water. Ready-made sirup is mean to pack around.

Sweet chocolate (not too sweet) has remarkable sustaining power. It will be mentioned further in Volume II, under EMERGENCY RATIONS.

When practicable, take along some jam and marmalade. The commissaries of the British army were wise when they gave jam an honorable place in Tommy Atkins' field ration. Yes: jam for soldiers in time of war. So many ounces of it, substituted, mind you, for so many ounces of the porky, porky, porky, that has ne'er a streak of lean. So, a little currant jelly with your duck or venison is worth breaking all rules for. Such conserves can be repacked by the buyer in pry-up cans that have been sterilized as recommended under the heading *Butter*.

Fresh Vegetables.— The only ones worth taking along are potatoes and onions. Choose potatoes with small eyes and of uniform medium size, even if you have to buy half a bushel to sort out a peck. They are very heavy and bulky in proportion to their food value; so you cannot afford to be burdened with any but the best. Cereals and beans take the place of potatoes when you go light.

Fresh onions are almost indispensable for seasoning soups, stews, etc. A few of them can be taken along almost anywhere. I generally carry at least one, even on a walking trip. Onions are good for the suddenly overtaxed system, relieve the inordinate thirst that one experiences the first day or two, and assist excretion. Freezing does not spoil onions if they are kept frozen until used.

Beans.— A prime factor in cold weather camping. Take a long time to cook ("soak all day and cook all night" is the rule). Cannot be cooked done at altitudes of five thousand feet and upward. Large varieties cook quickest, but the small white navy beans are best for baking. Pick them over before packing, as there is much waste.

Split Peas.— Used chiefly in making a thick, nourishing soup.

Dehydrated Vegetables.— Much of the flavor of fresh vegetables is lost when the juice is expressed or evaporated, but all of their nutriment is retained and enough of the flavor for them to serve as fair substitutes when fresh vegetables cannot be carried. They help out a camp stew, and may even be served as side dishes if one has butter and milk to season them. Generally they require soaking (which can be done overnight); then they are to be boiled slowly until tender, taking about as much time as fresh vegetables. If cooking is hurried they will be woody and tasteless.

Dehydrated vegetables are very portable, keep in any climate, and it is well to carry some on trips far from civilization.

Canned Vegetables.— In our table of food values it will be noticed that the least nourishing article for its weight and bulk is a can of tomatoes. Yet these "airtights" are great favorites with outdoorsmen, especially in the West and South, where frequently they are eaten raw out of the can. It is not so much their flavor as their acid that is grateful to a stomach overtaxed with fat or canned meat and hot bread three times a day. If wanted only as an adjuvant to soups, stews, rice, macaroni, etc., the more concentrated tomato purée will serve very well.

Canned corn (better still, "kornlet," which is

the concentrated milk of sweet corn) is quite nourishing, and everybody likes it.

A few cans of baked beans (*without* tomato sauce) will be handy in wet weather. The B. & M. ¾-lb. cans are convenient for a lone camper or for two going light.

Nuts.— A handful each of shelled nuts and raisins, with a cake of sweet chocolate, will carry a man far on the trail, or when he has lost it. The kernels of butternuts and hickory nuts have the highest fuel value of our native species; peanuts and almonds are very rich in protein; Brazil nuts, filberts, and pecans, in fat. Peanut butter is a concentrated food that goes well in sandwiches. One can easily make nut butter of any kind (except almonds or Brazil nuts) for himself by using the nut grinder that comes with a kitchen food-chopper, and can add ground dates, ground popcorn, or whatever he likes; but such preparations will soon grow rancid if not sealed air-tight. Nut butter is more digestible than kernels unless the latter are thoroughly chewed.

Fruits.— All fruits are very deficient in protein and (except olives) in fat, but dried fruit is rich in carbohydrates. Fruit acid (that of prunes, dried apricots, and dehydrated cranberries, when fresh fruit cannot be carried) is a good corrective of a too fatty and starchy or sugary diet, and a preventive of scurvy. Most fruits are laxative, and for that reason, if none other, a good proportion of dried fruit should be included in the ration, no matter how light one travels; otherwise one is likely to suffer from constipation when he changes "from town grub to trail grub."

Among canned fruits, those that go farthest are pineapples and blackberries.

Excellent jelly can be made in camp from dried apples (see recipe in Chapter XXII).

There is much nourishment in dates, figs (those dried round are better than layer figs) and raisins.

Pitted dates and seedless raisins are best for light outfits. And do not despise the humble prune; buy the best grade in the market (unknown to landladies) and soak overnight before stewing: it will be a revelation. Take a variety of dried fruits, and mix them in different combinations, sweet and tart, so as not to have the same sauce twice in succession; then you will learn that dried fruits are by no means a poor substitute for fresh or canned ones.

In hot weather I carry a few lemons whenever practicable. Limes are more compact and better medicinally, but they do not keep well. Lime juice in bottles is excellent, if you can carry it.

Citric acid crystals may be used in lieu of lemons when going light, but the flavor is not so good as that of lemonade powder that one can put up for himself. The process is described by A. W. Barnard: "Squeeze out the lemons and sift into the clear juice four to six spoonfuls of sugar to a lemon; let stand a few days if the weather is dry, or a week if wet, till it is dried up, then pulverize and put up into capsules." Gelatin capsules of any size, from 1-oz. down, can be procured at a drugstore. They are convenient to carry small quantities of spices, flavorings, medicines, etc., on a hike.

Vinegar and pickles are suitable only for fixed camps or easy cruises.

Fritures.— Lard is less wholesome than olive oil, or "Crisco," or the other preparations of vegetable fat. Crisco can be heated to a higher temperature than lard without burning, thus ensuring the "surprise" (see Chapter XVI), which prevents getting a fried article sodden with grease; it does as well as lard for shortening; and it can be used repeatedly without transmitting the flavor of one dish to the next one. Olive oil is superior as a friture, especially for fish, but expensive.

Beverages.—The best coffee can only be made from freshly roasted berries. Have it roasted and ground the day before you start, and put up in small air-tight canisters. It loses strength rapidly after a tin has been opened. If you are a connoisseur you will never be tempted more than once by any condensed coffee or substitute.

Tea is a better pick-me-up than coffee or liquor. Even if you don't use it at home, take along on your camping trip enough for midday meals. Tea tabloids are not bad, but I advise using the real thing. On a hike, with no tea-ball, I tie up enough for each pint in a bit of washed cheesecloth, loosely, leaving enough string attached whereby to whisk it out after exactly four minutes' steeping.

However it may be with you at home, leading a sedentary life, you probably will find that tea and coffee do you a world of good when working heartily out-of-doors.

There are exceptions, to be sure; but old campaigners generally will agree with Dr. Hutchinson when, having discussed the necessary solids for a soldier's ration, he says this:

"But is even this dietetic trinity of bread, beef and sugar, with greens and dessert on the side, sufficient? The results of a hundred campaigns have shown that it is not. Man is not merely a stomach and muscles — he is also a bundle of nerves; and they require their share of pabulum. In the early days the nerve-steadier in the soldier's diet used to be supplied in the form of grog, beer, wine, whisky; and up to about one hundred years ago alcohol in some form was considered to be an absolutely indispensable part of the army ration.

"Gradually, however, and by bitter experience, it was realized that alcohol's way of steadying and supporting the nerves was to narcotize them, which practically means poison them; that it gave no nourishment to the body and, instead of improving the digestion and utilization of food, really hindered and interfered with them. Man must have something to drink as well as to eat; but what can be found as a substitute?

"About two centuries ago two new planets swam into our human ken above the dietetic horizon — tea and coffee. They were looked on with great suspicion at first, partly because they were attractive and partly because they were new. They were denounced by the Puritan because they were pleasant, and by the doctor because they were not in the pharmacopœia; but, in spite of bitter opposition, they won their way.

"It is doubtful whether any addition to the comfort of civilized man within the last two hundred years in the realm of dietetics can be mentioned that equals them. Certainly, if we take into consideration the third new article of food, which came in and still goes down with them — sugar — it would be impossible to match them with anything of equal value."

Cocoa is not only a drink but a food. It is best for the evening meal, because it makes one sleepy, whereas tea and coffee have the opposite effect.

Get the soluble kind, if you want it quickly prepared.

Condiments.— Do not leave out a small assortment of condiments wherewith to vary the taste of common articles and serve a new sauce or gravy or pudding now and then.

Salt is best carried in a wooden box. The amount used in cooking and at table is small, but if pelts are to be preserved or game shipped out, considerably more will be needed.

White pepper is better than black. Some Cayenne or Chili should also be taken. Red pepper is not only a good stomachic, but also is fine for a chill (made into a tea with hot water and sugar).

Among condiments I class beef extract, bouillon cubes or capsules, and the like. They are of no use as food, except to stimulate a feeble stomach or furnish a spurt of energy, but invaluable for flavoring camp-made soups and stews when you are far away from beef. The powder called Oystero yields an oyster flavor.

When one is not going into a game country, it is worth while to carry Worcestershire sauce and pure tomato catchup, to relieve the monotony of cured and canned meats or of too much fish.

Mustard is useful not only at table but for medicinal purposes; cloves, not only for its more obvious purposes, but to stick in an onion for a stew, and perchance for a toothache.

Celery and parsley can now be had in dehydrated form. Some sage may be needed for stuffing.

If you aim at cake-making and puddings, ginger and cinnamon may be required. Curry powder is relished by many; its harshness may be tempered with sweet fruits or sugar.

Finally, a half-pint of brandy is worth its weight, for brandy-sauce — but keep it where it can't be filched, or somebody will invent a bellyache instanter.

On short trips, salt and pepper will meet all requirements.

RATION LISTS.— A ration list showing how much food of each kind is required, per man and per week, cannot be figured out satisfactorily unless one knows where the party is going, at what season of the year, how the stuff is to be carried, whether there is to be good chance of game or fish, and something about the men's personal tastes. Still, I may offer some suggestions.

Our army garrison ration often is used as a guide. Introducing the permissible substitutions in ratios given below, it works out as follows: —

U. S. ARMY GARRISON RATIONS
FOR ONE MAN ONE WEEK

Meats, Etc.:

	Lbs.	Oz.		
(½ time) Fresh meats, @ 20 oz. per day	4	6		
(½) Cured or canned, @ 12 oz.	2	10		
Lard, @ 0.64 oz.		4½		
Milk, evaporated, @ 0.5 oz.		3½		
Butter, @ 0.5 oz.		3½		
			7 lbs.	11½ oz.

Bread, Etc.:

	Lbs.	Oz.		
(¼) Hard bread, @ 16 oz.	1	12		
(¾) Flour, meal, @ 18 oz.	5	14½		
Baking powder, @ 1 oz. per lb. flour		6		
(½) Rice, hominy, @ 1.6 oz.		5½		
			8 lbs.	6 oz.

Vegetables:

	Lbs.	Oz.		
(½) Beans, @ 2.4 oz.		8½		
Potatoes, canned tomatoes, etc., @ 20 oz.	8	12		
			9 lbs.	4½ oz.

Fruits, Etc.:

	Lbs.	Oz.		
Prunes, dried apples or peaches, jam, @ 1.28 oz.		9		
Vinegar, @ 0.16 gill		4½		
				13½ oz.

Sugar, Etc.:

	Lbs.	Oz.		
Sugar, @ 3.2 oz.	1	6½		
Sirup, @ 0.32 gill		10		
			2 lbs.	½ oz.

Beverages:

	Lbs.	Oz.	
(⅔) Coffee, @ 1.12 oz.........		5¼	
(⅓) Tea, @ 0.32 oz.		¾	
			6 oz.

Condiments:

	Lbs.	Oz.	
Salt, @ 0.64 oz.		4½	
Pepper, @ 0.04 oz.		¼	
Spices, @ 0.014 oz............		¹⁄₁₀	
Flavoring extracts, @ 0.028 oz.		⅕	
			5 oz.

One man one week..................	28 lbs. 15 oz.
One man one day	4 lbs. 2 oz.

This is a very liberal ration, but would be so monotonous, if strictly adhered to, that much of it would be unused. Accordingly the soldier's mess is allowed to commute its surplus of staples for luxuries in which the ration is deficient.

For some years it was my practice to weigh personally, and note down at the time, the amount of provisions taken on my camping tours, and often I recorded the quantities left over at the end of the trip. I have also collected many ration lists compiled by practical woodsmen, and have spent considerable time in studying and comparing them. These varied remarkably, not so much in aggregate weights as in the proportions of this and that.

Still, a few general principles have been worked out:

1. When going as light as practicable, and taking the most concentrated (water-free) foods that will digest properly and sustain a man at hard work in the open air, the ration should not be cut down below 2¼ pounds (a ration being one man's food for one day). This is the minimum for mountaineering, arctic exploration, and wherever equipment must be "pared to the bone." This sort of provisioning will be considered in Volume II.

2. People leading an easy life in summer camp do not require so much actual nutriment as those engaged in hard travel, big game hunting, and the like; but they should have plenty of fruits and vegetables, and these things are heavy and bulky.

3. Men working hard in the open, and exposed to the vicissitudes of wilderness life, need a diet rich in protein, fats (especially in cold weather), and sweets. This may not agree with theories of dieticians, but it is the experience of millions of campaigners who know what their work demands. A low-proteid diet may be good for men leading soft lives, and for an occasional freak outdoorsman, but try it on an army in the field, or on a crew of lumberjacks, and you will face stark mutiny.

As a basis upon which the supplies for a party may be calculated, I offer, in the following table, two ration lists, called "light" and "heavy," for one man, one week. The first figures out about 4,900 calories, and the second about 5,300 calories, per man, per day. Either of these is sufficient for a man engaged in hard outdoor work; so the terms "light" and "heavy" do not refer to food values but to actual weights, the first being 3 pounds, aud the second a bit over 5 pounds, per man, per day. The difference is due chiefly to canned goods and fresh vegetables.

Observe that both of these lists include fresh

PROVISIONS

meat. It is assumed that the travelers will go either where they can supply this with game killed or where they can buy fresh meat as it is needed. Otherwise, substitute two-thirds its weight in cured meat.

For men not undergoing great strain, the "light" ration may be reduced, say to 2½ pounds a day.

CRUISER'S AND CAMPER'S RATIONS
FOR ONE MAN ONE WEEK
(Weights are *net*, not including tins, bags, wrappers.)

	LIGHT		HEAVY		
Meats, Etc.:	Lbs.	Oz.	Lbs.	Oz.	
Fresh meat	3	..	3	..	
Bacon	2	..	2	..	
Canned meat, poultry, fish	..	4	..	4	
Cured fish	..	4	..	4	
Canned soups	..	..	..	10	(1 can)
Dried soups	..	2	..	..	
Fresh eggs	..	..	1	8	(1 doz.)
Dried eggs	..	4	..	..	
Butter	..	8	..	8	
Cheese	..	4	..	4	
Crisco	..	4	..	4	
Evaporated milk	..	6	..	12	
	7	4	9	6	
Bread, Etc.:	Lbs.	Oz.	Lbs.	Oz.	
Biscuits (crackers) or fresh bread	1	..	1	..	
Wheat flour	4	..	4	..	
Corn meal	1	..	1	..	
Baking powder	..	4	..	4	
Macaroni, etc.	..	4	..	4	
Rice	..	6	..	6	
Other cereal	..	8	..	8	
	7	6	7	6	
Vegetables:	Lbs.	Oz.	Lbs.	Oz.	
Fresh potatoes	..	..	5	..	
Fresh onions	..	8	..	8	
Canned tomatoes	..	..	2	..	(1 can)
Canned corn	..	..	..	10	(½ can)
Dried beans	..	8	..	8	
Dehydrated vegetables	..	8	..	..	
	1	8	8	10	

Fruits, Acids, Nuts:	LIGHT Lbs.	LIGHT Oz.	HEAVY Lbs.	HEAVY Oz.	
Fresh lemons	..	..	1	..	(½ doz.)
Lemonade capsules	..	6	..	..	
Canned fruits	..	..	4	..	(2 cans)
Dried apples, apricots, prunes, cranberries	..	12	..	..	
Raisins, dates, figs........	..	8	..	8	
Pickles (sour)	..	..	..	6	
Shelled nuts, or nut butter	..	4	..	4	
	1	14	6	2	

Sweets:	Lbs.	Oz.	Lbs.	Oz.
Sugar (granulated)	..	14	..	14
Maple sugar (soft)........	..	8	..	8
Chocolate (medium sweet)	..	12	..	8
Jam, jelly, marmalade....	..	..	..	12
	2	2	2	10

Beverages:	Lbs.	Oz.	Lbs.	Oz.
Coffee	..	8	..	8
Tea	..	1	..	1
	..	9	..	9

Condiments:	Lbs.	Oz.	Lbs.	Oz.
*Salt	..	4	..	4
White pepper	..	¼	..	¼
Red pepper	..	⅛	..	⅛
Mustard (mixed).........	..	....	..	1
Celery, parsley (dehydrated)	..	⅜	..	⅜
Bouillon cubes	..	1	..	1
Nutmeg, cloves, cinnamon, ginger, curry powder...	..	¼	..	¼
Worcestershire sauce.....	..	..	..	2
Tomato catsup	..	..	..	2
	..	6	..	11
One man one week	21	1	35	6
One man one day.......	3	..	5	1

If butter is not carried, its weight in bacon should be added to the list; similarly other substitutions can be made to suit taste and circumstances. The second list provides enough eggs and milk

* Not allowing for preparing skins and salting horses.

to allow their use liberally in cooking. Its ration is of about the same weight as that of the U. S. Navy.

PACKING FOOD.— Meat of any kind will quickly mould or spoil if packed in tins from which air is not exhausted. Wrap your bacon, pork, etc., in parchment paper, which is grease-proof (you can buy it from a mail-order house — for small quantities get parchment paper ice blankets and cut to suit), then enclose the meat in loose cheesecloth bags that can be hung up in camp, secure from insects.

Flour should not be carried in the original sacks: they wet through or absorb moisture from the air, snag easily, and burst under the strain of a lash-rope. Pack your flower, cereals, vegetables, dried fruits, etc., in the round-bottomed paraffined bags sold by outfitters (various sizes, from 10 lbs. down), which are damp-proof and have the further merit of standing up on their bottoms instead of always falling over. Put a tag on each bag and label it in *ink*. These small bags may then be stowed in 9-inch waterproof canvas provision bags (see outfitter's catalogues), but in that case the thing you want is generally at the bottom. A much handier pack for horse or canoe is the side-opening one shown in Fig. 101.

Butter, lard, ground coffee, tea, sugar, jam, matches, go in pry-up tin cans, sold by outfitters (small quantities in mailing tubes), or in common capped tins with tops secured by surgeon's plaster. Get pepper and spices in shaker-top cans, or, if you carry common shakers, cover tops with cloth and snap stout rubber bands around them.

Salt, as it draws moisture, is best carried in a wooden box or in mailing tubes.

Often it is well to carry separately enough food to last the party between the jumping-off place and the main camp site, as it saves the bother of breaking bulk *en route*.

206 CAMPING AND WOODCRAFT

When transportation is easy it pays to pack the bread, bags of flour, etc., in a tin wash-boiler or two, which are wrapped in burlaps and crated. These make capital grub boxes in camp, securing their contents from wet, insects and rodents. Ants in summer and mice at all times are downright pests of the woods, to say nothing of the wily coon, the predatory mink, the inquisitive skunk, and the fretful porcupine. The boilers are useful, too, on many occasions, to catch rain-water, boil clothes, waterproof and dye tents, and so forth. After all these things have been done in them they are properly seasoned for cooking a burgoo.

Camp chests are very convenient when it is practicable to carry them. In fixed camp an old trunk will do; but if you are traveling from place to place, the boxes should be small, weighing not over fifty or sixty pounds each when packed, so that one man can easily handle them unassisted. If they are specially made, cottonwood is the best material (if thoroughly seasoned boards can be had—otherwise it warps abominably). It is the strongest and toughest wood for its weight that we have, and will not splinter. For the ends and lids of small chests, ⅝-inch stuff is thick enough, and ⅜-inch for the sides, bottoms and trays. The bottom should have a pair of ⅝-inch cleats for risers and the top a similar pair to keep it from warping, unless the chests are to go on pack animals. Strap-hinges and hasp, a brass padlock and broad leather end-straps (not drop-handles) should be provided, and the chest painted.

The best size is 24 x 18 x 9 inches, this being convenient for canoes and pack-saddles. A pine grocery box of this size, with ¾-inch ends and ⅜-inch sides, top, and bottom, weighs only 10 pounds, and will answer the purpose very well. Screw a wooden handle on each end, say 5 x 2 inches, with a hand-hold gouged out of the under side.

PROVISIONS

Chests intended to be used as hanging cupboards in camp should have shelf boards packed in them, and a bread board for rolling out biscuit dough and pastry. One box should be selected with a view to using it as a camp refrigerator or spring box (see Chapter XII). For a trip by wagon a regular "chuck box" may be built, with a drop front for serving table (held by light chains when open). This box is carried upright at the rear end of the wagon *à la* cow outfit.

When cruising where there are no portages it saves lots of time and bother if you build beforehand a light mess chest partitioned to hold utensils and all the food needed for, say, a week. This may be fitted with detachable legs, and the lid so fitted that it is supported level when opened, forming a table.

A LAST LOOK AROUND.— Check off every article in the outfit as it is stowed, and keep the inventory for future reference. Then note what is left over at the end of the trip. This will help in outfitting for the next season.

There are several things to be looked after in good season before starting on a camping trip. If your shoes are new, oil them and break them in. If your rifle is new, do not dream of carrying it into the wilderness until you have "sighted it up," testing the elevations at various ranges, and making sure that the sights are accurately aligned. If your fishing tackle is old, overhaul and test it thoroughly. If you have a hollow tooth, get it filled. Pare your nails closely, or they will soon be badly broken. Get your hair cropped short. See that you have a good supply of small change when you start. Don't carry off your bunch of keys. Be on hand early at the station and see to it personally that your humble but precious duffel all gets aboard.

And now, *bon voyage!*

CHAPTER XII
CAMP MAKING

As a rule, good camp sites are not found along the beaten road. Of course, water is the prime essential, and in a country where water is scarce, you will stop at an old camping ground; otherwise it is best to avoid such a place: for one thing, you don't want to be bothered with interlopers, and for another, the previous occupants will have stripped the neighborhood of good kindling and downwood, and may have left a legacy of rubbish and fleas.

A pleasant stopping-place is seldom far to seek in a hilly country that is well wooded. There are exceptions, as in the Ozarks, where the rock is a porous limestone, the drainage mostly is underground, and there are no brooks, nor are springs as common as one would expect, though when you do strike one it is a big one. Here a traveler must depend for water chiefly on the creeks and rivers, which may be miles apart.

In a level region, whether it be open plain or timbered bottom land, good water and a high and dry site may be hard to find.

In any case, when men are journeying through a wild country that is strange to them, they should begin at least two hours before sunset to keep a bright lookout for a good place on which to spend the night, and when such is found they had better accept it at once than run the risk of "murdering a night" farther on, wherever the powers of darkness may force them to stop.

CAMP SITES.— The essentials of a good camp site are these:

CAMP MAKING

1. Pure water.
2. Wood that burns well. In cold weather there should be either an abundance of sound downwood or some standing hardwood trees that are not too big for easy felling.
3. An open spot, level enough for the tent and campfire, but elevated above its surroundings so as to have good natural drainage. It must be well above any chance overflow from the sudden rise of a neighboring stream. Observe the previous flood marks.
4. Grass or browse for the horses (if there are any) and bedding for the men.
5. Straight poles for the tent, or trees convenient for attaching the ridge rope.
6. Security against the spread of fire.
7. Exposure to direct sunlight during a part of the day, especially during the early morning hours.
8. In summer, exposure to whatever breezes may blow; in cold weather, protection against the prevailing wind.
9. Privacy.

Water, wood, and good drainage may be all you need for a " one-night stand," but the other points, too, should be considered when selecting the site for a fixed camp.

WATER.— Be particularly careful about the purity of your water supply. You come, let us say, to a mountain brook, that issues from thick forest. It ripples over clean rocks, it bubbles with air, it is clear as crystal, and cool to your thirsty throat. " Surely that is good water." But do you know where it comes from? Every mountain cabin is built close to a spring-branch. Somewhere up that brook there may be a clearing; in that clearing, a house; in that house, a case of dysentery or typhoid fever. I have known several cases of infection from just such a source. It is not true that running water purifies itself.

When one must use well-water let him note the

surrounding drainage. If the well is near a stable or outhouse, or if dishwater is thrown near it, let it alone. A well in sandy soil is more or less filtered by nature, but rocky or clayey earth may conduct disease germs a considerable distance underground. Never drink from the well of an abandoned farm: there is no telling what may have fallen into it.

A spring issuing from the living rock is worthy of confidence. Even if it be but a trickle you can scoop out a basin to receive it that soon will clear itself.

Sometimes a subaqueous spring may be found near the margin of a lake or river by paddling close inshore and trailing your hand in the water. When a cold spot is noted, go ashore and dig a few feet back from the water's edge. I have found such spring exits in the Mississippi some distance from the bank, and, by weighting a canteen, tying a string to it and another to the stopper, have brought up cool water from the river bed.

Disease germs are of animal, not vegetable, origin. Still waters are not necessarily unwholesome, even though there be rotting vegetation in them: the water of cedar and cypress swamps is good to drink, wherever there is a deep pool of it, unless polluted from some outside source. Lake water is safe if no settlements are on its border; but even so large a body as Lake Champlain has been condemned by state boards of health because of the sewage that runs into it.

When a stream is in flood it is likely to be contaminated by decayed animal matter.

Alkaline Water.— When traveling in an alkali country, carry some vinegar or limes or lemons, or (better) a glass-stoppered bottle of hydrochloric acid. One teaspoonful of hydrochloric (muriatic) neutralizes about a gallon of water, and if there should be a little excess it will do no harm, but rather assist digestion. In default of acid, you may

CAMP MAKING

add a little Jamaica ginger and sugar to the water, making a weak ginger tea.

Muddy Water.— I used to clarify Mississippi water by stirring cornmeal in it and letting it settle, or by stirring a lump of alum in it until the mud began to precipitate, and then decanting the clear water. Lacking these, one can take a good handful of grass, tie it roughly in the form of a cone six or eight inches high, invert it, pour water slowly into the grass, and a runnel of comparatively clear water will trickle down through the small end.

The following simple method of purifying muddy water is recommended by H. G. Kegley:

"Dip up what is needed, place it in such vessels as are available, and treat it to condensed milk, in the proportion of two tablespoonfuls of milk to five gallons of water. The sediment settles in a very short time. Next morning, if you desire to carry some of the water with you through the day, pour it from the settlings, and then boil the water and skim it. In that way the cream and any possibility of sourness will be removed. Water thus clarified remains palatable so long as it lasts."

Stagnant Water.— A traveler may be reduced to the extremity of using stagnant or even putrid water; but this should never be done without first boiling it. Some charred wood from the camp fire should be boiled with the water; then skim off the scum, strain, and set the water aside to cool. Boiling sterilizes, and charcoal deodorizes.

I quote the following incident from Johnson's *Getting Gold.*—

"I once rode forty-five miles with nearly beaten horses to a native well, or rock hole, to find water, the next stage being nearly fifty miles further. The well was found, but the water in it was very bad; for in it was the body of a dead kangaroo, which had apparently been there for weeks. The wretched horses, half frantic with thirst, did manage to drink a few mouthfuls, but we could not. I filled our largest billycan, holding about a gallon, slung it over the fire and added, as the wood burnt down, charcoal, till the top was covered to a depth of two inches. With the charcoal there was, of course, a little ash containing bi-carbonate of potassium. The effect was marvellous. So soon as the horrible soup came to the boil, the impurities coagulated, and after keeping it at boiling temperature for about half an hour, it was removed from the fire, the cinders skimmed out, and the water allowed to settle, which it did very quickly. It was then decanted off into an ordinary prospector's pan, and some used to make tea (the flavor of which can be better imagined than described); the remainder was allowed to stand all night, a few pieces of charcoal being added. In the morning it was bright, clear, and absolutely sweet."

Filters are not to be depended upon to purify water. At best they only clarify; they do not sterilize it. A filter, to be of any use, must be cleaned out every day or two, and the sand forming the upper layer must be thoroughly washed or replaced; otherwise the filter itself becomes a breeding-place for germs.

To Cool Water.— Travelers in arid regions carry water bags of heavy canvas or linen duck. These, when filled, constantly "sweat" or exude enough moisture to cool the contents of the bag by evaporation. Wet canteens do the same. A covered pail or other vessel can be used: wrap cloths around it, keep them wet, and hang in a current of air.

FUEL.— In summer camping little firewood is used, but in cold weather an abundance is required. Some kinds of wood make fine fires, others are poor fuel or worthless: they are classified in the next chapter. In any case there should be plenty of sound dead wood to cook with.

When traveling with a team where fuel is scarce, make a practice of tossing into the wagon any good chunks that you may find along the road.

TENT GROUND.—Avoid low ground. Seek an open spot that is level enough for the purpose, but one that has good natural drainage. Wherever you may be, pitch your tent on a rise or slight slope instead of in a depression where water will gather if it rains. Don't trust a fair sky.

If you camp on the bank of a stream, be sure to

get well above the flood-marks left by previous freshets or overflows. Observe the more or less continuous line of dead grass, leaves, twigs, mud, and other flotsam or hurrah's-nests left in bushes along the water-front.

Precautions as to elevation and drainage are especially needful in those parts of our country that are subject to cloudbursts. I have seen a ravine that had been stone-dry for months fill fifteen feet deep, in a few minutes, with a torrent that swept trees and bowlders along with it; and it is quite common in many parts of the West for wide bottoms to be flooded in a night. When I was a boy in Iowa, a "mover" camped for the night on an island in Coon River, near our place. He had a bag of gold coin, but was out of rations. A sudden flood left him marooned the next morning on a knoll scarce big enough for his team and wagon. He subsisted for a week, like his horses, on the inner bark of cottonwood, and when a rescue party found him he was kicking his bag of gold over the few yards of dry ground that were left of his domain.

Bottom lands, and deep woods where the sun rarely penetrates, should be avoided, when practicable, for they are damp lairs at best, and in warm weather they are infested with mosquitoes. Keep away from thickets in summer: they are stifling and "buggy."

A ravine or narrow valley between steep hills is a trap for fog, and the cold, heavy air from the head of the hollow pours down it at night, while an undertow of warmer air drawing upward now and then makes the smoke from one's camp-fire shift most annoyingly. Besides a ravine gets too little sunlight.

New clearings in the forest are unhealthy, for the sun gets in on plants that are intolerant of strong light, they rot, and poisonous gases arise from their decay, as well as from the recently disturbed soil.

If one is obliged to camp in a malarial region he should not leave the camp-fire until the sun is up and the fog dispelled.

Sandy beaches, and low, gravelly points, are likely to swarm in summer with midges.

Sandy soil does not afford good holding-ground for the tent pegs; neither does a loamy or clayey soil after it gets soaked from rain. The best ground is gravelly earth: it holds well, and permits the rapid filtering through of surface water. A clay top-soil holds water and is soon trodden into sticky mud after a rain.

PRECAUTIONS AGAINST FIRE.— If the camp site is strewn with leaves, cut an evergreen branch, or, with some other makeshift broom or rake, clear all the ground of leaves, pile them in the bare spot, and burn them, lest a spark set the woods afire. In evergreen or cypress forests there is often a thick scurf on the ground (dead needles, etc.) that is very inflammable. Always scrape this away before building a fire. In a dry forest carpet, or in a punky log, fire may smoulder unnoticed for several days; then, when a breeze fans it into flame, it may start a conflagration. *One can't be too careful about fire in the woods.* Never leave a camp fire or a cooking fire to burn itself out. Drench it with water, or smother it absolutely by stamping earth upon it.

NEIGHBORHOOD OF TREES.— It is a common blunder to pitch the tent directly under the " natural shelter " of a big tree. This is pleasant enough at midday, but makes the tent catch drip from dew and keeps it from drying after a rain; besides, it may be positively dangerous. One of the first things to do in choosing the tent site is to see that it is not within reach of falling limbs. A tree branch falling forty or fifty feet, and striking a tent at night, is something to be remembered — if you survive. Shun the neighborhood of tall trees that are shallow-rooted, and of those with brittle limbs (the aspens,

CAMP MAKING

poplars, cottonwood, catalpa, butternut, yellow locust, silver maple), and any with unsound branches.

Dead trees are always unsafe. Every woodsman has often known them to come thundering down without the least warning when there was not so much as a zephyr astir. A tree that leans toward camp from a steep hillside hard by is a menace, and so is any near-by tree with a hollow butt.

TREES AND LIGHTNING.—I have never seen, nor heard of, a beech tree that had been struck by lightning, although beeches are plentiful on many battle-scarred mountains where stricken trees of other species can be noted by the score. Miss Keeler says on this point: " There was so firm a belief among the Indians that a beech tree was proof against lightning that on the approach of a thunder-storm they took refuge under its branches with full assurance of safety. . . . This popular belief has recently had scientific verification. . . . The general conclusion from a series of experiments is that trees ' poor in fat ' like the oak, willow, poplar, maple, elm and ash, oppose much less resistance to the electric current than trees ' rich in fat ' like the beech, chestnut, linden and birch."

In this connection I may note that there is no truth in the old adage that "lightning does not strike twice in the same place." At Takoma Park, a suburb of Washington, on July 19, 1915, a bolt of lightning struck an oak tree standing in the garden before the administration building of the Seventh-Day Adventists. After the storm had passed, several people went out from the building to view the damage done to the tree. Three of them lingered. A second bolt, from a clear sky, struck the same tree, killed two of the people under it, and knocked the other unconscious.

Electricity follows not only the trunk of a tree but also the drip that falls from it in a rain.

SHADE.— In summer it is well to camp where one's tent will be shaded from the afternoon sun, as otherwise it will get very hot, but morning sun should strike the tent fairly, to dry it, lest the canvas mildew and the interior get damp and musty. The wetter the climate, and the thicker the surrounding forest, the greater need of such exposure. Mildew attacks leather first, then woolens, and cottons last of all.

EXPOSURE.— As a general rule, an easterly or southeasterly frontage is best, not only to admit early sunlight and rouse you betimes, but also because, in most regions, it is the quarter least given to high winds and driving rains. Sudden and violent storms usually come up out of the southwest. This is true nearly everywhere: hence the sailor calls his tarp hat a " sou-wester."

Other considerations may govern the case. In hot weather we want exposure to whatever cool breezes may blow, and they are governed by local features. Late in the season we will take advantage of whatever natural windbreak we can find, such as the edge of a forest, the lee of a cliff, of a large rock, or of an evergreen thicket. This may make a difference of 10° or 15° in temperature. A rock absorbs the sun's heat slowly all day and parts with it slowly at night.

A grassy glade or meadow is colder than bare earth, sand, or rock. The air on a knoll is considerably warmer than that of flat land only a few feet below it.

PRIVACY.— A camp should not be exposed to view from a public road nor be in the track of picnickers, idle countrymen, vagabonds, or other unwelcome guests. One can save much annoyance by a little forethought in this matter.

GOOD CAMP SITES.— Often in traveling a party must put up for the night on unfavorable ground; but granting that there is much choice in the matter, then select, in summer, an open knoll, a low ridge, or, better, still, a bold, rocky point jutting out into a river or lake. A low promontory catches the

CAMP MAKING

breezes from both sides, which disperse fog and insects, and it is soon dried whenever the sun shines.

In cold weather seek an open, park-like spot in the forest, where surrounding trees will break the wind; or a "bench" (natural terrace backed by a cliff) on the leeward side of a hill. In the latter case, build your fire against the cliff, and shield the tent with a wind-break. The rock will reflect heat upon the tent, and will serve as a smoke-conductor as well.

On a hillside that is mostly bare, if there be a thicket or a cluster of evergreen trees, get on the downhill side of it. The stream of cold air from above will jump this obstacle and will leave an eddy of comparatively warm, still air immediately below it.

The best site for a fixed camp is near a river or lake, or on a bold, wooded islet, with a bathing beach, boating and fishing waters. A picturesque outlook is desirable, of course, but not if it makes the camp too prominent a landmark and so robs it of the privacy that refined people appreciate in camp as anywhere else.

SYSTEM IN CAMPING.— The celerity with which a camp is made depends upon the training and willingness of the men, and the system by which their duties are parceled. Let us suppose that there are four in the party, besides the teamster or packer. Then let No. 1, who is cook, get out the provisions and utensils, rig up the fireplace, build a fire, and prepare the food for cooking, while No. 2 is rustling wood and water. Meantime Nos. 3 and 4 clear the ground and smooth it off, cut tent pegs and poles, unpack the tent, and summon all hands for a minute, if they are needed, to assist in raising the tent and pegging it "square." Then the cook goes on with his proper duties, the axeman cuts and beds a chopping-block and gets in night-wood, and the canvas-men turn bed-makers. Thus, by the time supper is ready, which will be within an hour, or less, the camp will be properly made, and every one's work is done save the unfortunate scullion's.

When camping with a pack-train, pile the packs neatly together and cover them with canvas, and similarly pile and protect the saddles, making especially sure that the lash ropes cannot get wet, and that nothing will be buried out of sight, off somewhere by itself, if snow falls during the night. Soldierly system in all such matters pays a big dividend in time and good temper.

Even when stopping overnight, have a place for everything and let everything be in its place. Novices or shiftless folk strew things about and can't find them when needed. That is one reason why it takes them twice as long as it should to make or break camp, and it is why they are forever losing this and that, or leaving them behind and forgetting them till they reach the next stopping place.

If obliged to pitch the tent where there is not good natural drainage, trench it, if the weather be at all dubious. It is miserable business to crawl out into a driving storm at night and dig a ditch by lantern-light — worse still to awake to a realization that trenching is too late to save your soaking possessions. "Make yourself ready in your cabin for the mischance of the hour, if so it hap."

DINING PLACE.— It is wearisome to eat from the ground; and as Thoreau says, "None is so poor that he need sit on a pumpkin — that is shiftlessness." If stopping more than a day in one place, set up a rustic table and benches, away from the tent and near the cooking fire. Drive four stakes into the ground for legs, nail cleats across the ends, and cover the top with boards or straight sticks. If you have no nails, use forked stakes.

By the way, nearly every made-up picture of a camp shows crotches cut like Fig. 109. Why, good artists — why? You may hunt half a day in the woods to find such a natural crotch, and, if you should find it, the thing would be good-for-nothing

CAMP MAKING 219

as a stake, because you couldn't drive it without splitting it. A fork like Fig. 110 can be found anywhere; cut it as shown by the dotted lines, and

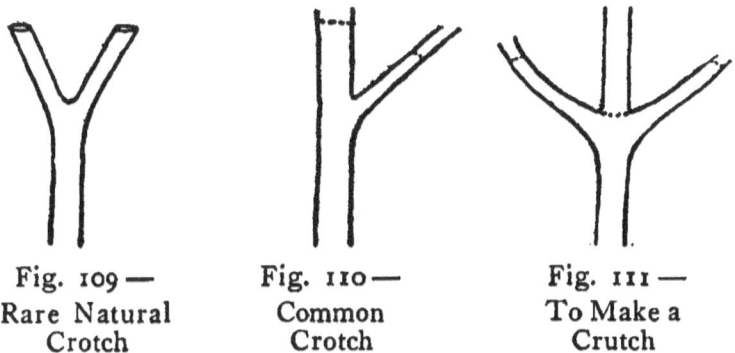

Fig. 109 —
Rare Natural
Crotch

Fig. 110 —
Common
Crotch

Fig. 111 —
To Make a
Crutch

it will drive all right. If somebody is injured and needs a crutch, pick out a sapling with limbs growing opposite, as in Fig. 111, cut out the central stem, trim, and shave down.

A comfortable height for the table is 30 inches, for the benches 18 inches. The latter are made in the same way as the table. Three widths of 10-inch boards make a good table top, and one suffices for each bench.

If you have a spare tent fly or tarpaulin, rig it over the dining table as a canopy. If no trees stand convenient for stretching it, set up two forked posts, lay a ridge pole on them, and guy out the sides to similar frames or to whatever may grow handy. To set a long stake, sharpen the butt end, hold the pole vertically, and make a hole in the ground by working the stick up and down as a quarryman does a long drill.

A table, bench, or shelf, can easily be set up wherever two trees grow close enough together. Nail a cross-piece from one to the other, and a similar one at same level on the other side, then cover with straight sticks or pieces of board.

COMMISSARIAT.— If food is carried in side-opening bags, suspend them from a horizontal pole run from tree to tree or from forked stakes. A cupboard made from packing boxes can be hung up in the same way, to keep vermin out. If ants are troublesome, the edibles can be hung up by wires, in a place where they will be sheltered from sun and rain.

In a stationary camp there should be a separate commissary tent, preferably of the baker style, as its door makes a good awning to work under in wet weather. Do not set boxes or bags of provisions on the ground, but on sticks, to keep dampness away from them.

RACKS or hangers for utensils, dish towels, etc., are improvised in many ways: a bush trimmed with stubs left on, and driven in the ground where it is wanted, inverted crotches nailed to a tree, and so on. Pegs of hard wood whittled to a blunt point can be driven into the trunk of a softwood tree by first making a vertical axe gash at the spot where the peg is to go.

COLD STORAGE.—Butter and milk should not be stored near anything that has a pronounced odor, for they would be tainted. As soon as the camp ground is reached the butter tin or jar should be placed in a net or bag and sunk in the spring or cold brook, the string being tied to the bank so that a freshet may not carry the food away or bury it out of sight. Later, if you stay in that place, a little rock-lined well can be dug near the spring, and covered securely so that 'coons and porcupines cannot plunder it.

Meat and fish may be kept fresh until consumed by digging a hole and putting a packing box in it, surrounding the sides and bottom of the box with six inches or more of gravel, and covering top of box with burlap or something similar. Keep the gravel and the burlap wet, and cover all with wet evergreen boughs.

If you have ice, a refrigerator can be made like the fireless cooker described in Chapter IV; or bore a few holes for drainage in the bottom of a box

CAMP MAKING

or barrel, sink it in the ground to its top, and cover with burlap or a blanket.

At a cabin in the Smokies, where I lived alone for three years, I had a spring box like the one shown in Fig. 112, which kept things cool and safe in the warmest weather, yet was easy for me to get

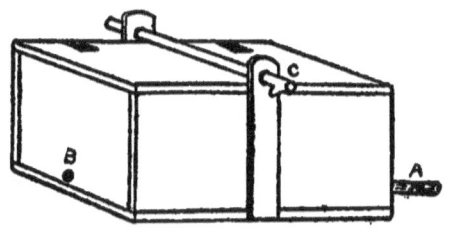

Fig. 112 — Spring Box

into. A short iron pipe at A entered the spring; the box inclined slightly toward the outlet B; pails and jars sat on flat rocks inside; the top was fastened by the round stick C passing through auger holes in the upright cleats.

Caches for provisions and other articles will be described in Volume II.

TENT FURNISHINGS.— If staying more than a night in one place, fit up the tent with hangers from which spare clothing, knapsacks and pouches, wall pockets, lantern, guns, and other loose articles may be suspended where they are kept dry, out of the way, and handy to get at. In a wall tent, plant a forked stake at each corner and lay a pole on them along each side, with nails in it. Guns are laid on shorter stakes underneath these. At the rear end you may set up a set of shelves for odds and ends.

If you have candles and no lantern, cut a stick long enough to hold the light as high as you want it, sharpen one end to shove in the ground, split the other end a little, put a loop of bark horizontally in the cleft, the candle in the loop, and draw tight against the stick. Half a potato, with a hole scooped in it, or a small can filled with earth, makes a portable candlestick.

FENCE.— Wild hogs are literally the *bêtes noires* of southern campers. Your thin-flanked, long-legged, sharp-nosed razorback, with tusks gleaming from his jaws — he or she of the third or further removed generation of feral lawlessness — is the most perverse, fearless, and maliciously destructive brute in America, wolverines or "Indian devils" not excepted. Shooting his tail off does not discourage him, rocks and clubs are his amusement, and no hint to leave that is weaker than a handful of red pepper baked inside a pone o' bread will drive him away. A hog-proof fence around camp, unsightly though it be, is one's only safeguard in southern wildwoods.

WASH-STAND.— A shelf between two trees, made as previously described, is best for this purpose. It should be so situated that wash-water will be thrown directly into a stream, or at least where it will quickly drain away from the camp, so as not to attract flies.

If one's ablutions are performed in the stream itself, drive a stick in the ground and nail the lid of a tin box to the top of it for a soap-dish.

CAMP SANITATION.— Nothing is cleaner, sweeter, wholesomer, than a wildwood unspoiled by man; and few spots are more disgusting than a "piggy" camp, with slops thrown everywhere, empty cans and broken bottles littering the ground, and organic refuse left festering in the sun, breeding disease germs, to be spread abroad by the swarms of flies. I have seen one of Nature's gardens, an ideal health resort, changed in a few months by a logging crew into an abomination and a pest-hole where typhoid and dysentery wrought deadly vengeance.

Destroy at once all refuse that would attract flies, or bury it where they cannot get at it.

Fire is the absolute disinfectant. Burn all solid kitchen refuse as fast as it accumulates. When a can of food is emptied toss it on the fire and burn it out, then drop it in a sink-hole, that you have

CAMP MAKING 223

dug for slops and unburnable trash, and cover it with earth or ashes so no mosquitoes can breed in it after a rainfall.

The sink should be on the downhill side of camp, and where it cannot pollute the water supply. Sprinkle kerosene on it, or burn it out frequently with a brush fire.

A latrine, as substitute for a closet, is one of the first things to be provided. A rude but sanitary

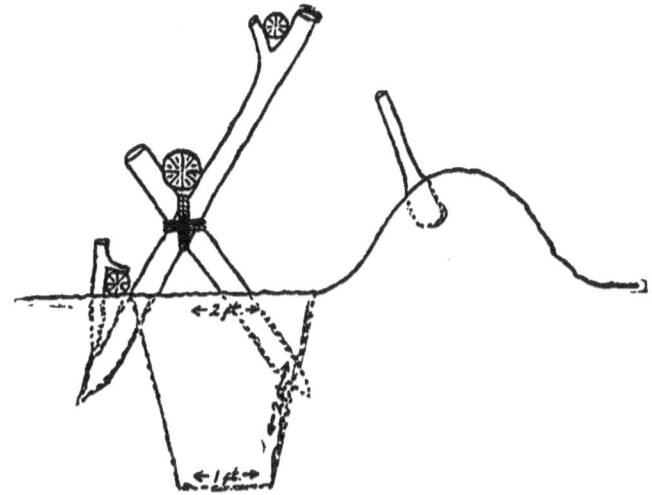

Fig. 113 — Latrine

one that can be made in a short time is shown in Fig. 113. The excavated earth is piled at the rear, and a paddle is left in it to cover excreta every time the place is used. (Whoever wrote Deuteronomy was a good camper.) The log used as seat, and the back-rest, are removable, so that a fire can be built in the trench every now and then from dead brush. Ashes and charcoal are good disinfectants in themselves. Dry earth does very well; but the trench should be burnt out after a rain.

A muslin or brush screen six feet high may be set around the latrine on stakes. A bathing screen can be similarly arranged at the water's edge.

CAMP CONVENIENCES.— A chopping-block is the first thing needed about a camp. The axe, when not in use, should always be stuck in that particular block, where any one can find it when wanted, and where it will not injure men or dogs.

Do not let the axe lie outdoors on a very cold night; the frost would make it brittle, so that the steel might shiver on the first knot you struck the next morning.

Stretch a stout line between two trees where the sunlight will strike, and air your blankets on it every day or two when the weather is pleasant. Against a straight tree near the tent make a rack, somewhat like a billiard-cue rack, in which fishing rods can be stood, full rigged, without danger of being blown down.

Of course, it takes time and brisk work to make everything snug and trim around camp; but it pays, just the same, to spend a couple of days at the start in rigging up such conveniences as I have described, and getting in a good supply of wood and kindling. To rush right off hunting or fishing, and leave the camp in disorder, is to eat your dough before it is baked.

CHAPTER XIII

THE CAMP-FIRE

"I am a woodland fellow, sir, that always loved a great fire."—*All's Well that Ends Well*.

> Cold night weighs down the forest bough,
>   Strange shapes go flitting through the gloom.
> But see — a spark, a flame, and now
>   The wilderness is home!
>
>   — *Edwin L. Sabin.*

The forest floor is always littered with old leaves, dead sticks, and fallen trees. During a drought this rubbish is so tinder-dry that a spark falling in it may start a conflagration; but through a great part of the year the leaves and sticks that lie flat on the ground are too moist, at least on their under side, to ignite readily. If we rake together a pile of leaves, cover it higgledy-piggledy with dead twigs and branches picked up at random, and set a match to it, the odds are that it will result in nothing but a quick blaze that soon dies down to a smudge. Yet that is the way most of us tried to make our first outdoor fires.

One glance at a camper's fire tells what kind of a woodsman he is. It is quite impossible to prepare a good meal over a heap of smoking chunks, a fierce blaze, or a great bed of coals that will warp iron and melt everything else.

If one would have good meals cooked out of doors, and would save much time and vexation — in other words, if he wants to be comfortable in the woods, he must learn how to produce at will either (1) a quick, hot little fire that will boil water in a jiffy, and will soon burn down to embers that are not too ardent for frying; or (2) a solid bed of long-lived coals that will keep up a steady, glowing, smokeless heat for baking, roasting, or slow boiling; or (3) a big log fire that will throw its heat forward on the ground, and into a tent or lean-to, and will last several hours without replenishing.

LUNCHEON FIRE.— For a noonday lunch, or any other quick meal, when you have only to boil coffee and fry something, a large fire is not wanted. Drive a forked stake in the ground, lay a green stick across it, slanting upward from the ground, and weight the lower end with a rock, so you can easily regulate the height of the pot. The slanting stick should be notched, or have the stub of a twig left at its upper end, to hold the pot bail in place, and should be set at such an angle that the pot swings about a foot clear of the ground.

Then gather a small armful of sound, dry twigs from the size of a lead pencil to that of your finger. Take no twig that lies flat on the ground, for such are generally damp or rotten. Choose hardwood, if there is any, for it lasts well.

Select three of your best sticks for kindling. Shave each of them almost through, for half its length, leaving lower end of shavings attached to the stick, one under the other. Stand these in a tripod, under the hanging pot, with their curls down. Around them build a *small* conical wigwam of the other sticks, standing each on end and slanting to a common center. The whole affair is no bigger than your hat. Leave free air spaces between the sticks. Fire requires air, and plenty of it, and it burns best when it has something to climb up on; hence the wigwam construction. Now touch off the shaved sticks, and in a moment you will have a small blast furnace under the pot. This will get up steam in a hurry. Feed it with small sticks as needed.

Meantime get two bed-sticks, four or five inches

THE CAMP-FIRE

thick, or a pair of flat rocks, to support the frying pan. The firewood will all drop to embers soon after the pot boils. Toss out the smoking butts, leaving only clear, glowing coals. Put your bedsticks on either side, parallel and level. Set the pan on them, and fry away. So, in twenty minutes from the time you drove your stake, the meal will be cooked.

A man acting without system or forethought, in even so simple a matter as this, can waste an hour in pottering over smoky mulch, or blistering himself before a bonfire, and it will be an ill mess of half-burned stuff that he serves in the end.

DINNER FIRE.— First get in plenty of wood and kindling. If you can find two large flat rocks, or several small ones of even height, use them as andirons; otherwise lay down two short cuts off a five- or six-inch log, facing you and about three feet apart. On these rocks or billets lay two four-foot logs parallel, and several inches apart, as rests for your utensils. Arrange the kindling between and under them, with small sticks laid across the top of the logs, a couple of long ones lengthwise, then more short ones across, another pair lengthwise, and thicker short ones across. Then light it. Many prefer to light the kindling at once and feed the fire gradually; but I do as above, so as to have an even glow under several pots at once, and then the sticks will all burn down to coals together.

This is the usual way to build a cooking fire when there is no time to do better. The objection is that the supporting logs must be close enough together to hold up the pots and pans, and, being round, this leaves too little space between them for the fire to heat their bottoms evenly; besides, a pot is liable to slip and topple over. A better way, if one has time, is to hew both the inside surfaces and the tops of the logs flat. Space these supports close enough together at one end for the narrowest pot and wide enough apart at the other for the frying-pan.

If you carry fire-irons, as recommended in a previous chapter, much bother is saved. Simply lay down two flat rocks or a pair of billets far enough apart for the purpose, place the flat irons on them, and space them to suit the utensils.

If a camp grate is used, build a crisscross fire of short sticks under it.

Split wood is better than round sticks for cooking; it catches easier and burns more evenly.

CAMP CRANE.— Pots for hot water, stews, coffee, and so on, are more manageable when hung above the fire. The heat can easily be regulated, the pots hanging low at first to boil quickly, and then being elevated or shifted aside to simmer.

Set up two forked stakes about five feet apart and four feet to the crotches. Across them lay a green stick (lug-pole) somewhat thicker than a broomstick. Now cut three or four green crotches from branches, drive a nail in the small end of each, or cut a notch in it, invert the crotches, and hang them on the lug-pole to suspend kettles from. These pot-hooks are to be of different lengths so that the kettle can be adjusted to different heights above the fire, first for hard boiling, and then for simmering. If kettles were hung from the lug-pole itself, this adjustment could not be made, and you would have to dismount the whole business in order to get one kettle off. *

---

* It is curious how many different names have been bestowed upon the hooks by which kettles are suspended over a fire. Our forefathers called them pot-hooks, trammels, hakes, hangers, pot-hangers, pot-claws, pot-crooks, gallows-crooks, pot-chips, pot-brakes, gibs or gib-crokes, rackan-crooks (a chain or pierced bar on which to hang hooks was called a rackan or reckon), and I know not what else besides. Among Maine lumbermen, such an implement is called a lug-stick, a hook for lifting kettles is a hook-stick, and a stick sharpened and driven into the ground at an angle so as to bend over the fire, to suspend a kettle from, is a wambeck or a spygelia — the Red Gods alone know why! The frame built over a cooking-fire is called by the Penobscots *kitchi-plak-wagn*, and the Micmacs call the lug-stick a *chiplok-waugan*, which the white guides have partially anglicized into waugan-stick. It is well to know, and heresy to disbelieve, that, after boiling the kettle, it brings bad luck to leave the waugan or spygelia standing.

If this catalogue does not suffice the amateur cook to express his ideas about such things, he may exercise his jaws with the Romany (gipsy) term for pot-hook, which is *kekauviscoe saster*.

THE CAMP-FIRE 229

If forked stakes are not readily found in the neighborhood, drive straight ones, then split the tops, flatten the ends of the cross-poles and insert them in the clefts of the stakes.

You do not want a big fire to cook over. Many and many a time I have watched old and experienced woodsmen spoil their grub, and their tempers, too, by trying to cook in front of a roaring winter camp-fire, and have marveled at their lack of common-sense. Off to one side of such a fire, lay your bed-logs, as above; then shovel from the camp-fire enough hard coals to fill the space between the logs within three inches of the top. You now have a steady, even heat from end to end; it can easily be regulated; there is level support for every vessel; and you can wield a short-handled frying-pan over such an outdoor range without scorching either the meat or yourself.

FIRE FOR BAKING.— For baking in a reflector, or roasting a joint, a high fire is best, with a backing to throw the heat forward. Sticks three feet long can be leaned against a big log or a sheer-faced rock, and the kindling started under them.

Often a good bed of coals is wanted. The camp-fire generally supplies these, but sometimes they are needed in a hurry, soon after camp is pitched. To get them, take *sound hardwood*, either green or dead, and split it into sticks of uniform thickness (say 1¼-inch face). Lay down two bed-sticks, cross these near the ends with two others, and so on up until you have a pen a foot high. Start a fire in this pen. Then cover it with a layer of parallel sticks laid an inch apart. Cross this with a similar layer at right angles, and so upward for another foot. The free draft will make a roaring fire, and all will burn down to coals together.

The thick bark of hemlock, and of hardwoods generally, will soon yield coals for ordinary cooking.

To keep coals a long time, cover them with ashes,

or with bark which will soon burn to ashes. In wet weather a bed of coals can be shielded by slanting broad strips of green bark over it and overlapping them at the edges.

FIRE IN A TRENCH.— In time of drought when everything is tinder-dry, or in windy weather, especially if the ground be strewn with dead leaves or pine needles, build your fire in a trench. This is the best way, too, if fuel is scarce and you must depend on brushwood, as a trench conserves heat.

Dig the trench in line with the prevailing wind. The point is to get a good draught. Make the windward end somewhat wider than the rest, and deeper, sloping the trench upward to the far end. Line the sides with flat rocks, if they are to be found, as they hold heat a long time and keep the sides from crumbling in. Lay other rocks, or a pair of green poles, along the edges to support vessels. A little chimney of flat stones or sod, at the leeward end, will make the fire draw well. If there is some sheet-iron to cover the trench a quite practical stove is made, but an open trench will do very well if properly managed.

THE HUNTER'S FIRE.— Good for a shifting camp in the fall of the year, because it affords first a quick cooking fire with supports for the utensils, and afterwards a fair camp-fire for the night when the weather is not severe. Cut two hardwood logs not less than a foot thick and about six feet long. Lay these side by side, about fifteen inches apart at one end and six or eight inches at the other. Across them lay short green sticks as supports, and on these build a crisscross pile of dry wood and set fire to it. The upper courses of wood will soon burn to coals which will drop between the logs and set them blazing on the inner sides. (If the bed logs were elevated to let draught under them they would blaze all around, and would not last long.)

After supper, lay two green billets, about eight inches thick, across the bed logs, and put night-wood

THE CAMP-FIRE

on it, to be renewed as required. In the morning there will be fine coals with which to cook breakfast.

WINTER CAMP-FIRE.— Let " Nessmuk " describe how he and a companion kept an open camp comfortably warm through a week in winter, with no other cutting tools than their hunting hatchets:

"We first felled a thrifty butternut tree ten inches in diameter, cut off three lengths of five feet each, and carried them to camp. These were the back-logs. Two stout stakes were driven at the back of the fire, and the logs, on top of each other, were laid firmly against the stakes. The latter were slanted a little back, and the largest log placed at bottom, the smallest on top, to prevent tipping forward. A couple of short, thick sticks were laid with the ends against the bottom log by way of fire-dogs; a fore-stick five feet long and five inches in diameter; a well built pyramid of bark, knots and small logs completed the camp-fire, which sent a pleasant glow of warmth and heat to the furthest corner of the shanty. For night-wood we cut a dozen birch and ash poles from four to six inches across, trimmed them to the tips, and dragged them to camp. Then we denuded a dry hemlock of its bark by aid of ten-foot poles flattened at one end, and packed the bark to camp. We had a bright, cheery fire from the early evening until morning, and four tired hunters never slept more soundly.

"We stayed in that camp a week; and, though the weather was rough and cold, the little pocket-axes kept us well in firewood. We selected butternut for back-logs, because, when green, it burns very slowly and lasts a long time. And we dragged our smaller wood to camp in lengths of twenty to thirty feet, because it was easier to lay them on the fire and 'nigger' them in two than to cut them shorter with light hatchets. With a heavy axe we should have cut them to lengths of five or six feet."

The first camp I ever made was built exactly after the " Nessmuk " pattern, shanty-tent, camp-fire with butternut back-logs, and all (see chapters III. and IV. of his *Woodcraft*). My only implement, besides knives, was a double-bitted hatchet just like his, of surgical instrument steel, weighing, with its twelve-inch handle, only eighteen ounces. I was alone. I stayed in that camp five weeks, in October and November; and I was snug and happy all the time. But then I was camping just for the fun of it. It is quite a different matter to come in at nightfall, dog-tired, and have to get in night-wood with a mere hatchet. Don't try that sort of camping without a full-size axe.

If there is a big, flat-faced rock or ledge on the camp site, take advantage of it by building your fire against it, with the tent in front. Or build a wall of rocks for a fire-back, with stone "andirons." Wooden ones must be renewed every day or so. But if logs must be used, and you have an axe, cut the back-logs from a green tree at least a foot thick, choosing wood that is slow to burn. Plaster mud in the crevices between the logs, around the bottom of stakes, and around the rear end of "handjunks" or billets used as andirons; otherwise the fire will soon attack these places. The fire-back reflects the heat forward into the tent, conducts the smoke upward, and serves as a windbreak in front of camp; so the higher it is, within reason, the better.

Novices generally erect the fire-back too far from the tent. Conditions vary, but ordinarily the face of the back-logs should not be more than five feet from the tent front; with a small fire, well tended, it need not be over four feet.

THE INDIAN'S FIRE.— Best where fuel is scarce, or when one has only a small hatchet with which to cut night-wood. Fell and trim a lot of hardwood saplings. Lay three or four of them on the ground, butts on top of each other, tips radiating from this center like the spokes of a wheel. On and around this center build a small, hot fire. Place butts of other saplings on this, radiating like the others. As the wood burns away, shove the sticks in toward the center, butts on top of each other, as before. This saves much chopping, and economizes fuel. Build a little windbreak behind you, and lie close to the fire. Doubtless you have heard the Indian's dictum (southern Indians express it just as the northern

THE CAMP-FIRE

and western ones do): "White man heap fool; make um big fire — can't git near: Injun make um little fire — git close. Uh, good!"

KINDLING.—The best kindling is fat pine, or the bark of the paper birch. Fat pine is found in the stumps and butt cuts of pine trees, particularly those that died on the stump. The resin has collected there and dried. This wood is usually easy to split. Pine knots are the tough, heavy, resinous stubs of limbs that are found on dead pine trees. They, as well as fat pine, are almost imperishable, and those sticking out of old rotten logs are as good as any. In collecting pine knots go to fallen trees that have almost rotted away. Hit the knot a lick with the poll of the axe and generally it will yield; if you must chop, cut deep to get it all and to save the axe edge. The knots of old dead balsams are similarly used. Usually a dead stump of pine, spruce, or balsam, all punky on the outside, has a core very rich in resin that makes excellent kindling.

Hemlock knots are worthless and hard as glass — keep your axe out of them.

The thick bark of hemlock is good to make glowing coals in a hurry; so is that of hardwoods generally. Good kindling, sure to be dry underneath the bark in all weathers, is procured by snapping off the small dead branches, or stubs of branches, that are left on the trunks of small or medium-sized trees, near the ground. Do not pick up twigs from the ground, but choose those, among the downwood, that are held up free from the ground. Where a tree is found that has been shivered by lightning, or one that has broken off without uprooting, good splinters of dry wood will be found. In every laurel thicket there is plenty of dead laurel, and, since it is of sprangling growth, most of the branches will be free from the ground and snap-dry. They ignite readily and give out intense heat.

The bark of all species of birch, but of paper birch especially, is excellent for kindling and for torches. It is full of resinous oil, blazes up at once, will burn in any wind, and wet sticks can be ignited with it.

Tinder, and methods of getting fire without matches, will be considered in Volume II.

MAKING FIRE IN THE WET.— It is a good test of one's resourcefulness to make a fire out-of-doors in rainy weather. The best way to go about it depends upon local conditions. If fat pine can be found the trick is easy: just split it up, and start your fire under a big fallen log. Dry fuel and a place to build the fire can often be found under big uptilted logs, shelving rocks, and similar natural shelters, or in the core of an old stump. In default of these, look for a dead softwood tree that leans to the south. The wood and bark on the under side will be dry — chop some off, split it fine, and build your fire under the shelter of the trunk.

LIGHTING A MATCH.— When there is nothing dry to strike it on, jerk the tip of the match forward against your teeth.

To light a match in the wind, *face* the wind. Cup your hands, with their backs toward the wind, and hold the match with its head pointing toward the rear of the cup — *i. e.*, toward the wind. Remove the right hand just long enough to strike the match on something very close by; then instantly resume the former position. The flame will run up the match stick, instead of being blown away from it, and so will have something to feed on.

FIRE REGULATIONS.— On state lands and on National forest reserves it is forbidden to use any but fallen timber for firewood. Different States have various other restrictions, some, I believe, not permitting campers to light a fire in the woods at all unless accompanied by a registered guide.

In New York the regulations prescribe that "Fires will be permitted for the purpose of cooking, warmth, and insect smudges; but before such fires are kindled sufficient space around the spot where the fire is to be lighted must be cleared from all combustible material; and before the place is abandoned, fires so lighted must be thoroughly quenched."

In Pennsylvania forest reserves no fire may be made except in a hole or pit one foot deep, the pit being encircled by the excavated earth. In those of California, no fire at all may be lighted without first procuring a permit from the authorities.

Fire regulations are posted on all public lands, and if campers disregard them they are subject to arrest.

These are wise and good laws. Every camper who loves the forest, and who has any regard for public interests, will do his part by obeying them to the letter. However, if he occupies private property where he may use his own judgment, or if he travels in a wilderness far from civilization, where there are no regulations, it will be useful for him to know something about the fuel value of all kinds of wood, green as well as dead, and for such people the following information is given:

The arts of fire-building are not so simple as they look. To practice them successfully in all sorts of wild regions we must know the different species of trees one from another, and their relative fuel values, which, as we shall see, vary a great deal. We must know how well, or ill, each of them burns in a green state, as well as when seasoned. It is important to discriminate between wood that makes lasting coals, and such as soon dies down to ashes. Some kinds of wood pop violently when burning and cast out embers that may burn holes in tents and bedding or set the neighborhood afire; others burn quietly, with clear, steady flame. Some are stubborn to split, others almost fall apart under the axe. In wet weather it takes a practiced woodsman to find tinder and dry wood, and to select a natural shelter where fire can be kept going during a storm of rain or snow, when a fire is most needed.

There are several handy little manuals by which

one who has no botanical knowledge can soon learn how to identify the different species of trees by merely examining their leaves; or, late in the season, by their bark, buds, and habit of growth.

But no book gives the other information that I have referred to; so I shall offer, in the present chapter, a little rudimentary instruction in this important branch of woodcraft.

It is convenient for our purpose to divide the trees into two great groups, hardwoods and softwoods, using these terms not so loosely as lumbermen do, but drawing the line between sycamore, yellow birch, yellow pine, and slippery elm, on the one side, and red cedar, sassafras, pitch pine and white birch, on the other.

As a general rule, hardwoods make good, slow-burning fuel that yields lasting coals, and softwoods make a quick, hot fire that is soon spent. But each species has peculiarities that deserve close attention. The knack of finding what we want in the woods lies a good deal in knowing what we *don't* want, and passing it by at a glance.

UNINFLAMMABLE WOODS.— The following woods will scarcely burn at all when they are green: basswood, black ash, balsam, box elder, buckeye, cucumber, black or pitch pine and white pine, poplar or aspen, yellow poplar or tulip, sassafras, service berry, sourwood, sycamore, tamarack, tupelo (sour gum), water oak. Butternut, chestnut, red oak, red maple, and persimmon burn very slowly in a green state. Such woods, or those of them that do not spit fire, are good for backlogs, hand-junks or andirons, and for side-logs in a cooking fire that is to be used continuously. Yellow birch and white ash, on the contrary, are better for a campfire when green than when seasoned. A dead pine log seldom burns well unless split. The outside catches fire readily, but it soon chars and goes out unless a blazing fire of sticks is kept up against it.

THE CAMP-FIRE

GREEN WOOD burns best in autumn and winter, when the sap is down. Trees that grow on high, dry ground burn better than those of the same species that stand in moist soil. Chestnut cut on the summits of the Appalachians burns freely, even when green, and the mountain beech burns as ardently as birch. Green wood growing along a river bank is very hard to burn.

SPITFIRE WOODS.— Arbor-vitæ (northern " white cedar ") and chestnut burn to dead coals that do not communicate flame. They, as well as box elder, red cedar, hemlock, sassafras, tulip, balsam, tamarack, and spruce, make a great crackling and snapping in the fire. All of the soft pines, too, are prone to pop. Certain hardwoods, such as sugar maple, beech, white oak, and sometimes hickory, must be watched for a time after the fire is started, because the embers that they shoot out are long-lived, and hence more dangerous than those of softwoods; but they are splendid fuel, for all that.

STUBBORN WOODS.— The following woods are very hard to split: Blue ash, box elder, buckeye, cherry, white elm, winged elm, sour gum, hemlock (generally), liquidambar (sweet gum), honey locust, sugar maple, sycamore, tupelo. Some woods, however, that are stubborn when seasoned are readily split when green, such as hickory, beech, dogwood, sugar maple, birch, and slippery elm.

THE BEST FUEL.—Best of all northern firewoods is hickory, green or dry. It makes a hot fire, but lasts a long time, burning down to a bed of hard coals that keep up an even, generous heat for hours. Hickory, by the way, is distinctly an American tree; no other region on earth produces it. The live oak of the South is most excellent fuel, so is holly. Following the hickory, in fuel value, are chestnut oak, overcup, white, blackjack, post and basket oaks, pecan, the hornbeams (ironwoods), and dogwood. The latter burns finally to a beautiful white ash that is characteristic; apple wood does the same. Black birch also ranks here; it has the advantage of "doing its own blowing," as a Carolina mountaineer said to me, meaning that the oil in the birch assists its combustion so that the wood needs no coaxing. All of the birches are good fuel, ranking in about this order: black, yellow, red, paper, and white. Sugar maple was the favorite fuel of our old-time hunters and surveyors, because it ignites easily, burns with a clear, steady flame, and leaves good coals.

Locust is a good, lasting fuel; it is easy to cut, and, when green, splits fairly well; the thick bark takes fire readily, and the wood then burns slowly, with little flame, leaving pretty good coals; hence it is good for night-wood. Mulberry has similar qualities. The scarlet and willow oaks are among the poorest of the hardwoods for fuel. Cherry makes only fair fuel. White elm is poor stuff, but slippery elm is better. Yellow pine burns well, as its sap is resinous instead of watery like that of the soft pines.

In some respects white ash is the best of green woods for campers' fuel. It is easily cut and split, is lighter to tote than most other hardwoods, and is of so dry a nature that even the green wood catches fire readily. It burns with clear flame, and lasts longer than any other free-burning wood of its weight. On a wager, I have built a bully fire from a green tree of white ash, one match, and no dry kindling whatever. I split some of the wood very fine and "frilled" a few of the little sticks with my knife.

SOFTWOODS.— Most of the softwoods are good only for kindling, or for quick cooking fires, and then only when seasoned. For these purposes, however, some of them are superior, as they split and shave readily and catch fire easily.

Liquidambar, magnolia, tulip, catalpa, and willow are poor fuel. Seasoned chestnut and yellow poplar make a hot fire, but crackle and leave no coals. Balsam fir, basswood, and the white and loblolly pines make quick fires but are soon spent. The gray (Labrador) pine or jack pine is considered good fuel in the far North, where hardwoods are scarce. Seasoned tamarack is good. Spruce is poor fuel, although, being resinous, it kindles easily and makes a good blaze for "branding up" a fire. Pitch pine, which is the most inflammable of all woods when dry and "fat," will scarcely burn at all in a green state. Sycamore and buckeye, when thoroughly seasoned, are good fuel, but will not split. Alder burns readily and gives out considerable heat, but is not lasting.

The dry wood of the northern poplar (large-toothed aspen) is a favorite for cooking fires, because it gives an intense heat, with little or no smoke, lasts well, and does not blacken the utensils. Red cedar has similar qualities, but is rather hard to ignite and must be fed fine at the start.

The best green softwoods for fuel are white birch, paper birch, soft maple, cottonwood, and quaking aspen.

As a rule, the timber growing along the margins of large streams is softwood. Hence driftwood is generally a poor mainstay, unless there is plenty of it on the spot; but driftwood on the seacoast is good fuel.

PRECAUTIONS.— I have already mentioned the necessity of clearing the camp ground of inflammable stuff before starting a fire on it, raking it toward a common center and burning all the dead leaves, pine needles, and trash; otherwise it may catch and spread beyond your control as soon as your back is turned. Don't build your fire against a big old punky log: it may smoulder a day or two after you have left, and then burst out into flame when a breeze fans it.

Never leave a spark of fire when breaking camp, or when leaving it for the day. Make absolutely sure of this, by drenching the camp-fire thoroughly, or by smothering it completely with earth or sand. Never drop a lighted match, a burning cigar stub, or the hot residue of your pipe, on the ground without stamping it out. Have you ever seen a forest fire? It is terrible. Thousands of acres are destroyed, and many a time men and women and children have been cut off by a tornado of flame and burned alive. The person whose carelessness starts such a holocaust is worse than a fool — he is a criminal, and a disgrace to the good earth he treads.

CHAPTER XIV
PESTS OF THE WOODS

Summer twilight brings the mosquito. In fact, when we go far north or far south, we have him with us both by day and night. Rather I should say that we have *her;* for the male mosquito is a gentleman, who sips daintily of nectar and minds his own business, while madame his spouse is a whining, peevish, venomous virago, that goes about seeking whose nerves she may unstring and whose blood she may devour. Strange to say, not among mosquitoes only, but among ticks, fleas, chiggers, and the whole legion of bloodthirsty, stinging flies and midges, it is only the female that attacks man and beast. Stranger still, the mosquito is not only a bloodsucker but an incorrigible wine-bibber as well — it will get helplessly fuddled on any sweet wine, such as port, or on sugared spirits, while of gin it is inordinately fond.

Such disreputable habits — the querulous singsong, the poisoned sting, the thirst for blood, and the practice of getting dead drunk at every opportunity, are enough of themselves to make the mosquito a thing accursed; but these are by no means the worst counts in our indictment against it. We have learned, within the past few years, that all the suffering and mortality from malaria, yellow fever, and filariasis (including the hideous and fatal elephantiasis of the tropics) is due to germs that are carried in no other way than by mosquitoes. Flies spread the germs of typhoid fever and malignant eye diseases; fleas carry the bubonic plague;

the sleeping-sickness of Africa is transmitted by insects. There is no longer any guesswork about this: it is demonstrated fact. Professor Kellogg, summing up what is now known of the life history of malaria-bearing mosquitoes (*Anopheles*) says: "When in malarial regions, avoid the bite of a mosquito as you would that of a rattlesnake — one can be quite as serious in its results as the other."

The worst of it, from a sportsman's view-point, is that the farther we push toward the arctics or the tropics, the worse becomes the pest of dangerous insects. It is into just such countries that, nowadays and in future, we must go in order to get really first-class hunting and fishing. Consequently the problem of how best to fight our insect enemies becomes of ever increasing importance to all who love to hunt over and explore the wild places that are still left upon the earth.

Mosquitoes are bad enough in the tropics, but they are at their worst in the coldest regions of the earth.

MOSQUITOES.— Harry de Windt reports that at Verkhoyansk, in Siberia, which is the arctic pole of cold (where the winter temperature often sinks to −75° Fahr., and has been known to reach −81°) the mosquitoes make their appearance before the snow is off the ground, and throughout the three summer months, make life almost unbearable to the wretched natives and exiles. The swamps and shoaly lakes in the surrounding country breed mosquitoes in such incredible hosts that reindeer, sledge-dogs, and sometimes even the natives themselves, are actually tormented to death by them.

Throughout a great part of central and western Canada, and Alaska, there are vast tundras of bog moss, called by the Indians muskegs, which in summer are the breeding-grounds of unending clouds of mosquitoes whose biting powers exceed those of any insects known in the United States. Even if the muskeg land were not a morass, this plague of

PESTS OF THE WOODS 243

mosquitoes would forever render it uninhabitable in summer. The insects come out of their pupæ at the first sprouting of spring vegetation, in May, and remain until destroyed by severe frosts in September. In Alaska, all animals leave for the snow-line as soon as the mosquito pest appears, but the enemy follows them even to the mountain tops above timber-line. Deer and moose are killed by mosquitoes, which settle upon them in such amazing swarms that the unfortunate beasts succumb from literally having the blood sucked out of their bodies. Bears are driven frantic, are totally blinded, mire in the mud, and starve to death. Animals that survive have their flesh discolored all through, and even their marrow is reduced to the consistency of blood and water. The men who penetrate such regions are not the kind that would allow toil or privation to break their spirit, but they become so unstrung from days and nights of continuous torment inflicted by enemies insignificant in size but infinite in number, that they become savage, desperate, and sometimes even weep in sheer helpless anger.

In regions so exceptionally cursed with mosquitoes no mere sportsman has any business until winter sets in. But even in the more accessible woodlands north and south of us the insect pest is by far the most serious hardship that fishermen and other summer outers are obliged to meet. Head-nets and gauntlets are all very well in their way, but one can neither hunt, fish, paddle, push through the brush, nor even smoke, when so accoutered. Consequently everybody tries some kind or other of "fly-dope," by which elegant name we mean any preparation which, being rubbed over the exposed parts of one's skin, is supposed to discourage insects from repeating their attacks.

The number of such dopes is legion. They may be classified in three groups:

(1) Thick ointments that dry to a tenacious glaze on the skin, if the wearer abstain from washing;

(2) Liquids or semi-fluid unguents that are supposed to protect by their odor alone, and must be renewed several times a day;
(3) Insecticides, which poison the little beasts.

Glazes.— Among the glazes, Nessmuk's recipe, published in his *Woodcraft,* is perhaps as well known and as widely used as any. He says this about it:

"I have never known it to fail: 3 oz. pine tar, 2 oz. castor oil, 1 oz. pennyroyal oil. Simmer all together over a slow fire, and bottle for use. You will hardy need more than a 2-oz. vial full in a season. One ounce has lasted me six weeks in the woods. Rub it in thoroughly and liberally at first, and after you have established a good glaze, a little replenishing from day to day will be sufficient. And don't fool with soap and towels where insects are plenty. A good safe coat of this varnish grows better the longer it is kept on — and it is cleanly and wholesome. If you get your face or hands crocky or smutty about the camp-fire, wet the corner of your handkerchief and rub it off, not forgetting to apply the varnish at once wherever you have cleaned it off. Last summer I carried a cake of soap and a towel in my knapsack through the North Woods for a seven weeks' tour, and never used either a single time. When I had established a good glaze on the skin, it was too valuable to be sacrificed for any weak whim connected with soap and water. . . . It is a soothing and healing application for poisonous bites already received."

Aside from my personal tests of many dopes, I have had some interesting correspondence on this topic with sportsmen in various parts of the world. I quote from one letter received from Norman Fletcher, of Louisville:

"Upon the swampy trout streams of Michigan on a warm May day . . . when the insects are abundant and vicious . . . pure pine tar is by far the best repellent when properly used. I give two recipes:

(1) Pure pine tar.......... 1 ounce,
    Oil pennyroyal .... 1 ounce,
    Vaseline .... 3 ounces.

Mix cold in a mortar. If you wish, you can add 3 per cent. carbolic acid to above. Sometimes I make it 1½ oz. tar.

(2) Pure pine tar.......... 2 ounces,
    Castor oil .... 3 ounces,

PESTS OF THE WOODS 245

Simmer for half an hour, and when cool add
Oil pennyroyal   1 ounce.
There are many others of similar nature, but the above are as good as any. Now as to use of above: apply freely and frequently to all exposed parts of person, and *do not wash off until leaving* the place where the pests abound. You can wash your eyes in the morning, and wash the palms of your hands as often as may be necessary, but if you wish to be immune, don't wash any other exposed parts. When you get accustomed to it you will find some compensating comfort.... I have had to contend with mosquitoes, deer-flies, black-flies, and midges and have found "dope" with tar in it the best. I know that where mosquitoes are not very bad, oil of citronella, oil of verbena or of lemon-grass or of pennyroyal mixed with vaselin will keep them off, if the mixture is applied frequently. These essential oils are quickly evaporated, however, by the heat of the body. Camphorated oil is also used by some; this is simply sweet oil with gum camphor dissolved in it: the camphor is volatile and soon evaporates.
. Now I don't much like tar dope because I can not wash my face and hands as often as I could wish; but when it is necessary to get some trout, without being worried too much by the insects, I can stand the tar for a few days."

Doctor L. O. Howard, Chief of the Bureau of Entomology, U. S. Department of Agriculture, recommends the following tar dope:

"Fishermen and hunters in the North Woods will find that a good mixture against mosquitoes and black-flies can be made as follows: Take 2½ pounds of mutton tallow, melt and strain it. While still hot add ½ pound black tar (Canadian tar), stir thoroughly, and pour into the receptacle in which it is to be contained. When nearly cool stir in 3 ounces of oil of citronella and 1½ ounces of pennyroyal."

It is my own experience that tar glazes do the work when the weather is comparatively cool, but when it is so hot that one perspires freely both by night and day there is no chance for a glaze to be established. The stuff melts and runs in your eyes. A hard rain will wash it off. Thick dopes, more or less sticky, are unpleasant at all times, and especially at night. For these reasons, and for appearance sake, most people will prefer to use a fluid or unguent that is less disagreeable, even though it must be renewed every hour or two.

Essential Oils.— As for protective liquids, it is safe to say that everything in the pharmacopœia that seemed the least promising has been tried. The oils of pennyroyal, cloves, lavender, citronella, eucalyptus, cedar and sassafras are used singly or in combination. Spirits of camphor is offensive to insects but soon evaporates.

Citronella is the favorite. All insect pests dislike it; but some people, too, find the odor intolerable. The oil of lavender flowers (genuine) has a pleasant odor, and is equally effective, but it is quite expensive. Both of these oils are bland, whereas most of the others are irritant and will make the eyes smart if the least bit comes in contact with them. Artificial oil of lavender is worthless.

The protection afforded by a given oil depends somewhat upon locality (number, species, persistence of insects), and, apparently, the personal equation cuts some figure, for what works satisfactorily with one man affords no immunity to another. Hence the more popular dopes are "shot-gun prescriptions," compounded on the principle that if one ingredient misses another may hit.

The trouble with all the essential oils is that their protective principles are volatile. To retard evaporation, add double or treble the amount of castor oil, which has a good body and is itself repugnant to the whole created kingdom. After mixing, put up some of this thick liquid in a small capped oil can (bicycle oiler), to carry in the field.

Thicker dopes, which can be put up in collapsible tubes like artists' colors, are made by mixing the oil with carbolated vaseline, or with borated lanolin. The latter is a particularly good base because it is not only antiseptic but it is also the best preventive of sunburn, excellent for blistered feet, and a particularly good application for slight wounds and abrasions. Add enough oil of lavender flowers

PESTS OF THE WOODS 247

to give it a strong odor, and put it up in tubes to keep out moisture. I know nothing better in the line of "elegant preparations" to keep off mosquitoes.

Insecticides.— One of these is creosote. Another is the tincture of *ledum palustre* (wild rosemary, a European relative of our Labrador tea). Oil of cassia (i.e., oil of cinnamon) is said to be an irritant poison to all kinds of insects, and "its power remains a long time after it has dried."

Another thing that flies of all sorts find bad for their systems is quassia. It is used as an ingredient of fly poisons, as a parasiticide, and in some fly dopes. Either the fluid extract or the solid may be employed, according to the base.

Carbolic acid in sweet oil (1 to 16) is often used where insects are very insistent. It has the obvious advantage of being a good antiseptic as well. On a trip to Hudson Bay, Dr. Robert T. Morris employed a very strong solution, of which he reported:

"We depended upon the mixture of one part of carbolic acid and nine parts of sweet oil to keep off various things that sought our acquaintance. A very little of this mixture on the face and hands was effective. It is a preparation that I learned to use in Labrador, where none of the common applications would suffice."

Doctor Durham, of the English Yellow Fever Commission, Rio de Janeiro, told Dr. L. O. Howard that

"He and the late Dr. Myers found that a 5 per cent. solution of sulphate of potash prevented mosquitoes from biting, and that they were obliged to use this mixture while at work in their laboratory in Brazil to prevent themselves from being badly bitten."

I judge this would also be a good preventive of attacks from ticks and chiggers, as they cannot stand sulphur.

Plain kerosene is certain death to all sorts of insect pests, so long as they have not burrowed beneath the skin, and one of the best preventives of their attacks. It is used everywhere by men whose constant exposure renders them less fastidious about personal greasiness and aroma than they are solicitous for comfort and health. Dr. W. H. Dade, an army surgeon in the Philippines, found that the addition of one part oil of bergamot to sixteen of kerosene made the odor less disagreeable and added enough body to prevent evaporation in less than six to eight hours. I have used Japanese oil of camphor for the same purpose.

Some Dopes.— The following mixtures may be particularly recommended:

Mr. C. A. Nash's.
Oil of citronella	1 oz.
Spirits of camphor	1 oz.
Oil of cedar	½ oz.

Doctor Howard says this is the most effective mixture he has tried. " Ordinarily a few drops on a bath towel hung over the head of the bed will keep *Culex pipiens* away for a whole night. Where mosquitoes are very persistent, however, a few drops rubbed on the face and hands will suffice."

Dr. Edward Beck's.
Pine tar	3 oz.
Olive (or castor) oil	2 oz.
Oil pennyroyal	1 oz.
Oil citronella	1 oz.
Creosote	1 oz.
Camphor (pulverized)	1 oz.
Carbolated vaseline	large tube.

Heat the tar and oil and add the other ingredients; simmer over slow fire until well mixed. The tar may be omitted if disliked, or for ladies' use. Above will rather more than fill a pint screw-top tin flask. This mixture not only discourages insect attacks but is also a good counter-irritant after being bitten. One may substitute for the olive oil its weight in carbolated vaseline and thus make an unguent that can be carried in collapsible tubes, and the Doctor now recommends this.

Col. Crofton Fox's.
Oil pennyroyal	1 dram.
Oil peppermint	1 dram.
Oil bergamot	1 dram.

PESTS OF THE WOODS

Oil cedar	1 dram.
Quassia	1 dram.
Gum camphor	4 drams.
Vaseline, yellow	2 drams.

Dissolve camphor in vaseline by heat; when cold add remainder.

I doubt if peppermint adds anything to the efficacy of this formula, and would substitute citronella or lavender.

The principles to be observed in compounding a dope of one's own are (1) choose your repellents or insecticides, or both; (2) add enough lanolin, vaseline, castor oil, or other base to give the desired " body." It is well to incorporate some good antiseptic with the stuff, to relieve irritation and poisoning from bites already received, and to serve as a healing ointment for abrasions, bruises, and other injuries, as already mentioned. Any ingredient that irritates the skin or makes the eyes smart should be avoided, except where insects are so bad that such addition may be necessary.

BITES AND STINGS.— To relieve the itching of insect bites the common remedies are ammonia or a solution of baking soda. A better one is to cover each bite with flexible collodion (" New Skin "); but be sure the bottle is always securely stoppered, for the ether of the solvent evaporates very quickly and then the stuff is useless.

A bee leaves its sting in the wound, and this of course should be removed; a wasp, hornet, or yellow-jacket can sting repeatedly. For the pain, apply ammonia or baking powder solution, or a weak solution of carbolic acid, or wet salt, moistened clay, a mud poultice, a slice of raw onion, or a moist quid of tobacco.

FLEAS.— In the high mountains of North Carolina and adjoining States there are no mosquitoes, at least none that sing or bite; but if a man sits down on a log, it may be five miles from any house, the chance is good that he will arise covered with fleas. I have been so tormented by these nimble allies of Auld Reekie, when spending a night in a herder's cabin on the summit of the Smokies, that I have arisen in desperation and rubbed myself from head to foot with kerosene. That settled the fleas. Citronella will do as well.

If you catch a flea, don't try to crush it, for you can't, but roll it between the fingers; that breaks its legs; than you can open your fingers and kill it. A good way, if water is handy, is to keep a tight grip until you get your thumb and finger into some water — a flea can't swim — then, if it is not already filled with blood, it will sink, and drown, and go to meet its reward, which, let us hope, is a hot one.

When you have to occupy a cabin infested with fleas, scrub it out with hot soapsuds, and see that the site is well wet beneath the floor. Fleas will not stay in a wet place.

BLOOD-SUCKING FLIES.—In northern forests we have several species of flies that attack man. The deer-fly or "bull-dog" is a small gad-fly that drives her dagger-like mandibles into one's skin so viciously that she takes out a bit of flesh and makes the blood flow freely. The black-fly (*Similium molestum*) is a stout, hump-backed, black termagant with transparent wings, from one-sixth to one-quarter inch long. This creature is a common nuisance of the forests and along the streams of northern New England, the Adirondacks, the Lake region, and Canada. She keeps busy until late in the afternoon, poisoning everything that she attacks, and raising a painful lump as big as a dime at every bite. Closely related species are the buffalo-gnat and turkey-gnat of the South, which sometimes appear in incredible numbers, driving animals frantic and setting up an inflammatory fever that may prove fatal. Black-flies and their ilk are easily driven away by smudges. Mosquito dopes will protect one from them.

BLOW-FLIES.— Worst of all flies, though fortunately rare in the North (it has been known to reach Canada), is the screw-worm fly (*Compsomyia macellaria*), a bright metallic-green insect with golden re-

PESTS OF THE WOODS 251

flections and four black stripes on the upper part of the body. This is a blow-fly which has the sickening habit of laying its eggs in wounds, and even in the nostrils of sleeping men. Several fatalities from this cause have been reported in our country; they have been much more numerous in South America. The *gusanéro* of tropical America is described by a traveler as "a beast of a fly that attacks you, you know not when, till after three or four months you know that he has done so by the swelling up of the bitten part into a fair-sized boil, from which issues a maggot of perhaps an inch and a half in length." Another Amazonian fly of similar habits is the *birni,* whose larva generates a grub in one's skin that requires careful extraction, lest it be crushed in the operation, "and then," said a native, "gentlemen often go to *o outro mundo*" (the other world). The *motûca* of Brazil has ways similar to those of our black-fly, and, like it, can easily be killed with one's fingers.

PESTS OF THE TROPICS.—While I am on this topic, it may add a little to the contentment of those outers who are unable to seek adventure in faraway lands, but must needs camp within a hundred miles or so of home, if I transcribe from the pages of a well-known naturalist the following notes on some of the impediments to travel in the tropics:

"But the most numerous and most dreaded of all animals in the middle Amazons are the insects. Nearly all kinds of articulate life here have either sting or bite. The strong trade wind keeps the lower Amazons clear of the winged pests; but soon after leaving Manãos, and especially on the Marañon in the rainy season, the traveler becomes intimately acquainted with half a dozen insects of torture:

(1) The sanguinary mosquito. . . . There are several species, most of them working at night; but one black fellow with white feet is diurnal. Doctor Spruce experimented upon himself, and found that he lost, by letting the blood-letters have their own way, three ounces of blood per day. . . . The ceaseless irritation of these ubiquitous creatures makes life almost intolerable. The great Cortez, after all his victories, could not forget his struggles with

these despicable enemies he could not conquer. Scorpions with cocked tails, spiders six inches in diameter, and centipedes running on all dozens, are not half so bad as a cloud of mosquitoes. . . .

(2) The *pium*, or sand-fly, a species of *trombidium* called mosquito in Peru. It is a minute, dark-colored dipter with two triangular, horny lancets, which leave a small, circular red spot on the skin. It works by day, relieving the mosquito at sunrise. It is the great scourge of the Amazons. Many a paradisiac spot is converted into an inferno by its presence. There are several species, which follow one another in succession through the day, all of them being diurnal. Their favorite region is said to be on the Cassiquiare and upper Orinoco.

(3) The *maruim*, which resembles the *pium*. They are infinitely numerous on the Juruá. Humboldt estimated there were a million to a cubic foot of air where he was.

(4) The *motúca*, called *tábono* on the Marañon (*Hadrus lepidotus*), resembling a small horse-fly, of a bronze-black color, with the tips of the wings transparent, and a formidable proboscis. . . .

(5) The *moquím* . . . a microscopic scarlet *acarus*, resembling a minute crab under the glass. It swarms on weeds and bushes, and on the skin causes an intolerable itching. An hour's walk through the grassy streets of Teffé was sufficient to cover my entire body with myriads of *moquíms*, which it took a week, and repeated bathing with rum, to exterminate.

(6) *Carapátos*, or ticks (*ixodes*), which mount to the tips of blades of grass, attach themselves to the clothes of passersby, and bury their jaws and heads so deeply in the flesh that it is difficult to remove them without leaving the proboscis behind to fret and fester. In sucking one's blood they cause no pain; but serious sores, even ulcers, often result. . . .

These few forms of insect life must forever hinder the settlement of the valley. . . . Besides there are ants . . . innumerable in species and individuals, and of all sizes, from the little red ant of the houses to the mammoth *tokandéra*, an inch and a half long. . . . The latter . . . bites fiercely, but rarely causes death. Doctor Spruce likens the pain to a hundred thousand nettles. . . . On the Tapajós lives the terrible fire-ant . . . whose sting is likened to the puncture of a red-hot needle. The *saübas* are not carnivorous, but they make agriculture almost impossible. . . . There are black and yellow wasps. . . . The large, hairy caterpillars should be handled with care, as the irritation caused by the nettling hairs is sometimes a serious matter. Cockroaches are great pests in the villages. Lice find a congenial home on the unwashed Indians of every tribe, but particularly the Andean. Jiggers and fleas prefer

PESTS OF THE WOODS 253

dry, sandy localities; they are accordingly most abounding on the mountains. The Pacific slope is worthy of being called flea-dom."— ORTON, *The Andes and the Amazons*, pp. 484-487.

NORTHERN CHIGGERS.— The *moquim* mentioned above answers the description of our own chigger, jigger, red-bug, as she is variously called, which is an entirely different beast from the real chigger or chigoe of the tropics. I do not know what may be the northern limit of these diabolic creatures, but have made their acquaintance on Swatara Creek in Pennsylvania. They are quite at home on the prairies of southern Illinois, exist in myriads on the Ozarks, and throughout the lowlands of the South, and are perhaps worst of all in some parts of Texas. The chigger, as I shall call it, is invisible on one's skin, unless you know just what to look for. Get it on a piece of black cloth, and you can distinguish what looks like a fine grain of red pepper. Put it under a microscope, and it resembles, as Orton says, a minute crab. It lives in the grass, and on the under side of leaves, dropping off on the first man or beast that comes its way. Then it prospects for a good place, where the skin is thin and tender, and straightway proceeds to burrow, not contenting itself, like a tick, with merely thrusting its head in and getting a good grip, but going in body and soul, to return no more. The victim is not aware of what is in store for him until he goes to bed that night. Then begins a violent itching, which continues for a week or two. I have had two hundred of these tormenting things in my skin at one time.

If one takes a bath in salt water every night before retiring, he can keep fairly rid of these unwelcome guests. A surer preventive is to rub kerosene on the wrists, neck, ankles, and abdominal region. Powdered sulphur dusted into one's drawers and stocking legs will do if one keeps out of the bushes. Naphthaline may be used successfully in the same manner.

The country people sometimes rub themselves

with salty bacon-rind before going outdoors, and claim that this is a preventive; also that kerosene will do as well. If one keeps an old suit of clothes expressly for chigger-time, puts the suit in a closet, and fumigates it thoroughly with the smoke of burning tobacco stems, no chigger will touch him. Alas! that the preventives should all be so disagreeable.

When chiggers have burrowed underneath the skin, neither salt, nor oil, nor turpentine, nor carbolized ointment, nor anything else that I have tried will kill them, save mercurial ointment or the tincture of stavesacre seed, both of which are dangerous if incautiously used. After much experiment, I found that chloroform, dropped or rubbed on each separate welt, will stop the itching for several hours. It is quite harmless, and pleasant enough to apply.

Moderately strong ammonia, or a saturated solution of baking soda, will suffice if applied as soon as the itching is felt, but they are useless if treatment is delayed. In the latter case, I would use tincture of iodine. It is said that collodion brushed over each welt will act as a specific, but I have had no chance to try it.

The chigger seems particularly fond of the butterfly-weed or pleurisy-root. It is seldom much of a nuisance until the middle of June, and generally disappears in the latter part of September.

TROPICAL CHIGOES.—The chigoe or sand-flea of Mexico, Central America, and South America, is a larger and more formidable pest than our little redbug. It attacks, preferably, the feet, especially under the nail of the great toe, and between the toes. The insect burrows there, becomes encysted, swells enormously from the development of her young, and thus sets up an intolerable itching in the victim's skin. If the female is crushed or ruptured in the tumor she has formed, the result is likely to be amputation of the toe, if nothing worse. She should be removed entire by careful manipulation with a needle. This chigoe is a native of tropical America, but seems to be gradually spreading northward.

About 1872 it was introduced into Africa, and spread with amazing rapidity over almost the entire continent. It will probably soon invade southern Europe and Asia.

TICKS.—The wood-ticks that fasten on man are, like the chiggers, not true insects, but arachnids, related to the scorpions and spiders. They are leathery-skinned creatures of about the same size and shape as a bedbug, but of quite different color and habits. They " use " on the under side of leaves of low shrubs, and thence are detached to the person of a passer-by just as chiggers are. They also abound in old mulchy wood, and are likely to infest any log that a tired man sits on. They hang on like grim death, and if you try to pull one off your skin, its head will break off and remain in the epidermis, to create a nasty sore. The ticks that infest birds, bats, sheep, and horses, are true insects, in no wise related to the wood-ticks, dog-ticks, and cattle-ticks. The cattle-tick is responsible for the fatal disease among cattle that is known as Texas fever.

Preventive measures are the same as for chiggers.

To remove a tick without breaking off its head, drop oil on it, or clap a quid of moistened tobacco on it, or touch it with nicotine from a pipe, or stand naked in the dense smoke of a green-wood fire, or use whiskey externally, or hot water, or flame; in either case the tick will back its way out. The meanest ticks to get rid of are the young, which are known as " seed-ticks." They are hard to discover until they have inflamed the skin, and then are hard to remove because they are so small and fragile. A man may find himself covered with hundreds of them. In such case let him strip and rub himself with kerosene, or, lacking that, steep some tobacco or a strong cigar in warm water and do the same with it. They will drop off.

PUNKIES.—The punkie or " no-see-um " of our northern wildwoods, and its cousins the biting gnats and stinging midges of southern and western forests, are minute bloodsuckers that, according to my learned friend Professor Comstock, live, "under the bark of decaying branches, under fallen leaves, and in sap flowing from wounded trees."

With all due deference to this distinguished entomologist, I must aver that they don't live there when I am around; they seem particularly fond of sap flowing from wounded fishermen. Dope will keep them from biting you, but it won't keep them out of your eyes. Punkies are particularly annoying about sunset. They seem to know just when and where you will be cleaning the day's catch of trout, and that you will then be completely at their mercy. At such times you will agree that they beat all creation for pure, downright cussedness. Oil of citronella will protect your face and neck, but you can't have it on your hands when cleaning the fish. Punkies can't stand a smudge.

INSECTS IN CAMP.— The common house-fly, which, as Dr. Howard suggests, should be called the typhoid-fly, is often a great nuisance in camps. Screening of tents and of food supplies is the only sure remedy. Burning insect powder (pyrethrum) will drive them out of a tent or cottage, and that is also a good way to get rid of the wood cockroaches that sometimes are attracted by the lights of the camp and proceed to make themselves offensively at home.

Sometime you may elect to occupy an abandoned lumber camp while on an outing. My advice is, pass it by: not all its inhabitants have moved away. Any shack in the woods may harbor bed-bugs. If you must use such a place, don't forget the kerosene can.

If ants are troublesome about camp, try to find the nest by following the workers; then pour kerosene or boiling water into it. Red pepper or oil of sassafras sprinkled about may discourage them, but repellent substances are not to be depended upon. Kerosene is the sovereign remedy.

SMUDGES.— A good smudge is raised by using cedar "cigars," made as follows: Take long

PESTS OF THE WOODS 257

strips of cedar bark and bunch them together into a fagot six or eight inches in diameter, about one strip in three being dry and the others water-soaked; bind them with strips of the inner bark of green cedar. Ignite one end at the camp-fire, and set up two or more such cigars on different sides of the camp, according as the wind may shift. Punky wood piled on a bed of coals is also good. The ammoniacal vapors from a smudge of dried cow-dung is particularly effective. I have elsewhere referred to smudges made of dried toadstools; these are peculiarly repellent to punkies. A toadstool as large as one's two fists will hold fire for six or eight hours. A piece of one can be carried suspended by a string around one's neck, the burning end out. If the fungus is too damp at first, it can soon be dried out by placing it before the fire.

SCORPIONS.— Scorpions are not uncommon as far north as Missouri. I often used to find them in the neighborhood of St. Louis — little red fellows about 4 inches long. In the southwest, where they abound, they grow to a length of 6 or 7 inches. They hide by day under flat rocks, in dead trees, and in moist, dark places generally, and do their foraging at night. They are very belligerent, always fighting to the death. They carry their tails curled upward and forward, and can only strike upward and backward. They are sometimes unpleasantly familiar around camp, especially in rainy weather, having a penchant for crawling into bedding, boots, coat sleeves, trousers legs, etc.

The sting of a small scorpion is about as severe as that of a hornet; that of a large one is more serious, but never fatal, so far as I know, except to small children. After a person is stung a few times he is inoculated, and proof against the poison thereafter. If you get stung, take a hollow key or small tube, press the hollow with force over the puncture, causing the poison and a little blood to exude, hold firmly in place for several minutes, and, if the scorpion was a large one, you have a good excuse for drinking all the whiskey you want. Ordinarily a quid of moist tobacco locally applied eases the pain and reduces the swelling. Tobacco juice, by the way, is fatal to scorpions, tarantulas, and centipedes, and will set a snake crazy.

An uncommonly severe bite should be treated like snake-bite (see Volume II).

TARANTULAS.— I first witnessed the leaping powers of a tarantula one night when I was alone in a deserted log cabin in southern Missouri. The cabin had not been occupied for fifteen years, and there was no furniture in it. I had scarcely made my bed on the board floor when a tornado struck the forest. It was a grand sight, but scared me stiff. Well, the electric plant was working finely, just then, the lightning being almost a continuous glare. A tarantula that spread as broad as my hand jumped out of the straw that I was lying on and — it was hard to tell which was quicker, he or the lightning. He seemed disturbed about something. Not being able to fight the tornado, I took after the big spider with an old stumpy broom that happened to be in the cabin. When the broom would land at one side of the room, the tarantula would be on the other side. I was afraid he would spring for my face, but presently he popped into a hole somewhere, and vanished. The cabin somehow stuck to terra firma, and I returned to my pallet.

The tarantula's habits are similar to the scorpion's. The fangs are in its mouth. The bite is very severe, but not fatal to an adult. Cases of men being injured by either of these venomous arachnids are extremely rare, considering the abundance of the pests in some countries, and their habit of secreting themselves in clothes and bedding. If you want to see a battle royal, drop a scorpion and a tarantula into the same box. They

PESTS OF THE WOODS 259

will spring for each other in a flash, and both are absolutely game to the last.

CENTIPEDES.— I have had no personal experience with centipedes. Paul Fountain says:

"The centipedes were an intolerable nuisance for they had a nasty habit of hiding among the bed-clothes and under the pillows, attracted there to prey on the bugs, as I suppose; one evil as a set-off to another. But the centipedes were something more than a mere nuisance. It is all very well to be blandly told by gentlemen who think they know all about it that the bites of centipedes and scorpions are not dangerous. It may not be particularly dangerous to have a red-hot wire applied to your flesh, but it is confoundedly painful. Yet that is to be preferred to a centipede bite, which will not only make you dance at the time of infliction, but leave a painful swelling for many days after, accompanied by great disturbance of the system."

The cowpunchers' remedy for centipede bites, according to Mr. Hough, was " a chaw of tobacco on the outside and a horn of whiskey on the inside, both repeated frequently."

PORCUPINES.—In northern woods the porcupine is a common nuisance. It is a stupid beast, devoid of fear, and an inveterate camp marauder. You may kick it or club it unmercifully, yet it will return again and again to forage and destroy. The " porky " has an insistent craving for salt, and will gnaw anything that has the least saline flavor, anything that perspiring hands have touched, such as an axe-handle, a gunstock, a canoe paddle, and will ruin the article. He is also fond of leather, and will chew up your saddle, bridle, shoes, gloves, belts, the sweat-band of your hat, or any sweaty cloth or rope. Foodstuffs that are salty or greasy are never safe from him unless hung up on wires.

Porcupine quills, being barbed, are hard to extract. When they break off they work deep into the flesh. They are poisonous, in a way, and cause severe pain.

The porcupine is not found south of the Canadian faunal zone, which extends well down into our northern States.

SKUNKS.— Another notoriously fearless pest is the skunk. It will turn tail quickly enough, but nothing on earth will make it run. If a skunk takes it into his head to raid your camp he will step right in without any precautions whatever. Then he will nose through all of your possessions, walk over you if you be in his way, and forty men cannot intimidate him.

Once when I was spending the summer in a herders' hut, on a summit of the Smoky Mountains, a skunk burrowed under the cabin wall and came up through the earthen floor. It was about midnight. My two companions slept in a pole bunk against the wall, and I had an army cot in the middle of the room. It 'vas cold enough for an all-night fire on the hearth.

I awoke with the uneasy feeling that some intruder was moving about in the darkness. There was no noise, and my first thought was of rattlesnakes, which were numerous in that region. I sat up and lit the lantern, which hung over my head. One glance was enough. "Boys," I warned in a stage whisper, "for the love of God, don't breathe: there's a skunk at the foot of my bed!"

The animal was not in the least disconcerted by the light, but proceeded leisurely to inspect the premises. It went under my cot and nosed around there for five mortal minutes, while I lay rigid as a corpse.

Then Doc sneezed. I heard Andy groan from under his blanket: "You damn fool: now we'll get it!"

But we didn't. Madame Polecat waddled to their bunk, and I had a vision of two fellows sweating blood.

Then she moved over to the grub chest, found some excelsior lying beside it, and deliberately went to work making a nest.

An hour passed. I simply had to take a smoke. My tobacco was on a shelf right over the skunk. I risked all, arose very quietly, reached over the

PESTS OF THE WOODS 261

beast, got my tobacco, and retired like a ghost to the other end of the cabin to warm myself at the fire. We were prisoners; for the only door was a clapboard affair on wooden hinges that skreeked like a dry axle.

The visitor, having made its bed, did not yet feel like turning in, but decided to find out what for a bare-legged, white-faced critter I was, anyhow. It came straight over to the fireplace and sniffed my toes. The other boys offered all sorts of advice, and I talked brimstone back at them — we had found that pussy didn't care a hang for human speech so long as it was gently modulated.

That was a most amiable female of her species. True, she investigated all our property that was within reach, but she respected it, and finally she cuddled up in the excelsior, quite satisfied with her new home.

To cut an awfully long story short, the polecat held us spellbound until daybreak. Then she crawled out through her burrow, and we instantly fled through our skreeky door. Doc had a shotgun in his hand and murder in his heart. Not being well posted on skunk reflexes, he stepped up within ten feet and blew the animal's head clean off by a simultaneous discharge of both barrels. Did that headless skunk retaliate? It did, brethren, it did!

Many methods have been reported effective in deodorizing clothing that has been struck by the skunk's effluvium. Burying the clothes in earth is of no use unless they are left there long enough to rot them (they will smell again every time they get wet). Chloride of lime is objectionable for the same reason. Ammonia is said to neutralize the odor, and benzine or wood alcohol to extract it. An old trappers' remedy is to wrap the clothes in fresh hemlock boughs and leave them out-of-doors for twenty-four hours. A writer in one of the sportsmen's magazines states that, having met disaster in the shape of a skunk, he took an old farmer's advice, put some cornmeal on top of a hot stove, and, when it began to char and smoke, he held the clothes in the smoke for somewhat less than five minutes, by which time the scent was gone, nor did it ever reappear, even when the clothes were damp. Personally I never have had occasion to try any of these remedies.

The belief that skunk-bite is likely to cause hydrophobia is common in the Southwest, and to some extent it is borne out by the reports of army surgeons. A considerable number of soldiers and plainsmen bitten by the spotted or rock skunk of that region, which is a particularly aggressive creature, have undoubtedly died of hydrophobia. Yet the facts seem to be, as explained by W. Wade in the *American Naturalist,* that although men and other animals have been stricken mad by skunk-bite and have died therefrom, still this has only happened during an epidemic of rabies, in which skunks, being slow-moving and utterly fearless creatures, fell easy prey to rabid dogs or wolves. Becoming mad, in their turn, they would bite men sleeping in the open, and their bites would usually be inflicted upon the men's faces, hands and other exposed parts of their persons. In such cases, since none of the poisonous saliva was wiped off by clothing, the result was almost certain death. But rabies is very exceptional among skunks, and the bite of a healthy animal is not a serious matter.

The best insurance against skunks and predatory beasts in general is a good camp dog.

WOLVERINES.— The wolverine, also called glutton, carcajou, skunk bear, and Indian devil, is the champion thief of the wilderness. Lacking the speed of most of his family, the weasel and marten tribe, and devoid of special means of defence such as have been given the skunk and the porcupine, he has developed a diabolic cunning, which, coupled with his great strength and dogged persistence, makes him detested beyond all other creatures in the wild Northland that he inhabits. He systematically robs hunters of their game, trappers of

PESTS OF THE WOODS 263

their bait, and breaks into caches that defy almost any other animal. If he finds more food than his capacious paunch will hold, he defiles the rest so that no beast, however hungry, will touch it. So far as I know, the wolverine is practically extinct in our country except in the northwestern States bordering on Canada.

OTHER CAMP THIEVES.—The bushy-tailed pack rat of the West is noted for carrying off any and everything that he can get away with, but the eastern wood rats and wood mice seldom do much damage about a camp beyond chewing up canvas or other cotton goods to build nests with — a trick that flying-squirrels also are prone to play.

I have never been bothered by 'coons, although living where they are abundant. But "Nessmuk" had a different experience. Many years ago he told in *Forest and Stream* of his troubles with them in northern Pennsylvania.—

"A strong cache . . . is indispensable in this region, for there is not a night during the open season in which you can lay by meat, fish, or butter, where hedgehogs and 'coons will not find it. Their strength and persistence in digging out your larder is something surprising. I have a butter cup with a tight-fitting cover, and a square tin case for keeping pork, also with a tight cover. Time and again I have had these tins raided by raccoons, nosed around, wallowed in the mud, and moved yards away from the cache; but the covers stuck like burs, and it must drive a 'coon frantic to work half the night in unearthing a butter cup, and then, with only one thickness of tin between his nose and the longed-for butter, be unable to get a taste of it. Unless the 'coon dialect has plenty of cuss-words I don't see how he could ever get over it."

CHAPTER XV

DRESSING AND KEEPING GAME AND FISH

Butchering is the most distasteful part of a hunter's work—a job to be sublet when you can; but sometimes you can't.

When an animal is shot, the first thing to do is to bleed it, unless the bullet itself has gone clean through and left a large hole of exit through which much blood has drained.

Even birds and fish should be bled as soon as secured. The meat keeps better, and, in the case of a bird, the feathers are more easily plucked. Speaking, now, of large game, do not drop your gun and rush in on a dying beast to stick it, for it might prove an ugly customer in its death struggle. First put a bullet through its heart or spine.

To cut a deer's throat would ruin the head for mounting. Twist its head to one side, with the throat downhill, if possible, so that blood will not flow over the hide; then stick your knife in at the point of the breast, just in front of the sternum or breastbone, and work the point of the knife two or three inches back and forth, close up to the backbone, so as to sever the great blood-vessels. Then if you must hurry on, perhaps after another animal, toss some brush over the carcass, or hang a handkerchief over it, to suggest a trap, and *make a brush blaze* here and there as you go along, to guide you back to the spot.

If practicable, remove the entrails at once. To do this, it is not necessary to hang the animal up.

If you are in a hurry, or if the camp is not far away, it will do merely to take out the paunch and intestines; but if this is neglected gas will accumulate and putrefaction will soon set in. A bear, especially, will soon spoil, because the fur keeps in the vital heat, so that the body will smoke when opened, even after it has lain a long time in hard-freezing weather.

If the animal is not to be butchered on the spot, slit the skin only from vent to stomach, using the point of the knife, and taking care not to rupture the paunch. Sever the intestine at the rectum, cut the genitals free, then cut off the gullet as high as you can above the stomach, and pull all out. The carcass should lie so that this is done toward the downhill side.

DRAGGING A DEER.— If the ground is not too rough, nor the distance too great, a deer may be dragged to camp over the snow or leaves; but drag it head-foremost; if pulled the other way every hair will act as a barb against the ground. Before starting, tie the front legs to the lower jaw. The carcass will slide easier, and the hide will not be so disfigured, if you first drop a bush or small tree by cutting through the roots, leaving a stub of a root projecting for a handle, then tie the animal on the upper side of the bush, and drag away.

PACKING DEER ON A SADDLE.— To pack a deer on horseback: first, if your horse is green in the business, let him smell the deer, pet him, and, if necessary, blindfold him until you get the carcass lashed in place. Even then you may have trouble. I have seen a mule get such a conniption fit at the smell of blood that he bucked himself, deer, and saddle, off a cut-bank into a swift river; the girth broke, and that saddle is going yet.

It may be necessary to smear some of the deer's blood on your horse's nose to kill the scent.

If the animal is antlered, remove the head and make a separate parcel of it.

Re-cinch your saddle, and, if the deer is too

heavy to lift upon the horse's back, fasten your picket-rope to the deer's hind legs, throw the line over the saddle, get on the other side, and haul away until the deer's hocks are up even with the saddle; then quickly snub the rope around the saddle-horn, go around, swing the burden over the saddle, balancing it evenly, and lash it fast. Or, if you wish to ride, move the deer behind the saddle and lash it there, bringing the legs forward on either side and tying them to the rings of the cinch. For thongs, if the saddle has none, cut strips from the skin of the deer's fore legs. Be sure to fasten the load securely, so that it cannot slip, or you will have a badly frightened horse. By skinning the legs from hoofs to ankles, partly disarticulating the latter, and then tying the legs snugly, they will not dangle and scare the horse, nor catch in underbrush.

Another way is to place the deer in the saddle seat, back to horn, legs to rear. Tie one end of a short rope to latigo ring, pass rope around deer back of shoulders and once more through the ring. Bring rope out in front of deer's breast, take a half turn with it in rope back of shoulders, and pull all tight. Take two half hitches on saddle horn. Repeat on opposite side, but bring rope up between hind legs of deer, take the half turn, and fasten to saddle horn as before. Now tie deer's head on top of load. This method of packing is recommended by W. G. Corker, who says "no horse alive can buck it off."

A simpler but secure way is to cut slits for thongs above the hocks and knees and another slit along the brisket. Place the deer on the saddle in such manner that the saddle horn sticks through the slit brisket. Tie down the legs at their middle joints to the cinch-ring on each side. (Emerson Hough.)

CARRYING ON A LITTER.— Two men can carry a deer on a pole by tying its legs together in pairs, slipping the pole through, and tying the head to the pole. Unless the carcass is tied snugly to the pole,

DRESSING GAME AND FISH 267

such a burden will swing like a pendulum as you trudge along, especially if the pole is at all springy.

A more comfortable way is to make a litter of two poles by laying them parallel, about two and one-half feet apart, and nailing or tying cross-pieces athwart the poles. Whittle the ends of the poles to a size convenient for your hands, and fasten to each end of the litter a broad strap, in such a way that it may pass over the shoulders of the carrier and thus take up much of the weight. Then lash the animal securely to the top of the litter.

CARRYING SINGLE-HANDED.—One man can carry a small deer entire by dragging it to a fallen tree, boosting it up on the log, lengthwise and back down, then grasping one or both hind legs with one hand and the fore legs with the other, and carrying the load so that its weight is on the back of his neck and shoulders.

Or you may prop the deer on the log breast down, squat with back of your neck against the body, put one arm under near front leg, the other under near hind leg, get the carcass on your shoulders, and arise.

A better scheme is to cut a slit through the lower jaw and up through the mouth, and another slit through each of the legs between the tendons, just above the hoof; tie the head and legs together, but not too close, and then, by the loop thus formed, swing the burden over your shoulder.

To carry a larger animal pickaback: gut it, cut off the head and hang it up to be called for later, skin the legs down to the knees and hocks, cut off the shinbones, tie the skin of each fore leg to the hind leg on the same side, put the arms through the loops thus formed, and "git ep!" Or, remove the bones from the fore legs from knee to foot, leaving the feet on, tie the hind legs together and the fore legs to them, thrust your head and one arm through, and carry the burden as a soldier does a blanket-roll.

THE INDIAN PACK.— When one has a long way

to go, and can only carry the hide and the choicer parts of the meat, the best way is to make up an Indian pack, as shown in Fig. 114. Skin the deer, place a stick athwart the inside of the skin, pack

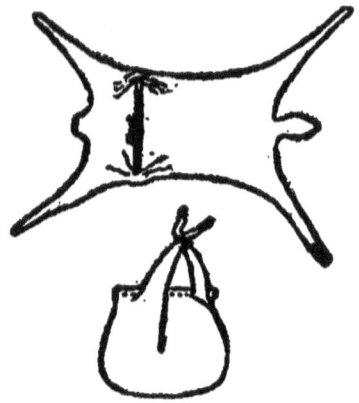

Fig. 114 — Indian Deer Pack

the saddles, hams, and tid-bits in the latter, and roll up and tie in a convenient bundle.

HANGING TO BUTCHER.— It is not necessary to hang a deer up to skin and butcher it; but that is the more cleanly way. One man, unassisted, can hang a pretty heavy animal in the following way: Drag it headforemost to a sapling that is just limber enough to bend near the ground when you climb it. Cut three poles, ten or twelve feet long, with crotches near the ends. Climb the sapling and trim off the top, leaving the stub of one stout branch near the top. Tie your belt, or a stout withe or flexible root, into a loop around the deer's antlers or throat. Bend the sapling down until you can slip the loop over the end of the sapling. The latter, acting as a spring-pole, will lift part of the deer's weight. Then place the crotches of the poles under the fork of the sapling, butts of poles radiating outward, thus forming a tripod. First push on one pole, then on another, and so raise the carcass free from the ground. If you do not intend to butcher it immediately, raise it up out of reach of roving dogs and "varmints."

DRESSING GAME AND FISH

It is common practice to hang deer by gambrels with the head down; but, when hung head up, the animal is easier to skin and to butcher, drains better, and does not drop blood and juices over the head and neck, which you may want to have mounted for a trophy. Dried blood is very hard to remove from hair or fur. If the skin is stripped off from rear to head it will be hard to grain. And if the animal is not to be skinned for some time it is best hung by the head, because the slope of the hair then sheds rain and snow instead of, holding them, and the lung cavity does not collect blood, rain, or snow.

The more common way of skinning a deer, when the head is not wanted for mounting, is to hang it up by one hind leg and begin skinning at the hock, peeling the legs, then the body, and finally the neck, then removing the head with skin on (for baking in a hole), after which the carcass is swung by both legs and is eviscerated.

If there is no time to hang the deer, open it, throw the entrails well off to one side, then cover the carcass with boughs as if it were a trap, or hang a handkerchief, or the blown-up bladder of the animal, over it, to scare away marauders. Place the deer so it will drain downhill. And don't neglect to blaze your way out, so you can find it again.

BUTCHERING DEER.— Now let us suppose that you have killed a deer far away from camp, and that you wish to skin and butcher it on the spot, saving all parts of it that are good for anything. You are alone. You wish to make a workmanlike job of it. You carry only the choicer parts with you that evening, and must fix the rest so it will not be molested overnight.

Of course, you have a jack-knife, and either a pocket hatchet or a big bowie-knife — probably the latter, if this is your first trip. First hang the deer, as described above. By the time you are through cutting those poles with the knife your hand will ache between thumb and forefinger; a tomahawk would have been better.

SKINNING.— This is your first buck, and you wish to save the head for mounting. For this the skin of the whole neck must be preserved, clear back to the shoulders. Cleanse away any blood that may have issued from the nose and mouth, and stuff some dry moss, or other absorbent, in the beast's mouth. Stick your big knife into a log alongside; it is only to look at, for the present.

Open your jack-knife, insert the point, edge up, where the neck joins the back, and cut the skin in a circle around the base of the neck, running from the withers down over the front of the shoulder-blade to the brisket or point of the breast on each side. Do not skin the head at present—you may not have time for that. Insert the point of the knife through the skin over the paunch, and, following the middle line of the chest, slit upward to meet the cut around the neck. Then reverse, and continue the slit backward to the end of the tail, being careful not to perforate the walls of the belly. Then slit along the inside of each leg from the hoof to the belly-slit. If you wish to save the feet for mounting, be particular to rip the skin in a straight line up the *under* side of the leg, starting by inserting the point of the knife between the heel-pads.

Now comes a nice trick, that of severing the shanks. Nearly every inexperienced person starts too high. Study the accompanying illustrations

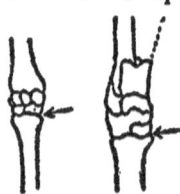

Fig. 115 — The Place to Use Your Knife. From *Forest and Stream*

of these joints, noting where the arrow points, which is the place to use your knife. In a

DRESSING GAME AND FISH

deer the joint is about an inch and a half below the hock on the hind leg, and an inch below the knee on the fore leg. Cut square across through skin and muscles, in front, and similarly behind; then, with a quick pull backward against your knee, snap the shank off. The joint of the fore leg is broken in a similar manner, excepting that it is snapped forward.

Having stripped the vertebræ from the tail, now peel the skin off the whole animal, from the shoulders downward, assisting with your closed fist, and, where necessary, with the knife; but wherever the knife is used be careful to scrape the skin as clean as you can, without cutting it, for every adhering bit of fat, flesh, or membrane must be thoroughly removed before the skin is ready for tanning, and that is easier to do now than after it dries. The whole operation of skinning is much easier while the animal is still warm than after the body has become cold. To skin a frozen animal is a desperately mean job. I have known four old hunters to work nearly a whole afternoon in skinning a frozen bear.

The skin of the body and limbs having been removed, stretch it out flat, hair side down, alongside of you to receive portions of the meat as it is butchered.

GRALLOCHING.— Now take up your big knife, insert its point alongside the breastbone, and cut through the false ribs to the point of the sternum. In a young animal this is easy; but in an old one the ribs have ossified, and you must search for the soft points of union between the ribs and the sternum, which are rather hard to find. Here your knife's temper, and perhaps your own, will be put to the test. The most trifling-looking pocket hatchet would do the trick in a jiffy.

Open the abdominal cavity, taking care not to rupture anything, and prop the chest open a few inches with a stick, or by merely pulling the ribs away from each other. Cut the diaphragm free at both sides and at the back. (It is the membrane that separates the organs of the chest from those of the abdomen.) Everything now is free from the body except at the throat and anus. Reach in and take in your grasp all the vessels that run up into the neck. With knife in the other hand, cut them across from above downward, taking care that you do not cut yourself. Now pull away gradually, helping a little here and there with the knife until all the contents of the visceral cavity lie at your feet, save the lower end of the rectum, which is still attached. With a hatchet, if you had one, you would now split the pelvis. The thing can be done with a large knife, if the animal is not too old, by finding the soft suture at the highest part of the bone and rocking the knife-edge on it. But you may not be able to accomplish this just now. So reach in with the jack-knife, cut carefully around the rectum and urinary organs, keeping as close to the bone as possible, and free everything from the cavity. If water is near, wash out the cavity and let it drain, or wipe with a dry cloth if you have one. Be particular to leave no clotted blood.

To remove the head; flay back the skin for several inches at base of neck, cut through flesh, etc., to the backbone. Search along this till you find the flat joint between the faces of two vertebræ, separate these as far as you can; then twist the attached part of the body round and round, until it breaks off.

Directions how to skin a head for mounting are given in Volume II.

In butchering, save the liver, heart, brain, milt (spleen), kidneys, and the caul fat. The caul is the fold of membrane loaded with fat that covers most of the intestines. In removing the liver you need not bother about a gall-bladder, for a deer has none. Many a tenderfoot has been tricked into looking for it. In the final cutting up, save the marrow-bones (especially of elk) for eating;

DRESSING GAME AND FISH

the ligaments that lie on either side of the backbone, from the head backward, for sinew thread; the hoofs for glue (if you are far from supply-stores and expect to remain a good while); and perhaps the bladder, paunch, large intestine, and pericardium (outer skin) of the heart, for pouches and receptacles of various kinds, and to make catgut. The scrotum of a buck, tanned with the hair on, makes a good tobacco-pouch.

BUTCHERING ON THE GROUND.— If one is in a hurry, and is not particular about the hide, he can do his butchering on the ground. In that case, lay the animal on sloping ground, with its head uphill; or bend its back over a log or rock; or turn it on its back with its head twisted around and wedged under one side. The old-time way of butchering a buffalo was to turn the carcass on its belly, stretching out the legs on either side to support it. A transverse cut was made at the nape of the neck; then the workman, gathering the long hair of the hump in one hand, separated the skin from the shoulder, laid it open to the tail, along the spine, freed it from the sides, and pulled it down to the brisket. While the skin was thus still attached to the belly it was stretched upon the ground to receive the dissected meat. Then the shoulder was severed, and the fleece, which is the mixed fat and lean that lies along the loin and ribs, was removed from along the backbone, and the hump ribs were cut off with a tomahawk. These portions were placed on the skin, together with the *boudins* from the stomach, and the tongue. The rest of the meat was left to feed the wolves.

ELK AND MOOSE.— Such large animals are generally butchered on the ground. If the beast has antlers, first remove the head. Then turn the body on its back and prop it in position with a couple of three-foot stakes sharpened at both ends, a hole being dug for a moose's withers. Sometimes only the haunches, sirloins and tongue are saved, these being cut away without skinning or gutting the carcass.

If there is a horse, or several men with a rope, to elevate the body, the animal's lower legs are skinned, the shanks removed, the hide split from throat to tail, the sides skinned free, the windpipe and gullet raised, the pleura and diaphragm cut loose, and the carcass then raised high enough so that the hide can be removed from the rump and back. The rectum, small intestines, and paunch are then loosened and allowed to roll out on the ground. The gullet is cut, the liver taken out, and the diaphragm, lungs and heart removed. Then the skinning is finished over the shoulders and fore legs.

It is best not to cut up the meat until it is quite cold and firm. Then split the carcass in halves along the backbone, and quarter it, leaving one rib on each hind quarter. The meat may then be put on a scaffold, and covered with the skin to protect it from moose-birds.

Two men can raise a very heavy animal clear of the ground with three stiff poles, say twelve feet long, which are sharpened at the butts and notched at the tips. Lay these on the ground with notched ends together over the animal's hind quarters and the sharpened ends radiating outward and equidistant from each other. Tie the notched ends rather loosely together with a short piece of rope, the other end of which is tied to a gambrel thrust through the hind legs under the hamstrings (or attach to antlers, nose, or through lower jaw). Lift the tripod until the rope is taut, shove one pole forward a few inches, then another, sticking the butts in the ground as you progress, until the hindquarters are raised, and so on until the beast swings free.

BEARS.— These beasts, too, are generally butchered on the ground. In skinning, begin the incisions at the feet, and leave at least the scalp, if not the skin of the whole head, attached. It is

DRESSING GAME AND FISH

quite a task to skin a bear, as the beast usually is covered with fat, which adheres to the hide and must be scraped free. All of the caul fat should be saved for rendering into bear's oil, which is better and wholesomer than lard. The brain, liver, and milt (spleen) are good eating.

Owing to its greasiness, the skin of a bear is very likely to spoil unless carefully scraped, especially at the ears. Slit the ears open on the inside, skin them back almost to the edge, and fill with salt; also salt the base of the ears. The feet likewise must be skinned out and well salted.

PRESERVING SKINS.— If a hide is to be preserved for some time in a green state, use nothing on it but salt. Spread it out flat, hair side down, stretch the legs, flanks, etc., and rub all parts thoroughly with salt, particular pains being taken to leave no little fold untreated. A moose-hide will take ten or even fifteen pounds of salt. As soon as the salting is done, fold in the legs and roll the hide up.

Methods of tanning, and of making buckskin and rawhide, will be discussed in Volume II.

CARE OF MEAT.— When a deer has merely been eviscerated and is hung up to be skinned, and cut up at a more convenient season, prop open the abdominal cavity with a stick, so that it may dry out quickly. If the weather is warm enough at any hour of the day for flies to come out, keep a smudge going under the carcass.* It takes flies but a few minutes to raise Ned with venison. If blows are discovered on the meat, remove them, looking especially at all folds and nicks in the meat, and around the bones, for the blows work into such places very quickly. So long as they have not bored into the flesh they do it no harm.

A surer way is described by Doctor Breck:

---

* This means in camp, where there is someone to look after it. Do not leave a smudge to take care of itself out in the woods: a wind springing up in your absence may cause it to set the forest afire.

"It is my practice to carry with me three or four yards of cheesecloth (which has been dipped in alum-water at home), and this I wrap closely round whatever parts of the animal I especially wish to preserve. If a round of venison is thus done up, preferably with a needle and thread, it is safe from fly-blows, which are the bane of hunters. If unskinned, a head may also be kept clean in like manner. The cheesecloth takes up little more room than a napkin, and amply repays the small bulge in the coat-pocket."—*The Way of the Woods.*

I always carry cheesecloth on fishing trips, too.

It may be said here that even smoked bacon is not immune from blows, and it should not be hung up without a cheesecloth cover. The fly that blows meats is the common "blue-bottle." Its eggs hatch into "skippers" within twelve hours.

CURING VENISON.— Venison keeps a long time without curing, if the climate is cool and dry. To cure a deer's ham, hang it up by the shank, divide the muscles just above the hock, and insert a handful of dry salt. The meat of the deer tribe gets more tender and better flavored the longer it is hung up. In warm weather dust flour all over a haunch or saddle of venison, sew it up in a loose bag of cheesecloth, and hang it in a shady place where there is a current of air. It will keep sweet for several weeks, if there is no crevice in the bag through which insects can penetrate. Ordinarily it is best not to salt meat, for salt draws the juices. Bear meat, however, requires much salt to cure it — more than any other game animal.

Hornaday recommends the following recipe for curing venison:—

The proportions of the mixture I use are:
Salt .... 3 lbs.
Allspice .... 4 table-spoonfuls,
Black Pepper .... 5 table-spoonfuls,
   all thoroughly mixed.

Take a ham of deer, elk, or mountain sheep, or fall-killed mountain goat, and as soon as possible after killing, dissect the thigh, muscle by muscle. Any one can learn to do this by following up with the knife the natural

DRESSING GAME AND FISH 277

divisions between the muscles. With big game like elk, some of the muscles of the thigh are so thick they require to be split in two. A piece of meat should not exceed five inches in thickness. Skin off all enveloping membranes, so that the curative powder will come in direct contact with the raw, moist flesh. The flesh must be sufficiently fresh and moist that the preservative will readily adhere to it. The best size for pieces of meat to be cured by this process is not over a foot long, by six or eight inches wide and four inches thick.

When each piece has been neatly and skilfully prepared rub the powder upon every part of the surface, and let the mixture adhere as much as it will. Then hang up each piece of meat, by a string through a hole in the smaller end, and let it dry in the wind. If the sun is hot, keep the meat in the shade; but in the North the sun helps the process. Never let the meat get wet. If the weather is rainy for a long period, hang your meat rack where it will get heat from the campfire, but no more smoke than is unavoidable, and cover it at night with a piece of canvas.

Meat thus prepared is not at its best for eating until it is about a month old; then slice it thin. After that no sportsman, or hunter, or trapper can get enough of it. . . .

No; this is *not* "jerked" meat. It is many times better. It is always eaten uncooked, and as a concentrated, stimulating food for men in the wilds it is valuable.

(*Camp-fires in the Canadian Rockies,* 201–203.)

It is a curious fact that blow-flies work close to the ground, and will seldom meddle with meat that is hung more than ten feet above the ground. Game or fish suspended at a height of twenty feet will be immune from "blows," if hung on a trimmed sapling well away from any foliage.

JERKED VENISON.—"Jerky" or jerked meat has nothing to do with our common word "jerk." It is an anglicized form of the Spanish *charqui,* which is itself derived from the Quichua (Peruvian) *ccharqui,* meaning flesh cut in flakes and dried without salt. It is the same as the African *biltong.* Those who have not investigated the matter may be surprised to learn that the round of beef is 61 per cent. water, and that even the common dried and smoked meat of the butcher shops contains 54 per cent. water. To condense the nutritive properties of these substances, the water, of course, must be exhausted. In ordinary dried beef this is only partially done, because the pieces are too thick.

In the dry air of uninhabited plains, meat does not putrefy, even when unsalted, and it may be dried in the sun, without fire. Elk flesh dried in the sun does not keep as well as that of deer.

As I have said, real jerky has been dried without salt; but it is common practice nowadays to use some salt in the process, proceeding as follows:—

If you can afford to be particular, select only the tender parts of the meat; otherwise use all of the lean. Cut it in strips about half an inch thick. If you have time, you may soak them a day in strong brine. If not, place the flakes of meat on the inside of the hide, and mix with them about a pint and a half of salt for a whole deer, or two or three quarts for an elk or moose; also some pepper. These condiments are not necessary, but are added merely for seasoning. Cover the meat with the hide, to keep flies out, and let it stand thus for about two hours to let the salt work in. Then drive four forked stakes in the ground so as to form a square, the forks being about four feet from the ground. Lay two poles across from fork to fork, parallel, and across these lay thin poles about two inches apart. Lay the strips of meat across the poles, and under them build a small fire to dry and smoke the meat. Do not let the fire get hot enough to cook the meat, but only to dehydrate it, so that the flesh becomes dry as a chip. The best fuel is birch, especially black birch, because it imparts a pleasant flavor. Only a thin smoke is wanted. To confine it, if a breeze is stirring, put up some sort of wind-break. This will reduce the weight of the meat about one-half, and will cure it so that it will keep indefinitely. You may have to keep up the fire for twenty-four hours. The meat of an old bull will, of course,

DRESSING GAME AND FISH 279

be as tough as sole leather; but, in any case, it will retain its flavor and sustenance. When pounded pretty fine, jerky makes excellent soup; but it is good enough as it is, and a man can live on it exclusively without suffering an inordinate craving for bread.

The breasts (only) of grouse and other game birds can be cured in the same way, and are good.

Some do not like their meat smoked. A way of jerking without smoking was described by "an old-timer" for the *New York Sun:*

"Cut the choicest of the meat into strips ten inches long and two inches square. Sprinkle them quite liberally with salt, but not enough to make them bitter. Let the salt work on them for a couple of hours. While it is doing it you go and put down two logs a foot or so in diameter side by side and about the same distance apart. Between the logs make a fire of dry hemlock bark.

"Hemlock, or a relative of hemlock, is always apt to be found in deer hunting regions, and I never go into camp without taking pains to gather up a lot of hemlock bark for use. It is the best material for the purpose because it will make a fire of hot coals without running to blaze or smoke. Birch bark would be ideal for the purpose, but it is all blaze with birch bark. Hickory wood couldn't be beat for jerking venison, but hickory wood would smoke the meat, and jerked venison isn't smoked venison, as a good many folks suppose it is, not by a long shot.

"Having got your bed of hemlock bark coals in fine shape, and having driven at the inside edge of the ends of each log a crotched stick long enough after it is securely driven to have the crotch perhaps a foot above the logs, and having extended from crotch to crotch in these sticks two poles that are thus suspended above the fire, cut as many half inch hardwood sticks as you need, long enough to reach across from one pole to another and rest securely on them. On these sticks string your strips of deer meat by thrusting them through the meat near one end of the strips, the sticks being sharpened at one end to facilitate that operation.

"This will leave the strips hanging from their sticks much as the candles used to hang from theirs in the old fashioned moulds, if any hunter of this generation is happy enough to have recollections of the days when we made our own candles. Place the sticks with their pendent meat over the coals. Turn the concave sides of lengths of hemlock bark over the top of the sticks. This will keep in the steam that will presently begin to rise from the meat, as the coals get their gradual but effective work in on it. Keep the fire down there between the logs so it won't make too rapid a heat, for if it does the juice will ooze out of the meat and be lost, and that would detract from the excellence of the finished product.

"If during the process of jerking your venison the meat is taken off the coals before it is done it will be soft and flabby. If it is hard when taken off it will be overdone. In either case your jerked venison might much better have remained unjerked, for it will be a failure. To prevent either of these catastrophes the meat should be tested frequently by pushing a sharp knife blade or other convenient probe into and through the strips. The moment it requires more than ordinary force to push the probe through, your venison is thoroughly and properly jerked. Then shove the coals from under the strips and let them cool with the dying embers."

COMPUTING WEIGHT.— Hornaday gives the following rule, in his *Natural History*, for computing the live weight of deer from the dressed weight: Add five ciphers to the dressed weight in pounds, and divide by 78,612; the quotient will be the live weight in pounds.

SMALL MAMMALS.— Now for what Shakespeare calls "small deer." The easiest way for a novice to skin a squirrel is the one described by "Nessmuk."—

"Chop off head, tail, and feet with the hatchet; cut the skin on the back crosswise, and, inserting the two middle fingers, pull the skin off in two parts (head and tail). Clean and cut the squirrel in halves, leaving two ribs on the hind quarters." The objection is that, in this case, you throw away the best part of the squirrel, the cheek meat and brain being its special tid-bits.

A better way is this: Sever the tail from below, holding your left forefinger close in behind it, and cutting through the vertebræ close up to the body, leaving only the hide on the top side. Then turn the squirrel over and cut a slit down along each ham. Put your foot on the tail, hold the rear end of the squirrel in your hand, and pull, stripping the skin off to the fore legs. Peel the

DRESSING GAME AND FISH 281

skin from the hind legs, and cut off the feet. Then cut off the fore feet. Skin to the neck; assist here a little with the knife; then skin to the ears; cut off the butts of the ears; then skin till the blue of the eyeballs shows, and cut; then to the nose till the teeth show, and cut it off. Thus you get no hair on the meat, and the whole thing is done in less than a minute, when you have gained deftness.

In dressing mammals larger than squirrels be particular to remove the scent glands. Even rabbits have them. Cut directly between the fore leg and body and you will find a small waxy " kernel " which is a gland. The degree to which this taints the flesh depends a good deal on the season; but in most of the fur-bearers it is always objectionable.

Dan Beard gives the following directions for dressing small animals:

"To prepare a musquash or any other small fur-bearing animal for the table, first make *a skinning stick* of a forked stick about as thick as your finger. Let the forks be about one inch to each branch, and the stick below long enough to reach up between your knees when the sharpened lower end is forced into the ground. If you squat on the ground the stick should be about a foot and one-half long, but longer if you sit on a camp stool, stump or stone. Hang the muskrat on the forks of the stick by thrusting the sharpened ends of the fork through the thin spot at the gambrel joints of the hind legs, that is, the parts which correspond with your own heels. Hung in this manner (with the one and one-half foot stick), the nose of the animal will just clear the ground. First skin the game, then remove all the internal organs, and, if it be a muskrat, not only remove all the musk glands, but cut into the inside of the forearms and the fleshy part of the thighs, and take out a little white substance you will find there which resembles a nerve. This done and the meat well washed, it may be cooked with little fear of the food retaining a musky flavor." — (*Field and Forest Handy Book.*)

To skin a 'coon: begin with the point of the knife in the center of one hind foot and slit up the inside of the leg to the vent and down the other leg in a like manner. Cut carefully around the vent, then rip from it up to the chin. Strip the skin from the bone of the tail with a split stick gripped firmly in the hand. Then flay the animal, scrape the pelt clean, and put it on a stretcher to dry.

DRESSING BIRDS.— Turkeys, geese, ducks, and grouse are usually dry picked. If this could be done while the bodies were still warm, it would be no job at all; but after they are cold it generally results in a good deal of laceration of the skin — so much so that sometimes the disgusted operator gives up and skins the whole bird. It would be better to scald them first, like chickens. In dry picking, hang the bird up by one leg, pluck first the pinions and tail feathers; then the small feathers from shanks and inside of thighs; then the others. Grasp only a few feathers at a time between finger and thumb, as close to the skin as possible, and pull quickly toward the head. Then pick out all pin-feathers and quills. Singe the down off quickly, so as not to give an oily appearance to the skin. Ordinarily the down can be removed from a duck's breast by grasping the bird by the neck and giving one sweep of the open hand down one side of the body and then one down the other. In plucking geese or ducks some use finely powdered resin to remove the pin-feathers. The bird is plucked dry, then rubbed all over with the resin, dipped in and out of boiling water seven or eight times, and then the pin-feathers and down are easily rubbed off.

To draw a bird: cut off the head, and the legs at the first joint. Make a lengthwise slit on back at base of neck and sever neck bone close to body, also the membrane which holds the windpipe. Make a lengthwise incision from breastbone to (and around) the vent, so you can easily draw the insides, which must be done carefully, so as not to rupture the gall-bladder (pheasants have none).

The idea that ducks and other game birds should hang until they smell badly is monstrous. If you

DRESSING GAME AND FISH

want to know where such tastes originated, read the annals of medieval sieges.

Small game birds, such as snipe and plover, can be cleaned very quickly by pressing a thumb on each side of their breasts, and, with a swift push, break the skin back, carrying feathers, backbone and entrails with it, and leaving only the breast. Grouse can be treated in the same way if the skin of the breast is first slit. The legs and rump, if wanted, can be removed separately.

KEEPING SMALL GAME.— To ship rabbits, squirrels, etc.: do not skin them, but remove the entrails, wipe the insides perfectly dry, wrap in paper, and pack them back down.

Never pack birds in straw or grass without ice, for in damp or warm weather this will heat or sweat them. If they freeze they must be kept so, as they will quickly spoil after thawing. Food in a bird's crop soon sours; the crop should be removed.

To preserve birds in warm weather for shipment: draw them, wash the inside perfectly clean, dry thoroughly, and then take pieces of charcoal from the fireplace, wrap them in a thin rag, and fill the abdominal cavity with this. Also fill the bill, ears, eyes, and anal opening with powdered charcoal, to keep off flies and prevent putrefaction. Reject all pieces of charcoal that are only half-burnt or have the odor of creosote. Birds stuffed in this way will keep sweet for a week in hot weather.

CLEANING TROUT.— Brook trout have no noticeable scales, but they should be scraped free of slime. Rainbow trout need scaling.

Remove the vent, cut the gills free from the lower jaw and back of head, and slit open from head to anal fin. Draw the inside out by the gills, and scrape the clotted blood away from the backbone. If the fish are only for the pan, not to be exhibited, cut the heads off; then they are easier to clean. Large ones, anyway, should have heads and tails cut off before frying.

A small trout may be cleaned without splitting, by cutting out the vent, tearing out the gills with the fingers, and drawing the entrails with them.

CLEANING SCALY FISH.— To scale a fish: grasp it by the head (or lay it on a board and drive a fork through its tail), and, using a knife that is not over-keen, scale first one side and then the other, with swift, steady sweeps. The scales below the gills, and those near the fins, are removed by moving the point of the knife crosswise to the fish's length. Next place the knife just below the belly fin and with a slant stroke cut off this, the side fins, and the head, all in one piece. Then remove the back fin, and the spines beneath it, by making a deep incision on each side of the fin and pulling the latter out. The ventral part is removed in the same way. Open the fish, wash it in cold water, scrape off the slime, and then wipe it *dry* with a clean cloth or towel. Large fish, for broiling, should be split open along the back and the spine removed.

A special fish knife, with saw-tooth back for scaling, can be bought at a sporting-goods store. A good scaler is extemporized by nailing a common bottle cap on the flattened end of a stick.

A slippery, flabby fish is more easily handled for scaling if you sharpen one end of a stick as thick as your little finger and run it down through the fish's mouth about two-thirds the length of the body.

Fish taken from muddy or mossy water, or from cedar swamps, taste strong if cleaned in the ordinary way, unless special precautions are taken in cooking (see Chapter XVIII). The taint is not removed by scaling, for its cause is hidden deep in the roots of the scales. Such fish should be skinned. That is also the best way to prepare yellow perch.

SKINNING FISH.— Grasp the fish firmly, belly down. Cut across the nape of the neck, run the point of the knife along the back to the tail, and

DRESSING GAME AND FISH 285

on each side of the back fin. Remove the fin by catching lower end between thumb and knife blade and pulling smartly upward toward the head. Skin each side by seizing between thumb and knife the flap of skin at nape and jerking outward and downward; then the rest, by grasping skin as near the vent as possible and tearing quickly down to the tail, bring away the anal fin. Remove the head and the entrails will come with it. Trout and pickerel should be scraped free of slime.

Large fish for frying are best steaked. Robert Pinkerton gives the following directions:

"Cut off the head, run the knife down either side of the bones of the back the entire length. Cut down to the backbone and continue along the ribs. This gives you two slabs of boneless meat and leaves the entrails in the skeleton. Lay the pieces, skin side down, on a paddle blade and run a sharp knife between the flesh and skin. You now have boneless, scaleless, skinless fish, which may be rolled in flour or cornmeal, fried in bacon grease, and eaten with as little difficulty as though it were moose steak."

To skin a catfish or bullhead, do not scald it, for that makes the meat flabby and robs it of its fresh flavor. Cut off the ends of the spines, slit the skin behind and around the head, and then from this point along the back to the tail, cutting around the back fin. Then peel the two corners of the skin well down, sever the backbone, and, holding to the corners of the skin with one hand, pull the fish's body free from the skin with the other. A pair of pliers will be appreciated here.

Or, cut through the skin clear around the neck near the gills. Stick a large table fork into the gills and pin the fish to a board by its backbone. Then catch the skin at neck between thumb and knife-blade, and strip it off by a steady pull.

To skin an eel: drive a fork through the back of his neck (if you have no fork, roll him in ashes or dust and use a swab in the left hand), slit the skin around his neck with a sharp knife, make a longitudinal slit half the length of the body, peel the skin back at the neck until you get a good hold, and then strip it off.

Another way is to rub the tail under your foot until the skin splits, or nail the eel up by the tail, cut through the skin around the body just forward of the tail and work its edges loose, then draw the skin off over the head; this takes out all of the fin bones, and strips off the skin entire.

To KEEP FISH.— It is very bad practice to string fish together through the gills and keep them in water till you start for home. It makes them lose blood and torments them till they die of suffocation. Why sicken your fish before you eat them? If you must use a stringer, push its point through the fish's lower jaw. Then it can breathe freely. A single fish on a good length of line, strung in this way, can fight off turtles till you notice the commotion.

If you are not fishing from a boat, with live box or net, then by all means kill your fish as fast as you catch them. Some do this by giving the thing's head a quick jerk backward, breaking its neck; others hit it a smart rap on the back of the head with the handle of a sheath-knife (many English fishermen carry a "priest," which is a miniature bludgeon, for this very purpose). It is better to break the fish's throat-latch (the cord that joins head to body on the under side), because that not only kills the fish but bleeds it, and one's finger does the trick in a second.

The reason for killing fish at once is two-fold; first, it is humane; second, it keeps the meat firm, as it should be for the pan, and it will not spoil so soon as if the fish smothered to death.

Fish spoil from exposure to sun and moisture, especially the latter. They keep much better if wiped dry before carrying away. Never use fish that have been lying in the sun or that have begun to soften. Ptomaines work in a mysterious but effectual way.

DRESSING GAME AND FISH 287

To keep fish in camp: scale, behead, and clean them; then string them by a cord through their tails and hang them, head down, in a shady, breezy place. They drain well when hung in this way, and that is important.

If you stay long in one place, it will pay to sink a covered box in the sloping bank of a stream, to keep your fish in. Such a bank is always cool. Hang the fish up separately in the box with rods or cords. If you lack a box, make a rock-lined cache, covered with flat stones to keep out mink and other robbers.

Trout may be kept bright, with their spots showing lively, for many hours, if each is wiped and wrapped separately in some absorbent paper, such as toilet paper, as soon as caught.

To keep fish that must be carried some distance, in hot weather: clean them as soon as you can after they are caught, and *wipe them dry*. Then rub a little salt along their backbones, but nowhere else, for salt draws the juices. Do not pile them touching each other, but between layers of paper, cheesecloth, basswood leaves, or ferns.

If you are to pack fish in ice, the best way is to have with you some parchment paper (any mail-order house) to keep them from direct contact with the ice. This paper is strong and waterproof. Everybody ought to know that when fish get wet from ice the best of their flavor is stolen. For the same reason it is bad practice to carry fish in damp moss or grass. Keep them dry, whether you have ice or not.

There is a very good thing called a refrigerator grip, to be bought of dealers in sporting goods. Outside it looks like a common handbag. Within are two metal compartments. The upper section is filled with cracked ice and the cover is screwed on. The lower one contains food and drink for an outing, and holds your fish on the trip home. It is surrounded by a metal shell into which the water drips as the ice melts. No ice or water comes in contact with what you carry.

If you have no ice, and yet wish to transport your catch a considerable distance, try the following method recommended a good many years ago by Colonel Park (he says it is also a good way to pack venison). Some of my correspondents have enthusiastically given me credit for inventing it, but I got it out of a little *Sportsmen's Handbook* by the above-named gentleman, printed, as I remember, in Cincinnati, of which I have seen but one copy. For brevity's sake, I paraphrase the description.—

> Kill the fish as soon as caught; wipe them clean and dry; remove the entrails; scrape the blood off from around the backbone; remove the gills and eyes; wipe dry again; split the fish through the backbone to the skin, from the inside; fill this split with salt; spread the fish overnight on a board or log to cool. In the morning, before sunrise, fold the fish in dry towels, so that there is a fold of towel between each fish and its neighbor; carefully wrap the whole package in a piece of muslin, and sew it up into a tight bag, and then in woolen blanketing, sewing up the ends and sides. Now put the roll in a stout paper bag, such as a flour sack. "Fish prepared in this way can be sent from Maine to New Orleans in August, and will remain fresh and nice."

Sugar, as it has antiseptic qualities, is a good preservative. Doctor O. M. Clay gives the following process for keeping trout a week or two:

> "Clean well; remove heads; wash thoroughly; dry with cloth. Cook a syrup of sugar and water until it begins to candy. In this dip the fish, one at a time, and lay them on a board to glaze. Pack in a box. Before using, soak overnight in cold water."

To dry fish for future use: split them along the back, remove the backbones and entrails, and soak them in a weak brine overnight. Make a conical teepee of cloth or bark, suspend the fish in it, and dry and smoke them over a small fire for a couple of days. This is tedious, as the fire requires close

DRESSING GAME AND FISH

attention; but it pays when many fish are to be dried.

To salt fish: dress them as above, wash clean, and roll in salt. " Place them in a wooden vessel in a cool place for several days; then turn them out and let the brine drain off. Clean the vessel and put the fish back. Cover them with brine made strong enough to carry an egg or potato. Trout preserved in this way are excellent." (E. Kreps, *Camp and Trail Methods.*)

The following method of preserving fish is quoted from *Outdoor Life:*

"Put two handfuls of salt in two or three quarts of water. Let it come to a boil. Then put fish on a piece of cheesecloth or other white cloth so as to be able to handle them, and dip them in this water, allowing them to remain in it five to seven minutes, according to size of fish. Water should not boil after the fish are put in. Then put them in vinegar, allspice, cloves and bay leaves — using enough vinegar to submerge the fish. Leave them in this solution until used. We believe you will find fish preserved in this way the sweetest-tasting that you ever ate."

CHAPTER XVI
CAMP COOKERY

MEATS

The main secrets of good meals in camp are to have a proper fire, good materials, and then to imprison in each dish, at the outset, its natural juice and characteristic flavor. To season fresh camp dishes as a French chef would is a blunder of the first magnitude. The raw materials used in city cuisine are often of inferior quality, from keeping in cold storage or with chemical preservatives; so their insipidity must be corrected by spices, herbs, and sauces to make them eatable. In cheap restaurants and boarding houses, where the chef's skill is lacking, " all things taste alike " from having been penned up together in a refrigerator and cooked in a fetid atmosphere.

In my chapter on PROVISIONS I advised that a few condiments be taken along, but these are mostly for seasoning left-overs or for desserts — not for fresh meat, unless we have but one kind, to the surfeiting point. In the woods our fish is freshly caught, our game has hung out of doors, and the water and air used in cooking (most important factors) are sweet and pure. Such viands need no masking. The only seasoning required is with pepper and salt, to be used sparingly, and not added (except in soups and stews) until the dish is nearly or quite done. Remember this: salt draws the juices.

The juices of meats and fish are their most palatable and nutritious ingredients. We extract them purposely in making soups, stews, and gravies,

MEATS

but in so doing we ruin the meat itself. Any fish, flesh, or fowl that is fit to be eaten for the good meat's sake should be cooked succulent, by first coagulating the outside (searing in a bright flame or in a very hot pan, or plunging into smoking hot grease or furiously boiling water) and then removing farther from the fire to cook gradually till done. The first process, which is quickly performed, is "the surprise." It sets the juices, and, in the case of frying, seals the fish or meat in a grease-proof envelope so that it will not become sodden but will dry crisp when drained. The horrors of the frying-pan that has been unskillfully wielded are too well known. Let us campers, to whom the frying-pan is an almost indispensable utensil, set a good example to our grease-afflicted country by using it according to the code of health and epicurean taste.

Meat, game, and fish may be fried, broiled, roasted, baked, boiled, stewed, or steamed. Frying and broiling are the quickest processes; roasting, baking, and boiling take an hour or two; a stew of meat and vegetables, to be good, takes half a day, and so does soup prepared from the raw materials. Tough meat should be boiled or braised in a pot.

Do not eat freshly killed meat if you can help it. Game should hang at least two days; otherwise it will be tough and tasteless. Venison eaten before it has completely cooled through will cause diarrhœa and perhaps nausea.

FRYING.— Do not try to fry over a flaming fire or a deep bed of coals; the grease would likely burn and catch aflame. Rake a thin layer of coals out in front of the fire; or, for a quick meal, make your fire of small dry sticks, no thicker than your finger, boil water for your coffee over the flame, and then fry over the quickly formed coals.

If you have a deep pan and plenty of frying fat, it is much the best to immerse the material completely in boiling grease, as doughnuts are fried.

Let the fat boil until little jets of smoke arise (being careful not to burn the grease). When fat begins to smoke continuously it is decomposing and will impart an acrid taste. When a bread crumb dropped in will be crisp when taken out, the fat is of the right temperature. Then quickly drop in small pieces of the material, one at a time so as not to check the heat. Turn them once while cooking. Remove when done, and drop them a moment on coarse paper to absorb surplus grease, or hang them over a row of small sticks so they can drain. Then season. The fry will be crisp, and dry enough to handle without soiling the fingers. This is *the* way for small fish.

Travelers must generally get along with shallow pans and little grease. To fry (or, properly, to sauté) in this manner, without getting the article sodden and unfit for the stomach, heat the dry pan very hot, and then grease it only enough to keep the meat from sticking (fat meat needs none). The material must be dry when put in the pan (wipe fish with a towel) or it will absorb grease. Cook quickly and turn frequently, not jabbing with a fork for that would let juice escape. Season when done, and serve piping hot.

Lard used for frying fish must not be used again for anything but fish. Crisco does not transmit the flavor of one food to another. Surplus fat can be kept in a baking powder can, sealed, for transit, with surgeon's plaster.

Chops, fat meats, squirrels, rabbits, and the smaller game birds are best sautéd or fricasseed and served with gravy. A fricassee is made of meat or birds cut into small pieces, fried or stewed, and served with gravy. Sausage should be fried over a very gentle fire.

Bear meat is best braised (see under that heading); if to be fried, it should first be soaked for an hour in a solution of one tablespoon baking soda to a quart of water, then parboiled until tender.

BROILING.— Fresh meat that is tender enough to

MEATS

escape the boiling pot or the braising oven should either be broiled or roasted before a bed of clear, hard coals. Both of these processes preserve the characteristic flavor of the meat and add that piquant, aromatic-bitter "taste of the fire" which no pan nor oven can impart. Broil when you are in a hurry, but when you have leisure for a good job, roast your meat, basting it frequently with drippings from the pan below, so as to keep the surface moist and flexible and insure that precise degree of browning which delights a gourmet.

For broiling, cut the meat at least an inch thick. Only tender pieces are fit for broiling. Venison usually requires some pounding, but don't gash it in doing so. Have a bed of bright coals free from smoke, with clear flaming fire to one side. Sear outside of meat by thrusting for a moment in the flame and turning; then broil before the fire, rather than over it, so as to catch drippings in a pan underneath. Do not season until done, or, if you do salt it, observe the rule for chops, given below. A steak 1 inch thick should be broiled five minutes, 1½ inches ten minutes, 2 inches twenty minutes. Serve on hot dish with drippings poured over, or buttered.

To broil on a forked, green stick, tie the split-open bird, or whatever it be, to the fork with hemlock rootlets or others that do not burn easily.

To broil enough for a party, when you have no broiler, clean the frying-pan thoroughly and get it almost red hot, so as to seal pores of meat instantly. Cover pan. Turn meat often, without stabbing. A large venison steak will be done in ten minutes. Put on hot dish, season with pepper and salt, and pour juices over it. Equal to meat broiled on a gridiron, and saves the juices. To broil by completely covering the slice of meat with hot ashes and embers is a very good way.

To grill on a rock, take two large flat stones of a kind that do not burst from heat (not moist or seamy ones), wipe them clean of grit, place them one above the other, with a few pebbles between to keep them apart, and build a fire around them. When they are well heated, sweep away the ashes, and place your slices of meat between the stones.

Before broiling fish on an iron they should be buttered and floured to prevent sticking; or, grease the broiler.

There is no chop like an English mutton chop. It should be cut *thick*. How to cook it is told by an English camper, Mr. T. H. Holding, in his *Camper's Handbook:*

"First let the pan get warm, then rub with a piece of the fat from the meat. As this fat warms and melts on the bottom, put in the chop and slightly increase your flame [he is assuming that you cook on a Primus stove], and let it cook rapidly. Put a very free sprinkling of salt on the *top* of the chop. I will explain this. The salt that is so distributed melts, and runs into the pores of the meat and gets through it. As the heat forces up the blood, so the salt in melting trickles down till it fills the chop, so to say. Directly the latter begins to look red on the top, turn it over smartly and cleanly. Now the heat will drive back the blood to meet the fresh supply of salt that is put on the 'new' side. Cook it gently, moving it at intervals. Presently this salt will disappear, and in its place blood will begin to make its appearance and show the chop is cooked.

"Now, the hungry one who knows how to enjoy a chop, will be delighted with one thus cooked. It will be tender, tasty, and soft, if the meat is good. A chop should not be cooked till it is pale inside; if it loses its redness it loses its character and its flavor.

"The fat of a chop should not be cut off, unless there is too much of it. It will pay to cook it and so help to make gravy, into which a piece of bread or slices of potato may be put and fried. . . .

"If a couple of potatoes be peeled and washed, cut in slices not more than an eighth-of-an-inch in thickness, put in the pan around the chop, and the whole covered over with a plate, they will be cooked by the time the chop is done. I am free to say from experience that never do potatoes taste so sweet as when cooked under these conditions. . . . But to cut these potatoes thick is to foil the object, because they have not time then to cook through."

Chops of mountain sheep and other game may be cooked in the same way.

ROASTING.— To roast is to cook by the direct

MEATS

heat of the fire, as on a spit or before a high bed of coals. Baking is performed in an oven, pit, or closed vessel. No kitchen range can compete with an open fire for roasting.

Build a rather large fire of split hardwood (softwoods are useless) against a high backlog or wall of rocks which will reflect the heat forward. Sear the outside of the roast (not a bird or fish) in clear flames until outer layer of albumen is coagulated. Then skewer thin slices of pork to upper end; hang roast before fire and close to it by a stout wet cord; turn frequently; catch drippings in pan or green-bark trough, and baste with them. This is better than roasting on a spit over the fire, because the heat can be better regulated, the meat turned and held in position more easily, the roast is not smoked, and the drippings are utilized.

Just before the meat is done, baste it and sprinkle with flour, then brown it near the fire, and make gravy as directed on page 303.

A whole side of venison can be roasted by planting two stout forked stakes before the fire, a stub of each stake being thrust through a slit cut between the ribs and under the backbone. The forward part of the saddle is the best roasting piece. Trim off flanky parts and ends of ribs, and split backbone lengthwise so that the whole will hang flat. To roast a shoulder, peel it from the side, cut off leg at knee, gash thickest part of flesh, press bits of pork into them, and skewer some slices to upper part.

When roasting a large joint, a turkey, or anything else that will require more than an hour of steady heat, do not depend upon adding wood from time to time, unless you have a good supply of sound, dry hardwood sticks of stove-wood size. If green wood or large sticks must be used, build a bonfire of them at one side of your cooking-fire, and shovel coals from it as required. It will not do to check the cooking-fire.

Kabobs.— When in a hurry, cut a 1½ or 2 inch portion from the saddle or other tender part, break up the fiber by pounding, unless the animal was young, and divide the meat into several small fragments. Impale one of these on a sharpened stick, salt and pepper it, plunge it for a moment into a clear bright flame, then toast it slowly over the embers. Salt, in this case, is glazed on the surface and cannot draw the juice. While eating one bit, toast another.

Roasting in the Reflector.— Pin thin slices of pork or bacon over the roast. Put a little water in the bake-pan, lay the meat in, and set the baker before the fire. Baste occasionally. When the front is done, reverse the pan. Make gravy from the drippings.

Barbecueing.— To barbecue is to roast an animal whole, and baste it frequently with a special dressing, for which the following recipe is borrowed from Frank Bates:

"One pint of vinegar, half a can of tomatoes, two teaspoonfuls of red pepper (chopped pepper-pods are better), a teaspoonful of black pepper, same of salt, two tablespoonfuls of butter. Simmer together till it is completely amalgamated. Have a bit of clean cloth or sponge tied on the end of a stick, and keep the meat well basted with the dressing as long as it is on the fire."

Dig a pit somewhat longer and wider than the spread-out carcass of the animal. Build a log fire in it of hardwood. When this has burned to coals, place a green log at each end of the pit and one on each side of it, near the edges. Over the side logs lay green poles to support the meat, thick enough not to burn through (when it can be procured, a sheet of wire netting is laid over this frame). Tough meat is previously parboiled in large pots.

BRAISING.— Tough meat is improved by braising in a Dutch oven, or a covered pot or saucepan. This process lies between baking and frying. It is pre-eminently the way to cook bear meat, venison shoulders and rounds. Put the meat in the oven or

MEATS

pot with about two inches of hot water in the bottom, and a bit of bacon or pork (but not for bear). Add some chopped onion, if desired, for seasoning. Cover and cook about fifteen minutes to the pound. A half hour before the meat is done, season it with salt and pepper.

The gravy is made by pouring the grease from the pot, adding a little water and salt, and rubbing flour into it gradually with a spoon.

BAKING MEAT.— *Baking in a Hole.*—This is a modification of braising. Dig a hole in the ground, say 18 x 18 x 12 inches. Place kindling in it, and over the hole build a cob house by laying split hardwood sticks across, not touching each other, then another course over these and at right angles to them, and so on till you have a stack two feet high. Set fire to it. The air will circulate freely, and the sticks, if of uniform size, will all burn down to coals together.

Cut the fowl, or whatever it is, in pieces, season, add a chunk of fat pork the size of your fist, put in the kettle, pour in enough water to cover, put lid on kettle, rake coals out of hole, put kettle in, shovel coals around and over it, cover all with a few inches of earth, and let it alone over night. It beats a bake-oven. In case of rain, cover with bark.

Experiment with this two or three times before you risk much on it; for the right heat and the time required can only be learned by experience.

Grouse and the like can be cooked nicely by putting one in the bean-pot when baking beans.

Baking an Animal in Its Hide.— If the beast is too large to bake entire, cut off what you want and sew it up in a piece of the hide. In this case it is best to have the hole lined with flat stones. Rake out embers, put meat in, cover first with green grass or leaves, then with the hot coals and ashes, and build a fire on top. When done, remove the skin.

A deer's head is placed in the pit, neck down,

and baked in the same way: time about six hours.

Baking in Clay.— This hermetically seals the meat while cooking, and is better than baking in a kettle, but requires experience. Draw the animal, but leave the skin and hair on. If it be a large bird, as a duck or goose, cut off head and most of neck, also feet and pinions, pull out tail feathers and cut tail off (to get rid of oil sac), but leave smaller feathers on. If a fish, do not scale. Moisten and work some clay till it is like softened putty. Roll it out in a sheet an inch thick and large enough to completely encase the animal. Cover the latter so that no feather or hair projects. Place in fire and cover with good bed of coals and let it remain with fire burning on top from ¾ of an hour, for a small bird or medium trout, to two hours for a pheasant or duck. Larger animals require more time, and had best be placed in bake-hole over night.

When done, break open the hard casing of baked clay. The skin peels off with it, leaving the meat perfectly clean and baked to perfection in its own juices. This method has been practiced for ages by the gipsies and other primitive peoples.

Frank Bates recommends another way: " Have a pail of water in which stir clay until it is of the consistency of thick porridge or whitewash. Take the bird by the feet and dip into the water. The clay will gather on and between the feathers. Repeat till the bird is a mass of clay. Lay this in the ashes, being careful to dry the outside. Bake till the clay is almost burned to a brick."

Baking in the Embers.— To bake a fish, clean it — if it is large enough to be emptied through a hole in the neck, do not slit the belly — season with salt and pepper, and, if liked, stuff with Indian meal. Have ready a good bed of glowing hardwood coals; cover it with a thin layer of ashes, that the fish may not be burnt. Lay the fish on this, and cover it with more ashes and coals. Half an hour, more or less, is required, according to size.

MEATS

On removing the fish, pull off the skin, and the flesh will be found clean and palatable.

A bird, for example a duck, is baked in much the same way. Draw it, through a small slit at the vent, but do not remove the feathers. If you like stuffed duck, stuff with bread crumbs or broken biscuit, well seasoned with salt and pepper. Wet the feathers by dipping the bird in water; then bury it in the ashes and coals. A teal will require about half an hour; other birds in proportion.

BOILING.— The broader the pot, and the blacker it is, the quicker it boils. Fresh meats should be started in boiling water; salt or corned meats, and those intended for stews or soups, in cold water. The meat (except hams) should be cut into chunks of not over five pounds each, and soup bones well cracked. Watch during first half hour, and skim off all scum as fast as it rises, or it will settle and adhere to meat. Fresh meat should be boiled until bones are free, or until a fork will pierce easily (ten pounds take about two and a half hours). Save the broth for soup-stock, or make gravy of it by seasoning with pepper and thickening with flour. (See page 303.)

Meat that is to be eaten cold should be allowed to cool in the liquor in which it was boiled. A tablespoonful or two of vinegar added to the boiling water makes meat more tender and fish firmer. Turn the meat several times while boiling. If the water needs replenishing, do it with boiling, not cold, water. Season a short time before meat is done. If vegetables are to be cooked with the meat, add them at such time that they will just finish cooking when the meat is done (potatoes twenty to thirty minutes before the end; carrots and turnips, sliced, one to one and a half hours).

Remember this: put fresh meat in hard boiling water for only five minutes, to set the juices; then remove to greater height over the fire and boil very slowly — to let it boil hard all the time would make it tough and indigestible. Salt or corned meats go in cold water at the start and are gradually brought to a boil; thereafter they should be allowed barely to simmer.

Fish go in boiling salted water. Boiling meat must be kept covered.

In heating milk beware that you do not burn it. Bring it gradually to the simmering point, but do not let it actually boil.

At high altitudes it is impossible to cook satisfactorily by boiling, because water boils at a lower and lower temperature the higher we climb. The decrease is at the rate of about one degree for every 550 feet up to one mile, and one degree for 560 feet above that, when the temperature is 70°. With the air at 32° F., and the barometer at 30 inches, water boils at 212° at sea-level, 202.5° at 5,000 feet, 193.3° at 10,000 feet, and 184.5° at 15,000 feet. These figures vary somewhat according to the purity of the water, the material of the vessel, etc.

To parboil is to boil only until tender, before cooking in some other way.

STEWING.— This process is slow, and should be reserved for tough meats. Use lean meat only. First brown it with some hot fat in a frying-pan; or put a couple of ounces of chopped pork in a kettle and get it thoroughly hot; cut your meat into small pieces; drop them into the fat and "jiggle" the kettle until the surface of the meat is coagulated by the hot fat, being careful, the while, not to burn it. Add a thickening of a couple of ounces of flour and mix it thoroughly with the fat; then a pint of water or soup-stock. Heat the contents of the kettle to boiling and season with salt, pepper, and chopped onion. Curry powder, if you like it, is proper in a stew. Now cover the kettle closely and hang it where it will only simmer for four or five hours. Stews may be thickened with rice, potatoes, or oatmeal, as well as with flour. Add condiments to suit the taste. A ragout is nothing but a highly seasoned stew. The greater the variety

MEATS 301

of meats and vegetables, the better. Rice and tomatoes are especially suitable. Macaroni, spaghetti, vermicelli, and noodles, are fine in stews; you will need little or no bread if you have such pastes or some dumplings in the stew. To vary the flavor of game stews, add beef extract, such as Steero or other beef cubes, or Oysters. Desiccated vegetables may be used instead of fresh ones.

The method given above is the one I usually follow; but I take the liberty of adding another by Captain Kenealy:

"Stewing is an admirable way of making palatable coarse and tough pieces of meat, but it requires the knack, like all other culinary processes. Have a hot fry-pan ready, cut the meat up into small squares and put it (without any dripping or fat) into the pan. Let it brown well, adding a small quantity of granulated sugar and sliced onions to taste. Cook until the onions are tender and well colored. Then empty the fry-pan into a stew-pan and add boiling water to cover the meat, and let it simmer gently for two or three hours. Flavor with salt, pepper, sweet herbs, curry powder or what you will. The result will be a savory dish of tender meat, called by the French a ragout. It is easy to prepare it this way. Do not boil it furiously as is sometimes done, or it will become tough. This dish may be thickened with browned flour, and vegetables may be added — turnips, carrots, celery, etc., cut into small pieces and browned with the meat. The sugar improves the flavor vastly. The only condiments actually necessary are pepper and salt. Other flavorings are luxuries."

STEAMING.— To steam meat or vegetables: build a large fire and throw on it a number of smooth stones, not of the bomb-shell kind. Dig a hole in the ground near the fire. When the stones are red hot, fork them into the hole, level them, cover with green or wet leaves, grass, or branches, place the meat or potatoes on this layer, cover with more leaves, and then cover all with a good layer of earth. Now bore a small hole down to the food, pour in some water, and immediately stop up the hole, letting the food steam until tender. This is the Chinook method of cooking camass. Shellfish can be steamed in the same way.

MEAT GRAVIES AND SAUCES.— A gravy is seasoned with nothing but salt and pepper, the object being to preserve the flavor of the meat. A sauce is highly seasoned to disguise poor meat, or made-over dishes, or whatever has been served so often that it begins to pall on the appetite.

An abundance of rich gravy is relished by campers who do not carry butter. They have nothing else to make their bread "slip down." Good gravy cannot be made from meat that has been fried properly or broiled, because the juice is left in the meat. Our pioneer families seldom had butter, yet they had to eat a much larger component of bread than we do, from lack of side dishes. Hence the "fried-to-a-chip" school of cookery.

In such case, the right way is obvious, granting that you have plenty of meat. Fry properly enough meat for the party and leave enough more in the pan to make gravy. Gash or mince this remainder, cook all the juice out of it without scorching, throw out the refuse meat, rub in a thickening prepared in advance as directed below, salt and pepper, then thin to the desired consistency with boiling water. The thickening is made by rubbing cold milk, or water, or broth, a little at a time, into a spoonful of flour, until a smooth paste is formed that will just drop from a spoon; or thicken with roux. Chopped liver improves a gravy.

Roux (pronounced "roo") is a thickening for gravy or soups that can be prepared at any time and kept ready for emergencies. It will keep good for months in a covered jar. A teaspoonful thickens half a pint of gravy, or a pint of soup.

Brown roux is made thus: Melt slowly ½ lb. of butter, skim it well, let it stand for a minute to settle, and pour it off from the curd. Put the clear oily butter into a pan over a slow fire, shake into it enough sifted flour (7 or 8 oz.) to make a thick paste. Stir constantly and heat slowly and evenly until it is very thick and of a bright brown color. Put it into a jar. White roux is made in

MEATS

the same way except that it is stirred over a very gentle fire until it is thoroughly baked but not browned. It is used for white gravy on fish, etc.

Gravy for Boiled Meat.— Some of the liquor in which the meat was cooked can be thickened by melting a piece of butter the size of a small egg, mixing with it very smoothly a tablespoonful of flour, heating until lightly browned, adding the meat liquor and letting it boil up. Flavor to taste and serve separately from the meat.

Gravy for Roast Meat.— Use the drippings as above, and thin with boiling water in which half a teaspoonful of salt has been dissolved.

Dripping is the fat that drops from meat when roasting.

Gravy from Extract of Beef.— When there is no venison in camp, it will not be long before the men crave the taste of beef. Liebig's extract, or Bovril, or Steero, dissolved in boiling water and liberally salted will make a good beef gravy by letting it boil up, then simmer, and thicken in one of the ways described above.

Onion Gravy.— Rub up flour in water to a batter; salt it. Chop some onion very fine and fry it a little in the meat juice. Pour the batter on this, and stir till the flour is done.

Cream Gravy for Meat or Fish.—

> ½ pint milk.
> 1 tablespoonful butter.
> ½ tablespoonful flour.
> ½ tablespoonful salt.
> ⅛ tablespoonful pepper.

Heat butter in frying-pan. Add flour, stirring until smooth and frothy. Draw pan back and gradually stir in the milk. Then return the pan to the fire. Add salt and pepper. Stir until sauce boils. This must be used at once, and everybody's plate should be hot, of course.

Sauces.— A camp cook nearly always lacks the sweet herbs, fresh parsley, mushrooms, capers, anchovies, shrimps, tarragon, wine, and many other condiments to which standard sauces owe their characteristic flavors. He must make shift with spices and perhaps lemon, Worcestershire, vinegar, mustard, curry powder, or celery seed. How to use these to the best advantage cannot be taught in a book. Personal tastes and the materials at hand must govern. I give here the recipes for three simple sauces for meat. Others will be found in the chapters on GAME, FISH, and DESSERTS.

Mustard Sauce.— Brown two teaspoonfuls of flour in a pan with a little butter. Put two tablespoonfuls of butter on a plate and blend with it the browned flour, a teaspoonful of mustard, and a little salt. When these are smoothly mixed stir them into ¼ pint boiling water. Simmer five minutes. Add enough vinegar or lemon juice to flavor.

Venison Sauce.— Stir together one tablespoonful of butter with a teaspoonful of mustard and three tablespoonfuls of jelly (preferably currant). When these are well blended, add three tablespoonfuls of vinegar, some grated nutmeg, and a dash of Cayenne pepper. Heat together. When the sauce boils add three tablespoonfuls chopped pickles. Serve at once. Currant jelly alone goes well with venison.

Sauce for Broiled Venison.— Make the steak-dish very hot. Put on it for each pound of venison ½ tablespoonful of butter, a tablespoonful of currant jelly, one of boiling water, and a little pepper and salt. Turn the broiled steaks in the sauce once or twice and serve very hot.

Parsley Butter.— I confess to a weakness for the flavor of parsley. The fresh herb, of course, we cannot have in camp, but the dehydrated kind, or C. & B. dried parsley, will do very well. Make a thin mixture of flour and water, salt it, and add a pat of butter (not really necessary). Boil this until the rawness is gone from the flour, and use it with fish, flesh, or fowl, particularly the latter.

CHAPTER XVII
CAMP COOKERY

GAME

The following additional details are supplementary to what has gone before, and presuppose a careful reading of the preceding pages.

Game and all other kinds of fresh meat should be hung up till they have bled thoroughly and have cooled through and through — they are tenderer and better after they have hung several days. Venison especially is tough until it has hung a week. In no case cook meat until the animal heat has left it: if you do, it is likely to sicken you. This does not apply to fish. Frozen meat or fish should be thawed in very cold water and then cooked immediately — warm water would soften it and steal its flavor.

All mammals from the 'coon size down, as well as duck and grouse, unless young and tender, or unless they have hung several days, should be parboiled (gently simmered) from ten to thirty minutes, according to size, before frying, broiling, or roasting. The scent glands of mammals and the oil sacs of birds should be removed before cooking. In small mammals look for pea-shaped, waxy or reddish kernels under the front legs and on either side of the small of the back.

As game has little natural fat, it requires frequent basting and the free use of butter or bacon grease in cooking.

VENISON.— *(Deer of all species, elk, moose, caribou.)*

Fried Venison.— See page 291.
Boiled Venison.— See page 292.
Roast Venison.— See page 294.
Braised Venison.— See page 296.
Baked Venison.— See page 297.
Boiled Venison.— See page 299.
Stewed Venison.— See page 300.
Steamed Venison.— See page 301.
Baked Deer's Head.— See page 297.
Braised Bear.— See page 296.
Fried Bear.— See page 292.
Brains.— Clean and wash them well. Fry; or boil slowly half an hour.

Brains and Eggs.— Desiccated eggs will do as well as fresh ones. Soak them as directed on can.

Chop fine some bacon and enough onion to season. Dice the brains into about ½-inch cubes. Fry bacon and onion together until brown. Add the brains, and cook until nearly done; then add the eggs, beaten slightly, and fry until they are scrambled. Season with salt and pepper.

Heart.— Remove valves and tough, fibrous tissue; then braise, or cut into small pieces and use in soups or stews.

Kidneys, Fried.— Halve them, slit twice the long way on the inside, but do not cut clear through; leave the fat on the kidneys. Fry until all blueness has disappeared.

Kidneys, Stewed.— Soak in cold water one hour. Cut into small pieces, and drop each piece into cold water, as cut. Wash well; then stew, seasoning with onion, celery (dehydrated), cloves, salt and pepper.

Liver.— Carefully remove the gall-bladder if the animal has one — deer have not. Parboil the liver and skim off the bitter scum that rises. Slice rather thin; put one slice of bacon in the pan and fry from it enough grease to keep liver from sticking. Salt the liver and fry until half done; then add more bacon and fry all until done. Liver should be thoroughly cooked; if you put all the bacon in with it at the start the latter would be ruined before the liver was done.

Another way: cut liver into slices ¼-inch thick, soak it one hour in cold salt water, rinse well in warm water, wipe dry, dip each slice in flour seasoned with salt and pepper, and fry as above.

If in a hurry, put the liver on a green hardwood stick for a spit, skewer some of the caul fat around it, and roast before the fire.

Marrow Bones.— Cover ends with small pieces of plain dough made with flour and water, over which tie a floured cloth; place bones upright in kettle, and cover with boiling water. Boil two hours. Remove cloth and paste, push out marrow, and serve with dry toast.

Milt (Spleen).— Skewer a piece of bacon to it, and broil.

Moose Muffle (nose and upper lip).— Boil like pig's head. Add an onion.

Tongue.— Soak for one hour; rinse in fresh water; put in a kettle of cold water, bring to a boil, skim and simmer two hours, or until tender. A blade of mace and a clove or two improve the gravy; so also Worcestershire sauce.

Croquettes.— Two cups minced meat or game of any kind, ½ cup bread or cracker crumbs, 1½ egg, melted butter. Roll meat, seasoning, and enough of the butter to moisten, into pear-shaped balls. Dip in beaten eggs and crumbs. Fry, with enough butter, to a nice brown.

Venison Sausages.— Utilize the tougher parts of the deer, or other game, by mincing the raw meat with half as much salt pork, season with pepper and sage, make into little pats, and fry like sausages. Very good.

Game Pot Pie.— Take ½ teaspoonful baking powder to ½ pint of flour, sift together, and add a teaspoonful lard or butter by rubbing it in, also a pinch of salt. Make a soft biscuit dough of this, handling as little as possible and being careful not to mix too thin. Roll into a sheet and cut into strips about 1½ inches wide and 3 inches long, cutting two or three little holes through each to let steam escape. Meantime you have been boiling meat or game and have sliced some potatoes.

When the meat is within one-half hour of being done, pour off the broth into another vessel and lift out most of the meat. Place a layer of meat and potatoes in bottom of kettle, and partially cover with strips of the dough; then another layer of meat and vegetables, another of dough, and so on until the pot is nearly full, topping off with dough. Pour the hot broth over this, cover tightly, and boil one-half hour, without lifting the pot cover, which, by admitting cold air, would make the dough "sad." Parsley helps the pot, when you can get it.

Dumplings.— These add zest to a stew or to boiled meat of any kind. Plain dumplings are made of biscuit dough or the batter of dropped biscuit (recipes in chapter on BREAD). Drop them into the pot a short time before meat is done. See also page 358.

Bear, Braised.— See page 296.

SMALL GAME.—

Jambolaya.— This is a delicious Creole dish, easily prepared. Cut up any kind of small game into joints, and stew them. When half done, add some minced ham or bacon, ¼ pint rice, and season with pepper and salt. If rabbit is used, add onions. Serve with tomatoes as a sauce.

Curry of Game.— Cut some birds or other small game into rather small joints. Fry until lightly browned. Score each joint slightly, place a little curry powder in each opening, and squeeze lemon juice over it. Cover the joints with brown gravy and simmer gently for twenty minutes. Serve with rice around the dish. (See also *Curry Sauce*, page 320.)

Game Pie.— Make a plain pie crust as directed in the chapter on DESSERTS. Cut the game into joints. Season rather highly. Moisten the joints with melted butter and lemon juice, or put a few thin strips of bacon in with them. Cover with top crust like a fruit pie and bake not too long; time according to size.

Squirrels, Fried.— Unless they are young, parboil them gently for ½ hour in salted water. Then fry in butter or pork grease until brown. A dash of curry powder when frying is begun improves them, unless you dislike curry. Make gravy as directed on page 303.

Squirrels, Broiled.— Use only young ones. Soak in cold salted water for an hour, wipe dry, and broil over the coals with a slice of bacon laid over each squirrel to baste it.

Squirrels, Stewed.— They are best this way, or fricasseed. For directions see pages 300 and 292.

Squirrels, Barbecued.— Build a hardwood fire between two large logs lying about two feet apart. At each end of the fire drive two forked stakes about fifteen inches apart, so that the four stakes will form a rectangle, like the legs of a table. The forks should all be about eighteen inches above the ground. Choose young, tender squirrels (if old ones must be used, parboil them until tender but not soft). Prepare spits by cutting stout switches of some wood that does not burn easily (sassafras is best — beware of poison sumach), peel them, sharpen the points, and harden them by thrusting for a few moments under the hot ashes. Impale each squirrel by thrusting a spit through flank, belly, and shoulder, on one side, and another spit similarly on the other side, spreading out the sides, and, if necessary, cutting through the ribs, so that the squirrel will lie open and flat.

Lay two poles across the fire from crotch to crotch of the posts, and across these lay your spitted squirrels. As soon as these are heated through, begin basting with a piece of pork on the end of a switch. Turn the squirrels as required. Cook slowly, tempering the heat, if needful, by scattering ashes thinly over the coals; but remove the ashes for a final browning. When the squirrels are done, butter them and gash a little that the juices may flow.

Rabbit, or Hare.— Remove the head; skin and draw, cut out the waxy glands under the front legs where they join the body; soak in cold salted water for one hour; rinse in fresh cold water and wipe dry. It is better, however, unless the animals are quite young, to parboil them for about fifteen minutes with salt, pepper, and an onion. Rabbits are not really good to eat until several days after killing.

To fry: parboil first, cut off legs at body joint, and cut the back into three pieces. Sprinkle with flour and fry brown on both sides. Remove rabbit to a dish kept hot over a few coals. Make a gravy as follows: Put into the pan a small onion previously parboiled and minced and add one cup boiling water. Stir in gradually one or two tablespoonfuls of browned flour; stir well, and let it boil one minute. Season with pepper, salt, and nutmeg. Pour it over the rabbit.

To roast in reflector: cut as above, lay a slice of pork on each piece, and baste frequently. The rabbit may be roasted whole before the fire.

To bake in an oven: stuff with a dressing made of bread crumbs, the heart and liver (previously parboiled in a small amount of water), some fat salt pork, and a small onion, all minced and mixed together, seasoned with pepper, salt, and nutmeg, and slightly moistened with the water in which heart and liver were parboiled. Sew up the opening closely; rub butter or dripping over rabbit, dredge with flour, lay thin slices of fat pork on back, and place it in pan or Dutch oven, back uppermost. Pour into pan a pint or more of boiling water (or stock, if you have it), and bake with very moderate heat, one hour, basting every few minutes if in pan, but not if in Dutch oven. Prepare a gravy with the pot juice, as directed above.

Rabbit is good stewed with onion, nutmeg, pep-

GAME

per, and salt for seasoning. Also curried, after the manner already described.

"The rabbity taste can be eliminated by putting a tablespoonful of vinegar in the water in which the rabbit is boiled. Hard boiling will toughen the meat; allow it to simmer gently for one or two hours. When tender add a minced onion and some bacon grease to the liquor and place in the baker to brown.

"The Germans prepare rabbit in a more ambitious manner, but one that well repays. The disjointed rabbit is simmered until tender. Pour the meat and liquor into a dressing made as follows: Fry until brown three or four pieces of bacon which have been diced. Add to this a tablespoonful of flour, a teaspoonful each of sugar and salt, a tablespoonful of vinegar, and a few cloves if possible. Stir well to keep from burning.

"In both cases time can be saved by simmering the rabbit in the evening, and, on the following day, browning in a baker or serving with the German dressing." (*Kathrene Pinkerton.*)

Rabbits are unfit to eat in late summer, as their backs are then infested with warbles, which are the larvæ of the rabbit bot-fly.

Possum.— To call our possum an opossum, outside of a scientific treatise, is an affectation. Possum is his name wherever he is known and hunted, this country over. He is not good until you have freezing weather; nor is he to be served without sweet potatoes, except in desperate extremity. This is how to serve "possum hot." —

Stick him, and hang him up to bleed until morning. A tub is half filled with hot water (not quite scalding) into which drop the possum and hold him by the tail until the hair will strip. Take him out, lay him on a plank, and pull the hair out with your fingers. Draw, clean, and hang him up to freeze for two or three nights. Then place him in a 5-gallon kettle of cold water, into which throw two pods of red pepper. Parboil for one hour in this pepper-water, which is then thrown out and the kettle refilled with fresh water, wherein he is boiled one hour.

While this is going on, slice and steam some sweet potatoes. Take the possum out, place him in a large Dutch oven, sprinkle him with black pepper, salt, and a pinch or two of sage. A dash of lemon will do no harm. Pack sweet potatoes around him. Pour a pint of water into the oven, put the lid on, and see that it fits tightly. Bake slowly until brown and crisp. Serve hot, *without* gravy. Bourbon whiskey is the orthodox accompaniment. If you are a teetotaler, any plantation darky can show you how to make "ginger tea" out of ginger, molasses, and water. Corn bread, of course.

It is said that possum is not hard to digest even when eaten cold, but the general verdict seems to be that none is ever left over to get cold.

When you have no oven, roast the possum before a high bed of coals, having suspended him by a wet string, which is twisted and untwisted to give a rotary motion, and constantly baste it with a sauce made from red pepper, salt, and vinegar.

Possum may also be baked in clay, with his hide on. Stuff with stale bread and sage, plaster over him an inch of stiff clay, and bake as previously directed. He will be done in about an hour.

Coon.— It is likewise pedantic to call this animal a raccoon. Coon he always has been, is now, and shall ever be, to those who know him best.

Skin and dress him. Remove the "kernels" (scent glands) under each front leg and on either side of spine in small of back. Wash in cold water. Parboil in one or two waters, depending upon the animal's age. Stuff with dressing like a turkey. If you have a tart apple, quarter it and add to the dressing. Bake to a delicate brown. Serve with fried sweet potatoes.

Porcupine.— I quote from Nessmuk: "And do not despise the fretful porcupine; he is better than he looks. If you happen on a healthy young specimen when you are needing meat, give him a show before condemning him. Shoot him humanely in the head, and dress him. It is easily done; there are no quills on the belly, and the skin peels as freely as a rabbit's. Take him to camp, parboil him for thirty minutes, and roast or broil him to a rich brown over a bed of glowing coals. He will need no pork to make him juicy, and you will find him very like spring lamb, only better."

The porcupine may also be baked in clay, without skinning him; the quills and skin peel off with the hard clay covering. Or, fry *quickly*.

As I have never eaten porcupine, I will do some more quoting — this time from Dr. Breck: "It may be either roasted or made into a stew, in the manner of hares, but must be parboiled at least a half-hour to be tender. One part of the porcupine is always a delicacy — the *liver,* which is easily removed by making a cut just under the neck into which the hand is thrust, and the liver pulled out. It may be fried with bacon, or baked slowly and carefully in the baker-pan with slices of bacon."

Muskrat.— You may be driven to this, some day, and will then learn that muskrat, properly prepared is not half bad. The French-Canadians found that out long ago. Remove the musk glands and the white stringy substance found on the inside of the forearms and thighs. I do not remember where I picked up the following recipe:

" Skin and clean carefully four muskrats, being particular not to rupture musk or gall sac. Take the hind legs and saddles, place in pot with a little water, a little julienne (or fresh vegetables, if you have them), some pepper and salt, and a few slices of pork or bacon. Simmer slowly over fire until half done. Remove to baker, place water from pot in the baking pan, and cook until done, basting frequently. This will be found a most toothsome dish."

Muskrat may also be broiled over the hot coals, basting with a bit of pork held on a switch above the beastie.

Woodchuck.— I asked old Uncle Bob Flowers,

one of my neighbors in the Smokies: "Did you ever eat a woodchuck?"

"Reckon I don't know what them is."

"Ground-hog."

"O la! dozens of 'em. The red ones hain't good, but the gray ones! man, they'd jest make yer mouth water!"

"How do you cook them!"

"Cut the leetle red kernels out from under their forelegs; then bile 'em, fust — all the strong is left in the water — then pepper 'em and sage 'em, and put 'em in a pan, and bake 'em to a nice rich brown, and — then I don't want nobody there but me!"

According to J. Alden Loring, "The only way to cook a woodchuck properly is to roast him whole on a stick over a camp-fire, turning him from time to time until he is well done. The skin keeps the fat from broiling out, and enough sinks into the flesh to make it tender and juicy."

Beaver Tail.— This tid-bit of the old-time trappers will be tasted by few of our generation, more's the pity. Impale the tail on a sharp stick and broil over the coals for a few minutes. The rough, scaly hide will blister and come off in sheets, leaving the tail clean, white, and solid. Then roast, or boil until tender. It is of a gelatinous nature, tastes somewhat like pork, and is considered very strengthening food. A young beaver, stuffed and baked in its hide, is good; old ones have a peculiar flavor that is unpleasant to those not accustomed to such diet.

Beaver tail may also be soused in vinegar, after boiling, or baked with beans. It makes a good soup if part of the backbone is added.

The liver, broiled on a stick and seasoned with butter, salt, and pepper, is the best part of the animal.

BIRDS.— If game birds are not hung a few days after killing they are likely to be tough; but, as I have remarked elsewhere, this should not be overdone.

GAME

Game Birds, Fried.— Birds for frying should be cut in convenient pieces, parboiled until tender in a pot with enough water to cover, then removed, saving the liquor. Sprinkle with salt, pepper, and flour (this for the sake of the gravy), fry in melted pork fat, take out when done, then stir into the frying fat one-half cupful dry flour till a dark brown, add parboiling liquor, bring to a boil, put game in dish, and pour gravy over it, or serve with one of the sauces described below.

Game Birds, Broiled.— Split them up the back, broil over the coals, and baste with a piece of pork on tined stick held over them. Fillets of ducks or other large birds may be sliced off and impaled on sticks with thin slices of pork.

Game Birds, Fricasseed.— Any kind of bird may be fricasseed as follows: Cut it into convenient pieces, parboil them in enough water to cover; when tender, remove from the pot and drain. Fry two or three slices of pork until brown. Sprinkle the pieces of bird with salt, pepper, and flour, and fry to a dark brown in the pork fat. Take up the bird, and stir into the frying fat half a cup, more or less, of dry flour, stirring until it becomes a dark brown; then pour over it the liquor in which the bird was boiled (unless it was a fish-eater), and bring the mixture to a boil. Put the bird in a hot dish, and serve with the gravy poured over it.

Wild Turkey, Roasted.— Pluck, draw, and singe. Wipe the bird inside and out. Rub the inside with salt and red pepper. Stuff the crop cavity, then the body, with either of the dressings mentioned below, allowing room for the filling to swell. Tie a string around the neck, and sew up the body. Truss wings to body with wooden skewers. Pin thin slices of fat pork to breast in same way. Suspend the fowl before a high bed of hardwood coals, as previously described, and place a pan under it to catch drippings. Tie a clean rag on the end of a stick to baste with. Turn and baste frequently. Roast until well done (two to three hours). (See also page 294.)

Meantime cleanse the gizzard, liver, and heart of the turkey thoroughly in cold water; mince them; put them in a pot with enough cold water to cover, and stew gently until tender; then place where they will keep warm until wanted. When the turkey is done, add the giblets with the water in which they were stewed to the drippings in pan; thicken with one or two tablespoonfuls of flour that has been stirred up in milk or water and browned in a pan; season with pepper and salt, and serve with the turkey. If you have butter, the fowl may be basted with it (melted, of course), and when stewing the giblets add a tablespoonful of butter and half a teacupful of evaporated milk.

Stuffing for Turkey.— (1) If chestnuts are procurable, roast a quart of them, remove shells, and mash. Add a teaspoonful of salt, and some pepper. Mix well together, and stuff the bird with them.

(2) Chop some fat salt pork very fine; soak stale bread or crackers in hot water, mash smooth, and mix with the chopped pork. Season with salt, pepper, sage, and chopped onion. No game bird save the wild turkey should be stuffed, unless you deliberately wish to disguise the natural flavor.

Wild Turkey, Boiled.— Pluck, draw, singe, wash inside with warm water, and wipe dry. Cut off head and neck close to backbone, leaving enough skin to turn over the stuffing. Draw sinews from legs, and cut off feet just below joint of leg. Press legs into sides and skewer them firmly. Stuff as above. Put the bird into enough hot water to cover it. Remove scum as it rises. Boil gently one and one-half to two hours. Serve with giblet sauce as above.

Waterfowl have two large oil glands in the tail, with which they oil their feathers. The oil in these glands imparts a strong, disagreeable flavor to the bird soon after it is killed. Hence the tail should always be removed before cooking.

To cook a large bird in a hurry.— Slice off several fillets from the breast; impale them, with slices of pork, on a green switch; broil over the coals.

Wild Goose, Roasted.— A good way to suspend a large bird before the fire is described by Dillon Wallace in his *Lure of the Labrador Wild:*

" George built a big fire — much bigger than usual. At the back he placed the largest green log he could find. Just in front of the fire, and at each side, he fixed a forked stake, and on these rested a cross-pole. From the center of the pole he suspended a piece of stout twine, which reached nearly to the ground, and tied the lower end into a noose.

" Then it was that the goose, nicely prepared for the cooking, was brought forth. Through it at the wings George stuck a sharp wooden pin, leaving the ends to protrude on each side. Through the legs he stuck a similar pin in a similar fashion. This being done, he slipped the noose at the end of the twine over the ends of one of the pins. And lo and behold! the goose was suspended before the fire.

" It hung low — just high enough to permit the placing of a dish under it to catch the gravy. Now and then George gave it a twirl so that none of its sides might have reason to complain at not receiving its share of the heat. The lower end roasted first; seeing which, George took the goose off, reversed it, and set it twirling again."

Time-table for Roasting Birds.— A goose or a middling-sized turkey takes about two hours to roast, a large turkey three hours, a duck about forty-five minutes, a pheasant twenty to thirty minutes, a woodcock or snipe fifteen to twenty minutes.

Wild Duck, Baked.— The bird should be dry-picked, and the head left on. Put a little pepper and salt inside the bird, but *no other dressing.* Lay the duck on its back in the bake-pan. Put no water in the pan. The oven must be hot, but not hot enough to burn; test with the hand. Baste frequently with butter or bacon. A canvasback requires about thirty minutes; other birds according to size. When done, the duck should be plump, and the flesh red, not blue.

This is the way to bring out the distinctive flavor

of a canvasback. Seasoning and stuffing destroy all that. A canvasback should not be washed either inside or outside, but wiped clean with a dry cloth. Duck should be served with currant jelly, if you have it. (See also page 297.)

Wild Duck, Stewed.— Clean well and divide into convenient pieces (say, legs, wings, and four parts of body). Place in pot with enough cold water to cover. Add salt, pepper, a pinch of mixed herbs, and a dash of Worcestershire sauce. Cut up fine some onions and potatoes (carrots, too, if you can get them). Put a few of these in the pot so they may dissolve and add body to the dish (flour or corn starch may be substituted for thickening). Stew slowly, skim and stir frequently. In forty-five minutes add the rest of the carrots, and in fifteen minutes more add the rest of the onions and potatoes, also turnips, if you have any. Stew until meat is done.

A plainer camp dish is to stew for an hour in water that has previously been boiled for an hour with pieces of salt pork. (See also page 300.)

Fish-eating Fowls.— The rank taste of these can be neutralized, unless very strong, by using plenty of pepper, inside and out, and baking with an onion inside. Or, skin, draw, and immerse overnight in a solution of ½ small teacup of vinegar to a gallon of water; then fry or bake.

Coots, sheldrake or old-squaw are rid of their fishy taste, without sacrificing the game flavor, by a process described by Mary Walsh:

"Pluck and draw the birds immediately; don't allow them to hang with the entrails in. Wash thoroughly with cold water both outside and in. Cut off the tail for about one inch with the fatty tissue at the base. Sprinkle with pungent white pepper both inside and out, using two teaspoonfuls to each bird. Place in the ice-box but not touching the ice, and keep for at least one week, better ten days. Then wash with salt water (handful to the pint), dry and roast for twenty minutes with an apple placed in each bird. Then serve, removing the apple before placing on the table."

The breast of a coot or rail may be broiled over the embers. Cut slits in it, and in these stick slices of fat salt pork. The broiled breast of a young bittern is good.

Grouse, Broiled.— Pluck and singe. Split down the back through the bone, and remove the trail. Wipe out with damp towel. Remove head and feet. Rub inside with pepper and salt. Flatten the breast, brush over with melted butter, or skewer bacon on upper side, and grill over a hot bed of coals.

Grouse, Roasted.— Dress and draw, but do not split. Place a piece of bacon or pork inside, and skewer a piece to the breast. Roast before the fire as described for turkey, or in a reflector.

Deviled Birds.— If drumsticks and breasts of birds are left over, they are better deviled than served cold. Mix up with a knife half an ounce of butter, half a teaspoonful each of mustard and salt, some white or black pepper, and enough cayenne or chile to give it " snap." Slit the meat, and insert this mixture, or chop the meat fine and add the seasoning. Heat well in the frying-pan, and serve.

Small Birds (quail, woodcock, snipe, plover, etc.).— These are good roasted before a bed of coals, searing them first as in broiling meat. Impale each bird on a green stick, with a slice of bacon on the point of the stick over the bird. Thrust butt of stick into the ground, and incline stick toward the fire. Turn frequently.

When a number of birds are to be roasted, a better way is to set up two forked stakes and a cross-pole before the fire. Hang birds from the pole, heads downward, by wet strings. Baste as recommended for turkey, and turn frequently. Serve very hot, without any sauce, unless it be plain melted butter and a slice of lemon.

To grill in a pan: pin a bit of bacon to the breast of each bird with a sliver like a toothpick; hold the pan close over the coals at first for searing;

then cook more slowly, but not enough to dry out the meat.

Such birds can also be served in a ragout. (See page 300.)

Woodcock are not drawn. The trail shrivels up and is easily removed at table.

SAUCES FOR GAME. (See also page 303.)—

Giblet Sauce.— See under *Wild Turkey, Roasted.*

Celery Sauce.— Having none of the vegetable itself, use a teaspoonful of celery seed freshly powdered, or five drops of the essence of celery on a piece of sugar. Flavor some melted butter with this, add a little milk, and simmer ten minutes.

Cranberry Sauce.— Put a pound of ripe cranberries in a kettle with just enough water to prevent burning. Stew to a pulp, stirring all the time. Then add syrup previously prepared by boiling a pound of sugar in ⅔ pint of water. Canned or dehydrated cranberries will answer.

Curry Sauce.— This is used with stewed small game or meat (especially left-overs) that is served in combination with rice. (See page 308.)

Put a large spoonful of butter in a pan over the fire; add one onion cut into slices; cook until the onion is lightly browned. Then stir in one teaspoonful of curry powder and add gradually a generous cup of brown gravy, or soup stock, or the broth in which meat has been stewed, or evaporated milk slightly thinned. Boil fifteen minutes, and strain. Curry may be varied indefinitely by further flavoring with lemon juice, red pepper, nutmeg, mace, or Worcestershire sauce.

CHAPTER XVIII
CAMP COOKERY

FISH AND SHELLFISH

Fish of the same species vary a great deal in quality according to the water in which they are caught. A black bass taken from one of the overflow lakes of the Mississippi bears no comparison with its brother from a swift, clear, spring-fed Ozark river. But however pure its native waters may be, no fish is good to eat unless it has been properly cared for after catching (see Chapter XV); and the best of fish is ruined if fried soggy with grease (see Chapter XVI under FRYING).

Fish, Fried.— Small fish should be fried whole, with the backbone severed to prevent curling up; large fish may be steaked (see Chapter XV); medium ones should have heads and tails removed so they will lie flat in the pan, and have the backbone cut in two or three places.

It is customary to roll fish in cornmeal or bread crumbs, thinly and evenly, before frying. That browns them, and keeps them from sticking to the pan; but it is best only for coarse fish; trout is of better flavor if simply wiped dry.

Fry in plenty of very hot grease to a golden brown, sprinkling lightly with pepper and salt just as the color turns. If the fish is not naturally full-flavored, a few drops of lemon juice will improve it.

Olive oil is best to fry fish in, especially small ones that can be quite immersed in it; but Crisco, bacon, salt pork, butter, or lard will do very well.

When butter is used, less salt is required. If the fish has not been wiped dry it will absorb too much grease. If the frying fat is not very hot when fish are put in it they will get soggy with it: put the pieces in one at a time so as not to check the heat.

Fish, Broiled.— (See also Chapter XVI.) If a broiling iron is used, first rub it with fat bacon to prevent fish from sticking to it. When broiling large fish, remove the head, split down the back instead of the belly, and lay on the broiler with strips of bacon or pork laid across. Broil over a rather moderate bed of coals so that the inside will cook done, but beware of cooking dry and " chippy." Small fish are best broiled quickly over ardent coals. They need not have heads removed.

When done, sprinkle with salt and pepper, spread with butter (unless you have been basting with bacon), and hold again over fire until butter melts.

If you have no broiler, sharpen a small green stick, thrust this through the mouth and into the body, and keep turning over the coals while you baste with the drippings from a bit of bacon held on another stick above the fish.

Fish, Skewered.— Small fish may be skewered on a thin, straight, greenwood stick, sharpened at the end, with a thin slice of bacon or pork between every two fish, the stick being constantly turned over the coals like a spit, so that juices may not be lost.

Another way is to cut some green hardwood sticks, about three feet long, forked at one end, and sharpen the tines. Lay a thin slice of pork inside each fish lengthwise, drive tines through fish and pork, letting them through between ribs near backbone and on opposite sides of the latter — then the fish won't drop off as soon as it begins to soften and curl from the heat. Place a log lengthwise of edge of coals, lay broiling sticks on this support, slanting upward over the fire, and lay a small log over their butts. Large fish should be planked.

FISH AND SHELLFISH

Fish Roasted in a Reflector.— This process is simpler than baking, and superior in resulting flavor, since the fish is basted in its own juices, and is delicately browned by the direct action of the fire. The surface of the fish is lightly moistened with olive oil (first choice) or butter; lacking these, use drippings, or bacon grease, or lard. Then place the fish in the pan and add two or three morsels of grease around it. Roast in front of a good fire, just as you would bake biscuit. Be careful not to overroast and dry the fish by evaporating the gravy. There is no better way to cook a large fish, unless it be planked.

Fish, Planked.— More expeditious than baking, and better flavored. Split and smooth a slab of sweet hardwood two or three inches thick, two feet long, and somewhat wider than the opened fish. Prop it in front of a bed of coals till it is sizzling hot. Split the fish down the back its entire length, but do not cut through the belly skin. Clean and wipe it quite dry. When plank is hot, grease it, spread fish out like an opened book, tack it, skin side down, to the plank and prop before fire. Baste continuously with a bit of pork on a switch held above it, or with butter. Reverse ends of plank from time to time. If the flesh is flaky when pierced with a fork, it is done. Sprinkle salt and pepper over the fish, moisten with drippings, and serve on the hot plank. No better dish ever was set before an epicure. Plenty of butter improves it at table.

Fish, Stuffed and Baked.— Clean, remove fins, but leave on head and tail. Prepare a stuffing as follows: put a cupful of dry bread-crumbs in a frying-pan over the fire with two tablespoonfuls of drippings, or the equivalent of butter, and stir them until they begin to brown. Then add enough boiling water to moisten them. Season this stuffing rather highly with salt, pepper, and either celery seed, or sage, or a teaspoonful of finely chopped onion. Stuff the fish with this and sew up the opening, or wind string several times around the fish. Lay several strips of salt pork or bacon in the pan, and several over the top of the fish. Sprinkle over all a little water, pepper, salt, and bread crumbs (or dredge with flour). Bake in a hot oven, basting frequently. When flakes of fish begin to separate, it will be done. This is best for coarse fish.

Fish, Steamed.— Smear some tissue Manila paper with butter. Clean the fish, leaving head and fins on. Season with salt and cayenne pepper. Roll each fish separately in a piece of the buttered paper. Place the fish in a pile and envelop them in a large sheet of paper. Then wrap the bundle in a newspaper, and dip this in water for five minutes, or long enough to saturate the newspaper. Scrape a hole in the middle of a bed of coals, and bury the package in the embers. Leave it there ten to twenty minutes, depending upon size. The newspaper will scorch, but the inner wrappers will not. The result is a dish fit for Olympus. (*Up De Graff.*)

Doctor Breck says of this dish:

"I am so fond of steamed trout that I never fail to take with me a dozen sheets of parchment paper (the kind in which butter is sold) in which to wrap my fish. . . . 'Steam-baked' trout are the *ne plus ultra* of woods cookery."

Small fish can be steamed in wet basswood leaves, or other large leaves, without buttering. For another method of steaming, see page 301.

Fish, Boiled.— None but fish of good size should be boiled. If the fish is started in cold water and not allowed to boil hard, it will be less likely to fall apart, but the flavor will not be so good. It is better to wrap the fish in a clean cloth and drop it into boiling water well salted. A tablespoonful of vinegar, or the juice of a lemon, improves the dish. Leave the head on, but remove the fins. Boil very gently until the fish will easily part from the bones. Skim off the scum as it rises. Time

FISH AND SHELLFISH 325

depends on species; from eight to ten minutes per pound for thick fish, and five minutes for small ones.

Boiled fish require considerable seasoning and a rich sauce, or at least melted butter, to accompany them. Besides vinegar or lemon, onions, carrots, cloves, etc., may be used in the water. Recipes for sauces follow. (See also pages 303 and 304.)

Butter Sauce.—

> 2 heaped tablespoonfuls butter.
> 1 heaped tablespoonful flour.
> 1 teaspoonful salt.
> ⅛ teaspoonful pepper.

Put the butter in a cold pan, and rub into it the flour, salt, and pepper, beating well. Then pour on a scant half-pint boiling water. Cook two minutes. Use immediately.

White Sauce.—

> 2 tablespoonfuls butter.
> 2 heaped tablespoonfuls flour.
> 1 pint milk.
> ½ teaspoonful salt.
> ⅛ teaspoonful pepper.

For two, use half this.

Cook butter until it bubbles. Add flour, and cook thoroughly, until smooth. Remove from direct heat of fire, but let it simmer, and add the milk in thirds, rubbing into a smooth paste each time as it thickens. Season last. Thick white sauce is made by doubling the flour.

Cold fish that has been left over is good when heated in this sauce. It can be served thus, or baked and some chopped pickles sprinkled over the top.

India Sauce.— Make a white sauce as above, add a teaspoonful of curry powder, and some pickles, chopped small, with a little of the vinegar.

Lemon Sauce.—

> 1 lemon.
> 3 tablespoonfuls sugar.
> ½ pint milk.
> 1 scant tablespoonful butter.

Put the milk, sugar, and thin rind of the lemon into a pan and simmer gently ten minutes. Then add the juice of the lemon and the butter rolled in flour. Stir until butter is dissolved and strain or pour off clear.

Mustard Sauce (best for coarse fish).—Melt butter size of large egg in pan and stir in 1 tablespoonful flour and ½ teaspoonful mustard. Boil up once, and season (*Breck*).

Fish Chowder.—Cut the fish into pieces the right size for serving, and remove all the bones possible. For 5 or 6 lbs. of fish take ¾ lb. clear fat salt pork, slice it, and fry moderately. Slice two good-sized onions and fry in the fat. Have ready ten potatoes pared and sliced. Into your largest pot place first a layer of fish, then one of potatoes, then some of the fried onion, with pepper, salt, and a little flour, then a slice or two of the pork. Repeat these alternate layers until all has been used. Then pour the fat from the frying-pan over all. Cover the whole with boiling water, and cook from twenty to thirty minutes, according to thickness of fish. Five or ten minutes before serving, split some hard crackers and dip them in cold water (or use stale bread or biscuits similarly), add them to the chowder, and pour in about a pint of hot milk.

The advantage of first frying the pork and onion is that the fish need not then be cooked overdone, which is the case in chowders started with raw pork in the bottom of the kettle and boiled.

Another Fish Chowder.—Clean the fish, parboil it, and reserve the water in which it was boiled. Place the dry pot on the fire; when it is hot, throw in a lump of butter and about six onions sliced finely. When the odor of onion arises, add the fish. Cover the pot closely for fish to absorb flavor. Add a very small quantity of potatoes, and some of the reserved broth. When cooked, let each man season his own dish. Ask a blessing and eat. (*Kenealy.*)

FISH AND SHELLFISH 327

Fish Cakes.— Take fish left over from a previous meal and either make some mashed potatoes (boil them, and mash with butter and milk) or use just the plain cold boiled potatoes. Remove bones from fish and mince it quite fine. Mix well, in proportion of one-third fish and two-thirds potato. Season with salt and pepper. Then mix in thoroughly a well-beaten egg or two (or equivalent of desiccated egg). If it seems too dry, add more egg. Form into flat cakes about 2½ x ¾ inches, and fry with salt pork, or (preferably) in deep fat, like doughnuts.

Fish, Creamed.— See page 337. A good way of utilizing fish left over.

Fish from Muddy Waters.— To clean them properly, see directions in Chapter XV. Another method is here copied from the *Outer's Book:*

" Remove the scales, head, fins and intestines, wash and clean well, then place the fish in a large dishpan and pour boiling water over them, let them remain in this water for one minute, two minutes if the fish are very large, take them out of the water and remove the skin. When the skin is removed the meat will be clean and free from moss, mud or tule taste. All fish caught from lakes or streams where fish frequent places where moss or tules grow, will taste of the moss unless they are scaled and the skin removed; the moss taste is under the scales and in the skin. Fish that live in swift running water will not have the moss taste, and will not have to be scalded."

When it is necessary to eat fish caught in muddy streams, rub a little salt down the backbone, lay them in strong brine for a couple of hours before cooking, and serve with one of the sauces described above. Carp should have the gills removed, as they are always muddy from burrowing.

Eel, Broiled.— Skin, clean well with salt to remove slime, slit down the back and remove bone, cut into good-sized pieces, rub inside with egg, if you have it, roll in cornmeal or dry breadcrumbs, season with pepper and salt, and broil to a nice brown. Some like a dash of nutmeg with the seasoning.

Eel, Stewed.— Skin the eel, remove backbone, and cut the eel into pieces about two inches long; put in the stew-pan with just enough water to cover, and add a teaspoonful of strong vinegar or a slice of lemon, cover stew-pan and boil moderately until flesh will leave the bones (20 minutes to half an hour). Then remove, pour off water, drain, add fresh water and vinegar as before, and stew until tender. Now drain, add cream enough for a stew, season with pepper and salt (no butter), boil again for a few minutes, and serve on hot, dry toast. (*Up De Graff.*)

Parsley butter (see page 304) is a good dressing. Stew the eel until done, add parsley butter, and continue stewing until it thickens and the parsley is cooked.

An eel is too oily for direct frying; but after stewing until quite done it may be put in a pan and fried to a nice brown.

A plain stew is made by adding only a little salt and a bit of butter, simmer gently till done, then put enough fine bread or cracker crumbs in the water to make a thick white sauce.

Fish Roe.— Parboil (merely simmer) fifteen minutes; let them cool and drain; then roll in flour, and fry.

MISCELLANEOUS.— *Frog Legs.*— First, after skinning, soak them an hour in cold water to which vinegar has been added, or put them for two minutes into scalding water that has vinegar in it. Drain, wipe dry, and cook as below:

To fry: roll in flour seasoned with salt and pepper and fry, not too rapidly, preferably in butter or oil. Water cress is a good relish with them.

To grill: Prepare three tablespoonfuls melted butter, one-half teaspoonful salt, and a pinch or two of pepper, into which dip the frog legs, then roll in fresh bread crumbs, and broil for three minutes on each side.

To cream: same process as for codfish (page 336) except stir cream until simmering, season with pep-

FISH AND SHELLFISH 329

per, salt, and nutmeg, cover and cook twenty minutes.

Turtles.— All turtles (aquatic) and most tortoises (land) are good to eat, the common snapper being far better than he looks. Kill by cutting or (readier) shooting the head off. This does not kill the brute immediately, of course, but it suffices. The common way of killing by dropping a turtle into boiling water I do not like. Let the animal bleed. Then drop into a pot of boiling water for a few seconds. After scalding, the outer scales of shell, as well as the skin, are easily removed. Turn turtle on its back, cut down middle of under shell from end to end, and then across. Throw away entrails, head, and claws. Salt and pepper it inside and out. Boil a short time in the shell. Remove when the meat has cooked free from the shell. Cut up the latter and boil slowly for three hours with some chopped onion. If a stew is preferred, add some salt pork cut into dice, and vegetables. (See page 300.)

Crayfish.— These are the "craw-feesh!" of our streets. Tear off extreme end of tail, bringing the entrail with it. Boil whole in salted water till the crayfish turns red. Peel and eat as a lobster, dipping each crayfish at a time into a saucer of vinegar, pepper, and salt.

SHELLFISH.— *Oysters, Stewed.*— Oysters should not be pierced with a fork, but removed from the liquor with a spoon. Thoroughly drain the juice from a quart of shelled oysters. Add to the juice enough water (if needed) to make one-half pint. Place juice over fire, and add butter the size of a walnut. Remove all scum that arises when the juice boils. Put in the oysters. Let them cook quickly until the beards wrinkle, but not until oysters shrivel— they should remain plump. Add two-thirds pint of milk, let all scald through, remove from fire, and season to taste. Never boil oysters in milk.

Oysters, Fried.— Drain the oysters, and dry

them on a soft cloth (then they will not absorb grease). Have some desiccated egg prepared, or beat light the yolks of two or three eggs. Have enough smoking hot grease in the pan to cover all the oysters. Dip an oyster into the egg, then into rolled cracker or dry crumbs, and repeat this. Lay oysters in the pan one at a time, so as not to check the heat. When one side is brown, turn, and brown the other side. Serve piping hot.

Oysters, Scalloped.— Cover bottom of greased bake-pan with a layer of drained oysters, dot thickly over with small bits of butter, then cover with finely crumbled stale bread, and sprinkle with pepper and salt. Repeat these layers until the pan is full, with bread and butter for top layer. The bread crumbs must be in very thin layers. Bake in reflector or oven until nicely browned.

Oysters, Sauté.— Drain the oysters. Melt a little butter in the frying-pan, and cook the oysters in it. Salt when removed from pan.

Oysters, Roasted.— Put oysters unopened on broiler, and hold over the coals. When they open, put a little melted butter and some white pepper on each oyster, and they are ready.

Clams, Baked.— Lay down a bed of stones in disk shape, and build a low wall almost around it, forming a rock oven open at the top. Build a big fire in it and keep it going until the wood has burned down to embers and the stones are very hot. Rake out all smoking chunks. Throw a layer of sea-weed over the embers, and lay the clams quickly on this. Roasting ears in the husks, or sweet potatoes, are a desirable addition. Cover all with another layer of sea-weed, and let steam about forty minutes, or until clams will slip in the shell. Uncover and serve with melted butter, pepper, salt, and perhaps lemon or vinegar.

Clam Chowder.— Wash the clams, put them in a kettle, and pour over them just enough boiling water to cover them. When the shells open, pour off the liquor, saving it, cool the clams, and shell

FISH AND SHELLFISH 331

them. Fry two or three slices of pork in bottom of kettle. When it is done, pour over it two quarts of boiling clam liquor. Add six large potatoes, sliced thin, and cook until nearly done. Turn in the clams, and a quart of hot milk. Season with salt and pepper. When this boils up, add crackers or stale bread, as in fish chowder. Remove from fire and let crackers steam in the covered pot until soft.

Fried sliced onion and a can of tomatoes will improve this chowder. Cloves, allspice, red pepper, Worcestershire sauce, and other condiments, may be added according to taste.

Shellfish, Steamed.— See page 301.

Crabs, Deviled.— Boil hard-shell crabs a few minutes until red. Remove the back shells, and shred out the white meat. Meantime make a paste of flour rubbed up in cold water, to which add a few drops of olive oil and some chopped green peppers. Mix swiftly with the crab meat, add a dash of cayenne, and stuff back into the shells. Bake until done. (*Fortiss.*)

CHAPTER XIX
CAMP COOKERY

Cured Meats, Etc.— Eggs

Bacon, Fried.— Slice quite thin. Remove the rind, as it not only is unsightly but makes the slices curl up in the pan. Put pan half full of water on fire; when water is warm, drop the bacon in, and stir around until water begins to simmer. Then remove bacon, throw out water, fry over very few coals, and turn often. Remove slices while still translucent, and season with pepper. They will turn crisp on cooling. Some prefer not to parboil.

Bacon, Broiled.— Slice as above. Turn broiler repeatedly until bacon is of a light brown color. Time, three to four minutes.

Bacon, Boiled.— Put in enough cold water to just cover. Bring to a boil very gradually. Remove all scum as it arises. Simmer gently until thoroughly done. Two pounds take $1\frac{1}{2}$ hours; each additional pound, $\frac{1}{2}$ hour.

Bacon, Toasted.— Cut cold boiled bacon into thin slices. Sprinkle each with fine bread crumbs peppered with cayenne. Toast quickly in wire broiler.

Bacon and Eggs.— Poach or fry the eggs and lay them on fried bacon.

Bacon Omelet.— See *Ham Omelet,* near end of chapter.

Bacon Gravy, Thin.— Pour off the fat and save it for future use. Pour in enough water to supply the quantity of gravy desired. Add the juice of a lemon. Boil and pour upon the bacon. If a

CURED MEATS

richer gravy is desired, follow recipe given below.

Pork Gravy, Thickened.— This can be made with ham or salt pork, as well as with bacon. To make gravy that is a good substitute for butter, rub into the hot grease that is left in the pan a tablespoonful of flour, keep on rubbing until smooth and brown; then add two cups boiling water and a dash of pepper. A tablespoonful of catchup may be added for variety. If you have milk, use it instead of water (a pint to the heaping tablespoonful of flour), and do not let the flour brown; this makes a delicious white gravy.

Salt Pork, Fried.— Same as fried bacon, above. Pork should be firm and dry. Clammy pork is stale.

Salt Pork, Broiled.— Same as bacon; but it is usually so salty that it should be parboiled first, or soaked at least an hour in cold water.

Salt Pork, Boiled.— Nearly always cooked with vegetables or greens; hence need not be soaked or parboiled. See page 299.

Pork Fritters.— Make a thick batter of cornmeal one-third and flour two-thirds, or of flour alone. Fry a few slices of salt pork or bacon until the fat is tried out. Then cut a few more slices, dip them in the batter, drop them in the bubbling fat, season with salt and pepper, fry to a light brown, and eat while hot. It takes the stomach of a lumberjack to digest this, but it is a favorite variant in frontier diet.

Pork and Hardtack.— Soak hardtack in water until it is partly softened. Drop it into hot pork fat, and cook. A soldier's resource.

Ham, Fried.— Same as bacon. Parboil, first, for eight or ten minutes, if hard and salty.

Ham and Eggs.— Same as bacon and eggs.

Ham, Broiled.— If salty, parboil first. Cut rather thick slices, pepper them, and broil five minutes. Ham that has been boiled is best for broiling. A little mustard may be spread on the slices when served.

Ham, Boiled.— Wash the ham, and let it soak over night in cold water. In the morning, cover it well with fresh water, bring to a boil, and hang the kettle high over the fire where it will boil gently until dinner time. When the bone on the under side leaves the meat readily, the ham is done. If you have eggs, the nicest way to serve a boiled ham is to remove the skin, brush over the top of ham with yolk of egg, sprinkle thickly with finely grated crumbs or cracker-dust, and brown in an oven.

Ham and Macaroni.— " Boil an inch-thick slice of ham half an hour, at the same time boiling the required amount of macaroni in salted water. When the macaroni is done, drain off the water and put in a baking dish and pour over it a can of tomatoes, which should be seasoned with salt and pepper. Place slice of ham on top, and bake half an hour. A little grated cheese is an improvement when mixed with the macaroni, before adding the tomatoes." (*Arthur Chapman.*)

Ham Chow.— Slice the required amount of potatoes in thin slices, season with salt and pepper, and place in baking dish. Add one can of tomatoes. Cover and cook for an hour. Then place slices of boiled ham, or some well seasoned chops, over the potato and tomato mixture, return to the oven without the cover, and bake half an hour. Thinly sliced bacon will take the place of ham or chops, but must only be left in the oven a few minutes. (*Same.*)

Pork Sausages.— Cut links apart, prick each with a fork so it will not burst in cooking, and broil on forked stick; or, lay in cold frying-pan, and fry fifteen to twenty minutes over a slow fire, moving them about so they will brown evenly all over. Serve with mashed potatoes, over which pour the fat from the pan. Apples fried to a light brown in the sausage grease are a pleasant accompaniment.

Corned Beef, Boiled.— Put the ham into enough

CURED MEATS 335

cold water to cover it. Let it come slowly to a boil, and then merely simmer until done. Time, about one-half hour to each pound. Vegetables may be added toward the end, as directed on page 299. If not to be used until the next day, leave the meat in its liquor, weighted down under the surface by a clean rock.

Corned Beef Hash.— Chop some canned corned beef fine with sliced onions. Hash up with freshly boiled potatoes, two parts potatoes to one of meat. Season highly with pepper (no salt), and some mustard if liked. Put a little pork fat in a frying-pan, melt, add hash, and cook until nearly dry and a brown crust has formed. Dehydrated potatoes and onions can be used according to directions on packages.

Stew with Canned Meat.— Peel and slice some onions. If the meat has much fat, melt it; if not, melt a little pork fat. Add onions, and fry until brown. Mix some flour into a smooth batter with cold water, season with pepper and salt, and pour into the camp kettle. Stir the whole well together. Cut meat into slices, put into the kettle, and heat through.

Lobscouse.— Boil corned beef as above (if very salty, parboil first, and then change the water). About thirty minutes before it is done add sliced potatoes and hardtack.

Slumgullion.— When the commissariat is reduced to bacon, corned beef, and hardtack, try this sailor's dish, described by Jack London: Fry half a dozen slices of bacon, add fragments of hardtack, then two cups of water, and stir briskly over the fire; in a few minutes mix in with it slices of canned corned beef; season well with pepper and salt.

Dried Beef, Creamed.— Slice 3 oz. of dried beef into thin shavings, or chop fine. Pour over it a pint of boiling water, and let it stand two minutes. Turn off water, and drain beef dry. Heat a heaped tablespoonful of butter in the frying-pan;

then add the beef. Cook three minutes, stirring all the time. Then pour on ¼ pint cold milk. Mix 4 tablespoonfuls milk with 1 teaspoonful flour, and stir into the beef in the pan. Add an egg, if you have it. Cook two minutes longer and serve at once.

Canned Meats.— Never eat any that has been left standing open in the can. It is dangerous. If any has been left over, remove it to a clean vessel and keep in a cool place.

Canned corned beef and the like should not be eaten cold out of the can if you can help it. Place the can in water and boil it about ten minutes: the meat is more wholesome this way.

Cured Venison.— " Cut off the worst of the blackened casing and slice into steaks an inch thick. Dredge these with flour, salt, and pepper, and lay in hot bacon grease in a frying-pan. Pour in a small cup of water, cover tightly, and allow to steam until the water is gone. Then remove the cover, and brown." (*Kathrene Pinkerton.*)

CURED FISH.— *Salt Fish* requires from twelve to thirty-six hours' soaking, flesh downward, in cold water before cooking, depending on the hardness and dryness of the fish. Change the water two or three times to remove surplus salt. Start in cold water, then, and boil until the flesh parts from the bones. When done, cover with bits of butter, or serve with one of the sauces given in the chapter on FISH.

Broiled Salt Fish.— Freshen the flakes of fish by soaking in cold water. Broil over the coals, and serve with potatoes.

Stewed Codfish.— Soak over night in plenty of cold water, or one hour in tepid water. Put in pot of fresh, cold water, and heat gradually until soft. Do not boil the fish or it will get hard. Serve with boiled potatoes, and with white sauce made as directed under FISH.

(2) Put two tablespoonfuls of butter in a pan; when melted add one tablespoonful of flour, stir-

CURED MEATS 337

ring constantly; then a cup of rich milk and some pepper; then half a pint of desiccated codfish. Stir until boiling. Serve on toast, if you have light bread.

Codfish Hash.— Prepare salt codfish as above. When soft, mash with potatoes and onions, season with pepper, and fry like corned beef hash.

Codfish Balls.— Shred the fish into small pieces. Peel some potatoes. Use one pint of fish to one quart of raw potatoes. Put them in a pot, cover with boiling water, cook till potatoes are soft, drain water off, mash fish and potatoes together, and beat light with a fork. Add a tablespoonful of butter and season with pepper. Shape into flattened balls, and fry in very hot fat deep enough to cover.

Smoked Herrings.— (1) Clean, and remove the skin. Toast on a stick over the coals.

(2) Scald in boiling water till the skin curls up, then remove head, tail, and skin. Clean well. Put into frying-pan with a little butter or lard. Fry gently a few minutes, dropping in a little vinegar.

Smoked Sprats.— Lay them on a slightly greased plate and set them in an oven until heated through.

Canned Salmon, Creamed.— Cut into dice. Heat about a pint of them in one-half pint milk. Season with salt and Cayenne pepper. Cold cooked fish of any kind can be served in this way.

Canned Salmon, Scalloped.— Rub two teaspoonfuls of butter and a tablespoonful of flour together. Stir this into boiling milk. Cut two pounds of canned salmon into dice. Put a layer of the sauce in bottom of a dish, then a layer of salmon. Sprinkle with salt, Cayenne pepper, and grated bread crumbs. Repeat alternate layers until dish is full, having the last layer sauce, which is sprinkled with crumbs and bits of butter. Bake in very hot oven until browned (about ten minutes).

Canned Salmon on Toast.— Dip slices of stale bread in smoking-hot lard. They will brown at once. Drain them. Heat a pint of salmon, picked into flakes, season with salt and Cayenne, and turn into a cupful of melted butter. Heat in pan. Stir in one egg, beaten light, with three tablespoonfuls evaporated milk not thinned. Pour the mixture on the fried bread.

Sardines on Toast.— Fry them and give them a dash of red pepper. They are better if wiped free of oil, dipped into whipped egg, sprinkled thickly with cracker crumbs, fried, and served on buttered toast.

(2) Drain and remove skins from one dozen sardines, put a tablespoonful of butter in the pan, with two teaspoonfuls anchovy paste, and a little tabasco. Lay the sardines carefully in the pan. When well heated through, serve each on a tiny strip of toast.

EGGS.—

Desiccated Egg.— The baker's egg mentioned in the chapter on PROVISIONS is in granules about the size of coarse sand. It is prepared for use by first soaking about two hours in cold or one hour in lukewarm water. Hot water must not be used. Solution can be quickened by occasional stirring. The proportion is one tablespoonful of egg to two of water, which is about the equivalent of one fresh egg. Use just like fresh eggs in baking, etc., and for scrambled eggs or omelets. Of course, the desiccated powder cannot be fried, boiled, or poached.

Fried Eggs.— Have the frying-pan scrupulously clean. Put in just enough butter, dripping, or other fat, to prevent the eggs sticking. Break an egg with a smart but gentle crack on the side of a cup, and drop it in the cup without breaking yolk. Otherwise you might drop a bad one in the pan and spoil the whole mess. Pour the egg slowly into the pan so that the albumen thickens over the yolk instead of spreading itself out like a pancake. The fire should be moderate. In two or three minutes they will be done. Eggs fried longer than this, or on both sides, are leathery and unwholesome.

Scrambled Eggs.— Put into a well-greased pan as many eggs as it will hold separately, each yolk being whole. When the whites have begun to set, stir from bottom of pan until done (buttery, not leathery). Add a piece of butter, pepper, and salt. Another way is to beat the eggs with a spoon. To five eggs add one-fourth teaspoonful salt. Heat one tablespoonful butter in the frying-pan. Stir in the eggs, and continue stirring until eggs set. Before they toughen, turn them out promptly into a warm dish.

Scrambled Eggs, Fancy.— After turning in five eggs as above, add a cupful of canned tomatoes, drained and chopped quite fine; or, chopped ham or bacon instead of tomatoes.

Plain Omelet.— It is better to make two or three small omelets than to attempt one large one. Scrape the pan and wipe it dry after each omelet is made. Use little salt: it keeps the eggs from rising. Heat the fat in the pan very gradually, but get it hot almost to the browning point.

Beat four eggs just enough to break them well; or, break into a bowl with four tablespoonfuls milk, and whip thoroughly. Add a little salt. Put two heaped teaspoonfuls of butter in the pan and heat as above. Pour egg into pan, and tilt the pan forward so that the egg flows to the far side. As soon as the egg begins to set, draw it up to the raised side of the pan with a knife. Beginning then at the left hand, turn the egg over in small folds until the lower part of the pan is reached, and the omelet has been rolled into a complete fold. Let the omelet rest a few seconds, and then turn out into a hot dish. Work rapidly throughout, so that the omelet is creamy instead of tough. It should be of a rich yellow color.

Ham Omelet.— Cut raw ham into dice. Fry. Turn the beaten eggs over it and cook as above. Bacon can be used instead of ham.

Fancy Omelets.— Take tender meat, game, fish, or vegetable, hash it fine, heat it in white sauce (see page 325), and spread this over the omelet before you begin to fold it; or they can be put in with the eggs. Jam, jelly, or preserved fruit may be used in a similar way (two tablespoonfuls, say, of marmalade to six eggs).

Rum Omelet.— Beat three eggs, add a very small pinch of salt, a teaspoonful of powdered sugar, a slice of butter, and a tablespoonful of rum. Fry as described above. Lay the omelet on a hot dish, pour around it one-half tumberful of rum that has been warmed in a pan, light it, and serve with its blue flame rising round it.

Poached Eggs.— Put a pint of water in the frying pan, with one-half teaspoonful of salt. If you have vinegar, add two teaspoonfuls to the water: it keeps the whites from running too much. Bring the water to a gentle boil. Break the eggs separately into a saucer and slide them into the water. Let the water simmer not longer than three minutes, meantime ladling spoonfuls of it over the yolks. Have toast already buttered on a very hot plate. Lay eggs carefully on it. Eat at once. This may be varied by moistening the toast with hot milk.

Eggs, Boiled.— Eggs are boiled soft in two and one-half to three minutes, depending upon size and freshness. If wanted hard boiled, put them in cold water, bring to a boil, and keep it up for twenty minutes. The yolk will then be mealy and wholesome. Eggs boiled between these extremes are either clammy or tough, and indigestible. To boil eggs, soft, if you have no watch: put them in *cold* water and set the pot over the fire. Watch the water; when it begins to sing slightly, or when the first little bubbles arise, the eggs are done to a turn.

Eggs, Roasted.— This can be done by covering the eggs with hot ashes and embers, but the shells must be cracked a little at one end to prevent them exploding.

Eggs, Stirred.— Make half a cup of rich gravy. Melt a tablespoon of butter in a pan and add the gravy. When hissing hot, stir in five beaten eggs

CURED MEATS

until they thicken. Season with half a teaspoonful of salt, a dash of pepper, sprinkle with parsley, and serve on toast.

CHAPTER XX
CAMP COOKERY

BREADSTUFFS AND CEREALS

When men must bake for themselves they generally make biscuit, biscuit-loaf, flap-jacks, or corn bread. Bread leavened with yeast is either beyond their skill or too troublesome to make out of doors; so baking powder is the mainstay of the camp. Generally the batch is a failure. To paraphrase Tom Hood,

> Who has not met with camp-made bread,
> Rolled out of putty and weighted with lead?

It need not be so. Just as good biscuit or johnny cake can be baked before a log fire in the woods as in a kitchen range. Bread making is a chemical process. Follow directions; pay close attention to details, as a chemist does, from building the fire to testing the loaf with a sliver. It does require experience or a special knack to *guess* quantities accurately, but none at all to *measure* them.

In general, biscuit or other small cakes should be baked quickly by ardent heat; large loaves require a slow, even heat, so that the outside will not harden until the inside is nearly done.

The way to bake in a reflector or in a "baker" has been shown in the chapter on MEATS. If you have neither of these utensils, there are other ways.

Baking in a Dutch Oven.— This is a cast-iron pot with flaring sides and short legs, fitted with a thick iron cover, the rim of which is turned up to

BREADSTUFFS

hold a layer of coals on top. If it were not for its weight it would be the best oven for outdoor use, since it not only bakes but cooks the meat or pone in its own steam.

Place the Dutch oven and its lid separately on the fire. Get the bottom moderately hot, and the lid very hot (but not red, lest it warp). Grease the bottom and sprinkle flour over it, put in the bread or biscuits, set cover on, rake a thin layer of coals out in front of the fire, stand oven on them, and cover lid thickly with more live coals. Replenish occasionally. Have a stout pot-hook to lift lid with, so you can inspect progress of baking once or twice.

The sheet-steel oven mentioned in Chapter VII can be used in a similar way, or one of the pots made for fireless cookers, or a pudding pan inverted over a slightly smaller one; but with such thin utensils you must use a more moderate heat, of course, and watch the baking carefully lest you burn it.

Baking in a Kettle.— Every fixed camp that has no stove should have a bake-hole, if for nothing else than baking beans. The hole can be dug anywhere, but it is best in the side of a bank or knoll, so that an opening can be left in front to rake out of, and for drainage in case of rain. Line it with stones, as they hold heat and keep the sides from crumbling. Have the completed hole a little larger than your baking kettle.

Build a hardwood fire in and above the hole and keep it going until the stones or earth are very hot (not less than half an hour). Rake out most of the coals and ashes, put in the bake-pot, which must have a tight-fitting lid, cover with ashes and then with live coals; and, if a long heating is required, keep a small fire going on top. Close the mouth of the oven with a flat rock. This is the way for beans or for braising meat.

Bread is not to be baked in the kettle alone, because the sides are vertical and you would have a sweet time getting the bread out; but if you have a pudding-pan that will go inside the kettle, well and good. Put three or four pebbles in the bottom of the kettle for the pan to rest on, so the dough will not burn.

A shifty camper can make bread in almost anything. I have even baked beans to perfection in a thin, soldered lard-pail, by first encasing it in clay.

Baking in the Ashes.— Build a good fire on a level bit of ground. When it has burned to coals and the ground has thoroughly heated, rake away the embers, lightly drop the loaf on the hot earth, pat it smooth, rake the embers back over the loaf (some hot ashes first), and let it bake until no dough will adhere to a sliver thrust to the center of the loaf. This is the Australian damper. Ash cakes are similarly baked (see page 352). Dirty? No it isn't; try it.

Baking in a Frying-pan.— Grease or flour a frying-pan and put a flat cake of biscuit-dough in it. Rake some embers out in front of the fire and put pan on them just long enough to form a little crust on bottom of loaf. Then remove from embers, and, with a short forked stick, the stub of which will enter hole in end of handle, prop pan up before fire at such angle that top of loaf will be exposed to heat. Turn loaf now and then, both sidewise and upside down. When firm enough to keep its shape, remove it, prop it by itself before the fire to finish baking, and go on with a fresh loaf. A tin plate may be used in place of the frying-pan.

If you have in your kit a shallow pudding-pan of the right size, invert it over the dough in the pan and heap embers on top; or a second frying-pan can be used in the same way. Another way, with one pan and no cover, is described by Kathrene Pinkerton:

"Make a rich, moist baking-powder biscuit dough, using double the amount of lard. The dough should be so thin it can be smoothed with a knife. Heat a little lard in a frying-pan and pour in the dough. A bannock should never be baked in less than twenty-five minutes.

BREADSTUFFS 345

With a good cooking fire, the pan should be held three feet above the blaze until the bannock has risen to twice its original height. Then lower the pan and brown. Shake the pan occasionally to see that the bannock is not burning. When one side is done, slide the bannock onto a plate, heat more lard in the pan, gently replace the bannock upside down and brown again. The result is a golden-brown loaf."

Baking on a Slab.— Heat a thick slab of non-resinous green wood until the sap simmers. Then proceed as with a frying-pan.

Baking on a Stick.— Work dough into a ribbon two inches wide. Get a club of sweet green wood (birch, sassafras, maple), about two feet long and three inches thick, peel large end, sharpen the other and stick it into ground, leaning toward fire. When sap simmers wind dough spirally around peeled end. Turn occasionally. Several sticks can be baking at once. Bread for one man's meal can be quickly baked on a peeled stick as thick as a broomstick, holding over fire and turning. This is " corkscrew bread."

Clay Oven.— In fixed camp, if you have no oven, a good substitute can soon be made in a clay bank or steep knoll near by. Dig down the bank to a vertical front. Back from this front, about 4 feet, drive a 4 or 5-inch stake down to what will be the bottom level of the oven. Draw the stake out, thus leaving a hole for flue. It is best to drive the stake before excavating, as otherwise it might cause the roof of your oven to cave in from the shock of driving. Now, from the bottom of the face, dig a horizontal hole back to the flue, keeping the entrance as small as you can, but enlarging the interior and arching its top. When the oven is finished, wet the whole interior, smooth it, and build a small fire in the oven to gradually dry and harden it.

To bake in such an oven: build a good fire in it of split hardwood sticks, and keep it burning hard for an hour or two; then rake out the embers, lay your dough on broad green leaves (basswood, from choice) or on the naked floor, and close both the door and the flue with flat stones or bark.

If no bank or knoll lies handy, build a form for your oven by first setting up a row of green-stick arches, like exaggerated croquet wickets, one behind the other, and cover with sticks laid on horizontally like a roof. At the rear, set up a round stake as core for the chimney. Now plaster wet clay thickly over all except the door. Let this dry naturally for a day in hot sunlight, or build a very small fire within and feed it only as needed to keep up a moderate heat. When the clay has hardened, give it another coating, to fill up the cracks that have appeared. Then give it a final firing.

To Mix Dough Without a Pan.— When bark will peel, use a broad sheet of it (paper birch, basswood, poplar, cottonwood, slippery elm, etc.). It is easy to mix unleavened dough in the sack of flour itself. Stand the latter horizontally where it can't fall over. Scoop a bowl-shaped depression in top of flour. Keep the right hand moving round while you pour in a little water at a time from a vessel held in the left. Sprinkle a little salt in. When a thick, adhesive dough has formed, lift this out and pat and work it into a round cake about $2\frac{1}{2}$ inches thick.

WHEAT BREAD AND BISCUITS.— When baking powder is used, the secret of good bread is to *handle the dough as little as possible*. After adding the water, mix as rapidly as you can, not with the warm hands, but with a big spoon or a wooden paddle. To knead such bread, or roll it much, or even to mould biscuits by hand instead of cutting them out, would surely make your baking " sad." As soon as water touches the flour, the baking powder begins to give off gas. It is this gas, imprisoned in the dough, that makes bread light. Squeezing or moulding presses this gas out. The heat of the hands turns such dough into Tom Hood's " putty."

Biscuit Loaf.— This is a standard camp bread, because it bakes quickly. It is good so long as it

BREADSTUFFS

is hot, but it dries out soon and will not keep. For four men:

   3 pints flour,
   3 heaping teaspoonfuls baking powder,
   1 heaping teaspoonful salt,
   2 heaping tablespoonfuls cold grease,
   1 scant pint cold water.

Amount of water varies according to quality of flour. Baking powders vary in strength; follow directions on can.

Mix thoroughly, with big spoon or wooden paddle, first the baking powder with the flour, and then the salt. Rub into this the cold grease (which may be lard, cold pork fat, drippings, or bear's grease), until there are no lumps left and no grease adhering to bottom of pan. This is a little tedious, but don't shirk it. Then stir in the water and work it with spoon until you have a rather stiff dough. Have the pan greased. Turn the loaf into it, and bake. Test center of loaf with a sliver when you think it probably done. When no dough adheres, remove bread. All hot breads should be broken with the hands, never cut.

To freshen any that is left over and dried out, sprinkle a little water over it and heat through. This can be done but once.

Biscuit.— These are baked in a reflector (12-inch holds 1 dozen, 18-inch holds 1½ dozen), unless a camp stove is carried or an oven is dug. Build the fire high. Make dough as in the preceding recipe, which is enough for two dozen biscuits. Flop the mass of dough to one side of pan, dust flour on bottom of pan, flop dough back over it, dust flour on top of loaf. Now rub some flour over the bread board, flour your hands, and gently lift loaf on board. Flour the bottle or bit of peeled sapling that you use as rolling-pin, also the edges of can or can cover used as biscuit cutter. Gently roll loaf to three-quarter-inch thickness. Stamp out the biscuit and lay them in pan. Roll out the culls and make biscuit of them, too. Bake until edge of front row turns brown; reverse pan and continue until rear row is similarly done. Time, twenty to twenty-five minutes in a reflector, ten to fifteen minutes in a closed oven.

Dropped Biscuit.— These do away with bread-board, rolling-pin, and most of the work, yet are about as good as stamped biscuit. Use same proportions as above, except turn in enough water to make a *thick batter* — one that will drop lazily from a spoon. In mixing, do not stir the batter more than necessary to smooth out all lumps. Drop from a big spoon into the greased bake-pan.

Army Bread.— This is easier to make than biscuit dough, since there is no grease to rub in, but it takes longer to bake. It keeps fresh longer than yeast bread, does not dry up in a week, nor mould, and is more wholesome than biscuit. It is the only baking-powder bread I know of that is good to eat cold — in fact, it is best that way.

> 1 quart flour,
> 1 teaspoonful salt,
> 1 tablespoonful sugar,
> 2 heaped teaspoonfuls baking powder.

Mix the dry ingredients thoroughly. Then stir in enough cold water (about 1½ pints) to make a thick batter that will pour out level. Mix rapidly with spoon until smooth, and pour at once into bake-pan. Bake about forty-five minutes, or until no dough adheres to a sliver. Above quantity makes a 1½-pound loaf (say 9x5x3 inches).

For variety, substitute for the sugar two or three tablespoonfuls of molasses, and add one to two teaspoonfuls of ginger.

Breakfast Rolls.—

> 1 quart flour,
> 2 level tablespoonfuls butter,
> 1 egg,
> 1 teaspoonful baking powder,
> 1 pint cold milk (or enough to make a soft dough).

Rub butter and flour well together, add beaten

BREADSTUFFS

egg, a pinch of salt, and the milk, till a soft dough is mixed. Form into rolls and bake quickly.

Salt-rising Bread.— This smells to heaven while it is fermenting, but is a welcome change after a long diet of baking-powder breadstuffs. For a baking of two or three loaves take about a pint of moderately warm water (a pleasant heat to the hand) and stir into it as much flour as will make a good batter, not too thick. Add to this one-half teaspoonful salt, not more. Set the vessel in a pan of moderately warm water, within a little distance of a fire, or in sunlight. The water must not be allowed to cool much below the original heat, more warm water being added to pan as required.

In six to eight hours the whole will be in active fermentation, when the dough must be mixed with it, and as much warm water (milk, if you have it) as you require. Knead the mass till it is tough and does not stick to the board. Make up your loaves, and keep them warmly covered near the fire till they rise. They must be baked as soon as this second rising takes place; for, unless the rising is used immediately on reaching its height, it sinks to rise no more.

Sour-dough Bread.— Mix a pail of batter from plain flour and water, and hang it up in a warm place until the batter sours. Then add salt and soda (not baking powder) and a spoonful of sugar, thicken with flour to a stiff dough, knead thoroughly, work into small loaves, and place them before the fire to rise. Then bake.

The following is by Mrs. Pinkerton:

"The sour-dough can ranks high in the list of woods time-savers. It is easy to manipulate, will supply yeast for both cakes and bread, and requires only one start, for it improves with age. Our sour-dough pail has now been going continuously for nine months and is getting better all the time.

"To make the 'sourings,' stir two cups of flour, two tablespoons of sugar and one of salt in sufficient water to make a creamy batter. Stir in a tablespoonful of vinegar and set near a fire or in the sun to sour. One author has said 'it requires a running start of thirty-six hours.' Two days' souring is better. Do not be dismayed by the odor. The woods axiom is, 'the sourer the better,' and it will not be at its best the first few days. Its great advantage for campers lies in the fact that it will raise either bread or pancakes in any temperature above freezing.

"Pancakes should be set in the evening. Beat until smooth; water and flour in proper proportions for batter. Stir this into the 'sourings' in the sour dough can. This rises overnight. In the morning the amount of batter necessary for breakfast should be taken out, leaving enough yeast for the next day. Into enough batter for two we stir two tablespoons of molasses, one teaspoon of salt, and one half teaspoon of soda, the last two dissolved in hot water. Then, small cakes are better and more easily handled than those the size of the frying pan.

"A quick, hot fire is necessary for pancakes, although, when frying in a pan, care must be taken or they will burn. Once a cake has burned to the pan you may as well stop and clean the pan thoroughly or every succeeding cake will be spoiled.

"Uneaten pancakes should be broken up and dropped into the sourings. It improves the cakes. Some woodsmen are almost superstitious about the mixture, and, with them, the sour dough pail rivals the garbage can as a receptacle for uneaten foods. When the yeast loses its sourness from overwork a tablespoon of vinegar will revive it. The 'sourings' can be carried in a pail or in a push-top tin. If you use the latter be sure to allow plenty of room for expansion. We still carry on a blanket evidences of too active 'sourings.'"

To Raise Bread in a Pot.— Set the dough to rise over a very few embers, keeping the pot turned as the loaf rises. When equally risen all around, put hot ashes under the pot and upon the lid, taking care that the heat be not too fierce at first.

Lungwort Bread.— On the bark of maples, and sometimes of beeches and birches, in the northern woods, there grows a green, broad-leaved lichen variously known as lungwort, liverwort, lung-lichen, and lung-moss, which is an excellent substitute for yeast. This is an altogether different growth from the plants commonly called lungwort and liverwort — I believe its scientific name is *Sticta pulmonacea.* This lichen is partly made up of fungus, which does the business of raising

BREADSTUFFS 351

dough. Gather a little of it and steep it over night in lukewarm water, set near the embers, but not near enough to get overheated. In the morning, pour off the infusion and mix it with enough flour to make a batter, beating it up with a spoon. Place this "sponge" in a warm can or pail, cover with a cloth, and set it near the fire to work. By evening it will have risen. Leaven your dough with this (saving some of the sponge for a future baking), let the bread rise before the fire that night, and by morning it will be ready to bake.

It takes but little of the original sponge to leaven a large mass of dough (but see that it never freezes), and it can be kept good for months.

Unleavened Bread.— Quickly made, wholesome, and good for a change. Keeps like hardtack.

> 2½ pints flour,
> 1 tablespoonful salt (scant),
> 1 tablespoonful sugar.

Mix with water to stiff dough, and knead and pull until lively. Roll out thin as a soda cracker, score with knife, and bake. Unleavened bread that is to be carried for a long time must be mixed with as little water as possible (merely dampened enough to make it adhere), for if any moisture is left in it after baking, it will mould.

A teaspoonful of lard worked in with the flour improves the taste, but the bread will not keep forever, as it would without the lard. If lard is used, you may as well make a good imitation of Maryland biscuit while you are about it. Lay the dough out on a board and beat it lustily with a paddle until it becomes elastic, then bake.

Dough Gods.—" Take ⅔ cupful of flour, 1 small teaspoonful of baking powder, ¼ teaspoonful of salt, and a slice of fat bacon minced fine as possible. Mix thoroughly in your bread-pan and add water slowly, stirring and working till you have a fairly stiff dough. Flour the loaf, top and bottom, flour your hands and pat the dough out into a couple of big cakes about half an inch thick. Bake in the ashes, or in the frying-pan. . . . This is the old way of baking with bacon instead of rendered grease or lard, used by men who carried nothing they could do without, and whose only food staples were flour, bacon, baking-powder, and salt." (*Edward Cave.*)

CORN BREAD.— Plain corn bread, without flour, milk, or egg, is hard to make eatable without a Dutch oven to bake it in. Even so, it is generally spoiled by being baked too fast and not long enough to be done inside.

Corn Pone.—

- 1 quart meal,
- 1 teaspoonful salt,
- 1 pint *warm* (but not scalding) water (1½ pints for old meal).

Stir together until light. Bake to a nice brown all around (about forty-five minutes), and let it sweat fifteen minutes longer in the closed oven, removed from the fire. Yellow meal generally requires more water than white. Freshly ground meal is much better than old.

Corn Dodgers.— Same as above, but mix to a stiff dough, and form into cylindrical dodgers four or five inches long and 1½ inches diameter, by rolling between the hands. Have frying-pan very hot, grease it a little, and put dodgers on as you roll them out. As soon as they have browned, put them in oven and bake thoroughly.

Ash Cake.— Same kind of dough. Form it into balls as big as hen's eggs, roll in dry flour, lay in hot ashes, and cover completely with them.

Johnny-cake.— "Mix at home, before starting, 1 quart of yellow, granulated corn meal, 1 pint of white flour, ½ cup of sugar, 1 teaspoonful of salt, 4 teaspoonfuls of baking-powder. In camp it should be mixed in the pan to make a fairly heavy batter and allowed to stand for a few minutes before frying so that it becomes light and puffy. It should then be dropped by spoonfuls, without further stirring,

BREADSTUFFS

into the hot, greased pan, and not turned until the top has begun to set. The bacon grease takes the place of butter.

"If less water is used, the entire mixture may be put in the frying-pan at once, baked from the bottom up over coals until the top has set, and then turned. It makes delicious johnny-cake. Try rolling the trout in a little of the dry mixture." (*Warwick S. Carpenter.*)

Corn Bread (Superior).—

>   1 pint corn meal,
>   1 pint flour,
>   3 tablespoonfuls sugar,
>   2 heaped tablespoonfuls butter,
>   3 teaspoonfuls baking powder,
>   1 teaspoonful salt,
>   2 eggs,
>   1 pint (or more) milk.

Rub butter and sugar together. Add the beaten eggs; then the milk. Sift the salt and baking powder into the meal and flour. Pour the liquid over the dry ingredients, beating well. Pour batter into well-greased pan, and bake thirty to forty minutes in moderately hot oven. Can also be made into muffins.

Corn Batter Bread.—

>   1 pint corn meal,
>   2 pints milk (or water),
>   2 eggs,
>   1 teaspoonful salt.

Beat the eggs light; add the salt; then the meal and milk, gradually, until well blended. Bake about thirty minutes. This is the standard breakfast bread of the South, easily made, and (if the meal is freshly ground) delicious. A little boiled rice, or hominy grits, may be substituted for part of the meal.

Snow Bread.— After a fall of light, feathery snow, superior corn bread may be made by stirring together

1 quart corn meal,
½ teaspoonful soda,
1 teaspoonful salt,
1 tablespoonful lard.

Then, in a cool place where the snow will not melt, stir into above one quart light snow. Bake about forty minutes in rather hot oven. Snow, for some unknown reason, has the same effect on bread as eggs have, two tablespoonfuls of snow equaling one egg. It can also be used in making batter for pancakes, or puddings, the batter being made rather thick, and the snow mixed with each cake just before putting in the pan.

Substitute for Baking Soda.— Take the *white* of wood ashes, same quantity as you would use of soda, and mix dry with the flour. It makes bread rise the same as soda, and you can't tell the difference. The best ashes are those of hickory, dogwood, sugar maple, and corncobs; but the ashes of beech, ash, buckeye, balsam poplar, and yellow poplar are also good.

"*Gritted Bread.*"— When green corn has just passed from the tucket, or soft and milky stage, and has become too hard for boiling, but is still too soft for grinding into meal, make a "gritter," as follows: Take a piece of tin about 7 x 14 inches (unsolder a lard pail by heating, and flatten the sides); punch holes through it, close together, with a large nail; bend the sheet into a half cylinder, rough side out, like a horseradish grater; nail the edges to a board somewhat longer and wider than the tin. Then, holding the ear of corn pointing lengthwise from you, grate it into a vessel held between the knees.

The meal thus formed will need no water, but can be mixed in its own milk. Salt it, and bake quickly. The flavor of "gritted bread" is a blend of hot pone and roasting ears — delectable! Hard corn can be grated by first soaking the ears over night.

BREADSTUFFS

PANCAKES.—

Plain Flapjacks.—
1 quart flour,
1 teaspoonful salt,
2 teaspoonfuls sugar, or 4 of molasses,
2 level tablespoonfuls baking powder.

Rub in, dry, two heaped tablespoonfuls grease. If you have no grease, do without. Make a smooth batter with cold milk (best) or water — thin enough to pour from a spoon, but not too thin, or it will take all day to bake enough for the party. Stir well, to smooth out lumps. Set frying-pan level over thin bed of coals, get it quite hot, and grease with a piece of pork in split end of stick. Pan must be hot enough to make batter sizzle as it touches, and it should be polished. Pour from end of a big spoon successively enough batter to fill pan within one-half inch of rim. When cake is full of bubbles and edges have stiffened, shuffle pan to make sure that cake is free below and stiff enough to flip. Then hold pan slanting in front of and away from you, go through preliminary motion of flapping once or twice to get the swing, then flip boldly so cake will turn a somersault in the air, and catch it upside down. Beginners generally lack the nerve to toss high enough. Grease pan anew and stir batter every time before pouring. This is the "universal pancake" that "Nessmuk" derided. Much better and wholesomer are:

Egg Pancakes.— Made same as above excepting that you add two eggs, or their equivalent in desiccated egg.

Snow Pancakes.— Instead of eggs, in the above recipe, use four tablespoonfuls of freshly fallen snow. Make the batter rather thick, and add some clean, dry snow to each pancake before putting it in the pan.

Mixed Cakes.— When cold boiled rice is left over, mix it half and half with flour, and proceed as with flapjacks. It makes them tender. The batter is best mixed with the water in which the rice was boiled. Oatmeal, grits, or cold boiled potatoes, may be used in the same way. Stewed dried fruit is also a good addition; mix the flour with their juice instead of water.

Corn Batter Cakes.—

> ½ pint corn meal,
> ¼ pint flour,
> 1 heaped teaspoonful baking powder,
> 1 heaped teaspoonful sugar or 2 molasses,
> 1 level teaspoonful salt.

After mixing the dry ingredients thoroughly, add cold water, a little at a time, stirring briskly, until a rather thick batter results. Bake like flapjacks. Wholesomer than plain flour flapjacks. These are better with an egg or two added, and if mixed with milk instead of water. Snow can be substituted for eggs, as described above.

Buckwheat Cakes.—

> 1 pint buckwheat flour,
> ½ pint wheat flour,
> 2 tablespoonfuls baking powder,
> ½ teaspoonful salt.

Mix to a thin batter, preferably with milk. A couple of eggs make them light, or make snow cakes.

Syrup.— Mix maple or brown sugar with just enough water to dissolve it, and heat until clear. If white sugar is used, caramel it by putting it dry in a pan and heating until browned; then add water to dissolve it.

TOAST, FRITTERS, DUMPLINGS, ETC.—

Stale Bread.— Biscuit or bread left over and dried out can be freshened for an hour or two by dipping quickly in and out of water and placing in the baker until heated through; or, the biscuit may be cut open, slightly moistened, and toasted in a broiler.

If you have eggs, make a French toast by dipping the slices in whipped eggs and frying them.

With milk, make milk toast: heat the milk, add a

BREADSTUFFS 357

chunk of butter and some salt, toast the bread, and pour milk over it. Heat the milk gradually to the simmering point, but do not let it boil, lest it burn.

Stale bread may also be dipped into smoking hot grease. It will brown immediately. Stand it edgewise to drain, then lay on hot plate. Cut into dice for soups.

Fried Quoits.— Make dough as for biscuit. Plant a stick slanting in the ground near the fire. Have another small, clean stick ready, and a frying-pan of lard or butter heated sissing hot. There must be enough grease in the pan to drown the quoits. Take dough the size of a small hen's egg, flatten it between the hands, make a hole in the center like that of a doughnut, and quickly work it (the dough, not the hole) into a flat ring of about two inches inside diameter. Drop it flat into the hot grease, turn almost immediately, and in a few seconds it will be cooked.

When of a light brown color, fish it out with your little stick and hang it on the slanting one before the fire to keep hot. If the grease is of the right temperature, the cooking of one quoit will occupy just the same time as the molding of another, and the product will be crisp and crumpety. If the grease is not hot enough, a visit from your oldest grandmother may be expected before midnight. (Adapted from *Lees and Clutterbuck.*)

Fritters.— A dainty variety is added to the camp bill-of-fare by fritters of fruit or vegetables, fish, flesh, or fowl. They are especially relished in cold weather, or when the butter supply is low. Being easily made and quickly cooked, they fit any time or place.

The one essential of good and wholesome fritters is plenty of fat to fry them in, and fat of the right temperature. (The best friture is equal parts of butter and lard.) Set the kettle where the fat will heat slowly until needed; then closer over the fire until a bluish smoke rises from the center of the kettle. Drop a cube of bread into it; if it turns golden-brown in one minute, the fat is right. Then keep the kettle at just this temperature. Make batter as follows:

Fritter Batter.—
  1 pint flour,
  4 eggs,
  1 tablespoonful salt,
  1 pint water or milk,
  3 tablespoonfuls butter or other grease.

Blend the salt and the yolks of the eggs (or desiccated egg). Rub the butter into this; then the flour, a little at a time; then the water. Beat well, and, if you have time, let it stand a while. If fresh eggs are used, now beat the whites to a stiff froth and stir them in. When using, drop even spoonfuls into the fat with a large spoon. When golden-brown, lift fritter out with a forked stick (not piercing), stand it up to drain, and serve very hot. The base may be almost anything: sliced fruit, minced game or meat, fish or shellfish, grated cheese, boiled rice, grated potato or green corn, etc. Anything cut to the size of an oyster is dipped in the batter and then fried; if minced or grated it is mixed with the batter. Jam is spread on bread, covered with another slice, the sandwich is cut into convenient pieces, and these are dipped in the batter. Plain fritters of batter alone are eaten with syrup. Those made of corn meal instead of flour (mixed with *warm* milk and egg) are particularly good. The variety that can be served, even in camp, is well-nigh endless.

Dumplings.— Those of biscuit dough have already been mentioned. When specially prepared they may be made as follows:

  ½ pint flour,
  1 teaspoonful baking powder,
  ¼ teaspoonful salt,
  ½ teaspoonful sugar,
  ⅙ pint milk.

The stew that they are to be cooked with should

BREADSTUFFS

be nearly done before the dumplings are started. Then mix the dry ingredients thoroughly. Wet with the milk and stir quickly into a smooth ball. Roll into a sheet three-quarters of an inch thick, and cut like biscuit. Meantime bring the stew to a sharp boil. Arrange dumplings on top of it, cover the vessel, and cook exactly ten minutes.

MACARONI.—

Boiled Macaroni.— For one-half pound macaroni have not less than three quarts of salted water boiling rapidly. Break the macaroni into short pieces, and boil thirty-five minutes for the small, forty-five minutes for the large. Then drain, and pour sauce over it, or bake it. It is better if boiled in good broth instead of water.

Tomato Sauce.—

    1 quart can tomatoes,
    1 tablespoonful butter,
    2 tablespoonfuls flour,
    1 teaspoonful salt,
    ⅛ teaspoonful pepper,
    1 teaspoonful sugar.

Rub the flour into the butter until they blend. Brown this in a pan. Add the tomatoes and simmer thirty minutes. Stir frequently. Add the seasoning, along with spices, if you wish. This makes enough sauce for 1½ pounds macaroni, but it keeps well in cold weather, and can be used with other dishes. Good in combination with the following:

Macaroni with Cheese.— After the macaroni is boiled, put it in a pan with a little butter and some grated cheese. Stir gently, and as soon as the cheese is melted, serve; or, pour the above sauce over it.

Macaroni, Baked.— Boil first, as above. Drain. Place in a deep pan, add a cupful of cold milk, sprinkle in three tablespoonfuls grated cheese and one tablespoonful butter. Then bake until brown.

Spaghetti.— This has the advantage over macaroni of not being so bulky to carry; but some do not like it so well. Speaking of bulk, if you cannot carry canned tomatoes, a very good sauce is made of Franco-American tomato purée (usually listed under SOUPS in grocers' catalogues) which is put up in cans as small as ½ pint.

"Dice one large onion and ¼ lb. of bacon and cook in a frying-pan until the onion is a light brown. Mix with this one small can of tomato purée, and, if you have it, a half cup of grated cheese. Season well and combine this with the spaghetti, which has been boiled, and blanched in cold water. Place in the baker in moderate heat for an hour. We buy plain American cheese and grate after drying: it should be packed in a push-top tin well lined with oiled paper." (*Mrs. Pinkerton.*)

PORRIDGE.—

Corn Meal Mush.— Mix two level tablespoonfuls salt with one quart meal. Bring four quarts of water (for yellow meal, or half as much for fresh white meal) to a hard boil in a two-gallon kettle. Mix the salted meal with enough *cold* water to make a batter that will run from the spoon; this is to prevent it from getting lumpy. With a large spoon drop the batter into the boiling water, adding gradually, so that water will not fall below boiling point. Stir constantly for ten minutes. Then cover pot and hang it high enough above fire to insure against scorching. Cook thus for one hour, stirring occasionally, and thinning with *boiling* water if it gets too thick.

Fried Mush.— This, as Father Izaak said of another dish, is "too good for any but very honest men." The only drawback to this gastronomic joy is that it takes a whole panful for one man. As it is rather slow to fry, let each man perform over the fire for himself. The mush should have been poured into a greased pan the previous evening, and set in a cool place over night to harden. Cut into slices one-third of an inch thick, and fry in very hot grease until nicely browned. Eat with syrup, or *au naturel*.

Polenta.— An Italian dish made from our native corn and decidedly superior to plain boiled mush. Cook mush as above for one hour. Partly fill the bake-pan with it, and pour over it either a good brown gravy, or the tomato sauce described under macaroni. Then sprinkle with grated cheese. Set the pan in the oven three minutes, or in the reflector five minutes, to bake a little.

Oatmeal Porridge.— Rolled oats may be cooked much more quickly than the old-fashioned oatmeal; the latter is not fit for the human stomach until it has been boiled as long as corn mush. To two quarts boiling water add one teaspoonful of salt, stir in gradually a pint of rolled oats, and boil ten minutes, stirring constantly, unless you have a double boiler. The latter may be extemporized by setting a small kettle inside a larger one that contains some water, with a few pebbles at the bottom to keep them apart.

CEREALS.—

Rice, Boiled.— Good precedent to the contrary notwithstanding, I contend that there is but one way to boil rice, and that is this (which is described in the words of Captain Kenealy, whose *Yachting Wrinkles* is a book worth owning):

" To cook rice so that each grain will be plump, dry, and separate, first, wash the measure of rice thoroughly in cold, salted water. Then put it in a pot of *furiously boiling* fresh water (1 cupful to 2 quarts water), no salt being added. Keep the pot boiling hard for twenty minutes, but *do not stir.* Then strain off the water, place the rice over a very moderate fire (hang high over camp-fire), and let it swell and dry for half an hour, in an uncovered vessel. Remember that rice swells enormously in cooking."

Plain boiled rice is not an appetising dish, particularly when you have no cream to eat it with; but no other cereal lends itself so well to varied combinations, not only as a breakfast food but also in soups and stews, in puddings, cakes, etc. Boiled rice with raisins is a standard dish; other dried fruit may be used. As a left-over, rice can be fried, made into pancakes or muffins, or utilized in a score of other ways, each dish tasting different from the others.

Rice, Fried.— When boiled rice is left over, spread it in a dish. When cold, cut it into cakes and fry it, for a hasty meal. It is better, though, in muffins.

Rice Muffins.— Mash very smooth half a pint boiled rice. Add slowly, stirring to a thinner paste, half a pint of milk, three beaten eggs, salt. Then make into a stiff batter with flour. Bake like dropped biscuits.

Rice with Onions.— A very good dish, quickly made, is boiled rice mixed with onions which have been chopped up and fried.

Spanish Rice.—" Mix two cupfuls of boiled rice, a large diced onion, and a can of tomato purée. Season with plenty of cayenne pepper and bake in the reflector for an hour." (*Mrs. Pinkerton.*)

Risotto.— Fry a sliced onion brown in a tablespoonful of butter. Add to this a pint of hot water and half a pint of washed rice. Boil until soft, adding more hot water if needed. Heat half a pint canned tomatoes, and stir into it a teaspoonful of sugar. When the rice is soft, salt it; add the tomato; turn into a dish and sprinkle over it a heaped tablespoonful of grated cheese.

Rice, Curried.— Same as Risotto, but put a teaspoonful of curry powder in the tomatoes and omit cheese.

Grits, Boiled.— Put in plenty of boiling unsalted water. Boil about thirty minutes; then salt and drain.

Grits, Fried.— Same as fried rice.

"Breakfast Foods."— According to directions on packages.

Left-over Cereals.— See MIXED CAKES, page 355.

CHAPTER XXI
CAMP COOKERY

Vegetables.— Soups

Fresh Vegetables.— Do not wash them until just before they are to be cooked or eaten. They lose flavor quickly after being washed. This is true even of potatoes.

Fresh vegetables go into plenty of fast-boiling salted water. Salt prevents their absorbing too much water. The water should be boiling fast, and there should be plenty of it. They should be boiled rapidly, with the lid left off the pan. If the water is as hot as it should be, the effect is similar to that which we have noted in the case of meats: the surface is coagulated into a waterproof envelope which seals up the flavor instead of letting it be soaked out. In making soup, the rule is reversed.

Dried Vegetables.— Beans and peas are to be cooked in unsalted water. If salted too soon they become leathery and difficult to cook. Put them in cold, fresh water, gradually heat to the boiling point, and boil slowly.

Dehydrated Vegetables.— When time permits they should first be soaked in cold water, according to directions on package; this makes them more tender. The onions and soup vegetables, however, can be boiled without previous soaking. Heat gradually to the boiling point and cook slowly in a covered vessel until done. When served alone they require butter for seasoning.

Canned Vegetables.— The liquor of canned peas, string beans, etc., is unfit for use and should be thrown away; this does not apply to tomatoes.

Cleaning Vegetables.— To clear cabbage, etc., from insects, immerse them, stalk upward, in plenty of cold water salted in the proportion of a large tablespoonful to two quarts. Vinegar may be used instead of salt. Shake occasionally. The insects will sink to bottom of pan.

Storing Vegetables.— To keep vegetables, put them in a cool, dry place (conditions similar to those of a good cellar). Keep each kind away from the other, or they will absorb each other's flavor.

Potatoes, Boiled.— Pick them out as nearly as possible of one size, or some will boil to pieces before the others are done; if necessary, cut them to one size. Remove eyes and specks, and pare as thinly as possible, for the best of the potato lies just under the skin. As fast as pared, throw into cold water, and leave until wanted. Put in furiously boiling salted water, then hang kettle a little higher where it will boil moderately, but do not let it check. Test with a fork or sliver. When the tubers are done (about twenty minutes for new potatoes, thirty to forty minutes for old ones) drain off all the water, dust some salt over the potatoes (it absorbs the surface moisture, and keeps leftovers from souring early), and let the pot stand uncovered close to the fire, shaking it gently once or twice, till the surface of each potato is dry and powdery. Never leave potatoes in the water after they are done; they become watery.

Potatoes, Boiled in Their Jackets.— After washing thoroughly, and gouging out the eyes, snip off a bit from each end of the potato; this gives a vent to the steam and keeps potatoes from bursting open. I prefer to put them in cold water and bring it gradually to a boil, because the skin of the potato contains an acid poison which is thus extracted. The water in which potatoes have been boiled will poison a dog. Of course we don't " eat 'em skin and all," like the people in the nursery rhyme; but

VEGETABLES

there is no use in driving the bitterness into a potato. Boil gently, but continuously, throw in a little salt now and then, drain, and dry before the fire.

Potatoes, Steamed.— Old potatoes are better steamed. A rough-and-ready method is shown on page 30.

Potatoes, Mashed.— After boiling, mash the potatoes with a peeled stub of sapling, or a bottle, and work into them some butter, if you have it, and milk. "The more you beat 'em, the better they be." Salt and pepper.

Potato Cakes.— Mould some mashed potato into cakes, season, and fry in deep fat. Or add egg and bake them brown.

Potatoes, Baked.— Nessmuk's description cannot be improved: "Scoop out a basin-like depression under the fore-stick, three or four inches deep, and large enough to hold the tubers when laid side by side; fill it with bright hardwood coals and keep up a strong heat for half an hour or more. Next, clean out the hollow, place the potatoes in it, and cover them with hot sand or ashes, topped with a heap of glowing coals, and keep up all the heat you like. In about forty minutes commence to try them with a sharpened hardwood sliver; when this will pass through them they are done and should be raked out at once. Run the sliver through them from end to end, to let the steam escape, and use immediately, as a roast potato quickly becomes soggy and bitter."

Potatoes, Fried.— Boiled or steamed potatoes that have been left over may be sliced one-quarter inch thick, and fried.

Potatoes, Fried, Raw.— Peel, and slice into pieces half an inch thick. Drop into cold water until frying-pan is ready. Put enough grease in pan to completely immerse the potatoes, and get it very hot, as directed under FRYING. Pour water off potatoes, dry a slice in a clean cloth, drop it into the sizzling fat, and so on, one slice at a time.

Drying the slices avoids a splutter in the pan and helps to keep from absorbing grease. If many slices were dropped into the pan together, the heat would be checked and the potatoes would get soggy with grease. When the slices begin to turn a faint brown, salt the potatoes, pour off the grease at once, and brown a little in the dry pan. The outside of each slice will then be crisp and the insides white and deliciously mealy.

Potatoes, Lyonnaise.— Fry one or more sliced onions until they are turning yellowish, then add sliced or diced potatoes, previously boiled; keep tossing now and then until the potatoes are fried somewhat yellow; salt and pepper to taste; you may add chopped or dehydrated parsley. Drain and serve.

Potatoes, Creamed.— Cut 1 pint cold potatoes in cubes or thin slices; put in pan and cover with milk; cook gradually until milk is absorbed. Then add 1 tablespoon butter, ½ teaspoonful salt, some pepper, and parsley. Stir a few moments, and serve.

Potatoes au Gratin.—" Chop cold boiled potatoes rather fine. Rub a tablespoonful of butter with one of flour, add ½ pint of milk, and season with salt and pepper. When this mixture has boiled, mix it with potatoes and turn into a baking dish. Sprinkle grated cheese over the top, pressing it down into the cream sauce. Bake in a quick oven until a golden brown." (*Arthur Chapman.*)

Potatoes, Stewed.— Cut cold boiled potatoes into dice, season with salt, pepper, butter, and stew gently in enough milk to cover them. Stir occasionally to prevent scorching. Or, peel and slice some raw potatoes. Cover with boiling water and boil until tender. Pour off the water. Roll a large piece of butter in flour, heat some milk, beat these together until smooth, season with salt and pepper, and bring to a boil. Then stew together five minutes. Serve very hot.

Sweet Potatoes, Boiled.— Use a kettle with lid.

VEGETABLES 367

Select tubers of uniform size; wash; do not cut or break the skins. Put them in boiling water, and continue boiling until, when you pierce one with a fork, you find it just a little hard in the center. Drain by raising the cover only a trifle when kettle is tilted, so as to keep in as much steam as possible. Hang the kettle high over the fire, cover closely, and let steam ten minutes.

Sweet Potatoes, Fried.— Skin the boiled potatoes and cut them lengthwise. Dust the slices with salt and pepper. Throw them into hot fat, browning first one side, then the other. Serve very hot.

Potatoes and Onions, Hashed.— Slice two potatoes to one onion. Parboil together about fifteen minutes in salted water. Pour off water, and drain. Meantime be frying some bacon. When it is done, remove it to a hot side dish, turn the vegetables into the pan, and fry them to a light brown. Then fall to, and enjoy a good thing!

Beans, Boiled.—Pick out all defective beans, and wash the rest. It is best to soak the beans over night; but if time does not permit, add one-quarter teaspoonful of baking soda to the parboiling water. In either case, start in fresh cold water, and parboil one quart of beans (for four men with hearty appetites) for one-half hour, or until one will pop open when blown upon. At the same time parboil separately one pound fat salt pork. Remove scum from beans as it rises. Drain both; place beans around pork, add two quarts boiling water, and boil slowly for two hours, or until tender. Drain, and season with salt and pepper.

It does not hurt beans to boil all day, provided boiling water is added from time to time, lest they get dry and scorch. The longer they boil the more digestible they become.

Left-over beans heated in a frying-pan with a little bacon grease have a pleasant and distinctive flavor.

Beans, Baked.— Soak and parboil as above, both the beans and the pork. Then pour off the water from the pork, gash the meat with a knife, spread half of it over the bottom of the kettle, drain the beans, pour them into the kettle, put the rest of pork on top, sprinkle not more than one-half teaspoonful of salt over the beans, pepper liberally, and if you have molasses, pour a tablespoonful over all; otherwise a tablespoonful of sugar. Hang the kettle high over the fire where it will not scorch, and bake at least two hours; or, add enough boiling water to just cover the beans, place kettle in bake-hole as directed on page 297, and bake all night, being careful that there are not enough embers with the ashes to burn the beans.

If a pail with thin lid must be used for a bean-pot, cover its top with a two or three-inch layer of browse or green twigs before shoveling on the embers.

Baked beans are strong food, ideal for active men in cold weather. One can work harder and longer on pork and beans, without feeling hungry, than on any other food with which I am acquainted, save bear meat. The ingredients are compact and easy to transport; they keep indefinitely in any weather. But when one is only beginning camp life he should be careful not to overload his stomach with beans, for they are rather indigestible until you have toned up your stomach by hearty exercise in the open air.

Baked Beans for Transport.—" Cook the amount thought necessary and, when finished, pour off every last drop of water, spread them out on plates, and let them dry over a slow fire, stirring constantly. When dried they can be carried in a sack or any other receptacle, and can be prepared to be eaten within five minutes by the addition of hot water. If the weather is cold, do not dry them, but spread them out and stir around with a stick. They will freeze, and if constantly stirred will be so many individual beans, hard and frozen; they can be handled or carried like so many pebbles, and will keep indefinitely. Add hot water and, as soon as thawed out, they are ready to eat." (*Edward Ferguson.*)

VEGETABLES

Onions, Boiled.— More wholesome this way than fried or baked. Like potatoes, they should be of as uniform size as possible, for boiling. Do not boil them in an iron vessel. Put them in enough boiling salted water to cover them. Cover the kettle and boil gently, lest the onions break. They are cooked when a straw will pierce them (about an hour). If you wish them mild, boil in two or three waters. When cooked, drain and season with butter or dripping, pepper, and salt. Boiled milk, thickened, is a good sauce.

Green Corn.— If you happen to camp near a farm in the "roasting-ear" season, you are in great luck. The quickest way to roast an ear of corn is to cut off the butt of the ear closely, so that the pith of the cob is exposed, ream it out a little, impale the cob lengthwise on the end of a long hardwood stick, and turn over the coals.

To bake in the ashes: remove one outer husk, stripping off the silk, break off about an inch of the silk end, and twist end of husks tightly down over the broken end. Then bake in the ashes and embers as directed for potatoes. Time, about one hour.

To boil: prepare as above, but tie the ends of husks; this preserves the sweetness of the corn. Put in enough boiling salted water to cover the ears. Boil thirty minutes. Like potatoes, corn is injured by over-boiling. When cooked, cut off the butt and remove the shucks.

Cold boiled corn may be cut from the cob and fried, or mixed with mashed potatoes and fried.

Kedgeree.— Soak 1 pint split peas overnight; drain them, add 1 pound rice, some salt, pepper, and ½ teaspoonful ginger. Stir, and cover with 1 quart water. Stir and cook slowly until done and almost dry. Make into a mound, garnished with fried onions and sliced hard-boiled eggs.

Greens.— One who camps early in the season can add a toothsome dish, now and then, to his menu by gathering fresh greens in the woods and marshes.*

As a salad (watercress, peppergrass, dandelion, wild mustard, sorrel, etc.): wash in cold salted water, if necessary, although this abstracts some of the flavor; dry immediately and thoroughly. Break into convenient pieces, rejecting tough stems. Prepare a simple French dressing, thus:

- 1 tablespoonful vinegar,
- 3 tablespoonfuls best olive oil,
- ½ teaspoonful salt,
- ¼ teaspoonful black pepper.

Put salt and pepper in bowl, gradually add oil, rubbing and mixing till salt is dissolved; then add by degrees the vinegar, stirring continuously one minute. In default of oil use cream and melted butter; but plain vinegar, salt, and pepper will do. Pour the dressing over the salad, turn the latter upside down, mix well, and serve.

A scalded salad is prepared in camp by cutting bacon into small dice, frying, adding vinegar, pepper, and a little salt to the grease, and pouring this, scalding hot, over the greens.

Greens may be boiled with salt pork, bacon, or other meat. To boil them separately: first soak in cold salted water for a few minutes, then drain well, and put into enough boiling salted water to cover, pressing them down until the pot is full. Cover, and boil steadily until tender, which may be from twenty minutes to an hour, depending upon kind of greens used. If the plants are a little older than they should be, parboil in water to which a little baking soda has been added; then drain, and continue boiling in plain water, salted.

Some greens are improved by chopping fine after boiling, putting in hot frying-pan with a tablespoonful of butter and some salt and pepper, and stirring until thoroughly heated.

Poke stalks are cooked like asparagus. They

* Nearly a hundred edible wild plants, besides mushrooms and fruits, are discussed in Volume II, under head of EDIBLE PLANTS OF THE WILDERNESS.

VEGETABLES 371

should not be over four inches long, and should show only a tuft of leaves at the top; if much older than this, they are unwholesome. Wash the stalks, scrape them, and lay in cold water for an hour; then tie loosely in bundles, put in a kettle of boiling water, and boil three-fourths of an hour, or until tender; drain, lay on buttered toast, dust with pepper and salt, cover with melted butter, and serve.

Jerusalem artichokes must be watched when boiling and removed as soon as tender; if left longer in the water they harden.

Dock and sorrel may be cooked like spinach: pick over and wash, drain, shake, and press out adhering water; put in kettle with one cup water, cover kettle, place over moderate fire, and steam thus twenty minutes; then drain, chop very fine, and heat in frying-pan as directed above.

Mushrooms.— Every one who camps in summer should take with him a mushroom book, such as Gibson's, Atkinson's, or Nina Marshall's. (Such a book in pocket form, with *colored* illustrations, is a desideratum.) Follow recipes in book. Mushrooms are very easy to prepare, cook quickly, and offer a great variety of flavors. The following general directions are condensed from McIlvaine's *One Thousand American Fungi:*

To Cleanse Mushrooms.— As they are found, cut loose well above attachment. Keep spore surface *down* until top is brushed clean and every particle of dirt removed from stem. If stem is hard, tough, or wormy, remove it. Do all possible cleaning in the field.

When ready to cook, wash by throwing into deep pan of water. Pass fingers quietly through them upward; let stand a moment for dirt to settle; then gather them from the water with fingers as a drain. Remove any adhering dirt with rough cloth. Thus wash in two or three waters. Lay to drain.

The largest amount of flavor is in the skin, the removal of which is seldom justifiable.

Concise Rule.— Cook in any way you can cook an oyster.

Broiling.— Use well-spread caps only. Place caps on double broiler, gills down. Broil two minutes. Turn and broil two minutes more. While hot, season with salt and pepper, butter well, especially on gill side. Serve on toast.

Frying.— Heat butter boiling hot in frying-pan. Fry five minutes. Serve on hot dish, pouring over them the sauce made by thickening the butter with a little flour.

Hunter's Toast.— Carry a vial of olive oil, or a small can of butter, and some pepper and salt mixed. Make fire of dry twigs. Split a green stick (sassafras, birch, or spicewood, is best) at one end; put mushroom in the cleft, broil, oil or butter, and eat from stick.

Camp Bake.— Cover bottom of tin plate with the caps, spore surface up. Sprinkle with salt and pepper. Place a bit of butter on each. Put another tin plate on top. Set on coals, or on a heated stone, fifteen minutes. No better baking will result in the best oven.

All mushrooms on the following list are delicious:

Coprinus comatus.	Lactarius volemus.
Hypholoma appendiculatum.	" deliciosus.
Tricholoma personatum.	Russula alutacea.
Boletus subaureus.	" virescens.
" bovinus.	Cantharellus cibarius.
" subsanguineous.	Marasmius oreades.
Clavaria botrytes.	Hydnum repandum.
" cinerea	" Caput-Medusæ.
" vermicularis.	Morchella esculenta.
" inæqualis.	" deliciosa.
" pistillaris.	

Canned Tomatoes.— To a pint of tomatoes add butter twice the size of an egg, some pepper, very little salt, and a tablespoonful of sugar. Boil about five minutes. Put some bread crumbs or toast in a dish, and pour tomatoes over them. Butter can be omitted. Some do not like sugar in tomatoes.

Canned Corn.— Same as tomatoes; but omit sugar and bread. Add a cup of milk, if you have it.

Miscellaneous Vegetables.— Since campers very seldom have any other fresh vegetables than potatoes and onions, I will not take up space with special recipes for others. The following timetable may some time be useful:

VEGETABLES 373

Boiling of Vegetables.

Asparagus	20 to 25 minutes
Cabbage	20 to 25 minutes
Carrots	30 to 40 minutes
Cauliflower	20 to 25 minutes
Corn (green)	15 to 20 minutes
Beans (string)	25 to 30 minutes
Beans (Lima)	30 to 35 minutes
Beans (navy, dried)	2½ to 4 hours
Beets	30 to 40 minutes
Onions	30 to 40 minutes
Parsnips	30 to 35 minutes
Peas (green)	20 minutes
Potatoes (new)	20 minutes
Potatoes (old)	30 to 40 minutes
Spinach	20 to 25 minutes
Turnips	30 to 35 minutes

SOUPS.— When Napoleon said that " soup makes the soldier," he meant thick, substantial soup — soup that sticks to the ribs — not mere broths or meat extracts, which are fit only for invalids or to coax an indifferent stomach. " Soup," says " Nessmuk," " requires time, and a solid basis of the right material. Venison is the basis, and the best material is the bloody part of the deer, where the bullet went through. We used to throw this away; we have learned better. Cut about four pounds of the bloody meat into convenient pieces, and wipe them as clean as possible with leaves or a damp cloth, but don't wash them. Put the meat into a five-quart kettle nearly filled with water, and raise it to a lively boiling pitch."

Here I must interfere. It is far better to bring the water gradually to a boil and then at once hang the kettle high over the fire where it will only keep up a moderate bubbling. There let it simmer at least two hours — better half a day. It is impossible to hasten the process. Furious boiling would ruin both the soup and the meat.

" Nessmuk " continues: " Have ready a three-tined fork made from a branch of birch or beech, and with this test the meat from time to time; when it parts readily from the bones, slice in a large onion. Pare six large, smooth potatoes, cut five of them into quarters, and drop them into the kettle; scrape the sixth one into the soup for thickening. Season with salt and white pepper to taste. When, by skirmishing with the wooden fork, you can fish up bones with no meat on them, the soup is cooked, and the kettle may be set aside to cool."

Any kind of game may be used in a similar way, provided that none but lean meat be used. Soup is improved by first soaking the chopped-up meat in cold water, and using this water to boil in thereafter. Soup should be skimmed for some time after it has started simmering, to remove grease and scum.

To anyone who knows *petite marmite* or *poule-au-pot,* these simple directions will seem barbarous — and so they are; but barbarism has its compensations. A really first-class soup cannot be made without a full day's previous preparation and the resources of a city grocery. Mulligatawny, for example, requires thirty-two varieties of spices and other condiments. No start can be made with any standard soup until one has a supply of "stock" made of veal or beef, mutton or poultry, by long simmering and skimming and straining.

In camp, stock can be made expeditiously by cutting one or two pounds of venison into thin slices, then into dice, cover with cold water, boil gently twenty minutes, take from the fire, skim, and strain. A tolerable substitute is Liebig's beef extract, or beef cubes, dissolved in water.

Onion, cloves, mace, celery seed, salt, and red or white pepper, are used for seasoning. Sassafras leaves, dried before the fire and powdered, make the gumbo *filé* of the creoles. Recipes for a few simple, nourishing soups, are given below:

Venison Soup.—"Put 4 or 5 lbs. of deer ribs in a bucket of water. Cook slowly until only half a bucket of 'stock' remains. Add 1 can tomatoes, ¼ cup rice, and salt to taste. Cook until these are done." (*Dr. O. M. Clay.*)

VEGETABLES

(2) Take 4 lbs. of lower leg bones of deer, or moose, caribou, sheep, goat, elk, etc., 2 lbs. of the meat, a large handful each of julienne and rice, a few pieces of pork, 1 teaspoonful of salt, pepper to taste, and 4 quarts of water. Crack the soup bones so that the marrow will run out, place in a large pot with the meat, water, and julienne, and boil slowly until the meat is shredded. Take out bones, add the rest of the ingredients, add hot water to make the desired quantity of soup, and boil until rice is cooked. (*Abercrombie.*)

Squirrel Soup.— Put the squirrels (not less than three) in a gallon of cold water, with a scant tablespoonful of salt. Cover the pot closely, bring to the bubbling point, and then simmer gently until the meat begins to be tender. Then add whatever vegetables you have. When the meat has boiled to a rag, remove the bones. Thicken the soup with a piece of butter rubbed to a smooth paste in flour. Season to taste.

Croutons for Soup.— Slice some stale bread half an inch thick, remove crust, and cut bread into half-inch dice. Fry these, a few at a time, in deep fat of the "blue smoke" temperature, until they are golden brown. Drain free from grease, and add to each plate of soup when serving. (See also page 356.)

Tomato Soup.— Take a quart can of tomatoes and a sliced onion. Stew twenty minutes. Meantime boil a quart of milk. Rub to a paste two tablespoonfuls each of flour and butter, and add to the boiling milk, stirring until it thickens. Now season the tomatoes with a teaspoonful of sugar, a little salt, and pepper. Then stir into the tomatoes one-half teaspoonful baking soda (to keep milk from curdling), add the boiling milk, stir quickly, and serve.

Bean Soup.— Boil with pork, as previously directed, until the beans are tender enough to crack open; then take out the pork and mash the beans into a paste. Return pork to kettle, add a cup of flour mixed thin with cold water, stirring it in slowly as the kettle simmers. Boil slowly an hour longer, stirring frequently so that it may not scorch. Season with little salt but plenty of pepper.

Pea Soup.— Wash well one pint of split peas, cover with cold water, and let them soak over night. In the morning put them in a kettle with close-fitting cover. Pour over them three quarts cold water, adding one-half pound lean bacon or ham cut into dice, one teaspoonful salt, and some pepper. When the soup begins to boil, skim the froth from the surface. Cook slowly three to four hours, stirring occasionally till the peas are all dissolved, and adding a little more boiling water to keep up the quantity as it boils away. Let it get quite thick. Just before serving, drop in small squares of toasted bread or biscuits, adding quickly while the bread is hot. Vegetables may be added one-half hour before the soup is done.

Turtle Soup.— Clean the turtle as directed in Chapter XV, leaving legs on, but skin them and remove the toes, as well as outer covering of shell. Place remaining parts, together with a little julienne, in fresh, hot water and boil until all the meat has left the bones. Remove bones, add hot water for required quantity of soup. Salt and pepper to taste. A tablespoonful each of sherry and brandy to each quart of liquid improves the flavor.

Condensed Soups.— Follow directions on wrapper.

Skilligalee.— The best thing in a fixed camp is the stock-pot. A large covered pot or enameled pail is reserved for this and nothing else. Into it go all the clean fag-ends of game — heads, tails, wings, feet, giblets, large bones — also the leftovers of fish, flesh, and fowl, of any and all sorts of vegetables, rice, or other cereals, macaroni, stale bread, everything edible except fat. This pot is always kept hot. Its flavors are forever changing, but ever welcome. It is always ready, day or night, for the hungry varlet who missed connections or who wants a bite between meals. No cook who values his peace of mind will fail to have skilly simmering at all hours.

CHAPTER XXII
BEVERAGES AND DESSERTS

Coffee.— To have coffee in perfection the berry must be freshly roasted and freshly ground. This can be done with frying-pan and pistol-butt; yet few but old-timers take the trouble.

There are two ways of making good coffee in an ordinary pot. (1) Put coffee in pot with cold water (one heaped tablespoonful freshly ground to one pint, or more coffee if canned ground) and hang over fire. Watch it, and when water first begins to bubble, remove pot from fire and let it stand five minutes. Settle grounds with a tablespoonful of cold water poured down spout. Do not let the coffee boil. Boiling extracts the tannin, and drives off the volatile aroma which is the most precious gift of superior berries. (2) Bring water to hard boil, remove from fire, and quickly put coffee in. Cover tightly and let steep ten minutes. A better way, when you have a seamless vessel that will stand dry heat, is to put coffee in, place over gentle fire to roast until aroma begins to rise, pour boiling water over the coffee, cover tightly, and set aside.

Tea is best made in a covered enameled pail. Leave the lid off until the water boils hard, then drop the tea in (one heaped teaspoonful to the pint is a common rule, but it depends on the strength of the brand you use), remove from the fire at once, stir it to make tea settle, cover tightly, and steep *away* from fire *four minutes by the watch.* Then strain into a separate vessel. A better way is to use a tea-ball, or put the tea in a small square

BEVERAGES AND DESSERTS

of cheesecloth, tie it up in loose bag form, and leave some string attached to remove it with.

A good deal of the aroma escapes from a teapot, but little from a covered pail.

If tea is left steeping more than five or six minutes the result is a liquor that would tan skin into leather. To boil is — well, it is like watering a rare vintage. You know what the old Colonel said: " My friend, if you put water in that wine, God'll never forgive you!"

Chocolate.— For each quart of boiling water scrape up four tablespoonfuls of chocolate. Boil until dissolved. Then add half a pint milk. Stir with a peeled stick until milk has boiled up once. Let each man sweeten his own cup.

Cocoa.— Follow directions on can.

DESSERTS.— *Dried Fruit.*— Evaporated or dried apples, apricots, peaches, prunes, etc., are misprized, under-rated, by most people from not knowing how to prepare them. The common way is to put the fruit on to stew without previous soaking, and then boil from one-half hour to two hours until it is more or less pulpy. It is then flat and insipid, besides unattractive to the eye.

There is a much better way. Soak the fruit at least over night, in clear cold water — just enough to cover — with or without spices, as you prefer. If time permits, soak it from twenty-four to thirty-six hours. This restores the fruit to its original size and flavor. It is good to eat, then, without cooking. To stew, merely simmer gently a few minutes in the water in which the fruit was soaked. This water carries much of the fruit's flavor, and is invaluable for sauce.

California prunes prepared in this way need no sugar. Dried apples and peaches have none of the rank taste by which they are unfavorably known, but resemble the canned fruit. Apricots properly soaked are especially good.

Jelly from Dried Fruit.— I was present when a Southern mountain woman did some " experiencin'," with nothing to guide her but her own wits. The result was a discovery of prime value to us campers. Here are the details — any one can follow them:

Wash one pound of evaporated apples (or common sun-dried apples of the country) in two waters. Cover with boiling water, and put them on to stew. Add boiling water as required to keep them covered. Cook until fruit is soft (about half an hour). Strain off all the juice (cheesecloth is convenient), and measure it. There will be, probably, a quart. Put this juice on the fire and add half its own measure of granulated sugar (say a scant pound — but measure it, to make sure of the proportion).

Now boil this briskly in a broad, uncovered vessel, without stirring or skimming, until the juice gets syrupy. The time varies according to quality of fruit — generally about twenty minutes after coming to a full boil. When the thickened juice begins to "flop," test it by letting a few drops drip from a spoon. When the drops thicken and adhere to the spoon, the syrup is done. There will be a little more than a pint. Pour it out. As soon as it cools it will be jelly, as good as if made from fresh fruit and much better than what is commonly sold in the stores.

The apples remaining can be spiced and used as sauce, or made into pies or turnovers, or into apple butter by beating smooth, adding a teacupful of sugar, spicing, and cooking again for fifteen or twenty minutes.

If preferred, a second run of jelly can be made from the same apples. Cover again with boiling water, stew about fifteen minutes, add sugar by measure, as before. This will take less boiling than the first juice (about seven minutes). Enough jelly will result to make nearly or quite a quart, all told, from one pound of dried apples and about one and one-half pounds of sugar.

Apricots or any other tart dried fruit can be used

BEVERAGES AND DESSERTS 381

instead of apples. Sweet fruit will not do, unless lemon juice or real apple vinegar is added.

Wild Fruits.— The time of ripening of American wild fruits is given in Volume II, under the heading EDIBLE PLANTS OF THE WILDERNESS.

Pie.— It is not to be presumed that a mere male camper can make a good pie-crust in the regular way; but it is easy to make a wholesome and very fair pie-crust in an irregular way, which is as follows: Make a glorified biscuit dough by mixing thoroughly 1 pint flour, 1 teaspoonful baking powder, ½ teaspoonful salt, rubbing in 4 heaped tablespoonfuls of lard (better still, half-and-half of butter and lard), and making into a soft dough with cold water. In doing this, observe the rules given under *Biscuit*. The above quantity is enough for a pie filling an 8 x 12 reflector pan. Roll the dough into a thin sheet, as thin as you can handle, and do the rolling as gently as you can.

From this sheet cut a piece large enough for bottom crust and lay it in the greased pan. The sheet should be big enough to lap over edge of pan. Into this put your fruit (dried fruit is previously stewed and mashed), and add sugar and spice to taste. Then, with great circumspection and becoming reverence, lay on top of all this your upper crust. Now, with your thumb, press the edges of upper and lower crust together all around, your thumb-prints leaving scallops around the edge. Trim off by running a knife around edge of pan. Then prick a number of small slits in the top crust, here and there, to give a vent to the steam when the fruit boils. Bake as you would biscuits.

Note that this dough contains baking powder, and that it will swell. Don't give the thing a name until it is baked; then, if you have made the crust too thick for a pie, call it a cobbler, or a shortcake, and the boys, instead of laughing at you, will ask for more.

Snits und Knepp.—This is a Pennsylvania-Dutch dish, and a good one for campers. Take some dried apples and soak them over night. Boil until tender. Prepare knepp as directed for potpie dough, only make a thick batter of it instead of a dough. It is best to add an egg and use no shortening. Drop the batter into the pan of stewing apples, a large spoonful at a time, not fast enough to check the boiling. Boil about ½ hour. Season with butter, sugar, and cinnamon.

Apple Dumpling.— Make a biscuit dough (see page 347) and roll out to ¼ inch thick. Peel and quarter some apples and remove the cores. Put four quarters together and cover it with a globe of dough. Put in a cloth and boil like pudding. (page 384) for 25 minutes.

To bake dumplings: roll the dough quite thin, cover as above, and bake.

Fruit Cobbler.— Make up your dough as directed under *Pie,* excepting omit baking powder, and use ½ pound of mixed butter and lard to 2 pints flour. Mix with coldest spring water, and have your hands cold. After putting under crust in greased pan, pour in scant 3 pints of fruit, which may be either fresh, canned, or evaporated (soaked as explained under *Dried Fruits*), leaving out the free juice. Cover with upper crust, bake brown, and serve with milk or pudding sauce.

Doughnuts.— Mix 1 quart of flour with 1 teaspoonful of salt, 1 tablespoonful of baking powder, and 1 pint of granulated sugar, and ½ nutmeg grated. Make a batter of this with 4 beaten eggs and enough milk to make smooth. Beat thoroughly and add enough flour to make a soft dough. Roll out into a sheet ½ inch thick and cut into rings or strips, which may be twisted into shape. Fry by completely immersing in very hot fat; turn when necessary. Drain and serve hot.

Gingerbread.— Mix 1 cup molasses, 1 tablespoonful ground ginger, ½ teaspoonful salt, ½ cup melted butter or drippings, 1 cup milk, 3 cups flour with 2 teaspoonfuls baking powder mixed in it. Bake ½ hour.

BEVERAGES AND DESSERTS 383

Cookies.— Mix 4 cups flour with 3 teaspoons baking powder and 1 cup sugar; pour into this 4 tablespoons melted butter or drippings; add 1 cup raisins and 1 teaspoon cinnamon and cloves or allspice. Mix with enough water to make of the consistency of biscuit dough. Roll out to about ½ inch thick (or thinner if raisins are omitted). Cut with top of baking powder can, and bake to a light brown.

Puddings are either baked in an oven or reflector, or boiled in a cloth bag. Baked puddings are quickest and easiest to manage. A few examples of simple puddings are given below. They may be varied indefinitely, according to materials available. Deep tin pudding pans are convenient to bake in. Snow may be substituted for eggs (see page 353).

Rice Pudding.— Mix 1 pint cold boiled rice with 1 quart milk and sugar to taste. Put in a well-greased pan, dust nutmeg or cinnamon over the top, and bake slowly one hour. Seeded raisins are an agreeable addition. Mix them in before baking. To stone them, keep them in lukewarm water during the process. A couple of eggs make the pudding richer.

Fruit Pudding.— Line a deep dish or pan, well greased, with slices of buttered bread. Then put in a layer of fruit, dusting it with sugar and dotting with small lumps of butter. Repeat these alternate layers until the dish is full, the last layer being bread. Bake ½ to ¾ hour, with moderate heat. Eat hot, with the sweet sauce given below.

Cottage Pudding.—

    1 pint flour,
    ½ pint sugar,
    ½ pint milk,
    2 heaped tablespoonfuls butter,
    1 egg,
    2 teaspoonfuls baking powder,
    Grated rind of a lemon,

Mix thoroughly the flour and baking powder. Rub the butter and sugar to a cream, add the milk and egg beaten together; then the lemon rind. Add this to the flour and mix well. Butter a pan well to prevent scorching and dredge it with flour or powdered bread-crumbs. Pour in the batter, and bake about half an hour in hot oven.

A richer pudding is made by using one-half pound butter and two eggs.

A cupful of stoned raisins, minced figs, or dates, added to the batter, converts this into a good fruit pudding. Nutmeg, cinnamon, or other flavoring may be substituted for lemon.

Batter Pudding.—

>½ pint flour,
>1 pint milk,
>1 heaped tablespoonful butter,
>6 eggs.

Beat flour and milk into a smooth batter. Then add the eggs, beaten light. Stir all well together, adding the butter in tiny lumps. Dip a clean cloth bag into hot water, dredge it with flour, pour the batter into this, tie up firmly, and put into plenty of boiling water. Keep this boiling steadily for an hour. Then dip the bag quickly in cold water and remove cloth with care not to break the pudding. Serve very hot, with a sauce.

Plain Plum Duff.—

>1 quart flour,
>1 heaped teaspoonful baking powder,
>2 tablespoonfuls sugar,
>1 ℔. seeded raisins.
>¾ ℔. suet (or see below).

Venison suet chopped fine, or the fat of salt pork minced up, will serve. Marrow is better than either. Mix the dry ingredients intimately. Then make up with half a pint of water. Put this into a cloth bag prepared as in the preceding recipe. Since suet puddings swell considerably, the bag must be large enough to allow for this. Place in enough boiling water to cover, and do not let it check boiling until done (about two hours). Add

BEVERAGES AND DESSERTS

boiling water as required to keep the bag covered. Turn the bag upside down when pudding begins to set, or the fruit will all go to the bottom; turn it around now and then to prevent scorching against sides of pot. When done, manipulate it like cottage pudding. Serve with sweet sauce.

A richer duff can be made by spicing and adding molasses, or the rind and juice of a lemon.

Sweet Sauce for Puddings.— Melt a little butter, sweeten it to taste, and flavor with grated lemon rind, nutmeg, or cinnamon.

Brandy Sauce.— Butter twice the size of an egg is to be beaten to a cream with a pint of sugar and a tablespoonful of flour. Add a gill of brandy. Set the cup in a dish of boiling water and beat until the sauce froths.

Fruit Sauce.— Boil almost any fresh fruit until it is quite soft. Squeeze it through cheesecloth, sweeten to taste, heat it, and pour the sauce over your pudding. Spices may be added during the final heating.

Hard Sauce.— Work 2 tablespoonfuls of butter with a small cupful of sugar to a cream. Flavor with a little nutmeg, lemon juice, brandy, or whatever may be your preference.

CHAPTER XXIII
COOK'S MISCELLANY

Dish Washing.— Gilbert Hamerton, in his *Painter's Camp*, dwells lovingly upon all the little details of camp life, excepting this:

5 P. M. Cease painting for the day. Dine. . . . After dinner the woeful drudgery of cleaning-up! At this period of the day am seized with a vague desire to espouse a scullery-maid, it being impossible to accommodate one in the hut without scandal, unless in the holy state of matrimony: hope no scullery-maid will pass the hut when I am engaged in washing-up, as I should be sure to make her an offer.

There is a desperately hard and disagreeable way of washing dishes, which consists, primarily, in " going for " everything alike with the same rag, and wiping grease off one dish only to smear it on the next one. There is another, an easier, and a cleaner way: First, as to the frying-pan, which generally is greasiest of all: pour it nearly full of water, place it level over the coals, and let it boil over. Then pick it up, give a quick flirt to empty it, and hang it up. Virtually it has cleaned itself, and will dry itself if let alone. Greasy dishes are scraped as clean as may be, washed with scalding water, and then wiped. An obdurate pot is cleaned by first boiling in it (if you have no soap powder) some wood ashes, the lye of which makes a sort of soap of the grease; or it may be scoured out with sand and hot water. Greasy dishes can even be cleaned without hot water, if first wiped with a handful or two of moss, which takes up the grease; use first the dirt side of the moss as a scourer, then the top. To scour greasy knives and forks, simply

COOK'S MISCELLANY

jab them once or twice into the ground. Rusty ones can be burnished by rubbing with a freshly cut potato dipped in wood ashes. The scouring rush (*Equisetum hymenale*), which grows in wet places and along banks throughout the northern hemisphere, has a gritty surface that makes an excellent swab. It is the tall, green, jointed, pipe-stem-like weed that children amuse themselves with, by pulling the joints apart. The sooty outside of a pot is readily cleaned with a bit of sod ("monkey soap").

In brief, the art of dish washing consists first in cleaning off nearly all the grease before using your dish-cloth on it. Then the cloth will be fit to use again. Dish-cloths are the supplies that first run short in an average outfit.

COOK'S MEASURES

45 drops water=1 teaspoonful=1 fluid dram.
2 teaspoonfuls=1 dessertspoonful.
4 teaspoonfuls=1 tablespoonful.
2 tablespoonfuls=1 fluidounce.
4 tablespoonfuls=1 wineglassful.
8 tablespoonfuls=1 gill.
2 gills=1 cup.
4 gills=1 pint (1 ℔. water).
2 pints=1 quart (1 ℔. flour).
4 quarts=1 gallon.
2 gallons (dry)=1 peck.
4 pecks (dry)=1 bushel.

OUTFITTER'S DATA

Baking powder .... 1 ℔.=1¼ pints.
Beans, dried .... 1 qt.=1¾ ℔s.
Coffee, roasted whole .... 1 qt.=10 oz.
Corn meal .... 1 qt.=1¼ ℔s.
Flour .... 1 qt.=1 ℔.
Macaroni .... 1 ℔.=8⅞x2⅜x2⅜ in.
Oatmeal .... 1 qt.=⅝ ℔.
Peas, split .... 1 qt.=1¾ lbs.
Rice .... 1 qt.=2 ℔s.
Salt, dry .... 1 qt.=1⅞ ℔s.
Soda crackers are about 3 times as bulky as bread, weight for weight.
Sugar, granulated .... 1 qt.=1¾ ℔s.
Tea .... 1 qt.=½ ℔.

388 CAMPING AND WOODCRAFT

Bacon, breakfast .... 1 flitch=5–8 lbs., average.
Salt pork .... 1 side=30–40 lbs., average.
Salt pork .... 1 belly=20 lbs., average.
Butter, closely packed ...... 1 lb.=1 pint.
Butter, creamery .... 1 lb.=4⅝x2½x2½ in.
Eggs, desiccated .... 1 lb.=6x3x3 in.=4 doz. fresh.
Eggs, fresh .... 1 doz. (average)=1½ lbs.
Lard .... 3 lb. pail=5x5 in.
Lard .... 5 lb. pail=6x6 in.
Milk, evaporated .... 7 oz. can=2½x2½ in.
Milk, evaporated .... 12 oz. can=3⅜x3 in.
Milk, evaporated .... 1 lb. can=4⅜x3 in.
Apples, evaporated .... 1 lb. (14 oz.)=7⅛x4½x2 in.
Apples, evaporated .... 1 peck=6 lbs
Corn, canned .... 1 can=2¼lbs.=4⅝x3⅜ in.
Fruit, canned, small can, same as corn.
Fruit, canned, large can, same as tomatoes.
Tomatoes, canned .... 1 can=2½ lbs.=4⅞x4⅛ in.
Lemons .... 1 doz.=2 lbs.=2 qts.
Raisins, stemmed .... 1 lb.=1⅓ pints.
Carrots .... 1 qt.=1¼ lbs.
Onions .... 1 qt.=1 lb.
Potatoes .... 1 peck=15 lbs.
Sweet potatoes .... 1 peck=14 lbs.

A TABLE

FOR READY REFERENCE IN CHOOSING WHAT TO COOK

All recipes in this book are here grouped under *Quick, Medium,* or *Slow,* according to the time they take. Everything under *Quick* can be prepared in less than 25 minutes, and so is specially suitable for breakfast or luncheon.

The table also shows at a glance what recipes call for milk, butter, or eggs, and what do not. The following abbreviations are used:

E = Eggs required (whole or desiccated).
B = Butter required.
M = Milk required (may be evaporated or powdered).
E^*= Eggs desirable, but may be omitted.
B^*= Butter desirable, but other fat may be substituted.
M^*= Milk desirable, but water may be substituted.
¶ = Made over from previously cooked material.

COOK'S MISCELLANY

Quick
(*Under 25 minutes*)

Fresh Meat, Game.
Broiled meat, game. *B.** 292
Fried meat, game 291
Chops 292
Kabobs 296
Brains, fried 306
Brains and eggs. *E.* 306
Liver, fried 306
Kidneys, fried 306
Milt, broiled 307
Venison sausages 307
¶Croquettes. *B, E.* 307
Small birds, roasted. *B.** 319
¶Deviled birds. *B.* 319
Frog legs, broiled or fried. *B.** 328

Fish.
Fish, fried 321
Fish, broiled. *B.** 322
Fish, skewered 322

Shellfish.
Oysters, stewed. *B, M.* 329
Oysters, fried. *E.* 329
Oysters, scalloped. *B.* 330
Oysters, sauté. *B.* 330

Cured Meat.
Bacon, broiled, fried, toasted 332
Salt pork, broiled or fried 333
Ham, broiled or fried 333
Bacon, or ham, and eggs. *E.* 332
Pork fritters 333
Pork sausages 334
Slumgullion 335
Dried beef, creamed. *M, B.** 335
Canned meat, heated 336

Cured or Canned Fish.
Smoked herring, toasted 337
Smoked herring, fried. *B.** 337
Sprats 337
Salmon, creamed. *M.* 337
Salmon, scalloped. *B, M.* 337
Salmon on toast. *B, E, M.* 337
Sardines, fried. *B,* E.** 338

Gravies.
Braising gravy 297
Frying gravy 302

Broiling gravy. B.* 292
Boiling gravy. B. 303
Roasting gravy 303
Beef extract gravy 303
Cream gravy. B, M. 303
Rabbit gravy 310
Bacon gravy, thin 332
Pork gravy, thick. M.* 333
Roux 302
Onion gravy 303

Eggs.
Eggs, poached (fresh). B,* E. 340
Eggs, boiled (fresh). E. 340
Eggs, fried (fresh). E. 338
Eggs, scrambled (fresh or desiccated). B,* E. .. 339
Omelets (fresh or desiccated). B,* E. 339
Eggs, stirred. B, E. 340

Bread.
Biscuit loaf 346
Biscuits 347
Dropped biscuits 348
Breakfast rolls. B, E, M. 348
Bannocks 344
Dough gods 351
Unleavened bread 351
French toast. E. 356
Milk toast. B, M. 356
¶Rice muffins. E, M. 362

Pancakes, etc.
Flapjacks, plain 355
Egg pancakes. E. 355
Snow pancakes 355
¶Mixed cakes 355
Corn batter cakes. E,* M.* 356
Buckwheat cakes. E,* M.* 356
Syrup 356
"Gritted" bread 354
Fried quoits 357
Fritters. B,* E, M.* 357
Dumplings. M.* 358

Porridge, etc.
¶Fried mush 360
¶Fried grits, rice 362
¶Rice with onions 362
Rolled oats 361
Breakfast cereals 362

Vegetables.
Potatoes, fried 365

COOK'S MISCELLANY

Potatoes, stewed. B, M.	366
¶Potato cakes. E,* M.*	365
¶Potatoes, mashed. B,* M.	365
¶Potatoes, lyonnaise	366
¶Potatoes, creamed	366
¶Sweet potatoes, fried	367
Potatoes and onions, hashed	367
Green corn, roasted. B.*	369
Greens, boiled (some kinds). B.*	369
Mushrooms. B.	371
Canned tomatoes, stewed. B.*	372
Canned corn, stewed. B,* M.*	372

Soups.

Condensed soups	376
Tomato soup. B, M.	375

Beverages.

Coffee	378
Tea	378
Chocolate. M.	379
Cocoa. M.	379

Sauces.

Barbecue sauce. B.*	296
Mustard sauce. B.	304
Venison sauce. B.	304
Broiled venison sauce. B.	304
Giblet sauce. B,* M.*	316
Celery sauce. B, M.	320
Cranberry sauce	320
Curry sauce. B, M.*	320
Butter sauce. B.	325
White sauce. B, M.	325
Lemon sauce. B, M.	325
Parsley sauce. B.*	304
India sauce. B, M.	325
Sweet sauce. B.	385
Brandy sauce. B.	385
Fruit sauce	385
Hard sauce. B.	385
Salad dressing	370

MEDIUM.

(25 to 45 minutes.)

Fresh Meat, Game.

Cured venison, steamed	336
Small mammals, roasted	294
Heart, braised	306
Liver, roasted	306
Game pot pie. B.*	307

Curry of game. B.* 308
Game pie 308
Small game, barbecued 309
Small game, fricasseed 315
Duck, roasted or baked 317
Grouse, roasted 319
Game birds, boiled 320

Fish.
Fish, baked 323
Fish, boiled. B. 324
Fish, roasted. B.* 323
Fish, planked. B.* 323
Fish, steamed 324
Fish chowder. B,* M.* 326
Fish cakes. E. 327
Fish roe 328
Eel, stewed. M. 328
Frog legs, creamed. B, M. 328

Shellfish, etc.
Clams, baked. B. 330
Clam chowder. M. 330
Crayfish, boiled 329
Crabs, deviled 331

Cured Meats.
Bacon and liver 306
Pork and hardtack 333
Corned beef hash 335
Canned meat stew 335

Cured Fish.
Salt fish, broiled 336
Codfish balls. B.* 337

Bread.
Army bread 348
Corn pone 352
Johnny-cake 352
Corn dodgers 352
Ash cake 352
Corn bread. B, E, M. 353
Corn batter bread. E, M. 353
Snow bread 353

Cereals, etc.
Rice, boiled 361
Rice, curried 362
Risotto 362
Grits, boiled 362
Macaroni, boiled 359

COOK'S MISCELLANY

Vegetables.
Desiccated vegetables 363
Potatoes, boiled 364
Potatoes, steamed 365
Potatoes, baked 365
¶Potatoes *au gratin*. B, M. 366
Sweet potatoes, boiled 366
Green corn, boiled 369
Kedgeree 369
Greens, boiled (some kinds). B.* 369

Desserts..
Pie. B.* 381
Doughnuts. E, M. 382
Snits und Knepp. B, E.* 381
Apple dumplings 382
Fruit cobbler. B. 382
Gingerbread. B,* M. 382
Cookies. B.* 383
Cottage pudding. B, E, M. 383

Sauces.
Tomato sauce. B. 359

SLOW.
(*Over 45 minutes.*)

Fresh Meat, Game.
Roasted meat, big game 294
Braised meat, big game 296
Baked meat, big game 297
Boiled meat, big game 299
Stewed meat, big game 300
Steamed meat, big game 301
Barbecued meat, big game 296
Kidneys, stewed 306
Marrow bones, boiled 307
Moose muffle, boiled 307
Tongue, boiled 307
Turkey, goose, roasted 315
Turkey, boiled 316
Jambolaya 308
Turtle, boiled 329

Cured Meat.
Lobscouse 335
Bacon, salt pork, ham, boiled 332
Ham and macaroni 360
Ham chow 334

Cured Fish.
Salt fish, boiled 336
Codfish, stewed 336

Codfish hash 337
Bread.
Sour-dough bread 349
Salt-rising bread 349
Lungwort bread 350
Porridge, etc.
Corn mush 360
Polenta 361
Macaroni, with cheese. B. 359
Macaroni, baked. B, M. 359
Spaghetti, baked 359
Rice, Spanish 362
Vegetables.
Beans, boiled 367
Beans, baked 367
Onions, boiled. B,* M.* 369
Green corn, baked 369
Greens, boiled (some kinds). B.* 369
Soups from raw materials. B.* 373
Desserts.
Dried fruit, stewed 379
Jelly from dried fruit 379
Rice pudding. E,* M. 383
Batter pudding. B, E, M. 384
Plum duff 384
Snow pudding 383

INDEX TO VOLUME I

Almanacs, 172
Ants, 220, 256
Apple dumpling, 382
Ash cake, 344, 352
Axes, 113
  Care of, 114, 115, 224

Bacon, 186
  and eggs, 332
  Boiled, 332
  Broiled, 332
  Fried, 332
  omelet, 332
  Toasted, 332
Baking bread, 342
  in a hole, 297
  ashes, 344, 352
  clay, 298
  clay oven, 345
  Dutch oven, 342
  embers, 298
  frying pan, 344
  kettle, 343
  reflector, 347
  the hide, 297
  meat, 297
  on a slab, 345
Baking powder, 346
Bandages, Triangular, 174
Bannocks, 344
Barbecuing, 296, 309
Bark as fuel, 230, 233
Bean soup, 375
Beans, 195
  Baked, 367
  and dried, 368
  with birds, 297
  Boiled, 367
Bear, Butchering, 274
  Cooking, 292, 296
Beaver tail, Cooking, 314
Bed-bugs, 256

Bed rolls, 136
Bed tick, 134
Bedding, 124
Beef extract, 199
  Gravy from, 303
Beef, Corned, 187, 334
  Hash, 335
Beef, Dried, 187
  Creamed, 335
Belts, 145
Benches, Rustic, 218
Beverages, 197, 378
Birds baked in clay, 299
  with beans, 297
  Broiled, 315
  Deviled, 319
  Fricasseed, 315
  Fried, 315
  Hanging to ripen, 282, 314
  Roasting, 317
  Small, To cook, 319
  To dress, 282
  dry, 279
  keep, 283
  ship, 283
Biscuit, 347
  Dropped, 348
  loaf, 344, 346
Bites and stings, 249, 257
Bittern, Cooking, 319
Blanket, To roll up in, 128
  To wear, 128
Blankets, 127
  Airing, 224
Blow-flies, 250, 275, 276
Boiling, 299, 324
  at high altitudes, 300
Boots, 156
  Felt, 161
Brains and eggs, 306
  Cooking, 306

INDEX

Braising, 296
Bread, 191
  Army, 348
  Baking, 342
  Corn, 352, 353
  Fried, 357
  Gritted, 352
  Lungwort, 350
  Raising in pot, 350
  Salt-rising, 349
  Snow, 353
  Sour-dough, 349
  Stale, To freshen, 347, 356
  Unleavened, 351
  Wheat, 346
Breakfast foods, 362
Breeches, 144
Broiling, 292, 322
Browse bag, 134
Buckskin jackets, 147
  moccasins, 158
Buckwheat cakes, 356
Bunks, 53
Butchering game, 264
Butter, 191
  Care of, 220
  Keeping, 191

Cakes, Mixed, 355
Calories, 181, 202
Cameras, 176
Camp conveniences, 223
  cookery, 290
  Exposure of, 216
  furniture, 53, 218
  making, 208
  pests, 241
  Privacy of, 216
  sanitation, 222
  sites, 208, 212, 216
Camp-fires, 101, 225, 230, 231
Camping, 20
  Preparations for, 207
  System in, 217
Candlesticks, Improvised, 221
Caps, 160
Capsules, 197
Carbohydrates, 179

Caribou hide, 131, 148, 158
Carryalls, 137
Catfish, To skin, 285
Celluloid varnish, 73
Centipedes, 259
Cereals, 185, 193
  Cooking, 361
  Left-over, 362
Chairs, Camp, 55
Cheese, 191
Chests, Camp, 206
Chocolate as a beverage, 379
  as food, 194
Chopping-block, 223
Chops, Cooking, 294
Chowder, Clam, 330
  Fish, 326
Chuck boxes, 207
Citric acid, 197
Clam chowder, 330
Clams, Baked, 330
  Stewed, 301
Cloth, Dyeing, 74
  Waterproofing, 72, 148
Clothes hangers, 58
  line, 224
Clothing, 138
  Colors, 143, 147, 162
  for cold weather, 162
  women, 163
Coals, To keep alive, 229
Coats, 146
  Mackinaw, 162
Cocoa, 199, 379
Codfish balls, 337
  hash, 337
  Stewed, 336
Coffee, 197
  Brewing, 378
Cold storage, 67, 220, 287
Comfort in camp, 124
Comforters, 126, 128
Compass, 168
Comrades and camp bores, 26
Condiments, 199
Cook's measures, 387
  miscellany, 387
  time-tables, 317, 373, 388
Cookers, Fireless, 66

INDEX

Cookery, Camp, 290
Cookies, 383
Cooking fires, 226
Cooking in the rain, 47
  utensils, 64, 118
  without utensils, 293, 295-299, 301, 309, 314, 315, 317, 319, 322-324, 330, 340, 344-346, 365, 369
'Coons, 263, 281
  Cooking, 312
Corn batter bread, 353
  batter cakes, 352, 356
  bread, 352, 353
  Canned, Cooking, 372
  dodgers, 352
  Green, 369
  meal, 192
  mush, 360
  pone, 352
Coots, Cooking, 318
Cot mattresses, 53
Cots, 53
Cow-bell for children, 60
Crabs, Deviled, 331
Crane, Cooking, 228
Crayfish, Cooking, 329
Crisco, 197, 292,
Croquettes, 307
Croutons, 375
Crotches, 218
Crutch, To make, 219
Curry of game, 308

Deer, Butchering, 264, 269
  Carrying on litter, 266
  pickaback, 267
  Dragging on ground, 265
  Hanging to butcher, 268, 274
  Packing on saddle, 265
  Skinning, 270
  skins, Preserving, 275
Desserts, 379
Dining place, 218
Dish washing, 386
Ditty boxes, 165
Dock, Cooking, 371
Dog trolley, 59

Dopes, Fly, 243
Dough, To mix without pan, 346
Dough-gods, 351
Doughnuts, 382
Drawers, 141
Dressing game and fish, 264
Driftwood, 239
Duck, Baked, 317
  in clay, 299
  Fish-eating, 318
  Stewed, 318
  To dress, 282, 316
Duck, Cotton, 32
Duff, Plum, 384
Dumplings, 308, 358
  Apple, 382
Dunnage bags, 164
Dutch ovens, 64
Dyeing cloth, 74

Economies, 24
Eel, Boiled, 327
  Stewed, 328
  To skin, 285
Eggs, 188
  Boiled, 340
  Desiccated, 189
  To cook, 338
  Fried, 338
  Frozen, 189
  Omelets, 339, 340
  Poached, 340
  Roasted, 340
  Scrambled, 339
  Snow as substitute for, 354
  Stirred, 340
  To pack, 189
    preserve, 189
    test, 189
Electric flashers, 173
Elk, Butchering, 273
Exposure of camp, 216
Eye glasses, 173

Fats, 179
Feet, Care of, 150
Fence, 222
Field glasses, 177
Filters, 212

Fire, Backlog, 231, 236
  Building, 235
  Camp, 225
  Cooking, 225
  Dinner, 227
  for baking, 229
  grates, 63
  Hunter's, 230
  in trench, 230, 235
    wet weather, 234
  Indian's, 232
  irons, 64, 228
  Luncheon, 226
  Precautions, 214, 234, 237, 239
  regulations, 234
  Starting in stove, 63
  Winter camp, 231
Fires, Forest, 214, 234, 239
Fireless cookers, 66
First aid, 59
  kits, 58, 174
Fish, Baked, 323
  in clay, 298
  Boiled, 300, 324
  Broiled, 294, 322
  cakes, 327
  Canned, 188
  chowder, 326
  Cooking, 321
  Creamed, 327, 337
  Cured, 188
    To cook, 336
  Fried, 321
  from muddy waters, 284, 327
  Frozen, 305
  Planked, 323
  Roasted, 323
  roe, Cooking, 328
  Salt, Cooking, 336
  Skewered, 324
  To clean, 283
    dry, 288
    keep, 286
    kill, 285
    salt, 289
    scale, 284
    ship, 288
    skin, 284
    steak, 285

Flapjacks, 355
Flashlights, 173
Fleas, 249
Flies, 222, 256
  Blood-sucking, 250, 255
  Blow, 250, 275, 276
Flies, Tent, 35, 51
Floss, Dental, 118
Flour, 192
Fly dopes, 243
Food, 178
  as a source of energy, 181
  Care of, 220, 259, 262, 263, 275, 364
  Digestibility, 185
  Nutritive values, 179, 182, 368
  Packing, 205
  Variety, 180
  Weights and measures, 387
Footwear, 150
  Rubber, 161
Fricassees, 292
Fritter batter, 358
Fritters, 357
  Pork, 333
Fritures, 197, 292, 321, 357
Frog legs, Cooking, 328
Fruit, 196
  cobbler, 382
  Dried, Cooking, 379
    Jelly from, 379
  Wild, 381
Frying, 291, 302, 321
Frying-pans, 120
Fuel, 212
  Best, 237
  Driftwood as, 239
  Hardwoods as, 236
  Softwoods as, 236, 238
Furniture, Camp, 53
  Rustic, 218

Gall-bladder, 272, 282
Game, Big, Cooking, 290
  birds. *See* Birds
  Cooking, 305
  Curry of, 308

INDEX

Game.— *Continued.*
  Dressing and keeping, 264
  Hanging to ripen, 274, 282, 291, 314
  pie, 308
  pot pie, 307
  Shipping small, 283
  Small, Cooking, 308
Gingerbread, 348, 382
Gloves, 160
Gnats, 255
Goggles, 173
Going light, 109
Goose, Roasted, 317
  To dress, 282
Gravy, 297, 302, 303
  Bacon, 332
  Cream, 303
  for boiled meat, 303
  roast meat, 303
  from beef extract, 303
  Onion, 303
  Pork, 333
Greens, Wild, 369
Grilling on a rock, 293
Grits, Boiled, 362
  Fried, 362
Gritted bread, 354
Groundhog, Cooking, 313
Ground sheets, 37, 107
Grouse, Baking with beans, 297
  Broiled, 319
  Roasted, 319
  To dress, 282, 283
  dry, 279
Guy frames, 46

Ham, 187
  and eggs, 333
  macaroni, 334
  Boiled, 333
  Broiled, 333
  chow, 334
  Fried, 333
Hardtack, 191, 333, 335
Hardwoods and softwoods, 236
Hare. *See* Rabbit

Hash, Codfish, 337
  Corned beef, 335
  Potato and onion, 367
Hat-bands, 139, 160
Hatchets, 165
Hats, 159
Head nets, 160
Headwear, 159
Heart, Cooking, 306
Herrings, Smoked, Cooking, 337
Hitch, Magnus, 47
Hobnails, 154
Hogs, 222
Horn, Huntsman's, 118

Ice, 220, 287
Insect bites and stings, 249, 257
Insecticides, 247
Insects in camp, 256
  Noxious, 241

Jackets, Leather, 147
Jackknives, 167
Jambolaya, 308
Jelly from dried fruit, 379
Jerusalem artichokes, Cooking, 371
Johnny-cake, 352

Kabobs, 296
Khaki, canvas, 33
Kedgeree, 369
Kidneys, Cooking, 306
Kindling, 233
Kit bags, 165
Knickerbockers, 145
Knives, Pocket, 167
  Sheath, 166

Lanolin, 149
Lanterns, 60, 117
Lard, 197
Larrigans, 157
Latrine, 223
Leather, To waterproof, 154
Left-overs, 307, 319, 355, 360, 362, 365, 366, 376

Leggings, 145
Lemonade powder, 197
Lightning, 215
Liver, Cooking, 306
Lobscouse, 335

Macaroni, 193
  Baked, 359
  Boiled, 359
  with cheese, 359
Mackinaws, 147, 162
Mammals, Small, To dress, 280
Mapping, 169
Map cases, 171
Maps, 170
Marrow-bones, 307
Match, To light in wind, 234
Matchboxes, 173
Matches, To waterproof, 173
Mattresses, 53, 134
  Air, 135
Measures, Cook's, 387
Meat, Canned, 187, 336
  Stewed, 335
  Care of, 220, 275
  Cooking, 290
  Cured, To cook, 332
  Curing, 276
  Frozen, 305
  "Jerked," 277
  Salt, Boiled, 299
Medical kits, 58
Mending canvas, 40
Mice, 263
Midges, 255
Milk, Condensed, 190
  Powdered, 190
  To heat, 300
Milt (spleen), To cook, 307
Moccasins, 157
Moose, Butchering, 273
  muffle, To cook, 307
Mosquito bars, 39, 55, 74, 106
  dopes, 243
Mosquitoes, 160, 241
Mulligan (skilly), 376

Munson shoe lasts, 151
Mush, Boiled, 360
  Fried, 360
Mushrooms, Cooking, 371
  Edible, 372
Muskrat, To cook, 313
  dress, 281

Neckerchiefs, 143
"No-see-ums," 255
Nut butter, 196
Nuts, 196

Oatmeal porridge, 361
Oil, Olive, 197
Oiled cloth, 71, 73
Oilskins, 160
  Care of, 161
Omelets. *See* Eggs
Onions, 194
  Boiled, 369
Opossum. *See* 'Possum
Outfits, Individual, 112
Outfitter's data, 387
Outfitting, 23, 109
Oven, Clay, 345
  Dutch, 64
    To use, 296, 342
  Reflecting, 121
    To use, 296, 323, 347
  Sheet steel, 122
Overalls, 160
Overshirts, 142, 162
Oysters, Fried, 329
  Roasted, 330
  Sauté, 330
  Scalloped, 330
  Steamed, 301
  Stewed, 329

Pack, Indian, 267
Packing, 113, 205
Pacs, Shoe, 157
Pancakes, Corn, 352, 356
  Egg, 355
  Snow, 355
Parboiling, 300, 305
Parsly butter, 304
Pea soup, 376
Peas, 195
Pegs, To drive in tree, 220

INDEX

Personal kits, 164
Pests of the woods, 241
Photography, 176
Pie, Fruit, 381
  Game, 308
  Pot, 307
Pillows, 135
Pine knots, 233
Plasmon, 192
Plaster, Adhesive, 116
Pliers, 115
Plover, Cooking, 319
  To dress, 283
Plum duff, 384
Poisoning, Ptomaine, 188, 286
Poke shoots, Cooking, 370
Polenta, 361
Ponchos, 146, 160
Porcupine, 259
  Cooking, 313
  To dress, 313
Pork and hardtack, 333
  fritters, 333
  Salt, 187
    Boiled, 333
    Broiled, 333
    Fried, 333
Porridge, 360
'Possum, Baked, 311
  Roasted, 312
  To dress, 311
Pot pie, Game, 307
Potatoes and onions hashed, 367
  au gratin, 366
  Baked, 365
  Boiled, 364
  cakes, 365
  Creamed, 366
  Fried, 365
  Lyonnaise, 366
  Mashed, 365
  Steamed, 365
  Stewed, 366
  Sweet, Boiled, 366
    Fried, 367
Pots, 119
Pouches, 165
Privacy of camp, 216
Protective coloration, 162

Protein, 179, 185, 202
Provisions. *See* Food
Ptomaine poisoning, 188, 286
Pudding, Batter, 384
  Cottage, 383
  Fruit, 383
  Rice, 383
  sauce, 385
  Suet, 384
Punkies, 255
Puttees, 145

Quail, Cooking, 319
Quilts, 126, 129
Quoits, Fried, 357

Rabbit, Baked, 310
  Fried, 310
  Roasted, 310
  Stewed, 310
  To dress, 281, 310
Raccoon. *See* 'Coon.
Ragouts, 300
Rail, Cooking breast of, 319
Ration lists, 200
  Cruisers' and campers', 203
  U. S. Army, 200
Rats, 263
Reflectors, 121
  Baking in, 347
  Roasting in, 296, 323
Refrigerators, 67, 220, 287
Refuse, Disposal of, 222
Repair kits, 116, 161, 176
Repairs, Quick, 116
Rice, 193
  Boiled, 361
  Curried, 362
  Fried, 362
  muffins, 362
  Spanish, 362
  with onions, 362
Risotto, 362
Roasting, 294
Roasting-ears, 369
Rolls, Breakfast, 348
Roughing it, 110, 124
Route sketching, 169

Roux, 302
Rubber clothing, 160
　footwear, 161

Saccharin, 193
Salad dressing, 370
Salads, Scalded, 370
　Wild, 370
Salmon, Creamed, 337
　on toast, 337
　Scalloped, 337
Salt, 199
Sandals for wading, 157
Sanitation, 222
Sardines on toast, 338
Sauce, 303
　Brandy, 385
　Butter, 325
　Celery, 320
　Cranberry, 320
　Curry, 320
　Fruit, 385
　Giblet, 316
　Hard, 385
　India, 325
　Lemon, 325
　Mustard, 304, 326
　Pudding, 385
　Tomato, 359
　Venison, 304
　White, 325
Sausage, Pork, 334
　Venison, 307
Saws, 59
Scales, 115
Scent glands, 305, 310, 312–314
Scorpions, 257
Shade, 215
Shear lashings, 47
Shears, Tent, 47
Sheath knives, 166
Shellfish, Cooking, 329
　Steamed, 301
Shelter-cloths, 97
Shelves, 58
Shipping fish, 288
　Game, 283
Shirts, 142
　Mackinaw, 147, 162
Shoe laces, 135, 151

Shoe-pacs, 157
Shoes, 151
　Breaking in, 152
　Canvas, 159
　Care of, 152
　Waterproofed, 153
Sink, Camp, 223
Sirup, 194
　To make, 356
Skilligalee, 376
Skins, Preserving, 275
Skunk-bite, 262
Skunks, 260
Sleeping bags, 126, 129, 131, 135
Slickers, 160
Slumgullion, 335
Smudges, 256
Sneakers, 159
Snipe, Cooking, 319
　To dress, 283
Snits und Knepp, 381
Snow bread, 353
　glasses, 173
　pancakes, 355
Soap, 119, 141, 176
Socks, 142
　German, 146, 161
Soda, Substitutes for, 354
Sod-cloths, 37, 74
Sorrel, Cooking, 371
Soup, 373
　Bean, 375
　Canned, 188
　Condensed (dry), 188
　Croutons for, 375
　Pea, 376
　Squirrel, 375
　stock, 374
　Tomato, 375
　Turtle, 376
　Venison, 374
Spades, 59, 115
Spaghetti, 359
Spleen, Cooking, 307
Sprats, Cooking, 337
Spring box, 221
Springs, 210
Squirrel, Barbecued, 309
　Broiled, 309
　Fried, 309

INDEX 403

Squirrel.— *Continued.*
  soup, 375
  Stewed, 309
  To dress, 280
Stakes, To drive, 219
Stationery, 172
Steaming fish, 324
  meat and vegetables, 301
Stewing, 300
Stings, 249, 257
Storm set, 45
Storms, 51
Stove-pipe holes, 40
  spark arrester, 63
Stoves, Cook, 60
  Heating, 63, 79
Stove-shield, 63
Stuffing for fish, 323
  rabbit, 310
  turkey, 315
Sugar, 193
Sweaters, 147
Sweets, 193
System in camping, 217

Table for choosing what to cook, 388
Tables, Camp, 56
  Rustic, 218
Tarantulas, 258
Tarp bed-sheet, 134
Tea, 198
  Steeping, 378
Tepees, 81
Tent, Action of wind on, 51
  canopies, 36
  Care of, 40
  door, 39
    weights, 39
  flies, 35, 51
  floors, cloth, 105, 107
    wooden, 49
  furnishings, 221
  furniture, 53
  ground, 212
  hangers, 58
  making, 88, 98
  materials, heavy, 31
    light, 69, 71
  mending, 40

Tent.— *Continued.*
  on rocky or sandy ground, 50
  shears, 46, 99, 106
  tripods, 83, 104
  parrels, 93, 96
  poles, 40, 45, 47, 78, 82, 94
  rental, 41
  ropes, 34, 75
  slides, 75
  stakes and pins, 40, 43, 50, 75
  striking, 43
  trenching, 49
  ventilation, 38
  windows, 38, 74
  with side bars, 48
  workmanship, 34, 74
Tents, "A," 92
  Alpine, 94, 96
  Baker, 98
  Bell, 78
Tents, Camp-fire, 100
  Canoe, 102
  Colored, 35
  Commissary, 101
  "Compac," 103
  Conical, 78
    To pitch, 79
  "Explorer's," 106
  for fixed camps, 29
    shifting camps, 68, 76
  Frazer, 84
  George, 85
  Hudson Bay, 95
  Insect-proof, 106
  Lean-to, 98
  Light, 68
  Marquee, 84
  Miner's, 82
  Pyramidal, 81
  Ross, 96
  Royce, 85
  Second-hand, 41
  Separable shelter, 96
  Semi-pyramidal, 84
  Shelter, 96
  Sibley, 78
  Snow, 105
  Tarpaulin, 98

Tents.— *Continued.*
　Tropical, 37
　Wall, heavy, 29
　　light, 76
　　To pitch, 41
　Waterproof, 34, 69
　Wedge, 92
　　To pitch, 92
　Whymper, 94
Ticks, 247, 255
Time-tables, Cook's, 388
　for boiling vegetables, 373
　roasting birds, 317
Toast, French, 356
　Milk, 356
Toilet articles, 176
Tomato soup, 375
Tomatoes, 195
　Cooking, 307
Tongue, Cooking, 307
Tools, 59, 113
Trees and lightning, 215
　Neighborhood of, 214
Tropics, Pests of, 251
Trousers, 144
Trout, To clean, 283
Turkey, Boiled, 316
　Roasted, 295, 315
　Stuffing for, 316
　To dress, 282
Turtle, Cooking, 329
　Soup, 376

Underclothing, 139
Union suits, 141

Vacations, 17
Vegetables boiled with meat, 299
　Canned, 195
　Cooking, 363
　Cleaning, 363
　Dehydrated, 195, 200
　　Cooking, 363
　Dried, Cooking, 363
　Fresh, 194
　Storing, 364
　Time-table for boiling, 373

Venison, Cooking, 305
　Cured, Cooking, 336
　Sauce for, 304
　sausages, 307
　soup, 374
　To cure, 276
　　hang for ripening, 274, 291
　jerk, 277
　ship, 288
Vests, 148

Waders, 157, 161
Wall pockets, 58, 137
Warbles, 311
Wash-boilers, 206
Wash-stand, 222
Washing clothing, 141, 142
　dishes, 386
Watches, 169
Water, 209
　Alkaline, 210
　To clarify, 211
　　cool, 212
　　purify, 211
Waterfowl, To dress, 282, 316
Waterproof cloths for tents, 34, 69
　tents, 34, 69
Waterproofing cloth, 72
　leather, 154
　matches, 173
　Woolens, 148
Waterproofs, 160
Weight of game, Computing, 280
Weights and measures of food, 387
Whistles, 170
Wild, Call of the, 17
Wilderness, Charm of, 21
Wind, Action of, on tents, 51
Wolverines, 262
Women, Clothing for, 163
Woodcock, Cooking, 319

Woodchuck, Cooking, 313
Woods as fuel, 236
  Green, as fuel, 237
  hard to split, 237
  Hardwoods and softwoods, 236
  Spitfire, 237
  Uninflammable, 236

Woodsman, Qualities of, 24, 110
Wool *vs.* cotton, 127, 128, 140, 144
Woolens, To waterproof, 148
Wounds, Treatment of, 175

CAMPING
AND
WOODCRAFT

A HANDBOOK FOR VACATION CAMPERS
AND FOR
TRAVELERS IN THE WILDERNESS

BY
HORACE KEPHART
Author of "Our Southern Highlanders," "Sporting
Firearms," "Camp Cookery," etc.

Vol. II
WOODCRAFT

NEW YORK
OUTING PUBLISHING COMPANY
1917

Copyright, 1917, by
OUTING PUBLISHING COMPANY

CONTENTS

CHAPTER		PAGE
I	WOODCRAFT	13
II	GETTING LOST—BIVOUACS	19
III	PATHFINDING	37
IV	NATURE'S GUIDE POSTS	49
V	BLAZES—SURVEY LINES—USE OF THE COMPASS	60
VI	ROUTE SKETCHING — MAPPING—MEASURING	80
VII	TRIPS AFOOT	97
VIII	PACKS FOR PEDESTRIANS	118
IX	HOW TO WALK—A HUNTER'S PACK—GOING ALONE	136
X	CONCENTRATED FOODS	150
XI	MARKSMANSHIP IN THE WOODS	173
XII	AXEMANSHIP — QUALITIES AND UTILIZATION OF WOOD	187
XIII	TOMAHAWK SHELTERS—AXEMEN'S CAMPS — CACHES — MASKED CAMPS	215
XIV	CABIN BUILDING—RUSTIC FURNITURE	236
XV	BARK UTENSILS—BAST ROPES AND TWINE—ROOT AND VINE CORDAGE—WITHES AND SPLITS	256
XVI	KNOTS, HITCHES AND LASHINGS	271

CONTENTS

XVII	Trophies—Pelts, Buckskin and Rawhide	298
XVIII	Tanning Skins—Other Animal Products	321
XIX	Cave Exploration	337
XX	Bee Hunting	354
XXI	Edible Plants of the Wilderness	367
XXII	Living off the Country—*In Extremis*	403
XXIII	Accidents and Emergencies: Their Backwoods Treatment	422
	Index	470

ILLUSTRATIONS

		PAGE
1	Following the Wrong Stream	22
2	Ox-bow Bends	23
3	Need of Base-line	39
4	One Blaze=*A*-way from Camp	41
5	Two Blazes=*To*-wards Camp	41
6	Bush Mark	42
7	Use of Divides	46
8	Numbering Sections of a Township	66
9	Subdivision of Sections	67
10	Compass Variation	74
11	Meridian by Sun	76
12	True North and South	77
13	Big Dipper and Pole Star	78
14	Route Sketch by Pacing	81
15	Map by Combining Route Sketches	83
16	Route Sketch, by C. H. Morrill	90
17	Hitches on Measuring Line	91
18	Laying Out a Right Angle	92
19	Width of River by Compass	93
20	Measuring Width without Compass	93
21	Measuring a Height	94
22	Extemporized Level	95
23	Pack Harness with Head Strap	119
24	U. S. A. Knapsack	123
25	Rucksack with Flap	123
26	Plain Rucksack	124
27	Rucksack in Use	125
28 29	Norwegian Knapsack	126
30	Tourist's Knapsack	127
31	Nessmuk Pack Sack	127
32	Duluth Pack Sack	129
33	Whelen Pack Sack	129
34	Pack Basket	132
35	Abercrombie Pack Frame	132
36	Felling Tree	190
37	Boggled Notch	190
38	True Notch	190
39	Logging Up	192

ILLUSTRATIONS

		PAGE
40	Scoring and Hewing	201
41	Maul	202
42	Gluts	202
43	Cross-section of Tree Trunk	203
44	Rail Splits	203
45	Splitting a Log	204
46	Splitting out Bolts	207
47	Block for Clapboards	207
48	Brake for Riving Boards	208
49	Splitting with a Froe	208
50	"Run-out" Rift	209
51	Springing the Rift	209
52	Double Bolting for Shingles	210
53	Shaving Horse	211
54	Spanish Windlass	213
55	Lopped Tree Den	217
56	Tripod Shelter Frame	217
57	Stake Frame for Lean-to	219
58	Shear Frame for Lean-to	219
59	Bark Tilt	222
60	Bark Lean-to	223
61	Beehive Lodge Frame	223
62	Beehive Lodge (covered)	223
63	Wikiup Frame	224
64	Wattled Work	224
65	Slab Camp	226
66	Log and Frame Camp	228
67	Camp Plan	230
68	Masked Camp	233
69	Log Cabin (ground plan)	237
70	Saddle Notch	242
71	Round Notch	242
72	Tenon-shaped End	242
73	"Trough" Corner	242
74	Fitting Joists	243
75	Log Cabin (end view)	244
76	Fireplace (vertical section)	246
77	Cabin Door	249
78	Pole Bunk	250
79	Table	251
80	Stool	252
81	Bench	252
82	Easy Chair	252
83	Split-bottom Chair	253
84	Fox Wedge	253
85	Bottoming Chair with Splits	254
86	Rustic Chair	254

ILLUSTRATIONS

PAGE

87	Folds for Water-tight Vessel	258
88	Bark Kettle	258
89	Bark Water Bucket	260
90	Bark Trough or Basin	260
91	Bark Barrel	261
92	Bark Berry Pail	261
93	Pocket Cup	261
94	Bark Dipper	263
95	Fold for Fish Bucket	263
96	Bark Fish Bucket	264
97	Becketing Hoops	269
98	Parts of Rope	272
99	Overhand Knot	272
100	Double Overhand Knot	272
101	Figure-of-Eight Knot	272
102	Thief Knot	272
103	Granny Knot	272
104	Reef Knot	272
105	Weaver's Knot	272
106	Double Bend	272
107	Carrick Bend	272
108	Lapped Overhand Knot	272
109	Water Knot	272
110	Double Water Knot	272
111	Leader Knot	276
112	Half Hitch	276
113	Two Half Hitches	276
114	Multiple Hitch	276
115	Rolling Hitch	276
116	Fisherman's Bend	276
117	Blackwall Hitch	276
118	Clove Hitch (over post)	276
119	Clove Hitch (overhand)	276
120	Clove Hitch and Half Hitch	276
121	Magnus Hitch	276
122	Cleat Tie	276
123	Timber Hitch	276
124	Killick Hitch	276
125	Ring Hitch	276
126	Lark's Head	276
127	Catspaw	276
128	Latigo Lash	280
129	Openhand Eye Knot	280
130	Midshipman's Hitch	280
131	Bowline Knot	280
132	Fisherman's Eye Knot	280

ILLUSTRATIONS

		PAGE
133	Loop Knot	280
134	Central Draught Loop	280
135	Slip Knot	280
136	Draw Knot	280
137	True Bow Knot	280
138	Slippery Hitch	280
139	Slippery Clove Hitch	280
140	Running Bowline	284
141	Running Noose with Stopper	284
142	Lark Boat Knot	284
143	Sheet Bend with Toggle	284
144	Hitching Tie	284
145	Hitching Tie (another)	284
146	Sheepshank	284
147	Bowline on a Bight	284
148	Man Sling	284
149	Boatswain's Chair	284
150	Plank Sling	284
151	Bale Hitch	284
152	Pack Sling	284
153	Harness Hitch	284
154	Can Sling	290
155	Parcel Lashing	290
156	Bottle Cork Tie	290
157	Handcuff Knot	290
158	Ledger Lashing	290
159	Putlog Lashing	290
160	Malay Hitch	290
161	Paling Hitch	290
162	Lever Knot	290
163	Necklace Tie	290
164	Pole Splice	290
165	Rod Winding	294
166	Loop Bend	294
167	Eight Bend	294
168	Jam Hitch	294
169	Double Hitch	294
170	Tiller Hitch	294
171	Double Loop	294
172	Loop to Line	294
173	Loop on Knot	294
174	Half Hitch Jam Knot	294
175	Common Dropper Loop	294
176	Jam Knot	294
177	Turle Knot	294
178	Eight Knot	294
179	Reverse Knot	294

ILLUSTRATIONS

		PAGE
180	Bow Knot	294
181	Taxidermist's Knife	299
182	Skinning a Head	300
183	Bear Skin Stretched to Dry	304
184	Pelt Stretcher	307
185	Splicing Thongs	316
186	Horn Cup	328
187	Lard Pail Lantern	334
188	Cross-section of Cavern	342
189	Map of Part of Mammoth Cave	345
190	Runway Snare	405
191	Baited Snare	406
192	Head of Rattlesnake	437
193	Surgeon's Knot	450

CAMPING AND WOODCRAFT

CHAPTER I

WOODCRAFT

From the autumn of 1903 to the winter of 1906 I lived, most of the time, alone in a little cabin on the Carolina side of the Great Smoky Mountains, surrounded by one of the finest primeval forests in the world. My few neighbors were born backwoodsmen. Most of them dwelt in log cabins of one or two rooms, roofed with clapboards riven with a froe, and heated by hardwood logs in wide stone fireplaces. Many had no cooking-stoves, but baked on the hearth and fried their meat over the embers.

Nearly every man in the settlement was a skilled axeman and a crack shot. Some of them still used home-made muzzle-loading rifles with barrels over four feet long. Some of the women still worked at home-made spinning-wheels and looms. Coonskins and ginseng passed as currency at the little wayside stores. Our manner of life was not essentially changed from that of the old colonial frontier.

To complete this historic setting, we had for neighbors the Eastern Band of Cherokees, who still hold a bit of their ancient patrimony, on the Okona Lufty. These Indians, while classed as civilized, have by no means forgotten all their aboriginal arts. You may find them, even now, betimes, slipping like shadows through the forest, killing small game with cane blow-guns, much longer than themselves, and small arrows with thistle-down wrapped round the butts so as to fit the bore.

To one coming from cities, it was a strange environment, almost as though he had been carried back, asleep, upon the wings of time, and had awakened in the eighteenth century, to meet Daniel Boone in flesh and blood.*

In such a situation it was natural, nay imperative, that one should pick up and practice certain arts long lost and forgotten by civilized communities but quite essential in our backwoods way of living. I began, to be sure, with the advantage of experience gained on many hunting and camping trips in other lands; but in this new field I had to make shift in a different way, and fashion many appliances from materials found on the spot. The forest itself was not only my hunting-ground but my workshop and my garden.

Into this novel and fascinating game I entered with keenest zest, and soon was going even "farther back" than the native woodsmen themselves. I gathered, cooked, and ate (with certain qualms, be it confessed, but never with serious mishap) a great variety of wild plants that country folk in general do not know to be edible. I learned better ways of dressing and keeping game and fish, and worked out odd makeshifts in cooking with rude utensils, or with none at all. I tested the fuel values and other qualities of a great many kinds of wood and bark, made leather and rawhide from game that fell to my rifle, and became more or less adept in other backwoods handicrafts, seeking not novelties but practical results.

To what degree I was reverting to the primitive came home to me one day when a white dame, find-

---

*For an account of this experience, with descriptions of the southern mountains and their primitive inhabitants, see *Our Southern Highlanders*, by Horace Kephart (Outing Publishing Co., New York).

ing Will Tallahlah giving me a lesson in Cherokee, remarked rather sourly to the redskin: "You needn't teach *him* anything; he's more of an Indian than you are."

Seldom during those three years as a forest exile did I feel lonesome in daytime; but when supper would be over, and black night closed in on my hermitage, and the owls began calling all the blue devils of the woods, one needed some indoor occupation to keep him in good cheer: and that is how I came to write my first little book on camping and woodcraft.

Since then I have spent several more years in "the sticks," at much the same kind of life, save that now I had as partner one of the best woodsmen in this country, a man so genuinely a scholar in his chosen lore that he could well afford to say, as once he did to me: "I've studied these woods and mountains all my life, Kep, like you do your books, and I don't know them all yet, no sirree." And I now say to the reader, for myself, just what Bob said to me about himself, save that my experience covers a less period of time.

In the school of the woods there is no graduation day. What would be good woodcraft in one region might be bad bungling in another. A Maine guide may scour all the forests of northeastern America, and feel quite at home in any of them; but put him in a Mississippi canebrake, and it is long odds that he would be, for a time,

> Perplexed, bewildered, till he scarce doth know
> His right forefinger from his left big toe.

And a southern can cracker would be quite as much at sea if he were turned loose in a spruce forest in winter. But it would not take long for either of these men to "catch on" to the new conditions; for both are shifty, both are cool-headed, and both are keen observers. Any man may blunder once, when confronted by strange conditions; but none will repeat the error unless he be possessed by the notion that he has nothing new to learn.

Woodcraft may be defined as the art of finding one's way in the wilderness and getting along well by utilizing Nature's storehouse. When we say that Daniel Boone, for example, was a master woodsman, we mean that he could confidently enter an unmapped wilderness, with no outfit but what was carried by his horse, his canoe, or on his own back, and with the intention of a protracted stay; that he could find his way through the dense forest without man-made marks to guide him; that he knew the habits and properties of trees and plants, and the ways of fish and game; that he was a good trailer and a good shot; that he could dress game and cure peltry, cook wholesome meals over an open fire, build adequate shelter against wind and rain, and keep himself warm through the bitter nights of winter—in short, that he knew how to utilize the gifts of Nature, and could bide comfortably in the wilderness without help from outside.

When one travels with a guide, it is the guide's woodcraft that pulls him through. When he goes on his own hook, he must play the woodsman himself. Woodcraft shows at its best when we "go light" through difficult and unknown country. Its supreme test is in an emergency, when the equipment, or essential parts of it, have been lost or destroyed through some disaster.

As for book-learning in such an art, it is useful only to those who do not expect too much of it. No book can teach a man how to swing an axe or follow a faint trail. Nor is it of much account to one who merely learns by rote, without using his own wits and common sense as he follows the pages. Yet a good book is the best stepping-stone for a beginner. Without it he might bog and flounder a long time without aim or method. It gives a clear idea of general principles. It can show, at least, how *not* to do a thing—and there is a good deal in that—half of woodcraft, as of any other art, is in knowing what to avoid. That is the difference between a true knot and a granny knot, and it can be shown by a sketch as well as with string in hand.

In this work I have preferred to give full details, so far as the book goes. One's health and comfort in the wilds very often depend upon close observance of just such details as breathless people would skip or scurry over. Moreover, since this is not a guide-book to any particular region, I have tried to keep in mind a variety of conditions existing in different kinds of country, and have suggested alternative methods or materials, to be used according to circumstances. One might, perhaps, compress into a vest-pocket manual all the expedients of woodcraft that would have to be practised in one certain locality, say the Adirondacks, but it would be of little use in a different sort of country.

Of course, no one person is likely to find all of this volume directly useful to himself. I must ask him to accept my assurance, based on a considerable correspondence with outdoor men in many countries, that there is no chapter in it but is of interest to somebody. Each reader is supposed to pick out for himself what bears on his own problems.

The first volume of this work, *Camping,* is intended mainly for parties who go well equipped and are guided by natives of the country, and who have adequate means of transportation, or for those who go into fixed camp and stay there until the vacation is over. This one, on *Woodcraft,* is for those who travel light, in the real wilderness, rove about a good deal, and sometimes scatter, every man for himself, with his life in his own hands.

In the following chapters I offer suggestions on forest travel, pathfinding, route sketching, what to do if lost, outfits for trips afoot, marksmanship in the woods, emergency foods, qualities and utilization of wood and bark, camp making with tomahawk or axe, cabins and rustic furniture, caches and masked camps, knots and lashings, buckskin and rawhide, tanning pelts, bee hunting, living off the country, cave exploration, first aid to the injured, and other shifts and expedients that are handy when one is far from shops and from hired help.

I have little to say, here, about the selection of arms and tackle, about hunting, fishing, trailing, trapping, mountaineering, and nothing about field photography, canoeing, snowshoeing, or the management of horses and pack trains, because each of these topics deserves a book by itself, and we now have good ones on all of them.*

Woodcraft properly relates only to the *forest* wilderness. The literature of outdoor sport is getting us used to such correlative terms as plainscraft, mountaincraft, and even icecraft and snowcraft. This sort of thing can be overdone; but we need a generic term to express the art, in general, of getting on well in wild regions of any and all kinds, whether in forests, deserts, mountains, plains, tropics or arctics; and for this I would suggest the plain English compound *wildcraft*.

If any one should get the impression from these pages that camping out with a light outfit means little but a daily grind of camp chores, questionable meals, a hard bed, torment from insects, and a good chance of starvation and broken bones at the end, he will not have caught the spirit of my intent. It is not here my purpose to dwell on the charms of free life in a wild country; rather, taking all that for granted, I would point out some short-cuts, and offer a lift, here and there, over rough parts of the trail. No one need be told how to enjoy the smooth ones. Hence it is that I treat chiefly of difficulties, and how to overcome them.

*See the series of *Outing Handbooks*, and lists of outdoor books in outfitters' catalogues.

CHAPTER II

GETTING LOST—BIVOUACS

When a man fixes up his pack and strikes out alone into strange woods, just for a little adventure, not caring where he may come out, he may be lost all the time, in one sense, but in a better sense he is at home all the time. Not for a moment does he worry about the future; he is exploring new territory —that is all.

But if one sets out for a certain destination, expecting to reach it by a given time, and loses the trail, he will be anxious at once, and the longer this continues, the more it will get on his nerves. Still we would hardly call him lost, so long as he retains a good idea of the general direction in which he should travel.

A man is really lost when, suddenly (it is always suddenly), there comes to him the thudding consciousness that he cannot tell, to save his life, whether he should go north, east, south or west. This is an unpleasant plight to be in, at any time; the first time that it is experienced the outlook will seem actually desperate.

Instantly the unfortunate man is overwhelmed by a sense of utter isolation, as though leagues and leagues of savage forest surrounded him on all sides, through which he must wander aimlessly, hopelessly, until he drops from exhaustion and starvation. Nervously he consults his compass, only to realize that it is of no more service to him now than a brass button. He starts to retrace his steps, but no sign of footprint can he detect. He is seized with a panic of fear, as irrational but quite as urgent as that which swoops upon a belated urchin when he is passing a country graveyard at night. It will take a mighty effort of will to rein himself in and check a headlong stampede.

PANIC.—In such predicament as this, a man is really in serious peril. The danger is not from the wilderness, which, pitiless niggard though it be to the weak-minded or disabled, can yet be forced to yield food and shelter to him who is able-bodied and who keeps his wits about him. No: the man's danger is from himself.

I have heard old woodsmen say that there is no use in offering advice to novices about what they should do if they get lost, because a lost man is an insane man, anyway, and will remember nothing that has been told him. Certainly it is true that if a man in such a strait permits panic to conquer him, he is likely either to perish or to come out of the woods a gibbering lunatic. There have been many such cases. But it is not true that they are the rule. Thousands of wayfarers have been lost for a day, two days, or longer, without losing their self-command. And there really is no valid excuse for an able-bodied person going out of his head from being bewildered in the big woods so long as he has a gun and ammunition, or even a few dry matches and a jackknife. The first time I was lost,* I was rattled and shook all over. Something seemed to tell me that camp lay in a certain direction, and I felt the same impulse to rush madly toward it that one feels to dash for the door when there is a cry of "fire!" in a theater. But I did remember what old Barnes had told me: "If you get lost, *sit down!*—sit down and give yourself half an hour to think it over." I sat down, and for five minutes could not think of anything, except cold, and rain, and hunger. Then

―――――
*When speaking of compasses, in Vol. I, p. 168, I said I was not frightened the first time I was lost. This was an inadvertence. The incident there mentioned occurred the second time.

I got to drawing diagrams on the ground. Making no headway at this, I began considering how to pass the night if I remained just where I was.

This cleared my mind, robbed the woods of their spooks, and presently I was myself again. Then the actual situation flashed upon me. I saw just how I had got into this scrape, and knew that if I made a circuit of 200 yards radius I would strike the trail. Before this it had seemed at least two miles away. Well, I found it, all right. Had I listened to the demon of flight, in the first place, I would have plunged into one of the worst canebrakes in all Arkansas, and might have struggled there till I died— all within a mile and a half of my own camp.

I have been lost several times: in canebrakes, in flat woods of the overflow country, in the laurel, in fog, above the clouds (in the sense that I did not know on which side to descend from an *aiguille* or bare pinnacle of rock), and in caverns. The cave experiences were hair-raising, but the others were only incidents to chuckle over in retrospect, although I have scorched the back of more than one coat from lying too near a bivouac fire. A bad record, you will say, for one who assumes to tell others how to keep from getting lost! Well, maybe so; but the fact that I am still on deck may be some excuse for offering a little counsel as to what to do if you should get lost.

I do not think that one can get the best of wild life if he does not often "go it alone." Men who are interested in the guiding business may say otherwise. If one does go it alone, he may as well take it for granted that, sooner or later, he will get lost and have to stay out over night, or for several nights, alone. There is no man, white or red, who is not liable to lose his bearings in strange woods if he is careless. If an Indian is seldom at fault as to his course it is because he pays close attention to business; he does not lose himself in reverie, nor is his mind ever so concentrated on an object that he fails to notice irregular or uncommon things along the way. And yet, even Indians and white frontiersmen sometimes get lost.

I have been with a first-class woodsman when he got mixed up on his own home hunting-ground—an overflow from the Mississippi, flooding sixty miles inland, had swept away old landmarks, replaced them with new ones, and changed the appearance of the country; then, subsiding, it had even altered the drainage of the land. At such a time the water of a tributary may actually run upstream. In fog or snowstorm anybody can get lost. You may take a professional guide from New Brunswick, let us say, or from Florida—it matters not where—place him in a new country where outlooks are few, and where the vegetation, the rocks and soil, and the general features of the country, are strange to him, and, if he does not get lost, it will be because he thinks more about avoiding it than he does about anything else.

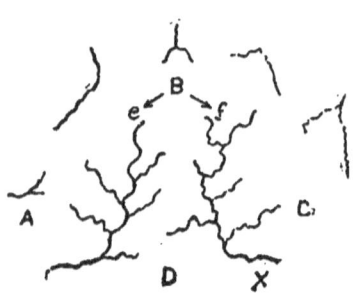

Fig. 1.—Following the Wrong Stream

Those who scout the idea of their ever losing bearings are such as have traveled little in strange lands, or have never ventured far without a native guide. Personally, I would rather get lost now and then than be forever hanging on to a guide's coat-tail. It is a matter of taste. Anyway, I shall never again have the willyjigs as I had 'em that first time, when I was actually within forty rods of a plain trail.

IN THE MOUNTAINS.—There is little excuse for getting lost, in fair weather, in a mountainous or undulating country where there are plenty of watercourses, unless one gets on the wrong side of a divide that separates two streams which do not run into each other. Thus, in Fig. 1, let ABC be a main

BIVOUACS

divide, *BD* a spur to the southward separating two streams that eventually flow in opposite directions, and let *X* be the location of the camp. A stranger who had spent the day on the upper mountains might return toward evening to *B,* and, thinking to follow the creek from *f* to *X,* might turn down at *e,* by mistake, and travel a considerable distance before he realized that he was going in the wrong direction.

FLAT WOODS.—In flat woods, where the watercourses are few and very meandering, the vegetation rank and monotonously uniform in appearance, and landmarks rare, a man may return within 200 yards of his own camp and pass by it, going ahead with hurrying pace as he becomes more and more anxious. In Fig. 2 a man leaves camp *X* in the morning, going in the direction indicated by the dotted line. He consults his compass at intervals during the day, tries to allow for his windings, and, returning in the evening, strikes the river at *Z.* If he follows its bank in either direction, he is likely to spend the night alone in the woods. If the camp were at *A,* and the homeward-bound hunter should reach the stream at *B,* he would be dumbfounded to find himself, apparently, on the wrong bank of the river.

Another easy way to get bewildered is as follows: In Fig. 2 we will assume that the current runs from *A* toward *Z,* that a party unfamiliar with the river is descending it in a boat, and that one of the men leaves the boat at *A,* going ashore to hunt along the bank. At *X* he comes to the mouth of a deep creek, or some other obstruction, or he starts game that

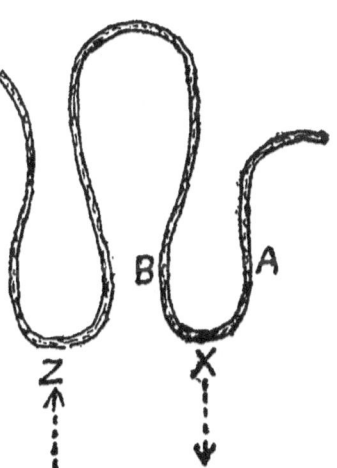

Fig. 2.—Ox-bow Bends

leads him back into the woods. Not long afterward he reaches the river again at Z, and, after hallooing and firing a shot or two, but getting no answer, he hurries on down-stream, thinking that the boat got ahead of him while he was making his detour. The boat, meanwhile, has been rounding a great ox-bow curve, and may be a couple of miles behind the man ashore.

In each of these examples the country is assumed to be fairly easy to traverse, and in each case the misadventure might have been avoided by a little forethought. A bush bent over, here and there, a blaze on a tree where the underbrush was dense, would have saved all that. Without such precautions, there are places where a man can get badly muddled in a forty-acre tract. This is no exaggeration. One of my companions once was lost from early morning until after nightfall in a thirty-acre patch of blue cane. He struggled until almost completely exhausted, and when we found him he looked like a scarecrow. At no time had he been half a mile from the cabin.

THICKETS.—A canebrake is bad enough, but it is not so bad as those great tracts of rhododendron which, in the region between Thunderhead and the Balsam Mountains (Tennessee and North Carolina) cover mile after mile of steep mountainside where few men have ever been. The natives call such wastes "laurel slicks," "woolly heads," "lettuce beds," "yaller patches," and "hells." The rhododendron is worse than laurel, because it is more stunted and grows much more densely, so that it is quite impossible to make a way through it without cutting, foot by foot; and the wood is very tough. Two powerful mountaineers starting from the Tennessee side to cross the Smokies were misdirected and proceeded up the slope of the Devil's Court House, just east of Thunderhead. They were two days in making the ascent, a matter of three or four miles, notwithstanding that they could see out all the time and pursued the shortest possible course. I asked one of them how they managed to crawl through the thicket. "We couldn't crawl," he replied, "we swum," meaning that they sprawled and floundered over the top. These men were not lost at all. In a "bad laurel" (heavily timbered), not very far from this, an old hunter and trapper who was born and bred in these mountains, was lost for three days, although the maze was not more than a mile square. His account of it gave it the name that it bears to-day, "Huggin's hell."

I could give many such instances, but these will suffice to show that there still is virgin ground in some of our oldest States. The far West and the far North present problems of their own. Extensive swamps are the worst places of all, above ground. As for caves, and how *not* to get lost in them, I will have something to say in another chapter.

WHAT TO DO.—No matter where, or in what circumstances, you may be, the moment you realize that you have lost your bearings, there is just one thing for you to do: *STOP!* Then sit down.

Now any man can remember that. It is a bit of "book learning" that no man can afford to despise. It is the one and only way to clear your wits, to drive off the demon of panic, and it is sure to help get you out of your predicament.

Then, if you are a smoker, light your pipe; if not, chew a twig. It won't take long for you to recover sense enough to know that if you stay right where you are until morning your companions, by that time, will be searching for you. They will be scouring the woods, hallooing, firing guns, scouting for your trail. Suppose you do have to stay out all night, alone in the woods; nothing will hurt you. The stories of bears or panthers pouncing on sleeping men are all tommyrot. So keep your shirt on.

How long has it been since you were where you *were* certain of your location? Probably not a long time. Suppose you have traveled half an hour after leaving a known landmark. What is half an hour in the woods? A mile, say; perhaps not so much; for one does not keep up a steady jog in the wilderness; he often pauses to look or listen, and is bound to move slowly when off a beaten path.

But you don't want to stay here like a numbskull and face the sly grins or open ridicule of a searching party? Very well, the bugaboos are fleeing. Now take a stick, make a bare spot on the ground, and try to trace your probable course from the time of leaving camp to the time you first suspected you might be wandering astray. Mark on it the estimated location of such landmarks as you noticed. If you are not altogether a tenderfoot, you will remember how many streams or ridges you have crossed. Anyway, you will recall some features of the country you traversed. Not unlikely, when your mind has recovered its equipoise, you will be able to "backtrack" without much difficulty.

But in any case, no matter how confident you may be, *don't* take ten steps from the place where you are until you have marked it. If the location is favorable for a smoke sign (in flat woods it is of no avail) build a fire, with enough damp or punky stuff on it to keep up a smoke for a good while, and bank it with earth so it cannot spread. Or, blaze a tree on four sides—make big blazes that can be seen from any direction. Do this even though there be several hours of daylight ahead, and although you have no present intention of staying here; for you do know that this spot is only so many hours from camp by back trail, and that you may have good reason to return to it. This blazed tree, moreover, will be of great assistance to your camp-mates in searching for you, if you should not turn up later.

Then take note of the lay of the land around you, the direction of its drainage, the character of its vegetation, and the hospitalities that it offers to a night-bound traveler, in the way of drinking-water,

BIVOUACS

sound down-wood for an all-night fire, natural shelter, and browse or other bedding.

Now when you start out to recover the trail, make bush-marks as you go along (see Chapter III, Fig. 6); otherwise it will be the easiest thing in the world to lose the way back to that blazed tree.

In trying to pick up your old footprints don't give much attention to dry ground, except where there may be dusty places, or rocks where your hobnails might have left scratches. Look for tracks (I don't mean run around hunting for them) in the damp places that you pass, mossy spots, swales, margins of brooks, and for "scrapes" on the tops of fallen logs.

When searching for a trail, do not look close to your feet, but three or four yards ahead of you; for a faint trail is more readily seen at that angle than by looking straight down upon it. Cast your eyes also from side to side, bearing in mind what a trail should look like when you walk parallel with it, as well as when approaching at right angles.

If you get a shot at a squirrel or other animal (of course, you don't wander around looking for them) kill it and tie it fast to you. It is one of the little ironies of wilderness life that food may be extraordinarily scarce when you most need it—and that may be to-morrow.

But if you don't soon find that back track of yours, and if no familiar landmark shows up before the sun is within an hour of setting, *QUIT IT* for the day. It is high time, now, that you go right to work to make yourself snug for the night. Your success or failure to-morrow will depend very much upon what kind of a night's rest you get.

BIVOUACS.—In nearly every story that you read of a lost man's misadventures you find him struggling desperately on until black night shuts down. Then he throws his exhausted body upon the cold, damp ground, soon to awaken in bitter misery, and back himself up against a tree, to droop there through the long, long hours; or, the cold being intense, and he without one dry match, the man totters crazily all night, 'round and 'round, to keep from freezing. What *could* he be fit for next day?

Of course, if the Swiss Family Robinson should get turned around in the forest primeval, they at once would find a shallow cave, a projecting ledge, a great hollow tree, or some other natural shelter ready-made on the spot. We often come across such natural harborages in the wilderness—when we don't need them. (Three of us hunters once spread our blankets inside a hollow cypress and had room to spare.) But no special providence looks after lost men.

It would be so easy to make a comfortable "one-night stand" if you had a knapsack of supplies on your back! Yes, you could get along very well if only you had a featherweight poncho, a 12-ounce tomahawk, and several big bites of grub (next time you go out alone you will have them). But to-day you just went off to one side after a crippled deer, or something, and your outfit comprises nothing but a gun and the contents of your pockets. Pretty prospect, isn't it?

"Under the greenwood tree,
Who loves to lie with me"

is all very nice on a summer's day; but under the greenwood tree on a cold night in the big sticks, and the Lord knows where, with no *me* to share *who's* troubles—oh, darn Shakespeare!

Well, you must rustle. Just now you need four things.—

(1) Water.
(2) A fire that won't go out till morning.
(3) A windbreak to keep the other side of you warm.
(4) A bed to rest your bones and to keep off the chill of the ground.

And, my friend, you want to get these things with the *least expenditure* of time and effort. Night ap-

BIVOUACS

proaches; to-morrow may be a hard day. Besides, you are quite too tired already to waste the crook of your finger on non-essentials, while aimless pottering would be your ruin. The job must be tackled methodically.

So think back along your recent route and recall the best place where all four of those things you need are to be found—that is, the raw materials—and go to it.

I am assuming that the night is likely to be cold, but that there is no indication of rain or snow—that contingency will be considered later.

In a primitive forest there are big fallen trees on nearly every acre. Find a *sound* one that lies flat on level ground. You might use it either as a backlog or as a windbreak; the latter in this case, since you are to erect no shelter. In summer, a bed of dead leaves piled against the log, with a small fire in front, would be a good cubby for the night. But we assume that there will be frost.

Select the spot that you intend to lie on (leeward side of the log, of course), cover it with dry brush, and set it afire. The object is to dry out the ground and heat it. If the tree is not punky it will stand a considerable blaze close to it without igniting more than little spots on the bark, which can be extinguished with a handful or two of dirt. But don't, on your life, kindle a fire against a decayed or hollow log—you never could be sure of putting it out. If there are no sound down-logs, build an artificial windbreak of poles laid on top of each other and chinked with earth.

You first have raked the leaves together toward the center so that the fire cannot spread. Don't make too big a blaze at a time. When the ground you are to sleep on is burned off, keep a fire of small sticks going on it for half an hour, the length and width you are to occupy. Meantime you will be dragging in, and piling on one side, all the sound, dry wood you can get, for the night's fuel. Get long sticks, as big as you can handle, and plenty of them. Perhaps there are some old pine stumps that you can uproot. Don't fool with soggy, decayed stuff. Probably the top of your fallen tree will furnish a lot of broken limbs that sprangle enough to have been kept mostly off the ground and have seasoned hard.

When you have plenty of night-wood piled up, take a pair of sticks and rake the embers of your brush fire forward to a place five or six feet in front of your bed. Build there your night fire. Tramp down all embers left by the first fire, and carefully extinguish any smoking spots on the tree. If the log does not quite meet the ground, chink the openings with dirt.

If there are evergreen bushes at hand, they make the best bedding (balsam, hemlock, spruce, in that order—even pine or cedar will do in a pinch). You won't have time to make a real browse bed (described in Chapter XIII of this book), but remember that the smaller the sticks under you, the better you will rest. If there are no evergreens, then use moss, ferns, grass, or whatever other soft stuff you may find. Dead leaves and pine needles are the last choice, as they are inflammable. If you have time, make that bed two feet deep.

The ground that you are going to sleep on is dry and hot, and will stay so a long time, being insulated by the bedding stuff. The log behind you is warm, and it will shield you from the wind. You have effected a double economy, because a small fire in front will suffice until the cold hours on the far side of midnight, for which time the bulk of your fuel is to be saved.

Don't fire any distress signals until shortly before dark; earlier ones would be attributed to some wandering hunter. But when the shadows begin to fall, and you have not shown up, your comrades will begin to grow uneasy and will listen for signals. The best signal with a gun is a shot, a pause of ten

BIVOUACS

seconds, and then two shots in quick succession. The first attracts attention, the others give the direction. If the men of your party hear you they will reply instantly. But if you hear no answer, do not try again for half an hour. *Save ammunition.* You will need it worse to-morrow, for signalling as you travel, and to get meat with.

If your camp-fire smokes badly, it is because it lies too flat on the ground for air to get under it. Build it on thick chunks, or on rocks if there are flat ones to be found.

So long as it does not rain, the problem of keeping warm without a blanket is not serious. If more covering is demanded, and there are enough small balsams in the neighborhood, one can make a deep bed of the browse, lay two or three poles over it, pile a lot of boughs on top, and then, by manipulating the poles, insinuate himself between the two layers. This will help very much to prevent too rapid radiation of the bodily heat. Another good kink is to get a number of stones, six to eight inches in diameter, heat them before the fire, and place them around you wherever the cold is felt. Have others heating in the meantime, and change from time to time. To lift and carry them, cut a small forked limb close to the joint, leaving two feet of each fork for handles, put the crotch over the rock, and press inward with the handles.

Perhaps, instead of a fallen tree, you may have the good luck to find a big uptilted rock with flat face, long enough to serve as windbreak, or a ledge, with enough level ground in front of it for your purpose. Rock holds heat a long time, yet generously radiates it. The warm air from the camp-fire will eddy around it.

A man without a blanket can bivouac in the way here described, and get a pretty good night's rest, even in freezing weather. If it snows, a browse bed-covering will help. But a chill fall rain is something else. Ugh! Maybe you can twist up enough evergreen shrubs with your hands to build a kennel of some sort, but its slope must be steeper than 45° to do any good. If you find old logs from which sheets of bark can be peeled with a stick whittled wedge-shape at one end, you can make a pent-roof over your bed. Slope some sticks from the far side of the big log that serves as windbreak, forward over your bed, weight them down with rocks or a heavy stick, and shingle the bark over the upper ends. But you are in for a night of it—the best you can do—all for the lack of what "Nessmuk's" scoffers called his "limber-go-shiftless pocket axe." With the like of it you could build a good shelter of bark or of browse, such as will be described in a future chapter.

Among my most valued possessions is a tiny Colclesser tomahawk, of 8-ounce head and 2½ inch bitt, which, with hickory handle and home-made sheath, weighs only three-quarters of a pound. I seldom go anywhere in the woods (unless in marching order with a heavier axe) without this little trick. It is all that is needed to put up a satisfactory shelter wherever there is hemlock or balsam, or bark that will peel, while for other service I use it oftener than I do my jackknife.

FIRE WITHOUT MATCHES.—So far I have taken for granted that you have matches and that they are dry. Damp ones, by the way, may be restored by rubbing through the hair; or, place a match between the palms of your hands, with its head projecting a trifle, and roll it briskly back and forth; in a short time it will be dry enough to light.

But suppose you have no matches. Well, with a shotgun the task of making fire is easy; with a modern rifle, or pistol, that uses jacketed bullets, it is not so easy, because the bullet is hard to get out of the shell—still you can manage it by cutting lengthwise through the neck of the shell and prying the bullet out.

First make all preparations needed to ensure success when you get the flame. Build up your **wood**

BIVOUACS

ready to light, the kindling being stood up on end against the larger sticks in a half-cone shape, with opening at the bottom, in front, for tinder. This last may be very dry shredded bark, fine slivers of fat pine, or any dry splinters, pounded between two rocks until the fibers separate. In a rain you can get dry stuff from the inside of a hollow tree.

Worry the bullet out of the cartridge; sprinkle most of the powder (smokeless, I assume) on the tinder, leaving only *a few grains* in the shell. Then tear a bit of dry *cotton* cloth (lining from your clothing, for instance) with fluffy edges, and with this loosely fill the nearly emptied cartridge. Put it in your gun, and fire straight up into the air. The cloth will drop close to you, and either will be aflame or, at least, burning so that you can blow it into a blaze. Drop this quickly on your tinder, and the trick is done. Remember, you want only enough powder in the cartridge to blow the bit of rag a few feet into the air. Very little will do.

Sparks may be struck from flint, quartz, or pyrites, by striking a glancing blow with the back of a knife or other piece of hard steel. The chief difficulty is to *catch* the sparks. Hold the flint between thumb and finger of left hand, and some tinder in the hollow of the same hand. Tinder for this purpose is made by tearing (not cutting) cotton cloth into a long, narrow strip, and rolling it up like a roller bandage, but a bit spirally, so that the fluffy edge will overlay a little at each revolution, thus forming a nest of lint at one end of the roll, into which the sparks are to be struck. As soon as it catches, blow it into a flame.

The lens of a field-glass, or the outer lens of a camera, may do service as a burning glass; but it is another of the little ironies that the sun probably isn't shining when you get lost.

As for the fire-drill so dramatically exploited by popular lecturers, who make fire with sticks in less than a minute, it is all right provided you have the right material, which must be soft, non-resinous wood, thoroughly seasoned, brash, but not the least punky. In most situations it would be accidental if a lost man should find such wood. As a matter of fact, savages carry their fire-sticks with them, as we do matches.

NEXT MORNING.—A night's rest, even though fitful, will have cleared your mind a good deal. By this time you probably will have a definite theory of location, based upon what you know of the relation of the camp site to the surrounding country, and the general course of your wanderings. And you will feel much better at having a whole day of sunlight ahead of you.

The first effort will be to get an outlook over the surrounding country. In the hills this is easy, but in a level country heavily timbered it is difficult. If you are a good climber, pick out a tall tree and go up as high as you can get. Where the trunks are too thick for climbing, select a big tree that has a slender one growing beside it from which you can clamber into the lower limbs of the old one. But don't risk a broken limb of your own—that might be fatal.

Having gained your outlook, note the compass direction of watercourses and other landmarks, mapping them on a piece of paper; for a lost man's memory is treacherous. The courses of small streams show where the main valley lies. Look for smoke. Your comrades will have raised one, if there be a woodsman among them.

Now decide whether to try to reach camp or to "break out" to a known road or settlement. If still completely bewildered, then there is but one thing to do: work *down country,* either along a stream or a divide. If you do this, even in a remote district, it cannot be more than a few days until you reach habitations of men. In the meantime you may suffer, but you certainly need not starve nor freeze. If you have no one definite objective, but are merely going down country, do not try to steer a straight course, but save your strength by following the easiest way, being careful merely to keep the general direction. Follow divides, rather than streams, for reasons that will be given in the next chapter.

But we will assume that you have an idea which way camp lies. Take the compass direction from your outlook, note how the sun bears as you face that way, pick out a mark in line with the course, and steer for it— then from this to another, and so on. But, before leaving the site of your bivouac, blaze a tree and pencil on it the time of your start and the direction you intend to travel in. This will be invaluable to your mates if they track you up. At intervals of half an hour or so, fire a distress signal, if you can spare the ammunition—*don't waste it*.

As you travel, make bush marks and blazes along the course. It may be necessary to return; others can follow your trail by them; and, if you should circle, you will know it when you come across your old marks.

CIRCLING.—When a man travels where there is no outlook over the surrounding country, he is apt to "circle." In going around obstacles he may choose habitually the same side, and not make enough allowance for this tendency when averaging up his windings. But many men have an unconscious *leaning* toward one side or the other, even in open country, even on horseback, and will tend to travel in a circle unless they frequently check their course by compass or landmarks. Just why, we do not know. It is said that only an ambidextrous man goes straight naturally. Most men swerve to the right, and, since most of us are right-handed, it may be that when there is nothing else to guide us we incline toward the stronger side.

I offer this explanation for what it may be worth. Anyway, the tendency to travel in a circle is common to most men when they are lost. Mr. C. C. Filson says that a lost man once came to his camp who had walked continuously for six days and nights and was only about six miles from his starting point. Five hours of travel in any one direction would have taken him out of the woods and saved him the subsequent loss of both feet by freezing.

To avoid circling, one must travel by landmarks, or, where none are visible, as in thick woods, then by compass. Consult the instrument every two or three minutes, for a slight deviation, persisted in, soon swings you far aside. After going around an obstacle to the right, even up, by walking as far to the left. Don't travel too fast—it would excite you, wear you out, and keep you from marking your trail as you went along. Keep a stiff upper lip, and assure yourself that this is not a tragedy but only an interesting adventure—then it will turn out so.

How to live off the country, in case of being out a long time, will be discussed hereafter.

By the time you get out of this predicament you will agree that the art of *not* getting lost is worth studying. Let me now direct our attention to it.

CHAPTER III
PATHFINDING

I never knew a native of the wilderness who used a compass to guide him. The born backwoodsman relies upon the sun and stars, the direction of the wind, the courses of streams, prominent landmarks, and other natural signs of direction. That kind of pathfinding will be discussed later. It is essential in the education even of an amateur woodsman that he should learn to steer a course, over average ground and under ordinary conditions, without recourse to map or compass; for one can't be pottering over them when hunting or doing anything else of absorbing interest. Yet he should never be without them in the field; in emergencies they are simply invaluable.

On a windless, cloudy day, when boring through new country, especially if it be heavily timbered, it is quite too easy to lose one's bearings if the compass has been left behind. In thick fog or fast-falling snow, the best of men may go astray for lack of the faithful needle. Make it a rule, then, an iron rule, of wilderness life, never to leave your bed in the morning without compass, jackknife, and waterproof matchbox *filled* (fill it, as a matter of habit, every time you wind your watch). A small section of map showing the principal features of the country round about is another mighty good thing to have always on your person, no matter how you may be dressed for the day or what you may be intending to do. There is no telling when you may be called off on the keen jump, nor whither you may have to go.

For instance: one time a big buck ran right through camp while we were cooking dinner; in the flurry, everybody grabbed some other fellow's gun, somebody wounded the beast, and there was a long chase without the least preparation in the world. Again, we we're all out picketing the mountain for a bear drive; the bear avoided all the likely crossings and slipped by within fifty yards of camp. Now suppose you had been left there as camp-keeper for the day. You snatch up a gun, fire, find blood on the trail, follow it a couple of hours, and then—"where are you at?"

Aside from their value in emergencies, the compass and map are particularly useful to *keep you out* of trouble. The best advice in the world is "Don't get lost." The only way to make reasonably sure of that is to mind your P's and Q's (or rather your *N* and *S*) in advance. For example:

BASE LINES.—You have camped in a pleasant bit of flat-woods, on the margin of a stream, at *A* (Fig. 3). In the morning you decide to go out by yourself for a look-see, not hunting, of course, but just to get a good idea of the lay of the land. You know that the river runs north and south. Simplest thing in the world, then, to tramp eastward a couple of hours, and return in time for dinner. You can't cross that river without knowing it, and camp is right on the river bank, you know.

The forest is fairly open for the first mile or so and you steer an approximately straight course. Then you strike bogs and thickets, not bad ones nor big ones, but just enough to make you average your windings by glancing at the compass now and then. Presently the going is better, and you continue nearly straight east until you reach *B*, when it is time to return. You are sure that your course has been almost due east, and that you are about four miles from camp. You take compass bearings due west as far as you can see out, and back you go. But

PATHFINDING 39

you can't trail your own foot-prints. It would take one of Fenimore Cooper's redskins to do so over this firm ground covered with dry fallen leaves. No matter: you have a compass, haven't you?

Soon, at a point where your outbound course bore a bit northerly, you pass it, unknowingly, by going straight back west. You feel certain that you are steering right; for that compass is in your hand half the time.

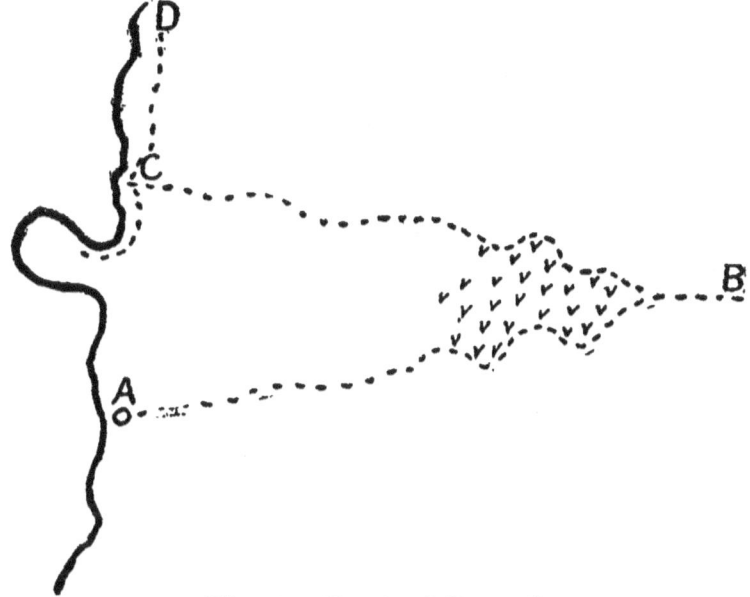

Fig. 3.—Need of Base line

Hang it! here is a bog. To the left it looks impracticable. You go around to the right, and then carefully even up the winding by swerving left an equal distance. Some lesser curves hereafter are allowed for in the same way. Finally you come out on the river. You *know* your return course has been very nearly due west. But the confounded river doesn't look a bit like it did at camp! You struggle to the bank through thick undergrowth, and when you get there you can't see two hundred yards of the stream in either direction. There is a jungle to the water's edge.

Well, you are either above or below camp. But which? Maybe old Leatherstocking could tell; but you can't, to save your life. You might as well pitch a penny for it. At random you turn downstream. Very soon you come to an abrupt bend going westward. There was no indication of such a bend close to camp. Probably the tents are upstream, you say. So you turn about-face and go north. Still an utterly strange river.

By one o'clock you realize that you are going wrong. Camp *couldn't* be so far off from where you struck the river. So you turn wearily back downstream, and, late in the afternoon you reach camp, feeling like a fool, and silently swearing never to tell a soul the true story of your misadventure.

This is one of the simplest cases of "bumfuzzlement" that I can think of. It might have been complicated by any of a hundred difficulties or mishaps that are common in the wilderness. Yet, simple as it was, it gave you no little anxiety and it ended in humiliation.

The trouble was that you started out in the wrong way. You should have explored a few miles of the river first. This would have given you a known *base-line,* to which you could return with perfect confidence from any direction. You could have marked that base-line with blazes every half-mile or thereabouts, on which were penciled the number of minutes' travel each location was from camp, the arrangement of blazes showing which way camp lay.

Where there is no river, road, or range of hills, running in a long continuous line to serve as base—nothing, say, but trackless forest—the first thing to do is to run such a line by compass, spotting the trees, as will be described hereafter. I am assuming, here, that camp is to remain in one place for some time.

TRAIL MAKING.—Various kinds of blazed trails will be described in the next chapter. There is a

PATHFINDING

way that I consider better for a man or a party venturing into strange woods where there are few if any old trails—better because it always shows which way camp lies, and because it takes much less labor than spotting trees so close together that the next blaze ahead can always be seen from the one preceding it. At such intervals as may be required, blaze a tree here and there along the course, with one spot on the side away from camp (Fig. 4) and two on the opposite side (Fig. 5). Even when a

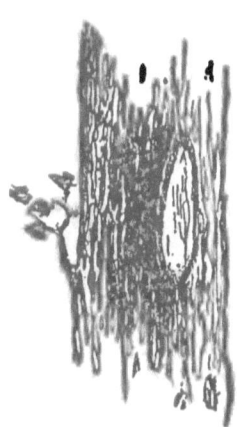

Fig. 4.—One Blaze
A-way from Camp

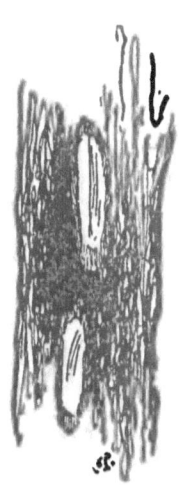

Fig. 5.—Two blazes
To-ward Camp

man is bewildered he can remember "*A* blaze means *a*-way from, *two* blazes means *to*-ward."

A blaze with a hack below it (simply drive the hatchet into the bark and draw it out) is easier and quite as effective. And between the blazed trees, at such intervals that you can see one from another, or as circumstances may require, make bush marks (Fig. 6). A bush mark is made by bending over the top of a green and leafy bush in the direction you are going, snapping the stem (if necessary clipping it half through with knife or hatchet) but letting it adhere by part of the wood and bark so that the under side of the bushy top will "look at you" when you return. The under side of the leaves, being of lighter shade than the upper, makes such a bush sign conspicuous in the woods. Marks like these can be made without slacking one's pace.

Where a bend in the trail is made, the blazes, instead of being opposite, should follow the bend, of course.

Blazing trees is prohibited on public lands, and the practice should be limited to remote regions where there are no regular trails. A blaze is everlasting, so long as the tree stands, and may cause trouble over land boundaries in years to come. Where underbrush is scarce, it may be necessary to spot the trees, but generally it will suffice merely to hack off a bit of the outer bark as big as your hand, without cutting into the sapwood.

Fig. 6.—Bush Mark

The snow-laden limbs of low evergreen trees may droop so low as to conceal blazes on the trunks, and driving snow may cover them anyway, on any kind of tree. Consequently bush marks are more reliable than blazes in winter, if the snow is not too deep.

In average country, bush marks alone will suffice.

When going out on an old trail for the first time make such a mark wherever you might be in doubt on the return, as where the trail forks, or where it is overgrown or faint. If there are no bushes, jab a stick into the side of the trail, sloping toward camp, or arrange a few stones in the form of an arrow-head, pointing the way.

Of course, such precautions as these are only to be taken on new ground, and then only according to circumstances. Nowadays our wilderness travel

PATHFINDING 43

is usually in regions where there are regular trails that are soon learned and which serve then as baselines, or where mountains, streams, lakes, and other physical features are so prominent that it is easy to learn the lay of the land.

In thick woods, canebrakes, swamps, big thickets, and other places where the course is necessarily very tortuous, a compass is of little use while one is on the march. Wherever the traveler can get an outlook he fixes on some landmark in advance, notes how the sun strikes him when facing the mark, and thenceforth averages up his windings as well as he can. The compass is only of service when he can no longer see the sun, and is in doubt as to the direction he is traveling in.

In the wilderness one never knows when he may want to retrace his steps. Hence, when passing anything that has particularly caught his eye, let him turn and see how it looks *from the other side.*

ROUGH TRAVEL.—The way to find game, or to get the best of anything else that the forest hides, is not to follow well-beaten paths. One must often make his own trails, and go where the going is hardest. As he travels through the unbroken woods he may come, now and then, to a glade where the trees do not crowd each other, where the undergrowth is sparse, and the view so unobstructed that he can see to shoot for a hundred yards in any direction; such spots may be about as common, relatively, as are safe anchorages and deep-water harbors along the coast. But part of the time, a wanderer in the forest primeval must pick a way for his feet over uneven ground that is covered with stubs, loose stones, slippery roots, crooked saplings, mixed downwood, and tough, thorny vines. He is forever busy seeking openings, parting bushes, brushing away cobwebs, fending off springy branches, crawling over or under fallen trees, working around impenetrable tangles, or trying to find a foot-log or a ford. There is no such thing as a short-cut. It is beyond the power of man to steer a straight course, or to keep up a uniform cadence of his steps.

Unless the traveler knows his ground there is no telling when he may come to a "windfall" where several acres of big timber have been overthrown by a hurricane and the great trees lie piled across each other in an awkward snarl. Or maybe there is an alder or spruce thicket or a cedar swamp in the way, or a canebrake or a cypress slough, or a laurel or rhododendron "slick," wherein a man will soon exhaust his strength to no purpose, if he be so unwise as to try to force a passage.

A *brule* or burnt-wood is a nasty place to pass through. Every foot of ground that is not covered by charred snags, or fallen trunks and limbs, bristles with a new growth of fireweed, blackberry and raspberry briers, young red cherries, white birches, poplars, quaking aspens, scrub oaks, or gray pines. Where the fire has occurred on one of those barren ridges that was covered with dwarfish oaks (post, black, or blackjack), the sharp, fire-hardened stubs of limbs protrude, like bayonets, at the height of one's face, menacing his eyes.

An old "lumber works," where the trees have been chopped out, leaving nothing but stumps, treetops, and other debris, grows up with the same rank tenants as a burnt-wood, and is as mean to flounder through. As a general rule, a mile and a half an hour of actual progress is "making good time" in the woods.

CROSSING STREAMS.—If you have to cross a deep, rocky ravine or dangerous mountain stream by passing over a high foot-log or fallen tree, then, if the log is tilted at an uncomfortable angle, or if its surface is wet, or icy, or treacherous with loose bark, or if, for any reason, you fear dizziness or faintness, don't be ashamed to get down and straddle the log, and "coon it," hunching yourself along with hands and thighs. Let your companions laugh, if they will. It is not nice to break a limb when you are

PATHFINDING

in a country so rough that your comrades may have to pack you out, by each, in turn, carrying you on his own back and crawling with you.

Where there is no foot-log, a narrow stream may be crossed by using a jumping-pole, or, if it is too deep for that, by a rope or vine swung from an overhanging tree and doubled back.

Before fording, if the weather is cold, take off trousers and drawers and tie them to your pack, but keep your shoes on, lest you slip on smooth rocks. If the stream is swift, cut a stout pole, longer than yourself, with which to sound ahead of you and to brace yourself against the current by planting it downstream at each step.

In flat country the shallowest part of a stream is usually where the near bank makes the longest, sharpest point, and it runs diagonally toward a projection of the opposite bank, either up or downstream. The widest part of a river generally is the shallowest. The inside of a sharp bend is deep. In swift-flowing streams look for fords above the riffles.

Fording swift water is easiest with a heavy pack to help hold one down; but sling it so it will slip off if you stumble—otherwise it may drown you. Several men in company can cross a stream too swift for one at a time, if they cut a long pole and cross abreast, holding the pole horizontally in front of them with each man grasping it. The heaviest man should be on the downstream side.

To avoid mud and quicksand, look for pebbles on the bottom.

USE OF DIVIDES.—Rivers are often spoken of as having been man's natural highways in the days before roads. This was true only to a limited extent. A few great rivers such as the Hudson, the Ohio, the Mississippi, and the Missouri, were highways for down-stream travel, and smaller waterways were, and still are, used in summer in the *muskeg* country of the North, where land travel is imprac-

46 CAMPING AND WOODCRAFT

ticable until everything freezes up. But the general rule of aboriginal travel was to keep away from streams and follow the ridges between them. This rule still holds good when a party travels afoot or with pack-train in a country where there are no

Fig. 7.—Use of Divides

bridges. A glance at the accompanying diagram (Fig. 7) will show why.

In this figure, AG represents a river, and CF the main divide or summit of watershed separating it from another river basin. It is assumed that a party afoot or with horses desires to advance from A to G. Evidently, if they try to follow either bank of the main stream, they will have many fords to make, not only crossing tributaries here and there, but fording or swimming the main stream itself, many times, where cliffs, bogs, or impenetrable thickets make one of the banks impassable.

If the region through which the river runs is wide bottom-land, the mouths of its tributaries are likely to be deep, or to run over fathomless mud as dangerous as quicksand, and this will necessitate long detours. The vegetation up to the very bank of the river will be exceedingly rank, a wretched tangle of bushes, vines, briers, and tall grass, and fallen trees will be plentiful and large. At any time a heavy rainstorm may send the river out of its banks, and the party may find itself marooned where it can neither go forward nor backward. On the other hand, if the river runs through a mountainous country, it is probable that the travelers will come to a cañon that will compel them to retreat. In any case, the party will never have an outlook; it will never know what lies beyond the next bend of the river.

A comparatively easy way around all of these difficulties is shown by the dotted line *ABDEG*. Leaving the river by a ridge that leads to the main divide, and following the crest to a similar abutting ridge that runs down to the valley at the objective point, there will be no fords to make, the footing will be much better because vegetation is thinner on the more sterile, wind-swept heights, the fallen trees will be smaller, there will be no mud or quicksand or miry bogs, and every here and there a coign of vantage will be climbed from which a far outlook can be had over the surrounding country.

The chief precaution to be observed in trying to follow a divide where there is no trail, or where there are many intersecting trails, is not to stray off on some abutting ridge. Thus, at the points *B* and *D* there may be in each case a gap between knolls or peaks, and the lead to the left might easily be mistaken for the main divide. If the party were enticed along either of these leads, on account of its trending in the desired direction, it would soon find itself in a *cul de sac.*

CELESTIAL GUIDES.—The sun by day and the stars by night are Nature's chief guides for the traveler. So long as the sun is visible anyone can tell, in a general way, the direction in which he is going. To find the sun on a cloudy day: hold a knife-blade or other thin, flat article perpendicularly on the thumb-nail, watch-case, or any glossy surface, and slowly twirl it around. It will cast a faint shadow, unless the day is very dark. Choose an open spot in the woods for this, rather than under the trees, and don't try it near noon, when little shadow would be cast anyway.

How to find the North Star is shown at the end of Chapter V.

CHAPTER IV

NATURE'S GUIDE-POSTS

SAMENESS OF THE FOREST.—All dense woods look much alike. Trees of most species grow very tall in a forest that has never been cut over, their trunks being commonly straight and slender, with no branches within, say, forty feet of the ground. This is because they cannot live without sunlight for their leaves, and they can only reach sunlight by growing tall like their neighbors that crowd around them. As the young tree shoots upward, its lower limbs atrophy and drop off. To some extent the characteristic markings of the trunk that distinguish the different species when they grow in the open, and to a greater extent their characteristic habits of branching, are neutralized when they grow in dense forest. Consequently a man who can readily tell one species from another, in open country, by their bark and branching habits, may be puzzled to distinguish them in aboriginal forest. Moreover, the lichens and mosses that cover the boles of trees, in the deep shade of a primitive wood, give them a sameness of aspect, so that there is some excuse for the novice who says that "all trees look alike" to him.

The knowledge of trees that can be gained, first from books and secondly from studies of trees themselves in city parks or in country wood-lots, must be supplemented by considerable experience in the real wilderness before one can say with confidence, by merely glancing at the bark, "that is a soft maple, and the other is a sugar-tree." And yet, I do not know any study that, in the long run, would be more serviceable to the amateur woodsman than to get a good manual of American trees and then go about identifying the species in his neighborhood. Having gained some facility in this, then let him turn to studying peculiarities of individual growth. Such self-training, which can be carried out almost anywhere, will make him observant of a thousand and one little marks and characteristics that are sign-boards and street-numbers in the wilds.

WHAT TO NOTICE.—After a novice has had some preliminary training of the kind I have indicated, so that all things in the woods no longer look alike to him, he will meet another difficulty. His memory will be swamped! It is utterly impossible for any man, whether he be red, white, black, or yellow, to store up in his mind all the woodland marks and signs that one can see in a mile's tramp, to say nothing of the infinite diversity that he encounters in a long journey. Now, here is just where a skilled woodcraftsman has an enormous advantage over any and all amateurs. He knows what is common, and pays no attention to it; he knows what is uncommon, it catches his eye at once, and it interests him, so that he need make no effort to remember the thing. This *disregard for the common* eliminates at once three-fourths, yes, nine-tenths, of the trees, plants, rocks, etc., from his consideration; it relieves his memory of just that much burden. He will pass a hundred birch trees without a second glance, until his eye is riveted by a curly birch. Why riveted? Because curly birch is valuable. In the bottom lands he will scarcely see a sour gum, or a hundred of them; but let him come across one such tree on top of the ridge, and he will wonder how it chanced to stray so far from home. And so on, through all categories of woodland features. A woodsman notices such things as infallibly, and with as little conscious effort, as a woman notices the crumbs and lint on her neighbor's carpet.

THE HOMING INSTINCT (?)—We hear much

about the "innate sense of direction," the "extraordinary bump of locality," of savages and of certain white woodcraftsmen. "A good woodsman," we are told, "finds his way, just as an animal does, by a certain kind of instinct." If by this is meant that some men are born with a "gift," a sixth sense or homing instinct comparable to that of a carrier pigeon, I am more than sceptical. In the art of wilderness travel, as in other things, some men are more adept than others who have had equal advantages, and a few possess almost uncanny powers, amounting to what we call genius. To my notion this means little more than that some individuals are quicker to observe than others, reason more surely from cause to effect, and keep their minds more alert; and I believe that this is far more due to their taking unusual interest in their surroundings than to any marked partiality of Mother Nature in distributing her gifts. Instinct will work as well in one place as in another, but human "sense of direction" will not.

This is not saying that all men are born equal as regards the faculty of orientation; some have a knack; but that knack is not an instinct; it is worthless until sharpened and trained by experience.

Let me illustrate.—In the Great Smoky Mountains, which separate part of North Carolina from Tennessee, the "standers" in a bear drive are stationed along the main divide, or near it, at elevations of from 4,000 to 6,000 feet. We are out in all sorts of weather. The chase may continue from dawn until midnight, the bear perhaps running ten or fifteen miles through the roughest of all this rough country. At almost any time clouds may descend upon us, or ascend from below, and the fog, as we call it, is sometimes so thick that a man cannot see thirty feet in any direction. It may lift in five minutes, or it may continue for a day, two days, three days—there is no foretelling. It may be accompanied by drenching rain, or by a keen wind, or may turn into a snowstorm; so we cannot sit around waiting on the chance of its rising.

Below the balsam zone (5,000 to 6,000 feet) the leaves, in autumn and early winter, lie very thickly upon the ground, so that a scurry of wind may at any moment obliterate the trail for some distance. When a cloud settles upon the mountain, a man hurrying along to get into the valley before nightfall, and over-confident, perhaps, of his bearings, may easily miss the trail and find himself on the wrong ridge—where? Once off the trail, there are no blazes to guide him, and the going gets worse and worse until it becomes damnable. If one only could see out, he would not hesitate; but he cannot see a tree two rods away.

In such case, it is of serious import for a man to decide, rather promptly, upon which particular ridge he may have straggled; for many of these ridges are very thickety, some of them lead into laurel "hells," and on others one's progress is impeded by cliffs. To descend immediately into a creek valley would be the worst thing he could do, for the headwaters generally rise in almost impenetrable thickets of laurel and rhododendron, and their beds are rough and steep.

Now, what does a mountaineer do in such dilemma? Trust to instinct? Not a bit of it. Our strayed man might not be able to explain the process, he probably would not even be conscious of the infinitude of details involved, he might lay it all to "woods sense" and let you credit him with a mysterious "gift"; but this is what he would do: first, he would scan the trees and shrubs, closely observing their prevailing habit of growth; then he would examine the ground itself; he would move about like a dog scenting for a track; presently he would find evidence, not single, but collective—gathered from many sources—which his memory and reasoning powers would combine into a theory of locality, and, five times out of six, his theory would prove correct.

I have known a mountaineer, on a pitch-dark night, to identify the ridge he was on by feeling the trees; and there were no blazes on those trees, either.

Our mountaineers know the peculiarities and variations of their home hunting-grounds most thoroughly, so far as they relate to the hunter's and herdsman's arts, and from this intimate local knowledge they have gained certain general signs of direction that are fairly reliable throughout all the main ranges of the Southern Appalachians (mountains densely covered with more varied forest growth than any others in the world). So they have not the least hesitation about traveling into unknown parts for a week at a stretch, and without a compass, even though they may get into fog so thick that, as they quaintly say, "You could nigh stick your butcher-knife into it and hang up your shot-pouch."

But there is no dog-like or pigeon-like instinct about this. I can take one of these same men to the city of Boston and get him thoroughly lost within half a mile of his hotel. If he had the homing instinct he could find his own way back on the city streets; but he has not the ghost of such endowment. He is bewildered by the maze of things new to him, as a city man is in the forest. His attention is attracted to other things than signs of direction: so he goes astray.

NATURE'S GUIDE-POSTS.—There are two questions that woodsmen will argue, I suppose, until doomsday. Having given my views on one of them, I may as well tackle the other, and then have done with controversy. Are there any natural signs of direction that will give a man his bearings when the sky is obscured? Every one has heard, for example, that "moss grows thickest on the north side of a tree," and nearly every one has heard this as flatly contradicted. The general opinion seems to be that such signs are "important if true." The Indians and white frontiersmen of fiction never have any difficulty in finding their way by noting where moss grows thickest on the trees; but when our novel-reader goes into the woods, compass in hand, and puts the thing to actual test, he probably will be disgusted to find that, in densely shaded primeval forest, there seems to be no regularity in the growth of moss, one tree having a thick layer of it on the north side, another on the east, another on the south, and so on. He is then ready to declare that the old saying is a "fake."

I shall endeavor to show that there is more in this matter than is generally credited. There are certain signs of direction that are fairly constant in given regions, so that by their help a native, or even a stranger who has good powers of observation, some patience, and a fair knowledge of the life habits of trees and plants, can steer his course without a compass, and without help from sun or stars. But let us clearly understand what is involved in this use of nature's compass-marks.

No universal rule can be established from such signs as the growth of moss on trees, the preponderance of branches on one side of a tree, or the direction toward which the tips of tall conifers point. Such things are modified by prevailing winds, shadows and shelter of nearby mountains, depth or sparseness of forest growth, and other local conditions. Everywhere exceptions will be found; if there were none, it would be child's play, not woodcraft, to follow such signs.

No one sign is infallible. A botanist can tell the north side of a steep hill from the south side by examining the plant growth; but no one plant of itself will tell him the story. So a woodsman works out his course by a system of *averaging* the signs around him. It is this averaging that demands genuine skill. It takes into account the prevailing winds of the region, the lay of the land, the habits of shade-loving and moisture-loving plants (and their opposites), the tendency of certain plants to point their leaves or their tips persistently in a certain direction, the growth of tree bark as influenced by sun and shade, the nesting habits of certain animals, the morning and evening flight of birds, and other natural phenomena, depending upon the general character of the country traversed. Moreover, in studying any one sign, a nice discrimination must be exercised. Let us glance at a few examples:

Moss ON Trees.—First, as to the time-honored subject of moss—not confusing real moss with the parasitic lichens that incrust rocks and trees. Moss favors that part of a tree that holds the most moisture; not necessarily the part that receives the most moisture, but the part that *retains* it longest. Consequently it grows more abundantly on the upper side of a leaning tree than on the under side, on rough bark than on smooth bark, on top of projecting burls rather than on the lower side, and in the forks of trees, and on their buttressed bases. These factors are, of course, independent of the points of the compass.

Does it follow, then, that exposure has nothing to do with the growth of moss? Not at all. It merely follows that a competent woodcraftsman, seeking a sign of direction from the moss on trees, would *ignore* leaning trees, uncommonly rough bark, bossy knots, forks of limbs, and the bases of tree trunks, just as he would give no heed to the growth on prostrate logs. He would single out for examination the straight shafted old trees of rather smooth bark, knowing that on them there would be fairly even lodgment for moisture all around, and that the wet would evaporate least from the north and northeast sides of the tree, as a general rule, and, consequently, that on those sides the moss would preponderate. He would expect to find such difference more pronounced on the edge of thick forests than in their densely shaded interior. He would give special heed to the evidence of trees that were isolated enough to get direct sunlight throughout a good portion of the day, while those that were in the shade of cliffs or steep mountains so that they could only catch the sunbeams in the morning or the afternoon would be ruled out of court.

You see how much more swiftly and surely such a man would reach a decision than could one who tried to take into account all kinds and conditions of trees, regardless of surroundings, and how much less he would have to puzzle over contradictory evidence. Among a hundred trees he might only examine ten, but those ten would be more trustworthy for his purpose than their ninety neighbors. This is woodcraft—the genuine article—as distinguished from the mysterious and infallible "sixth sense" of direction that, I think, exists nowhere outside of Leatherstocking Tales.

TIPS OF CONIFERS.—A rule that holds good in the main, wherever I have had a chance to study it, is that the feathery tip, the topmost little branch, of a towering pine or hemlock, points toward the rising sun, that is to say, a little south of east. There are exceptions, of course, but I have generally found this to be the case in three-fourths of the trees examined, leaving out of consideration those growing in deep, narrow valleys, or on wind-swept crests. I do not know whether it is characteristic of all conifers, throughout their ranges; but I commend this peculiar phenomenon to travelers, for observation.

BARK AND ANNUAL RINGS.—The bark of *old* trees is generally thicker on the north and northeast sides than on the other sides. A more reliable indicator of direction, though one that a traveler seldom has opportunity to test, is the thickness of annual rings of wood growth, which is more pronounced on the north than on the south side of a tree. This has been noted in widely separated parts of the earth, and has been known for many centuries. More than four hundred years ago it was mentioned by Leonardo da Vinci, that universal genius who was scarcely less celebrated as an engineer and scientist than as an artist and litterateur. "The rings of

NATURE'S GUIDE-POSTS

trees," wrote Leonardo, "show how many years they have lived, and their greater or smaller size shows whether the years were damper or drier. They also show the direction in which they were turned, because they are *larger on the north side than on the south,* and for this reason the center of the tree is nearer the bark on the south than on the north side." In 1893 this matter was put to a definite test by the New York State Forest Commission, which directed its foresters to examine the regularity of the northward thickening of annual rings in the black spruce of the Adirondacks. The foresters examined 700 trees, of varying exposure, noting in each case the compass-point toward which the longest radius of wood growth pointed. The result was:

North	471	South	1
Northeast	81	Southeast	0
East	106	West	27
		Southwest	6
Total north and east.	658	Northwest	8
	94%		
		Total south and west.	42
			6%

These figures deserve more than a passing glance.

COMPASS-PLANTS.—Some plants show a decided polarity in their habit of growth. The compass-plant or rosin-weed (*Silphium laciniatum*) that once abounded on the prairies of the Mississippi valley, from Minnesota to Texas, is a conspicuous example. It is a tall plant with long, stiff leaves, that do not grow horizontally but with their edges perpendicular. Its natural habitat is the open, shadeless prairie. If plants are examined that grow thus in the open, especially those in the little swales where they are not fully exposed to fierce winds, it will be found that the great majority of them present their radical leaves *north and south.* The large flower heads on short, thick stems point, like the hemlock's "finger," to the eastward, and show no such tendency to follow the sun toward the west as is characteristic of many plants. I have often used the compass-plant as a guide, and never was led astray by it; in fact, the old settlers on the prairies, if they chanced to get lost on a dark night, would get their bearings by feeling the leaves of the compass-plant.

The closely related prairie dock (*Silphium terebinthinaceum*) and that troublesome weed known as prickly lettuce (*Lactuca scariola*), show a similar polarity. This characteristic is lost if the plants are grown where they receive much shade. Of course, terrestrial magnetism has nothing to do with the polarity of plants; it is the sunlight, received on the two sides of the leaves alternately, that determines their position.

But what think you of plant *roots* that persistently grow north and south? The woodsmen of the Great Smoky Mountains declare that there is a "north-and-south plant," as they call it, with two long roots that grow respectively north and south. Doctor Davis of Ware's Valley, on the Tennessee side described it to me as follows: "It resembles wild verbena, grows 'thigh-high, is a rare plant, and generally is found in hollows on the south side of mountains, in rocky neighborhoods, near trickling streams. Its leaf is serrated, 1½ by 1 inch, or larger, with purple heart, yellow edges, and the rest a bright red. Its roots usually do grow north and south. The plant is one of the most valuable medicinally that I know of, particularly for syphilitic affections. I do not know it by any other name than the native one of North-and-South. I gather it when I can find it, and use it in my practice." Many others have given me similar reports. I do not know the plant; have never hunted systematically for it.

LOST ARTS.—I am of the opinion that there are natural compass-signs in the forest, and on the plain, that we are ignorant of, but that were well known to savages in a state of nature. Such men, dependent from childhood upon close observation of their environment, but observation urged by entirely different motives from those of our naturalists, and directed toward different ends, would inevitably acquire a woodland lore different from ours, but quite as thorough in its own way. That they should develop keen perceptive faculties is no more remarkable than that a carpenter should hit a nail instead of the thumb that steadies it. That they should notice and study signs that no modern hunter or scientist would bother his head about is a matter of course. Unquestionably we have lost many arts of wildcraft that were daily practised by our ancestors of the stone age, just as we have lost their acquaintance with the habits of animals now extinct. Probably no white man of the future will ever equal Jim Bridger as a trailer; and it is but natural to suppose that Bridger himself had superiors among the savages from whom he learned his craft. It is a superficial judgment to rate as an old-wives' tale every story of exploits in the past that we cannot at present duplicate. However, we need not go to novelists to find out how such things were done. There is much pleasure to be gained in seeking to recover some of the lost arts of a primitive age; and, I believe, some profit as well.

But facts such as I have cited regarding the compass-signs of the woods are of practical value only to men who spend much of their time in the forest, rely wholly on themselves as guides, seldom or never use instruments, and so have their perceptive faculties sharpened beyond any keenness that average sportsmen are likely to acquire. Carry a compass.

CHAPTER V

BLAZES—SURVEY LINES—USE OF THE COMPASS

The chief difficulty in forest travel, especially in flat lands that are heavily timbered, is the lack of natural outlooks from which one could get a view of distant landmarks. Although there are plenty of marks in the woods themselves by which a trained woodsman can follow a route that he traversed not long before, yet these signs are forever changing, vanishing, being superseded by others. Not only do new growths spring up, but old ones are swept away, sometimes suddenly, as by flood or fire. Hence, when men have once picked out a course through the woods that they intend to follow again, they leave permanent marks along the way for future guidance. The most conspicuous and durable waymarks that can easily be made are blazes on the trees. It is of no little consequence to a traveler in the wilds that he should know something about blazes and the special uses made of them in the backwoods.

BLAZES.—On a thin-barked tree, a blaze is made by a single downward stroke, the axe being held almost parallel with the trunk; but if the bark is thick, an upward and a downward clip must be made, perhaps several of them, because, in any case, the object usually is to expose a good-sized spot of the whitish sapwood of the tree, which, set in the dark framework of the outer bark, is a staring mark in the woods, sure to attract attention, at least while fresh. Outside of white birch forests, white is the most conspicuous color in the woods, until snow falls.

USE OF THE COMPASS 61

If a blaze is made merely on the outer bark, it will not show so plainly by contrast. This kind of blaze, however, may be preferred for some purposes; for example, by a trapper who does not want to call everybody's attention to where his traps are set. A bark-blaze has the peculiarity that it lasts unaltered, so long as the bark itself endures, preserving its original outlines and distinctness, no matter how much the tree may grow. But if a wound, however slight, be made through the bark into the sapwood of the tree, so that the sap, which is the tree's blood, exudes, a healing process will at once set in, and the injury, in time, will be covered over. So, as soon as a blaze is made that exposes the wood, the tree begins at once to cover up its scar. This is a slow process. First the edges of the cut will widen, then a sort of lip of smooth new inner bark will form, and this will gradually spread inward over the gash. Once this new skin has formed, the wound will be covered by new annual layers of wood, as well as by new outer bark. Years after the blaze was made, nothing will show on the surface but a slight scar, a sign that takes practised eyes to detect and read.

A blaze always remains at its original height above the ground, and, where two or more spots have been cut in the same tree, they will always stand at the same distance apart. This is because a tree increases its height and girth only by building on top of the previous growth, not by stretching it.

AGE OF BLAZES.—The age of a hack or blaze in a marked tree is determined by chopping out a billet of the wood containing the mark and counting the annular rings of growth from bottom of scar outward, allowing one year for each ring. In counting annular growth, some begin with the first soft lamina (porous part of year's growth), jumping the first hard layer, to the second lamina, and so on. It is more accurate to count the hard strata, for the following reasons: Soft laminae are formed in the spring, when the sap is rising. If a hack is made at that time it may not show until a hard ring forms over it the next fall or winter, when the sap is down. If the season has been very dry, there may be two runs of sap, hence a double soft ring that year. A mark made in wood when the sap is down (after the fall of leaves) can have its age determined very positively, but if made when the fresh sap is up it may be hard to say whether the mark goes through that year's growth or only to it.

On some kinds of trees, if a blaze goes through to the sap wood, the scar on the bark is hard to identify as an ax mark, because the wood, in growing, spreads it.

The age of an axe mark is hard to determine in birch, and impossible in tupelo or winged elm, owing to irregularity of fiber.

A blaze on a frozen tree makes a bad wound.

A mark on the sheltered side of a tree does not look nearly so old as one opposite, because moisture accumulated makes the bark rot off from the weather side.

Blazes on the bark of chestnut, tulip poplar, young white oak, many locusts, and some other trees, are not apt to be permanent because these trees shed their bark more or less and do not retain marks so well as beech, black birch, Spanish oak, mountain oak, and other close-barked trees. Bark that scales does not hold moss.

FOLLOWING A LINE.—Most old woods trails are blazed on only one side of the tree, the side facing the trail, so as to be seen from either direction. Spotted trails (opposite sides blazed as previously described) are seldom made by professional woodsmen except where there is unusual danger of losing the way.

An old line of blazes on spruce or pine trees is much easier to follow than if made on non-resinous trees, because the resin deposited by the oozing sap leaves a very noticeable and durable mark. Similarly, when an inscription has been penciled or

USE OF THE COMPASS 63

painted on a fresh blaze on a pine tree, the sap glazes over the mark and makes it almost imperishable.

In searching out a line of blazes, one should keep his eyes glancing horizontally along a plane about breast-high, because that is the height at which surveyors leave their marks, and others usually follow the custom, unless the line has been spotted by a man on horseback, or from a boat during time of overflow.

When a blazed line turns abruptly, so that a person following might otherwise overrun it, a long slash is made on that side of the tree which *faces* the new direction.

It is difficult to follow a line of blazes when snow is falling, because the wind drives the damp flakes against the tree, where they adhere, and must be brushed away to find the blaze.

Now, it is often of much consequence to a traveler to remember such facts as these. For example, there is nothing more common in the annals of misadventure than for a novice to stray off on a deer trail, or, in southern forests, on a cattle trail, which, although seductively plain at first, leads nowhere in particular and soon dwindles to nothing. When undecided, look for blazes along the path. In heavily timbered regions, such as we are now considering, any trail that is, or ever has been, used as a highway by white men is likely to have been blazed.

Again, it is often of moment to determine, when one strikes a strange trail, what its nature is—for what purpose it was made—and thus be able to figure out whether it is likely to lead directly to a settlement or camp. This ought not to be very difficult when one knows what classes of men have preceded him in this particular forest. Generally speaking, a line spotted in a wide forest that as yet has no farmers' clearings is likely to have been made by either (1) a trapper, (2) a lumberman or timber-looker, or (3) a surveyor.

A TRAPPER'S LINE usually leads from one stream

or lake to another. The blazes are likely to be inconspicuous. The line probably meanders a good deal, but not to escape ordinary obstacles, not disdaining a steep climb for a short-cut. Along its course, at intervals of eight or ten miles, there are probably rude shanties containing supplies or the ruins of such shacks, if the line is no longer used. Such a line does not lead to any settlement, and can seldom be of any use to a wayfarer.

A LUMBERMAN'S LINE.—Timber-lookers may or may not leave evidence of their wanderings—more likely not, for, like other seekers after bonanzas, they may have excellent reasons for not doing so. At most, they would merely mark the easiest route for a prospective road from the river to some "bunch" of timber. Where logging operations have already begun, then, wherever a stump stands it will not be hard to determine the direction in which the logs were twitched to the nearby "lizard road," where they were loaded on lizards (forks of timber used as sleds), or on wagons, and dragged to the river or saw-mill. (I am assuming primitive operations in a remote wilderness.) The lizard road was blazed when first laid out. Logs are never dragged uphill if that can be avoided; consequently the trend of the road will be downhill, or on a level. The lizard road will show ruts, trees barked along the way by whiffle-trees, and other characteristic marks. Wherever there is a bridge or a corduroyed road the timbers will be worn most on the side opposite the camp, because heavy loads were drawn toward camp, not away from it. Once the old lumber-camp site is reached, even though it be long deserted, the signs of an old "tote road" can be discerned, leading toward a settlement from which supplies were transported.

A SURVEYOR'S LINE is absolutely straight (with exception noted below). When it reaches an impassable obstacle, such as a swamp or a cliff, an offset is made to right or left; but this offset is also

USE OF THE COMPASS 65

a straight line, at right angles, of course, to the main one, the latter being continued in the original direction as soon as the obstacle has been passed. For this, and other reasons that presently will appear, a surveyor's line can never be mistaken for any other.

Surveyors are careful to space their marks more uniformly than hunters and trappers and loggers. They cut rather square into the tree, at right angles, so that the weather may not wear away the marks nor the tree become diseased and so obliterate them.

OLD SURVEYS.—The old states of the East and South were surveyed before there were any Government regulations for such work, and had methods of their own for marking lines and corners, varying from place to place. In the rougher regions such work was likely to be slipshod. Old-time surveyors in the mountains often ran lines that were winding, because they had no flagmen to keep the line straight. It was difficult to keep sight marks. Measurements often were inaccurate. The chain was likely to go too low up a ridge and too high in crossing hollows. Mere surface surveying was practised over logs, rocks, etc. Chains were intentionally made over-length to allow for this.

The practice of measuring by half-chains in rough country led to many errors of counting, by dropping a link, and so on. Few of the old surveyors were careful about variations of the compass. In fact, I have known backwoods surveyors who were ignorant of the change in magnetic meridian.

MODERN SURVEYS.—Throughout most parts of the West, the method of numbering, subdividing, and marking township sections is that adopted by the public land surveys, a brief description of which is given below. If one understands the merest rudiments of public surveying, and has a township map of the locality, then, whenever he runs across a section line, he can soon tell exactly where he is, and what is the most direct route to any other point in the neighborhood.

66 CAMPING AND WOODCRAFT

It is common practice, wherever a regular trail crosses one of these lines, to square or face on four sides a tree or two standing close by, drawing the traveler's attention to the line. These survey lines may be of practical use to him in various ways. By them he can determine exactly the position of his camp with reference to the surrounding country. He can locate any point that he desires to visit or revisit, such as a cache, a mineral deposit, a piece of land that he may wish to purchase, and so on. If he gets lost, it is somewhere within half a mile, or less, of a survey line, which will take him to a marked corner from which he can learn his position.

6	5	4	3	2	1
7	8	9	10	11	12
18	17	16	15	14	13
19	20	21	22	23	24
30	29	28	27	26	25
31	32	33	34	35	36

Fig. 8.—Plan for Numbering Sections of a Township

TOWNSHIP AND SECTION LINES.—The public lands of the United States are divided into townships, usually of six miles square (23,040 acres), as nearly as convergence of meridians allows. A township is sub-divided into thirty-six sections, each one mile square, as nearly as may be, which, as a general rule, are numbered as shown in Fig. 8, and are legally subdivided as indicated in Fig. 9.

Starting from an established corner, all trees that stand directly on the line of survey have two chops or notches cut on each side of them, without any other marks whatever. These are called "sight trees" or "line trees" (sometimes "fore and aft trees"). Since there may not be enough trees actually intercepting the line of sight to make such a line conspicuous, a sufficient number of other trees standing within not more than two rods of the line,

USE OF THE COMPASS 67

on either side of it, are blazed on two sides diagonally, or quartering toward the line, or coinciding in direction with the line where the trees stand very near it. Blazes are not omitted where trees two inches or more in diameter are found on or near the line.

Where trees are scarce, bushes on or near the line are bent at right angles therewith, and receive a blow with the axe at the usual height of blazes from the

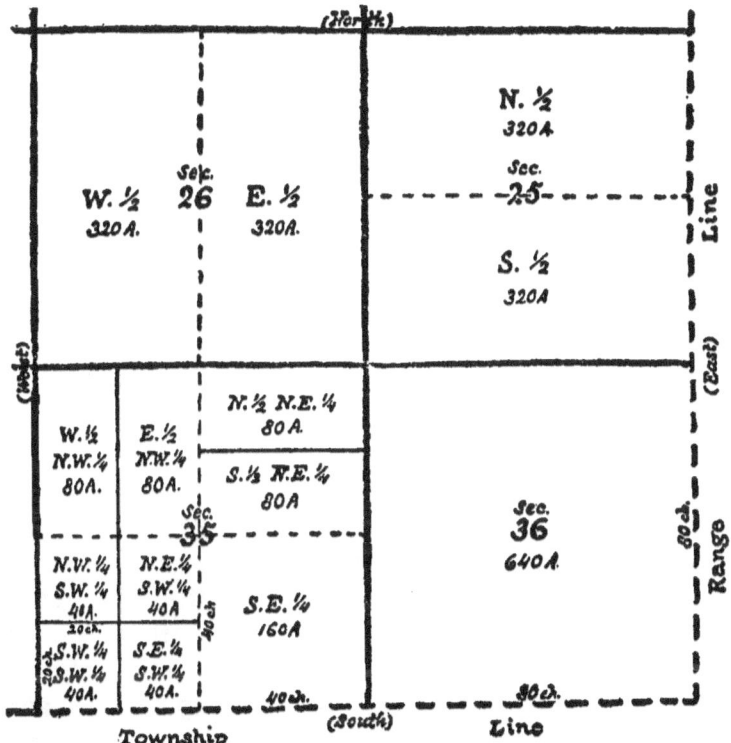

Fig. 9—Subdivision of Sections

ground, sufficient to leave them in a bent position, but not to prevent growth.

When the course is obstructed by swamps, lakes, or other impassable objects, the line is prolonged across by taking the necessary right angle offsets, or by traverse, etc., until the line is regained on the opposite side. At the intersection of lines on both margins, a post is set for a witness point, and two trees on opposite sides of the line are here marked with a blaze and notch facing the post; but on the margins of navigable rivers or lakes the trees are marked with the number of the fractional section, township, and range. Arabic figures are used exclusively.

CORNER MARKS.—The following corners are marked:

(1) For township boundaries, at intervals of every six miles.

(2) For section boundaries, at intervals of every mile.

(3) For quarter-section boundaries, at intervals of one-half mile (with exceptions).

(4) Meander corners, wherever lines intersect banks of rivers, etc., directed to be meandered.

Witness corners bear the same marks as those of true corners, plus the letters *W. C.*

Four different modes of perpetuating corners are employed, in the following order of choice:

(1) Corner trees, when a tree not less than five inches in diameter stands immediately in place.

(2) Stone corners, where procurable. These must be at least 14 inches long. Stones 14 to 18 inches long are set two-thirds and larger ones three-fourths of their length in the ground.

(3) Posts and witnesses. The latter are trees adjacent, in opposite directions, each with a smooth blaze facing the corner, with a notch at the lower end, and with the number of township, range, and section; below this, near the ground, on a smooth blaze are marked the letters *B. T.* ("bearing tree"). Blazes may be omitted from smooth-barked trees. Where there are no trees, witness pits are dug, two feet square, and at least one foot deep.

(4) Posts and mounds. A mound is erected around the corner post, and a marked stone, or some charcoal, or a charred stake, is deposited a foot below the surface on the side toward which the line runs.

Township Corner Post.—This projects two feet above the ground, the projecting part being squared.

USE OF THE COMPASS 69

When the corner is common to four townships, the post is set cornerwise to the lines, and on each flattened side is marked the number of the township, range, and section, thus: *T. 1 S.; R. 2 W.; S. 36.*

This example reading "Township 1 South, Range 2 West, Section 36." *Six notches* are cut on each of the four edges.

If the post is on a closing corner, where the line does not continue straight ahead, but is offset to allow for convergence of meridians, this closing corner being common to two townships south of the base line, six notches are cut on each of the east, south, and west sides, but none on the north, and *C. C.* ("closing corner") is cut on the surface.

The position of *all* township corner posts is witnessed by four "bearing trees," or pits, or stones. Bearing trees are marked like the post; stones are merely notched.

Section Corners.—When the corner is common to four sections, the post is set cornerwise to the lines, the numbers of sections being marked on the surfaces facing them, and on the northeast face the number of township and range is inscribed. All mile-posts on township lines have as many notches on the two corresponding edges as they are miles distant from the respective township corners. Section posts in the interior of a township have as many notches on the south and east edges as they are miles from the south and east boundaries of the township, but none on the north and west edges. All section posts are "witnessed" as above. Section corner stones are merely notched.

Quarter-section Corners.—These are merely marked ¼ and "witnessed."

Red chalk is used to make marks more conspicuous.

USE OF THE COMPASS.—In Volume I (pp. 168-169) some advice was given as to selecting a compass. Let me repeat that it should be of hunting case pattern, not only because an open faced one is easily broken, but because a cover helps to exclude dust and moisture. The least moisture under the glass will cause the needle to stick (if dampness gets inside anyway, dry the compass by a gentle heat: too much heat will destroy the magnetism). And there is another reason: the friction of one's pocket on the glass of a compass may magnetize it and attract the needle (touching the glass with a wet finger will remedy this).

You may have a pocket compass of surveyor's pattern, such as the common military compass in a square wooden box, used in our army. Observe that on a surveyor's compass the E and W marks are transposed, and don't let this fool you in the field.

In using a compass look out for local attraction. Put your gun or axe aside; a knife, or belt buckle, or other piece of metal may deflect the needle. If there is anything in your equipment that might do this, test the instrument first on the ground a pace away, and then in your hand. The compass should not be kept near iron, even when not in use, as the needle is likely to be demagnetized.

A compass needle may be demagnetized when traveling in an electric car if carried in a valise or knapsack and set down on the floor over a powerful motor, if the needle is clamped, as it should be when not in use. To strengthen the magnetism of a compass needle, unclamp it and lay the instrument near a motor or generator or strong magnet; then, when it has stopped quivering, clamp it again and leave it under the influence of the magnetic current for a short time.

A compass may become bewitched by a body of ore that you may be passing over, but such experiences are rare. If you suspect something of the sort, carry the instrument away, it need not be far, and test again. You are far more likely to be bewitched yourself.

THE COMPASS IN CAMP.—No compass can tell

USE OF THE COMPASS 71

you which way camp lies when you are lost. So the first and best place to use it is in camp, before you go anywhere. If there are landmarks visible from camp, take their bearings, and locate them on a sheet of paper or in your notebook. Then, if you are in a flat country, run a base-line as described in Chapter III. If in a hilly region, climb the nearest height, and from it make a sketch map of the surrounding country, with streams and prominent landmarks noted and their bearings shown. Carry that map always with you, and add to it as you learn the country. No matter how rude it may be, it is likely to come in mighty handy.

An experienced woodsman may photograph the landscape on his brain, but not one city man in a hundred can do so with certainty that it will not have blurred or faded away when he gets bewildered. So don't let any false modesty keep you from using your pencil: the man who laughs at an amateur (or anybody else) for doing so is most likely a Reub who never has been a hundred miles from his own front door.

KEEPING A COURSE.—When traveling in a region where there are plenty of outlooks, the weather being clear, the sun and visible landmarks are sufficient guides. When you do use a compass on the march, and the country is not too difficult, it will be enough to hold the instrument in one hand, and, without waiting for the needle to stop swinging, note the point midway of the limits of its motion and take that for north, unless the magnetic declination is considerable (see below).

In level, heavily timbered country, one must take greater pains if he wants to reach a definite point. Lay the compass on the ground, or on any higher object that will hold it level. Or, if both hands are free, hold it in both of them at half-arm's length, with elbows resting on your sides, so as to bring the instrument straight in front of the center of your body. Then face some tall tree or other conspicuous feature of the landscape in direct line with your objective and as far off as you can see. Check the vibration of the needle by quickly tipping the compass until the end of the needle touches the glass, and repeat until needle stops quivering. Now level the box and take the bearing of your landmark. Walk to it, and take a sight on something else in the same line.

Where you cannot see out to take bearings in this way, consult the compass every two or three minutes; for it is the easiest thing in the world to get off a true course at such times, and a few degrees' swerve, if not soon detected, will carry you far astray.

When some obstacle obliges you to make a detour, sight some landmark ahead, if you can, before you go around. If there be none visible, then estimate your winding with great care, and get back in line again as soon as you can. It is rarely the case that one can travel any distance in the wilderness without swerving very often from a true course; so the art of averaging windings should be practiced until one becomes adept.

When following a stream, note how many tributaries you cross. When following a divide, note how many abutting ridges you pass on each side. You will need that knowledge when you return, and it must be *exact*.

MAGNETIC VARIATION.—The north end of a compass needle *does not point to the true north,* except in certain places as noted below. It points to the *magnetic pole,* which lies far south of the north pole and about seven degrees west of the meridian of 90°W.

The places where a compass does point to the geographic north are those situated along what is called the "agonic line," or "zero curve," or "line of no variation." This is not a straight line from north to south like a meridian on the map, but has many waves and loops, and runs in the main easterly

USE OF THE COMPASS 73

of south. At present the agonic line runs from Mackinac Island, in Lake Michigan, loops west and then diagonally through eastern Michigan to central Ohio, makes a big loop north toward Lake Erie and back, south to the Ohio River, makes two big loops east and west in eastern Kentucky, runs south through western Virginia, loops west in eastern Tennessee and then far back east, goes down through western North Carolina, loops east again, and then runs diagonally down through Georgia and out into the Atlantic. This line is not stationary, but has a slow movement westward called the "annual change." Nobody knows the cause of these vagaries: magnetic variation is a mystery as yet unsolved.

Now note this: at *all places east* of the agonic line the north end of a compass needle *points to the west* of true north (more and more as the distance increases), and everywhere *west* of this line it *points easterly*.

For instance, at New York City the compass now points 10°W; at Eastport, Me., 20°W; at Lincoln, Neb., 10°E; at Helena, Mont., 20°E. This "declination" or "variation of the compass" must be allowed for when running a true course, or when plotting one by map.

A line passing through all places that show the same compass variation is called a "line of equal magnetic variation." Such lines do not by any means run straight like meridians, but are wavy and looped and run off at strange angles, like the agonic line, though none of them correspond to its meanders; and they, too, shift slowly westward from year to year.

Now for the practical application. Suppose you are on the line of magnetic variation that runs through Ogden, Utah, where the declination is 18E°. To find true north, you set your compass so that the needle points 18°E, as in Fig. 10. Then the *N* mark on the dial points due north.

To lay out a course by map: spread the sheet out

74   CAMPING AND WOODCRAFT

flat and lay the compass on it with *N-S* line of dial exactly parallel with *N-S* line on map. Then revolve map until needle shows proper number of degrees allowance for local variation, if any. All meridians on the map will then be parallel with the lines they represent on the ground. Now you can take the bearings of your objective, and if the instrument has a movable course arrow (see Vol. I., p. 169) set it accordingly.

The following table of declinations, prepared by the U. S. Coast and Geodetic Survey, is copied from the *World Almanac* of 1916. By adding or subtracting, as the case may be, the "annual change" multiplied by the number of years after 1916, you will get a close approximation to the variation for a future date, although the annual change is not constant.

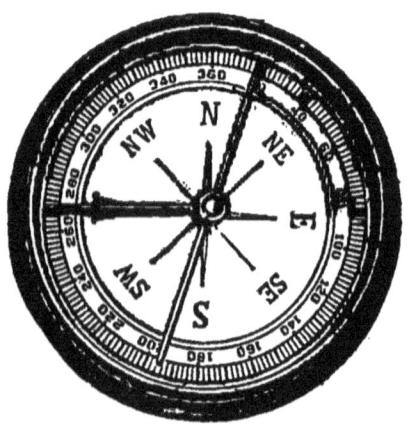

Fig. 10.—Compass Variation

USE OF THE COMPASS

MAGNETIC DECLINATIONS

Or Variations of Compass for January, 1916—With the Annual Change between 1910 and 1915 for the Principal Places in the United States

State or Territory	Station	Variation January, 1916	Annual Change	State or Territory	Station	Variation January, 1916	Annual Change
Ala	Montgomery	2 51 E	+1	Mo	Jefferson City	7 45 E	+1
	Mobile	4 45 E	+1		St. Louis	5 07 E	0
	Huntsville	3 59 E	0		Kansas City	9 24 E	+2
Alaska	Sitka	30 25 E	+2	Mon	Helena	20 16 E	+3
	Kodiak	24 00 E	−2	Neb	Lincoln	10 00 E	+2
	St. Michaels	21 12 E	−4		Omaha	9 51 E	+3
	Dutch Harbor	18 40 E	−4	Nevada	Carson City	17 44 E	+3
	Kiska	7 12 E	−5		Eureka	17 44 E	+3
Ariz	Prescott	14 45 E	+3	N. H	Concord	14 11 W	+6
	Yuma	14 51 E	+4	N. J	Trenton	9 04 W	+5
	Nogales	13 34 E	+4	N. Mex	Santa Fé	13 29 E	+3
Ark	Little Rock	7 00 E	+2	N. Y	Albany	12 11 W	+6
Cal	Sacramento	17 24 E	+3		New York	10 00 W	+5
	San Francisco	18 09 E	+3		Ithaca	8 16 W	+5
	Los Angeles	15 55 E	+3		Buffalo	6 57 W	+4
	San Diego	15 26 E	+3	N. C	Raleigh	2 56 W	+3
Col	Denver	14 45 E	+3		Wilmington	4 43 W	+3
Conn	Hartford	11 44 W	+6	N. Dak	Bismarck	15 11 E	+2
	New Haven	11 13 W	+6		Pembina	11 35 E	+1
Del	Dover	7 42 W	+5	Ohio	Columbus	1 29 W	+3
Dist. of Col	Washington	5 50 W	+4		Cleveland	3 58 W	+3
					Cincinnati	0 43 E	−2
Florida	Tallahassee	2 20 E	0	Okla	Atoka	8 48 E	+2
	Jacksonville	0 58 E	−1		Guthrie	10 02 E	+3
	Key West	2 30 E	0	Oregon	Portland	23 30 E	+3
Georgia	Atlanta	1 33 E	−1	Pa	Harrisburg	7 28 W	+5
	Savannah	0 19 E	−2		Philadelphia	8 37 W	+5
Idaho	Boisé	19 48 E	+3		Allegheny	4 41 W	+5
Illinois	Springfield	4 18 E	0	R. I	Providence	13 15 W	+6
	Chicago	3 35 E	−1	S. C	Columbia	0 23 W	+2
Indiana	Indianapolis	0 59 E	−1		Charleston	1 13 W	+2
	Fort Wayne	0 13 W	+2	S. Dak	Pierre	13 07 E	+2
Iowa	Des Moines	8 03 E	+1		Yankton	11 36 E	+2
	Keokuk	6 03 E	0	Tenn	Nashville	3 55 E	0
Kansas	Topeka	9 32 E	+2		Knoxville	0 26 W	+1
	Ness City	11 40 E	+2		Memphis	5 35 E	+1
Ky	Lexington	0 13 E	+1	Tex	Austin	8 55 E	+3
	Paducah	4 24 E	0		San Antonio	9 31 E	+3
	Louisville	1 11 E	−1		Houston	8 24 E	+3
La	Baton Rouge	6 14 E	+2		Galveston	8 03 E	+3
	New Orleans	5 45 E	+2		El Paso	12 46 E	+4
	Shreveport	7 30 E	+2	Utah	Salt Lake	17 21 E	+3
Maine	Bangor	18 25 W	+6		Ogden	18 17 E	+3
	Portland	15 55 W	+6	Vt	Montpelier	15 16 W	+6
	Eastport	20 30 W	+6		Burlington	13 48 W	+6
Md	Annapolis	6 31 W	+4	Va	Richmond	4 37 W	+4
	Baltimore	6 42 W	+4		Norfolk	5 22 W	+4
Mass	Boston	14 00 W	+6		Lynchburg	3 27 W	+3
	Pittsfield	12 21 W	+6	Wash	Olympia	23 30 E	+3
Mich	Lansing	0 40 E	+2		Walla Walla	22 02 E	+3
	Detroit	1 55 W	+3	W. Va	Charleston	2 53 W	+3
	Marquette	1 51 E	−2		Wheeling	1 56 W	+3
Minn	St. Paul	8 50 E	0	Wis	Madison	4 45 E	−1
	Duluth	8 35 E	−1		Milwaukee	3 04 E	−1
Miss	Jackson	6 18 E	+1		La Crosse	6 25 E	0
	Oxford	5 45 E	+1	Wyo	Cheyenne	15 29 E	+2

A plus (+) sign to the annual change denotes that the declination is increasing, and a minus (−) sign the reverse.

MERIDIAN BY WATCH.—One's watch, if it be keeping correct time, and the sun is shining, can be used as a compass (Fig. 11). The watch being set by local (sun) time, turn the face of the watch to the sun in such position that the hour-hand shall point to the sun. Half-way between the hour-hand and 12 o'clock will then be the *south* point (south of the equator, the north point). Of course, when the sun is near the zenith this trick will not work.

To do the thing accurately, hold a grass stem

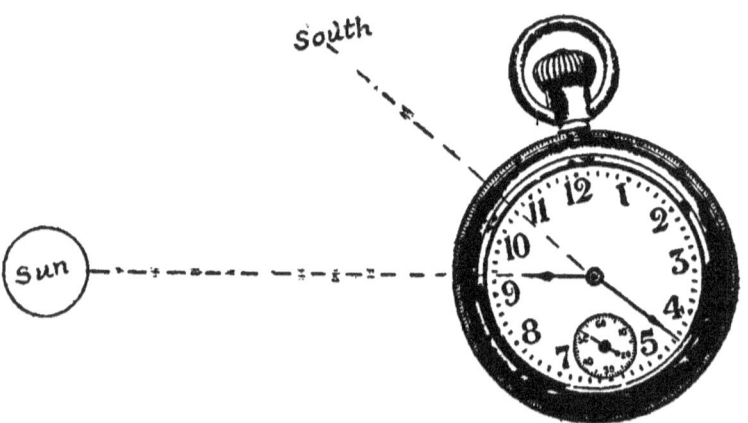

Fig. 11.— Meridian by Sun

or other small object vertically so its shadow will be cast across the face of the watch, and then bring the hour-hand into this shadow.

By laying the watch on a level place and sighting across it at a pole, the true meridian may be established closely enough for most purposes.

MERIDIAN BY SHADOW.—When rough-and-ready methods are not precise enough for one's purpose, the following method will give a true meridian by which variation of the compass may be corrected (Fig. 12): On a smooth and level piece of ground lean a pole toward the north and rest it in a crotch or on shears as shown. Make a plummet with string and stone or other weight, and suspend it from the end of the pole so that the plumb-bob nearly touches the ground.

USE OF THE COMPASS 77

Drive a peg (*S* in the figure) directly under the plummet. Then, an hour or two before noon, attach a string to the peg and, with a sharpened stick tied to the other end of the string, describe a semicircle, or arc of a circle, with a radius equal to the distance from the peg *S* to the shadow of the tip of the pole. Drive a peg on the arc where the shadow of the tip of the pole rested. About an hour after noon, watch the shadow of the tip as it approaches the eastern side of the arc, and drive another peg at the point

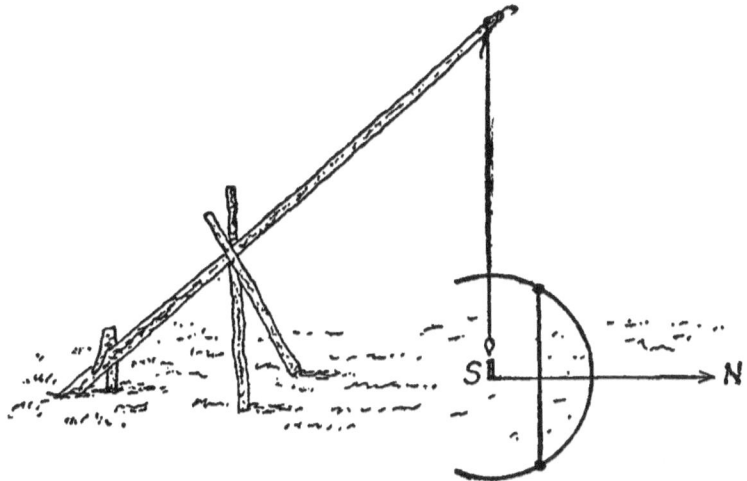

Fig. 12.—True North and South

where it crosses. Then with a string find the middle point of the straight line joining the last two pegs mentioned. A straight line joining this middle point and the peg under the plummet will lie in the true meridian.

To get the variation of the compass needle, set up a pole exactly in line with the short line mentioned above, and sight back from the pole to the tip of the slanting stick that holds the plummet. Make a note of the variation, so many degrees east or west, and use this when running a line by compass.

MERIDIAN BY POLE STAR.—Everybody knows the "Dipper" in the constellation of the Great Bear (Fig. 13). Its stars never set but revolve around

78   CAMPING AND WOODCRAFT

the North Star. The two stars forming the front of the Dipper's bowl (*a* and *b* in the figure), called the "pointers," point toward a conspicuously bright

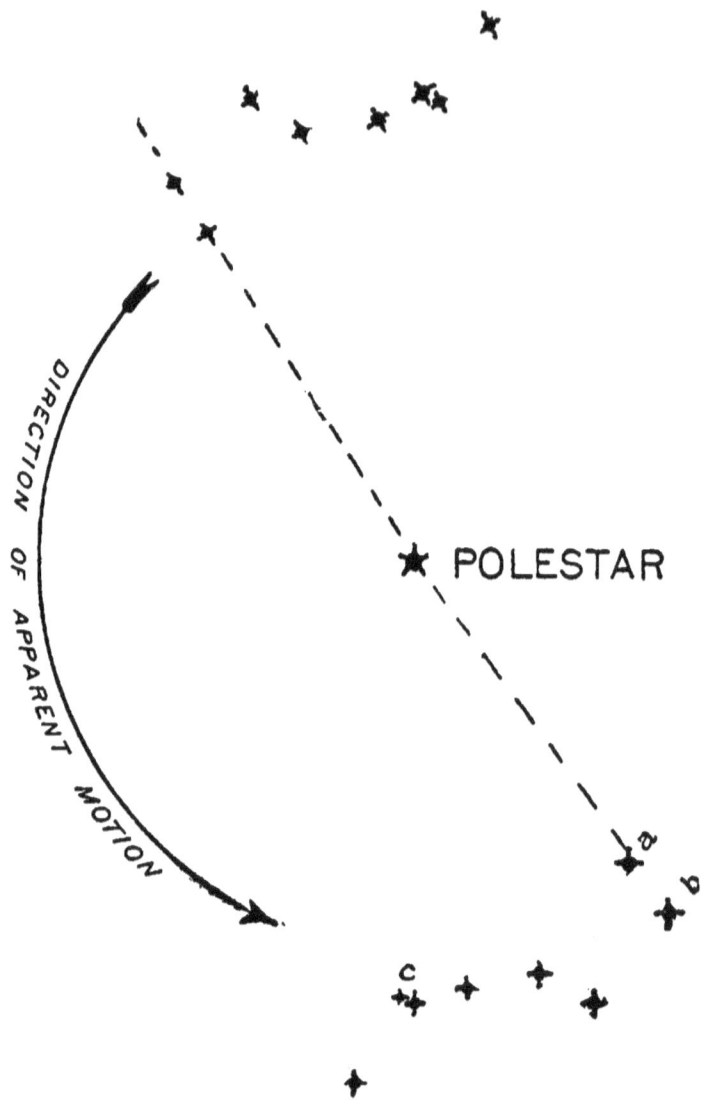

Fig. 13—Position of Big Dipper above or below the Pole Star when the Pole Star is due North.

star which is Polaris, the North or Pole Star.

The North Star bears exactly due north only twice a day. It is always close enough to steer by, but if one wishes to correct his compass by it he must

USE OF THE COMPASS

do so at a time when the double star in the middle of the Dipper's handle (c in the figure) is either directly above or directly below the North Star, for that is when the bearing is correct. At all other hours Polaris bears somewhat east or west of true north.

To find the true meridian: set up two poles ten or twelve feet apart and exactly in line with the North Star, at such time as mentioned above. The front pole should be illuminated by a lantern or candle so that correct sight can be taken. Next day the line of sight can be prolonged, and the compass variation determined.

CHAPTER VI

ROUTE SKETCHING—MAPPING— MEASURING

Among the pleasures of life in a wild country I count first the thrill of exploring new ground. "Something hidden: go and find it!" He who does not respond to that mainspring is out of order— his works need looking into.

Of course, the whole earth has been rambled over by somebody before our time; but it suffices one of us to bore into some wild region that is unknown to himself, unknown to his companions, and which never has been mapped in detail.

I used to go hunting, every fall, with two or three comrades who felt as I did about such matters. We never hired a guide. On arriving at a blank spot we would spend the first day or two scouting. We would scatter, scour the country, and then, around the camp fire at night, we would describe, in turn, what we had found.

Verbal reports, such as these, are more entertaining than useful. The crudest sort of a sketch on paper would have taught us much more. By combining our route sketches we might have produced a serviceable map of the country for miles around. I wish we had made such maps. I would love to pore over them in these later years.

We thought that route sketching would take too much time and trouble. That was a mistake. Anybody who can read a compass and draw lines of direction can make a practical route sketch without losing more than twenty-five per cent of a steady

ROUTE SKETCHING 81

jog. The only instruments and materials needed are a pocket compass, a watch, a lead pencil, and a notebook, or a bit of paper tacked on a piece of thin board.

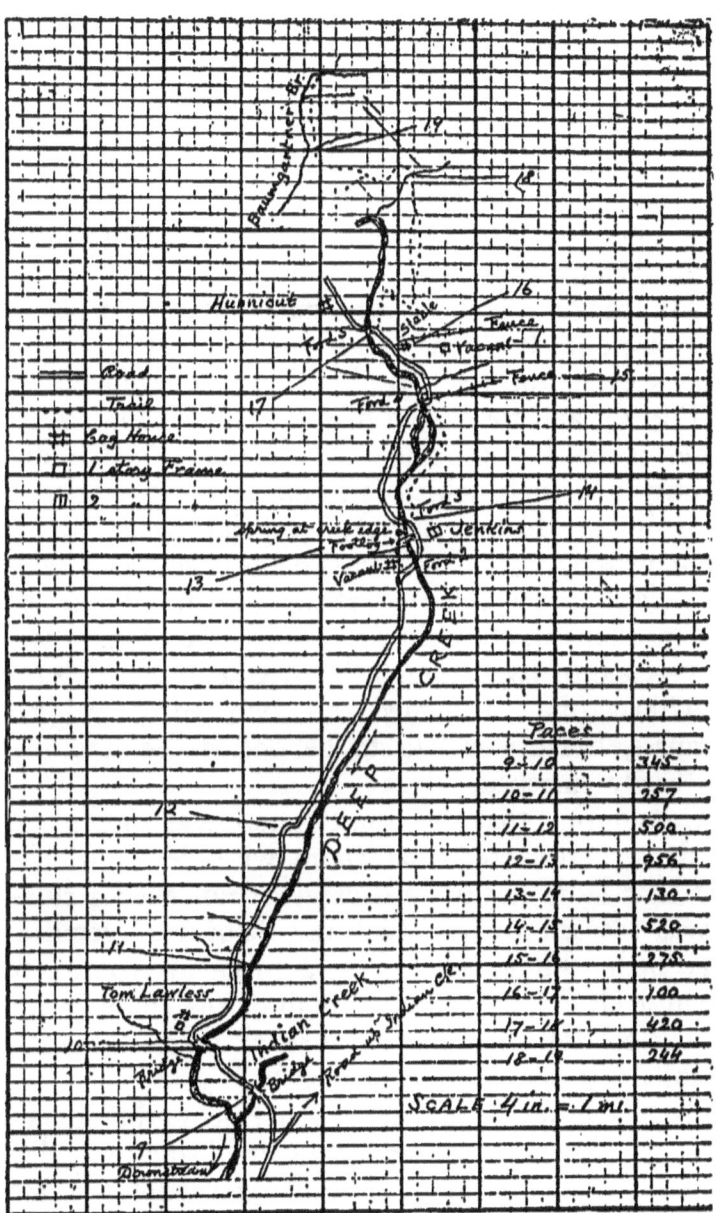

Fig. 14—Route sketch map showing method of computing distances by counting paces from point to point

As examples, I give here a couple of sketches (Figs. 14 and 15) showing, respectively, the backwoods half of the wagon road and the over-mountain trail to "the last house up Deep Creek," where I once lived for a year or so. I made these while still new to the country, without losing more than half an hour from regular marching time. First, I walked in to the railway station, pacing and sketching the trail as I went. The next day I returned by wagon, mapping the road and the creek, without once checking the horses, and judging distances altogether by eye.

My rough sketches were made in a vest-pocket memorandum book that was quadrille ruled. Mere lines showed the road, trail, creek, and branches, as in Fig. 14, and the sketch map was finished on larger paper when I got home. My compass had a dial of only $1\frac{1}{8}$ inch, which is small for such work. I wore it in a leather strap on my left wrist, like a wrist watch; so it never was in the way, yet always was right under the eye when needed. To orient the instrument, it could be slipped out of its guard in a second or two, though this was seldom necessary.

Afterwards I discarded this way of carrying a compass, because it had to be open-faced and was too easily smashed.

Considering that the country here was rough, and so densely timbered that there were few outlooks, and that I did not use a protractor nor even a ruler, I was pleased to find that my "closures" required very little "humoring in," as a surveyor would say. I had a U. S. topographical map of the country, but it was so defective that it was of no use, save in establishing one or two "controls."

In sketching a route it is convenient, though not necessary, to use paper ruled in little squares. Any dealer in draughting materials can supply cross-section paper ruled ten lines to the inch. A piece of such paper, about 7 x 10 inches, tacked on a thin board and carried in the hand, is a good way. If this is too cumbersome, use a notebook, as I did, and, when you come to an edge of the paper, start anew on a fresh page. If you have nothing but plain

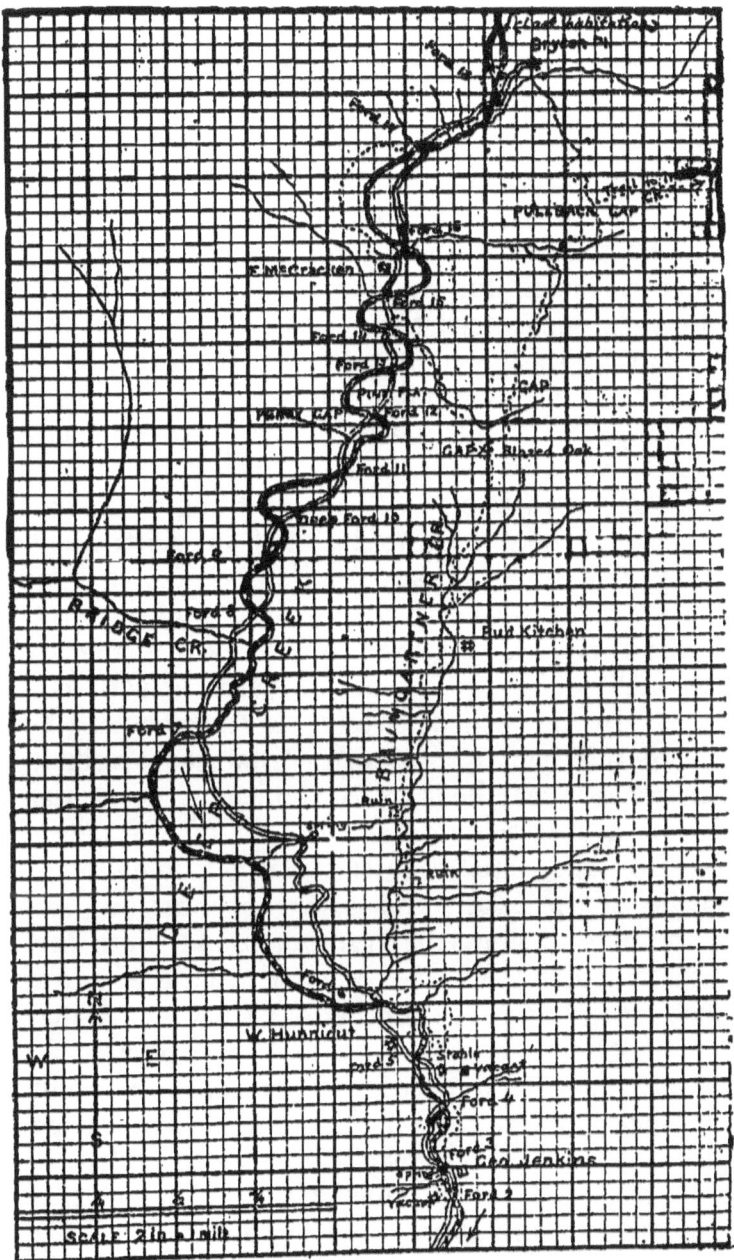

Fig. 15.—Map made by combining two route sketches

paper, a measuring instrument must be used, which need be no more than your octagonal lead pencil on which you have scored two or three inches with their subdivisions.

If you are merely plotting a course, it is not necessary to sketch in so many topographic features as are shown in these examples. In any case it is a mistake to crowd the sheet with details, as they might be confusing. In the present instance the route ran through a mountainous country, but I made no attempt to show contours, nor even to note the steep slopes, for there was a trail all the way. I did note, separately, the marching time from point to point (not shown in sketches), and that is important. The time table of actual marching, in connection with the plotted route, showed plainly enough where the going was slow.

SCALE OF SKETCH.—The first thing to do is to fix on a certain scale to be used in plotting. In Fig. 14 it is four inches to a mile, meaning that four inches on the map corresponds to a mile on the ground itself. Therefore a side of each of the little 1-10 inch squares represents 44 yards of actual distance. In Fig. 15 it is two inches to the mile. (The cuts in this book are reduced from the originals). Sometimes it may be more convenient to use a man's pace or a horse's stride as the unit of a scale. In any case, the scale adopted must be noted on the margin of the paper, and an arrow must be drawn on the map to show the true north and south line.

PACING DISTANCES.—When traveling afoot, distances are judged by counting one's paces. A man's normal stride varies from 27 to 33 inches, according to individuals and nature of ground. Woodsmen commonly exceed this, owing to their rolling gait. The conventional surveyor's pace is 30 inches, and so is that of infantry "quick time." Do not try to pace yards, or any other arbitrary distance. That is unnatural, fatiguing, distracts your attention, and cannot be kept up on a long hike. Walk at your

ROUTE SKETCHING

natural stride back and forth over a measured distance, and average the results. Do this after a long walk, for by that time you will have "struck your gait." Practice first over fairly level ground, and then up and down steep places, learning to make allowances, by lengthening out a little when going up-hill and shortening the stride when going downhill.

One's stride on the march, after he has settled down to it, is likely to be longer than it is in town. In my own case, on a hike over fair road, I find that my pace is about 33 inches (three inches longer than it is around home), and the cadence of a steady jog is 100 steps to the minute. This makes 1,920 paces to the mile. Allowing for uneven ground, I figure on 2,000 paces to the mile, and three miles an hour. This happens to be convenient in plotting, for, when mapping on a scale of, say, four inches to the mile, each of the 1-10 inch squares on my cross-section paper represents just 100 paces of 31.68 inches average, and on a scale of two inches to the mile it is 50 paces. Timber cruisers figure on 2,000 paces to the mile, or 1,000 "cruiser paces" (double paces, as explained below).

THE APPLICATION.—At the start, take the bearings by compass of some object that you can see in advance. Then jog along, counting *every other pace* (left or right foot only) as you go. To count every single pace would be needlessly wearisome. Where there is a long distance between bearing points, drop a pebble into your pocket for every hundred double paces.

When the object you sighted is reached, mark its location on the paper, as nearly as you can, according to compass bearing and distance traversed. Until you become skilful at this without sight compass and protractor, check your first reading by turning around and taking the bearing back to your starting point.

Having located the object, draw a line from the

starting point corresponding to your course, number this first stop "1," and note on the margin the number of paces from 0 to 1, as well as the time between them. Then take a fresh bearing on some other object ahead, and continue the same way.

TIME.—In the wilderness, where roads generally are bad, if there are any at all, the distance traversed is of less consequence, for a mere route sketch, than the time taken to cover it. Your estimates of distance may be faulty, but your watch can be relied upon.

Time measurements also are good enough for rough mapping of open country and fairly straight courses, where it is not necessary to count paces in order to keep the general bearings correct.

JUDGING DISTANCES BY EYE.—In thickets, swamps, blow-downs, steeps, and other places so rough that one can neither pace steadily nor judge distance by time, a man going alone must estimate by eye only. It is remarkable how skilful men can become at this by assiduous practice. Riflemen generally are good judges of distances by eye. Timber cruisers are better still. Amateurs should seldom trust their estimates of distance in the woods and mountains, or over water, for intervals of over 100 yards.

When two men travel together they can assist each other in estimating. Let your partner walk away 100 paces, then hold your pencil at arm's length, and measure his apparent height on it from pencil tip down with your thumb-nail, as an artist does in landscape sketching. Mark that point with your knife. Then let him go another 100 paces; measure and mark again. This scale can be used thereafter wherever his full height is visible.

PEDOMETERS save considerable trouble where trails are good or the country is fairly level and open, but they are of no use in rough country, since they record every step taken, regardless of whether it is in the course or not.

ROUTE SKETCHING

PACES OF ANIMALS.—The paces of saddle animals vary according to individuals, but can soon be determined by test. This should be done both at walk and trot, counting only the double pace, like that of a man, when walking, or the rise when trotting. The pace of a horse is as uniform as that of a man. A mule's gait is still steadier and the stride is more even.

DISTANCE BY SOUND.—In mapping a considerable territory in the mountains, where pacing is unreliable and may be impracticable, two men can work to advantage if one carries a gun or pistol and the other a stop-watch. For example, you wish to know the distance from camp to a certain peak. The man with the gun climbs the peak, and fires a shot when he gets there, to call his comrade's attention. Then he ties his neckerchief on a stick, and, stepping out in plain view, signals with the extemporized flag, and fires at the same instant. The man in camp times, with his stop-watch, the interval between signal and arrival of the gun's report. Sound travels, in quiet open air, approximately at the following rates, according to temperature:

VELOCITY OF SOUND

At—	30° Fahr.,	1030 ft. per sec.	=1 mile in	5.13 secs.
" —	20° "	1040 "	=1 "	5.08 "
" —	10° "	1050 "	=1 "	5.03 "
" —	0° "	1060 "	=1 "	4.98 "
" —	10° "	1070 "	=1 "	4.93 "
" —	20° "	1080 "	=1 "	4.88 "
" —	32° "	1092 "	=1 "	4.83 "
" —	40° "	1100 "	=1 "	4.80 "
" —	50° "	1110 "	=1 "	4.78 "
" —	60° "	1120 "	=1 "	4.73 "
" —	70° "	1130 "	=1 "	4.68 "
" —	80° "	1140 "	=1 "	4.63 "
" —	90° "	1150 "	=1 "	4.59 "
" —100° "		1160 "	=1 "	4.55 "
" —110° "		1170 "	=1 "	4.51 "
" —120° "		1180 "	=1 "	4.47 "

When the air is calm, fog or rain does not appreciably affect the result; wind does, of course. The report of a gun, being sharp and loud, travels considerably faster than this for a *short* distance, but the above table is a close enough approximation for the purposes of sketch mapping.

DISTANCES ON RIVERS.—Floating down a river of fairly regular current, one may estimate distances pretty closely by keeping his boat in midstream and timing it from point to point.

LANDMARKS.—My sketches show how landmarks are noted along the route. In the wild and uninhabited country beyond our house I would have noted old camp grounds, gaps, bad thickets, cliffs, etc., in a similar way. Where the forest and contours are of uniform character, one should establish here and there, some artificial marks. Where tree blazing is not permitted, blazed stakes may be driven, bush-marks made, stones piled, and so on, according to circumstances.

Written notes will help anyone who is to follow the route. The examples here printed were made for a friend who wanted to visit me, but who could not foretell, a day in advance, when he could get away from business. After directing him to get a U. S. Geological Survey topographical sheet for the country south of us, which was accurate up to the place where my sketch map began, I wrote him:

>There are two ways to our place. One is a wagon road over which a team can haul one thousand pounds when Jupiter isn't pluviating. There are eighteen fords in the last six miles. The creek is impassable for a few hours after a smart rain. Ford 10 ("the deep ford") always wets a wagon bed. Ford 12, at the Perry gap, is dangerous when there is ice. No footbridge between Hunnicut's and McCracken's, nor any habitation.
>
>The other way is by trail across the mountain from Hunnicut's. This is always practicable for a mountain-bred horse or mule with light pack, but he must do some sliding down from either the McCracken gap or the Pullback.
>
>Trail at Hunnicut's stable swerves sharply to the right, up a steep bank, and thence onward goes through thick forest. At McCracken gap our fork

ROUTE SKETCHING 89

of the trail is marked by a small oak, with burl at height of your head, blazed last year with a cross, and pencil-marked with arrow. The trail to Indian Creek and the Cherokee reserve on Lufty is much fainter than ours.

MAPPING.—Observe that a mere route sketch is only intended to show the way from one point to another, and tell the user where he is at any stage of the journey. Hence it need not be mathematically accurate, and hence it can be made swiftly, with crude instruments. Mapping proper is much slower work. Still, a very useful and practical map of a region several miles square can be made in a few days by one man, combining his route sketches, provided he takes a little more pains in locating a few prominent landmarks as "controls."

In the example already given the country was so heavily timbered that there were few outlooks from which mountain tops or other features could be observed from different points on the journey. If there had been such, I would have noted their bearings from different positions, and thus would have had a series of positive checks or controls by which to regulate my sketches. How this is done is shown in Fig. 16, which is reproduced from an article in *Outing,* by C. H. Morrill. In this case a 4 x 7 notebook was used, the left-hand page being ruled for notes on compass bearings, distances (a pedometer was carried), time, etc., while the sketch was drawn on the right-hand page. Notice the compass bearings of mountains, brooks and pond.

If a similar trip had been made a few miles away, and bearings taken on objects visible on the first route, the two sketches could be combined into a map, as in Fig. 15. Where there were discrepancies they could be humored in by "splitting the difference," and the finished work would be true enough for practical purposes.

If one has a reliable map of the region he is in, but on too small a scale to show the details that he

90 CAMPING AND WOODCRAFT

wants to record, he can use some of the major features on the map as controls, and thus make his sketch map pretty accurate.

A method of making more accurate sketch maps with an improvised plane table, or with a cavalry sketching case carried on the left wrist, is given in a handy little pocket manual of *Military Map Reading; Field, Outpost and Road Sketching,* by Major Wm. D. Beach, U. S. A. (Hudson Publishing Co., Kansas City, Mo.).

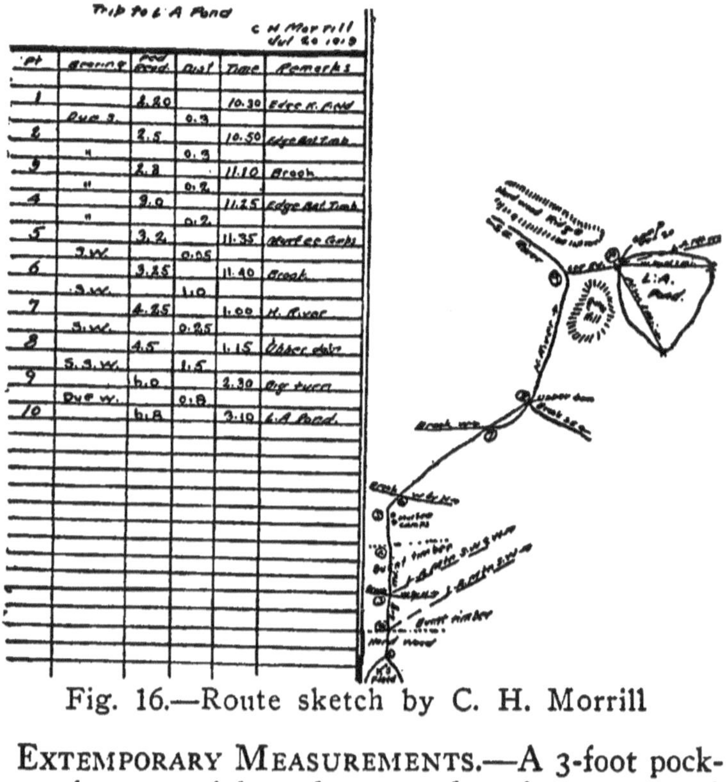

Fig. 16.—Route sketch by C. H. Morrill

EXTEMPORARY MEASUREMENTS.—A 3-foot pocket steel tape weighs only a couple of ounces and takes up no more room than a watch. It is a good thing for a woodsman to carry, as he often has occasion to take measurements. Where the tape is inconvenient to use, he can measure with it a certain length on a straight pole, or on a fish line. Lacking this, he should have a measure scored on his pencil, hatchet handle (if straight), inside of waist

ROUTE SKETCHING 91

belt, or some other article of equipment that he constantly carries.

He should also know some of the measurements of his body. The first joint of the little finger, for instance, may be one inch, or the thumb an inch wide. Clench both fists, making the extended thumbs meet: this may be just one foot. Measure the span of thumb and little finger and the height of your eye from the ground. The full stretch of the extended arms is often used, but is unreliable on curved surfaces, as in measuring the girth of a tree, since it will be several inches shorter than if one stood with his back to a flat wall and stretched his arms horizontally.

To measure successive lengths with a stout cord, such as a fishing line: Knot the line two or three feet from one end, measure off, say, 100 feet from this, and knot again, leaving a stray end beyond the second knot. One end could be looped, as in Fig. 17a, in which case you stick a smooth peg in the ground, put the loop over the peg, carry out the hundred feet, set a peg there, and then jerk the line upward, which, if the ground is smooth, will cause a wave to run along it that will lift the loop off the first peg. But a permanent loop is too likely to catch in bushes, etc.: so it is better to leave plain ends as I have described, and make your loop each time with a hitch (Fig. 17b) so it may shake out as it comes off the peg, leaving only a free end to be hauled in. A sheepshank (Fig. 17c) may be used for the same purpose.

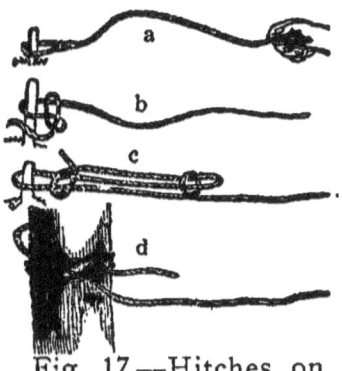
Fig. 17.—Hitches on Measuring Line

However, in the woods, it is better to fasten your line with a signal halyard hitch (Fig. 17d) to any convenient small tree or bush that stands fairly in the line you wish to measure. Pass the end of the line twice round the stem or peg, then, taking the end and a small bight of the measuring part, hitch them as if you were going to tie a reef knot, pull the first hitch tight, but do not complete the knot by making the second hitch; this will hold quite fast enough, and a slight jerk will be sufficient to set it free when you wish to haul in the end.

A measuring line should merely be straight upon the ground, not drawn taut; still less should it be lifted up and then pulled to a straight line in the air. Cords of any kind are too easily stretched to be trusted for measuring if there is any strain on them.

To SET OUT A RIGHT ANGLE.—Any triangle the sides of which are in the proportion of 3, 4, and 5, is a right angled triangle. For example: Measure 40 feet on a line that you wish to run at right angles, Peg A and B (Fig. 18). Fasten end of tape at A, take 80 feet, and fasten 80-foot mark at B. Then, taking tape in hand, walk aside till BC and AC are taut. BC is then perpendicular to AB, and B is a right angle.

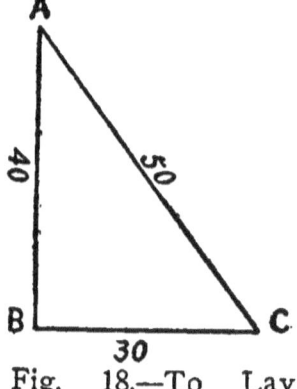

Fig. 18.—To Lay Out a Right Angle

To MEASURE AN INACCESSIBLE DISTANCE.— The width of a river, for instance, may be measured with the aid of a pocket compass. Say the river runs east and west, and you are on the south side. Choose a tree (A, Fig. 19), or other well defined mark on the opposite shore, and bring it to bear due north of you. Mark your position with a peg at B; turn to one side, say the left, and walk westward till A bears exactly northeast, and put a peg there, C; then CB will equal BA, the breadth of the river, because CB and BA subtend an angle of 90°, or a

ROUTE SKETCHING

right angle, and must therefore be of equal length.

Since your readings on a small compass may not be quite true, check them, if the ground permits, by walking east till *A* bears northwest from *D*. If the

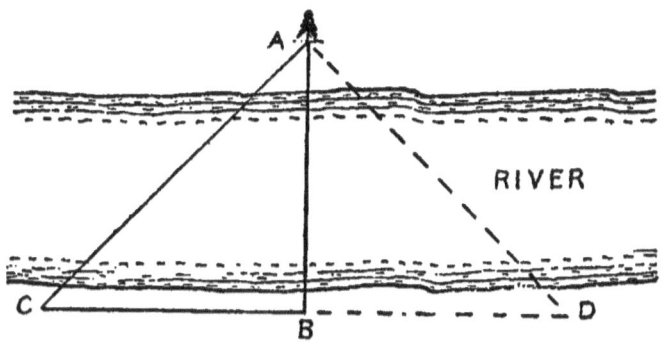

Fig. 19.—Measuring Width of River by Compass.

two observations do not quite coincide, the mean of the two will be approximately correct.

If you have no compass, there are many ways of measuring an inaccessible distance by angles otherwise determined, provided there is enough level land on your side for the purpose. One of these is shown in Fig. 20. Sight a conspicuous object, as before. Plant a stake about 5 feet high at *A*, as nearly oppo-

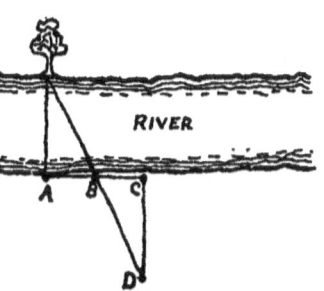

Fig. 20.—Measuring Width without Compass

site and "square" as you can judge. Set up another stake at *B,* as nearly at a right angle as you can, and at about one-half the estimated distance to your mark. Continue *AB* straight to *C* and plant another stake. *AB* must equal *BC*. Now set a stake at *D,* at right angle to base, wherever the line *DB* continued will strike the object across the river that you have been sighting at. Then *DC* equals the width across.

TO MEASURE AN INACCESSIBLE HEIGHT OR DEPTH.—Suppose you wish to measure the height of a cliff, a tree, or other object the base of which you can reach, and with fairly level ground in front of it. In Fig. 21, the man wants to know the length of the merchantable "stick" below the tree branches. He estimates the height by eye, then paces off that distance and marks it at C. He cuts a stake about as long as himself, stands it in front of him and marks on it with his knife the height of his eye, then sharpens the few inches remaining. At C he drives

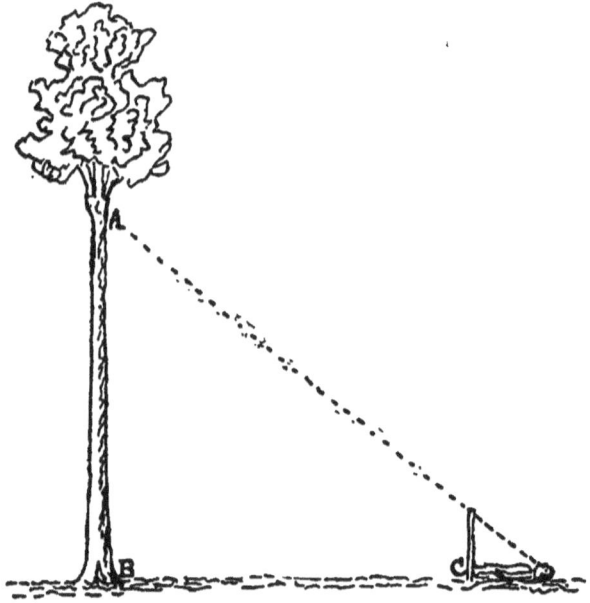

Fig. 21.—Measuring a Height.

the stake perpendicular, with the knife mark level with the ground. Then he lies down with feet against the stake, as shown, and sights at the tree. If the line of sight over the top of stake does not strike the point A, he shifts, and tries again, until the alignment is correct. The height AB then equals the distance BC.

Some backwoodsmen have a rough-and-ready way of estimating the height of a tree. They walk off until its topmost branches or first fork can be viewed by looking backwards between the outstretched legs;

ROUTE SKETCHING 95

with practice this method may become pretty accurate.

On level open country a height can be measured by shadow. Set up vertically a stick of known length; measure the length of its shadow, and that of the object whose height is required. As the length of stick's shadow is to stick's length, so is that of the object's shadow to the object's height. For example: the stick is 5 feet long and its shadow 7, while the shadow of the tree is 70 feet; then 7:5::70:x, and x=50 feet.

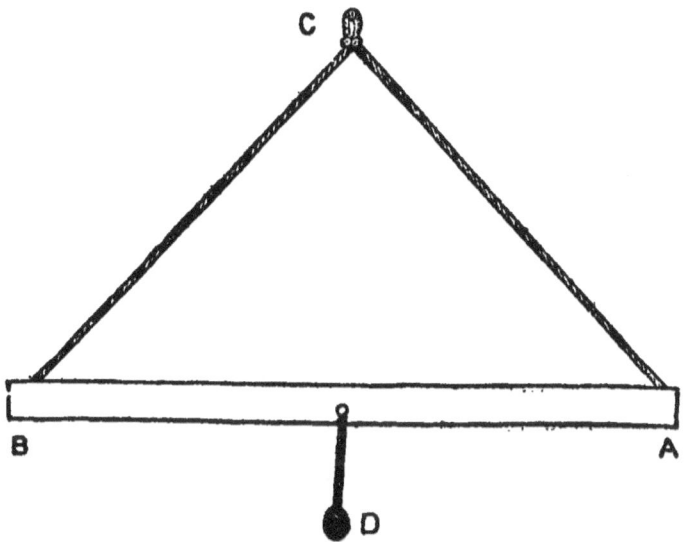

Fig. 22.—Extemporized Level

To measure a depth with the watch: square the number of seconds a stone takes to reach the bottom, and multiply by 16: the result is the depth in feet.

LEVELING.—Take a short straight stick or ruler, AB in Fig. 22, mark it exactly in the middle, and suspend it with a string with loop at C directly over the middle of the stick, from which latter a little weight D is suspended to keep the wind from shaking the level. To use the instrument: hold it from C above your head so that top of stick is in line with your eye, and sight along the surface, noting at what point of the ground the line of sight corresponds.

Going there, you have ascended a distance equal to the height of your eye from the ground. Many applications of this method will suggest themselves.

I do not give more elaborate processes of measuring and leveling, because the simple ones here described are accurate enough for a woodsman's purposes, and they take little time or trouble.

TIME.—A leaf of an almanac for the month you are out is useful in case your watch runs down. The *World Almanac* shows the time of rising and setting of sun and moon for four different zones from the Atlantic to the Pacific. These, of course, are dependable only when you can observe them on a level horizon; but the time when the sun is in the zenith (directly overhead) is also given for every day in the year, on the meridian of Washington, and you can allow for the difference in time wherever you may be. The sun is in the zenith when a straight pole casts its shortest shadow.

A practical sundial is easily extemporized by sweeping off a level place and planting in it a 5-foot stick slanted toward the north by compass. Nail the stick to a stout stake driven under it, so it cannot be moved, and sharpen the upper end so as to cast a finely tapered shadow. When the sun shines, take your watch and stick a peg at the end of the shadow for each even hour. Subdivisions of the hour can be marked by shorter pegs. In a fixed camp such a sundial is handy near the cook's fire. Often I have boiled my three-minute eggs by one. If the pegs are altered every week they will indicate near enough actual sun time for practical purposes.

CHAPTER VII

TRIPS AFOOT

Quand na pas choual, monté bourique;
Quand na pas bourique, monté cabri;
Quand na pas cabri, monté jambe.
(When you have no horse, you ride a donkey;
When you have no donkey, you ride a goat;
When you have no goat, you ride your legs.)
—*Creole Saying.*

The man who goes afoot, prepared to camp anywhere and in any weather, is the most independent fellow on earth. He can follow his bent, obey the whim of the hour, do what he pleases whenever he pleases, without deference to anybody, or care for any beast of burden, or obedience to the course of any current. He is footloose and free. Where neither horse nor boat can go, he can go, seeing country that no other kind of traveler ever sees. And it is just these otherwise inaccessible places that have the strongest lure for anyone who delights in new discovery, in unspoiled nature, and in the charms of primitive society.

The man with the knapsack is never lost. No matter whither he may stray, his food and shelter are right with him, and home is wherever he may choose to stop. There is no anxiety about the morrow, or the day after. Somewhere he will come out—and one place is as good as another. No panic-stricken horse, or wrecked canoe, can leave him naked in the wilderness.

But how to do it? This is the hardest problem in outfitting. To equip a pedestrian with shelter, bedding, utensils, food, and other necessities, in a pack so light and small that he can carry it without overstrain, is really a fine art. One can't enjoy wild scenery and backwoods characters if bending and chafing under a load of fardels, all the time conscious that he is making a pack animal, a donkey, of himself.

Consider, then, your personal equation. If you are a middle-aged city man, soft from a year or more of office work, about twenty pounds on your back is all the weight that you ought to carry. Even that little will be burdensome the first day out; but soon you will be striding along all day hardly knowing it is there. A younger man, or one who gets a good deal of daily exercise in the open air, can do the same with thirty pounds, until he gets in training, and then go considerably more.

I am speaking of all-day hikes, across country, through the woods, uphill and down dale. In untracked wilderness, especially if it be mountainous, it takes a husky fellow, in good form, to pack fifty pounds without over-exertion. Yes, infantrymen carry seventy, sometimes, but they don't do it through thickets, over rocks and down-logs, up and down ravines, where there are no trails—nor are they out for the fun of the thing. The personal equation, then—your own—regardless of what other folks do, or think you ought to do. Find out what is light and easy for you, and then *GO LIGHT*.

Weigh the essentials. Are you to sleep out? You need a comfortable bed, shelter from rain, and security against venomous insects. Food, then, for how many meals? Choose what can be cooked with the simplest and lightest utensils, and what will give you the most nourishment for its weight and bulk, and such as does not require more than half an hour to make ready and fit for the stomach. Bedding, shelter, food and something to prepare it in: those are the essentials, besides the clothes on your back and the contents of your pockets. Anything else is dispensable, to be picked with care and weighed with scales, and balanced against some other thing that might be of more real use or pleasure.

Then how is the weight to be carried? A great

TRIPS AFOOT 99

deal depends on getting a pack so adjusted that it will "ride" just right, shoulders and hips each bearing their due part of the strain, with as little binding and chafing as possible.

Finally, will you go in company or alone? A party of three or four uses the same tent, utensils, and some other articles in common. That means less weight for each man to carry. Two in a bed require less bedding than if they slept separately. A satisfactory kit for one man who goes alone and afoot is the last refinement in camp equipment. Because this is a particularly difficult problem I shall give it special attention. Whoever masters it will have little trouble in getting up a squad outfit.

CLOTHES.—This topic has been considered in detail in Vol. I. (pp. 138-163). Little need be added. Footwear is the most important item. Shoes and socks must *FIT*, or you will be made miserable by blisters. For dry weather and fair roads, the standard U. S. Army shoes are excellent; but for rough country, heavier ones, made over the Munson last, are required. In the wilderness there is considerable wading to do, sometimes over the shoe tops. The only shoes that will stand it are those that are waterproofed and have no lining whatever: they dry out soon on the march, and do not get hard or "bowed up." Buy them of some firm that makes a specialty of sportsmen's footwear.

Up to the season when Mackinaws are needed, do not carry a coat. You would not wear it on the march, and, when the cool of evening comes, a sweater coat or a Mackinaw stag shirt is more comfortable, besides being a good night garment, which the coat distinctly is *not*. Then have a light-weight rubber cape reaching just to the knee. From the knee down you will get wet anyway, even though you wear a long poncho or rain coat, and any garment that flops against the legs at every stride is a positive nuisance; besides, it will soon tear when you thrash through brush, and it will trip you at every step in climbing. A cape has the merits of a poncho, in that it is airy underneath, and it can be slipped on over the pack-sack, while it has the advantage of leaving your arms free to fend off bushes, to climb with, to shoot, paddle, and so on.

There is a pattern called the "Fairy," 34 inches long, that weighs only 21 ounces and takes up hardly any room when packed. It and a medium-weight sweater coat together weigh only about six ounces more than a duxbak hunting coat. Worn together, they form good protection against a cold, keen wind.

Carry a change of underwear. When on a hike, take your bath or rub-down at close of day, instead of in the morning; then change to fresh underwear and socks, and put on your sweater and trousers to sleep in. Fresh dry underclothes are as warm as an extra blanket would be if one slept in the sweaty garments he wore during the day—to say nothing of cleanliness.

SHELTER.—Rain is the campaigner's worst enemy. Jack Frost can be kept at bay, in a timbered region, though you be bivouacing under the stars; but you require a waterproof roof to defy Jupiter Pluvius. The kind will depend chiefly on whether you go alone or in company. For two or more, choose one of the very light tents described in Vol. I. (pp. 76-108). When going alone, in summer, a simple shelter cloth and small mosquito bar are sufficient. They can easily be made at home. Take, for example, seven yards of the green waterproof material called verdalite, which comes in 38-inch width, and weighs $4\frac{1}{4}$ ounces to the running yard. Sew up three widths of seven feet length, and hem all around, making a rectangle very nearly 7 x 9 feet. Put small grommets or eyelets around all four edges, for tie-strings. The completed shelter cloth, in this material, will weigh about $2\frac{1}{4}$ pounds, in waterproofed "balloon silk," or similar stuff, about $2\frac{1}{2}$ pounds.

Such a cloth may be set up in various ways. One of the quickest is to tie or nail a pole horizontally from one sapling to another, four feet from the ground, for a ridge, and tie one of the 9-foot sides of the cloth to it. Tie the other side of the cloth to another straight pole, draw out to an angle of 45°, and pin the pole down with an inverted crotch at each end. That is all. You have a shed roof sheltering a space 5¾ by 9 feet, and 4 feet high in front. Under this you sleep parallel with the fire, instead of feet toward it. If no small trees stand in the right place, set up a pair of forked stakes, or, on rocky ground, shears (Vol. I., p. 46). Sharpen both ends of a pliant green stick, bend it into a bow, and drive the ends into the ground on either side at the head of your bed, to support your mosquito netting; crawl under, and tuck the edges of the net under your bedding.

Smoke from the camp-fire does not hang under such a shelter, as there is free draught through it. If the wind shifts lean a pole against the ridge, on the windward side, and stack some boughs against it. Nothing could be simpler, cheaper, lighter, more compact, nor, in the long run, more satisfactory for the lone forest cruiser in summer, than this plain rectangle of thin but close-woven waterproof cloth. One of its advantages is that a stretcher-bed, if you carry such a thing, can be set up under it without bother about the length of poles. With the cloth set up over a big fallen log for windbreak, as already described under BIVOUACS, there is plenty of headroom. If you wish to stay a few days in one place, the cloth can be used as a roof over a frame of baker tent form. I carry a few wire nails and tacks for making such a structure.

For a mosquito bar, take two yards of the fine mesh that comes in 68-inch width, and hem the ends, or use bobbinet, which is stronger and a better protection.

BEDDING.—Don't bed down on the cold, hard earth. And, unless you know the country to be traversed, don't depend on finding balsam or hemlock for a browse bed wherever you may spend a night. In Vol. I. (p. 134) I have spoken of the bed tick. One that I now have, made of romper cloth, is a bag 32 x 78 inches, to be filled with dry leaves, if nothing better is found, and closed with horse-blanket pins; it weighs just one pound, and takes up very little space in the knapsack. The leaves, being in a bag, cannot spread from under you; they cushion the body and keep off the chill of the ground. A 3-pound blanket on top of such a mattress is warmer than a 5-pound one without it, and a pound weight is saved, to say nothing of bone-ache. That is enough for summer camping, unless you are at a considerable altitude.

A 20 x 30-inch pillow-bag will weigh 3 ounces. Stuff it with leaves or other soft material, before you turn in at night, close the end with safety pins, and pin your towel over it if the surface is not soft enough.

COOKING KIT.—It is easy to make up a good light-weight set of utensils for two or more men (see Vol. I. pp. 118-123), but a satisfactory one-man kit is another matter. The Boy Scout sets do fairly well for a short outing when baked bread is carried, but are inadequate for baking on the journey. A reflector is too cumbersome for a lone woods-cruiser. Let him bake his bread and cakes in a frying-pan (see Vol. I, pp. 344-345). This calls for an 8 or 9-inch pan. Get one with folding handle (detachable ones are easily lost), or take a common one, cut off all of the handle but about $1\frac{1}{2}$ inches, and rivet on this stub a semi-circular socket into which you fit your stick for a handle when you go to cooking. For general use I do not like aluminum frying pans, but when traveling afoot they are satisfactory. A deep aluminum plate fits inside the pan in my kit, along with an aluminum fork, white-metal dessert spoon, and a dish towel. When tied up tightly in a light bag they do not rattle around. You want two little kettles for cereals, dried fruit, tea or coffee, to mix dough in, and the like. A pot that is broad and shallow boils water much sooner than one that is deep and narrow, and it is easier

TRIPS AFOOT

to clean. The kettles must not be too big to stow in the knapsack. Anyway, when one is going afoot he does not want to bother with food that takes long boiling, and so has no use for a large kettle I choose two 1-quart aluminum buckets, which can be bought through any dealer in kitchen ware, fill them with part of my foodstuffs, set them bottom to bottom, and tie them tightly in a bag so that the covers will not come off. So there is no waste space, for the food must go somewhere, anyway. The kettles are good protection for perishables. Thus no sooty vessel goes inside another, and you have a package of small diameter.

A seamless tin cup is carried wherever convenient, generally outside the pack, where it can be got at when one is thirsty. Aluminum is much too hot for cup and spoon. The complete kit weighs just 2 lbs. 2 oz. including bags. No table knife is carried, as I wear a sheath knife.

TOOLS, ETC.—In summer the little 12-ounce tomahawk already mentioned is all that is needed in that line, its chief uses being to get kindling in wet weather, provide poles and thatch for shelter, blaze a trail, and so on. A small pair of side-cutting pliers is well worth its weight, if you are a fisherman.

The first aid kit mentioned in the following lists is made up as described in Vol. I. (p. 175), with the addition of a "snake doctor" which consists of a hard rubber tube, about half the size of a fountain pen, in one end of which is a lancet (very dull as you buy it) and in the other a receptacle containing potassium permanganate in crystals ready to be rubbed into the incision. There is also a pair of splinter forceps. The whole goes in a tin tobacco box, $4\frac{3}{8} \times 3\frac{1}{4} \times 1\frac{1}{8}$ inches, sealed airtight with adhesive plaster, and weighs 5 ounces.

Other small "icta" will vary according to one's personal taste and requirements. The point is to have them compact and of unnoticeable weight. For a trip afoot there is no need of a whole spool of thread, for example, or of wire, or a quarter-pound mirror, or a large towel, or a whole cake of soap.

ONE-MAN KIT FOR SUMMER.—As an example, to be modified each for himself, I list below a summer marching and camping outfit (good also as a canoeing kit) complete for a man going alone. It is enough in most parts of our country, but warmer bedding would be required at high altitudes, and perhaps a closed tent, such as the "Compac" or one of the semi-pyramid type, weighing $3\frac{1}{2}$ to 4 pounds, instead of the one-pound shelter cloth. The total weight of the pack, as here given, including two days' full rations, is 23 pounds 2 ounces. The whole equipment, except the few light articles worn on the person, stows *inside* a pack sack of moderate dimensions. There is nothing exposed to advertise your mission; so you give the idle curious something to puzzle and fret over—which is good for them.

With such an outfit and his gun or fishing tackle, camera, or whatever may be the tools of his outdoor hobby, anyone of average physique and a little gumption can fare very well in the open, and enjoy absolute independence.

It will be noticed that little is carried on the person. Such things as are used many times a day are right where they can be reached without fumbling or pulling out the wrong article. Very little weight is carried on the belt. Comfort and suppleness of movement have been studied. There is no "ditty bag"; I discarded such a pouch long ago. If worn on the left side it often is in the way, and it dangles provokingly when you lean over or get down to crawl. If carried on the belt it is too heavy there. When I go out just for a day, I carry on my back a miniature knapsack containing the cape, lunch, tea pail, and such other things as I need for the work at hand. Five or six pounds on the back is less burdensome than half that weight in a ditty bag, and it is out of the way.

TRIPS AFOOT

It is important in marching that the trousers should be held snug up in the crotch, or there will be chafing. They should not be tight around the abdomen, as that would constrict blood-vessels and interfere with digestion. Stout men, and those with narrow hips, cannot depend on a belt, unless it is drawn very much too tight. Ordinary suspenders are best for them, but many object to their appearance, and so the "invisible" kind is specified in this check-list, although it is hard on buttons.

SUMMER EQUIPMENT FOR BACK-PACKING

WEAR
Woolen gauze undershirt.
Woolen gauze (or balbriggan) drawers.
Woolen socks, winter weight, natural color.
Army overshirt, olive drab chambray (or flannel).
Silk neckerchief, 27 x 27 in.
Khaki trousers, extra suspender buttons.
Invisible suspenders.
Leather belt, narrow.
Army shoes, cone-headed Hungarian nails.
Army leggings, canvas.
Felt hat, medium brim, ventilated, felt sweat-band.

IN POCKETS
Left shirt.—Map sections, in cover. Leaf of almanac. Note book and pencil.
Right shirt.—Compass.
Left trousers.—Purse. Waterproof match box, flat pattern (as reserve).
Right trousers.—Pocket knife.
Fob.—Watch.
Left hip.—Pipe. Tobacco.
Right hip.—Bandanna handkerchief.

ON BELT
Right side, front.—Waterproofed matches (50) in leather belt-pocket.
Right side, rear.—Sheath knife.

ON BACK

	lbs.	oz.
Duluth pack sack, 24 x 26 in. (see Fig. 32)..	2	4
Shelter cloth, 7 x 9 ft., waterproof	2	4
Mosquito net, 68 x 72 in.		4
U. S. A. blanket, summer weight, 66 x 84 in. ...	3	
Browse bag, 32 x 78 in.	1	
Pillow bag, 20 x 30 in.		3

CAMPING AND WOODCRAFT

Rubber cape, 34 in.	1	5
Stag shirt	1	8
Spare suit underwear and socks, as above	1	2
Tomahawk, muzzled		12
Side-cutting pliers, 5 in.		4
Carborundum whetstone, 4 x 1 x ½ in.		2
Wallet fitted with small scissors, needles, sail needle, awl point, 2 waxed ends, thread on card, sail twine, buttons, safety pins, horse-blanket pins, 2 short rigged fish lines, spare hooks, minnow hooks with half barb filed off, sinkers, snare wire, rubber bands, shoe laces		6
Strong twine in bag		1
Aluminum frying-pan (8⅝ in.), plate, fork, white-metal dessert spoon, dish towel, in bag	1	1
2 Aluminum buckets (1 qt.), in bag		14
Tin cup, seamless (1 pt.)		3
Nails and tacks		3
Cheesecloth, 1 yd.		1
Fly dope, in pocket oiler		2
Talcum powder, in wpf. bag		1
Comb, tooth brush, tiny mirror, bit of soap in wpf. bag, rolled in small towel secured by rubber bands		6
Toilet paper		1
First aid kit		5
Spare matches, in tin box secured by adhesive plaster		2
Electric flasher, flat, round corners		5
Total pack without provisions	18	3

TWO DAYS' RATIONS

	lbs.	oz
Bread, or prepared flour, in wpf. bag ....*net*	1	
Cereal, in bag	"	8
Milk powder, in bag (=1 qt. milk)	"	4
Butter, in tin	"	4
Bacon, sliced and trimmed, in waxed paper	"	12
Cheese, in waxed paper	"	4
Egg powder, in bag (=9 eggs)	"	3
Raisins, in bag	"	4
Dried apricots, prunes, or cranberries, in bag	"	4
Sugar, in bag	"	6
Chocolate (for eating), in waxed paper	"	4
Coffee, ground, in bag	"	2
Tea, in bag	"	1

TRIPS AFOOT

Salt, in bamboo tube	"	2
		4 10
Bags, paper, tin, tube		5
		4 15
	Pack complete..23	2

The articles in the main pack suffice for an indefinite period. If one is going out only for a couple of days he will not carry all of them. The provisions afford a varied diet, yet weigh no more than "iron rations" of hardtack, bacon, and coffee, and they keep as well. They are very nourishing for their weight, being almost water-free (except fresh bread, if taken instead of flour). Since one usually travels either where fish or game can be secured, or where farm produce can be bought, the food packed along may last longer than two days. If such rations as those here listed were carried sufficient for a week, the whole burden would still be only about 35½ pounds, allowing for a larger pack sack.

When bread is to be baked on the journey, I make up a mixture beforehand of wheat flour (2 parts), cornmeal (1 part), a little egg powder, and some baking powder sifted in. This makes a fine johnny-cake, lighter than common frying-pan bread, wholesomer, and better tasting.

Abjure all canned stuffs on a marching trip. If you test the canned meats, etc., that are put up in tins small enough for one man, you will find that nearly or quite half of the weight is *in the* tin.

The little bags mentioned above are made of the thin but stout paraffined cloth called by tent makers "balloon silk." Salt draws too much moisture to be carried in a bag, and it quickly rusts tin; so cut a joint of bamboo to proper length, put in the salt, and secure the cork with a strip of adhesive plaster. Such tubes are useful for various purposes, being very light and unbreakable.

In Vol. I. (p. 190), I spoke of the difficulty in getting milk powder made of anything richer than skim milk. Since then I have learned that a certain New York outfitter keeps in stock milk powder that contain 27½ per cent. of butter fat, which is the U. S. Government standard for whole milk, cream included, and it is good.

A waterproof match box is good for emergencies, but not for a smoker's daily supply. For this I waterproof the matches themselves, as described in Vol. I. (p. 173) and carry them on my belt in a snap-buttoned pigskin case that came originally with a round carborundum whetstone. This is the handiest way I know of when one does not wear a coat or vest. A similar pocket will carry thirty .22-caliber cartridges for your rifle or pistol.

A bag of the cheesecloth is used to carry fish in, or to hang up game in when flies are about, and a little square of it serves as substitute for a tea-ball.

Nails are not needed unless you expect to stay several days in one place and wish to put up a lean-to of baker tent shape, with shelter cloth for roof, and thatched sides and back—then they are useful in making the frame. In that case you will want half a dozen each of 6d and 3d wire nails, and some galvanized tacks (they do not rust the cloth). A few 1-inch wire brads are handy to hang kettles on pot-hooks, as they do not split the end of a green stick, but simple notches will do.

When traveling in company through a thickly wooded region, where the men may have to scatter to find a trail or a divide, it is good forethought for each of them to carry a whistle, the army pattern being a good one. Its note carries better than the voice, and it saves breath. Have a pre-arranged code of signals, such as *one note*: "I am here," *two*: "Come this way," and so on.

FEATHERWEIGHT KITS.—The outfit already listed may be considered of medium weight. A heavier one, for cold weather camping, will be suggested in Chapter IX. But what is the lightest equipment that will serve for tramping and camping, decently, in civilized country? Many summer outers who enjoy walking and like to explore out-of-the-way places are interested in that question.

Well, what would you say of a ready-made camping outfit that weighs just 7 pounds? Tent, jointed poles, pegs, ground sheet, sleeping bag, air pillow, toilet articles, canvas bucket and wash-basin, spirit stove, cooking utensils—seven pounds to the very ounce; and the whole kit is so compact that it stows in a light rucksack, or a bicycle pannier, with room left for spare clothing and such food as is not bought along the route of travel. Total burden about 10 pounds, with which the lone pedestrian or cycle tourist is independent of hotels and boarding-houses!

I first heard of this campestral marvel in 1910, when a young Londoner wrote me for a dimensional sketch of a tomahawk I had recommended. A chatty correspondence followed that introduced me to a new Old World scheme of tent life very different from what I was used to, but one developed to the last line of refinement and full of canny tricks of the outers' guild.

For me it was an eye-opener to find the lightest camp equipments of the world in England, a nation I had always associated with one-ton "caravans" at home and five-ton "safaris" abroad. Verily here was the art of open-air life evolved to a type undreamed of in our own country.

Back of this development, I learned, were years of patient, thoroughgoing experiment by scores of men and women whose one fad (if it be a fad) was to perfect a camping kit that should be light, lighter, lightest, and yet right, righter, rightest. Then it came to me from faraway years that the father of modern lightweight camping was not the Yankee "Nessmuk," but the Scotchman Macgregor, who in 1865, built the first modern canoe, *Rob Roy,* and cruised her a thousand miles with no baggage but a black bag one foot square and six inches deep. It was said of Macgregor that he would not willingly give even a fly deck passage,

Featherweight camping in "civilized" fashion began with the *Rob Roy*, progressed with the flotillas of British and American canoeists who followed its skipper's example, was refined by the squadrons of cycle tourists and the pedestrian campers who scour the highways and byways of all Christendom in their yearly holidays.

To one whose camps have always been pitched in the wilderness the seven-pound English kit seems amusingly frail and inadequate. Such a one might exclaim in mock reverence, as my partner used to when he caught me modeling some new-fangled "dingbat": "Great and marvelous art thy works, Lord Geeminy Criminy!" But such an outfit is not meant for the wilderness. It is for the independent vacationist who wants to ramble off the beaten track, to see what conventional travelers always miss: the most interesting and picturesque places and peoples in their own and foreign countries.

European outfitters have been catering for years to this class of trade; but what have we done for it? Precious little. Whoever goes in for that sort of vacation must either pack around with him twice as much weight and bulk as there is any sense in, if he buys his kit ready made, or he must build an equipment for himself, which few tourists have either the time or the skill to do. Perhaps, then, this foreign cult may be worth looking into.

First, the featherweight kit already alluded to. It was designed by Owen G. Williams, and marketed by J. Langdon & Sons, Duke St., Liverpool. The constituent parts, with their weights, and prices before the war, are given below. If ordered together the price of complete outfit was £4 4s, or about $21.00.

SINGLE OUTFIT FOR PEDESTRIAN OR CYCLING TOURS

	Price	Weight
"Featherweight" tent complete	£1 10 0	2 8
Ground sheet and pegs for same	0 4 3	15

TRIPS AFOOT

"Comfy" sleeping-bag (eiderdown)...2   2 0   1   4
Compact brush and comb and mirror.0   1 9   2
Japanese rubbered air cushion 0   1 6   2
"Compleat" cooking outfit and stove.0   3 6   15
Aluminum knife, fork and spoon.....0   1 4   2
¼ pint aluminum flask and egg cup...0   2 8   3
Enamelled cup, plate, and mop, per set 0   0 9   5
Canvas bucket and wash basin 0   2 3   6
Pole clips and candle holder 0   0 6   2

£4 10 6   7 lbs.

The tent is barely large enough for one man to sleep in: 3 feet high, 6 feet long, 3 feet wide on the floor, with front and rear extensions of 32 inches and 36 inches respectively. It is a modification of the common "A" or wedge pattern. The doorways are cut so as to peg out straight in front, affording an outside windshield for cooking. The back end is rounded for storage accommodation and to provide in the worst of weather for cooking without risk of spilling foodstuff on the ground sheet.

The top, which shields the sleeper, is made of "swallow-wing," unprocessed but rain-proof. The bottom portion of the tent is of a lighter material that helps ventilate, but still is spray-proof. The tent alone weighs 22 ounces, poles and case 10 ounces, pegs and lines 8 ounces. The tent rolls into a package 8½ inches long by 4 inches thick. The poles unjoint to a length of 23 inches.

I am assured that this midget shelter will stand up in a hurricane that overthrows wall tents, marquees, and the army bell tent. Enthusiastic campers use it even in winter, sleeping out without a fire when the tent sags heavily with snow. They find it satisfactory protection in torrents of gusty rain so fierce as to wet through a common tent in spite of the fly, by driving through the material of back or front. It has stood nine months' continuous service in Canada.

The ground sheet is of a special fawn waterproof sheeting, 5 feet by 3 feet, eyeletted at each corner, and with pegs to hold it down.

The sleeping-bag is shaped narrow at the foot to save weight and bulk, and is of the old-fashioned pattern closed with a draw-string. It is stuffed thinly with eiderdown, the warmest of all known materials for its weight and (rolled up) bulk. It has a thin rubbered cover bag, waterproof and windproof. For those who dislike the stuffiness of so small a "sleeping-pocket" the same outfitters provided down quilts of two sizes, the 6 x 4 foot size, with valance, weighing $3\frac{1}{4}$ pounds.

The air-pillow is a Japanese contrivance, incredibly light and compact. A reeded form, more comfortable than the plain oblong one listed with the set, is 12 x 10 inches, weighs only $2\frac{1}{2}$ ounces, and three of them can be carried in a coat pocket when deflated.

Since the English camper seldom could get wood for fuel, or permission to make a fire in the open, he was obliged to carry a miniature stove and some alcohol or kerosene. In this instance it is an alcohol burner of common pad form, which is wasteful of spirits, but less likely to get out of order than an alcohol vapor stove. The cooking outfit is made up of two little kettles or deep stew-pans with handles, a miniature frying-pan, a toaster, a tea-ball, and the stove, all nesting in the outer kettle, which has a cover.

Another one-man outfit was designed and is (or was—I know not what the war may have done there) manufactured by that veteran camper and outdoor writer, T. H. Holding, of 7 Maddox St., London, W. It includes the following articles:

Tent	13 ounces
Poles (3)	15 "
Pegs	10 "
Ground sheet	10 "
Ground "blanket"	8 "
Down quilt	20 "
Cooking kit	16 "

6 pounds

The "Wigwam," as Mr. Holding calls his tiny tent, is of ordinary "A" shape and is made of Japanese silk, 5 ft. 11 in. long, 4½ ft. wide, and 4 ft. high, giving sufficient headroom to lounge in comfortably. When rolled up it can be carried in an ordinary pocket. It will be noticed that the poles and pegs weigh practically twice as much as the tent itself. This is due partly to the use of shear poles in front, instead of a single vertical pole, giving freer entrance and egress, besides supporting the tent better. A ridge pole, weighing 10 ounces, is supplied extra, and is recommended for the sake of trim setting. The poles are of jointed bamboo, and the pegs of aluminum, flattened at the ends instead of pointed, to give a good grip in the ground.

Of the silk tent Mr. Holding says: "Such is its toughness that I have seen a pair of the strongest fingers try to tear the material, and fail. For its weight and thickness it is the most powerful stuff in the world in the shape of textile goods. I have put several tents I possess to protracted and severe tests, and I have never had one to tear. One has stood some of the heaviest rains, in fact, records for thirty hours at a stretch, without letting in wet, and I say this of an 11-ounce silk one.

"What, however, silk does not stand well is *friction*. As an instance, open your silk umbrella and look down the folds, half way between each rib. The parts of a tent, therefore, which show the wear are at the pegging and head places, where the fingers touch it in erecting. To this end I recommend they should not be rolled up, as cotton fabrics, but rucked, like a pocket handkerchief."

The "Wigwam" is also furnished ready-made in various other materials, cheaper but heavier than silk, of which the next lightest is lawn, weighing 1 pound 8 ounces.

The ground sheet is of light mackintosh. Over it goes a little "ground blanket" of thin cashmere, with eyelets at the corners, so that it may be pegged down. This is not only for the sake of warmth, but also to save wear on the mackintosh, which has to be very thin.

Mr. Holding's eiderdown quilt is only to cover with, not to roll up in. The Wigwam size is 5 ft. 10 in. by 4 ft., to which is added a foot of cloth valance all around, which is pegged or weighted down so that the sleeper will not kick off his covering. These quilts are thinner than the domestic ones of down, and roll up into remarkably small compass.

The cooking kit is made of thin copper. It includes a pad spirit stove with damper and windshield, a boiler 6 inches across, a porridge pan that fits inside, and a fry-pan that forms a cover for the boiler; also a separate handle for the various pans. The vessels are seamless.

Of course, this six-pound outfit does not include everything that a hiker requires in camp and on the march. Mr. Holding gives a list of articles recommended for two pedestrians traveling together:

	lbs.	oz.
"A" Tent, 6 ft. by 5 ft. 9 in. by 5 ft. 9 in.	2	0
Set of 2 tent poles	1	0
Set of pegs (ordinary skewers)		3
Oil stove—"Baby Primus"	1	3
Aluminum pans—"So Soon" pattern	1	1
Piece of waterproof for tent		2
2 Aluminum cups and saucers (plates)		4
2 sets Aluminum knife, fork, spoon		4
Candlestick and candle		2
Aluminum box of soap		1
	6	4

The piece of waterproof is two feet square. It is to roll up the tent in when wet, and serves otherwise as a wash-basin, seat, etc.

Each man carries half of this company kit, making his share 3 pounds 2 ounces. Adding his personal equipment, his burden becomes:

	lbs.	oz.
Share of baggage	3	2
Mackintosh coat	1	6
Air pillow		3

TRIPS AFOOT

Down pillow (a luxury)		1
Sweater	1	0
Sleeping stockings (long ones)		6
Extra walking socks		4
Down quilt	1	10
Thin extra vest (undershirt)		5
Scarf		2
Tooth brush, etc.		3
Hold-all with straps (under)		8
	9	2

For hiking instead of cycling, a rucksack should be substituted for the hold-all. Adding a towel, the weight, without food, is close to 10 pounds, with part food 12 pounds.

The "Baby" kerosene vapor stove here listed is like a regular Primus except that its valve is in different position, the pump is set in snugly at the side, it has rounded cone feet set inward, and it is of reduced size, weighing only 1 pound 3 ounces instead of 4 pounds. A still smaller stove of the same pattern, called the "Pocket Primus," measures $2\frac{3}{4}$ inches deep by 4 inches across, when packed, and weighs only 1 pound 1 ounce.

Another specialty is the "So-Soon" cooking kit. The lower vessel is a boiler $3\frac{3}{4}$ by $5\frac{1}{2}$ inches, the second is another boiler that fits inside the first, next is a stew or porridge pan which, inverted, makes a cover for the kit; on top is the frying-pan, 1 inch deep. All of these vessels are of stamped aluminum. A separate handle fits all of them. A "Baby Primus" stove fits inside the nested pans. The main boiler tapers narrower at the bottom, so as to keep the set from rattling when carried about. No part has any excrescence or projection to obstruct the packing. The whole set, omitting stove, weighs 1 pound 5 ounces.

There is a smaller "So-Soon" set made for the "Pocket Primus," which is $3\frac{1}{2}$ by $5\frac{1}{4}$ inches, and its three vessels weigh only 8 ounces.

Returning to the subject of tents: the English outfitters supply them of many shapes and sizes and in various lightweight materials, besides common tents, of course. It will strike American campers as peculiar that none of the extra thin materials used in tents up to 7 x 7 size are subjected to any waterproofing process whatever. For rain-shedding quality they depend solely, like an umbrella, upon the closeness with which the textile is woven. On examining these clothes one is surprised at their exceeding fineness of texture. Some of the cotton goods are woven almost twice as fine as our so-called "balloon silk" or the 4-ounce special Lowell cloth used for extra-light racing sails on small craft.

The best lawns, etc., are made from Egyptian cotton, which has a stronger and finer fiber than American cotton, and is said to be 15 per cent. stronger. In spite of this, I doubt if any thin, unprocessed tent is really rainproof unless it is stretched very taut and the occupant takes great pains to avoid touching it from the inside. In a shelter only three or four feet high, and wedge-shaped, one can hardly help rubbing against the interior, and then will come the *drip-drip* that we know too well. Even the rear wall, though vertical, will be rubbed by one's pillow in a very short tent, and then, if rain is driven by the wind, this wall will leak. The only remedy would be to waterproof the cloth or use a fly.

There is another objection to extremely thin tenting material: it requires tighter stretching, and hence more pegs, than stouter material would, or it will belly and sag. Moreover, it stretches excessively, and then the poles will no longer fit. Mr. Holding himself reports that a small tent stretches from three to nine inches, in service. Waterproofing would prevent nearly all of this, for it is the alternate tightening and loosening of the cloth from wetting and drying that makes the fiber of the material loosen up.

A feature of some of the English tents that deserves copying is the angular extension of lower edge of door flaps, so that the doors can be pegged out

TRIPS AFOOT

straight in line with sides of tent, forming windshields and protection against driving rain when one wants the door open. Another is that the ground sheet, instead of being made square or rectangular, has the sides and rear end cut in segments of a circle, so as to fit against the walls when they are drawn outward by sagging of ridge and stretching of sides.

The bedding here described would not suit us at all. The down sleeping-bag would be too stuffy. The Holding quilts are so narrow that they can only be used to cover with, and so the under side of the body is left unprotected by anything but cold mackintosh and a very thin sheet of cashmere. In England, I suppose, it is taken for granted that the camper will procure, for each night, a bedding of straw or hay; but in our country there are many places, even in "civilization," where the camper would have to chance it on the bare ground. In our climate (or climates) we need more bedding under than over us, if there is nothing to serve as mattress.

The English featherweight outfits, although not adapted to our needs, are very suggestive, and American pedestrian tourists will do well to study them. (Full details are given in Mr. Holding's *Camper's Handbook*). Not only lightness but compactness seem to have been brought to an irreducible minimum. For example, there is a complete cycle-camping outfit for two men, including tent, down quilt, toilet articles, cooking utensils, etc., that stows in a bag only 15 x 7 x 7 inches!

CHAPTER VIII

PACKS FOR PEDESTRIANS

The simplest way to carry a light marching kit is in a blanket roll. It is made up as follows: Spread the shelter cloth or tent on the ground, fold the blanket once, end for end, and place it on top, with same amount of cloth left uncovered at front and rear. Divide the other equipment into two piles of equal weight, arrange one of these along one end of blanket, the other along the other end. Fold free sides of shelter cloth over all. Roll the whole affair as tightly and smoothly as possible, and secure with straps or cords, one at middle and one half-way to either end, making a roll about six feet long. Then fasten each end tightly with a slip-knot, leaving enough free cord on each to tie the ends of the roll together in horse-collar form. It takes two men to make a neat job of this.

The roll is worn over one shoulder with ends over opposite hip. Some pedestrians like the blanket roll because it saves the expense and weight of a pack-sack or harness, and because it can be shifted from one side to the other. In reality nothing is gained in ease of carrying, but rather the contrary. All the weight is thrown on one shoulder at a time, and there is no help from the hips. A man can carry a heavier load in a pack-sack with less fatigue in the long run.

The blanket roll is oppressive in hot weather, and its pressure on the chest is a handicap at all times. It is much in the way when one has to climb or crawl, and even more so when you go to shoot. It will not hold half the equipment mentioned in

PACKS FOR PEDESTRIANS 119

my summer list, and if a haversack is added, you have a particularly irksome "flip-flop" to impede you, and the "advantage" of shifting weights is then lost. A blanket roll is suitable only for a day's hike and a one-night camp; even so, it is much less comfortable than a light pack on one's back.

PACK HARNESS.—I leave out of account simple tump lines and the like, because they are practical only for canoeists carrying heavy burdens across portages.

A pack harness is an arrangement of straps for carrying an outfit made up into a bundle inside the blanket, or for toting two duffel bags strapped side by side. The illustration (Fig. 23) shows one with tump or head-band added. If bags are not used, the bundle must be wrapped in a pack cloth of strong waterproof canvas (the tent or shelter cloth will not do, for it needs protection from rough usage).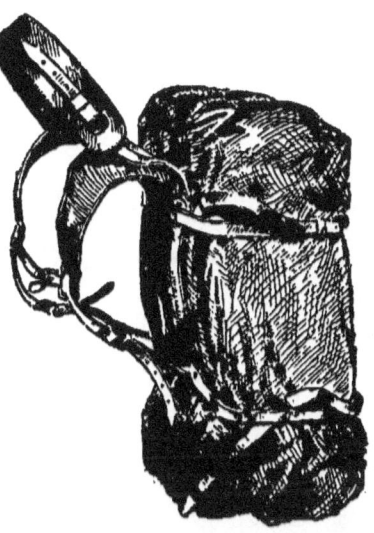

Fig. 23.—Pack Harness with Head Strap

As to this method of packing I quote from the book on *Winter Camping* (Outing Handbooks) by Warwick S. Carpenter, who has had more experience with it than I:

"The arrangement that I have frequently used is that of the pack cloth, with the outfit and blankets or sleeping bag folded inside. Its flexibility for various sizes of load commend it strongly, and the pack cloth may be used as shelter besides, or as a ground cloth in a lean-to or tent. The method of making this pack is to lay the pack cloth on the ground and place the blankets or sleeping bag folded once on top of the cloth. Place the outfit as compactly as possible on the blankets or bag and fold it tightly in, making the bundle considerably longer than it is wide and thick. Then take the end of the pack cloth which runs along the bottom of the pack, and bend it up over the folded bundle. Next take the sides of the pack cloth and fold them over, or if there is much cloth, roll the whole pack over from side to side, keeping everything snug and tight.

This will leave the bottom of the pack cloth folded inside and the sides of the cloth lapping all around so that no snow or wet will sift in at the bottom. Fold the still open top down as a flap, just as you would the end of a paper package, with the folded flap at the side of the pack away from the back. Pass a rope or a strap lengthwise around the whole and then attach the harness with its shoulder straps or tump line. Such a pack is absolutely secure against snow or rain.

The best form of pack-harness is that which is made with a broad shoulder piece shaped like a sailor's collar, the wide bands of which run well over the shoulders and about eight inches down in front. From the back of the collar, about five inches apart, two vertical straps run downward about fifteen inches to the small of the back and bend up under the arms to meet the broad bands in front. There they are fastened with buckles, and the straps are made long enough to permit considerable taking up or letting out. Riveted horizontally to the straps behind, one at the height of the collar piece and the other fifteen inches lower, are two straps six feet long, which go around the pack. This harness may be bought of any dealer in camping outfits, but the collar portion of all that I have seen is made of heavy canvas. This very quickly wrinkles and draws up and cuts the shoulders. It is far better to have it made of a very heavy piece of leather.

One of these that I put together myself has been used for years and the broad bands that go over the shoulders are still as smooth and comfortable as when new. To the back of the collar should be riveted two short straps about six inches long, extending upward, as the others go downward. To these can be buckled a broad tump which goes over the forehead. It will be adjustable with the buckles or can be removed entirely."

The chief merit of this kind of pack is its adaptability to any size or shape of bundle. On the other hand, the weight of harness and pack cloth together ($3\frac{1}{2}$ to 5 pounds) is considerably more

PACKS FOR PEDESTRIANS

than that of a roomy pack-sack. True, the cloth can be used as a ground sheet under the blanket at night, but that is not needed if one has a sleeping-bag, or a browse-bag (and rubber cape to go over it when things are wet) which weighs but a pound and makes a far better bed. Pack cloths are made from 5 x 6 to 6 x 7 feet, which is too small for a shelter cloth. Another disadvantage is that whenever you want to get at anything in the pack, the whole thing must be undone and repacked.

The tump or head-band is a good addition not only to a pack harness but to almost any other kind of pack used for carrying heavy weights. Generally it will not be used until the shoulders tire; then it relieves the strain. It is an advantage in climbing steep hillsides. When fording a swift stream, crossing on a foot-log or fallen tree, going over windfalls, crossing ice, or passing other dangerous places, the shoulder straps may be dropped, the head-strap alone being employed; then, if you slip or get overbalanced, the load can be cast off instantly by throwing back the head, and you save your bones or possibly your life. When the tump is not in use, drop it down over the chest.

MILITARY KNAPSACKS.—In most European armies the infantry carry small knapsacks made of leather, stiffened with a framework of wood or bamboo, or reinforced at the sides to give a certain rigidity. Inside the knapsack are stowed spare underwear, fatigue shoes (if any), a reserve ration, spare ammunition, and various small articles. The blanket, or overcoat, is rolled tightly in a shelter half and strapped around the top and sides, and a mess kettle generally is strapped on the outside. In some models, as the German, the interior is divided into compartments to separate and protect the different articles and to assure a constant distribution of the weight.

A military knapsack is too small for campers, it is much too heavy for its size, and it obliges the wearer to carry most of his outfit outside, attached to it, or strapped separately to the person. Such an arrangement is bad, for various reasons. A blanket roll strapped around the outside does not fit well on a soft sack. The knapsack must be stiff, therefore heavy, and it must be narrow, or the complete pack will project too much beyond the shoulders, worrying the bearer by preventing the free swing of his arms, and proving a serious obstacle when he has to go through the matted undergrowth of a forest. Besides, the blanket is needed as a soft pad against one's back. If worn on the outside, it must be protected by something. A thin tent or shelter cloth will not do, because it, too, needs protection against snags and abrasion. If a poncho or cape is used for the purpose, it must be a heavy one, to stand the wear, whereas it should be light from every other consideration; and your waterproof is best carried where you can get at it and don it quickly.

As for "flip-flops" and "stick-outs" in your equipment, they are anathema. Suppose you have to cross a stream or a deep gulley on a fallen tree. If there is a dangling article about you, such as a haversack, it will swing to one side and tend to throw you off balance. If anything sticks out of your pack, or is tied on the outside of it, the thing will everlastingly be catching in vines and bushes. Taking it day in and day out, in all kinds of country, the best pack is a commodious sack on your back that contains everything you carry except what goes in your pockets and in one hand.

The soft canvas knapsack formerly used by our own army has no compartments save a narrow outside pocket, under the flap, and is not stiffened. It is cheap (from dealers in second-hand military equipments), very strong, and serviceable as a carryall for one's personal duffel aside from shelter and bedding. This pattern, like most other military ones, is ill-suited to carrying heavy loads, because the points of suspension of the shoulder straps (see Fig. 24, *A, B*) are too near the outer edge of the knapsack

PACKS FOR PEDESTRIANS 123

and consequently drag on the weakest part of the shoulders, next to the arms. The strain should come nearer the neck, where the vertebral column will help to support it.

Old types of knapsacks had the straps crossed over the breast — about the worst arrangement that could be devised, since it compresses the bearer's chest and interferes with his breathing. A horizontal strap across the chest to keep shoulder straps from spreading is likewise oppressive, and bothersome because it must be unbuckled before the knapsack can be cast off.

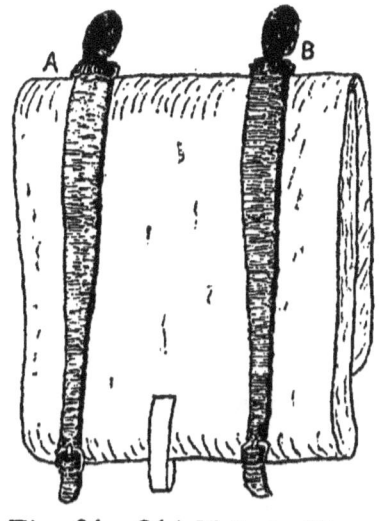

Fig. 24.—Old U. S. A. Knapsack (back). A. B. points of suspension

*RUCKSACKS.— From time immemorial the chamois hunters of the Alps have used a simple but ingenious pack sack for carrying light kits and game. This is called a rucksack. It is to-day the favorite packing device of European Alpinists and pedestrian tourists, is much used as a game bag, and, of late years, has

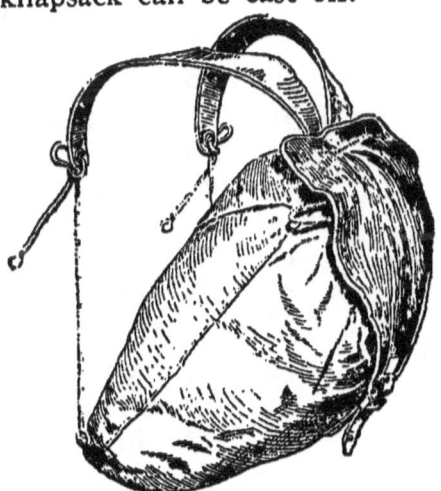

Fig 25.—Rucksack with Flap

Rucksack is a German word meaning "back-sack." In English the umlaut sign (two dots over u) is dropped and the pronunciation changed so that ruck rhymes with stuck.

come into vogue in our country for light mountaineering and for walking trips in settled regions. In tourists' patterns the opening is protected from dust and rain by a flap (Fig. 25), and one or two covered pockets may be added on the outside (Fig. 27) for such articles as may be wanted from time to time on the way. In its original form the rucksack is sketched in Fig. 26, which shows an open-mouthed bag of light cloth closed by a puckering cord.

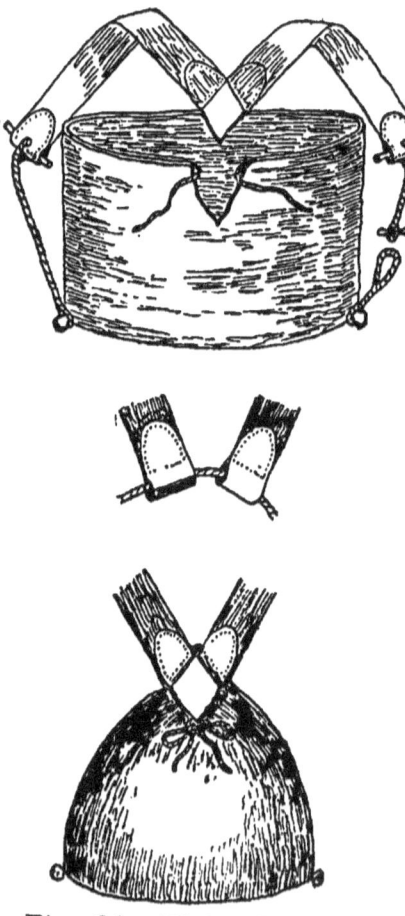

Fig. 26.—Plain Rucksack (after Payne-Gallwey)

The rucksack is distinguished from all other packs by the method of attaching its shoulder straps, which swing directly from the puckering cord at the top, and are fastened below by toggles, h o o k s, or buckles. (Fig. 25 shows another fastening by a cord tying into the shoulder strap with a looped knot; this is easily adjustable, and a tug at the end of the cord will loosen the p a c k instantly). The point of suspension, then, is in the center of the sack's top, instead of near the upper corners as on a military knapsack. T h i s brings the strain over the strongest part of the shoulders, where it is least felt.

Since the rucksack is made of light cloth, with no stiffening, it is very capacious for its weight: one that holds half a bushel can be rolled up and tucked into the pocket of a hunting coat. When filled with spare clothing and such other articles as would be carried by one who went afoot through well settled districts and put up for the night at inns or farmhouses, the weight of such a pack is hardly noticeable. On the hike, one's coat or cape, rolled up, may be carried under the flap. The plain rucksack, without flap, is easy to get into, since all you have to do is to pull one end of the puckering cord and the bag is wide open: this makes it handy as a game bag. The weight, being carried low and tight against the body, does not tend to overbalance one in difficult climbing—a point of consequence to mountaineers.

But the rucksack is a poor device for carrying such a kit as is required by one who sleeps out and totes his bed and shelter with him. Its contents bunch up into a rounded lump (see Fig. 27), and heavy articles work to the bottom. Everything gets jumbled up. Worse still, the pack "rides" so low that it presses hard against the small of the back, which is the worst of all places to put a strain on.

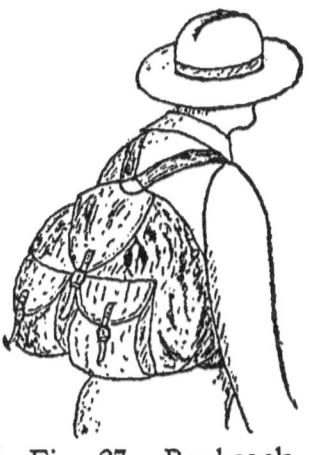

Fig. 27.—Rucksack in Use

I tried out the rucksack thoroughly, years ago. It is a good contrivance for carrying the day's necessities when you are reasonably sure of reaching a house or camp at night, being never in the way like a haversack or blanket-roll, yet more capacious. The one illustrated in Fig. 25, made of thin brown waterproof canvas, 21 inches wide by 22 inches high, weighs 12 ounces. Another outfitter supplies one of about the same size, in waterproofed olive-drab cloth, with an outside pocket, that weighs only 9 ounces. One of these is an excellent carrier for a featherweight camping kit, but for packs of over 15 pounds, I will have none of it.

An interesting modification of the rucksack, which brings the weight where it can best be borne, is the Norwegian army pack sack (Figs. 28, 29). In this the sack is united to a support of oak or ash, which comprises a horizontal wooden crosspiece (*A*) and two vertical pieces (*B, C*) curved to fit the back. Bag and frame are joined at the bottom by two rings, which are sewed on leather bands and attached to the horizontal piece of wood, at one end

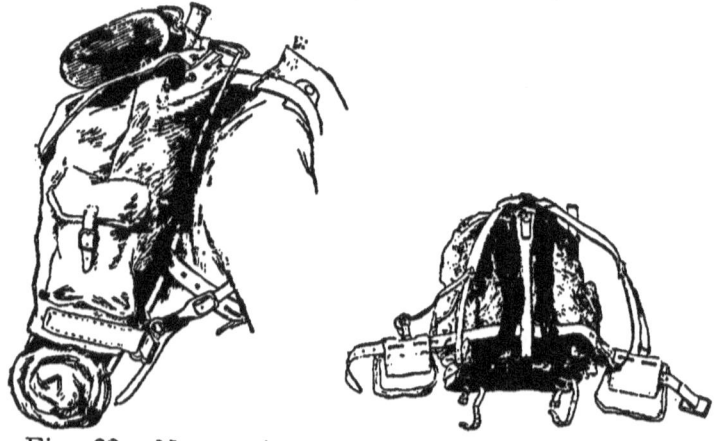

Fig. 28.—Norwegian Knapsack in Use

Fig. 29.—Norwegian Knapsack (Back)

by a spring placed on the traverse, and at the other by an eyebolt. At the top they are joined by a strap, one part of which is sewed on the middle of the back of the knapsack, the other, or free part, being passed through a slit made in the upper part of the support, and bent back and buttoned on itself.

The slings of the knapsack draw from the center, as in a rucksack, but are attached to a small arch-shaped brass piece riveted to the upper part of the support. Their free ends have hooks which engage in the eyes of eyebolts fixed at each end of the lower traverse of the frame. On each sling, at the height of the armpit, there is a double button on which is fixed a counter sling furnished with a brass hook,

PACKS FOR PEDESTRIANS 127

which latter is hooked to the belt from the under side, helping to support cartridge pouches. The knapsack is 17½ inches high, 14½ inches wide, and weighs 3½ pounds. I have seen lighter ones made for civilians. The lower crosspiece rests above the hips, on the pelvis, which, the designer says, "is the most suitable part of our framework to support burdens." The shoulder straps have little more to do than keep the pack against the back.

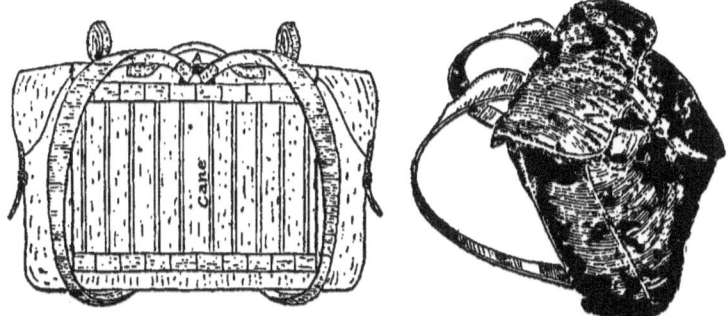

Fig. 30.—Tourist Knapsack (back)   Fig. 31.—Nessmuk Pack Sack

Another and lighter way of stiffening a knapsack is to reinforce the sides and insert pieces of cane vertically in small pockets on the back (Fig. 30). This also allows air to circulate between the pack and the bearer's back, preventing excessive sweating. (When our old army knapsack was worn, in summer, men would sweat clear through the heavy canvas). The tourist's knapsack here illustrated is pliable and yet has enough rigidity to maintain a neat form. Of course, it is not suitable for carrying a heavy weight. In this case the slings are suspended centrally from a D-ring (A in the figure). A handle like that of a shawl-strap is provided, so that the knapsack may be carried like a satchel when one is in town. Straps on top are provided to carry the coat or cape.

PACK SACKS.—I use this term specifically to denote sacks that are roomy enough to take inside a whole outfit for the pedestrian or canoeist who camps out. It would be a waste of space to describe half the patterns that are listed by outfitters, as there are so many that are ill-designed. Three examples that have good "points" will suffice:

The so-called "Nessmuk" pack sack (he did not design it) is shown in Fig. 31. It is made of medium-weight brown waterproof canvas. The bag has boxed sides that taper from about 5 inches width at bottom to 3 inches at top (not shown in illustration) and it is about 3 inches narrower at the top than at the bottom. To the top edge of the bag proper is sewed a throat piece like that of a duffel bag. When the bag has been packed, this throat piece is gathered together and tied like the mouth of a grain sack, so as to exclude water. You may take a header while fording a stream, or capsize your canoe, without getting water inside the pack. The extension also allows the sack to be packed fuller than normal, so that when carried the pack rises as high as one's collar. It is somewhat in the way when one is making up his pack, but, when tied, there is no risk of losing anything out of the bag.

This pack sack carries higher, and hence more comfortably, than a rucksack. It will contain a light camping equipment, say one of twenty pounds. The slings draw from the center, but are somewhat over 2 inches apart at top of pack, and so do not pucker the bag so much, nor throw its top so far backward, as if they drew straight from a D-ring.

The common pattern of "Nessmuk" pack has light web shoulder straps, which are an unmitigated nuisance: they wrinkle up and cut like ropes. Get the better grade with leather straps. I have one of this kind, 20 inches wide by 15 inches high, that weighs 2 pounds 2 ounces. It would be better if the throat piece were a couple of inches longer. The buckle for the flap strap should be placed as high as the upper hole of the strap. There is a similar sack 5 x 16 x 18 inches, with an outside pocket almost the size of the face of the pack, which, with leather slings, weighs only 24 ounces.

PACKS FOR PEDESTRIANS

For regular packing, when one sleeps out, the best pack sack at a moderate price that I know of is what is known as the Duluth, or, from its inventor, the Poirier pattern (Fig 32). Originally made for trappers, timber cruisers, and other professional woodsmen, it is now used by many sportsmen as well. The Duluth sack has no boxed sides, but is sewed up in the form of a simple bag, and so is made wider and higher than boxed ones of equal capacity.

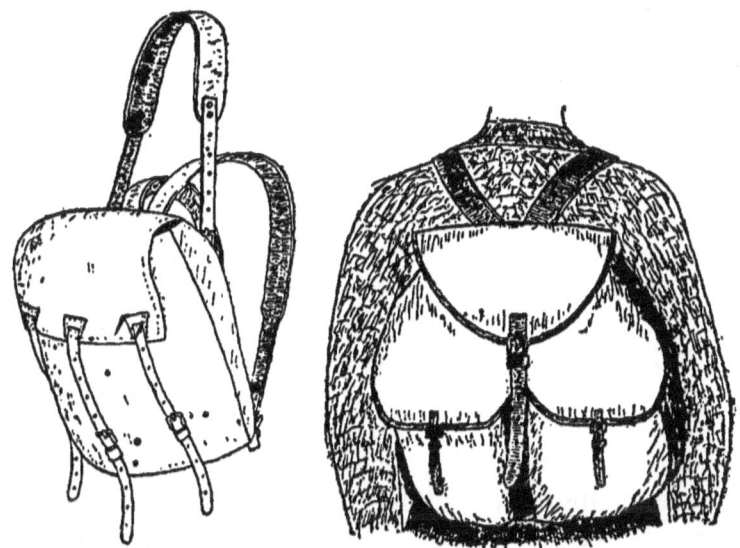

Fig. 32.—Duluth Pack Sack   Fig. 33.—Whelen Pack Sack

The advantage is that one's blanket, which goes in first, as a pad for the back, can be folded two feet square, or a little more, and consequently in fewer thicknesses; hence the bag packs flatter than a boxed one and does not bulge so far backward at the top. Poirier makes his pack sacks in three grades: (A) 12-oz. duck, heavy grain leather shoulder straps and canvas head strap, all straps and buckles fastened with copper rivets and burrs; (B) 10-oz. duck, canvas shoulder and head straps; (C) 10-oz. duck, canvas shoulder straps, no head strap. By all means get the A grade, as canvas slings will wrinkle when wet and cut the shoulders. The standard sizes and weights, in *A* grade, are as follows:

No. 1. 24 x 26 inches. 2¼ lbs.
No. 2. 26 x 28 inches. 2½ lbs.
No. 3. 28 x 30 inches. 2¾ lbs.

For a pedestrian the No. 1 or No. 2 is large enough. A canoeist will find one of the larger ones ample to hold all the duffel for a single-handed cruise, and a week's provisions; but if he chooses to carry more on the outside, then, when he comes to a portage, the surplus articles can be piled on top of the pack, the head strap will be put to use, and he can tote as much as with a tump line, or more, because the shoulders assist.

The shoulder straps of the Duluth sack start from a common center, where they are riveted to an inside piece of leather. They fork from between one's shoulder blades like a pair of suspenders. The flap is half as long as the sack, and it is fitted with three *long* straps whereby the sack may be adjusted snugly to a large or small load. As the sack has a wide mouth, it is easy to pack and to get into. The three straps hold down the flap closely at the corners as well as in the center, and so keep out rain and snow and prevent things spilling out. There is no throat piece; but a wise woodsman stows his perishables in light waterproof bags, anyway.

The pack designed by Captain Townsend Whelen, U. S. A., has an ingenious arrangement for regulating the size of the bag according to what is carried. It consists of a many-gored bag (Fig. 33), about 18 inches wide by 22 inches long without the gores. The bag can be let out enough to carry a small deer, feet up, or, by means of a strap that goes around it from top to bottom, it can be triced up, gores folded inside, until there is nothing of it but a little knapsack for carrying one's daily equipment. There are two roomy pockets on the outside, one of them, for the camera, made so that

PACKS FOR PEDESTRIANS 131

no water can get into it. The arrangement of straps is such that all the strain is put on them instead of on the canvas. Made of 12-oz. waterproof khaki duck, the Whelen pack sack weighs 2⅜ pounds.

COMBINATION PACK SACKS.—Since "an ounce in the morning is a pound before night" when one goes afoot, and "a mile uphill is five on the level," many ingenious contrivances have been devised to make one article in the outfit serve two or more purposes. So we have various combinations of pack and tent, pack and sleeping-bag, pack and stretcher-bed, and so forth. Though I do not go so far as the old-timer who averred that "all combination tricks are pizen," yet I am apt to be rather shy of them. An article can serve two purposes, but it can't do them both at the same time, and in either case it is likely to be a makeshift.

If a pack does not "ride" just right, or if it is not easy to fill and easy to get into at any time, it is faulty. If the tent, or the sleeping-bag, or the stretcher-bed, is altered from what it should be to accommodate it to some other use, it is vexatious. Most of these inventions defeat their own purpose by being almost, if not quite, as bulky and heavy as the separate articles would be if made right. For instance, you can use a sleeping-bag as a pack to stow your duffel in, but to carry it you must have a harness of some sort, and that harness will weigh over a pound. I would rather tote an extra pound and have a pack sack, for it is so much more convenient. The notion that a sack is good for nothing in camp is wrong; you need a receptacle for everything that is not in present use, lest things get scattered and lost. Or, if long training has made you habitually careful in such a matter, you may do with that sack as I often do; turn it inside out, stuff it with dry leaves, put it under your filled pillow-bag, and sleep with your head comfortably high.

PACK BASKETS.—In the forests of the northeastern states and in the maritime provinces of Canada, a favorite carrier is the pack basket, made smaller at the top than at the bottom, flattened on the back, and provided with a cover. An average size is about 18 inches high, 17 inches wide at the bottom and 15 at the top, by about 12 inches deep. Various sizes can be bought from outfitters in the cities, who also supply them with waterproof canvas covers (Fig. 34). One of the latter kind, holding 1¼ bushels, weighs 4¾ pounds. A larger one, 18¾ inches high by 18 by 14½ inches, weighs 7 pounds;

Fig. 34.—Pack Basket (covered)   Fig. 35.—Abercrombie Pack Frame

it fastens with lock-buckle and strap. Uncovered baskets weigh from 2½ to 5 pounds, according to size. Common ones generally are too small at the top for easy stowage of bulky articles; but if the basket is made more than 12 inches deep it will drag back unmercifully on the shoulders.

To my notion, the best that can be said of the pack basket is that it is a bully thing in which to carry canned and bottled goods—when some other fellow does the toting. It is too heavy, too abrasive, and too bothersome in the brush and thickets, for average foot travelers, and it does not stow so well in a canoe as a pack sack of equal capacity.

PACK FRAMES.—The far Northwest has another

PACKS FOR PEDESTRIANS

pet rig for the "human beast of burden": the pack frame. In its simplest form this consists of two vertical or slightly flaring pieces of wood joined by cross-bars near the top and bottom, covered with a sheet of canvas, and fitted on one side with broad straps for the shoulders, on the other with straps, ropes, or thongs, for tying on the load. One model has a little skeleton shelf on the back, near the bottom, for the pack to rest on, this shelf being fitted with hinged metal supports so it can be folded down when not in use. Such a frame leaves an air space between the body and the pack, and so does not sweat the carrier's back like a knapsack. A load of any size or shape can easily be fixed on it. The weight is comfortably balanced and divided between shoulders and hips. The upright pieces of wood are of such length that their lower ends support the whole load when the man sits down to rest, as on a log, for instance.

Figure 35 shows a new invention in pack frames, by D. T. Abercrombie. In this the frame, and consequently the load, is kept quite away from the lower part of the back, being joined to a hip strap by a rod with horizontal arm on each side. There is a tump strap, as well as shoulder straps. Heavy weights can be carried with this contrivance, and, no matter how hard or irregular the load may be, it cannot hurt the back. The frame complete weighs only 2½ pounds.

Pack frames are not suitable for ordinary pedestrian trips, of course, but have such merit for portaging heavy and hard or sharp-cornered baggage that I mention them here, while on the subject of packing on human backs and shoulders.

CANTEENS.—One may travel where water is hard to find, though this seldom is the case in a timbered region. The best canteen is one of aluminum, which neither leaks nor rusts like the old-fashioned tin affairs. It should have a canvas cover with felt lining. When the felt is wet its moisture cools the water in the canteen by evaporation. The canvas cover prevents too rapid evaporation, and keeps the canteen from wetting one's clothing. At night, or in case of illness, the thing can be used as a hot-water bottle, the insulation keeping the water hot for a considerable time. The best pattern is the present regulation army canteen, which is shaped like a flat flask, but with one side rounded a little and the other concaved to fit the body. It has a flat bottom, so you can stand it up. The aluminum screw-cap, held by a chain, cannot jolt out like the corks of common canteens.

To cleanse the vessel, boil it. To sterilize suspected water, fill the naked canteen and place it, unstoppered, on the fire till the water boils. The army model holds one quart, and weighs 11 ounces. It can be bought from some outfitters, either with or without an aluminum cup that fits over the bottom. It is rigged to carry on the belt, where it will not flop nor pound the wearer. To draw it from its cover, turn two little thumb-screw fasteners half a turn, and you can whisk it out almost as easily as you would a pistol.

Aluminum is not fit to carry liquor in; but, for that matter, neither is tin. One of my old partners and I, on a voyage to the Arkansas swamps, once hit upon what we conceived to be a brilliant scheme for transporting a gallon of whiskey inconspicuously in our John-boat. (You know whiskey warms the hearts of otherwise disobliging natives—yes indeedy). We got a new kerosene can, had a tinner remove the spout and solder a patch of tin over it; then in went Old Taylor. We didn't open that can for a week (hadn't seen any natives). Then along came the dickens of a cold rain, and, when it ceased, we declared an "emergency." Well, what do you think? That whiskey had turned as black as ink. *Potztausend himmel donnerwetter!* or words to that effect. If anybody doubts that we didn't open that stuff for a week, I refer him to S. D. Barnes, captain of said John-boat, of which I was crew.

In mountaineering it often happens that one plans

to camp on or near the summit, and wants to carry water with him from some head spring, to save a long climb down after it. A large canteen would be cumbersome. A half-gallon rubber water-bottle solves the problem. It weighs less than a pound, and takes up little room in the pack. In cold weather, such a bottle, filled with hot water, may save packing the weight and bulk of an extra blanket.

CHAPTER IX

HOW TO WALK—A HUNTER'S PACK—GOING ALONE

In walking through a primitive forest, an Indian or a white woodsman can wear out a town-bred athlete, although the latter may be the stronger man. This is because a man who is used to the woods has a knack of walking over uneven and slippery ground, edging through thickets, and worming his way amid fallen timber, with less fret and exertion than one who is accustomed to smooth, unobstructed paths.

How to Walk.—There is somewhat the same difference between a townsman's and a woodsman's gait as there is between a soldier's and a sailor's. It it chiefly a difference of hip action, looseness of joints, and the manner of planting one's feet. The townsman's stride is an up-and-down knee action, with rather rigid hips, the toes pointing outward, and heels striking first. The carriage is erect, the movement springy and graceful, so long as one is walking over firm, level footing—but beware the banana-peel and the small boy's sliding-place! This is an ill-poised gait, because one's weight falls first upon the heel alone, and at that instant the walker has little command of his balance. It is an exhausting gait as soon as its normally short pace is lengthened by so much as an inch.

A woodsman, on the contrary, walks with a rolling motion, his hips swaying an inch or more to the stepping side, and his pace is correspondingly long. This hip action may be noticed to an exaggerated degree in the stride of a professional pedestrian; but the latter walks with a heel-and-toe step, whereas

HOW TO WALK

an Indian's or sailor's step is more nearly flat-footed. In the latter case the center of gravity is covered by the whole foot. The poise is as secure as that of a rope-walker. The toes are pointed straight forward, or even a trifle inward, so that the inside of the heel, the outside of the ball of the foot, and the smaller toes, all do their share of work and assist in balancing. Walking in this manner, one is not so likely, either, to trip over projecting roots, stones, and other traps, as he would be if the feet formed hooks by pointing outward. The necessity is obvious in snow-shoeing.

A fellow sportsman, H. G. Dulog, once remarked: "If the Indian were turned to stone while in the act of stepping, the statue would probably stand balanced on one foot. This gait gives the limbs great control over his movements. He is always poised. If a stick cracks under him it is because of his weight, and not by reason of the impact. He goes silently on, and with great economy of force. . . . His steady balance enables him to put his moving foot down as gently as you would lay an egg on the table."

There is another advantage in walking with toes pointing straight ahead instead of outward: one gains ground at each stride. I have often noticed that an Indian's stride gains in this manner, as well as from the rolling motion of the hips. The white man acquires this habit, if he ever gets it, but an Indian is *molded* to it in the cradle. If you examine the way in which a papoose is bound to its cradle-board, this will be made clear. Immediately after birth the infant is stretched out on the board, its bowlegged little limbs are laid as straight as possible, and the feet are placed exactly perpendicular and close together before being swaddled. Often the squaw removes the bandages and gently drags and works on the baby's limbs and spine to make them as straight as possible. Then, in rebandaging, care is always taken that the toes shall point straight forward.

The woodsman walks with a springy knee action. There is a "give" at every step, and in going downhill the knees are bent a good deal, as they are when one carries a heavy burden. It is said of the Indian "he does not walk, he glides." No Indian glides in boots, but put him in moccasins and the word does express his silent, rhythmical, tireless, sure-footed progress, an admirable example of precision of movement and economy of effort. A white man acquires somewhat the same glide after getting used to moccasins, and especially after some experience on snowshoes, which compel him to walk with toes pointed straight ahead or a little inward.

OVER-STRAIN.—When carrying a pack on your back, do not over-exert yourself. Halt whenever your breathing is very labored or exertion becomes painful. Nobody who understands horses would think of driving them ahead when they show signs of distress, and there is quite as much common sense in treating yourself with the same consideration, if you want to travel far. Rig your pack at the start so it can be flung off whenever you sit down for a moment's rest; it pays. But don't halt more than three to five minutes. Long halts eat up daylight; they stiffen the muscles; and they cause chills and colds. Over-exertion is particularly disastrous in mountain climbing.

Not only in marching but in other labors, go steadily but moderately. Do not chop to the point of exhaustion, nor strain yourself in lifting or carrying. A feat of "showing off" is poor compensation for a lame back.

One who is unused to long marches may get along pretty well the first day, but on the second morning it will seem as if he could not drag one foot after the other. This is the time when the above remarks do not apply; for if one uses the gad and goes ahead he will soon limber up. But by the morning of the third day it is likely that complications will have set in. The novice by this time is worn, not only from unaccustomed exertion, but from loss of

HOW TO WALK

sleep—for few men sleep well the first night or two in the open. He is probably constipated from change of diet, and from drinking too much on the march. More serious still, he probably has sore feet. This latter ailment is not so much due to his feet being tender at the start as from his not having taken proper care of them. Aside from the downright necessity of seeing that one's shoes and stockings fit well, and that the shoes are well broken in before starting, there are certain rules of pedestrian hygiene that should be observed from the word "go."

CARE OF THE FEET.—"An ounce of prevention is worth a pound of cure." I have already said a good deal about the choice of shoes and stockings (Vol. I., Chapter IX). Let me add another reason for wearing heavy but soft woolen socks when you are in the wilderness, regardless of season; they ventilate the shoes. You probably will be wearing rather heavy shoes coated with some waterproofing preparation. The pores of the leather are filled so that no air can get through. But one's feet cannot be kept in good condition if the shoes are not ventilated somehow. Thick socks do it in this way: when your weight is thrown on one foot as in stepping forward, the air that was confined in the meshes of the fabric is forced out through the shoe tops (but not through a high laced boot); then, when the pressure is relieved, fresh air is sucked back to fill the partial vacuum. Thin socks, especially cotton ones, become saturated with perspiration, and little or no air can get into them at all: then the feet have their pores clogged and they become tender. Thin hose also admit sand and dirt more readily than thick ones.

One's feet can be toughened and hardened before starting on a hike by soaking them for some time, the night before, in a solution of alcohol and salt, or in one made by dissolving a tablespoonful of tannic acid in a wash-bowl of cold water. (*American Red Cross Text-Book on First Aid.*) A little alum in water may be substituted.

Every morning before starting on a hike, rub some talcum powder over the feet and dust some inside your shoes. One's underwear should also be dusted with it at all places where the garments are likely to chafe. If you have no talcum, then rub the feet with vaseline, melted tallow from a candle, or oil. Soap often is used for the purpose, but some soaps contain too much free alkali, which is bad for the skin; Castile or Ivory soap is not objectionable.

But the main thing is to keep the feet clean. Wash them well every evening, preferably in hot salted water. If they are strained, swollen, or hot, the best treatment is to rub them with alcohol or whiskey, but hot salted water and massage will do very well. Keep the nails cut close and square.

If the feet are washed in the morning, or when resting on the march, it should be done briskly, not by soaking, and they should be thoroughly dried, otherwise they will be tender. In winter, if water is hard to get, the feet may be cleansed by rubbing them with snow.

Should you step in water over your shoe-tops, or in any other way get the feet sopping wet, stop as soon as you can and wring out the hose; do not "walk them dry," for that makes the skin tender.

As soon as a blister is discovered, it should be opened *in the right way,* so that the skin may not be rubbed off and infection ensue. Sterilize a needle by holding it in the flame of a match. When it has cooled, prick the blister, not directly, but through the skin at the side, and gently press out the fluid till the blister is flat. Then put a light pledget of absorbent cotton on it, or a little square of sterilized gauze, and over this strap a bit of adhesive plaster. A second similar strap may be stuck on top of this in the opposite direction. Such a dressing keeps the skin from rubbing off, prevents infection, and enables you to travel on without inconvenience. A raw blister is treated in the same way, but a little Resinol or carbolized vaseline smeared on it with

HOW TO WALK

a clean splinter, before the pad is applied, will help it to heal.

When walking long distances, it is a wise plan to change feet with one's socks at noon.

Cramps in the leg muscles are best treated by massage.

THIRST.—In warm weather, one's first few days on the march will bring an inordinate thirst, which is not caused by the stomach's demand for water, but by a fever of the palate. This may be relieved somewhat by chewing a green leaf, or by carrying a smooth, non-absorbent pebble in the mouth; but a much better thirst-quencher is to suck a prune or carry a bit of raw onion in the mouth. One can go a long time without drinking if he has an onion with him; this also helps to prevent his lips from cracking in alkali dust.

Drink as often as you please, but only a sup or two at a time. Sip slowly, so as not to chill the stomach. If one drinks till he no longer feels thirst, he is likely to suffer first from "cotton mouth," and then from the cramp of acute indigestion.

Never try to satisfy thirst by swallowing snow or ice; melt the snow first by holding it in the mouth, if no fire can be had. It is best to eat a cracker or something with it, as snow water is bad on an empty stomach.

TO AVOID CHILL.—Wear a woolen undershirt (woolen gauze for summer). Do not sit around when overheated and damp from perspiration, unless you have a sweater or extra wrap of some sort to put on. Do the same when reaching the top of a mountain, or other place exposed freely to the wind. But do not muffle up on the march.

MOUNTAIN CLIMBING.—The city man's gait, to which I have already referred, is peculiarly exhausting in mountain-climbing. He is accustomed to spring from the toe of the lower foot, in going uphill. That throws nearly the whole weight of the body upon the muscles of the calf of the leg, a misadjustment of strain that would soon wear out even a native mountaineer. The latter walks uphill with a woodsman's gait, planting the whole foot on the ground, and swinging or rolling the hip at each stride, thus not only gaining an inch or two in his pace, but distributing the strain between several groups of muscles. When going downhill, bend the knees considerably so that the leg forms a spring to land on at each stride.

In Dent's *Mountaineering* are given some useful hints to climbers that I take the liberty of condensing here:

In walking up a steep hill, go slowly and steadily. If you cannot talk without catching your breath, it is a sure sign that you are going too fast.

If you slip on a loose stone, do not try to recover your lost ground quickly, but slip away until your foot is checked a few inches below. Thus keep up the rhythm of your footfall.

On an average mountain, where the slope is tolerably uniform, and the climber has no long journey before him, an ascent of 1,000 ft. in an hour is quick walking. In beginning a long climb, 800 ft. of vertical ascent in an hour is good work. On a good trail, for a moderate distance, 1,500 ft. an hour is quick walking. Under favorable conditions a good climber can ascend from a height of 7,000 ft. to 14,000 ft. in seven hours; at greater altitudes the pace will slacken.

In descending a mountain, the pace, however slow, should be continuous. To remain stationary, even for a moment, not only necessitates a fresh start, but demands an adjustment of balance which implies an unnecessary outlay of muscular effort. To descend rapidly and safely without exertion, a certain looseness of joints should be cultivated. On a steep slope one should descend sideways, so that the whole length of the foot can be planted fairly on any hold that offers.

A man will never sprain his ankle when he expects to do so at any moment, nor will he be likely to slip if he is always prepared to fall.

A HUNTER'S PACK.—Returning to the subject of outfitting: I have, so far, considered only summer travel afoot. There are many who go out in the

HOW TO WALK

fall of the year, hunters especially, and who may wish to make side trips on their own hook. Captain Whelen has stated their case convincingly:

"There is much to be said in favor of back-packing. It increases many fold that sense of absolute freedom which is one of the fundamental reasons why men try to escape from civilization for a time. There is none of that trouble and worry that we all experience when we have the responsibility of a pack-train. I admit that back-packing, especially in a mountainous country, is downright hard work; but it's work worthy of a man; and once you get into a game country, you have very much less work than has he who must be continually watching and caring for a band of horses. Moreover, the back-packer usually has better success. He drops into a new country quietly and unseen. There is none of that clatter of hoofs, jingle of horse-bells, and noise of chopping. Before the game comes to know that there is a human being in the country, he has had his pick. . . .

The problem of transportation on a western big-game hunt is a constant one. The country is open, and one locality soon becomes hunted out. The reports of the rifles, the sound of axes, and the shouts as the horses are daily driven to camp, soon cause the game to leave for more healthful country. Hence camp must be moved from ten to twenty miles every three or four days. It has always seemed that one could hunt longer in one locality, and make these short journeys more easily, if he could forsake the pack-train for the back-pack. The latter method is a necessity when one wants to hunt a country inaccessible to horses. On some of my most successful hunts, from the standpoints both of recreation and of heads, I have hired a packer to take me in and bring me out, but in the meantime have carried my entire hunting where I would."

We may add that back-packing is the cheapest possible way to spend one's vacation in the wilderness.

The man who goes out alone for a week or so in the fall of the year, or at an altitude where the nights always are cold, should be fit to carry on his back from 40 to 50 pounds at the outset—of course the pack lightens as he consumes rations. I am **not** including weight of gun, cleaning implements, and ammunition. He should wear woolen underwear of medium weight, thick and soft woolen socks, army overshirt, kersey or moleskin trousers, leather belt with pockets (not loops) for clips or loose cartridges, hunting shoes of medium height for ordinary use, felt hat, and, at times, buckskin gloves. In his pack there would be a spare suit of underwear and hose, a cruiser or "stag" shirt of best Mackinaw, moccasins or leather-topped rubbers, and German socks. In pockets and on the belt he would carry the same articles mentioned in my summer hiking list.

A mere shelter cloth is too breezy for this season (there will be no opportunity to build a thatched camp, as the hunter will be on the move from day to day). He needs a half-pyramid tent, say of the Royce pattern (Vol. I., pp. 85-91) but somewhat smaller, and weighing not over 4 pounds.

Bedding is the problem; a man carrying his all upon his back, in cold weather, must study compactness as well as lightness of outfit. Here the points are in favor of sleeping-bag *vs.* blankets, because, for a given insulation against cold and draughts, it may be so made as to save bulk as well as weight. For a pedestrian it need not be so roomy as the standard ones, especially at the foot end. Better design one to suit yourself, and have an outfitter make it up to order, if you have no skill with the needle. An inner bag of woolen blanketing, an outer one of knotted wool batting, and a separate cover of cravenetted khaki or Tanalite—the weight need not be over 8 pounds complete. Your campfire will do the rest. A browse bag is dispensed with, for you will carry an axe and can cut small logs to hold in place a deep layer of such soft stuff as the location affords.

The short axe may be of Hudson Bay or Damascus pattern. There should be a small mill file to keep it in order, besides the whetstone.

The ration list is based on the assumption that the

HOW TO WALK

hunter's rifle will supply him, after the first day or two, with at least a pound of fresh meat a day. If it does not, go elsewhere. There are plenty of good ways to cook without boiling, stewing, or roasting in an oven (see Vol. I.), which are processes that require vessels too bulky for a foot traveler to bother with.

Either the Whelen pack sack or a large Duluth one will carry the whole outfit. Both have the advantage that they can be drawn up to smaller dimensions as the pack decreases in size, or for carrying the day's supplies when most of the outfit is cached at or near camp.

The following outfit is complete, save for gun, ammunition and cleaning implements. For a longer trip than one week, a reserve of provisions can be cached at some central point in the hunting district.

AUTUMN OUTFIT

	bs.	oz.
Pack sack, with tump strap	2	12
Tent	4	
Sleeping-bag	8	
Pillow bag*		3
Rubber cape*	1	5
Mackinaw stag shirt	1	8
Spare underwear, 1 suit	1	8
Spare socks, 2 pairs		5
Moccasins	1	
German socks		12
Axe and muzzle	1	12
Cooking kit, dish towel, tin cup*	2	2
Cheese cloth		2
Mill file, 6 in.		2
Whetstone*		2
Pliers*		4
Wallet, fitted*		6
Twine*		2
Toilet articles*		6
Talcum powder*		2
Toilet paper*		1
First aid kit*		5
Spare matches, in tin		6
Alpina folding lantern		8
Candles, ½ doz.		8

Emergency ration 8
Tobacco, in wpf. bag 8
Spare pipe 3

Total pack without provisions..28 12

ONE WEEK'S RATIONS (not including fresh meat)
Flour 4
Baking powder 4
Meal, cereal 1 8
Milk powder 8
Butter 8
Bacon 2
Egg powder 8
Raisins 8
Dried apricots, prunes 1
Sugar 1
Chocolate 12
Coffee 8
Tea 2
Salt 4

13 6

Provision bags, etc. 10

14

Pack complete..42 12

The articles starred (*) are same as in summer hiking list already given.

Moccasins are to be large enough to fit over the German socks. This foot-gear is used in still hunting in dry weather, and on cold nights. The camper sleeps, when it is frosty, in fresh underwear and socks, army shirt (dried before the fire after the day's use), trousers, stag shirt, neckerchief rigged as hood, German socks, and moccasins. When he has to get up to replenish the fire, or in case of any alarm, he springs from his bed attired *cap-a-pie*.

Many a time I have gone for a week's hunt, high up in the mountains, in bleak November, with much less outfit than is here listed. My native companions went even lighter than I. Often they slept out on the mountainside without shelter or

HOW TO WALK

blanket, when the winter fog coated every twig in the forest with rime, and frost sprang up from the ground in feathery forms three or four inches high. We grinned at all that, and fancied that we were playing the game like men. So we were, but not like sensible men. We were sapping our vitality. Had we gone fixed to be well fed by day, warm and dry at night, and clean enough not to have smelt like a monkey's nest, we would have been playing a better game. *A-loo,* it is gone—and I am done.

GOING ALONE.—I have given a good deal of space to the subject of outfitting for single-handed cruising in the wilderness, because, as I have said, it is a difficult art, and anyone who masters it can easily fit up a company kit for two or more. But why go alone? To the multitude, whether city or country bred, the bare idea of faring alone in the wilds for days or weeks at a time is eerie and fantastic: it makes their flesh creep. He who does so is certainly an eccentric, probably a misanthrope, possibly a fugitive from justice, or, likely enough, some moonstruck fellow whom the authorities would do well to follow up and watch.

But many a seasoned woodsman can avow that some of the most satisfying, if not the happiest, periods of his life have been spent far out of sight and suggestion of his fellow men.

From a practical standpoint there are compensations in cruising the woods and streams alone, and even in camping without human fellowship. You get the most out of the least kit. It simplifies the whole business of camp routine. It would be piggish, for example, for two men to eat out of the same dish; there must be three at least, one to cook in and two for serving the food; but for one man to eat from his own frying-pan is not only cleanly but a sensible thing to do. It keeps the food hotter than if transferred to a cold plate, and saves washing an extra dish, an economy of effort that is the most admirable of all efficiencies!

The problem of cuisine is reduced to its lowest

terms. You cook what *you* like, and nothing else; you prepare what you need, and not one dumpling more. It is done precisely to your own taste—there is a world of gustatory satisfaction in that. You bake a corn pone, let us say, leaving the frying-pan clean of grease. You cut your venison (the flesh of all game is venison) into cubes and broil these on a sharpened stick, one at a time, just as you eat them, which is the best and daintiest cooking process in the world. Your coffee, settled by a dash of cold water, is drunk from the same cup you brewed it in.

Then comes the cleaning up. No more bugaboo of dishwashing, which all men so cordially despise. You give pan and pannikin a rinse and a wipe, jab your knife into the ground and draw it through some fresh leaves, chuck the broiling-stick into the fire, and—*voila,* the thing is done, thoroughly and neatly done, without rising from your seat!

So with other camp chores, from pitching the miniature tent to packing up for the march: everything is simplified, and time and effort are saved.

From a selfish standpoint, the solitary camper revels in absolute freedom. Any time, anywhere, he can do as he pleases. There is no anxiety as to whether his mates are having a good time, no obligation of deference to their wishes. Selfish? Yes; but, *per contra,* when one is alone he is boring nobody, elbowing nobody, treading on nobody's toes. He is neither chiding nor giving unasked advice. Undeniably he is minding his own business—a virtue to cover multitudes of sins.

A companion, however light-footed he may be, adds fourfold to the risk of disturbing the shy natives of the wild. By yourself you can sit motionless and mutely watchful, but where two are side by side it is neither polite nor endurable to pass an hour without saying a word. Lonesome? Nay indeed. Whoever has an eye for Nature is never less alone than when he is by himself. Should a strain of poetic temperament be wedded to one's

HOW TO WALK

habit of observing, then it is more than ever urgent that he should be undisturbed; for in another's presence
"Imagination flutters feeble wings."
Solitude has its finer side. The saints of old, when seeking to cleanse themselves from taint of worldliness and get closer to the source of prophecy, went singly into the desert and bided there alone. So now our lone adventurer, unsaintly as he may have been among men, experiences an exaltation, finds healing and encouragement in wilderness life.

When twilight falls, and shadows merge in darkness, the single-handed camper muses before the fire that comforts his bivouac and listens to the low, sweet voices of the night, which never are heard in full harmony save by those who sit silent and alone.

Then comes the time of padded feet. Stealthy now, and mute, are the creatures that move in the forest. Our woodsman, knowing the ways of the beasts, regards them not, but dreams before the leaping flames like any Parsee worshipping the fire.

Weird shapes appear in the glowing coals. Elves dance in the halo where night and radiance mingle.

Hark to Titania!
"Out of this wood do not desire to go:
Thou shalt remain here, whether thou wilt or no.
I am a spirit of no common rate;
The summer still doth tend upon my state;
And I do love thee."

Ah, precious even the ass's noll, if by that masque one shall enter the fairy realm!

CHAPTER X

CONCENTRATED FOODS

The first European settlers in this country were ignorant of the ways of the wilderness. Some of them had been old campaigners in civilized lands, but they did not know the resources of American forests, nor how to utilize them. The consequence was that many starved in a land of plenty. The survivors learned to pocket their pride and learn from the natives, who, however contemptible they might seem in other respects, were past masters of the art of going "light but right." An almost naked savage could start out alone and cross from the Atlantic to the Mississippi, without buying or begging from anybody, and without robbing, unless from other motives than hunger. This was not merely due to the abundance of game. There were large tracts of the wilderness where game was scarce, or where it was unsafe to hunt. The Indian knew the edible plants of the forest, and how to extract good food from roots that were rank or poisonous in their natural state; but he could not depend wholly upon such fortuitous findings. His mainstay on long journeys was a small bag of parched and pulverized maize, a spoonful of which, stirred in water, and swallowed at a draught, sufficed him for a meal when nature's storehouse failed.

PINOLE.—All of our early chroniclers praised this parched meal as the most nourishing food known. In New England it went by the name of "nocake," a corruption of the Indian word *nookik*. William Wood, who, in 1634, wrote the first topographical account of the Massachusetts colony, says of nocake

CONCENTRATED FOODS 151

that "It is Indian corn parched in the hot ashes, the ashes being sifted from it; it is afterwards beaten to powder and put into a long leatherne bag trussed at the Indian's backe like a knapsacke, out of which they take three spoonsful a day." Roger Williams, the founder of Rhode Island, said that a spoonful of nocake mixed with water made him "many a good meal." Roger did not affirm, however, that it made him a square meal, nor did he mention the size of his spoon.

In Virginia this preparation was known by another Indian name, "rockahominy" (which is not, as our dictionaries assume, a synonym for plain hominy, but a quite different thing). That most entertaining of our early woodcraftsmen, Colonel Byrd of Westover, who ran the dividing line between Virginia and North Carolina in 1728-29, speaks of it as follows:

"Rockahominy is nothing but Indian corn parched without burning, and reduced to Powder. The Fire drives out all the Watery Parts of the Corn, leaving the Strength of it behind, and this being very dry, becomes much lighter for carriage and less liable to be Spoilt by the Moist Air. Thus half a Dozen Pounds of this Sprightful Bread will sustain a Man for as many Months, provided he husband it well, and always spare it when he meets with Venison, which, as I said before, may be Safely eaten without any Bread at all. By what I have said, a Man needs not encumber himself with more than 8 or 10 Pounds of Provision, tho' he continue half a year in the Woods. These and his Gun will support him very well during the time, without the least danger of keeping one Single Fast."

The Moravian missionary Heckewelder, in his *History, Manners and Customs of the Indian Nations,* describes how the Lenni Lenape, or Delawares, prepared and used this emergency food:

"Their *Psindamóoan* or *Tassmanáne,* as they call it, is the most nourishing and durable food made out of the Indian corn. The blue sweetish kind is the grain which they prefer for that purpose. They parch it in clean hot ashes, until it bursts; it is then sifted and cleaned, and pounded in a mortar into a kind of flour, and when they wish to make it very good, they mix some sugar [*i.e.*, maple sugar] with it. When wanted for use, they take about a tablespoonful of this flour in their mouths, then stooping to the river or brook, drink water to it. If, however, they have a cup or other small vessel at hand, they put the flour in it and mix it with water, in the proportion of one tablespoonful to a pint. At their camps they will put a small quantity in a kettle with water and let it boil down, and they will have a thick pottage. With this food the traveler and warrior will set out on long journeys and expeditions, and as a little of it will serve them for a day, they have not a heavy load of provisions to carry. Persons who are unacquainted with this diet ought to be careful not to take too much at a time, and not to suffer themselves to be tempted too far by its flavor; more than one or two spoonfuls, at most, at any one time or at one meal is dangerous; for it is apt to swell in the stomach or bowels, as when heated over a fire."

The best of our border hunters and warriors, such as Boone and Kenton and Crockett, relied a good deal upon this Indian dietary when starting on their long hunts, or when undertaking forced marches more formidable than any that regular troops could have withstood. So did Lewis and Clark on their ever-memorable expedition across the unknown West. Modern explorers who do their outfitting in London or New York, and who think it needful to command a small army of porters and gun-bearers when they go into savage lands, might do worse than read the simple annals of that trip by Lewis and Clark, if they care to learn what real pioneering was.

It is to be understood, of course, that the parched and pulverized maize was used mainly or solely as an emergency food, when no meat was to be had. Ordinarily the hunters of that day, white and red, when they were away from settlements or trading posts, lived on "meat straight," helped out with nuts, roots, wild salads, and berries. Thus did Boone, the greater part of two years, on his first expedition to Kentucky; and so did the trappers of

CONCENTRATED FOODS 153

the far West in the days of Jim Bridger and Kit Carson.

Powdered parched corn is still the standby of native travelers in the wilds of Spanish America, and it is sometimes used by those hardy mountaineers, "our contemporary ancestors," in the Southern Appalachians. One of my camp-mates in the Great Smoky Mountains expressed to me his surprise that any one should be ignorant of so valuable a resource of the hunter's life. He claimed that no other food was so "good for a man's wind" in mountain climbing.

In some parts of the South and West the pulverized parched corn is called "coal flour." The Indians of Louisiana gave it the name of *gofio*. In Mexico it is known as *pinole*. (Spanish pronunciation, *pee*-no-lay; English, pie-*no*-lee.)

Some years ago Mr. T. S. Van Dyke, author of *The Still Hunter* and other excellent works on field sports, published a very practical article on emergency rations in a weekly paper, from which, as it is now buried where few can consult it, I take the liberty of making the following quotation:

"*La comida del desierto*, the food of the desert, or *pinole*, as it is generally called, knocks the hind sights off all American condensed foods. It is the only form in which you can carry an equal weight and bulk of nutriment on which alone one can, if necessary, live continuously for weeks, and even months, without any disorder of stomach or bowels. . . . The principle of *pinole* is very simple. If you should eat a breakfast of corn-meal mush alone, and start out for a hard tramp, you will feel hungry in an hour or two, though at the table the dewrinkling of your abdomen may have reached the hurting point. But if, instead of distending the meal so much with water and heat, you had simply mixed it in cold water and drunk it, you could have taken down three times the quantity in one-tenth of the time. You would not feel the difference at your waistband, but you would feel it mightily in your legs, especially if you have a heavy rifle on your back. It works a little on the principle of dried apples, though it is quite an improvement. There is no danger of explosion; it swells to suit the demand, and not too suddenly

Suppose, now, instead of raw corn-meal, we make

it not only drinkable but positively good. This is easily done by parching to a very light brown before grinding, and grinding just fine enough to mix so as to be drinkable, but not pasty, as flour would be. Good wheat is as good as corn, and perhaps better, while the mixture is very good. Common rolled oats browned in a pan in the oven and run through a spice mill is as good and easy to make it out of as anything. A coffee mill may do if it will set fine enough. Ten per cent. of popped corn ground in with it will improve the flavor so much that your children will get away with it all if you don't hide it. Wheat and corn are hard to grind, but the small Enterprise spice mill will do it. You may also mix some ground chocolate with it for flavor, which, with popped corn, makes it very fine . . Indigestible? Your granny's nightcap! . . You must remember that it is "werry fillin' for the price," and go slow with it until you have found your co-efficient. . .

Now for the application. The Mexican rover of the desert will tie a small sack of *pinole* behind his saddle and start for a trip of several days. It is the lightest of food, and in the most portable shape, sandproof, bug and fly proof, and everything. Wherever he finds water he stirs a few ounces in a cup (I never weighed it, but four seem about enough at a time for an ordinary man), drinks it in five seconds, and is fed for five or six hours. If he has jerky, he chews that as he jogs along, but if he has not he will go through the longest trip and come out strong and well on *pinole* alone."—*Shooting and Fishing*, Vol. xx, p. 248.

When preparing pinole for mountaineering trips, I used to pulverize the parched corn in a hominy mortar, which is nothing but a three-foot cut off of a two-foot log, with a cavity chiseled out in the top, and a wooden pestle shod with iron. The hole is of smaller diameter at the bottom than at the top, so that each blow of the pestle throws most of the corn upward, and thus it is evenly powdered. Two heaping tablespoonfuls was the usual "sup," and, if I had nothing else, I took it frequently during the day. With a handful of raisins, or a chunk of sweet chocolate or maple sugar, it made a square meal.

CONCENTRATED FOODS 155

But what is the actual food value of this Indian invention? I take the following figures from a bulletin of the Department of Agriculture on *Food Value of Corn and Corn Products*, by Dr. Charles D. Woods (Washington, 1907):

Kind of material	Protein	Fat	Carbo-hydrates	Mineral matter	Fuel value per pound
	%	%	%	%	Calories
Hominy, boiled	2.2	0.2	17.8	0.5	380
Hulled corn	2.3	0.9	22.2	0.5	490
Indian pudding (corn mush)	5.5	4.8	27.5	1.5	815
Hoecake	4.0	0.6	40.2	2.4	885
Boston brown bread	6.3	2.1	45.8	1.9	1,110
Johnnycake	7.8	2.2	57.7	2.9	1,385
Granulated cornmeal	9.2	1.9	75.4	1.0	1,655
Corn br'kfast foods, flaked (part cook'd at factory)	9.6	1.1	78.3	0.7	1,680
Corn br'kfast foods, flaked and parched (ready to eat)	10.1	1.8	78.4	2.4	1,735
Popped corn	10.7	5.0	78.7	1.3	1,880
Parched corn	11.5	8.4	72.3	2.6	1,915
Wheat bread (for comparison)	9.2	1.3	53.1	1.1	1,205

The remaining percentages are water.

Pulverized parched corn owes its "carrying power" not only to its relatively high nutritive value, as shown in this table, but largely to the fact that, when drunk with water instead of cooked, it swells in the stomach and gives it a comfortable feeling of fullness. That this is not an imaginary gain will be shown later in this chapter.

JERKED VENISON.—The "jerky" referred to by Mr. Van Dyke is jerked meat, usually venison: that is to say, lean meat cut in strips and dried over a slow fire or in the sun. It is very different from our commercial dried beef, less salty, more nourishing and appetizing, and one can subsist comfortably on it for some time with no other foodstuff at all. The process of jerking venison is described in Vol. I (pp. 277-280).

PEMMICAN.—The staple commissary supply of arctic travelers, and of hunters and traders in the far Northwest, is pemmican. This is not so palatable as jerky, at least when carelessly prepared; but it contains more nutriment, in a given bulk, and is better suited for cold climates, on account of the fat mixed with it.

The old-time Hudson Bay pemmican was made from buffalo meat, in the following manner: first a sufficient number of bags, about 2 x 1½ feet, were made from the hides of old bulls that were unfit for robes. The lean meat was then cut into thin strips, as for jerky, and dried in the sun for two or three days, or over a fire, until it was hard and brittle. It was then pounded to a powder between two stones, or by a flail, on a sort of hide threshing-floor with the edges pegged up. The fat and marrow were then melted and mixed with the powdered lean meat to a paste; or, the bags were filled with the lean and then the fat was run in on top. After this the mass was well rammed down, and the bags were sewed up tight. No salt was used; but the pemmican thus prepared would keep sweet for years in the cool climate of the North. A piece as large as one's fist, when soaked and cooked, would make a meal for two men. When there was flour in the outfit, the usual allowance of pemmican was 1¼ to 1½ pounds a day per man, with one pound of flour added. This was for men performing the hardest labor, and whose appetites were enormous. Service berries were sometimes added. "Officers' pemmican" was made from buffalo humps and marrow.

Pemmican nowadays is made from beef. Bleasdell Cameron gives the following details: A beef dressing 698 pounds yields 47 pounds of first-class pemmican, 47 pounds of second-class pemmican and 23 pounds of dried meat, including tongues, a total of 117 pounds, dried. The total nutritive strength is thus reduced in weight to one-sixth that of the fresh beef. Such pemmican, at the time he wrote, cost the Canadian government about forty

CONCENTRATED FOODS 157

cents a pound, equivalent to six pounds of fresh beef.

Pemmican is sometimes eaten raw, sometimes boiled with flour into a thick soup or porridge called *roboboo;* or, mixed with flour and water and fried like sausage, it is known as *rascho*. The pemmican made nowadays for arctic expeditions is prepared from the round of beef cut into strips and kiln-dried until friable, then ground fine and mixed with beef suet, a little sugar, and a few currants. It is compressed into cakes, and then packed so as to exclude moisture. It can be bought ready-made in New York, but at an enormous price when sold in small quantity, and the tins add considerably to the weight. If one has home facilities he can make it himself. Leave out the sugar, which makes meat unpalatable to most men. The sugar item should be separate in the ration.

Desiccated meat is disagreeable, and not nearly so nutritious as pemmican, which is already concentrated as much as meat should be, and has the advantage of containing a liberal amount of fat.

ARMY EMERGENCY RATIONS.—In 1870 there was issued to every German soldier a queer, yellow, sausage-shaped contrivance that held within its paper wrapper what looked and felt like a short stick of dynamite. No, it was not a bomb nor a hand grenade. It was just a pound of compressed dry pea soup. This was guaranteed to support a man's strength for one day, without any other aliment whatever. The soldier was ordered to keep this roll of soup about him at all times, and never to use it until there was no other food to be had. The official name of the thing was erbswurst (pronounced *airbs-voorst*) which means pea sausage. Within a few months it became famous as the "iron ration" of the Germans in the Franco-Prussian war.

Our sportsmen over here are well acquainted with erbswurst, either in its original form or, at present, as an American "pea soup with bacon" done up in cartons. For many it is the last call to supper when they have had no dinner and see slight prospect of breakfast. Besides, it is the lazy man's prop on rainy days, and the standby of inexperienced cooks.

Erbswurst is composed of pea meal mixed with a very little fat pork and some salt, so treated as to prevent decay, desiccated and compressed into rolls of various sizes. It is much the same thing as baked beans would be if they were dried and powdered, except that it tastes different and it contains much less fat. I understand that the original erbswurst, as prepared by its inventor, Grunberg, included a goodly proportion of fat; but the article of commerce that appeared later had so little of this valuable component (by analysis only 3.08%) that you could scarce detect it.

Nobody can spoil erbswurst in the cooking, unless he goes away and lets it burn. All you have to do is to start a quart of water boiling, tear off the cover from a quarter-pound roll of this "dynamite soup," crumble the stuff finely into the water with your fingers, and boil for fifteen or twenty minutes, stirring a few times to avoid lumps. Then let the mess cool, and go to it. You may make it thin as a soup or thick as a porridge, or fry it after mixing with a little water, granting you have grease to fry with.

It never spoils, never gets any "punkier" than it was at the beginning. The stick of erbswurst that you left undetected last year in the seventh pocket of your hunting coat will be just as good when you discover it again this year. Mice won't gnaw it; bugs can't get at it; moisture can't get into it. I have used rolls that had lain so long in damp places that they were all moldy outside, yet the food within was neither worse nor better than before.

A pound of erbswurst, costing from thirty-two to forty cents, is about all a man can eat in three meals straight. Cheap enough, and compact enough, God wot! However, this little boon has a string attached. Erbswurst tastes pretty good to a hungry man in the woods as a hot noonday snack, now and

CONCENTRATED FOODS 159

then. It is not appetizing as a sole mainstay for supper on the same day. Next morning, supposing you have missed connections with camp, and have nothing but the rest of that erbswurst, you will down it amid storms and tempests of your own raising. And thenceforth, no matter what fleshpots you may fall upon, you will taste "dynamite soup" for a week.

In its native land, this iron ration lost its popularity and was thrown out of the German army. Over here, we benighted wights keep on using it, or its American similitude, in emergencies, simply because we know of no better substitute, or because it is the easiest thing of the kind to be found on the market. We all wish to discover a ready-made ration as light and compact as erbswurst, as incorruptible and cheap, but one that would be fairly savory at the second and third eating, and polite to our insides (which "dynamite soup" is not).

Now I am not about to offer a new invention, nor introduce some wonderful good grub that has lately arrived from abroad. Before the outbreak of the present war, I believe, every army had discarded all the emergency rations it had tried. And yet all of them were searching for a better one. Which goes to prove that a satisfactory thing of this sort is most desirable, but the hardest thing in the world for a commissariat to find. We wilderness prowlers join heartily in praying that somebody will find it; for we, too, like the soldiery, may be cut off from supplies, no telling when, and with the added dilemma, perhaps, of being lost and alone in the "big sticks."

So it is quite worth while to review the best that has been done along this line, show wherein the most promising experiments have failed, and restate the problem anew—then let fresh inventive genius tackle it. And a few suggestions may not be out of place.

Beginning again with erbswurst, as prototype of such foods; theoretically it is highly nutritious, though less fit for continuous use as a sole diet than baked beans, even though the latter were desiccated. Practically it soon palls on the palate, upsets the stomach, and, like any other food composed almost wholly of legumes, causes flatulent dyspepsia or other disorders of the digestive tract.

The British army tried it, and Tommy Atkins let out a howl that reached from South Africa to London. The War Office replaced it with another German invention, Kopf's soup, which also had pea meal for its basis but had a higher content of fat (17.25%). This was superior in potential energy, but the after effects were similar to those of erbswurst. It was plain that an exclusive diet, if only for a day or two, of legumes and fat would soon put a man to the bad. England discarded the iron ration and placated Tommy with jam—a wise move, as we shall see.

In 1900 a new kind of emergency ration was introduced in our own army. This was made up of eight ounces of a meat-and-cereal powder, four ounces of sweet chocolate, and some salt and pepper; all put up in a tin can eight inches long and thin enough to slip easily into one's pocket. This pound of food was calculated to subsist a man in full strength and vigor for one day. Details of its preparation are here copied from official sources:

"The chocolate component consists of equal weights of pure chocolate and pure sugar molded into cakes of one and one-third ounces each. Three of these go into the day's ration.

"The bread and meat component consists of:

"(1) Fresh lean beef free from visible fat and sinew, ground in a meat grinder and desiccated so as to contain five per cent or less of moisture, the heat never being allowed to cook it in the slightest degree. The dried product is then reduced to powder and carefully sifted through a fine-meshed sieve, the resulting flour being the meat component.

"(2) Cooked kiln-dried wheat, the outer bran removed, is parched and then ground to a coarse powder. This yields the bread component. Sixteen parts of the meat, thirty-two parts of the bread, and one part of common salt, all by weight, are thoroughly mixed in such small quantities as to be entirely homogeneous and compressed into four-ounce cakes. Three of these go into the day's ration. The bread and meat may be eaten dry, or be stirred in cold water and eaten; or one cake may be boiled for five minutes in three pints of water, and seasoned [as soup]; or one cake may be boiled for five minutes in one pint of water to make a thick porridge and be eaten hot or cold. When cold it may be sliced, and, if fat is available, may be fried. Three-fourths of an ounce of salt and one gramme of pepper are in the can for seasoning."

At first glance it might seem that the bread and meat components of this ration were essentially the same as the pinole and jerked venison of our Indians and white frontiersmen—and it is quite likely that the inventors had those primitive foods in mind, seeking only to condense them still further without impairing their famous nutritive values. Practically, however, there is little resemblance. Jerky retains much of the meat juice, which gives it its pleasant flavor. Desiccated meat contains no juice, and its taste is altogether different. Pulverized, parched wheat is a sort of pinole, but in this case it was first cooked, then parched, and the flavor was inferior.

Finally the meat powder and grain powder were mixed and sifted into a homogeneous mass, compressed, and sealed up in an air-tight tin. One need not even taste such a product to know that it could not possibly satisfy the palate like the old-time preparations.

The emergency ration gave satisfaction for a time, but eventually there were many complaints that it was indigestible, or otherwise unwholesome. Scientists reported that it was lacking in nutrition. The troops did not like its taste, and their officers warned them to husband their hard bread and bacon as long as they could, since a very limited amount of either or both, taken with the emergency ration, made it far more palatable. Another fault of this "near-food" was that the can that held it was so thick and heavy that it made the gross weight of the article almost as great as that of the regular haversack ration, which cost much less and had a better taste.

In 1913 the Secretary of War ordered the discontinuance of this emergency ration, notwithstanding that great quantities of it still were in storage. The problem of getting up a better one was turned over to food experts of the Department of Agriculture. About a year later a new emergency ration was, I believe, adopted, composed of bean flour, lean meat, raisins, and a small percentage of wheat flour. This is said to be palatable and nutritious, but I do not know how well it may have stood the test of service.

THE PROBLEM of an emergency ration is not merely one of condensing the utmost nutriment into the least bulk and weight. One cannot live on butter or peanuts alone, however high their caloric value may be. The stuff must be digestible: it must neither nauseate nor clog the system. When a man is faint from hunger (and that is the only time he ever will need an emergency ration) his stomach must not be forced to any uncommon stunts. And so I hold that a half ration of palatable food that is readily assimilated does more good than a full quota of stuff that taxes a man's gastric strength or disorders his bowels. And there is a good deal to be said for mere palatability. Food that tastes bad *is* bad, for nobody can work well on it.

Of course, an emergency ration is not intended to be used long at a time. It is not meant to interchange with the regular reserve ration of hard bread, bacon, or preserved meat, dried vegetables, coffee, sugar, and salt, that soldiers carry on their persons during a campaign. The iron ration proper is a minimum bulk and weight of unspoilable food that is complete in itself, packed in a waterproof and insect-proof cover, and it is never to be opened save

CONCENTRATED FOODS 163

in extremity when reserve rations have run out and supply trains cannot connect with the troops. Yet this is the very time when men are likely to be exhausted and famished. It is the very time when their systems demand food that tastes good and that assimilates easily.

Again, an emergency ration should contain some component that digests rather slowly, or it soon will leave a feeling of emptiness in the stomach—it will not "stick to the ribs" like one that takes several hours to become assimilated. Moreover, the stomach craves bulk as well as nutriment—there should be something to swell up and distend it. This is important, for, if condensation be carried too far, it defeats its own purpose. If we could concentrate a thousand calories of food energy into a single tablet, a man would not feel that he had eaten anything after taking it.

BREAD SUBSTITUTES.—The main difficulty in compounding a good emergency ration is in getting a concentrated substitute for bread. The Germans have experimented with flour or grits made from peanuts. It is claimed that a pound of peanut flour contains as much nutritive material as three pounds of beef or two of peas. It can be made into porridge or into biscuits. Its flavor is pleasant in either a cooked or a raw state. Whether its nutrients are easily and completely utilized by the system has not, so far as I know, been proven.

As for meal made from beans or peas, it is not easily digested, and it tends to putrify in the alimentary canal. (A method of desiccating baked beans is given in Vol. I, p. 368).

Hardtack may be considered a proper component of an emergency ration, because it is a concentrated bread that does not spoil. The best way to use it, when facilities permit, is to break it up and add it to hot soup or coffee, or pour hot water over it, pepper and salt, and eat with bacon grease.

Plasmon biscuit (see Vol. I., p. 192) are more palatable than hardtack and more nutritious, but expensive. In appearance they resemble round Educator crackers. Half a dozen of them, with a small cake of chocolate, make a satisfying lunch. Plasmon itself is the proteid of milk in powdered form, containing 80% of pure protein. It may be used either dry or dissolved in water. When sprinkled dry over any kind of food, or cooked in with cereals, bread, soups, etc., it adds very much to the nutritive value without altering the flavor of the food.

Various kinds of meat biscuits have been tried out most thoroughly by troops and travelers, but without satisfaction. Kipling said, "compressed vegetables and meat biscuits may be nourishing, but what Tommy Atkins needs is bulk in his inside." In this he was doing the vegetables injustice, for, when cooked, they do swell up and fill one's inside.

CONDENSED SOUPS.—Nearly all go-light outfits include a supply of compressed soups. Some of these are of good flavor, others are of what Stewart Edward White calls the "dishwater brand." He recommends Knorr's pea, bean, lentil, rice, onion (none of the others), and particularly Maggi's green pea and lentil. Of bouillon capsules he says that "they serve to flavor hot water, and that is about all." I agree with him throughout. Maggi's soups are packed in tin-foil before putting on the paper wrapper. This excludes moisture, but I have found that it will not keep out the industrious weevil. Condensed soups have their uses, chiefly as pick-me-ups; but they do not by any means contain enough nourishment to furnish a hungry man's meal. I mention them here only as a warning against putting confidence in them for any such purpose.

Bouillon cubes, etc., are much worse, in this respect. Properly they are nothing but condiments or appetizers for healthy people and mild stimulants for the sick. Their actual food value has been determined by the Bureau of Chemistry of the U. S. Department of Agriculture, which was led to investigate the matter because "these articles are erroneously believed to be convenient forms of concentrated meat."

CONCENTRATED FOODS 165

Ten different brands of commercial bouillon cubes were analyzed, with the result that the best showed 62% salt, 5.25% water and fat, 28% meat extract, 4.75% plant extract, and from this they ranged on down to the poorest, with 72% salt, 8.5% water and fat, 8.17% meat extract, 11.33% plant extract. The plant extract " is useful because of its flavoring properties, but has slight, if any, nutritive value." As for the semi-solid meat extracts sold in jars, the chemist reported that they "are not concentrated beef. They are stimulants and flavoring adjuncts, and have only a slight food value, owing to the small amount of protein (muscle-building food) which they contain."

On the other hand, one can make for himself a real meat extract, in which much of the nourishment of beef or veal or venison is concentrated in the form of little cubes of a gluey consistency from which a strengthening soup can quickly be prepared.

Take a leg of young beef, veal, or venison (old meat will not jelly easily). Pare off every bit of fat and place the lean meat in a large pot. Boil it steadily and gently for seven or eight hours, until the meat is reduced to rags, skimming off, from time to time, the grease that arises. Then pour this strong broth into a large, wide stew-pan, place it over a moderate fire, and let it simmer gently until it comes to a thick jelly. When it gets so thick that there may be danger of scorching it, place the vessel over boiling water, and stir it very frequently until, when cold, it will have the consistency of glue. Cut this substance into small cubes and lay them singly where they can become thoroughly dry. Or, if you prefer, run the jelly into sausage skins and tie up the ends. A cube or thick slice of this glaze, dissolved in hot water, makes an excellent soup. A small piece allowed to melt in one's mouth is strengthening on the march.

This is a very old recipe, being mentioned in Byrd's *History of the Dividing Line*, and recommended along with rockahominy. The above can be made in camp, when opportunity offers, thus laying in enough concentrated soup stock to last a month, which is quite convenient, as it takes at least half a day to make good soup from the raw materials, and these are not always at hand when most wanted.

FATS.—In speaking of erbswurst I remarked on its deficiency in fat, which is an important component of field rations, especially in cold weather, since it is fuel for the body. Pemmican owes much of its efficiency to the large percentage of fat. Captain Scott had the pemmican for his antarctic expedition made with 50% lard, which is pure fat. Such a mixture would nauseate many a man, but nearly everybody likes butter, which is the next most concentrated form of fat. The best field luncheon for cold weather, when you can get it, is in the form of sandwiches of toasted bread, thick slices of butter, and brown or maple sugar. It is very nourishing, and it will not freeze up like plain bread, as there is practically no water in it. Outfitters supply excellent butter, in one-pound cans, that will keep in any climate.

Butter is out of the question in an emergency ration that is to be sealed up and kept indefinitely. There are, however, certain other fats that will take its place as fuel.

DESICCATED EGGS, if prepared from the whole egg, contain 36% of fat. They are also remarkably rich in protein. There is no good reason, except its cost and the fact that it requires cooking, why egg powder should not form a considerable constituent of an emergency ration, as it keeps perfectly when protected from moisture. (See Vol. I., pp. 183 and 189). Its fat content is nearly equal to that of full cream cheese, and its fuel value nearly a third more.

CHOCOLATE, in plain form, contains about 49% of vegetable fat; less, of course, when sweetened. It is necessary, however, for eating purposes, that chocolate should have considerable sugar added, and this is directly a gain, for sugar itself is stored energy, as we soon shall see. Chocolate never gets stale.

CONCENTRATED FOODS 167

It requires no cooking, can be eaten on the march, yet a stimulating hot drink can be prepared from it in a few minutes. It is the experience of Alpinists and other go-light artists that no other raw food of equal weight and bulk will carry a man so far under severe strain as a handful of raisins and a cake of chocolate. When eaten by itself, chocolate is constipating and cloying, at least to some people. Raisins eaten along with it prevent digestive troubles; a couple of crackers help the ration.

There is a "camper's emergency ration," carried in stock by outfitters, that contains chocolate, malted milk, egg albumen, casein, sugar, and cocoa butter, with added coffee flavor. Three cakes of it, each sufficient for a meal, are wrapped in paper and tin-foil and enclosed in a sealed box with key-opener, the box being 4½ x 3 x 1⅜ inches, and rounded for the pocket. The net weight of the ration is 8 ounces; gross weight of box filled, 11½ ounces. Chocolate is not to be recommended for hot weather.

NUTS.—The table of food values in Vol. I., pp. 182-184, shows that various nuts are very rich in vegetable fat, and so have high fuel values. They are discussed on page 196 of the same volume. Nuts should be chewed thoroughly, so as to be well mixed with saliva, or they will clog the digestive tract.

SWEETS.—Sugar has peculiar merit as a component of the emergency ration. All old-timers know from experience that one has an unusual craving for sweets when working hard afield. Hunters and lumberjacks and soldiers suffered from that craving long before scientists discovered the cause of it, which is that during hard muscular exertion the consumption of sugar in the body increases four-fold.

It may sound odd but it is true, that when hunters or explorers are reduced to a diet of meat "straight" the most grateful addition that they could have would be something sweet. Men can get along very well on venison, without bread, if they have maple sugar or candy and some citric acid (crystallized lemon juice) to go with it. And there is good reason for this. Sugars have about the same food uses as starches, because all starch must be converted into sugar or dextrin before it can be assimilated. Mark, then, that sugar needs no conversion; therefore it acts quickly as a pick-me-up to relieve fatigue, while bread or any other starchy food would have to go first through the process of changing into sugar before it could supply force and heat to the body.

A great advantage of sweets is that every normal person likes them. Another is that they are antiseptic and preservative, which adapts them perfectly to use in rations that may have to be stored or carried a long time before using.

These are not merely my own individual opinions, although all my experience backs them. Since the worth of sweets in a sportsman's or soldier's food supply is commonly underrated, or even ridiculed, through sheer crass ignorance, let me quote from Thompson, one of the most eminent of our dieticians:

"The value of sweets in the adult dietary has of late years found recognition in armies. The British War Office shipped 1,500,000 pounds of jam to South Africa as a four months' supply for 116,000 troops, and one New York firm, during the Spanish-American War, shipped over fifty tons of confectionery to the troops in Cuba, Porto Rico, and the Philippines. The confectionery consisted of chocolate creams, cocoanut macaroons, lemon and other acid fruit drops. . . .

"An old-time custom among soldiers in the field is to fill a canteen with two parts vinegar and one part molasses as an emergency sustaining drink. . . .

"Sugar furnishes, in addition to heat, considerable muscle energy, and it has been lately proved by Mosso, Vaughn Harley and others to have distinct power in relieving muscular fatigue.

"Vaughn Harley found that with an exclusive diet of $17\frac{1}{2}$ ounces of sugar dissolved in water he could perform almost as much muscular work as upon a full mixed diet. The effect in lessening muscle fatigue was noticeable in half an hour and reached a maximum in two hours. Three or four ounces of

CONCENTRATED FOODS 169

sugar taken before the expected onset of fatigue postponed or entirely inhibited the sensation.

"The hard-working lumbermen of Canada and Maine eat a very large quantity of sugar in the form of molasses. I have seen them add it to tea and to almost everything they cook. Sugar has also been found of much service upon polar expeditions."

Many of our sportsmen, when going light, substitute saccharin (saxin, crystallose) for sugar, thinking thereby to save weight and bulk. This is a grave error. It is true that saccharin has enormous sweetening power, and that moderate use of it on an outing trip, in one's tea and coffee, will do no harm. But the point overlooked is that sugar is a concentrated source of energy, easily and quickly assimilated, whereas saccharin produces no energy at all, being nothing but a coal-tar drug. It is the grape sugar in raisins, for example, that makes them so stimulating.

Sir Ernest Shackleton, in outfitting his party for their recent antarctic expedition, made sugar figure largely in the rations. On the previous exploring trip he and his companions each took two or three lumps of sugar every two or three hours, and he said that ten minutes after eating it they could feel the heat going through their bodies.

One at least of the nations engaged in the present war supplies its men in the trenches with a daily ration of ten ounces of sugar, which is over three times the allowance of sugar in the field ration of our own service. "It has been found, however," says *Outing,* "that this abundance of sweet not only gives the soldier added muscular strength but increases his resistance to cold and fatigue, both physical and nervous. The action of sugar is most effective when dissolved in some hot liquid: it is especially beneficial taken in chocolate."

FRUITS.—One fault of all the ready-made concentrated rations that I have seen was that they contained no acids. A fruit acid is needed, even in a food preparation that is to be used only for a day or two, in order to correct the ultra-sweet or fatty components, and is particularly desirable in summer. It is easy to supply the deficiency, in very concentrated form, by adding tablets of citric acid. This makes refreshing lemonade. Lime-juice tablets are good on the march, as they combine sugar with acid, and not only supply energy but ward off thirst. Fruit acid is supplied in very palatable form by dehydrated rhubarb and cranberries, which cook in a few minutes, and can scarcely be told from the fresh articles.

Raisins have already been mentioned several times. Their stimulating effect, due to the grape sugar in them, is felt ten minutes after eating. On the trail, when working hard, as in mountain climbing, it is a good rule to eat little and often. Raisins are particularly convenient for munching as one goes along. They have added value in that they are mildly laxative, and something of that sort is certainly needed in the ration. Figs have the same virtue. I imagine the seeds have something to do with this, and for that reason I do not use seedless or seeded raisins.

Dehydrated vegetables have no place in emergency rations simply because they require long cooking.

RATION PACKING.—The mere weight of the tin container of the discarded U. S. A. emergency ration was a serious objection. Such a box will weigh about a third as much as the food itself. Being made of heavy tin, it is hard to open. If a key opener is attached, it is likely to be lost. A cover of parchment paper, which is waterproof, dirt-proof, and insect-proof, like the erbswurst "sausage," is cheaper, easier to apply, weighs practically nothing, and can be torn off with the fingers.

I think it is a mistake to mix meat powder with legumes or cereals and seal the mass up in an airtight cover. In such case, each food taints the other. The combination has a stale, nondescript taste, whereas each component would preserve its natural flavor if packed separately. For woodsmen, if not for troops, it seems more practical to put up

CONCENTRATED FOODS 171

the emergency ration in two, or even three, separate packages, each containing only such articles as will not taint nor steal flavor from the others. This suggestion is made for rations to be carried in stock by outfitters, which are likely to be kept a good while in storage.

But when a camper puts up emergency grub for himself, there is a better way. Raisins, pinole, and the like, are best carried in little bags of thin paraffined cloth (the "balloon silk" of tent makers), tied low enough so that the top can be doubled over and tied again, making a water-tight package, very light, and soft enough to go into one's pocket, or anywhere. Chocolate (which I don't carry in hot weather) usually comes wrapped in tin-foil, and enclosed in paper. You will need salt, in a waterproof bag or a bamboo tube, to season such game or fish as you may get.

If you carry anything in which water can be boiled, put a dozen tabloids of tea in the ration, leave out chocolate and substitute sugar. A hot cup of sweetened tea is one of the best hearteners that I know of, and the tabloid tea sold by outfitters is pretty good. But what vessel to boil in? Water can be boiled in a bark cup, as I shall show hereafter; but maybe you can't find bark that will peel. A practical outdoorsman, C. L. Gilman, suggests that the emergency food be packed in a half-pound cocoa can, which is of handy shape for the pocket, seamed water-tight without solder, holds a pint, and has a cover that fits over the outside. Punch two holes near top edge of can, and make a removable wire bail that will stow inside. Steam escapes through bail holes when cover is on. Thus your grub has a light tin container that is good for something when it is opened.

For myself, I would fill that little kettle with pinole, sugar, tea, and salt, in "pokes," and would carry some raisins separately. One advantage of pinole, aside from those already mentioned, is that it is not, like chocolate and raisins, a confection that tempts one to draw on it when he does not need it, albeit the flavor is good, when the stuff is properly prepared, and does not pall on the appetite.

LIGHT TRAVELING RATIONS.—Many correspondents have asked me to suggest a "grub list" for men traveling light—one that should be complete in itself, without helping out by game or fish or articles purchased on the way. Tastes differ, and "what is one man's meat is another man's poison." Some assimilate their food more completely than others. I know of several experienced campers who seem to get along very well on a food allowance (their own choice) of from 1½ to 1¾ pounds a day. They are quite exceptional. An average man, engaged in hearty outdoor exercise, requires, on a trip of more than two or three days, about 2¼ pounds a day of carefully selected and varied food that is, nearly as practicable, water-free. Study the chapter on PROVISIONS in the first volume of this book, paying heed to the table of nutritive values.

As all-around advice, I can do no better than suggest, for a real light but adequate and wholesome ration, what I have given on the list of Summer Equipment for Back-packing in Chapter VII., omitting the cheese. This would make the ration 2 lbs. 3 oz. *net*. The tea (not tabloids) and salt are purposely in excess of what a man would likely consume. Admiral Peary's ration for arctic sledge journeys (2 lbs. 4¼ oz.) given in Vol. I., p. 190, may be regarded as a minimum for hard work in winter. It is a monotonous diet, deficient in sugar and in fruit acid, although his pemmican contained a little of both.

CHAPTER XI

MARKSMANSHIP IN THE WOODS

Never shall I forget the remark that a backwoodsman once made when I was trying to entertain him at a rifle match near St. Louis. I had shown him the shooting-house, the target-house, and their appurtenances; had explained our system of scoring and our code of rules; had told him the reasons for using such heavy rifles, sensitive triggers, pronged butt-plates, cheek-pieces, vernier and wind-gauge sights—all that; and then I bade him watch some of our experts as they made bullseye after bullseye, seldom missing a space the size of a man's head, shooting offhand, at 200 measured yards. I thought that my friend would be impressed. He was; but not quite as I had anticipated. After watching the firing for a long time in silence, he turned to me and remarked: "If it weren't for the noise and the powder smoke, this would be a very ladylike game."

Of course, I was piqued at this, and felt like giving the honest fellow a peppery reply. And yet, many a time since, as I have sat, chilled to the bone, on some crossing in the high Smokies, straining my ears for the bear-dogs far below; or, tired beyond speech and faint from hunger, as I lay down beside a log in the great forest, all alone; or, blown by hard climbing till my heart seemed bursting, as I wiped the mist from my eyes, and got down on all fours to follow a fresh spoor into the hideous laurel fastness of Godforsaken—aye, many a time I have looked backward and thought, "You were right, partner; it was a very ladylike game."

It was a long time ago—that shooting match. If

a city man, in those days, wanted to practice with a rifle at targets, he had to join a "schuetzen" society. (In Missouri the organized militia had no range, and never fired a rifle except with blanks!) So we had to fall back on a foreign system that never yet has found so much as an English name. The schuetzen method did teach a man to hold steadily and to let off delicately, and this is the A B C of marksmanship. But it stopped there. It taught the A B C forward and backward till the pupil became, perhaps, wonderfully expert in such exercise; but it never got beyond A B C and Z Y X. It taught him to drive a nail with a bullet, offhand; but nothing about quick firing with accuracy, nothing about hitting moving objects, nothing about judging distances and making true allowance for them, nothing about aiming at a neutral-colored object that blended with its surroundings. Our men were "crackajacks" at drilling a squirrel's head, but only the few who took regular hunting trips in the wilderness had any idea of what kind of a thing to look for if they went after deer or any other big game.

RIFLE PRACTICE.—Times have changed. Civilians now can join clubs that have the use of military ranges, where they can use practical weapons supplied by the Government, at known and unknown distances, deliberate fire and quick fire, resting at ease or after a skirmish run. They may, if they choose, rig up "running deer" targets. All this is excellent practice for one preparing to go after big game.

If you are so situated that you cannot join such a club, nor use a powerful rifle in your neighborhood, get a repeating .22, learn first to drive tacks with it (in a city basement, if need be), then take it out somewhere that is safe for the purpose, and shoot at miscellaneous objects, at unknown distances all the way from twenty to a hundred yards. If you can get a friend to roll a barrel for you down a bumpy hillside, try it at various angles—good training before you go to shoot at deer on the bound.

It is practice, intelligently varied practice, that

MARKSMANSHIP IN THE WOODS 175

makes a marksman. Without it, the keenest eye and the steadiest nerve are of no avail. I have associated intimately with expert riflemen for half a lifetime, and I know that every one of them would tell you that there "is no such animal" as a born marksman. There never was. If frontiersmen generally are good shots it is simply because they have had plenty of practice from their youth up. Some have natural advantages over others, to be sure, but nothing will take the place of training. It is like writing, for instance: anybody of average sense can learn to write correctly, many can write entertainingly, a few have genius and may become immortal—but no genius who ever lived has turned out first-class work at the first trial: he had to practice, practice, practice!

There is no room here to discuss the topic of hunting rifles. Get the best that you can, of course; but do not worship it. Bear in mind that, whatever its trajectory and smashing quality, it is only a gun, and can kill nothing that you miss with it. When you get into the real wilderness far away from rich men's preserves and summer hotels, you will find there some mighty hunters who make mighty kills with guns that would bring only the price of scrap-iron in New York.

Get sights that you can *see,* and such as you are not likely to overshoot with when taking quick aim. Take pains to get what suits your eyes, and spare no time in the adjustment. Never take an untried gun into the woods. That is no place to align sights and test elevations. Never trust the sights as they are placed on the gun at the factory. Test them not only from rest, but offhand, too; for a light rifle charged with high-power ammunition is likely to shoot several inches higher (or in some other direction) when fired from muzzle-and-elbow rest, than it does when shot offhand, albeit it may be an accurate weapon when rightly used.

SIGHT ADJUSTMENT.—Now, as for adjusting the elevation—a most important matter—first, by all means, find the "point-blank" of your weapon by actual test. If your dealer assures you that a certain rifle shoots practically point-blank up to 300 yards, "trust him not; he's fooling thee." Theoretically there is no such thing as a point-blank range. Practically, what we mean by it is the extreme distance to which a rifle may be sighted to strike center without overshooting at any intermediate distance the vitals of the animal to be hunted.

Why a bullet rises above the line of aim and stays above it until it reaches a point for which the sights were set, and then falls below it, if not stopped; how much it does so, at various ranges and with various types of ammunition; how to determine the best point-blank for different kinds of hunting: these are matters that would require a good many pages to explain. (See the writer's *Sporting Firearms,* in the series of "Outing Handbooks").

In the big-game fields of the East and South, which generally are thickly timbered or bushy cutover lands, it is seldom that one gets a shot at over 60 or 70 yards, unless he is in the mountains or on the margin of a lake or river. Even an old-fashioned rifle, using ammunition of, say 1,300 feet muzzle velocity per second, if sighted accurately for 50 yards, will not drop its bullet more than two inches at 75 yards, and at 25 yards you need only draw a wee bit fine to cut off the head of a grouse or squirrel. Fifty yards, then, is a good elevation at which to set the rear sight of such a gun. A .30-30, or other rifle of the 2,000 feet M. V. class, shoots to this same "practical point-blank" up to 100 yards when sighted for 75 yards.

In other words, the hunter need make no allowance for distance, in aiming, up to these respective ranges, except when shooting at small game close by. This is why so many old hunters east of the Mississippi take little or no interest in guns more powerful than the kinds here mentioned. They don't feel the need of anything better. If they should unexpectedly have to take a long shot, and do it quickly, they simply draw a coarse bead, or hold high, and take their chances.

MARKSMANSHIP IN THE WOODS 177

In the West it is different. Much of the game country is open. Often you can't get close by stalking. Shots at 200 yards are common, and much longer ones can be made successfully by a well-trained marksman armed with a very *accurate* rifle that drives its bullet at a high and *well-sustained* velocity. I emphasize the words "accurate" and "well-sustained" because there are many rifles that are inaccurate beyond 100 or 150 yards, and that start their bullets swiftly but do not maintain a high velocity beyond short range. Their trajectory figures are illusory, because trajectory means only the *average* or mean height of bullet flight above line of fire at such and such intermediate distances. Take, for example, a .30-30 sighted for 200 yards. Its trajectory at 100 yards is given in the tables as 5.79 inches above line of fire; but, as a matter of fact, the shots vary so much at 100 yards that they may go anywhere from 3.40 to 8.40 inches high; at 250 yards, with same aim, they may drop anywhere from 2.25 to 14.75 inches below line of fire. Yet the .30-30 is considered a fairly accurate cartridge: there are others, with short, snub-nosed bullets, that shoot much worse.

Now, by contrast, let us consider a gun that shoots swift and true at all ranges, for instance one using our Springfield ammunition. I take the liberty of quoting from Captain Whelen the following table of such a rifle's actual performance, with 150-grain bullet, when sighted for 200 yards, and some of his comments thereon:

Trajectory	Range in Yards			
	100	200	225	300
Above line of fire, in. ...	2.5	0	....	....
Below line of fire, in.		0	1.9	9.
Sight allowance, in.	.5	0	.12	..5
Above line of *aim*, in....	2.	0	....	....
Below line of *aim*, in.		0	2.02	9.5
Mean vertical deviation, inches	.8	1.6	1.8	2.4
Greatest deviation from point of *aim*, with range unestimated, in. ..	2.8	1.6	3.82	11.9

"From this table, with the sights adjusted correctly for 200 yards and using the service ammunition, we can arrive at the following facts: Suppose one has not time to think of estimating the exact range, or has not the talent to do so. But he thinks his quarry is about 200 yards off. He fires. If the game was at 100 yards the greatest error he need expect is a hit 2.8 inches above the point aimed at. If the game was exactly at 200 yards then only the error of the rifle and ammunition need be counted on which is 1.6 inches either above or below. If again the game was at 225 yards the greatest deviation would be a hit 3.82 inches below the point aimed at. In other words, with the sights thus adjusted one would be sure to hit within the vital 8-inch disk at all ranges up to 225 yards, provided always of course that his sights were correctly aligned at the center of the disk at the instant of discharge. At no point during its flight, would the trajectory and the accuracy error, together, carry the bullet over three inches above the line of aim, and at 225 yards it would hit but 3.82 inches low. Should the range be over 225 yards, the visual angle subtended by the game, that is its appearance, will be so small that the hunter will not risk a snap shot but will instinctively proceed to take all those precautions necessary for a long range shot including a careful estimate of the range and wind direction and velocity and an accurate setting of the sights for those estimates.

"Thus, for all around work in hunting with the Springfield rifle, using the service cartridge, in order to attain the highest efficiency and the greatest chance for a properly placed hit, we should use three adjustments of the rear sight, as follows:

For small game at close range .... 40 yards
For apparently easy shots at large game 200 yards
For apparently hard, long shots at any
    game   ..The estimated range."

The "vital 8-inch disk" refers to an expression I used in the book *Guns, Ammunition, and Tackle*:

MARKSMANSHIP IN THE WOODS 179

"Let us say that an 8-inch disk represents that part of a deer in which a bullet may be counted on to inflict a mortal wound; then the deer's killing zone would be that distance throughout which the trajectory of the bullet would cut an 8-inch disk. For open country, where long shots are the rule, the rifle may then be sighted for an extreme rise of 4 inches above line of *aim,* and the killing zone for deer will extend to that point where the descending bullet falls 4 inches below line of *aim.* Remember that line of aim or sight is different from line of fire (prolongation of axis of bore)." If the top of front sight stands one inch above axis of bore, then you subtract from the midway trajectory one-half inch, and make proportional allowances at other points intermediate or beyond the range sighted for. In all targeting to determine point-blank you must aim exactly *on* the point to be hit—not at lower edge of a bullseye, but at its center.

The old-fashioned practice of "drawing coarse" for a long shot is guesswork. A novice is almost sure to overdo it. An experienced hunter may do very well that way, so long as he uses rifle and ammunition that he is thoroughly familiar with; but let him change to something different and he must learn all over again. That is one reason why many expert hunters are old-fogyish about arms and ammunition. On the other hand, there is no guesswork in the system of determining a "practical point-blank" and then aiming straight at the spot you want to hit. It "gets the meat" with certainty—always provided, my brother, that you hold true and draw trigger without jerk or quiver.

It is not nearly so much the "make" of rifle as *the load it takes* that determines the gun's shooting qualities. So, choose first a cartridge, then a gun to handle it. For example, the Springfield cartridge is a good one for big game at all ranges; but you can use it in rifles of several different makes, and most of them will do the same work with it. The old .44-40 is still a good cartridge for brush-shooting at deer, but a mighty poor one beyond 100 yards, no matter what kind of a rifle it is shot out of. And so we might go on through the whole maze of ammunition lists. But how to choose a cartidge? Well, here are two rules that will help a good deal:

(1) No cartridge is accurate beyond a very moderate distance unless the bullet is at least

> 3 calibers long for .25 caliber bullets,
> 2½ calibers long for .30 to .35 caliber bullets,
> 2 calibers long for .40 to .45 caliber bullets,
> 1¾ calibers long for .50 caliber bullets.

(2) No bullet is accurate at high speed unless it either is long and heavy or has fine lines forward, as one would say of a boat.

HUNTERS' MAXIMS.—This is not an essay on hunting, but in trying to give an idea of how marksmanship in the woods differs from marksmanship on the range, it may help a beginner to understand just what is meant if I first state certain maxims of the still-hunter's craft:

(1) Hunt one kind of animal at a time, and think of *it*.
(2) Know its strong points and its weak ones.
(3) Know where to hunt and where not to.
(4) Choose favorable ground.
(5) Consider the animal's daily habits.
(6) Know just what to look for.
(7) Maneuver according to a definite plan.
(8) Work against the wind, or across it.
(9) Move noiselessly and reconnoiter carefully.
(10) Try to see the game before it sees you.
(11) Keep cool.
(12) Never fire at anything until you are absolutely *certain* it is not a human being.
(13) Never fire a shot that is not the best you can possibly do.
(14) After firing, reload instantly.
(15) If you wound an animal, don't follow immediately upon its track, unless you are sure it is shot through the heart.
(16) Be patient over ill-luck, and keep on trying.

MARKSMANSHIP IN THE WOODS 181

Serve your apprenticeship under a guide. He can teach you more in a week than you could learn by yourself in a year. There are, however, two books that every beginner ought to study before he goes to the woods: Van Dyke's *Still Hunter* and Brunner's *Tracks and Tracking,* both of them far and away ahead of anything else on their respective subjects. Don't try to memorize, but read and re-read until the lessons have soaked in. They will make it much easier for you to understand your guide's movements and directions (but don't quote your book-learning to him, or to anybody else).

After you have learned something of woodcraft by actual experience in company, make a practice of going alone and putting it to the proof. In still-hunting, two men working together make four times as much noise as one would by himself. They more than double the risk of alarming the game by their scent, as they seldom will be right together. And each relies too much on the other. "Tom may jump one to me" is a thought that has spoiled many a hunt (and hunter). You don't want any Tom to think about: you want to think *deer,* if that is what you are after.

WHAT TO LOOK FOR.—Wild animals in the woods do not look at all like the same species do in captivity or in picture-books. Only at rare intervals does one see a buck in the open posed like Landseer's "Stag at Bay," and when he does, the picture is altogether different. The buck's coloration blends with his surroundings. You never see him in stark relief unless he be on a ridge, outlined against the sky, or somewhere with a broad sheet of water for a background. Nor does he carry his head erect, unless suspicious, startled, challenging, or browsing on branches that hang above him.

A deer is always hard to see unless he be out in the open, or in the water, or on the jump. Generally its body is half hidden, or more than half, by underbrush or intervening trees. So what you want to look for is not an animal as a whole, but for *spots* of leaden gray (the "blue" coat of autumn and winter) of no particular shape. The spot may seem fairly vaporous, like fog. Of course if the animal moves, you will see it, but probably not until it is sneaking stealthily but swiftly away. Then there are trees in the way, and brush; your footing may not be secure; the light may be shining in your eyes; and, with it all, you must shoot quickly, or lose the opportunity. Under such circumstances it is absurdly easy to miss a full-grown deer at twenty paces. So *try* to see the game before it sees you. Quite likely you won't; but if you have maneuvered against the wind so that the animal has not caught your scent, it may stay quietly hidden, trusting in the cover of the shrubs, or it may hesitate long enough for you to raise your gun before it moves.

RUNNING SHOTS.—A deer does not gallop unless a dog is after it. When fleeing from a man it commonly goes at an indescribably easy and graceful lope, varied at every few bounds by a high, long leap. It does not seem to be exerting itself, yet it goes pretty fast. Having got out of the immediate neighborhood, it subsides into a trot or amble, and then stops, looks backward, and scents the air, to find if it is pursued.

Now a deer on the jump is hard to hit. The points to be observed are: To be as alert at all times as though you were hunting grouse without a dog; to get your gun in position the instant that you see the game; to pick out, as quick as lightning, a clear space through which to fire; but, *above all things,* not to shoot until you are absolutely certain that it is game you are shooting at; and then to dwell on the aim just long enough to see your bead clearly and to hold for a vital spot. Beyond that, do not hesitate the fraction of a second. To give a novice an idea, I would say that three or four seconds is a fair average interval between raising the rifle and firing, when a deer has been jumped in the forest. It is not so much the hands, but the eyes and brain, that must be quick, very quick.

MARKSMANSHIP IN THE WOODS 183

When a deer is running in the open, follow it with the rifle about as you would a bird with a shotgun, only don't "lead," that is, consciously. At a hundred yards, a high-velocity bullet will reach him in the time that it takes him to go, say, four feet. If your rifle is swinging with him, you don't have to hold ahead. And most shots at running deer are at a shorter distance than that. Try to catch him as he strikes the ground at the end of a jump. Anyway, beware of firing too high. Most of the time he is "hugging the ground" pretty close.

In thick timber, don't try to swing with him— you can't see him well enough. Pick out an opening that he will cross, and fire the instant his head crosses above your front sight (this is a general idea —"lead," in this case, depends on distance). Then you will, at least, not send your bullet *whack* into an intervening tree.

Although one may often get a chance for a standing shot, yet I think it is best to spend most of one's target ammunition (at home) in snap-shooting. By snap-shooting with the rifle I do not mean merely glancing along a barrel and disregarding the sights. You must see your bead, and, in case of open sights, you must see that the bead is well down in the notch; but it is snap-shooting to press the trigger instantly when it first touches, or rather when it swings close to, the object that you want to hit, instead of waiting to swing back and steady down, as one would do when aiming deliberately. To snap-shoot at the right instant, without pulling off to one side, is a fine art.

The main trouble, in such cases, is to select the right spot to shoot at, and then to find it over the sights. With a deer, for example, the color is so neutral and the outlines are so indistinct, even in good light, that a man's eyes can seldom distinguish the exact spot that he wants to hit. He judges where it must be, from the general bulk of the animal and the position in which it is presented.

WHERE TO AIM.—Standing shots, even at a considerable distance, call for no comment, as they are comparatively easy, in good light, for anyone who has been well trained on the rifle range at home—provided he does not get "buck ague."

For a broadside shot, the best point to aim at is immediately behind the shoulder and only one-third of the way up from breast to withers—that is, where the heart lies. When the body is presented in any other position, shoot, as a rule, at such a point that the bullet, in ranging forward, will pass through or close to the heart. When an animal stands looking at me as a deer often will when it comes in on a runway and one bleats or whistles at it, my favorite shot is the neck. A bullet passing through any animal's neck, near the center, is almost sure to strike a paralyzing, knock-out blow, because it can scarcely miss a vital part.

Aim low when shooting downhill, because then you see more of the upper side of the animal than you ordinarily would. A shot high up is seldom fatal, unless you hit the spine. In making long shots downhill, do not forget that the only distance to be allowed for is that from the mark to a point directly *under* you and *level with the mark*.

Aim dead-on when shooting uphill, unless the range is greater than your rifle is sighted for on a level. The extra allowance for "lift" is so trifling at ordinary ranges that you had better disregard it than overdo the matter.

Don't rely on "raining lead." The man who does his "darndest" with the first shot is the one who gets most venison in the long run. But reload instantly, and be ready, if necessary, to follow up without hesitation. Shoot until the animal is down, or while it remains in view.

If a deer is not hit, it goes off with its "flag" (white underside of tail) in the air. If hit, it may or may not clap its tail down. When struck in the rear half of the body (unless through the spine, which is a knock-out) it will likely kick out its hind legs, and there is some long trailing ahead of you.

MARKSMANSHIP IN THE WOODS 185

Even when shot through the heart, a deer may run a hundred yards or more; but when it drops it is dead. If you are sure that it was a heart shot, follow up at once, but if you are not, then wait a good while. A wounded deer, when it finds it is not followed, is likely to lie down; then it gets stiff and weak from loss of blood. Give it time for this before you go after it. Don't follow directly on its tracks, for it will watch backward as long as it can hold its head up, and will run again, if possible, the instant it finds itself followed. Go in half-circles, to one side, then in to the trail, out again, and so on, until you have headed it on the leeward side.

BUCK FEVER.—History mercifully does not record how many thousand big and bewhiskered armed men, at their first sight of big game, have stood or sat with mouth wide open, gazing at the thing, oblivious to everything else on earth, including the loaded gun in the hand. If a deer only could wink one eye!

Buck ague is different. With it, the victim knows it is a deer before him, and knows but too well that he has a gun. But he also has as bad a case of "shakes" as a toper after a long spree. This affliction may overcome a rifleman in any kind of hunting, but it is most likely to seize upon the novice when he is sitting on a stand and hears the dogs baying toward him. It is hard on a fellow's nerves to sit there, praying with all his soul that the bear may not run some other way, and yet half doubtful of his own ability to head it off if it does come his way. The chances are that it will by no means run over him, but that it will come crashing through the brush at some point on one side, toward which he will have to run with all his might and main before firing. Now if he does let that bear go through, after all the hard work of dogs and drivers, his shirt-tail will be amputated that night by his comrades and hung from a high pole in the midst of the camp—a flag of distress indeed! Who wouldn't get buck ague in the face of such alternative?

It is hard on a fellow's nerves, I say, to hear those dogs coming toward him, and to know from the racket that a bear is certainly ahead of them, but *not* to know where or when the brute may emerge, nor what infernal trees or thickets and downwood may be in the way. Can you hit him? That is the question. The honor of the camp is on your shoulders. Ah, me! it is easy to follow the pack on horseback—to chase after something that is running away. But to sit here clenching your teeth while at any moment a hard-pressed and angry bear may burst out of the thicket and find you in his way—nothing but you between him and near-by freedom—gentlemen, it tests nerve!

Buck ague is not the effect of fear. In fact, fear has nothing to do with it. It is a tremor and a galloping of the heart that comes from over-anxiety lest you should fail to score. Precisely the same seizure may come upon you on the target range. That is the only place that I ever experienced it. There is no telling when it may strike. I have known seasoned sportsmen to be victimized by it. Yet, when the critical moment does come, it often turns out that the man who has been shaking like a leaf from pent-up anxiety suddenly grows cold and steady as a rock. Especially is this apt to be the case when a fighting beast comes suddenly in view. Instantly the man's primeval instincts are aroused; his fighting blood comes to the surface; the spirit of some warrior ancestor (dead, maybe, these thousand years) possesses and sways your mild-eyed modern man, and he who trembled but a moment ago now leaps into the combat with a wild joy playing on his heart strings.

CHAPTER XII

AXEMANSHIP—QUALITIES AND UTILIZATION OF WOOD

Next to the rifle, a backwoodsman's main reliance is on his axe. With these two instruments, and little else, our pioneers attacked the forest wilderness that once covered all eastern America, and won it for civilization.

In the clearing and in lumber works the favorite axe is a double-bitt with 4½ to 5-pound head. One blade is ground thin and kept whetted keen, for chopping in clear timber. The other is left with more bevel, as that is advantageous in splitting, and the edge, although sharp, is rather stunt, so that it will not shiver against a knot, or nick badly when driven through into the earth, as may happen when cutting through roots. A professional chopper, who works only at felling trees and cutting off "lops" (the branching tops) will grind both blades thin. For him, too, the double-bitt is best, since most of its weight is back in line with the cutting edge, and so it bites deep, although driven with little force. The helve of such an axe, of course, is straight, and one bought at a store should be shaved considerably thinner on both sides; then it is not so clumsy, lies in the hands more compactly, does not cramp the fingers and will not jar the hands, as it has some spring.

A double-bitted axe is dangerous in any but expert hands—more so than a loaded gun—and would be a menace lying around in camp, for, even when stuck in a tree or chopping-block, one edge is always exposed. I have given elsewhere (Vol. I., pp.

113-114) other reasons why a light single-bitt is the best axe for a camper, and have told how to select such a tool and care for it.

GRINDING AXES.—A new axe must be ground before it is fit for use. Do this on a grindstone (or have it done where they have a power grindstone) using water freely so the steel will not overheat. The average "cutler and grinder" in a city would make a quick job of it on an emery wheel, and ruin the temper. Since you will do much more chopping than splitting, you want the blade thin. Start grinding well back on the blade, and work out to the edge until most of the bevel has been ground off, but leave a little of it between the center and the outside corner; that is, the blade should be thickest at a point a little beyond the center, so it will not "bind" (stick fast in wood) and so that it will spring a chip loose. Then whet off the wire edge with a stone. Make or buy a leather sheath for the axe-head, riveted to prevent cutting through (see illustrations in outfitters' catalogues).

FITTING AXE-HELVES.—A broken axe-helve is not an uncommon accident in the woods, and it is a very serious one until a new helve is made and fitted. Now it sometimes happens that the stub of the old handle cannot be removed by ordinary means: it must be burnt out. To do this without drawing the temper of the steel might seem impracticable; but the thing is as simple as rolling off a log, when you see it done. Pick out a spot where the earth is free from pebbles, and drive the blade of the axe into the ground up to the eye. Then build a fire around the axe-head—that is all. If the axe is double-bitted, dig a little trench about six inches deep and the width of the axe-eye, or a little more. Lay the axe flat over it, cover both blades with two inches of earth, and build a small fire on top.

In making a new axe-helve, do not bother to make a crooked one like the store pattern. Thousands of expert axemen use, from preference, straight handles in their axes—single-bitted axes at that.

AXEMANSHIP

I have seen such handles full four feet long, to be used chiefly in logging-up big trees. Two feet eight inches is long enough for ordinary chopping. To smooth any article made of wood, when you have no sandpaper, use loose sand in a piece of leather or buckskin.

Split the eye end of the helve before driving it in. Make the wedge thin, and of even taper. Leave a little of it protruding, at first, for green wood soon will shrink and you must tighten it up.

How To Chop.—To be expert with the axe, one must have been trained to it from boyhood. A novice, however, can learn to do much better than bungle if he observes a few simple directions, watches a good chopper, and uses his wits in trying to "catch on."

Practice until you can hit the same spot repeatedly. Precision, rhythmical strokes, good judgment as to where a cut will do the most good; these are the main points to strive after.

Beginners invariably over-exert themselves in chopping, and are soon blown. An accurate stroke counts for much more than a heavy but blundering one. A good chopper lands one blow exactly on top of the other with the precision and regularity of a machine; he chops slowly but rhythmically, and puts little more effort into striking than he does into lifting his axe for the blow. Trying to sink the axe deeply at every stroke is about the hardest work that a man can do, and it spoils accuracy.

Try your axe first on saplings up to six inches in diameter. A little one is downed with two strokes. Bend it over so its fiber is strained on one side, hit it a clip with the axe in one hand, then similarly on the other side. A larger one is notched on each side, like a tree (see below) but does not need to have the large notch blocked out.

When cutting saplings that are to be dragged to camp, throw them with tops in the opposite direction from camp, so they can easily be dragged out by the butts; otherwise you will have to slew them around so the branches will not catch in everything.

Before starting to fell a tree, clear away all underbrush and vines that are within reach of the extended axe, overhead as well as around you. Neglect of this precaution may cripple a man for life.

FELLING A TREE.—Before starting to chop down a tree, decide in which direction you wish it to fall. This will be governed partly by the lay of the ground and the obstacles on it. The tree should fall where it will be easy to log up. Most trees lean more or less out of plumb, or have a heavier growth of branches on one side than on the other. If there is nothing to interfere, drop it on the side

Fig. 36.—Felling Tree   Fig. 37.—Boggled Notch   Fig 38.—True Notch

toward which it is naturally inclined to fall. In a thick forest, throw it in such direction that it will not lodge on some other tree in falling. It is both difficult and dangerous for anyone but an expert to bring down a lodged tree. Don't try to throw a tree against the wind, if there is a strong breeze blowing.

Now, suppose you decide to throw the tree to the south. First cut a notch (kerf) on the south side of the tree, half way through the trunk (*A* in Fig. 36). A novice would make this notch by starting with a small nick and laboriously enlarging it by

AXEMANSHIP

whacking out from the upper side one layer of chips after another. Soon he would be driving his axe in at too sharp an angle, and his work would grow harder and harder as he got to cutting more and more nearly straight across the grain (Fig. 37). Finally the inside of the notch would get so narrow that he would wedge his axe fast. The right way is shown in Fig. 38. Make a nick at *a* as guide then another at *b,* a little higher above *a* than half the thickness of the tree. Chop alternately at these notches, and split out the block *c* with a downward blow of the axe. Proceed in this way until the notch is finished, making as big chips as you can. A green axeman is known by the finely minced chips and haggled stump that he leaves.

If the tree is of such wood as is easy to cut, make the cut *ae* as nearly square across the butt as you can. To do this keep the hand that holds the hilt of the axe-helve well down. But if the tree is hard and stubborn to fell, or if you are rustling firewood in a hurry, it is easier to make this cut in a slanting direction, so as not to chop squarely across the grain, and then make the opposite one diagonally across it.

Having finished this south kerf (which is two-thirds the labor of felling the tree), now begin the opposite one, *b,* at a point three or four inches *higher* than the other. By studying the diagram, and taking into account the tree's great weight, you can see why this method will infallibly throw the tree where you want it, if it stands anywhere near perpendicular, and if there is not a contrary wind blowing. Comparatively few blows are needed here. When the tree begins to crack, step to one side. Never jump in a direction opposite that in which the tree falls. Many a man has been killed in that way. Sometimes a falling tree, striking against one of its neighbors, shoots backward from the stump like lightning. Look out, too, for shattered limbs.

If a tree leans in the wrong direction for your purpose, insert a billet of wood in the kerf *B,* and drive a wedge or two above it in the direction of the kerf. A tree weighing many tons can be forced to fall in any desired direction by the proper use of wedges; and a good axeman, in open woods, can throw a tree with such accuracy as to drive a stake previously stuck in the ground at an agreed position. He can even do this when a considerable wind is blowing, by watching the sway of the tree and striking his final blow at the right moment.

LOGGING UP.—When the tree is down, trim off the branches for firewood, if the stuff is good for

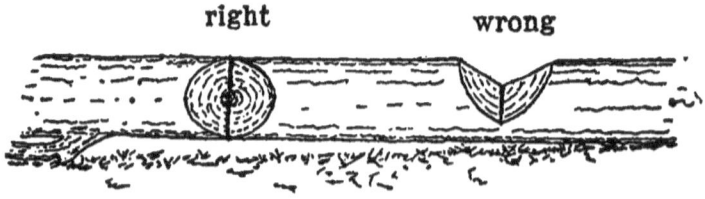

Fig. 39.—Logging Up

fuel (on the fuel values of trees see Vol. I., pp. 236-239). Then log up the trunk. When a novice tries to cut a log in two he stands in front of it and chops on the farther side until he has most of it and a good part of the top hacked out. Then he realizes that he is "up against it," for he cannot turn the tree over to get at the under side. The axeman must stand on the prostrate trunk, with his legs well apart, and cut down between his feet. This, to a beginner, looks like a risky performance; yet I have seen one of my woodland neighbors, who professes to be "only a triflin' hand with an axe," stand on a slender tree-trunk that was balanced about ten feet over a gulch, whack away between his feet, with the trunk swaying several inches at every stroke, nor did he step over on the main trunk until two or three light "draw cuts" sufficed to cut the end log free. But such a performance is tame compared with the feats of axemanship that regular choppers and river drivers do every day as a mere matter of course.

Make the outside chip not less in length than the

AXEMANSHIP

diameter of the log. This will seem absurdly long, until you have struggled futilely to "nigger" a log in two. Make two outside nicks, as in felling a tree, split out the block between them, and so go on, making big chips, and cutting at a considerable angle to the grain of the wood instead of across it. Chop straight down, so that when you get to the center of the trunk the bottom of your kerf will be perpendicular (Fig. 39). Usually the trunk is held a little off the ground by broken limbs on the under side of the top. If not, then, when you work close to the ground, look out for pebbles (rather scrape them away beforehand). A nick in the axe will make your work doubly hard. Before felling a tree on stony ground it is well worth while to place a small log across the way for the butt of the tree to fall on, so as to keep it off the ground.

Speaking of nicks in the axe, beware of cutting into hemlock or balsam knots; in trimming limbs close to such trees you can ruin the best steel that ever was made, for they are almost as hard as glass. If it must be done, strike gentle blows; hold the axe-head exactly perpendicular to the spot struck, and rigid, so it cannot glance in the least. The trick is similar to that of driving a bowie through a silver dollar without spoiling the knife's edge.

Having cut one notch half through the trunk, go on to the next ones until the end piece is reached; then turn around and work back until all cuts have been severed.

In working up crooked branches into firewood lengths, have something solid under the spot to be cut. If you don't, sometime a billet will fly up and hit you in the face. I have seen more than one man who had lost an eye in that way.

SAWING.—If there is a sharp and well set crosscut saw in the outfit, it makes the work of felling and logging a great deal easier. The veriest tyro can soon learn to saw tolerably well. Observe that your sole duties are to pull and help guide the saw straight. If you push, as one would with a bucksaw, the other fellow may let you do all the work. If you don't do your share of the pulling, your partner, if he be a woodsman, is apt to remonstrate "Say, you! I don't mind you riding the saw, but don't drag your feet."

To fell with a saw, first cut a small notch with the axe on the side toward which you want the tree to fall. Then saw from the opposite side, beginning a little higher than the notch, and sawing diagonally down to meet it. When the saw gets well into the wood it will begin to bind from the weight of the tree. Then relieve it by driving a wedge or glut into the kerf behind the saw. Drive the wedge in still farther as you progress, and it will tilt the tree in the right direction. When you hear the first premonitory crack, or see that the tree is near the toppling point, one man will quickly remove the handle at his end; the other will saw away until the tree sways, and then pull the saw out. A log should be laid for the butt to fall on.

In sawing up large logs, wedges are used in the same way to keep the saw running free.

QUALITIES OF WOODS.—The working qualities of common woods ought to be known by every one who has occasion to use timber, and especially by a woodsman, who may at any time be driven to shifts in which a mistake in choosing material may have disagreeable consequences. A few simple tables are here given, which, it is hoped, may be of assistance. Only common native trees are included. The data refer to the seasoned wood only, except where green is specified. Such tables might easily be extended, but mine are confined to the qualities of most account to campers and explorers, and to trees native to the region north of Georgia and east of the Rocky Mountains.

AXEMANSHIP

Very Hard Woods

Osage Orange (hardest),
Dogwood,
Black Haw,
Yellow Locust,
Post Oak,
Overcup Oak,
Sugar Maple,
Crab-Apple,
Persimmon,
Hickory,
Service-berry,
Black Jack Oak,
Chestnut Oak,
Mountain Laurel,
Winged Elm.

Hard Woods

Other Oaks,
Hornbeam,
Ash,
Elm,
Cherry,
Beech,
Tupelo,
Red-bud,
Red Maple,
Holly,
Sycamore,
Yellow Pine,
Pecan,
Black Birch,
Hackberry,
Plum,
Sourwood,
Sour Gum,
Walnut,
Silver Maple,
Mulberry,
Honey Locust,
Yellow Birch.

Very Soft Woods

Spruce,
Balsam Poplar,
White Pine,
Pawpaw,
Aspen,
Balsam Fir,
Catalpa,
Buckeye,
Basswood,
Arbor-vitae (softest).

(Common woods not mentioned above are of medium softness.)

Very Strong Woods

Yellow Locust,
Yellow Birch,
Shingle Oak,
Shellbark Hickory,
Yellow Pine,
Hornbeam,
Service-berry,
Big-bud Hickory,
Basket Oak,
Pignut Hickory,
Chestnut Oak,
Black Birch,
Spanish Oak,
Sugar Maple,
Beech,
Osage Orange,
Bitternut Hickory.

Strong Woods

Other Oaks,
Paper Birch,
Silver Maple,
Red Birch,
Dogwood,
Ash,
Rock Elm,
Water Locust,
Chinquapin,
Honey Locust,
Tamarack,
Loblolly Pine,

Persimmon,
Plum,
White Elm,
Cherry,
Red Pine,

Slippery Elm,
Black Walnut,
Sour Gum,
Red Maple.

Very Stiff Woods

Yellow Birch,
Sugar Maple,
Spanish Oak,
Hornbeam,
Paper Birch,
Tamarack.

Yellow Pine,
Black Birch,
Shellbark Hickory,
Overcup Oak,
Yellow Locust,
Beech.

Very Tough Woods

Beech,
Osage Orange,

Water Oak,
Tupelo.

Tough Woods

Black Ash,
Basswood,
Yellow Birch,
Dogwood,
Sour Gum,
Hornbeam,
Basket Oak,
Overcup Oak,
Yellow Pine,
Black Walnut,

White Ash,
Paper Birch,
Cottonwood,
Elm,
Hickory,
Liquidambar,
Bur Oak,
Swamp White Oak,
Tamarack.

(Saplings generally are tougher than mature trees of the same species.)

Woods that Split Easily

Arbor-vitae,
Basswood,
Cedar,
Chestnut,
Slippery Elm (green),
Hackberry,
The Soft Pines,
Spruce,
Ash,
Beech (when green),

White Birch,
Black Birch (green),
Dogwood (green),
Balsam Fir,
Basket Oak,
White Oak,
Red Oak,
Shingle Oak,
Black Oak,
Water Oak.

Woods Difficult to Split

Blue Ash (seasoned),
Buckeye,
White Elm,
Sour Gum,

Box Elder,
Wild Cherry,
Winged Elm (unwedgeable),

AXEMANSHIP

Liquidambar,
Sugar Maple (seasoned),
Tupelo (unwedgeable),
Hemlock,
Honey Locust (seasoned),
Sycamore.

Woods that Separate Easily into Thin Layers
Black Ash,
Basket Oak.

Flexible, Pliable Woods
Basswood,
Hackberry,
Red-bud,
Witch Hazel,
Elm,
Big-bud Hickory,
Yellow Poplar.

Springy Woods
Black Ash,
Hickory,
Honey Locust,
White Oak,
Service-berry,
White Ash,
Hornbeam,
Yellow Locust,
Osage Orange,
Spruce.

Woods Easily Wrought
Basswood,
Paper Birch,
Buckeye,
Catalpa,
Cherry,
Cottonwood,
Hackberry,
Silver Maple,
Yellow Poplar,
Black Birch,
Red Birch,
Butternut,
Cedar,
Chestnut,
Cypress,
Red Maple,
White Pine,
Black Walnut.

Compact Woods (Not Liable to Check)
Arbor-vitae,
The Ashes,
The Aspens,
Basswood,
Balsam Fir,
The Birches (except White Birch),
Box Elder,
Buckeye,
Butternut,
Catalpa,
The Cedars (very),
The Cherries,
Cucumber,
The Elms,
Hackberry,
Big Shellbark Hickory,
Water Hickory,
Red Mulberry,
Basket Oak,
Bur Oak,
Willow Oak,
Pecan,
Persimmon,
Gray Pine,
Jersey Pine,
Long-leaved Pine,
Pitch Pine,
Red Pine,
Short-leaved Pine,
White Pine,
The Poplars,
Red-bud,
Silver-bell,
Sorrel Tree,
The Spruces,

Holly (very),
Hop Hornbeam,
Laurel (very),
The Magnolias,
The Maples,
Tamarack,
The Thorns,
Witch Hazel,
Yellow Wood.

Woods Liable to Check in Seasoning

Beech,
Chestnut,
Dogwood,
Hickory (except Shellbark)
Yellow Locust,
Sassafras,
Black Walnut,
White Birch,
Crab-apple,
Sour Gum,
Hornbeam,
Most Oaks,
Sycamore.

Woods Liable to Shrink and Warp

Chestnut,
White Elm,
Hemlock,
Liquidambar,
Loblolly Pine,
Yellow Poplar,
Cottonwood,
Sour Gum,
Shellbark Hickory,
Pin Oak,
Sycamore.

Woods Difficult to Season

Beech,
Sour Gum,
Red Oak,
Water Oak,
Cottonwood,
Sugar Maple,
Rock Chestnut Oak,
Osage Orange,

Woods that Can Be Obtained in Wide Boards Free from Knots

Basswood,
Cypress,
Cottonwood,
Yellow Poplar,

Woods Durable in Soil, Water and Weather

Arbor-vitae,
Catalpa,
Cherry,
Cucumber,
Slippery Elm,
Juniper,
Honey Locust,
Mulberry,
Chestnut Oak,
Post Oak,
Swamp White Oak,
Osage Orange,
Pitch Pine,
Tamarack,
Butternut,
Cedar,
Chestnut,
Cypress,
Hop Hornbeam,
Kentucky Coffee Tree
Yellow Locust,
Bur Oak,
Overcup Oak,
Rock Chestnut Oak,
White Oak,
Yellow Pine (long leaved)
Sassafras,
Black Walnut.

AXEMANSHIP

Perishable Woods

White Birch,
Paper Birch,
Hackberry
Black Jack Oak,
Spanish Oak,
Loblolly Pine,
Service-berry,

Box Elder
Silver Maple,
Pin Oak,
Water Oak,
The Poplars,
Sycamore.

(Most woods are durable when not exposed to alternate wetting and drying. Sapwood is more liable to decay than heart-wood, as a rule, but this is not true of Paper Birch.)

Resinous Woods

Gray Pine (very),
Jersey Pine (very),
Long-leaved Pine (very),
Pitch Pine (very),

Red Pine,
Short-leaved Pine,
The Spruces.

Close-grained Woods

Blue Ash,
The Aspens,
Basswood,
Red Bay (very),
Beech, (very),
Black Birch,
Paper Birch (very),
Red Birch,
White Birch,
Yellow Birch,
Box Elder,
Buckeye,
The Cedars (very),
The Cherries,
Cottonwood,
Crab-apple (very),
Cucumber,
Cypress,
Dogwood,
Rock Elm (very),
Slippery Elm (very),
Winged Elm very),
Big Shellbark Hickory (very),
Bitter-nut Hickory,
Mocker-nut Hickory (very)
Pig-nut Hickory,
Water Hickory (very),
Holly (very),
Hornbeam (Ironwood),
Hop Hornbeam (very),

Laurel,
Liquidambar,
Yellow Locust,
Magnolia,
The Maples,
Basket Oak,
Bur Oak,
Chestnut Oak,
Overcup Oak,
Post Oak,
Rock Chestnut Oak,
Swamp White Oak,
White Oak,
Osage Orange (extremely),
Pecan,
Persimmon (very),
Short-leaved Pine (generally),
White Pine (very),
Plum,
The Poplars,
Service-berry,
Silver-bell,
Sorrel Tree (very),
The Spruces,
Sycamore (very),
The Thorns,
Tulip,
Witch Hazel (very),
Yellow Wood.

Very Heavy Woods

Chestnut Oak,
Shellbark Hickory,
Hop Hornbeam,
Overcup Oak,
Post Oak,
Flowering Dogwood,
Big Shellbark Hickory,
Pig-nut Hickory,
Mocker-nut Hickory,
Basket Oak,
Persimmon,
Service-berry,
Swamp White Oak,
Osage Orange.

Very Light Woods

White Basswood,
Box Elder ,
Sweet Buckeye,
Hemlock,
Yellow Poplar,
Quaking Aspen,
Butternut,
White Spruce,
Cottonwood,
Balsam Fir,
White Pine,
Balsam Poplar,
White Cedar,
Arborvitae.

The weight of seasoned wood is no criterion of the weight of the green wood, which must be learned by experience. For example, the dry wood of the Sequoia, or California Big Tree, is lighter than White Pine, but the freshly cut log is so heavy that it scarcely will float in water. Black Walnut and Sour Gum are only moderately heavy when seasoned, but the green logs will not float.

WOODS FOR SPECIAL PURPOSES.—These tables are only general guides. Individual trees of the same species vary much in their qualities. In selecting wood for a special purpose one will be governed, of course, by the material at hand. Suppose he wants a very hard and close-grained wood: He may choose, according to circumstances, beech, birch, dogwood, rock elm, mocker-nut (white-heart) hickory, holly, hornbeam, yellow locust, sugar maple, Osage orange, persimmon, service-berry, or whatever he can get on the spot that will answer his purpose. If it must also be strong, tough, elastic, or have some other merit, the choice will be narrowed.

Timber cut in the spring of the year, when the sap is up is much inferior in quality and durability to that which is cut in autumn and winter, when the sap is down. Sap softens the fibers, sours in cut timber, and carries the seeds of dry-rot or decay.

HEWING TIMBER.—To flatten a log, as for a

AXEMANSHIP 201

bench seat, if it will not split straight: Score the top of it with notches of uniform depth, like saw teeth, but as far apart as the stuff will block off evenly; then chop out the blocks, and hew smooth (along the dotted line $A\ B$ in Fig. 40).

When much hewing is to be done, a broadaxe or adze is used; but both of these tools are difficult and dangerous for an inexperienced man to handle, and neither of them will be obtainable except where skilled artisans can be hired to wield them.

Fig. 40.—Scoring and Hewing

SPLITTING TIMBER.—Logs split through the center into half-logs with one face flat are very useful in cabins and about camp, for tables, benches, shelves, and other rustic furniture. They also are employed in making slab camps, puncheons for flooring, and small enclosed cabins. In the latter case, split logs have certain advantages over round ones. They take only half as many trees, they are easier for one or two men to handle, easier to notch for the corners, make close joints without much, if any chinking, and leave a flat surface for the interior of the cabin. They may also be used vertically instead of horizontally, and in this way short logs can be utilized.

The only implements needed in splitting logs are an axe (single-bitted) and a maul and some wooden wedges made with the axe. The maul is made in club shape (Fig. 41). Beech, oak and hickory are good materials, but any hardwood that does not splinter easily will do. Choose a sapling about five inches thick at the butt, not counting the bark. Dig a little below the surface of the ground and cut the sapling off where the stools of the roots begin. (The wood is very tough here, and this is to be used for the large end of the maul, which should be about ten inches long). From this, forward, shave down the handle, which should be twenty inches long. Thus balanced, the maul will not jar one's hands.

Gluts (Fig. 42) are simply wooden wedges. The best woods for them are dogwood and hornbeam or ironwood, as they are very hard and tough, even when green; but use whatever is handy. Chop a sapling of suitable thickness, and make one end wedged-shaped; then cut it off square at the top; and so continue until you have all the gluts you

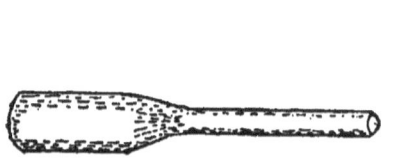 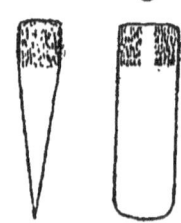

Fig. 41.—Maul   Fig. 42.—Gluts (edge and face)

want. It takes no mean skill to chop a glut to a true wedge shape, and much depends upon getting the angles and surfaces correctly proportioned. A novice is apt to make a glut too short and thick, but it must not be quite so slender as a steel wedge, for it would splinter too readily.

In splitting timber, one must observe the grain and structure of the wood. Naturally, he would select stuff that is straight-grained; but that is not all. Fig. 43 shows the end of a log that has been sawed off square. Observe that there are four kinds of structure to be considered: (1) the bark, (2) the light-colored sapwood next to the bark, (3) the mature wood, (4) the dark-colored heartwood. It is seldom that heartwood splits evenly. Outside of it we notice the concentric rings of annual growth; also the medullary rays, radiating from the center like spokes of a wheel. Both of these continue through the sapwood, though not so shown here, as they are less conspicuous in it.

Now the natural lines of cleavage are along the

AXEMANSHIP

medullary rays, which are pithy. Hence a log can be split straight through the center (if clear and straight-grained) from any point on the circumference, but if you try to make other splits *parallel* with this, you will have trouble, for you are attempting to cross the rays at an angle. Some trees can be split, by careful manipulation, into three slabs or four slabs with parallel faces, but usually it will not pay you to try it.

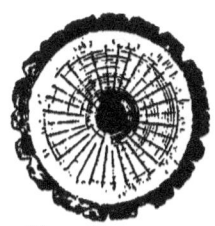 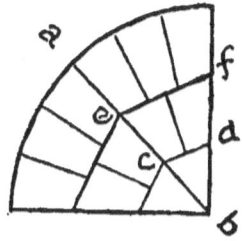

Fig. 43.—Cross-section of Tree Trunk   Fig. 44.—Rail Splits

The natural way of cleavage is shown in Fig. 44, which illustrates the method of splitting rails. First the log is split through the center, then each half similarly. Then one of the quarters is split through the line *ab,* following, as you see, a medullary ray. Next the point of the wedge is split off across *cd* (direction of annual rings), forming one rail. The remaining billet is again split in the same direction, *ef,* and its separate parts are now split along the rays, forming, in this instance, five rails. The number, of course, will depend upon the size of the log.

To split a log: Begin at the smaller or top end, because it splits easiest that way. Advantage may be taken of a natural crack or check, but if there is none, take axe in one hand, maul in the other, and start a crack. Into this drive two wedges, as in Fig. 45, and others into the longitudinal crack on top as it opens. To ensure a straight split: First score the log lengthwise with the axe, driving the bitt in with a moderate tap or two, at one place, then extending the cut backward with another, and so on. finally splitting this apart with gluts. A free-splitting log of moderate size can be split without wedges, by using two axes, one working behind the other.

Fig. 45.—Splitting a Log

Slabs for siding and puncheons for flooring are thus split out and then hewn smooth on the flat side. Almost any tree that splits straight will do. Those commonly used are chestnut, oak, ash, poplar, cedar, spruce and pine. A small tree is merely split through the center, and the halves laid with round side out, or down, as the case may be. A larger one is first halved, and then each half is split parallel with the flat side, if the grain permits, making four puncheons from each log. Very large ones are split into long bolts, in the same manner as clapboard bolts (see below), thus making a considerable number of narrow puncheons from each log, which are to be hewn of even thickness on both edges.

Puncheons usually are cut so that two lengths equal the length of the room—eight-foot puncheons for a sixteen-foot room, and so on. They are laid by fitting the rough side to the sleepers. It is best to leave them loose until they have seasoned; then true up their edges, spike them down, and you will have a tight floor of uncommon solidity and warmth.

SELECTING A "BOARD TREE."—If clapboards or

AXEMANSHIP 205

other thin pieces are to be riven, a nice judgment must be exercised in selecting the right kind of tree. Wood for this purpose must be sound, straight-grained and springy. If brash or doty, it will not do at all. Nor will "any old wood" do that splits easily; it must split straight and make thin boards.

The species of tree will depend, of course, on what growths one has to choose from. Cedar is best, as it is easily riven and is very durable. Boards from five to six feet long can be split out of cedar with no other tool than an axe, and a club or mallet to tap it. If the board shows a tendency to "run out," the workman changes ends and makes another split back toward the first one, or "coaxes" it after the manner to be described hereafter. Such axe-riven boards or shingles are commonly called "splits."

Here in the southern Appalachians, our first choice for clapboards is "mountain oak," when we can find one that splits well. Its wood resembles that of live oak in hardness and texture. Otherwise we take white, black, red, or water oak. White and yellow pines are much used; occasionally yellow poplar. A young, quick-growing chestnut tree makes good 18-inch shingles, but not the longer clapboards or "shakes," as chestnut is prone to "run out" when long splits are made. Mature chestnut trees generally are full of worm-holes. Sometimes a hemlock is found that will make clapboards, if split bastard (the way the rings run), but, as a rule, hemlock has a spiral grain.

When a suitable species is found, the next thing is to pick out a good "board tree." This takes an experienced eye, so leave it to a native woodsman, if you can. The way he does it is not easy to explain. First he looks for a straight trunk, free from knots, limbs, and dote. It should be not less than two feet thick. Then he scans the bark. If the ridges and furrows run straight, in a general way, parallel with the trunk, it is an indication of straight grain. An oak with a large fork is likely to split well.

But there is more than this in picking a board-tree: the wood should be not only separable but springy. The woodsman will tell you that he "senses" this; and he does, to the extent that his choice is guided by no rule nor process of reasoning. Twice out of three times he is right when he says "That tree 'll do;" nine times out of ten he is right when he says "That tree 's no good." Experience has taught me that a tree with a certain "look" is likely timber, but I can't, for the life of me, describe that look. You may have to split a big block out of a tree, test its cleavage, and try several other trees before you find a good one. This is bad practice, but not so bad as felling, sawing off a cut, and then leaving the tree to waste utterly.

CLAPBOARDS.—To rive clapboards or shingles from the green tree is now a lost art, outside of the backwoods. Not one carpenter in fifty, nowadays, can show you how. Yet it is an art well worth knowing for hunters and others who may want to go, season after season, to the same locality, and wish a snug shack on the place for regular quarters. Since good hunting seldom is found in the neighborhood of a sawmill, a lumber yard, or a wagon road, the crux of the cabin scheme is how to get roofing material. Bark is flimsy and will scarce outlast the season. Tarred paper—what is more hideously incongruous than tarred paper over honest log walls? Anyway, paper requires boards underneath.

The thing to do is to rive clapboards from trees that grow on the spot. A clapboard is simply a thin board, from two to four feet long, split or worked with a froe from straight-grained timber. It is a little thicker along one edge than the other, being split from bolts, as shown in Fig. 47. A clapboard roof is dependable. It harmonizes better than any other with the general woodsy effect. When properly laid, it is storm-proof, and will not cup. It will last a generation.

The tools required are few: An axe or two, a crosscut saw, a pair of steel wedges, and a froe. A maul for the wedges and gluts, and a mallet of similar

AXEMANSHIP

shape, but smaller, for the froe, are made on the spot. The froe is a tool that seldom is seen outside of the backwoods. Any blacksmith on the edge of the wilderness can make one for you. Its shape is shown in Fig. 49. The blade should be straight (old ones that have yielded to the mallet and become swaybacked are hard to manage). Let it be about 14 inches long, rather thick, and stunt-edged, as it is for splitting, not cutting. Its weight will be about five pounds. A green stick will do for the handle.

When the right tree is found, throw it in the best place for working up, and saw off a cut of 2½ to 3 feet. The butt cut usually is not so good as the upper ones, being tougher. Turn the cut up on end, and, with a single-bitt axe and mallet, mark an indentation straight across the center of the block.

Do not tap hard until you come to the end of the line; then strike vigorously, and the block will fall in halves. If you struck hard from the first, the split might run off to one side. In the same way, split the halves into quarters, and these into bolts or

Fig. 46.—Splitting Out Bolts

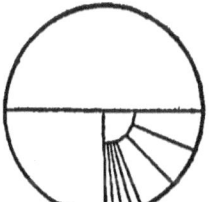

Fig. 47.—Block for Clapboards

billets of convenient size for riving (see Fig. 46). A bolt is usually of such thickness, that it will make eight boards or shingles—say five inches across the outside.

Now split out the heartwood of each bolt by laying the axe across and tapping it. Heartwood is useless, for it won't split well. In some trees the heart is so tough that it is advisable, instead of halving and quartering your cut, to just split in toward the cut, all around, to bolt size, and then knock out the bolts by driving the axe in at right angles to the cuts, leaving the heart as one solid core (Fig. 47). Skin off the bark, and your bolts are ready to rive.

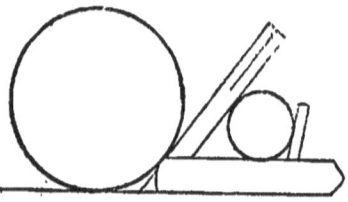

Fig. 48.—Brake for Riving Boards

The next thing is to make a brake. This may be simply the fork of a limb, as in Figs. 49 and 51. Another way is to lay two blocks against the prostrate trunk of your board tree, at right angles to it, like fire dogs, and a yard or so apart; on them lay a small log, parallel with the trunk, and drive stakes outside this "roller" to keep it from rolling more than six or eight inches away from the trunk (Fig. 48). The office of the brake is to clamp one end of the bolt while you are riving with the froe.

Fig. 49.—Splitting with a Froe

Now take up your froe. Stand one of the bolts on end, lay the froe's edge accurately along the center of one end, and split the bolt in twain by tapping with the mallet and springing your cleft

AXEMANSHIP

apart with the froe (Fig. 49). Take one of these halves and rive it similarly into two equal parts.

At this stage (more surely at the next one) you must learn a new trick—the difference between riving and mere splitting, and how to govern the rift. The wood has a tendency to "run out" more toward one side than the other. If you went on just forc-

Fig. 50.—"Run-out" Rift

ing the froe down, the result would be a botch (as in Fig. 50). To prevent this, turn the block so that *the thicker side is down,* lay its lower end in the brake, open the cleft until you can insert your flat left hand (the froe will prevent pinching), and then *bear down* hard on the bottom (*thicker*) section while you work the froe gently up and down.

Fig. 51.—Springing the Rift

This will make your split run back again into the thicker section.

Having quartered the bolt, now carefully rive each quarter into two clapboards or shingles (Fig. 51). You may have to turn the piece three or four times in order to get boards of uniform thickness. It is right here that judgment and skill are called for.

210   CAMPING AND WOODCRAFT

With good wood, already bolted, an experienced hand can turn out about one thousand clapboards, or four thousand shingles, in a day. Experts do better.

Clapboards, although slower to make than short shingles, save time and labor in the end, because of their extra span, and because they can be nailed directly to rib poles running lengthwise of the roof, whereas shingles require strips of board or flattened poles laid across rafters and close together. The rib pole construction makes a prettier gable end than the usual way of boxing up the gable with boards, because courses of logs are carried all the way up into the peak. Sawed boards break rustic effect.

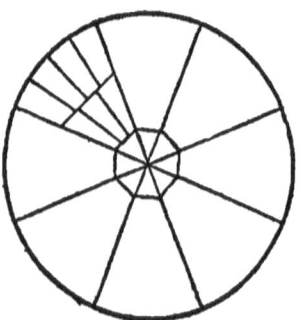

Fig. 52.—Double Bolting for Shingles

SHINGLES.—However, if shingles be preferred, they, too, can readily be made from the green tree. These hand-made shingles, if finished by shaving smooth with a drawing knife, are superior to the mill product.

To make them, a large tree is chosen, and the cuts are double bolted (as in Fig. 52). Since the sides of the outer bolts are almost parallel, the unshaved shingles will be of nearly even thickness on both edges. In riving shingles the bolt is turned end-for-end every time a shingle is struck off, and the shingles are allowed to run out a little so as to be thinner at one end than at the other.

A rude but efficient shaving-horse is shown in Fig. 53. My partner and I made such a one in an hour out of a chestnut log, a dogwood fork, two sticks for legs, and a hickory wand. The log ($A\ B$ in Fig. 53) is flattened on top to the rear of C. The far end rests on the ground and the near one is elevated on legs to such height that a man sitting in front of it will find A at the level of his elbows. The clamp

AXEMANSHIP

C D is pivoted in a slot by a wooden pin. (We had a chisel, but no auger; so we burned the hole out with a red-hot poker). Its head, *C,* may be cut as shown or formed of the stub of a natural fork. The end *D* is high enough to clear the ground, and at such distance from *A* that the operator can press against it with his foot, and thus clamp the head down on a shingle which is laid from *C* to *A*. A bowstring runs from *C* to the springy stick *E* inserted in the log a few feet back

Fig. 53.—Shaving Horse

of the clamp, to hold the latter back out of the way when not in use. For ordinary cabins, the clapboards or shingles do not require shaving.

Shingles are best made of soft wood (cedar is first choice). Then, if stacked and seasoned, they will not cup. If oak shingles are seasoned they will split in nailing; consequently they are used green. Moderate cupping does not necessarily mean a leaky roof, but it is unsightly. Clapboards, although always laid green, cannot cup, because they are nailed at both ends. They should be laid thick edge to thick and thin to thin. A thin board will outlast a thick one and makes tighter joints.

Speaking of cupping—it is universally believed by backwoodsmen that green shingles surely will cup if laid at any other time than "the old of the moon." Twice out of three times they will cup anyway—but it is heresy to say so.

LONG, SLENDER SPLITS.—When one is obliged to use wood that does not naturally split very straight, he still can rive out long and slender pieces of uniform thickness by careful manipulation. In his very practical little book on *Camp and Trail Methods,* Mr. Kreps describes the following method that he uses in getting material for snowshoe frames out of white birch, which is the only good wood for the purpose that is to be found in the far northern woods:

"Look along the edges of the swamps and you will find long, slender birches with smooth bark. Select one of about six inches in diameter, free of knots and flaws for about ten feet. It should be straight, and there must be no twist to the grain of the wood. If the limbs of the tree are drooping, so much the better, as it is stronger wood. Avoid the red-barked kind, with upright limbs.

"Having found a good tree, fell it, cut off about ten feet, and lay this piece in a notch cut in an old log or stump. Now carefully cut a groove the entire length of the stick, making it an inch or more deep. Do not strike hard when cutting this groove, or you will shatter the wood. When finished, turn the stick over and make a similar groove in the opposite side.

"Now go along the entire length and strike lightly with the axe in the bottom of the groove to start the split; turn the stick over and do the same with the other side.

"Next make two small wooden wedges, and, commencing at the end of the stick, driving one wedge in each groove, keep moving them along, and the stick will split nicely, following the grooves. If at any point the split is inclined to lead away from the groove, bring it back by cutting the contrary fibers.

"Now select the best of the two pieces and cut another groove the entire length, on tne bark side. Split this the same as before and you will have the wood for two frames."

QUICK SEASONING.—Green wood can be seasoned quickly, or rather have the sap driven out of it and the fibers hardened, by careful roasting in hot ashes or over the camp-fire. The old English word for such treatment of wood was "beathing." For the time being, this makes the wood soft and pliable, so that it can be bent into any required shape, or it can be straightened by hanging a weight from one end, or by fastening it to a straight form; but when the

AXEMANSHIP

wood has cooled, it becomes stiff, as if regularly seasoned.

One time when some of us were bivouacing in the mountains, Bob announced that he was going to catch a mess of trout in the morning. He had a line and some flies, but I wondered how he would extemporize a rod stiff and elastic enough for fly fishing. It didn't bother him a bit. The only straight and slender stick he could find right there was a box elder seedling. He trimmed it, removed the bark, and spent about an hour roasting it over the campfire, drawing it back and forth in his hands, so as not to overheat and crack it, and to temper the heat just right, according to thickness of the point treated. When the sap was roasted out, he hung the rod up to cool, and when that was done he had a one-piece trout rod with the necessary whippy action for fly fishing. Next morning he soon caught all we could eat.

BENDING WOOD.—Small pieces of green wood can be bent to a required form by merely soaking the

Fig. 54.—Spanish Windlass (for bending wood)

pieces for two or three days in water, but if it is desired that they should retain their new shape, they should be steamed. Small pieces can be immersed in a kettle of hot water. A long, slender one is suppled by laying it over the kettle, mopping it with boiling water, and shifting it along as required. Large pieces may be steamed in a trench partly filled with water, by throwing red-hot stones into it. Then drive stout stakes into the ground, in the outline desired, and bend the steamed wood over these stakes, with small sticks underneath to keep the wood from contact with the ground, that it may dry more readily. If a simple bow-shape is all that is wanted, it can be secured by merely sticking the two ends of the wood into the ground and letting the bow stand upright to dry; or, use the Spanish windlass, as shown in Fig. 54.

CHAPTER XIII

TOMAHAWK SHELTERS—AXEMEN'S CAMPS—CACHES—MASKED CAMPS

"The simplest and most primitive of all camps is the 'Indian camp.' It is easily and quickly made, is warm and comfortable, and stands a pretty heavy rain when properly put up. This is how it is made: Let us say you are out and have slightly missed your way. The coming gloom warns you that night is shutting down. You are no tenderfoot. You know that a place of rest is essential to health and comfort through the long, cold, November night.

"You dive down the first little hollow until you strike a rill of water, for water is a prime necessity. As you draw your hatchet you take in the whole situation at a glance. The little stream is gurgling downward in a half-choked frozen way. There is a huge sodden hemlock lying across it. One clip of the hatchet shows it will peel. There is plenty of smaller timber standing around: long, slim poles, with a tuft of foliage on top. Five minutes suffices to drop one of these, cut a twelve-foot pole from it, sharpen the pole at each end, jam one end into the ground and the other into the rough bark of a scraggy hemlock, and there is your ridge pole. Now go —with your hatchet—for the bushiest and most promising young hemlocks within reach. Drop them and draw them to camp rapidly.

"Next, you need a fire. There are fifty hard, resinous limbs sticking up from the prone hemlock; lop off a few of these, and split the largest into match timber; reduce the splinters to shavings, scrape the wet leaves from your prospective fire-place, and strike a match on the balloon part of your trousers. If you are a woodsman you will strike but one. Feed the fire slowly at first; it will gain fast. When you have a blaze ten feet high, look at your watch. It is 6 P. M. You don't want to turn in before 10 o'clock, and you have four hours to kill before bedtime. Now, tackle the old hemlock, take off every dry limb, and then peel the bark and bring it into camp. You will find this takes an hour or more.

"Next, strip every limb from your young hemlocks. and shingle them on your ridge pole. This will make a sort of bear den, very well calculated to give you a comfortable night's rest. The bright fire will soon dry the ground that is to be your bed, and you will have plenty of time to drop another small hemlock and make a bed of browse a foot thick. You do it. Then you make your pillow. Now, this pillow is essential to comfort, and is very simple. It is half a yard of muslin, sewed up as a bag, and filled with moss or hemlock browse. You can empty it and put it in your pocket, where it takes up about as much room as a handerchief.

"You have other little muslin bags—an' you be wise. One holds a couple of ounces of good tea; another sugar; another is kept to put your loose duffel in: money, match safe, pocket knife (when you go to bed). You have a pat of butter and a bit of pork, with a liberal slice of brown bread; and before turning in you make a cup of tea, broil a slice of pork, and indulge in a lunch.

"Ten o'clock comes. The time has not passed tediously. You are warm, dry, and well fed. Your old friends, the owls, come near the fire-light and salute you with their strange, wild notes; a distant fox sets up for himself with his odd barking cry, and you turn in. Not ready to sleep just yet.

"But you drop off; and it is two bells in the morning watch when you awaken with a sense of chill and darkness. The fire has burned low, and snow is falling. The owls have left, and a deep silence broods over the cold, still forest. You rouse the fire, and, as the bright light shines to the furthest recesses of your forest den, get out the little pipe. and reduce a bit of navy plug to its lowest denomination. The smoke curls lazily upward; the fire makes you warm and drowsy, and again you lie down —to again awaken with a sense of chilliness—to find the fire burned low, and daylight breaking. You have slept better than you would in your own room at home. You have slept in an 'Indian camp.'

"You have also learned the difference between such a simple shelter and an open-air bivouac under a tree or beside an old log."—("Nessmuk," *Woodcraft*.)

Why peel the old hemlock? Because the thick bark is resinous, is good to "brand up" a fire, and to

TOMAHAWK SHELTERS

cook over. Those hemlock stubs by themselves are rather poor fuel—you took what was handy—but, as I already have warned, chop them off well above their butts where they join the log, or you will have a nicked hatchet.

Fig. 55.—Lopped Tree Den

Nowadays it is prohibited, on public lands, to make a fire against the trunk of a tree, for it ruins the tree. The ridge pole can be supported by a low limb, or it can be set up on shears.

If one is alone, and needs nothing but a windbreak at night, a quick and easy way is to select a small, thick foliaged evergreen, cut the stem partly

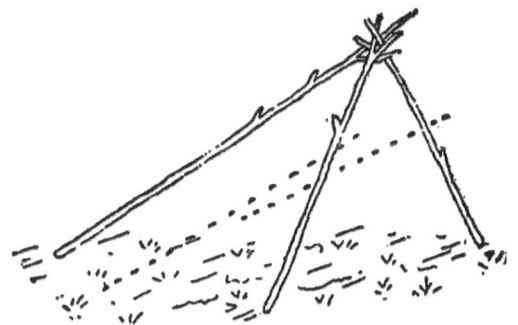

Fig. 56.—Straddle-bug Frame

in two at about five feet from the ground, then push the top over till it rests on the ground, the stem still being fast to the butt. Trim off the boughs from the inside, to use in thatching. Partially sever the upstanding limbs on the outside and let them hang down as part of the roof. Add your thatching, and branches from nearby small trees, as may be needed to make your den wind-proof (Fig. 55). This will be little protection, however, against rain, as the angle of the ridge is not steep enough, unless the tree be cut higher.

Where no tree grows on a favorable place, one can erect very quickly a tripod of poles (Fig. 56) secured at the apex by interlocking forks, or by tying. No triangular framework, however, is satisfactory for more than one occupant, because, if there be two or more of you, the den must be made so deep that the angle farthest from the fire is sure to be cold and dismal. The tripod frame is improved by tying one end of a pole to each leg of the shears, about two-thirds of the way to the top, and letting the other end rest on the ground, so that the rear of the shelter will be nearer a semi-circle than a triangle.

This is what I call a "straddle-bug" frame (see dotted lines in Fig. 56). It is economical of time and material, as it takes but five sticks. It is a particularly good frame to use if one has a poncho or pack cloth, which is spread over the top, tied to the side bars, and the whole is then covered with boughs. This ensures a dry spot to sleep on, and makes a very snug shelter in snowy weather, as no wind can get through, nor snow-water leak through from the top (snow does not melt at the sides) from the heat of the camp-fire.

BRUSH LEAN-TO.—If two trees happen to stand in the right position, run a stout ridge pole horizontally from one to the other, secured in forks of low limbs, or in notches cut in the trees, or by nailing, or tying (use twisted withes, pliable rootlets, or bark straps, if you have no cord). Against this lay poles sloping backward to the ground like a shed roof. Fasten a cross bar on the back, and one on each side, to stiffen the frame and to support thatching. Cover the roof and sides with evergreen boughs (balsam, hemlock, or spruce) hanging them from ridge and cross bars by stubs of their branchlets, trim them

TOMAHAWK SHELTERS

on the inside, and thatch them deeply outside with small boughs, beginning at the bottom, so that each layer will be overlapped by the one above it, like shingles. Lay the thatch with feathery tips down.

Fig. 57.—Stake Frame for Lean-to

When no trees grow where you want your bed, set up two forked stakes, slanting slightly outward at the butts so they will not need bracing, to hold your ridge pole (Fig. 57), and proceed as above. If the

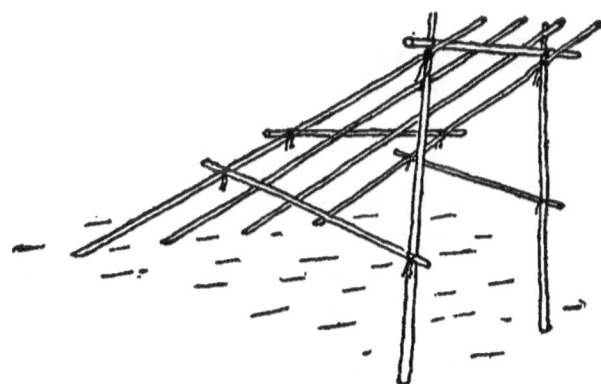

Fig. 58.—Shear Frame for Lean-to

ground is too stony or frozen to plant stakes in, use shear poles (Fig. 58), letting them flare outward so as to brace in every direction.

A frame must be stout enough, in winter, to hold up the weight of a snowfall. The lower the frame, the less material needed. Five feet to the ridge is high enough for a "one-night stand."

Any such bower is delightfully woodsy and sweet-scented, but it is not good protection against long or heavy rain. Of course, it lasts only so long as the browse remains green.

BOUGH BEDS.—Balsam makes the best bed, as it has thick, flat needles, soft and fragrant. Hemlock is next choice, then arborvitæ (white cedar) and spruce. Pine sprays are too scraggly. A bed of boughs or leaves will spread from under one if not held in place by something at the ends and sides; so, if practicable, cut four logs and stake them in a rectangle to keep the stuff in place. The fewer thick stems there are in your mattress, the easier you will sleep; but it takes a long time to make a browse bed of only the feathery tips; and you may be too hurried and weary.

For the first course use branchlets from eighteen inches to two feet long. Begin at the head end, lay them against the log, butts down, bottom or convex side up, and stick them in the ground with butts slanting only a little to the front, to make the bed springy. Then shingle another row of the fans in front of these, and so on down to the foot, leaving only the tips exposed. Then take smaller ones and stick them upright, tips inclined slightly to the head, all over the bed, as thickly as time and material will allow. Such a bed is luxurious in proportion to its depth and freshness. If the browse were merely laid flat on the ground it would pack hard and lumpy, and the sticks would soon find your ribs. The bed should be renewed with fresh stuff every two or three days.

Balsam twigs should not be cut, but snapped off. Grasp the stem with two front fingers underneath, pointing toward the tip, and thumb on top, then press downward with the thumb and give a quick twist of the wrist.

Where there are no evergreens, collect small green branches of willow, cherry, alder, or any tree or

TOMAHAWK SHELTERS

shrub that is springy and supple. Lay a course of these on the ground and cover with moss, dead grass, dry leaves, or whatever soft stuff you can find. Green leafy branchlets, ferns, rushes, herbage, and so forth, will do, if you can get nothing better. Even if such a bed is not soft, it will serve as insulation between your body and the cold, damp earth, and that is far better than none at all.

BARK SHELTERS.—Almost any bark will peel freely in the spring, when sap is rising, and several kinds will peel all summer. Elm peels through eight months of the year, and some young basswood trees may be peeled even in winter. But, as a rule, if one wishes to strip bark in cold weather he will have to roast a log carfully without burning the outside.

Barking a tree generally kills it, and is prohibited on public lands. But in the far wilderness such barking as campers would do is not detrimental to the forest, which generally needs thinning out, anyway.

The bark of the following trees makes good roofs and temporary shelters, and is useful for many other purposes: Paper birch, cedar, basswood, buckeye, elm, pig-nut hickory, spruce, hemlock, chestnut, balsam fir, white ash, yellow poplar and cottonwood. (That of the paper birch and of cedar, is quite inflammable). Select a tree with smooth and faultless trunk. If it is a birch, choose one with bark that is thick, with few and small "eyes." If it is of a species that has rough, hard, furrowed bark on old trees, pick out a young one that still is smooth on the outside, or treat as described below.

For a temporary roof it will be enough merely to skin the bark off in long strips eight to twelve inches wide, lay a course lengthwise with the slope of the roof, convex side up, and then another on top of this with concave side up, so that the first course will form troughs to run off the water that is shed by the second (Fig. 59). One axeman can erect a rain-proof shelter in this way, from the bark of young chestnut trees, for example, in less than an hour. It will not last long, however, as the sun will curl the troughs inward. If a tree is felled for the purpose of stripping its bark, first place a short log near the butt as a skid for it to fall on.

For neater and more permanent jobs the bark must be flattened, and the rough outer bark must be removed (except birch, which is always smooth) only the tough, fibrous, soft inner bark being used.

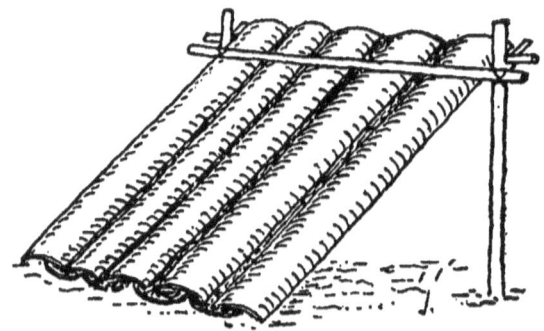

Fig. 59.—Bark Tilt

For rough work the outer bark may simply be "rossed" off with a hatchet, but for nice jobs the bark should be treated as described below.

If only a moderate-sized sheet is needed, the tree may not have to be felled. First girdle the tree just above the swell of the butt, by cutting through into the sapwood. Then girdle it again as high up as you can reach. Connect these two rings by a vertical slit through the bark. Now cut into wedge-shape the larger end of a four-foot length of sapling; this is your "spud" or barking tool. With it gently work the bark free along one edge of the upright slit, and thus proceed around the tree till the whole sheet falls off. If the girdles are 5 feet apart, a tree 2 feet in diameter will thus yield a sheet about $5 \times 6\frac{1}{3}$ feet, and a 3-foot tree will afford one $5 \times 9\frac{1}{2}$ feet. The bark is laid on the ground for a few days to dry in the sun, and is then soaked in water, which supples it and makes the inner bark easy to remove from the outer.

TOMAHAWK SHELTERS 223

The frame for a bark lean-to is like that in Fig. 57 or Fig. 58. The roof is laid in courses, beginning at the bottom, and overlapping like shingles. It is secured in place by weight-poles. The sheets of bark at the sides can be tied to stakes by using bark straps,

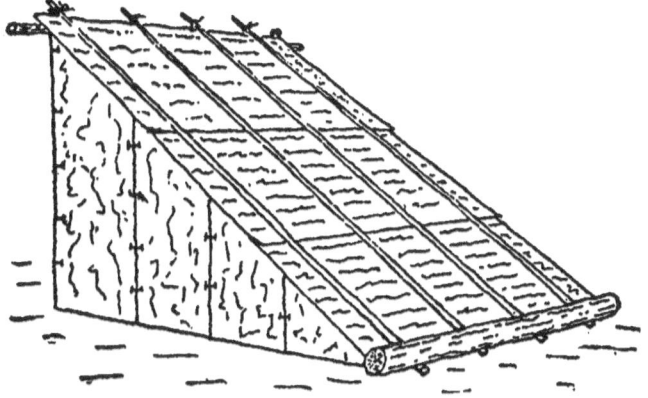

Fig. 60.—Bark Lean-to

or held in place by driving other slender stakes on the outside and tying them to the inner ones at the top (Fig. 60). Such a camp will last a whole season.

A bark teepee is made by lashing the tops of three poles loosely together, spreading them as a tripod,

Fig. 61.—Beehive Lodge Frame

Fig. 62.—Beehive Lodge (covered)

laying other poles against them with their butts radiating in a circle, covering with bark as above, and holding it in place with other poles laid against the outside. A more commodious circular lodge (more head-room for its size) was formerly used by the Algonquin tribes of the East. It was of beehive shape (Figs. 61 and 62), and was covered with skins or bark. The butts of the poles were driven into the ground and the tops bent over and tied together. Inner hoops were added as shown in the illustration, and the two crossed poles in front left openings for a doorway below and a smoke-vent above. If a rope or vine were run around near the top, pegged down at the bottom of the lodge on the opposite side, and a similar one used on the other side, such a structure would stand against a heavy gale. The Indians, so far as I know, did not do this, but I have shown the arrangement in Fig. 62.

A wikiup frame that is quickly set up can be made by driving six or more slender and flexible rods into the ground, in semi-circular or half-oval form, bending over those opposite each other, and twisting their

Fig. 63.—Wikiup Frame   Fig. 64.—Wattled Work

tops together so that they hold without tying. In a thicket of seedlings, I have cleared out a circular space, bent over some of the tall, slender ones on the margin of this space, trimmed off the lower branches, interwoven the others, and so, in a jiffy, have had a wikiup frame that no wind could blow down (Fig. 63). The covering would be bark, evergreen boughs, or whatever I could rustle that would serve the purpose. A small fire built close in front would soon warm the little cubby. If there are prospects of rain, the top should not be bent over so far, but sloped like the one in Fig. 61.

WATTLED WORK.—A frame of any shape may be wattled to serve as foundation for a lasting thatch, or for daubing with clay. Bed bottoms and other

TOMAHAWK SHELTERS 225

movable articles can be made in the same way. It also makes good fencing around a camp in a wild hog country. To illustrate the process, let us suppose you want to make a spring bed-frame to hold hay, browse, or whatever your mattress stuff may be. As many sticks as are required are driven firmly into the ground (make holes for them with a pointed stick). Then take willows or other flexible wands, previously suppled by soaking, and weave them in and out from stake to stake as shown in Fig. 64. To keep the outermost stakes from drawing together, cut a strong stick with a fork at one end and a notch cut in the other and set it between the stakes to keep them apart, shoving it higher up as the work progresses.

SLAB CAMPS.—In the mountains round about where I live there are many slab camps made by the native hunters and herdsmen. They last for years, and are welcome shelters for any wanderers who know their location or who chance to come upon them when the weather is bad. Very often the mountaineers go far up into the wilds without blankets or shelter cloths, carrying only their guns, ammunition, frying pan, tin cups, and "some rations in a tow sack." This, too, in freezing weather. But I omitted one thing that they always take along: a full-size axe. Having that indispensable tool, they can get along without tent or bedding, no matter what kind of weather may ensue. From chestnut, basswood, ash, spruce, pine, balsam, or other suitable wood, they split out, with axe and gluts a lot of 9-foot slabs. A stout ridge pole is laid across heavy forked posts or in notches cut in two adjoining trees to which the pole is withed fast. The slabs are laid, overlapping lengthwise, from ridge to ground. A big log fire is kept going all night in front of the shelter. Usually that is all. It must be bitter weather that would urge a southern mountaineer to enclose the sides of such a camp—in his vocabulary there's no such word as "draughts."

A slab camp may be made a very comfortable retreat by taking a little more pains, and it will last unimpaired for years, providing ready-made quarters for future trips. Instead of plain slabs, which let in more or less rainwater, owing to imperfect joining at the laps, use "scoops." These are simply slabs with the flat side hollowed out into shallow troughs or gutters. This is done by cutting a series of cross hacks a few inches apart along the core of the slab from end to end, then, splitting these out by chopping lightly lengthwise of the slab. Having

Fig. 65.—Slab Camp

set up your ridge pole, roll a good sized log to form a back for the camp, about seven feet from the ridge, and peg it in position. Lay the scoops overlapping from ridge to log (Fig. 65) and nail them fast, or drive stakes at the rear against ends of scoops. Then enclose the sides with splits or bark, and chink crevices around the log with moss or clay.

The siding may extend to the roof, being trimmed there to proper angle, or may rise little or no higher than the side bar shown in the illustration. The latter plan is best in localities where there are eddying and contrary winds, because it lets smoke out, instead of smoking out the occupants. It is the draught along the ground that chills sleepers, not what comes from above.

In a mountainous region it may be necessary to

TOMAHAWK SHELTERS

build the camp in a hollow between steep ridges. In that case, make it face across the hollow, not up nor down, because the night draughts sweep down a ravine and reverse currents draw up it.

To complete the slab camp, add side logs on the inside, and a foot-log for the bed, the latter being, say, fifteen inches thick, so as to serve as a "deacon's seat." The roof should project far enough in front to shelter the deacon and elders when they are busy holding down the aforesaid log.

Back of this a browse bed, not less than a foot deep; in front, a jolly fire of big logs: then who cares where the mercury may go?

In winter, cover the roof with a layer of evergreen boughs, so that snow shall not melt on it from the heat of the camp-fire. A drift six feet high would only make such a camp the snugger against wind and cold.

LOG CAMPS.—A favorite type of "open faced" camp, is shown in Fig. 66. Logs are laid on top of each other, at sides and rear of camp, to a height of about three feet, being flattened a little so as to make close joints. The back corners may be notched, as in a log house, but it is easier to butt the logs by halving their ends (Fig. 66*A*) and spiking them together. Two stakes are set up in front to hold the ridge pole, and the front ends of the logs are spiked to them. As many rafters as needed are nailed to the ridge pole in front and the top log at the rear. The roof usually is of canvas, but bark or splits may be used by adding cross pieces to hold them. The triangular sides may be enclosed, or left open as smoke vents, bushy boughs being leaned up against the windward side when desired.

The stakes need not be set in the ground, but if it is preferred to do so, the stakes being of green timber, select such poles as are durable in the soil, and roast the sap out of their lower ends until the surface is charred, as this will help keep them from rotting.

In covering such a shelter, put on the siding first

and the roof last, so as to overlap. A two or three-foot overhang sloping downward from the ridge is a desirable addition, to keep rain from driving in. A simple and effective way to rig it is shown by the dotted lines, which represent two forked poles slanting upward from the rear, outside of logs, nailed to logs and posts, and a cross bar laid in the forks to hold the font edge of tarpaulin or whatever else is used as roof. The most comfortable open-air camps that I have made were of this design. There is

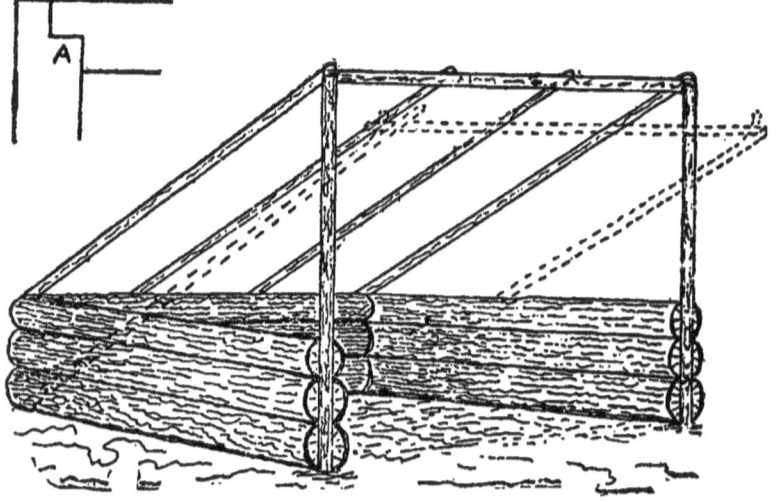

Fig. 66.—Log and Frame Camp

much more room than in a simple lean-to of the same ground dimensions, and heat from the camp-fire is reflected down on the occupants so that they are comfortable in zero weather, yet they have the fresh air of all outdoors.

I prefer such quarters to any tent that ever was made. In summer, the front and sides are easily screened with mosquito netting, a pole on the ground holding the front curtain down. If a little care is used in selecting wood that is durable (see table in Chapter XII) such a camp will last for several seasons, the tarpaulin, of course, being carried along on each trip. For two men and their duffel, a good size is 7 feet high, 7 feet wide, and 9 feet deep, inside measurement; for more, merely increase the width.

An excellent camp for a party is arranged by building two such shelters, facing each other, with a log fire between, and a "kitchen" with dining table, benches, and "pantry," at one side, as shown in the ground plan (Fig. 67). The fire is built by laying logs on thick "hand junks," and throws out heat in all directions. In bad, windy weather, the end opposite the kitchen is screened by setting up a row of bushy evergreens close together.

CACHES.—In a camp that is liable to be raided by 'coons, porcupines, or other predatory animals, the meat, fish, butter, lard, etc., should be cached under piles of stones twice as heavy as you think such beasts could move, for they are astonishingly strong and persistent. Bears will demolish any such pile that one man could build.

To cache provisions and other articles in trees: Fasten a strong peeled pole from the fork of one tree to another at fifteen to twenty feet from the ground, wrap up the parcel in canvas or oilskin so snugly that ants cannot get into it, and suspend it from the pole with ropes or wires. The trees should be too slender for a bear to climb, yet too stout for him to shake. The pole is peeled to give less secure footing for small animals, and to make it season into sound wood that will not rot and break. Canvas waterproofed with linseed oil is the best covering, as its odor and taste are offensive to animals of all kinds, great and small. A further precaution, in case of a light parcel, is to make a St. Andrew's cross (X-shaped), hang it from the pole, and suspend the package from the end of one arm of the cross, so that every puff of wind will set it swinging.

A good place for a cache is on an islet in a river or lake, so small that there are not likely to be any predatory animals living on it.

In the North, where wolves and wolverenes must be guarded against, the best cache for meat is made by cutting a hole through the ice of a stream or lake, fastening the sack of meat to a stick by a rope or hide thong, and letting it down into the water, the stick resting across the orifice. Lumps of ice are then piled into and over the hole, and water is poured on them, which freezes the mass together into a mound a foot or two high. Or a place may

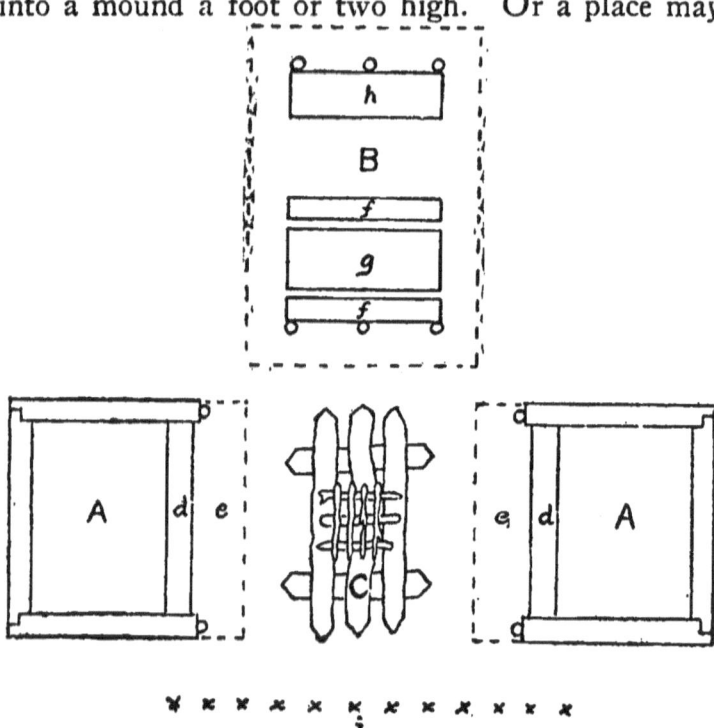

Fig. 67.—Camp Plan
AA—Log Lean-tos; B—Kitchen; C—Camp-fire; dd—Deacon Seats; ee—Overhangs; ff—Benches; g—Table; h—Pantry; j—Wind Screen

be chosen in shoal water where there is no current, a hole broken through, the meat dropped in, and the surface left to freeze over. Warburton Pike says that meat which he cached in this way was found fresh and palatable two months afterward, although the outside was discolored by its long soaking.

On the dry plains and prairies of the West, caches were made in the ground. How these subterranean hiding places were arranged was described by Lewis and Clarke, who, of course, adopted the method of the plains Indians:

TOMAHAWK SHELTERS

"In the high plain on the north side of the Missouri, and 40 yards from a steep bluff, we chose a dry situation; then describing a small circle of about 20 inches diameter, we removed the sod as gently and carefully as possible. The hole is then sunk perpendicularly for a foot deep, or more if the ground be not firm. It is now worked gradually wider as we descend, till at length it becomes six or seven feet deep, shaped nearly like a kettle, or the lower part of a large still, with the bottom somewhat sunk at the center. As the earth is dug, it is handed up on a vessel and carefully laid on a cloth, in which it is carried away, and usually it is thrown into the river, or concealed so as to leave no trace of it. A floor of three or four inches in thickness is then made of dry sticks, on which is thrown hay, or a hide perfectly dry. The goods, being well aired and dried are laid on this floor, and prevented from touching the wall by other dried sticks, in proportion as the merchandise is stored away. When the hole is nearly full, a skin is laid over the goods, and on this earth is thrown and beaten down until, with the additon of the sod first removed, the whole is on a level with the ground and there remains not the slightest appearance of an excavation."

Even after such precautions, caches sometimes were discovered and dug into by wolves or by Indians' dogs. Another trouble was that they were liable to cave in, if there were no trees with which to timber them. Of course, they had to be situated high enough to be out of reach of river overflows. Still, this method of storing supplies for the future was the best that could be devised in such a situation, and generally it turned out all right. Even such food as dried fish was kept a long time uninjured in underground caches lined with dead grass and hides.

In the far wilderness a cache is considered sacred by all woodsmen, white or red; hence it need not be concealed from prying eyes and itching fingers. But in woods that are frequented by all sorts of vagabonds and ne'er-do-wells, a hiding place for one's supplies must be well chosen to escape the attention of thieves or malicious people. For temporary concealment, a hollow log may do, in case of such articles as cannot be gnawed into by rodents or entered by insects. Anything that is not injured by dampness can be hidden more securely by digging under an old embedded log, laying it there, covering it up, and restoring the surface to its former appearance.

A secret storehouse for tools, utensils, etc., that you may wish to leave near the camp until next season may be dug in a dry bank and roofed over with logs, brush, and then a layer of earth, like a dug-out, the interior being lined with poles and dry grass, brush, or bark.

Another way, when you have a cabin, is to floor it with split puncheons conspicuously spiked to walls and sleepers. One or two of these puncheons have only spike *heads* driven in the usual places, and are removable. They are fitted with hidden fastenings to keep them firmly in place. This false flooring communicates with a miniature cellar, rock lined, under the middle of the cabin. Boxes are made that can be sealed air-tight (for example, with adhesive plaster). Articles to be stored are thoroughly dried, sealed up in the boxes, on a day when the air is not moist, and the chests are placed in the cellar, resting on flat rocks.

Generally I prefer to build the cache separate from the camp, and hidden at some distance from it. Then, in case the camp is entered by prowlers, or burned out, I will not be minus tools and bedding at the next visit. The cache may be built of rocks under the overhang of a ledge where nobody else is likely to go, or of notched logs with slab roof spiked down, or in other ways, according to circumstances. One will use his wits in utilizing such facilities as the country affords.

MASKED CAMPS.—I have had occasion to locate my lone camp where it would be out of the way of thieves or interlopers, beast or human, as I would be away a good part of the time. Such devices will vary, of course, with the locality one is in. Here are a few general principles to bear in mind,—

TOMAHAWK SHELTERS 233

The camp is to be situated where not only men but cattle and wild hogs are unlikely to go. There should be nothing in the neighborhood to attract any of the various classes of people who frequent the woods. Study each of these classes in turn, and their habits.

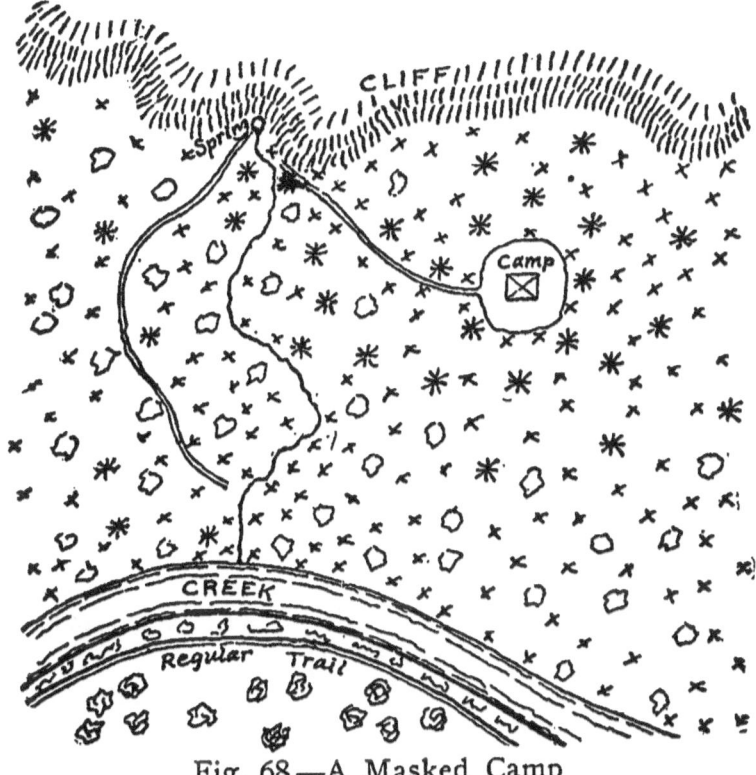

Fig. 68.—A Masked Camp

It should be invisible from trails, and from opposite ridges.

It should be screened by tall trees, preferably evergreens, so that the smoke of a properly fed fire will not betray it by day, nor its light do so at night.

There should be plenty of down-wood in the neighborhood, so that the noise of chopping may be reduced to a minimum.

It should be not far from a regular trail; because you must go back and forth yourself, and if you should make a new trail it soon would attract notice and speculation,

It is impossible for a man, even though he be alone, to camp more than a day or two in one place without leaving footprints that a woodsman would notice, unless the weather is extremely dry. The problem, then, is to mask the points of ingress and egress.

If your presence in the country is known to low characters, establish a woods alibi, by building another camp away from the real one, but somewhat more public. Build a fire there every day or two, freshen the browse bed now and then, and leave litter and footprints indicating recent occupancy. The more shrewdly this false camp is located the surer you are to lead busybodies to spy after you in the wrong places.

An example of a successful masked camp is illustrated in Fig. 68.

An old trail up the creek is used by herdsmen, hunters, and others going up into the mountains. Fishermen commonly wade the creek itself. On the south side of the stream is a forest mostly of oaks and chestnuts. On the north side is a laurel thicket in which stand numerous birches and hemlocks. To the north is a cliff or steep-sided ridge, at the base of which is a spring.

Neither hogs nor cattle will go over into that laurel thicket when there is an open forest of mast-bearing trees on the other side of the creek, and a regular trail running through it. Consequently nobody looking for his hogs or cattle will cross the stream at this point. Nor is there anything over there to attract game or its pursuers. About the only people who would be likely to go into such a place are timber cruisers, who, of late years, actually count every tree, or blockaders (moonshiners), or spies serving the revenue agents.

If you know those woods, you know how long it has been since its timber was "cruised," and the likelihood of it being gone over for that purpose this year. Anyway, cruisers are decent fellows. The spring branch and the solitude of that north side would be attractive to blockaders looking for a new location; but if they picked on it, they would erect their still on the branch itself, low enough down from the spring so that they could run water through a spout to the worm of the still. Spies searching for such gentry would go along the branch, and, finding no sign, would waste no more time there.

A man camping in that thicket would have to have some way of getting in and out. It would be much too wearisome to go a new way every time, crawling through the laurel. That means he will make a trail of his own. He leaves the regular trail and steps into the creek not far from a point opposite the mouth of the spring branch, and up that branch he wades a short distance until out of sight of the creek. Here he turns out into the thicket to the left and trims a trail to the spring, starting a few yards back from the branch so that no marks are visible from it. Directly below the spring he starts similarly a trail to the camp site, where he trims out as much space as he needs. Dead trees wind-thrown from the cliff supply him with almost smokeless fuel, and dead laurel, of which there is plenty in every thicket, gives him an abundance of excellent kindling that is really smokeless. When he chops, it will be so early in the morning that nobody else will be within sound of it, for it is an hour's walk, at least, from any house.

Whenever he goes to the spring, or returns from it, he drops a dead laurel bush at the entrance to the side trail leading to camp, the sprangling forks of the bush being thrown outward, which would deter any stranger from pushing through just at that point. The entrance to this side trail, like the one near the mouth of the branch, is "blind"; *i. e.*, not visible from the branch, as you have to part some bushes to find it.

CHAPTER XIV

CABIN BUILDING AND FITTING UP

Nobody knows what solid comfort means until he finds himself, snug and well fed, in a bit of a cabin, far away in the big sticks, while icy blasts rebound from his stanch roof and walls, to go howling away through a famine-stricken wilderness, thwarted by a woodsman's providence and skill.

Open the door: you are face-to-face with misery and death. Close it: the hearth-fire leaps, the kettle sings, you smoke contentedly, and all is well.

A tent, at best, is only a shelter: a cabin is a home. Log walls insure everything within against storms and prowling beasts. There are comfortable bunks for Partner and you, a table, benches and stools or chairs, a cupboard and bins with a good store of food, a chest or two, shelves and racks, a fireplace or stove. The weapons, tools, and utensils are hung just where they are handiest. Plenty of good wood is stacked in the dry. On wet days you can stay indoors without feeling cramped or jailed. And next season, when you come back again, how like an old friend the log hut twinkles welcome!

I shall describe only two types of simple one-room cabins, such as would be built by hunters or others who go pretty far back into the woods and require no more than a snug "home camp." For designs of more elaborate structures, to be used as summer homes in or near "civilization," the reader is referred to Kemp's *Wilderness Homes* (Outing Publishing Co., New York) and Wickes' *Log Cabins* (Forest and Stream Publishing Co., New York).

CABIN BUILDING

In the first example I will assume that there is a road or waterway to the camp site on which tools and some materials can be transported by wagon, boat, or raft; also that the cabin is to be large enough for four men, but planned to economize time and labor in construction, so that it may be finished in a week. You are supposed to hire a man with team to snake the logs in, unless enough suitable trees grow on the site itself.

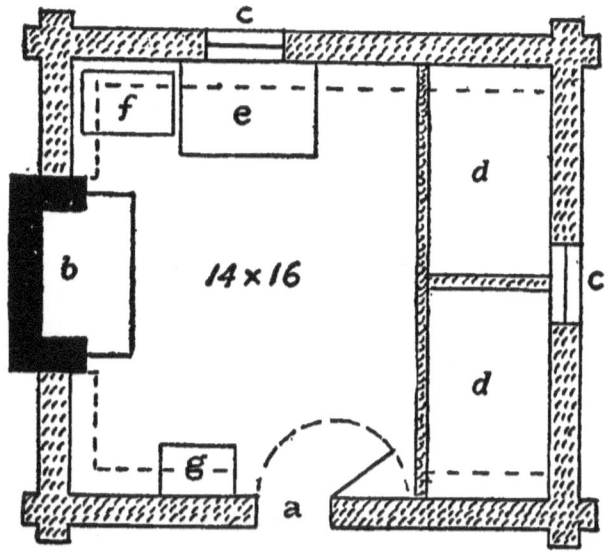

Fig. 69.—Log cabin (ground plan) a—door; b—fireplace, 4'; c, c—windows; d, d—bunks, 4½x6¾'; e—table, 3x4½'; f—grub chest, 2'x3'; g—wash stand, 1½'x2½'; straight dotted lines indicate high shelves

Decide beforehand what kind of roof you shall make. If it be of sawed shingles, or of roofing felt, then you must take along roof-boards as a foundation for them. A roof made simply of planks battened and painted will last several years without any covering, and it is easiest of all to build; but it is prone to warp or cup, under a summer sun, and then leak.

If roofing felt is used, carry along paint and brush to take the black "curse" off. Clapboards riven from neighboring trees are chosen in the present instance, as other methods of roofing are familiar to everybody. They call for no roof-boards, being nailed directly to the stringers (rafters that run parallel with the ridge). The way to make them has been described in Chapter XII.

A stone chimney, with fireplace not less than four feet wide, is ideal for heating a woodland home. Nothing is so jolly as an open fire of hardwood logs. With a Dutch oven or reflector, besides the ordinary utensils (see Vol. I., pp. 65-66), you can cook as well on the hearth and over the fire as in a stove. But if rocks are scarce about your building site, or if good fuel is not abundant, a stove will be required. It will save a good deal of labor in building, and much wood chopping thereafter. Choose for yourself.

Let us say that you decide on a clapboard roof and a stone chimney, the house to be 14 x 16 feet inside measurement, high enough for a porch in front and a lean-to kitchen in the rear, to be added in future. A ground plan is shown in Fig. 69. It may be modified, of course, according to frontage and other conditions.

The tools you ought to have for such a job are:

2 Axes,
2 Hatchets,
Crosscut saw (6 ft.) and handles,
Peavey, or cant hook,
Sledge hammer (8 lb.),
2 Steel wedges (5 lb.),
Froe,
Spade,
Mattock,
Hand saw,
Rip saw,
Compass saw,
Brace,
3 Auger bits (⅜, ¾, 1¼),
2 Drill bits (⅛, ¼),
Drawing knife,

Jack plane,
Framing chisel (1½),
Tape line,
2 ft. Rule,
Steel square,
Pocket level to screw on square,
T-bevel,
Plumb-bob,
Chalk line and chalk,
Crosscut saw file,
2 Triangular files (7 in. and 6 in. slim taper),
Mill file (8 in.),
Whetstone,
50 ft. Rope (1 in.).

CABIN BUILDING

I have helped to build two clapboard-roofed cabins with fewer tools than these, but the others would have come in handy. We had no need for any not mentioned on this list. Some of these are used only in making furniture. All of the light tools except the square go in a carpenter's shoulder chest. The crosscut saw should be tied between two thin boards, as shipped from the factory.

Materials to be "carried in" are $1\frac{1}{4}$-in. planks for flooring, dressed on one side; $\frac{7}{8}$-in. planks, dressed on both sides, for door, casings, shutters, furniture, and shelving; 2 glazed window sashes, single; wire nails (40d, 10d, 6d), wrought nails for door and hinges; strap hinges for door and cupboard and chests; door-lock; 2 flat steel bars for fireplace lintel; round steel rod for "crane" in fireplace; heavy wire for pot-hooks. A screen door, and wire screen cloth for windows, will add greatly to comfort.

SITE.—Build where there is good natural drainage, and below a spring, or near some other source of water supply that is beyond suspicion. Cut away all trees that would shade the cabin except from the afternoon sun. Forest air is nearly always damp, and you need plenty of sunshine up to the noon hour. If you are in an original forest of tall trees, bear in mind that such do not root nearly so firmly as trees growing alone in exposed positions. When a tree of the ancient forest is left standing by itself in a clearing, it is easily overthrown by wind; so do not leave one of these near enough to the house that it might crush your cabin.

The features of good and bad sites are discussed in Vol. I., pp. 208-214.

Do not dig a cellar under the house. A cellar not cemented is a trap for water, especially when the snow begins to melt. A small cache may be dug under the center of the floor, where it will stay dry.

TIMBER.—The logs should be straight and of slight taper, the best of the smaller ones being reserved for floor and roof timbers. Those for the sills should be at least a foot thick, but the upper courses may be smaller. The wood must be of some species that is light and easy to work. Choice will depend, of course, upon what is available. The best common woods are the soft pines, spruce, and young chestnut. Sills should be of wood that is stiff and durable (see tables in Chapter XII). They may be cut long enough to support the porch, if one is to be built. Tall, straight, slender trees are common among the younger growth wherever the stand of timber is dense.

Logs are best cut in spring or early summer, as the bark then can be peeled with ease. If it is left on, it soon begins to loosen, moisture and insects get under it, and decay sets in. Pine logs, even after they are peeled, are attacked by "sawyers" (wood-boring larvæ of beetles) which advertise their work by a creaking sound and by wood-dust dropped from their borings. They work just under the surface, in a girdling way, do no serious damage, and cease operations after the first season.

Cut the wall logs about three feet longer than the inside dimensions of the room, so as to allow eighteen inches at each end for jointing, unless you adopt one of the ways of building without notches to be described hereafter. I have already told how to select good board trees for the roofing.

CORNERS.—If the building site happens to be of sand or gravel, and is flat, the sills may be laid directly on the ground; but if the place is not level, or if there is soil on the surface, you should set them up on piers or posts.

Stake out the corners, and square them by the method shown in Fig 18. At each corner set up either a pier of flat rocks or a heavy post.

CABIN BUILDING

These should go down in the ground below frost-line, and project just enough to keep the sills off the ground all the way round. Lay the two sills and level them by hewing out underneath or blocking up, and testing with the level on your square. To make a good job of this, rip out two boards about six inches wide, nail them together for a straight-edge reaching from one corner to another diagonally opposite, and use your level on the center of the straight-edge, where it is most likely to sag. When the sills are level and squared, block them up near the center of each with rocks, to keep them from springing and sagging. The tops of the sills and floor joists are to be scored and hewn flat.

After laying the sills, dig down at the chimney end to a solid base and lay a rock foundation for chimney and hearth (Fig. 76d), the latter to project about two feet inward from front of fireplace. Make corbels or some other arrangement for inner ends of floor joists to rest on where they meet this foundation.

LOCKING CORNERS.—Wall logs usually are locked together at the corners by notching. There are several ways of doing this. The quickest is the saddle notch (Fig. 70) which has a wedge-shaped cut on top of lower log and a V-notch in bottom of the one that rides on it. This work is done by eye alone, and calls for expert axemen.

Another is the rounded notch (Fig. 71) cut nearly half-way through on under side of log. It takes some trouble to round out the notch, but a neat fit results. There might be a shallower rounded notch cut on both top and bottom of each log, to make the logs lie close together; but the upper one would collect moisture and then decay would set in.

A third way is to saw and split out one-fourth the diameter on each side of the end (Fig. 72), leaving the center like a tenon, and spike the ends together. This makes close joints, and shorter logs are used, as the ends do not project. It is best adapted to poles of six-inch diameter and under, which do not require large spikes.

Fig. 70.—Saddle notch   Fig. 71.—Round notch

A very good way, especially for amateurs, is to saw the logs to exact dimensions of *interior* of room designed, and spike the ends to an L-shaped "trough" of heavy plank (Fig. 73) which, when set on end, will reach to the height of the walls. First lay the four bottom logs, and spike the troughs upright

 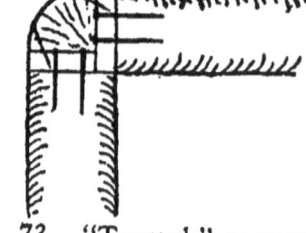

Fig. 72.—Tenon-shaped end   Fig. 73.—"Trough" corner

to the corners, having, of course, plumbed and braced them in position. Then proceed similarly with the other logs until walls are finished. This makes close joints that require little chinking, if the logs are straight. Finish the open corners by quartering a large log, or hewing four small ones, cut to height of walls, and nailing them to the troughs as shown. This is easier and quicker than notching. If you choose this plan, take along some 2-inch plank for the troughs, as thinner stuff is not stiff or strong enough; also some 60d nails or spikes.

JOISTS AND WALLS.—Having fitted cross logs to the sills, test again to insure that all is square. Then fit the ends of the joists into gains chiseled out of the sills (Fig. 74). The logs for joists

CABIN BUILDING

should be fully eight inches thick, or they will be too springy. They may be spaced about two feet apart from center to center. Different thicknesses can be allowed for in shaping them to the gains, so that all may be level.

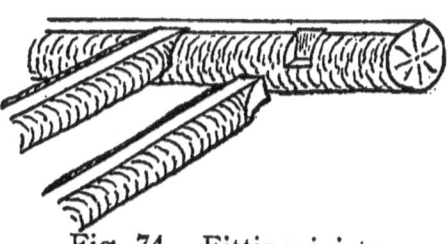

Fig. 74.—Fitting joists

Now go ahead with the walls. Lay the logs with butts and small ends alternating, so the walls may go up of even height. To raise the logs, as the work advances, lean two poles against the wall as skids. Near each end of the top log fasten a rope, pass the free ends of the ropes under and over the log to be lifted, and up to the corner men, who pull on these while other men push from below.

At the height of windows, door and fireplace, make saw cuts almost through the upper log, in each case, at proper distance apart, so that afterward the crosscut blade can be pushed through and the spaces sawed out.

ROOF.—For a clapboard roof the stringers or rafters run lengthwise of the cabin instead of from eaves to ridge (Fig. 75). The gables are built of logs notched for the stringers, spiked together, and cut to the proper pitch. Select straight, slender poles for stringers. The ridge pole should be heavier: say 8 or 10 inches thick.

The pitch of the roof will depend upon climatic conditions; rather flat for a dry region, and steeper for a wet one (not less than one foot rise to two of width for main building, and one to four for porch and kitchen). If there are heavy snowfalls, a steep pitch is required to stand the strain, and to keep snow-water from backing up under the shingles.

In laying the roof, begin at the eaves, letting several inches overhang. The clapboards should also project a little at the sides of the roof. When the first course is laid, take the straight-edge that

Fig. 75.—Log cabin (end view)

you used for leveling the sills and nail it lightly on top of this course as a guide for the next to butt against. Then lay the second course, breaking joints carefully; and so on to the top. If you finish the ridge with a saddle-board (inverted trough to shed water from the joint), or a log hewed out to serve as such, then the clapboards are sawed off to fit. Otherwise, let the top course on one side project, slanting upward over the other (this is not a reliable device for a very windy or snowy climate).

FLOOR.—In laying the floor, leave an open space in front of fireplace for the hearth. As the joists will shrink in seasoning, it is wise to use as few nails as practicable (only at ends of boards). Next year the planks may be taken up to be refitted where they have gaped apart, blocked up where the joists have sagged, driven tight together by an extra strip, and then nailed permanently in place.

DOOR AND WINDOWS.—Before sawing out the door space, tack a plank vertically on each side as a guide, and block or wedge the logs so they cannot

CABIN BUILDING

sag when cut through. Remove one handle from your crosscut saw, push the blade through the cut that you made when building the wall, attach handle again, and saw out. Snap a chalk-line along the log that comes directly over the doorway, and chisel out a section three or four inches deep for top of door frame to be nailed to. Spike the jambs to ends of abutting logs. Fit in a washboard beveled on both sides.

The door should swing inward; otherwise, if the cabin is occupied in winter, you may find your egress blocked by a snow-drift.

If you can bring in a screen door, by all means do so. In such case you may as well bring also a ready-made door and casing. If means of transportation do not permit this, then make a simple batten door. Use wrought nails, as they can be clinched more neatly and firmly than wire ones.

To hang a door: Place it exactly in position (shut) with bottom and sides wedged to give proper clearance. Set the top hinge so that its pin is just in line with crack between door and jamb, and nail it; so also with the lower one. Fit the lock, or make a wooden latch and attach hasp and padlock.

The windows, being only single sashes, may be hinged to their casings, like the door, or fitted on slides (Fig. 78). Shutters should be provided to close the openings when the cabin is left unoccupied. They may be fitted to bolt from the inside.

There may well be a third window in our design, alongside the door and over the washstand. If a kitchen is added, the rear window space will be sawed down for a doorway.

CHIMNEY.—Saw out of the end wall a space for the chimney, just as you did for the doorway. The opening between wing walls of fireplace should be about 4 feet wide, 18 inches deep, and 3 feet high. The sides of fireplaces often are built narrow within and flaring outward, so as to help throw the heat out into the room. This is well enough where fuel must be economized; but in the big forest, where there is abundance, it is best to build the fireplace with straight sides, so that backlogs of nearly 4-foot length can be used. This saves a lot of chopping.

If the back of the fireplace is built up straight into the flue, the chimney is very likely to smoke whenever the air is heavy or the winds contrary. To insure a good draught, build the upper part of the fireback with a forward slope, as shown in Fig. 76, forming a "throat" (*a*) about 5 inches *above* the front of arch or lintels and only 3 or 4 inches deep. The top of this throat forms a ledge (*b*) that checks wind from rushing down the flue.

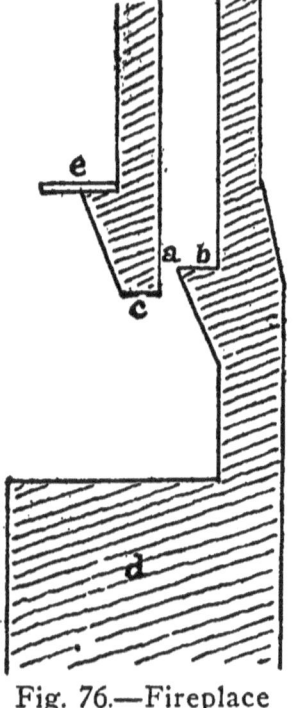

Fig. 76.—Fireplace (vertical section)

To support the rocks over the fireplace, instead of building an arch (which is likely to crack or give way from settling of chimney) set in two flat steel bars, 2½ x ¼ inch, as lintels (*c*).

Build the wing walls of the fireplace out into the cabin far enough to protect the ends of abutting logs, and to support a plank or puncheon for mantelshelf (*e*). The upper part of the chimney goes quite outside the cabin, and so requires no flashings.

In backwoods cabins the chimneys generally are built up without mortar, clay being used instead. As clay shrinks and loosens in drying, such a structure must be chinked over again at intervals. It is more satisfactory to take in with you a sack of

CABIN BUILDING

cement, if possible, and use around the joints of fireplace and hearth a mixture of one part cement to two of clean sand. Mix only a little at a time, as it soon sets. However, this may be deferred until the second season, by which time the chimney is likely to have settled and opened the joints here and there.

Wherever there is limestone, enough lime for mortar can be made without much trouble, by a process similar to that of burning charcoal. Enclose a circular space of 5 feet diameter by a rude stone wall 3 feet high; cover the bottom of this enclosure with brush to facilitate kindling the kiln; then fill with alternate layers of dry hardwood and limestone broken into moderate-sized pieces, piling the top into conical form. Light the pile, and when it is well going, cover the top with sods to make the calcination slow and regular. Keep it going for two days and nights. Lime can also be made from mussel shells or oyster shells. Slake the lime in a box some days before it is to be used, and cover with sand.

For mortar, work the lime into a paste with water and mix in with this, thoroughly, from $2\frac{1}{2}$ to 3 parts of sand. Thin with water until it mixes easily.

A pretty good substitute for mortar is blue clay (yellow will do) mixed intimately with wet sand. Another is a mixture of sand, salt, and wood ashes.

When laying a chimney or wall, see that no joint comes over or close to another joint. If a rock does not fit, turn it over and try again.

At the proper height in your fireplace (a little below level of lintels) insert a stout steel rod horizontally on which to hang wire pot-hooks when cooking. In place of andirons, select two rocks about 15 x 5 x 5 inches, to support the "fire irons" for frying-pan, etc. (See Vol. I, p. 64.) Never lay backlogs on them: they are only to be used when cooking, or to hold forestick in place.

CHINKING.—If there are large crevices between the logs they should be filled with quartered poles. Small ones are caulked with moss or clay. Mortar should never be used for this purpose until the logs have seasoned thoroughly and got their "set."

FITTINGS.—In Fig. 69, a pair of pole bunks are shown (d, d) across the end of the room opposite the fireplace, where they are least in the way. They are to be built high enough to store personal chests under. A high window at c lets in the morning light. Each bunk is roomy enough for two persons.

The table (e) is movable. The provision chest (f) may be lined with zinc to keep out rodents, although wire screen cloth is effective and easier to apply. It serves as a bin for flour, potatoes, etc. Over it hangs a cupboard for dishes and minor foodstuffs.

Dotted lines show high shelves around three sides of the room. At g is a stand for water pail and basin, with towel and mirror above and slop pail underneath. Dry wood is piled in the corner between this and the fireplace. A broom is hung behind the door. Chairs or stools go where most convenient at the time.

AXEMAN'S CABIN.—It is quite practicable to build a small cabin with no other tool than the axe, and out of no other materials than such as grow on or around the site. This often is done in remote forests where there is no road. In such case the shack is no larger than actually necessary—say 8 x 10 feet, or at most 10 x 12.

The roof may be of bark (see Chapters XII and XIII) held down by weight-poles running from ridge to eaves and tied together in pairs at the top to keep them from slipping down. However, a bark roof is flimsy. A much better arrangement is to "carry in" a ready-made paulin of 12-oz. canvas,

CABIN BUILDING

which can be bought of a tent maker or a mail order house, a can of paint, and a brush (or the paulin may be waterproofed before starting—see Vol. I., p. 72), and tack this to the rafters. Thus a durable and perfectly reliable roof is quickly made.

These small shacks are best heated by a folding stove of sheet iron, which can be carried in on a man's back. Take along, also, a collar for the pipe.

When there are only one or two men to do the work, the house may have to be built of poles. In such case I prefer a shed-roof construction, as it takes less material and is easier erected than one with a ridge. But if there are trees that split easily, it is better to build of logs split through the center. These half-logs are easy to handle, easy to notch and lock at the corners, make close joints and require little chinking; besides, since the walls are flat inside, there is less waste of space and material.

It is not necessary to floor such a shack. Some use poles for the purpose; but a pole floor is hard to keep clean and offers harborage for vermin. A hard-trodden earthen floor is easy to sweep and can be kept quite neat. It is warmer than an ill-fitting one of boards or puncheons.

The door can be made of boards riven with axe and wooden wedges, with wooden hinges and latch,

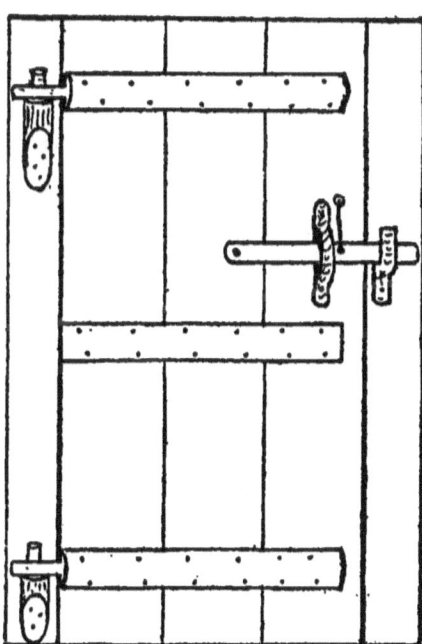

Fig. 77.—Cabin door (wooden hinges and latch)

as in Fig. 77. The hinge pins are made of cuts from a sapling, slightly flattened on the inner side and with tops whittled to fit holes in flattened ends of top and bottom door battens, which are half-round. The latch guard and catch are of naturally bent branches or roots, or may be whittled out. The end of latch string that hangs outside is knotted so it cannot pull through the hole.

Cabin windows, when glass is unobtainable, may be made of translucent parchment (recipes in Chapter XVII), but it is better to carry in with the outfit a sheet or two of transparent celluloid, such as is employed for automobile curtain windows. Lacking all such materials, cut out a window space, anyway, that can be left open in fair weather and closed with split boards at other times.

RUSTIC FURNITURE.—Boards riven like clapboards from green timber are likely to warp in seasoning unless stacked carefully, or held in forms

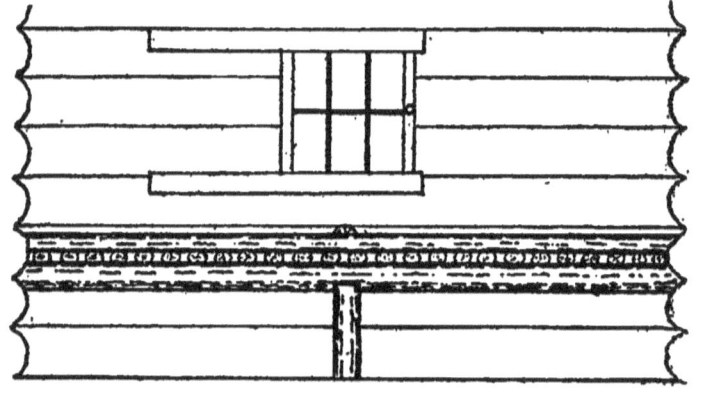

Fig. 78.—Pole bunk (for four men)

until they have dried through. If only one flat side is required, as in shelving, seats of stools and benches and so forth, split a small log in two and hew the flat side smooth. A number of these joined side by side, and cleated on the under side, will serve very well for a table top or other broad surface.

The bunk (Fig. 78), for four men, is made by running a pair of straight poles about 4½ feet apart, from side to side of cabin, fitting the ends in the joints between wall logs, and supporting the middle on posts. Athwart these are laid small poles to support the mattresses and on top of them, directly over the large poles, are fastened two other long poles as guards. The mattresses are simple bed ticks filled with fine browse or whatever other soft stuff is available. It pays to take ticks along, as they hold the stuff in place and are easy to refill.

Double berths, one above the other, are nuisances in every way. Folding cots are more cleanly than any kind of fixed berths, and they can be carried out of the house to sun and air while the floor is being swept.

The table (Fig. 79) has no rounds nor braces at the bottom, which would be in the way when people

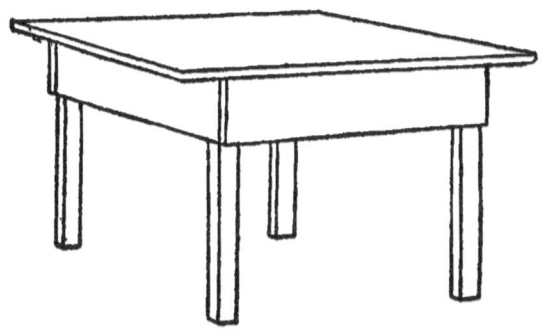

Fig. 79.—Table

were seated at dinner. The legs may be made of four pieces of sapling squared for nailing cleats at the top, and the lower parts may then be shaved round or tapered. Make the table 30 inches high.

The washstand is simply a broad shelf attached to a cleat on the cabin wall and supported further by brackets or diagonal braces, leaving the space underneath clear.

Regular chairs should not be made until proper

Fig. 80.—Stool

wood has been thoroughly seasoned for this purpose. If it is to be used with the bark on it must be cut in mid-winter. Meantime the occupants of the cabin can use stools (Fig. 80) and benches (Fig. 81) made of green wood by splitting out slabs and fitting natural round sticks in auger holes for legs, wedging these in like an axe helve so they can be refitted when the wood has shrunk in seasoning.

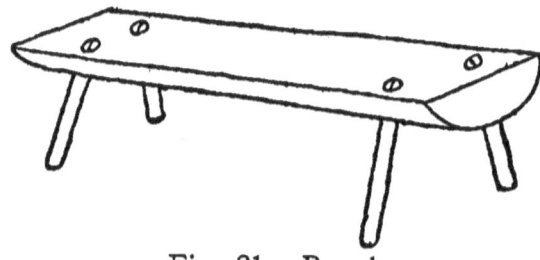

Fig. 81.—Bench

An easy chair is readily made, as shown in Fig. 82, by using a piece of canvas for seat and back.

Split-bottom chairs (Fig. 83) are particularly appropriate in a log cabin. Those common in the backwoods are generally made stumpy (only 16 inches high in front and 15 in the rear). It is better to make them 18 inches to top of seat, so they will be right for a 30-inch height of table. In making them you will need a drawing knife, a ¾-in.

Fig. 82.—Easy chair

CABIN BUILDING

bit and ¼-in. chisel to mortise slots for the three broad splits that connect the back posts (round sticks may be used instead of splits). A 60-cent hollow auger, commonly used for making tenons, is better than a spoke sizer to fit the ends of rounds to their holes. Besides gluing these ends, you can fox-wedge them (Fig. 84) in place by splitting each end a little and inserting a thin wedge before driving home.

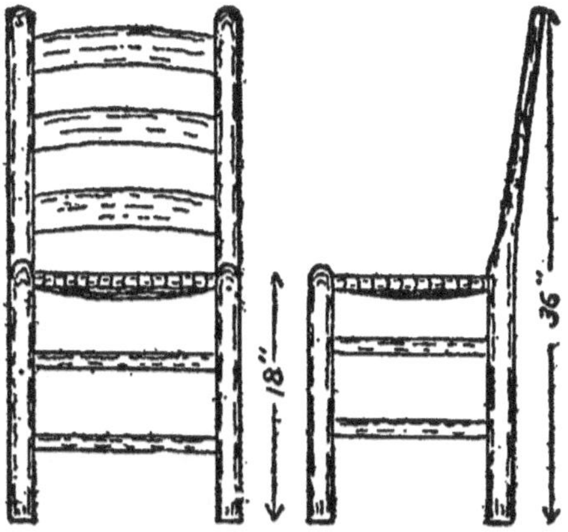

Fig. 83.—Split-bottom chair

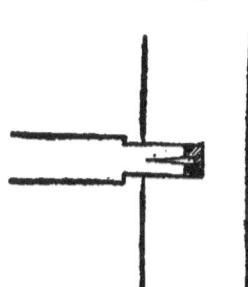

Fig. 84.—Fox-wedge

To fill the chair seat, use oak or other splits (see Chapter XIII) in the manner shown in Fig. 85. Cut the end of a split narrow enough to tie easily around the side bar at *a*. Then run it across and pass it under and back over the opposite bar, and so on, as the cut shows. When you get to the end of this split, tie another to it, keeping knots on under side of chair where they will not show. When the seat is filled up with the strips going one way, fasten the end, beginning at rear (*b*), and run others crosswise, in and out, until the seat is finished.

Instead of the plain pattern shown in this example, it is better to weave a diagonal one similar to that in the back of the rocking chair (Fig. 86). To do this, run the strands as follows:

1. Over two, under two, etc.
2. Under one, over two, under two, etc.
3. Under two, over two, etc.
4. Over one, under two, over two, etc.

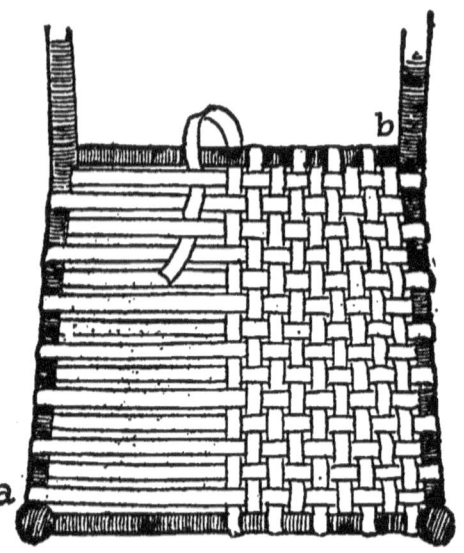

Fig. 85.—Bottoming chair with splits

Repeat in above order. Be sure to draw the split as tightly as you can every time it crosses the chair.

Raw deerskin, or other animal pelt, makes good chair seats.

Fig. 86.—Rustic rocker

Racks for guns, clothing, etc., are easily provided by cutting crotches of small limbs and nailing them up in convenient places. Wooden pins set in auger holes in the walls may be used for similar purposes. If you have no auger, a hardwood pin can be driven into a softwood log by trimming its point wedge-shape and starting it in a nick made with the corner of the axe blade.

Outside, under the projecting roof at a gable end,

CABIN BUILDING

fix a rack on which full-rigged fishing rods may be stood during the day (of course, you will unjoint them and take them in at night). This rack consists simply of a small shelf for the butts, and, high up a narrow shelf with auger holes bored close to the edge and a narrow slot cut out from each hole to the edge for a rod tip to slip through.

The first essential of good housekeeping is a broom. Tie together a round bundle of thin birch, willow, or other flexible twigs. Cut a broomstick, sharpen one end, and drive this pointed end into the center of the bunch—then it will hold fast.

Some rainy day you can make a really first-class broom from birch splints. Select a straight yellow birch five inches in diameter and cut off a six-foot length. At about fourteen inches from the big end cut a ring around the bark about two inches wide. Peel off all the bark below that ring. Then, working with a sharp jackknife, split small flat slivers from the butt end up to the bark ring. Continue until there is nothing left of the butt save a small core at the top, and cut this off carefully Then remove the bark above the ring and sliver the wood down until there is only enough left for a broom-handle. Tie this last lot of slivers tightly down over the others with a stout string. Trim off the slivers evenly. Then whittle off the handle, smooth it with glass, make a hole in its top and insert a hide loop to hang it up by. This is the famous splint broom of our foremothers, as described by Miss Earle in her *Home Life in Colonial Days*.

Don't crowd the cabin with decorations or "conveniences" that will be in the way and serve chiefly to collect dust and cobwebs. Let each and every article have a definite purpose, and show it by its perfect adaptability. The simplest contrivances generally are the best.

CHAPTER XV

BARK UTENSILS—BAST ROPES AND TWINE—ROOT AND VINE CORDAGE—WITHES AND SPLITS

Among the many interesting woodsmen that I have known was one who, years agone, had lived a long time alone in the forest, not far from where Daniel Boone's last cabin was built, in what is now St. Charles County, Missouri. I call him a woodsman, because he had to be, and loved to be, a real one; but beyond that he was a scholar. In his young manhood he took to the woods that he might gain first-hand knowledge of Nature, and have leisure for a colossal labor of love: that of translating into English, with his own exegesis, the works of the philosopher Hegel. When the Civil War broke out, this hermit abandoned his cabin and raised a body of volunteers to defend the Union. Afterward he became Lieutenant Governor of his State.

One day we were discussing those traits of our old-time frontiersmen that made them irresistible as conquerors of the West. The Colonel named, as one factor, their extraordinary shiftiness in shaping the simplest or most unlikely means to important ends, and he illustrated it with an anecdote.

"I knew an old man of the Leatherstocking type who once was far away and alone in the wilderness, hunting and trapping, when the mainspring of his flint-lock rifle broke. Now what do you suppose he did?"

"Made a new one out of an odd bit of steel."

"No, sir: he had no bit of steel."

BARK UTENSILS 257

"Then of seasoned hickory or *bois d'arc.*"

"No room for it in the lock. The old man had killed a turkey. He split several quills of its pinions, overlaid them one on another, bound them together with wet sinews that shrunk when they dried, and —there was his mainspring. It worked."

BOILING WATER IN A BARK KETTLE.—A competent woodsman can cook good meals without any utensils except what he makes on the spot from materials that lie around him, and he will waste no time at it. In the chapters on *Camp Cookery** I have shown how to broil, grill, roast, bake, barbecue, plank and steam without utensils. But, it may be asked, how would one *boil water* without a metal kettle? There is more than one way of doing this.

One of them, which many have read of, but few nowadays have seen, is to split a short log, chop out of it a trough, pour water in, heat a number of small round stones to a white heat, pick up one with a forked stick or extemporized tongs, drop it into the water, add another, and so on until the water boils, which will be very soon. To keep it boiling, remove the stones and add others from the fire. You must select such stones as will neither burst in the fire nor, like sandstone, shiver to pieces when dropped in the water.

Another way, which will be news to many, is to boil the water in a bark kettle by direct action of the fire. The thin inner bark of many species of trees will do, or a thin sheet of the bark of the paper birch, notwithstanding that it is so notoriously inflammable that we use it for kindling. No, this is not a trick; it is a practical expedient.

But first you must know how to make a watertight vessel out of nothing but a square sheet of pliable bark and a couple of thorns or splinters. Seems

---

*See Vol. I., pp. 293-299, 301, 309, 312, 315, 317, 319, 322-324, 330, 344-346, 352, 369.

impossible? Nay, very simple. Try it at home with a sheet of writing paper. Cut out a 12-inch square (or smaller—I give dimensions for a real bark kettle in which to boil a quart or more of

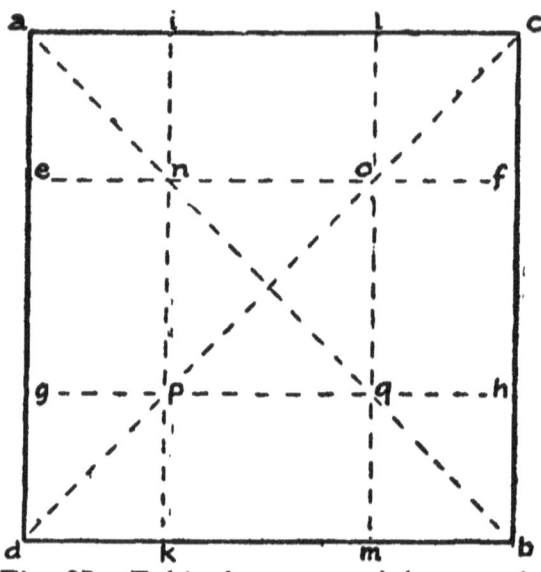

Fig. 87.—Folds for water tight vessel

water). Note the diagram (Fig. 87). Fold over from *d* to *c* making the points of triangle meet at *a*. Open up, and fold similarly from *a* to *b*. Open again, and you have the diagonal creases *ab* and *dc*. Turn the sheet over, and fold from *ad* along the line *ik*, which is to be 3½ inches from the margin. Similarly fold *cb, db,* and *ac*. You now have made all creases as in the figure. They are your guides in making a neat job.

Grasp the point *i* with one hand and *e* with the other, raise them, and bring them together: This throws *a* outward at an angle. Fold *a* over to right on the outside, and hold it there. Do the same at the corner *c*. These two corners now will overlap on the outside, as in Fig. 88. Fasten them with

Fig. 88.—
Bark kettle
(end)

BARK UTENSILS

a pin (with a splinter like a skewer, if you are using bark). In the same way fold the corners d and b, and pin them. The creases *no, pq, np, oq,* now are folded inward, instead of outward as they were originally. Here you have an open-top box 5 inches square and 3½ inches deep, with perfectly tight joints, which will hold water so long as it does not seep through the pores of the paper (would hold it till it evaporated, if you had used bark).

Now, if you are skeptical about boiling water in a bark kettle, suppose you try your paper one. Arrange a stand that will support it over a gas jet. Put the paper kettle on the stand and pour some water into it. Light the gas, raising the jet just high enough for it to play on the bottom of the vessel but not up the sides; for, mark you, if the flame touches the paper *anywhere above the waterline,* it will set the thing afire. Observing this precaution, you can boil water in the paper kettle quicker than you could in tin.

The reason that the paper is not even scorched is that the water inside instantly attracts the heat of the flame and absorbs it to itself. My partner, Bob, once told me he could take a boiling tea-kettle from the stove, put his naked hand on the bottom, and hold the thing out at arm's length. I smiled. He led the way to the kitchen, where an old-fashioned black kettle of cast-iron was steaming at a hard boil, did as he had offered, and sustained no injury whatever. Then I did it myself. The bottom of the kettle merely feels warm to the naked hand. But the water must be boiling, not just simmering. If one touches the vessel above the water-line, he will get a severe burn.

In making a bark kettle, the material must, of course, be quite free from holes or cracks. In the case of birch, select a sheet free from "eyes" and surface "curls." Supple it by roasting gently over the fire.

I have boiled water in such a vessel by setting it directly on the coals, and covering all around its bottom with ashes, so no flame could reach the sides. For your first trial it will be better to build a little circular fireplace of stones, with a draught hole at the bottom, and cover the top with flat rocks, leaving an opening of about three inches diameter for the bottom of your kettle. Fill this with live coals, and chink with mud, so that no flame can get out.

It might seem impossible to *melt snow* in such a bark utensil, but the thing can be done when you know how. Place the kettle in the snow before the fire, so it will not warp from the heat. In front of it set a number of little forked sticks, slanting backward over the kettle, and on each fork place a snowball. Thus let the snowballs melt into the kettle until the vessel is filled as nearly as you want it. Then set the kettle on the coals, cover around it with ashes to keep flame from the sides, and the water will boil in a few minutes.

BARK UTENSILS.—Vessels to hold water or other liquids can be made, as above, of any size, square or

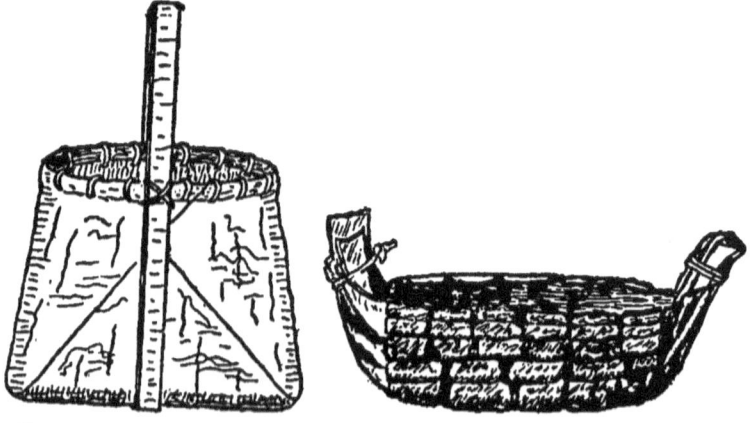

Fig. 89.—Bark water bucket

Fig. 90.—Bark trough or basin

rectangular. You soon will learn the trick of folding the corners without preliminary folding and creasing. Since the top of a cubical bark vessel

BARK UTENSILS

of this sort readily adapts itself to a circular shape, when softened by heating, one can make a water bucket, for example, by sewing a hoop or splint (like a basket splint) around the inside of the top edge, and adding another vertically for bail, like a basket handle, going clear around the bottom to take up

Fig. 91.—Bark barrel

Fig. 92.—Bark berry pail

the strain (Fig. 89). Punch the holes with a sharpened twig for awl, and use rootlets or bast fiber, soaked in water, for thread, or lace the loop in place with narrow strips of pliable bark.

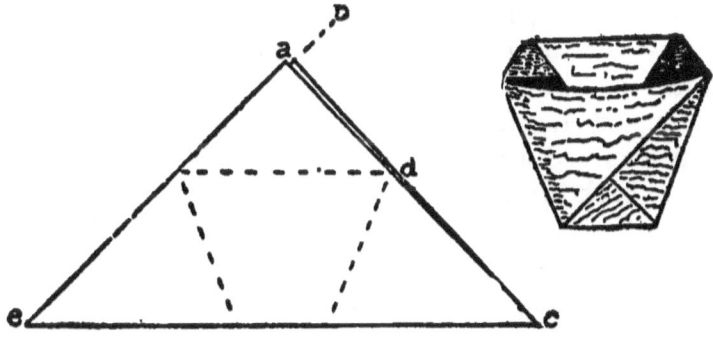

Fig. 93.—Pocket cup (folding)

Wash basins and the like are made in the same way, shallow without bails. A trough or tub, of any size, to hold liquids, is quickly made by rossing off the thick outer bark from the ends of a sheet of elm, basswood, poplar, cottonwood, or other suitable material, but leaving it on the middle part to stiffen the vessel; the rossed ends are then folded over in several overlaying laps, gathered in somewhat the shape of a canoe's bow and stern, and tied with bark straps (Fig. 90). The Indians used to make such troughs for collecting maple sap. They also made elm barrels (Fig. 91) that would last for years. Their bark buckets often were made with lapped seams, sewed together with bark or root twine (Fig. 92). The seams were closed with a mixture of pine resin or spruce "gum" and grease or oil, laid on while hot, and the upper edges were stiffened with hoops or splints of pliable wood.

To make a folding bark cup for the pocket: take a sheet of thin bark about 7 inches square and fold it diagonally (a to b, Fig. 93). Now fold the corner c over to the left so that its upper edge coincides with the dotted line that extends horizontally from d. Then fold, over this, the corner e straight to d. This leaves two triangular flaps standing out at the top, a and b. Slip the inner one, a into the outer pocket formed by e, and fold the flap b backward over the outside. You now have a flat cup that holds about a quarter of a pint. To open it, press against the outer edges with the thumb and finger. When carrying it in your pocket, slip the flap b in along with a, and the cup is closed against dirt.

A bark dipper is easily made. Take a sheet about 8 x 10 inches, trim it to spade shape (Fig. 94), fold it lengthwise from A to B, open it out, place the second finger behind A, and make the fold upward as shown at F. Cut a stick for handle, with stub of a fork at one end to hang it up by. Split the other end of the stick, insert F in the cleft, and bind it fast with a narrow strap of bark.

A strong and durable tray, dish pan, or similar utensil, is made like Fig 90, with the addition of a hickory or other rim like that of Fig. 92, sewed on

BARK UTENSILS

the outside. Leave the thick bark on the sides to stiffen them, but shave it off of the bottom, so that the vessel will stand upright.

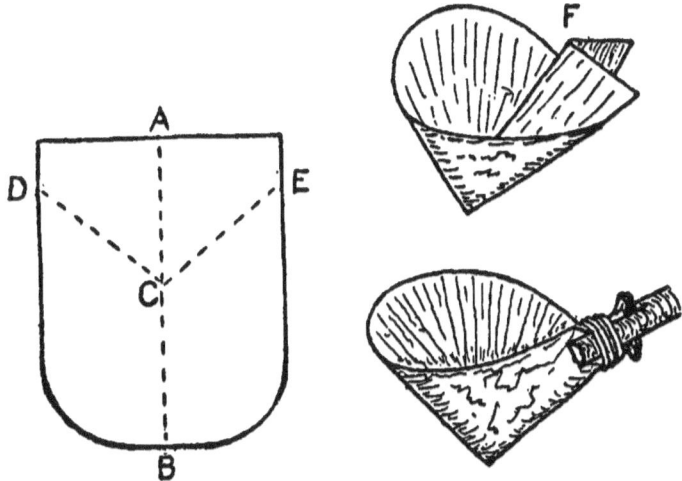

Fig. 94.—Bark dipper

BARK FISH BUCKETS AND CORSEAUX.—Every trout fisherman knows how bothersome a willow creel is when he is fishing the brushy head waters of a stream. And a creel is a nuisance not to be thought of when one is off on a hiking trip. A canvas bag, with or without rubber lining, is compact enough, but it is mussy and does not keep the fish in good order. To carry trout on a stringer is

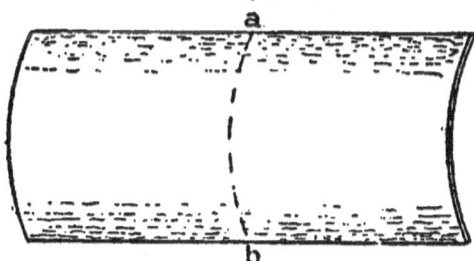

Fig. 95. Fold for fish bucket

barbarism. So, look for a young basswood, or poplar, or other smooth-barked tree that will peel. It need not be more than 9 or 10 inches thick. Strip from it a rectangular sheet about 12 x 22 inches.

Also cut a bark carrying strap about 4½ feet long, and a quite narrow one for thongs.

Fold the sheet of bark across the middle of the longer dimensions (*a--b*, Fig. 95), and bring the ends together, one overlapping the other. The natural convexity of the bark spreads it out into an oval at the top. If the bucket were to be used for berry picking, or the like, you would fasten the top by merely cutting holes through at *A*, Fig. 96, and the corresponding point on the opposite side, and tying with bark thongs.

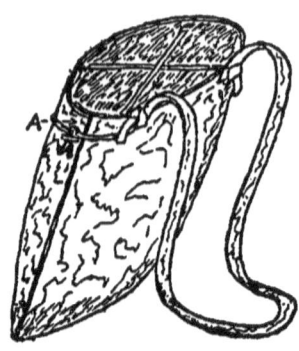

Fig. 96.—Fish bucket

For a fish basket, the thong is strung crisscross as shown in the illustration, as this keeps the fish from flopping out. Attach a bark shoulder strap through slits in the back, and the thing is done. You have a sweet, clean "bucket" that carries under the left arm without bulging so much as a creel, and no top is needed. Put clean ferns or grass over the fish when the sun is hot, and they will keep moist and firm and well-colored, all day. This bucket is easier to wash than a creel. In a week, if you are to stay longer, make a new one, as the old one will have warped.

Large packs for the back are made in the same way, from balsam or other bark, but laced up along the sides, stiffened by a couple of hoops on the inside, and fitted with a pack strap of bark or plaited fiber. A flap to cover it, if wanted, is provided by an extension of the bark at the top, which is rossed off to make it flexible. Such a carrier is called by the French Canadians a *corseau* (from *casseau*). In warm weather it is more comfortable to carry than a blanket pack, as it does not sweat the back.

BAST ROPES AND TWINE.—Straps, fish-stringers, etc., are made from the whole bark of pawpaw,

BARK UTENSILS 265

leatherwood (remarkably strong), and hickory shoots. Very good ropes and twine can be made from the fibers of the inner bark of the slippery, white, and winged elms, the pignut and other hickories, white oak, and buckeye, red cedar, yellow locust, red mulberry, and Osage-orange. One who has not examined the finished work would scarce believe what strong, soft, and durable cordage, matting, braided tump-lines, and even thread, fish-nets, and garments can be made from such materials by proper manipulation. The Indians first separate the bark in long strips, remove the woody outer layer, and then boil it in a lye of sifted wood ashes and water, which softens the fiber so it can be manipulated without breaking. After it is dried it can be separated into small filaments by pounding, the strings running with the grain for several feet. Slippery elm especially makes a pliable rope, soft to the touch; it can be closely braided, and is very durable. If the woody splinters and hard fragments have not been entirely removed by pounding, the shoulder blade of a deer is fastened to an upright post, an inch hole is drilled through it, and bunches of the boiled bark are pulled backward and forward through the hole. The filaments are then put up in hanks and hung aside for use, being boiled to supple them when needed.

Bark twine is made by holding in the left hand one end of the fiber as it is pulled from the hank, and separating it into two parts, which are laid across the thigh. The palm of the right hand is then rolled forward over both, so as to twist tightly the pair of strands, when they are permitted to unite and twist into a cord, the left hand drawing it away as completed. Other strands are twisted in to make the length of cord desired. Twine and thread are made from the bark of young sprouts.

The bast or inner rind of basswood (linden) makes good rope. More than a century ago, two Indians whose canoe had drifted, while they were in a drunken sleep, upon Goat Island, between the American and Canadian falls of Niagara, let themselves down over the face of the cliff by a rope that they made from basswood bark, and thus escaped from what seemed to the on-lookers as certain death by starvation.

Mulberry and Osage orange bast yield a fine, white, flax-like fiber, that used to be spun by squaws to the thickness of packthread and then woven into garments. The inner bark of Indian hemp (*Apocynum cannabinum*), collected in the fall, is soft silky, and exceedingly strong. The woody stems are first soaked in water; then the bast, with bark adhering, is easily removed; after which the bark is washed off, leaving the yellowish-brown fiber ready to be picked apart and used. A rope made from it is stronger, and keeps longer in water, than one made from common hemp. It was formerly used by the Indians, almost all over the continent, not only for ropes, but for nets, threads, and garments. The fibers of the nettle were also similarly used.

In the southern Appalachians, it is not many years since the mountain women used to make bedcords (perhaps you know how strong such cords must be) by twisting or plaiting together long, slender splits of hickory wood (preferably mockernut) that they suppled by soaking. Such bed-cords are in use to this day.

ROOT AND VINE CORDAGE.—The remarkably tough and pliable rootlets of white spruce, about the size of a quill, when barked, split, and suppled in water, are used by Indians to stitch together the bark plates of their birch canoes, the seams being smeared with the resin that exudes from the tree; also for sewing up bark tents, and utensils that will hold water. The finely divided roots are called by northern Indians *watab* or *watape*.

Twine and stout cords are also made of this material, strands for fish-nets being sometimes made

BARK UTENSILS

as much as fifty yards in length. The old-time Indians used to say that bark cords were better than hemp ropes, as they did not rot so quickly from alternate wetting and drying, nor were they so harsh and kinky, but, when damped, became as supple as leather. "Our bast cords," they said, "are always rather greasy in the water, and slip more easily through our hands. Nor do they cut the skin, like your ropes, when anything has to be pulled. Lastly, they feel rather warmer in winter."

The fibers of tamarack roots, and of hemlock, cedar, and cottonwood, are similarly used. Dan Beard says: "I have pulled up the young tamarack trees from where they grew in a cranberry 'mash' and used the long, cord-like roots for twine with which to tie up bundles. So pliable are these water-soaked roots that you can tie them in a knot with almost the same facility that you can your shoestring. . . . Each section of the country has its own peculiar vegetable fiber which was known to the ancient red men and used by them for the purposes named. . . . Dig up the trailing roots of young firs or other saplings suitable for your use, test them and see if they can be twisted into cordage stout enough for your purpose. Coil the green roots and bury them under a heap of hot ashes from your camp-fire, and there allow them to steam in their own sap for an hour, then take them out, split them into halves and quarters, and soak them in water until they are pliable enough to braid into twine or twist into withes. Don't gather roots over one and one-half inches thick for this purpose."

The long, tough rootstocks of sedge or saw-grass are much used by our Indians as substitutes for twine. Baskets made of them are the strongest, most durable and costliest of all the ingenious products of the aboriginal basket-maker. The fiber is strongest when well moistened. The stringy roots of the catgut or devil's shoe-string (*Cracca* or *Te-*

phrosia), called also goat's rue or hoary pea, are tough and flexible.

Grapevine rope is made in a manner similar to bark rope. The American wistaria (*Kraunhia frutescens*) is so tenacious and supple that it was formerly used along the lower Mississippi for boats' cables; it can also be knotted with ease.

WITHES.—A favorite basket plant of the Apaches and Navajos is the ill-scented sumac or skunk-bush (*Rhus trilobata*), which is common from Illinois westward. The twigs are soaked in water, scraped, and then split. Baskets of this material are so made that they will hold water, and they are often used to cook in, by dropping hot stones in the water. A southern shrub, the supple-jack (*Berchemia scandens*), makes good withes. The fibers of the red-bud tree are said by basket-makers to equal in strength those of palm or bamboo. For such purpose as basket-making, withes should be gathered in spring or early summer, when the wood is full of sap and pliable. If the material is to be kept for some time before weaving, it should be buried in the ground to keep it fresh. In any case, a good soaking is necessary, and the work should be done while the withes are still wet and soft. Other good woods for withes are ash, white oak, hickory, yellow birch, leatherwood, liquidambar, willow, and witch hazel. Large withes for binding rails, raft logs, etc., are made from tall shoots or sprouts of hickory or other tough wood, by twisting at one end with the hands until the fiber separates into strands, making the withe pliable so that it can be knotted. This usually is done before cutting off the shoot from its roots. A sapling as thick as one's wrist can be twisted by cutting it down, chopping a notch in a log (making it a little wider at the bottom than at the top) trimming the butt of the sapling to fit loosely, driving in a wedge, and then twisting.

A withe is quickly fastened in place by drawing

BARK UTENSILS 269

the two ends tightly together, twisting them on each other into a knot, and shoving them under, as a farmer binds a sheaf of grain.

HOOPS AND SPLITS.—The best hoops are made from hickory, white or black ash, birch, alder, arborvitæ or other cedar, dogwood, and various oaks. Take sprouts or seedlings and split down the middle, leaving the outer side round. Thin the ends a little, and cut notches as in Fig. 97. An inside

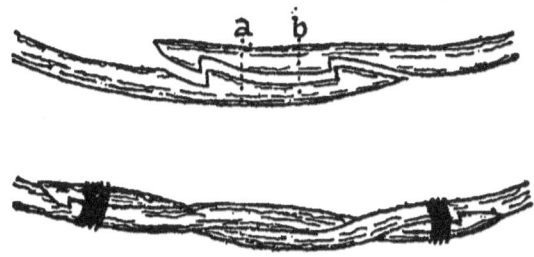

Fig. 97.—Becketing hoops

hoop, or any that is not subjected to much strain, is simply notched for a short overlap, as in the upper illustration; the ends are brought together, one on top of the other, and bound at a and b. A hoop to be driven on the outside of a keg or barrel has a long joint (lower figure); each end takes a half turn round the other, between notches, and the joint is then tied.

Splits for basket-making and similar purposes are commonly made of white oak, in spring or summer, when the sap is up. Select a straight-grained sapling, cut in lengths wanted, rive these into strips as wide as desired, then, with a knife, split these strips bastard (*i.e.*, along the rings of growth) to the proper thickness. Put them in water to soak until needed, if you want them pliable.

Splits are easily made from slippery elm, for instance, by taking saplings or limbs three or four inches in diameter, and hammering them with a wooden mallet until the individual layers of wood are detached from those underneath, then cutting these into thin narrow strips. The strips are kept in coils until wanted for use, and then are soaked.

Black ash and basket oak, when green, separate easily into thin sheets or ribbons along the line of each annual ring of growth, when beaten with mallets. The Indians, in making split baskets, cut the wood into sticks as wide along the rings as the splits are to be, and perhaps two inches thick. These are then bent sharply in the plane of the radius of the rings, when they part into thin strips, nearly or quite as many of them as there are rings of growth.

CHAPTER XVI
KNOTS, HITCHES, AND LASHINGS

Much depends on knowing how to tie just the right knot or other fastening for a certain job. In learning to tie knots, do not use small twine, but rope or cord at least an eight of an inch thick. Take plenty of it in hand, and do not begin too near the end.

The main part of a rope is called the "standing part" (Fig. 98). When the end is bent back toward the standing part, the loop thus formed is called a "bight," regardless of whether it crosses the rope, as in the illustration, or only lies parallel with it.

For the sake of clearness, in the accompanying illustrations, *ends* are shown *pointed* like thongs, and standing parts are left open to indicate that they extend indefinitely. Parts of the knots are shaded to show plainly how the convolutions are formed.

STOPPER KNOTS.—A plain knot tied anywhere on a rope to keep it from slipping beyond that point through a bight, sheave, ring, or other hole, is called a stopper knot. Such a knot often is used, too, at the end of a rope to keep the strands from unlaying.

OVERHAND KNOT (Fig. 99).—Simplest of all knots. Often used as component part of other knots. Jams hard when under strain, and is hard to untie.

DOUBLE OVERHAND KNOT (Fig. 100).—If the end is passed through the bight two or more times before hauling taut, a larger knot is made than the simple overhand.

FIGURE-OF-EIGHT KNOT (Fig. 101).—Also

272 CAMPING AND WOODCRAFT

98. Parts of Rope.

99. Overhand Knot.

100. Double Overhand Knot.

101. Figure-of-eight Knot.

102. Thief Knot. (will slip).

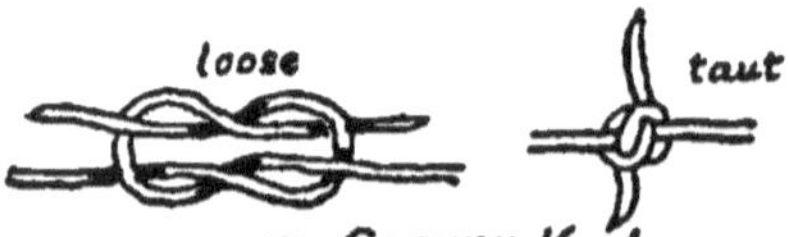

103. Granny Knot. (will slip).

104. Reef Knot (holds, does not jam, easy to untie).

105. Weaver's Knot.

106. Double Bend.

107. Carrick Bend.

108. Lapped Overhand Knot.

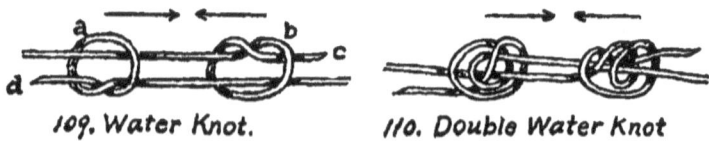

109. Water Knot.

110. Double Water Knot

KNOTS, HITCHES, LASHINGS 273

called Flemish or German knot. Used for the same purposes as the overhand knot, but more elegant and easier to untie.

KNOTS FOR JOINING ROPES, ETC.—First are given illustrations of two knots that *never* are to be used, because both are treacherous. The thief knot (Fig. 102), with ends pointing in opposite directions, is sure to slip. It is a bungled weaver's knot (compare Fig. 105).

The granny or lubber's knot (Fig 103) is formed by passing the end *a* in Fig. 104 *over* instead of under the end *b*, and then bending *b* down under it. The result is that the loops cross over and under on opposite sides, instead of the same way on both sides. Such a knot, when drawn taut, has its ends sticking out and away from the standing part, and it is very likely to slip.

REEF KNOT (Fig. 104).—Known also as square or true knot. Will not slip, *unless* used in tying a small cord or rope to a thicker one. So long as the two ends are of equal diameter this knot may be relied upon. It has the advantage of being easy to untie. To make it, cross the two ends, *a* under *b*, turn *a* over and under *b*, bring the two ends up away from you, cross *a* under *b*, turn *b* under *a*, and draw taut by pulling the ends.

To untie, if the rope or cord is stiff enough, seize the standing part on each side, just outside the knot, push the hands together, and the loops slip over one another. If the material is limber, take one end in left hand and the standing part of the same end in the other, pull hard on both, and the knot becomes dislocated so that it is easily undone.

SURGEON'S KNOT.—This is the same as a reef knot except that, in making it, the end *a* is turned twice around the standing part of *b* before proceeding with the loop, just as in the double overhand knot (Fig. 100). It is used by surgeons in drawing tissue together, to prevent slipping of the first turn of the knot (see Fig. 193).

WEAVER'S KNOT (Fig. 105).—Often called thumb knot, or, by sailors, becket bend or hitch, single or common bend. Almost the only knot by which two ropes of greatly differing sizes can be joined firmly together; also the quickest and most secure of all knots for joining threads or twine. Weavers tie it so deftly that the eye cannot follow their movements. To tie it as they do: (1) Cross the ends of two pieces of thread, the right one underneath the left, and hold them with thumb and finger where they cross; (2) with the other hand bring the standing part of right thread up over left thumb, down around its own end (which is projecting to the left), back in between the two ends, on top of the cross, and hold it there with left thumb; (3) slip the loop that is around thumb forward over end of left thread (which is projecting forward in line with thumb); (4) draw taut by drawing on both standing parts. The knack is in the third operation, which is done by raising knuckle of left thumb so that loop will slide forward, at the same time pushing end of left thread under it with right thumb (the two thumbs pointing straight toward each other). This can only be done with thread or soft twine.

This knot never slips, when properly made, but when ropes or cords of different thicknesses are joined with it, *make the eye on the stouter,* as shown in the figure. The weaver's knot is used in making nets, and has a great variety of other applications. When tied to a loop already made, such as the clew of a sail or a loop on a gut leader, the end is passed up through the loop, round the back of it, and under its own part.

DOUBLE BEND (Fig. 106) OR SHEET BEND.—Same as above, except that the end is passed twice around the back of the loop before putting it under its own part. This gives it additional security when one line is thicker than the other. Often

KNOTS, HITCHES, LASHINGS 275

used by fishermen in bending a line on the loop of a gut leader.

CARRICK BEND (Fig. 107).—Used for joining tow ropes together. Holds well, but is easily undone by pushing the loops inward toward each other. Lay the end of one rope *a* over the standing part *b;* put the end of another rope under the bight, over the other behind *a*, under the other at *b*, over at *c*, under its own part, out over the bight, and haul taut. Best of all knots for joining stiff ropes.

LAPPED OVERHAND KNOT (Fig. 108) OR OPENHAND KNOT.—A quick way of joining two lines or strands of gut together, and so used by fishermen to mend a broken cast when in a hurry, although it is not absolutely secure. Lay the two ends together and past each other about three inches; give these a turn over the right forefinger to form a loop; slip this off, and pass the two ends to the left through the loop and draw tight, snipping off the short end close to the knot. Rather clumsy, and more likely to break at the knot than elsewhere.

By passing the ends twice through the loop, as in Fig. 100, a very strong but bulky knot is formed.

WATER KNOT (Fig. 109) OR FISHERMAN'S KNOT.—A favorite knot for uniting strands of gut, in making leaders. (The strands should first be soaked several hours in tepid, soft water to make them soft and pliable.) Make a small overhand knot close to the end of one strand, *a*. Through this thrust the butt of another strand, and, close to the end of it, tie a similar knot around the first strand, *b*. Draw both of these knots pretty tight, and then pull them together by drawing on the two long ends. Tighten the two knots as much as possible, draw them together until they bed themselves in one knot, and snip off the protruding ends.

The water knot may be drawn apart by pulling on the ends *c* and *d*. This is an easy way to insert a dropper fly at any joint, as in Fig. 171.

276 CAMPING AND WOODCRAFT

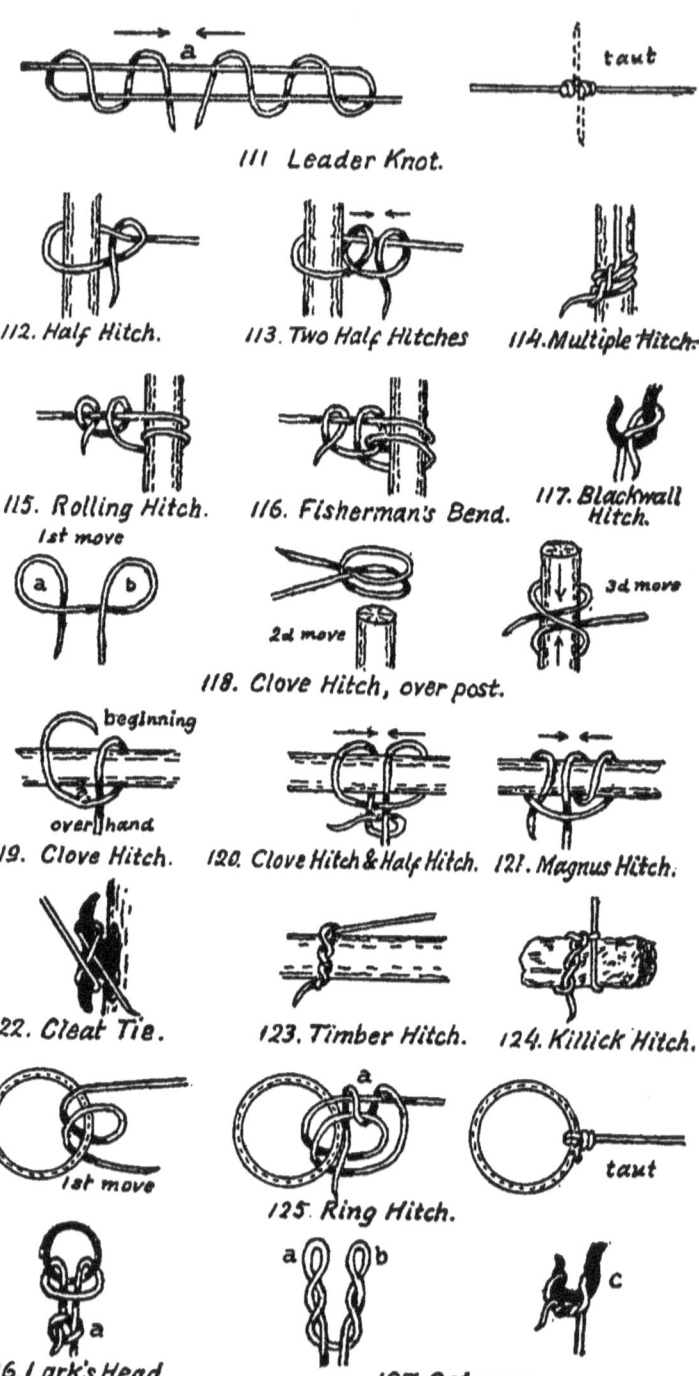

111. Leader Knot.

112. Half Hitch. *113. Two Half Hitches* *114. Multiple Hitch.*

115. Rolling Hitch. 1st move *116. Fisherman's Bend.* *117. Blackwall Hitch.*

118. Clove Hitch, over post.

119. Clove Hitch. *120. Clove Hitch & Half Hitch.* *121. Magnus Hitch.*

122. Cleat Tie. *123. Timber Hitch.* *124. Killick Hitch.*

125. Ring Hitch.

126. Lark's Head. *127. Catspaw.*

KNOTS, HITCHES, LASHINGS 277

For thin gut, especially, the double water knot (Fig. 110) is preferable, as it is stronger and less apt to pull out. It is made like the other, except that the short end is passed twice round the other long part, instead of once, and then through both loops thus formed.

LEADER KNOT (Fig. 111).—In this knot, the ends, when snipped off close, are firmly held in the middle and guarded on each side by two round turns of gut; consequently the leader slips smoothly over or through obstacles. To make it, overlap the ends of the gut, as in Fig. 108, turn one end twice around the other and slip it between the two strands; then, gripping between thumb and finger at *a,* reverse the ends and twist the second part in the same way; shove and humor the knot taut, in direction shown by the arrows, and cut the ends off close.

HITCHES.—A hitch is a twist, or combination of twists, to secure a rope or other line.

HALF HITCH (Fig. 112).—Simply a turning in of the end of a rope.

TWO HALF HITCHES (Fig. 113).—Another turn in the rope forms two half hitches, which, when drawn together, hold securely. This is the quickest and simplest way to make a rope fast to a post or ring. When subjected to heavy strain it is apt to jam so tight as to be hard to undo.

MULTIPLE HITCHES (Fig. 114).—Three or more half hitches bind so tightly on a pole that it can be hung vertically with a heavy weight on the lower end. Also used as an easy and pretty way of "serving" rope, and for covering bottles, jugs, etc., to preserve them from breaking.

ROLLING HITCH (Fig. 115).—The quickest way to make a rope fast when it is under strain, and without letting up the strain in the act of securing it. Take two or three turns around the stake, pole or ring, then make two half hitches round the standing part, and haul taut. There are other and more elaborate rolling hitches. This one is often called a "round turn and two half hitches," or simply a "sailor's knot." It is one of the most useful and easily made knots known.

FISHERMAN'S BEND (Fig. 116) OR ANCHOR BEND.—Take two turns round the object, as above, then make two half hitches, the first of which is *slipped under* both turns. A very secure fastening, but can only be made on a slack line. Chiefly used for bending a rope to a ring or to the shackle of an anchor, or for attaching a line to the bail of a bucket.

BLACKWALL HITCH (Fig. 117).—Simplest of all hitches. Used to attach the end of a rope to a hook, where the strain is steady. The strain on the first turn jams the end between it and the hook.

CLOVE HITCH (Figs. 118-120).—This is one of the simplest and yet most useful fastenings ever invented. It can be made under strain, will not slip on itself nor along the pole, and can easily be cast loose. It has numberless applications, from mooring vessels to setting up staging or reducing a dislocated thumb. Every woodsman should learn to make it in various positions.

To make it on a post, hold the rope in the left hand, give it a twist toward you with the right, and it automatically forms a loop (Fig. 118, *a*); hold this with the finger and thumb, give another twist in the same direction, and a second loop is formed (*b*); now, for the next move, bring *b* under *a*, as in the middle figure, slip them both over the post, shove them tight together, and haul taut. In this way a boat is moored, or a rope fastened to a tent pin, almost as quick as you would bat an eye.

Next learn to make the clove hitch on a long pole or other object that the loops cannot slip over: for instance, a horizontal rail. With rope coming from behind, pass the end forward over the rail, down and around it, back over the rope, up and over as in Fig. 119, and then bring the end out through the opening *a*.

KNOTS, HITCHES, LASHINGS 279

Then tie it in reverse position, end pointing toward you. Observe that, in any case, the end goes round the pole the second time *always in the same direction* as the first, and that the end and the standing part comes out on opposite sides.

Absolutely to prevent slipping, take a half hitch around the standing part (Fig. 120).

All of these illustrations show the hitch before being drawn taut, which is in the direction of the arrows.

A clove hitch may be used to secure a small line to a stout rope. Since this hitch it not apt to slip along a smooth timber, it is used by builders in fitting up scaffolding. Its advantage in setting a dislocated limb is that, while it cannot slip, yet no amount of pulling will tighten it so as to stop the current of blood.

MAGNUS HITCH (Fig. 121).—Another easily made hitch that will not slip along a pole. It can be made with a line that is under strain.

CLEAT TIE (Fig. 122).—A quick fastening for a rope that is under strain. Never use it to make fast the mainsheet of a sailboat (see SLIPPERY HITCH, Fig. 138).

TIMBER HITCH (Fig. 123).—For dragging logs over the ground, or towing them through the water, the timber hitch has even greater gripping power than any of those hitherto mentioned. It cannot be made while there is a strain on the rope.

Pass the end of the rope around the timber, then round the standing part, then twist it two or more turns under and over itself. The pressure of the coils gives remarkable holding power. A timber hitch can be cast off easily. It is not reliable with new rope, and is liable to come adrift if the strain is intermittent.

KILLICK HITCH (Fig. 124).— To secure a stone for a boat anchor, or for lifting similar objects, make a timber hitch, haul taut, and then make a single half hitch alongside it.

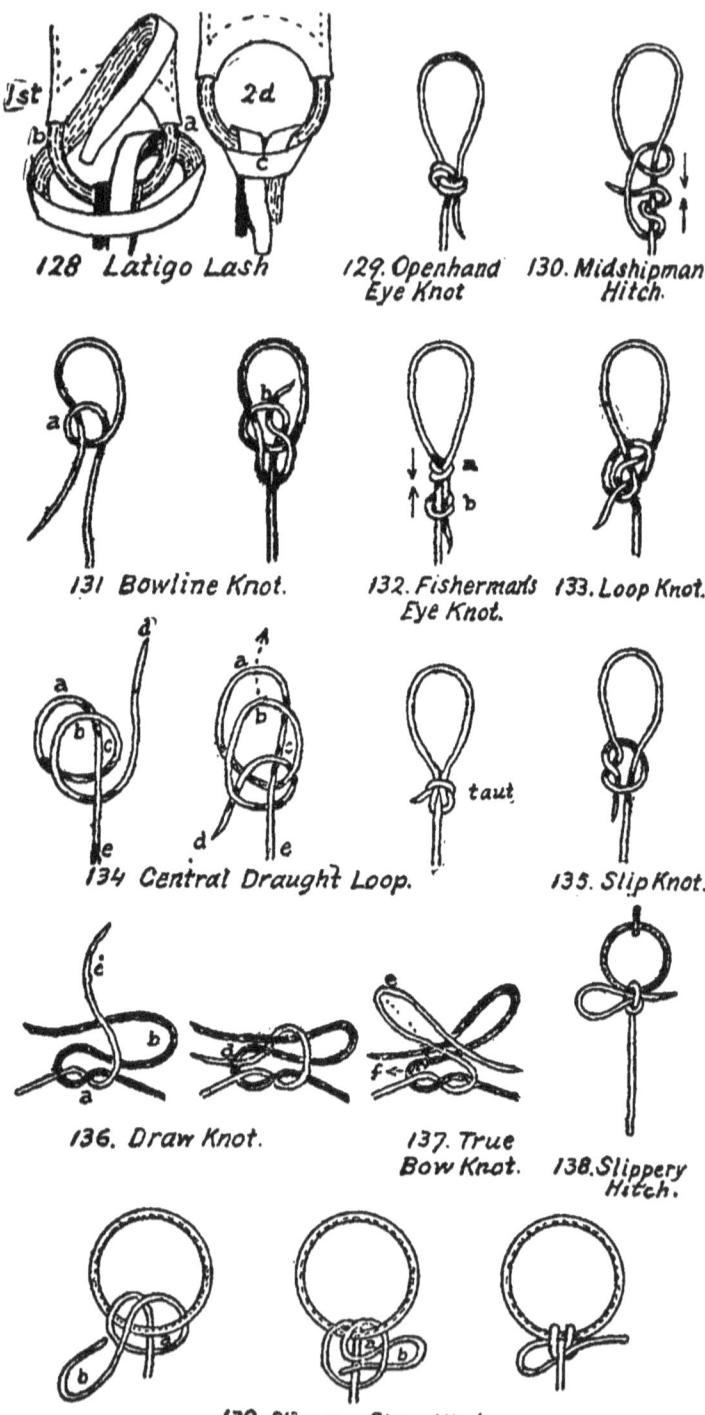

128 Latigo Lash. 129. Openhand Eye Knot. 130. Midshipman's Hitch. 131 Bowline Knot. 132. Fisherman's Eye Knot. 133. Loop Knot. 134 Central Draught Loop. 135. Slip Knot. 136. Draw Knot. 137. True Bow Knot. 138. Slippery Hitch. 139. Slippery Clove Hitch.

KNOTS, HITCHES, LASHINGS 281

For towing slimy and slippery logs the same method is used, except that the half hitch is made a couple of feet in front of the other instead of alongside.

RING HITCH (Fig. 125).—When tying a line or gut to a swivel ring, and for various other purposes, we want to secure attachment that is not clumsy and will not part at the knot. In the ring hitch the end fastening has no tendency to cut the line, and the draught is direct. If used in tying gut to a swivel, pass it twice around the swivel ring as shown in "first move"; pass the end over to the far side, and bring it through the double loop toward you at *a;* pass it over again and bring it through as before, but toward the swivel. See that these two turns are not too loose, and pull tight on the standing part first while still keeping a good strain on the standing part. With tweezers tighten the short end, then snip it off close. Cover the knot with a good blob of celluloid varnish (old photo films soaked in hot water, scrubbed with a stiff nail brush on exposed side, cut in pieces, and dissolved in acetone).

LARK'S HEAD (Fig. 126).—A bight of the rope is passed through the ring, and the ends are then drawn through the bight. To make this tie more secure a half hitch (*a*) may be added.

CATSPAW (Fig. 127).—This is for hitching a rope on to the hook of a block for hoisting. The simplest form is here shown. First you make two bights in a rope, then, with a bight in each hand, take two or three twists from you; bring the two bights side by side, and throw their loops (*a, b*) over the hook (*c*).

LATIGO LASH (Fig. 128).—Used in cinching a saddle, the latigo being the strap by which the girth is lashed to a ring at the other end of the girth. Pass the latigo through the ring from outside to inside; down to ring that holds latigo itself, and through that from inside to outside, and up; through upper ring from outside, passing under and out at the right (*a*). Then bring strap forward horizontally to the left; pass it around back of ring (*b*) and then out through ring to the front, as in first illustration. Now pass end of latigo down through the horizontal loop (*c*). Cinch and pull tight, as in second illustration.

LOOP KNOTS.—These are for forming eyes that will not slip, in the end of a rope or other line, or to make secure fastenings for various purposes.

OPENHAND EYE KNOT (Fig. 129).—Lay the end back along the standing part far enough to make an overhand knot with the doubled line, leaving a loop projecting. Very easy to make, and will not slip, but it does not give a direct pull, and one strand is likely to cut the other; hence a poor way to make, for instance, a loop at the end of a gut leader.

MIDSHIPMAN'S HITCH (Fig. 130).—Practically a loop secured by a magnus hitch. The strain is direct, and the knot easy to make and undo. Often used for attaching a tail-block to a rope.

BOWLINE KNOT (Fig. 131).—Pronounced *bo-lin*. Most important of all loop knots, as it is perfectly dependable, cannot slip, cannot jam, and is easily cast loose. It has innumerable uses.

Form a small bight (*a*) on the standing part, leaving the end long enough for the loop, and bring the end down through the bight; pass the end *under* and around the standing part, back *over* and then *under* the bight (*b*); draw loop snug, and pull on standing part to haul taut.

It is immaterial whether the bight is made to left, as here shown, or to right, provided the end is properly passed. Learn to tie the bowline both overhand and underhand, with loop toward you and with it away from you.

A quick way to tie a bowline around a post, or through a ring, is to pass the end of the rope round the post, then take the standing part of the rope in

KNOTS, HITCHES, LASHINGS 283

your left hand, the post being next to you, and the end of the rope in your *right* hand; lay the end over the standing part and make an overhand knot as if you were going to make a reef knot; then by a twist, capsize the knot so that it becomes a half hitch in the standing part. Now pass the end behind and around the standing part, away from the post, and back *down* through the same half-hitch. Then pull tight.

FISHERMAN'S EYE KNOT (Fig. 132).—A bight is first made, and an overhand knot is tied with the *standing part* around the other as in Fig. 135; the end is now passed round the standing part, and knotted in the same way. Thus there is a running knot *a* followed by a check knot *b,* which, when the loop is hauled on, jam tight against one another. The strain is divided equally between the two knots, and the loop will stand until the line parts. This is one of the best ways to make an eye on a fishing line or gut.

LOOP KNOT (Fig. 133).—Shown in the illustration as formed before drawing taut, which is done by pulling on the end with one hand and on left-hand side of loop with the other. Jams fast, but is not so strong as 131, 132, or 134.

CENTRAL DRAUGHT LOOP (Fig. 134).—Another excellent loop for lines or gut, as it will not give nor cut itself. Make the bight *a,* then *b* over it, and pass the end *d* under the standing part; then thread *d* through the opening *c,* over the standing part, and out between the bights *a* and *b*. Now draw the bight *b* under and *through* the bight *a,* in the direction of the arrow. Haul taut by pulling on *e* and *d.*

SLIP KNOTS.—A plain slip knot or running knot is made by first forming a bight and then tying a common overhand knot with the end around the standing part (Fig. 135). It is a common knot for forming a noose, but inferior to the running bowline (Fig. 140).

284 CAMPING AND WOODCRAFT

140. Running Bowline. *141. Running Noose with Stopper.* *142. Lark Boat Knot.* *143. Sheet Bend with Toggle.*

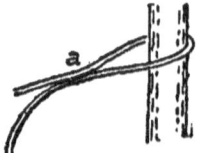 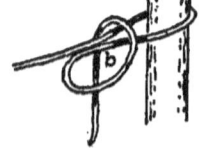 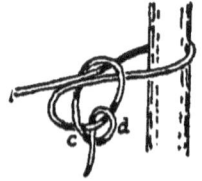

144. Hitching Tie.

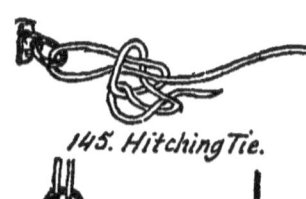 

145. Hitching Tie. *146. Sheepshank.*

 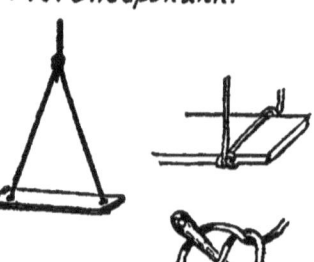

147. Bowline on a Bight. *148. Man Sling.* *149. Boatswain's Chair.* *150. Plank Sling (Marlinspike Hitch).*

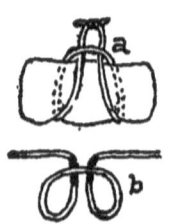  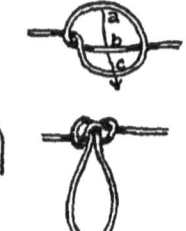
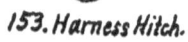

151. Bale Hitch. *152. Pack Sling.* *153. Harness Hitch.*

KNOTS, HITCHES, LASHINGS 285

DRAW KNOT (Fig. 136).—This is tied just like a reef knot, except that after crossing the ends at *a* the right-hand end is bent back on itself to form a loop (*b*); then pass the left-hand end (*c*) *over* the loop, draw it back down *under* it, and out *over* at *d*. Remember the sequence: over, under, over —to reverse it would produce a granny knot.

TRUE BOW KNOT (Fig. 137).—This is the same as the preceding save that both ends are doubled back, and the loop *e* is drawn down under and out over, in the direction of the arrow. This is the way to fasten your shoe laces securely.

SLIPPERY HITCH (Fig. 138).—This is a very common temporary fastening in tying up packages, fastening the painter of a boat to the ring of a pier, etc. A pull at the free end casts off the rope at once. Liable to come undone by accident.

SLIPPERY CLOVE HITCH (Fig. 139).—A very useful hitch for fishermen and others, as it can be employed on a ring, eye knot, plain rope or line, or a pole or post. A ring is here used for illustration. Pass end of line up through the ring, down over it and behind the standing part of line, up over ring again (to the right) leaving an open loop at *a;* bend the end into a bight *b,* pass it back through loop *a,* and draw taut. It holds against direct strain as firmly as a clove hitch, but is freed instantly by a tug at the free end.

RUNNING BOWLINE (Fig. 140). —This is merely a bowline with the main rope passed back through the large loop above *b* in Fig. 131. This forms a slip knot, its superiority to Fig. 135 being that its small loop cannot bind nor jam.

Two ropes may be joined together by making a bowline in the end of one and putting the end of the other through the bight, then forming with it another bowline on its own part—a method often used with heavy ropes or hawsers.

RUNNING NOOSE WITH STOPPER (Fig. 141).— A simple way of picketing a horse with a lariat, though the bowline is better. The noose is made of right size for the horse's neck, and the overhand knot at the end prevents it from drawing tighter. This loop may also be used at the end of a bowstring.

LARK BOAT KNOT (Fig. 142).—A means of mooring a boat whereby the painter can be cast off instantly. A bight of the rope is put through the ring and a stick is thrust through in the manner shown. When the stick is pulled out the painter comes adrift of its own accord.

SHEET BEND WITH TOGGLE (Fig. 143).—Two ropes are joined together by a sheet bend (weaver's knot, Fig. 105), but, instead of drawing them taut against each other, a stick (toggle) is inserted for the same purpose as in a lark boat knot.

HITCHING TIE (Fig. 144).—Commonly used in hitching a horse. Pass the halter strap or rope around the post from left to right; bring it together and hold in the left hand at *a*. With right hand throw the end across, in front of the left hand, thus forming the loop *b*. Now reach with the right hand in through this loop, grasp the part of strap hanging straight down on the far side, and pull enough of it through *b* to form a bight *cd*. and slip end through *cd*. Then draw taut, with the knot turned to the *right* of the post. If the knot were turned to the left, or drawn directly in front of the post, it would not pull tight and would slide down a smooth post.

Another hitching tie is shown in Fig. 145.

SHORTENING ROPES.—If a rope is too long for its purpose there are many ways of shortening it for the time being without cutting. I show only one, a form of sheepshank (Fig. 146) which has two advantages: first, it can be used even where both ends of the rope are fast; second, it is secure by itself, without seizing (whipping the twine). Make a simple running knot, push a bend of the rope

KNOTS, HITCHES, LASHINGS 287

through this loop, and draw the loop tight. The other end of the bend is fastened in a similar manner.

SLINGS.—These are used for a great variety of purposes. They must be absolutely secure, and yet, in many cases, they must be easy to undo.

BOWLINE ON A BIGHT (Fig. 147).—This is made like the common bowline except that the end is left long enough so that after it has passed out through the bight at *b* in Fig. 131 it is continued around the big loop and back around and out through *b* again, so as to double its course. When this is drawn taut you have two loops, instead of one as in the single bowline, and, like it, they cannot slip.

This is *the* sling for hoisting a man, or lowering him down a shaft, over a cliff, or out of a burning building. For this purpose, make one of the loops longer than the other, for him to sit in, while the shorter loop passes under his armpits and across his back, as in Fig. 148. The man grasps the ropes of the long loop, and is safely supported.

The bowline on a bight is also used in slinging casks or barrels, bales, etc. To untie it, draw the bight of the rope up on the standing parts until it is slack enough, then bring the whole of the other parts of the knot up through it.

BOATSWAIN'S CHAIR (Fig. 149).—A comfortable seat for painters or others working on the side of a building or for similar purposes. The rope goes through auger holes in the board and is secured above by a bowline knot.

PLANK SLING (Fig. 150).—Each end of a plank used as a stage is fastened to a rope by making a marlinspike hitch in the rope and running the end of the plank through it in the same way as the marlinspike in the lower figure.

BALE HITCH (Fig. 151).—Bend the middle of the rope over the back of the package as indicated by the dotted lines, bring the ends up over the front of it at *a,* and out under the bend, using the two long ends to hoist or lower by. A parcel can be carried easily by using a short rope in this way and knotting the ends together for a handle, forming an extemporized shawl-strap. In portaging, the two ends are brought forward over the man's shoulders and held in his hands; the pack can be dropped instantly if he should slip or stumble.

This hitch is used in another way to attach an article to a line that has both ends fastened, for example, a sinker to a fishing line. Gather a loop in the line and bend it back on itself, Fig. 151b, slip the sinker through the double loop thus formed, and tighten by hauling on the two ends.

PACK SLING (Fig. 152).—Make a loop a in the middle of a rope, with ends crossed as shown, b, c, and lay the rope on a log or stump. Place the folded pack on the rope. Back up to it and pull the loop a over your head and down under your chin. Pass the ends b, c, up through the loop, cinch them tight, and tie each with a slip knot.

HARNESS HITCH (Fig. 153) OR ARTILLERY KNOT.—Although not a sling, this hitch is introduced here for convenience sake. Enables one to make a loop quickly in a rope or line, the ends of which are already engaged. Derives its names from being the best way to harness men to a rope for towing boats, dragging guns, etc., where horses cannot be employed. The loop is thrown over a man's shoulder so he can exert his full strength. Make a large loop, laying the right end backward over the left. Pick up right side of loop and draw it toward you over the standing part in the position shown in upper diagram. Place the hand under b and grasp the rope at a. Draw a right through, as in lower diagram, and tighten.

Unless care is taken in drawing this knot close it is apt to turn itself in such manner as to slip, even though correctly made. It is best to put the right foot on the right hand part of the rope, or a foot on each side, to prevent slipping; then tighten.

KNOTS, HITCHES, LASHINGS 289

CAN SLING (Fig. 154) OR BUTT SLING.—To improvise a bucket or a paint pot out of a can: pass the end of the cord under the bottom of the can, bring the two parts over it and make with them a loose overhand knot (*b*); draw the two parts down until they come around the upper edge of the can; haul taut, and knot them together over the can (*a*). To sling a barrel or cask, draw the two parts around the swell of the cask, near the middle, and leave two ends free to haul by.

LASHINGS.—I have space to show only a few of the more useful lashings.

PARCEL LASHING (Fig. 155).—Make a bowline knot in end of rope and run the standing part through it, thus forming a running bowline. Pass this loop around one end of the parcel (*a*) and cinch up (*i.e.*, draw taut). Run the line to *b*, and there throw a loop around the other end of the parcel, crossing the rope as at *d* (not *b*). Run the rope on around to the other side and take a turn around the cross rope as at *b* (under, over, over, and under), cinch and do the same at the other cross rope opposite *a*. Bring the rope around the end to *c*, and there hitch it fast by passing end over the cross rope above bowline, under the part running lengthwise, over bowline (cinch up), back over and under itself; then make a similar hitch with it in the reverse direction, and, if extra security is needed, make a third over the first at *b*.

This lashing is easy to cinch up, easy to cast off, and leaves the rope then with no knot in it.

PACKING HITCHES.—The various hitches used in packing on animals, with aparejo, sawbuck saddle, riding saddle, or merely with a piece of rope, are so numerous and require so much description that there is no room for them in this book. See the excellent special treatise by Lieut. C. J. Post on *Horse Packing* (Outing Pub. Co., New York).

BOTTLE CORK TIE (Fig. 156).—Make a com-

290 CAMPING AND WOODCRAFT

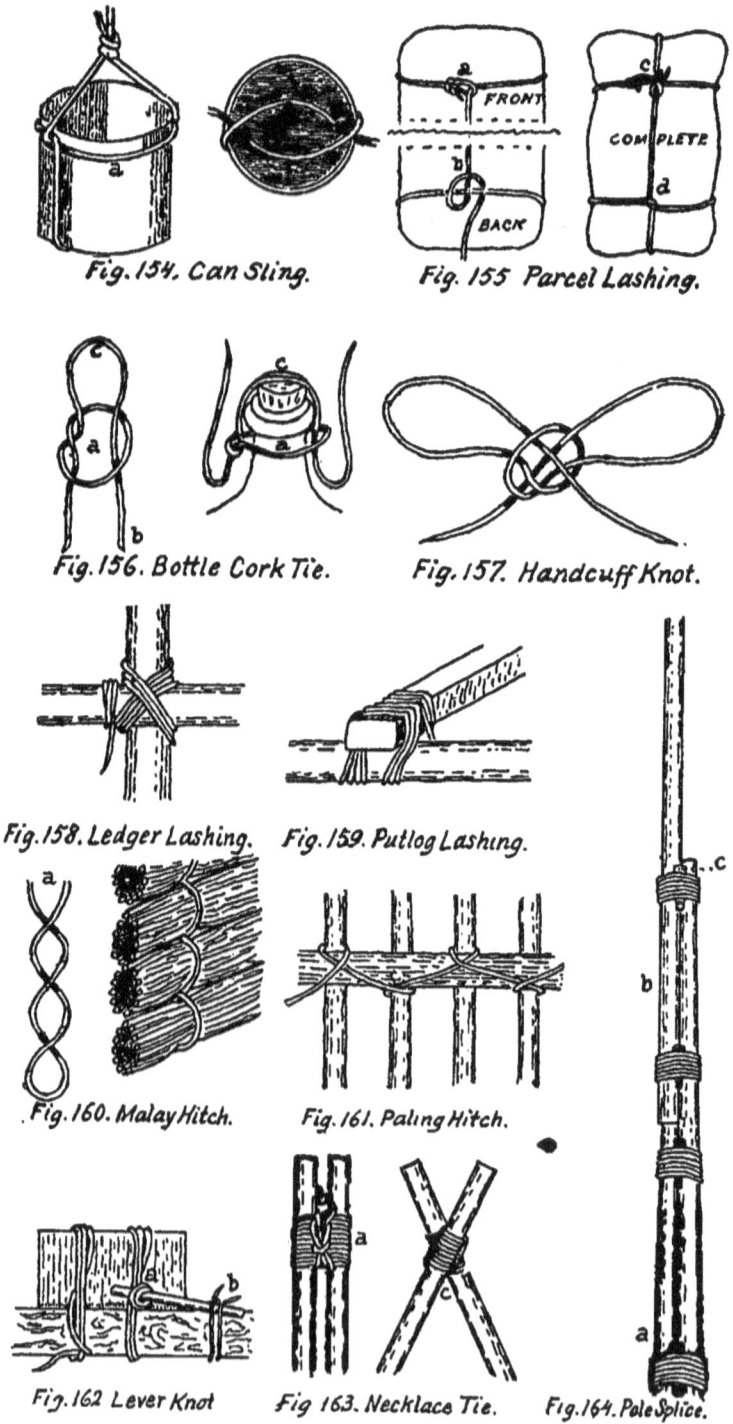

Fig. 154. Can Sling. Fig. 155 Parcel Lashing.

Fig. 156. Bottle Cork Tie. Fig. 157. Handcuff Knot.

Fig. 158. Ledger Lashing. Fig. 159. Putlog Lashing.

Fig. 160. Malay Hitch. Fig. 161. Paling Hitch.

Fig. 162 Lever Knot Fig 163. Necklace Tie. Fig. 164. Pole Splice.

KNOTS, HITCHES, LASHINGS 291

mon slip knot like Fig. 135 (start an overhand knot, *a,* Fig. 156, but instead of drawing the end *b* through, leave it inside *a,* forming the upper loop *c*). Put the lower loop *a* down over the neck of the bottle with *c* over top of cork, draw taut, run the free ends up over the cork and tie them alongside of *c.*

HANDCUFF KNOT (Fig. 157).—Make a slip knot like the first part of Fig. 156, but return the end *b* back through the open knot so as to form a double loop or bow. Slip these loops over a man's wrists, draw taut, tie the lose ends firmly around the central part with a reef knot and you have him secured in a way that would baffle a "handcuff king." A prisoner can be secured even with a piece of fishline by tying his thumbs together behind his back with this knot.

Never fasten a prisoner's single wrist to your own: that would place him on equal terms. If he protests that the cords hurt him, or feigns sickness, "watch well lest you cure him too quickly."

LEDGER LASHING (Fig. 158).— A scaffold ledger or other horizontal stick is lashed to a vertical timber in the way here shown.

PUTLOG LASHING (Fig. 159).—A putlog or other squared timber may be roped to a horizontal pole in the manner illustrated.

MALAY HITCH (Fig. 160).—This is a quick way to fasten together wisps of grass, reeds, etc., for matting, or poles, planks, or other material for siding of temporary quarters. The whole affair can be shaken apart in a few moments leaving no knots in the ropes.

PALING HITCH (Fig. 161).—Used by Indians of the olden time to set up the framework of their houses, rawhide ropes being employed, which were put on wet and shrank very tight in drying. With ropes or vines, it can be used to secure small poles as palings to horizontal ones between posts, in making a tight fence around camp.

LEVER KNOT (Fig. 162).—To secure large pieces of timber together, or to lash articles fast to logs, such as a box to a raft: take two or three turns of rope somewhat loosely round the article and its support, then insert a stiff stick under the coils (*a*) and twist round until all the slack is taken out and the cordage is taut; the end of the lever is then secured with cord (*b*).

A similar appliance may be used as a vice, or to get a powerful grip on a smooth round object, such as a large pipe. The degree of tension is limited only by the strength of the rope and the length of the lever.

NECKLACE TIE (Fig. 163) OR PORTUGUESE KNOT.—Used to hold two timbers or hawsers side by side, and for lashing shear legs. The lashing is passed round and round the two objects to be joined (*a*), only a few turns being taken in the case of shears, then the lashings are brought round across themselves, from opposite directions (*b*) and tied with a reef knot.

When employed as a lashing for shear legs (*e.g.*, supports for the ridge pole of a tent) the crossing of the two legs puts a strain on the knot, holding it in place (*c*), yet there is enough play for the legs to be spread as far apart as desired, since the rope has been wound rather loosely for that purpose.

POLE SPLICE (Fig. 164).—If it is desired to set up a tall pole, and there is no material at hand that is long enough for the purpose, erect as good a pole as you can get, lash a shorter one to its lower part (*a*), resting on the ground, and, above this, butting on the top of the short one, lash another pole (*b*). Tighten the lashings by driving a wedge into each (*c*). The wedges must be rounded on the outer side to avoid cutting the ropes.

To splice a broken pole or the like, bind on a splint and wedge it as above: the splice will be more rigid than if screwed.

WINDING (Fig. 165).—In winding a fishing rod,

KNOTS, HITCHES, LASHINGS 293

or other round object, we wish to leave no knot showing at either end. At the beginning, lay the end of the thread or twine lengthwise of the rod and take four turns around it (*a*) in the direction that the end points. Draw taut, and cut the projecting end off with a sharp knife. Then continue your winding almost as far as you wish it to go. Now make a loop of a bit of waxed thread (*b*), lay it lengthwise of the rod, as you did *a*, and wrap several turns over it. To finish this end, cut off your thread a few inches beyond the last turn, slip it through the end of the projecting loop (*c*), and pull back on *b* until the end of the thread has been drawn out at the point where the wrapping started around the loop; then snip it off close. During the winding, be careful to keep an even tension and the turns snug against each other. This is accomplished by turning the rod itself, instead of winding the thread round and round. It will help if you put the right-hand end of the rod against the far side of some support, so you can draw back on the thread while turning.

Another way is to wind over a needle, instead of a loop of thread, and, when you have gone far enough, pass the free end of your thread through the needle's eye and draw it back.

Either of these is a better way for *long* windings than the common one of laying a loop along the rod the whole length of the wrapping, as you did the end *a*, and drawing it back to finish off, as the loop gives considerable trouble.

In whipping the end of a rope so that the end may not unravel, begin the same as above. When within three or four laps of the finish, make a loop with the twine or yarn, holding the end firmly down with the thumb, wind three or four turns around the loop, then pull it back and cut off the end.

ANGLERS' KNOTS.—I have already described the best ways of joining lines together (Figs. 108-111) and of making loops on the ends of lines or leaders

294 CAMPING AND WOODCRAFT

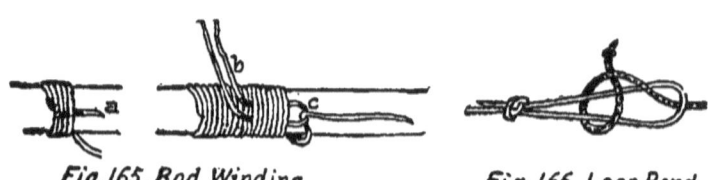

Fig. 165. Rod Winding.   Fig. 166. Loop Bend.

Fig. 167. Eight Bend.   Fig. 168. Jam Hitch.   Fig. 169. Double Hitch.

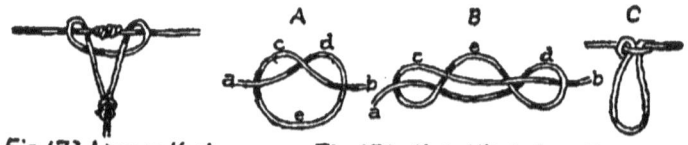

Fig. 170. Tiller Hitch.   Fig. 171. Double Loop.   Fig. 172. Loop to Line.

Fig. 173. Loop on Knot.   Fig. 174. Half Hitch Jam Knot.

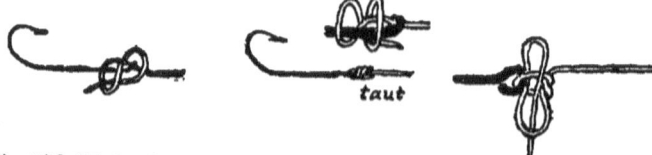

Fig. 175. Common Dropper Loop.   Fig. 176. Jam Knot.

Fig. 177. Turle Knot.

Fig. 178. Eight Knot.   Fig. 179. Reverse Knot.   Fig. 180. Bow Knot.

KNOTS, HITCHES, LASHINGS 295

(Figs. 129-134) Following are special knots for joining lines to loops, loops to loops, for making dropper loops, and for tying on hooks, sinkers, etc.

LOOP BEND (Fig. 166).—The quickest way to attach a line to a leader loop. Knot the end of the line, pass it through the loop, around the outside of it, back under itself, and draw taut, leaving nothing but the knot projecting. Fairly secure, compact, and easy to undo. Sometimes called jam hitch.

EIGHT BEND (Fig. 167).—Same as above but with the line carried back over itself and forward under the first formed loop. Really a figure-of-eight knot. More secure than the plain loop bend, and almost as easy to cast off.

JAM HITCH (Fig. 168).—A neat hitch, and quite safe. To loosen it, shove the loops apart.

DOUBLE HITCH (Fig. 169).—Very secure, and neat. To loosen, push forward on line.

TILLER HITCH (Fig. 170).—A bit clumsy, but reliable, and easiest of all to cast loose, which is done by a tug at *c,* when the line instantly comes adrift. This can be done in the dark.

Holding the leader loop in left hand, catch the main line within two inches of the end by the same finger and thumb, underneath the knot of the leader loop; pass the line across the loop, fetch the loose end up over it, and double it into a lopp, which is now passed into the head of the leader loop, and all drawn taut.

Another way to make this slip knot is first to bend the end of the line into the shape shown in the figure (*a, b, c*) ; now pass the leader loop *down* through *a,* raise it over the loop *b* and drop it down around it to the main line; then draw tight.

DOUBLE LOOP (Fig. 171).—The end of a leader usually is looped, and so is the gut of most flies and snelled hooks. To join these, push the loop of the snell through that of the leader, then the hook through the loop of its snell, and draw tight.

If there is no loop on the fly, the leader may be made with a loop at each end where the dropper fly is to be attached, these loops joined as above, a knot tied in the end of the dropper fly's snell, and this inserted like *a* in the figure, before drawing taut. A looped snell can be used in the same way, gripped in the joint, just below its knot, and with its own loop projecting above. This makes it easy to change flies.

LOOP TO LINE (Fig. 172).—A snelled hook can readily be attached to a line anywhere except at the end, by bending the line into a bight, slipping the loop of the snell over the bight, the hook up through as shown, and drawing tight. A dropper fly can be hitched to a leader that has no loop, in the same way, but the strain may eventually cut the leader.

LOOP OVER KNOT (Fig. 173).—In a similar way a looped snell is hitched over a knot in a leader when the leader has no dropper loop.

A split shot for sinker can be attached to a line or leader in the same way. Close it on a loop of thread just large enough for the shot to pass through, and loop the sinker on the leader just above a knot. The thread being relatively weak, it will break if the sinker gets caught, instead of breaking the gut.

HALF HITCH JAM KNOT (Fig. 174).—To make a dropper loop anywhere on a line or leader, this method may be employed. First make a common half hitch (*A*). Then spread *c* and *d* apart and bring *e* up between them (*B*). Now draw the ends *a* and *b* taut, and a loop is formed (*C*) which stands at right angle to the line or leader. If the dropper loop does not stand straight away from the leader, like this one, it is likely to cause a fine snell to foul in casting.

COMMON DROPPER LOOP (Fig. 175).—The usual way of tying a dropper loop is to bend the end of one strand back against itself (*a*) into the form of a loop, lay it alongside the next strand (*b*) which runs toward the main line, then make a common over-

KNOTS, HITCHES, LASHINGS 297

hand knot at *c* with all of them together. Of course, the gut must be well soaked and soft. Having drawn them tight, take the loop *a* in one hand and the upper end *b* in the other, and pull them strongly apart, so that the loop will point outward nearly at a right angle, instead of lying close along the line.

With light leaders it is better to make the loop of a separate piece of gut, somewhat heavier and stiffer than the main strands, lay it alongside a complete leader and tie as above. It will stand away at the proper angle.

JAM KNOT (Fig. 176).—To attach an eyed fly or hook to gut: Push one end of gut through the eye toward bend of hook; bring it back and make with it a slip knot around the gut, as in the figure, leave this open so it will pass forward over the eye of the hook, which is done by pulling at *a*. Draw tight, and clip off the protruding end.

TURLE KNOT (Fig. 177).—Pass end of gut through eye, and draw hook well up on gut to be out of the way. Make a running loop (*a*) with end of gut; draw the knot (*b*) nearly tight; pass hook through the loop thus made, and bring knot to eye of hook; draw tight by pulling first on *c,* then on *d,* and clip off end. This is particularly a good knot for eyed flies.

FIGURE-OF-EIGHT KNOT FOR HOOKS (Fig. 178). —A secure knot, more easily loosened than the turle knot.

REVERSE KNOT (Fig. 179).—Pass end of gut through eye of hook, take two turns with it around the leader, then stick it backward under the turn nearest the eye, draw taut, and clip off.

SINGLE BOW KNOT (Fig. 180).—Sometimes used for attaching hook to line when it is desired to change quickly.

CHAPTER XVII

TROPHIES.—PELTS, BUCKSKIN AND RAWHIDE

The preparation of game heads, or of entire skins, for subsequent mounting or tanning is not very difficult, even for an amateur, if one goes about it in the right way. A few simple rules may be given at the start:

1. Skin the specimen in such a way that the taxidermist can mount it in lifelike attitude and natural proportions. Make as few incisions as need be, and these in places where the seams will not show.

2. Remove every bit of fat, flesh and cartilage that you can. This is very important, but be careful not to cut through the skin.

3. Dry thoroughly *in the shade;* not in the sun nor before a fire.

4. Furred pelts are dried on stretchers, but specimens to be mounted by a taxidermist must *not* be stretched at all.

5. Pelts are to be dried without salt or other preservative, except under conditions mentioned below. Heads are best dried in the same way, unless the weather is damp, or you are collecting in a warm climate.

Many a fine head has been spoiled by not leaving enough of the neck skin attached to give it a good poise in mounting. Many more are ruined by skimped or boggled work about the eyes, lips, and ears, or by leaving fat on the skin so that it gets "grease-burnt," or by rolling up the skin and leaving it in a warm or moist place until decay sets in.

PELTS, BUCKSKIN, RAWHIDE 299

Remember that the taxidermist or furrier must soak the skin to soften it before he can do anything else with it, and if it has been allowed to decay at all the hair will come out when soaked.

To make a good job of skinning is somewhat tedious, and to make buckskin or tan pelts calls for plenty of elbow-grease. Amateurs are apt to be taken in by humbugs who profess to teach quick and easy ways of doing these things. There is no nostrum nor hocus-pocus that will save you the trouble of good knife work in the field, or of real labor if you do your own tanning.

In skinning out heads, or full pelts, one can do pretty fair work with no other tool than a jackknife with two blades, one of them thin and pointed, the other thicker edged for scraping and for working close to bones. It is best, however, to have two knives. For making incisions and for skinning out the more delicate parts a good instrument is the taxidermist's knife shown in Fig. 181. It has a

Fig. 181.—Taxidermist's knife

thin three-inch blade that takes a keen edge, weighs but two ounces, and costs 35 cents. Then have at hand a jackknife or a small hunting knife for the rougher work. You will need a whetstone, as skinning is hard on knife edges. When slitting a skin, use point of small blade, edge up, so you do not have to cut the hair.

When heads are to be skinned for mounting, one ought to have a pocket tape measure and make notes of actual dimensions on the animal itself. Since trappers and hunters of big game are afield only in cold weather, there is no need of arsenical soap or other chemical preservatives.

300 CAMPING AND WOODCRAFT

SKINNING A HEAD.—Begin at a point over the backbone, close to the shoulder, and run the point of the small knife, just under the skin, down to the throat, then down the other side in the same way (*AB* in Fig. 182). Make these cuts close to the body where the swell of the shoulders and brisket begins, as the skin of the whole neck is needed to mount the trophy true to life. Then from *C* run the knife straight up the back of the neck to *D,* midway between the ears. From *D* make incisions to *EE* at the bases of the two antlers. (If the animal has no antlers or horns, then the cut from *C* to *D* is sufficient.)

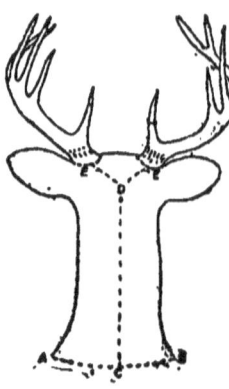

Fig. 182.—Skinning a head

Now begin to peel off the skin, working first from *C* down on each side. Pull away the skin with one hand while you assist with the knife in the other, cutting off the little ligaments as you go, so as to leave no flesh adhering to the skin, taking care not to cut the skin or rupture blood vessels. This kind of work is not to be done by a few heavy strokes, but by many light ones, holding the knife like a pencil. Peel forward to base of ears, and cut these off *close to the skull*. Then take up the V-shaped point between the ears (*D*) and skin off the scalp. Cut and pry the skin away from the base of each antler (*EE*) all around, working carefully and close to the base so as not to haggle edge of skin or leave hairs attached to antlers. It will help here to insert under the skin a small wedge-shaped stick, and pound a little on it.

Just above each eye is a depression in the skull, with no flesh between skin and bone, and the skin adheres tightly. Go slow here, cutting loose the skin to the very bottom of the cavities.

PELTS, BUCKSKIN, RAWHIDE 301

About the eyes you must proceed with great care, for if you cut the eyelids they cannot be repaired so as not to show the fault. Keep the blade close to bony rim of eye socket. Insert a finger into eye as guide, and cut through the membrane over the eye without puncturing the eyeball. Free the corners of the eyelids from the bone by neat work with the knife.

Pull off the skin as far as the nostrils and mouth. Here again you must work slowly and carefully. Sever the cartilage of the nose well back of the opening so the cut will not show from the front when head is mounted. When the lips are reached, cut close to the bone all around.

The skin being free from the skull, now proceed to remove the cartilage from the ears, so the taxidermist can insert metal forms that will preserve the natural contours. Many leave the cartilage in place, in ears, nose, and lips; but if this is done the parts will shrink and shrivel, besides being good prey for insects. Begin at the base of the *back* of the ear, separate the cartilage as far as you can with the knife, then start to turn the ear inside out, peeling as you go. Continue until you reach the point of the ear. Your wedge-shaped stick will come handy here. Having finished the back, then skin down the inside in the same way. Be careful not to cut the skin at the edge. Thus remove each cartilage entire.

Then pare away all the cartilage and flesh from the nose and lips, splitting them open for the purpose. If the head is that of a moose, the cartilage of its "bell" is to be removed.

Go over the entire skin and make sure that all fat and flesh have been removed, so it will keep well and so that when the taxidermist gets it his preservative will penetrate the skin evenly at all parts. Then wash it, inside and out, thoroughly, in cold or lukewarm water, to remove blood and dirt. Bloodstains are hard to remove from any kind of hair or fur, and on some, as the caribou's, they cause a rust that cannot be eradicated. Finally, turn the skin inside out and hang it up in a cool, *shady* place to dry, spreading its folds smoothly apart, not wrinkled, so that air can circulate freely over all parts. *Never* roll a fresh hide up, expecting it to dry that way; it would surely spoil.

A skin dried thus without any preservative at all will soak up better when the taxidermist gets it than if it had been salted. If, however, the weather be damp all the time, you will have to use salt. In this case rub *plenty* of fine salt over every inch of the inner surface of the skin; then roll the skin up and let it lie until morning; do not stretch it nor hang it up by the nose. Next morning examine it carefully for soft spots where the salt has not struck in; shave these down and rub salt into them. Do not use any alum, for it would shrink the skin.

Then immediately hang up the skin in a shady place, well out of reach of dogs and vermin.

Meantime you will have the skull to attend to. Before removing it, make the following measurements and note them down as a guide to the taxidermist:

1. Length from base of skull to where neck joins the body.
2. Girth of neck at throat.
3. Girth at center.
4. Girth around AB where neck joined body.

Turn the head to one side and insert the knife between the base of the skull and the first or atlas vertebra, severing the muscles and tendons; then turn the head in the opposite direction and perform a similar operation there; give a wrench, and the skull is detached. Cut and scrape all flesh, etc., from the skull.

Disarticulate the lower jaw so that you can work better, and clean it. Remove the tongue and eyes. Now get a stiff stick, small enough to enter the hole in the base of the skull, splinter one end by pound-

PELTS, BUCKSKIN, RAWHIDE 303

ing it on a rock, and work this end around inside the skull so as to break up and remove the brain, using water to assist you. Wash out the inside of the skull, and tie the lower jaw in place.

HIDES.—How to remove and care for the entire skins of large animals is described in Vol. I., pp. 270-275. If they are to be used in making buckskin or rawhide, do not salt them.

Skins of bears, cougars, etc., that are to be made up into rugs may be skinned with either the whole head or only the scalp attached—the former if wanted mostly for decorative purposes, but practical minded folk prefer the latter, as these are not so mean to stumble over. If the animal has a large tail, slit the tail skin on the under side, the whole length. The tail bone must be removed in any case.

In skinning a bear slit it along the belly from chin to tail, and up the inside of each leg from toes to the belly slit. Skin out each foot by peeling the skin down and severing each toe just above base of nail. Skin out the ears like those of a deer, and the muzzle the same way if the whole head is to be preserved. The skin, being very fatty, requires careful fleshing. As there probably will be no time for this until the next day, spread the skin out on the ground, rub salt into it, and roll it up for the night, flesh side to flesh side. Next morning fix up a sapling for a "beam," as described under the head of BUCKSKIN, throw the skin over it, rub some cornmeal or ashes on it, and thoroughly scrape off the fat. Then salt the skin again.

To stretch and dry a skin, set up a rectangular frame, well braced, which may be made of saplings lashed or nailed together. Lace the skin to this frame, drawing as taut and evenly all around as you can (Fig. 183). The best way is with a sacking or sail needle and heavy twine. If you must make slits along the edges, from lack of a needle, cut them as small as practicable. Use a separate length of twine or thong on each side, so that all four can be stretched or let out independently. This is far better than to tack the skin up on a door or the side of a barn, as it gives the air free access to both sides. Set the frame in an airy, shady place, out of reach of dogs and "varmints."

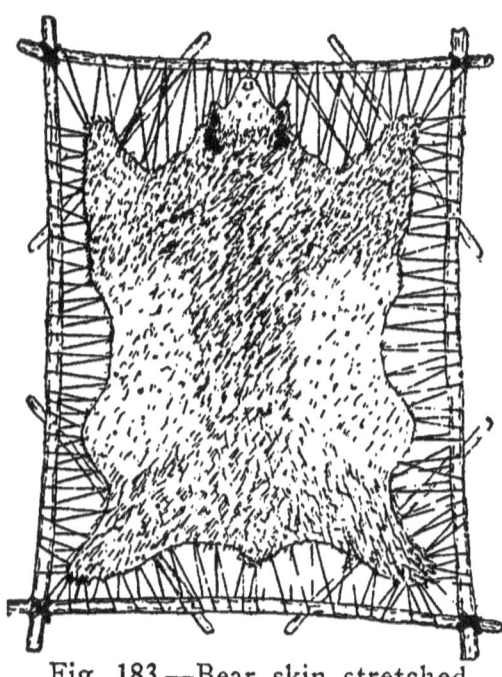

Fig. 183.—Bear skin stretched to dry

Another way to stretch a slit-open skin is to lace it up inside a hoop. Lay the skin out flat. Get a rod of elastic wood long enough to bend into a hoop that will go clear around the outside of the skin, or, if need be, splice two or more rods together for the purpose. Tie the skin to the hoop at opposite sides, then the other way, and so on until all loose parts are taken up and the skin is stretched tight as a drumhead.

The skull of a hornless animal is easily prepared for cleaning by simmering in water over the fire until the flesh begins to get tender (but beware of over-boiling, lest the sutures of the skull open and the teeth come loose); then remove the brain and scrape the skull.

SMALL PELTS.—Animals found frozen in the traps should be thawed out *gradually* before skinning—never by direct heat of the fire.

The wolf, coyote, wolverine, raccoon, and badger are skinned "open" and stretched square like a bear

PELTS, BUCKSKIN, RAWHIDE 305

skin. A beaver skin is slit open from chin to tail, but the legs are stripped out without slitting so that the skin may be stretched to oval form.

The lynx, wildcat, fox, otter, fisher, marten, mink, skunk, muskrat, and oppossum are skinned "cased," without slitting the belly. The skin, being now flesh side out, is dried on a stretcher as described hereafter. The reason for "casing" is that the furrier then can cut the pelt for himself to the best advantage, matching the best parts with those from other pelts, and making up separately the thin-furred or off-color parts.

In skinning a small animal "cased" it may be convenient to hang it up by the hind legs on a wooden gambrel thrust through the heel tendons, or on wire gambrel hooks, suspended by a short cord so that both hands can be used and the animal turned freely; but this is not necessary: if the beast is large, as a wolf or lynx, lay it on its back; if small, hold it on your knees.

Beginning at a hind foot, slit the skin along back of leg to base of tail, cutting carefully around the vent; then similarly along the other leg. If the feet are furred, skin them out with nails attached; if not, run the knife around the ankles. Peel the skin from the hind legs.

Tails of muskrat, beaver, and oppossum, being worthless, are chopped off where the fur ends, before skinning; those of other fur bearers are left on, the bone being completely removed, of course, or the tail would spoil. Cut a green stick about an inch thick and seven or eight inches long. Split it about half its length, work the skin loose from root of tail with finger and thumb until you can slip the split stick over the bone, then, pressing the sides of stick firmly so that the edges cannot slip over the skin, pull *hard* with it toward end of tail while your other hand pulls the body in the opposite direction, thus stripping the tail skin off "as slick as a whistle."

Make a small incision through tip of tail, and, before putting the pelt on a stretcher, run a switch through the tail sheath to open it up and allow the air to pass through it. If the tail sheath were left stuck together it would not cure properly and the fur would slip. This is the best way with mink and other animals that have tails more or less rat-like, and trappers generally practice it even on fox, raccoon, skunk, etc.; but if the animal has a thick, fleshy tail, the skin should rather be slit its entire length, on the under side, and spread flat for curing.

Next strip the skin down over the body. The front legs are easily worked out with the fingers. Sever the feet at the ankles, or skin them out with toes attached, as the case may require. Such skins as mink, marten, fisher, and fox may be slit up the back of the front legs to assure proper drying.

Peel the skin down over the head, using the knife gently. The ears are cut off not too close to the skull, the membranes cut through at the eyes, and the muzzle skinned off with lips and bare nose attached. The cartilage need not be removed, since the animal is not to be mounted.

Now go over the flesh side of the whole pelt and remove all adhering flesh and fat with the knife, but do not scrape thin at any place. Raccoon, skunk, and oppossum skins are fatty, like a bear's, and should be fleshed with particular care.

If the fur is dirty, or has blood spots on it, you must clean it with water and a rag (soap, too, if need be). A wet pelt should be dried by swinging it around in the air, before putting it on the stretcher.

As furs are of no value until freezing weather sets in, there is no need to salt the skins or use any other preservative; just dry them in the shade on stretchers.

Pelts of skunk, mink, etc., can be deodorized most effectively by soaking and washing them in gasoline

PELTS, BUCKSKIN, RAWHIDE

or benzine (away from a fire, of course); then wring out, and hang up in a current of air to dry, before stretching.

A "cased" skin is dried by slipping it over a thin board of proper shape and size so it is stretched tight like a drumhead. Stretchers are of various patterns. For muskrat the stretcher need be no more than a box board about 20 inches long, 5 or 6 inches wide at the base, and 4 or 5 inches at the shoulder, from which it is rounded off to the upper end. Dimensions depend, of course, on the size of the skin. The sides are chamfered so as to be thin along the edges, which are rounded.

To get the approximate size and shape for a stretcher, lay the animal on its back, on a board, and mark around it near the end of the fur. A fox skin will require a ½-inch board; otter, ¾-inch, and long enough so its tail can be spread out flat and tacked at full length. Slip the skin over the stretcher, fur side in, back on one side and belly on the other, and tack at the hind feet, or fasten to notches cut in edge of board. Then push in on each side a thin, narrow strip, or a stick to stretch the skin outward and let air get in. A few tacks at the base will complete the stretching. Then hang in some cool, dry, airy place until dry.

Fig. 184. Pelt stretcher (a, b, wedge) Another form of stretcher is shown in Fig. 184. The board is shaped as above, then a tapered piece is ripped from the center (*ab*), which, after the skin has been slipped on, is pushed forward like a wedge to stretch taut.

BIRD SKINS.—A sportsman may wish to save the skin of a particularly fine bird for mounting, and this can be done, in cool weather, without any preservatives or taxidermist's equipment at all. You are likely to have some absorbent cotton or gauze in your first-aid kit. With this, plug the bird's throat, nostrils, and vent, and wipe off any blood that may have escaped from shot holes. The feathers must be disarranged as little as possible, and must be kept clean.

Lay the bird on its back, head to one side, and bend the wings backward out of the way. Part the feathers from point of breastbone to vent, and make an incision straight from one point to the other, being careful not to cut through the abdominal wall. Lift edge of skin and peel from body until thigh joint is exposed. Sever leg from body. Work thigh gradually out of skin, cut tendons free just above knee, and strip all flesh from bone. Do the same with the other leg. Use cotton or corn meal if blood or juice starts.

Set bird on end, tail up. Bend tail backward, and cut through vent lining, tail muscles, and backbone, being careful not to cut butts of tail feathers, or through skin of back. Work the skin loose from back, sides, and breast, to the wings, turning it inside out as you go. If the bird is large, you can work better if you hang it up by a wire hook and cord, thrusting the hook into pelvis.

Press wings forward strongly to loosen joint muscles, and detach them at shoulder joints. Peel skin off the head. Then gently stretch and push the skin over the swell of skull, inverting it entirely to the beak, pulling out ear linings and working with knife to free eyelids without marring them or puncturing the eyeball. Cut off neck at base of skull, including enough of skull to leave a hole through which brain may be scooped out. If the bird's head is too large to skin in this way, slit the skin from middle of back of head down nearly half the length of neck, and, through this incision, turn and clean the head.

Now remove eyes, brain, tongue, and jaw muscles,

PELTS, BUCKSKIN, RAWHIDE 309

scrape off whatever fat is on the skin, and return skull to its natural position inside the skin. Cut away all meat from leg and wing bones, and from base of tail, but without loosening tail feathers. Turn the skin right side out, smooth the plumage, and fill the cavity loosely with cotton.

BUCKSKIN.—To make good buckskin takes considerable manual labor; otherwise it is not difficult, and one can turn out a good article if he follows closely the directions here given—the regular Indian way, which I myself have used. Whether you make your own or not, it is well to know how real buckskin is made, so you may not be humbugged into buying base imitations.*

Genuine Indian-tanned buckskin is, properly speaking, not tanned at all. Tanned leather has undergone a chemical change, from the tannin or other chemicals used in converting it from the raw hide to leather. Buckskin, on the contrary, is still a raw skin that has been made supple and soft by breaking up the fibers mechanically and has then merely been treated with brains and smoke to preserve its softness. In color and pliability it is somewhat like what is called chamois skin, but it is far stronger and has the singular property that although it shrinks some after wetting and gets stiff in drying, it can easily be made soft as ever by merely rubbing it in the hands.

For some purposes buckskin is superior to any leather. It was used by our frontiersmen, as well

---

*"Much 'buckskin' nowadays comes from a sheep's back. I will give an infallible rule by which to tell genuine buckskin that comes from a deer's back. After the skin is tanned by 'any old process,' you will observe on the flesh side little veins, or channels where they once were. They are spread like the veins on the back of one's hands, only smaller. Where these are found on a hide or skin, you may rest assured it is buckskin off a deer's back."—(Farnham, *Home Manufacture of Furs and Skins*.)

310 CAMPING AND WOODCRAFT

as by the Indians, for moccasins, leggings, hunting shirts, gun covers and numerous other purposes. It is warmer than cloth, pliable as kid, noiseless against bushes, proof against thorns, collects no burs, wears like iron and its soft neutral color renders the wearer inconspicuous amid any surroundings. When of good quality it can be washed like a piece of cloth.

Its only fault is that it is very unpleasant to wear in wet weather; but against this is the consideration that buckskin can be prepared in the wilderness, with no materials save those furnished on the spot by the forest, the stream, and the animal itself. Not even salt is used in its manufacture. Neither tannin, nor any substitute for it, has touched a piece of buckskin; its fibers have been loosened and rendered permanently soft and flexible, its pores have been closed up, but there has been little or no chemical change from the raw state of the skin and consequently it has no tendency to rot.

INDIAN TAN.—Different Indian tribes have different methods of making buckskin, but the essential processes are the same, namely: (1) soaking, (2) depilating and fleshing, (3) stretching and treating with brains, with repeated soaking and drying, (4) smoking. The skin of a deer, for example, is first soaked in water from three to five days, depending upon temperature. Elk or buffalo hides are immersed in a lye of wood ashes and water or rolled up in ashes moistened with warm water. After soaking, the hide is taken to a graining log, which is simply a piece of sapling or small tree about 8 feet long and 6 or 8 inches thick at the butt. The bark is removed from the thick end and the other end is stuck under a root or otherwise fastened in the ground at an angle, leaving the smooth end about waist high, like a tanner's beam. Or, a short log may be used—one that will reach to a man's chin when stood on end; in which case a notch is cut in the butt by which the stick is braced

PELTS, BUCKSKIN, RAWHIDE 311

against the limb of a small tree, with smooth surface facing the operator, and the small end sticking in the ground about two feet from the tree.

A graining knife is now required. It was formerly made of hardwood, of flint, of the sharpened rib or scapula of an animal, or of the attached bones of a deer's foreleg with the front end of the ulna scraped sharp, the latter instrument being used like a spoke-shave. Sometimes a large, strong mussel shell was used. A favorite instrument was an adze or hoe-shaped tool made from the fork of an elk antler. After they could get iron, the squaws made skin-scrapers shaped like a little hoe, the handle being about a foot long. A similar tool for scraping small skins can be bought from dealers in taxidermists' materials. In the backwoods, however, one must commonly use an extemporized instrument. The back of a thin butcher knife does well enough, if filed square across so as to give a scraping edge, and the point of the blade driven into a stick for a handle at that end. Or, one can take a large half-round file or a rasp, grind it to a square edge on each side, draw out the point into a tang, fit a short oval handle crosswise on this end and a common file handle on the regular tang at the other end. A skate blade does very well. In fact, almost anything with a scraping rather than a cutting edge will answer the purpose.

The skin is placed on the graining log with the neck drawn over the upper end of the log about six or eight inches; the operator places a flat stick between the neck and his body, to prevent slipping, and presses his weight against it. If the short notched log is used, the neck is caught between the notch and the limb. The hair and grain (black epidermis) are scraped off by working the knife down the skin the way the hair runs. If the hair is stubborn, a little ashes rubbed into such spots will offer resistance to the knife and will make the grain slip.

The hide is now turned over and fleshed with a sharp knife, by removing all superfluous tissue and working the skin down to an even thickness throughout. This operation must be performed with extreme care or the buckskin will have thick and stiff spots which make it comparatively worthless—a point to be considered in buying buckskin. In olden times, when a squaw wanted to make something particularly nice, she would patiently work down a deerskin until it was almost as thin and pliable as a piece of cotton cloth. After cleaning in this manner the skin is allowed to dry and then is re-soaked over night.

Softening the Skin.—Now comes the job of stretching and softening the hide. There is only one recipe for this: elbow-grease and plenty of it. The skin is pulled, twisted, and worked in every direction until it becomes white and soft, after which the operator rubs into it the brains of the animal, which have been removed by splitting the skull lengthwise half in two. Sometimes the brains are first dissolved in tepid water, being allowed to simmer over a slow fire while the lumps are rolled between the fingers till they form a paste which will dissolve more freely. This solution is then rubbed into the hide on the hair side, which is coarser than the flesh side. The brains act as a sort of dubbing; if there is not likely to be enough for the job, the macerated liver of the animal is added to the brains. Deer brains may be preserved by mixing them with moss so as to make the mass adhere enough to be formed into a cake which is hung by the fire to dry. Such a cake will keep for years. When wanted for dressing a hide, it is dissolved in hot water and the moss is removed.

A skin may be treated by soaking it in the solution, wringing out, drying and re-soaking till it is thoroughly penetrated. After this process the skin must again be pulled, stretched, kneaded, and rubbed, until the fiber is thoroughly loosened and

PELTS, BUCKSKIN, RAWHIDE 313

every part becomes as pliable as chamois skin. If two men are available they saw the hide back and forth over the sharpened edge of a plank or over a taut rope, lariat, or a twisted sinew as thick as one's finger. Large and refractory hides may be softened by stretching them firmly on elevated frames and dancing on them. It is a hard job for one man to soften a large hide, but he can accomplish it by throwing the wet skin over a convenient limb, forming a loop at the other end, passing a stout stick through it, and twisting into a hard knot—leaving it to dry; then he re-soaks it and repeats the operation as often as necessary. The oftener a skin is wet and softened, the more pliable it becomes.

Smoking the Skin.—The final process is smoking, which closes the pores, toughens the skin, gives it the desired color, and insures its drying soft after a wetting. Ordinarily the skin is made its own smoke-house. A small hole is dug in the ground and a smudge started in it. The best smudge is made from "dozed" wood, that is, from wood affected with dry rot until it is spongy; this, when dried, gives out a pale blue smoke without flame. If a particular shade of yellow or brown is desired, some discrimination must be used in selecting the fuel. Above all things, the smudge must not be allowed to break out in flame, for heating would ruin the skin. Several small poles are stuck around the hole and the skin is wrapped around them somewhat like a teepee cover, the edges being sewed or skewered together; it is best, when practicable, to smoke two or more skins at once, so as to have plenty of room around and above the smudge. When two skins of about equal size are ready, a good way to smoke them is to baste their edges together loosely in the form of a bag, the outside of the skins forming the inside of the bag and the after part of the skins forming its bottom, the neck end being left open; to the edges of the open end sew a cloth continuation, leaving it open. Suspend this bag from its bottom to a tree or pole. Bend a small green stick into a hoop and place it within the bottom of the bag; under the mouth of the bag place a pan containing the smouldering wood (the cloth mouth is to prevent the skin from heating). Inspect the inside of the skins from time to time and when they are smoked to a deep yellow or light brown the process is finished; sometimes both sides of the skins are smoked; otherwise, fold the skins with the smoked side within and lay them away for a few days to season. This sets the color, making it permanent. The skins of antelope or any of the deer tribe are treated in the same way. Antelope, deer, moose, and caribou hides make good buckskin, but elk hides are comparatively weak and inferior material.

RAWHIDE.—Rawhide is often useful in camp and is easily prepared. Soak the fresh hide in water, or in a weak lye made by adding wood ashes to water, until the hair will slip. The alkali is not necessary for deerskins. Then remove the hair and stretch the hide with great force on a frame or on the side of a building, extending it in all directions as tightly as possible, so that when it dries it will be as taut as a drumhead. Dry it in the shade. Use no salt or other preservative.

This is all, unless you wish to make the rawhide supple, in which case rub into it thoroughly a mixture of equal parts of neat's foot oil and tallow, and work it thoroughly over the edge of a plank. Butter, lard, or any kind of animal grease will do as a substitute for the above mixture. Viscol, rubbed in, not only softens but waterproofs the skin.

A convenient way of making a stretching frame in the woods is to go where two trees grow at the right distance apart; notch them at the proper height to receive a strong, stiff sapling that has been cut to fit the notches, the deep cut of the latter

PELTS, BUCKSKIN, RAWHIDE

being at the lower side so that no force can pull the pole down; similarly fit another pole into reversed notches just above the ground; cut slits in the edges of the hide and from them stretch thongs or very strong cords to the trees and poles, twisting them up tightly.

Parfleche.—The plains Indians used to make rawhide trunks or boxes which would stand any amount of abuse in packing and travel. These were called by the voyageurs *parfleche*. (Our dictionaries surmise that this is a French adaptation of some Indian word, but it is simply Canadian-French, meaning an arrow-fender, because it was from rawhide that the Indians made their almost impenetrable shields. The word is commonly pronounced by Americans "par-flesh," with the accent on the last syllable.) In making these rawhide receptacles the thickest hides of buffalo bulls were dehaired, cut into the required shapes and stretched on wooden forms to dry; they then retained their shapes and were almost as hard as iron. A hide bucket can be made by cutting off from the rawhide some thin strips for lacing, soaking the skin until it is quite soft, shaping from it a bag, sewing this up with the lace-leather, fitting to it a handle of twisted or plaited hide, then filling the bucket with dry sand or earth and letting it stand till dry.

WHANG LEATHER.—Woodchuck skins are proverbially tough, and are good for whangs or shoestrings. Squirrel skins can be used for thinner ones. An old summer coon's skin is very good for this purpose; wildcat's skin is better; eel skins make the strongest of all whangs.

Whang-leather is prepared just like rawhide, but the thongs are cut out before softening. It is common practice to tan the leather with alum, but this is objectionable for reasons given in the next chapter. Many farmers "tan" small skins for whang-leather by putting them in a tub of soft soap; or dissolve a bar of shaved-up laundry soap in a pail of hot water, let it cool, soak the skin in this solution until you can squeeze water through it, then wring it out, work by hand until dry, and finally smoke like buckskin. But such leather is of inferior strength, as the alkali weakens the fibers; it remains slippery; and it draws dampness till it rots. Plain rawhide, suppled with grease or oil, is stronger than any tanned leather.

Lace-leather is cut of uniform width by the following means. With a pair of compasses (a forked stick with pencil or metal scoring point attached to one leg will serve) draw a circle on a piece of hide; cut out this round piece with a keen knife; make a starting cut of the desired width on the edge of the circular piece of hide. Drive an awl or a slender round nail into a board, and alongside of it, at precisely the width of the lace, stick the knife, edge foremost, and inclining a little to the rear; then lay the round bit of hide in front of the knife, draw the cut strip between the awl and the knife and steadily pull away; the round leather will revolve as the knife cuts its way, and the awl, acting as a guage, will insure a uniform width of lacing. The same method is used in cutting shorter thongs from the side of a skin or piece of leather.

How to splice thongs is shown in Fig. 185. Cut a slit in the end of each, a little longer than width

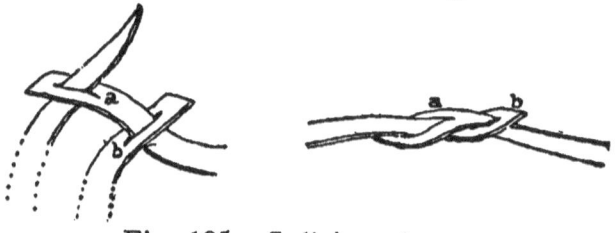

Fig. 185.—Splicing thongs

of thong, slip *b* over *a*, bring end of *b* up through the slit in *a*, and draw tight.

A RIATA.—To make a rawhide riata: select carefully skinned hides that have no false cuts in them. A 30-foot riata will require two large cowhides if it is to be made three-stranded, or four

PELTS, BUCKSKIN, RAWHIDE

small ones if four-stranded. Having removed the hair, stake the hides out on level ground, keeping them well stretched and constantly wetted so as not to harden; keep them pegged out two days. Cut up the hide in the manner of laces, the width of the strip not exceeding one-half inch; wet each strip, when cut, and wrap it around a stick; then fasten the strips to a tree and plait them to a uniform circumference and tightness of twist. Keep the strands and plaited portion wet; a Mexican fills his mouth with water which he squirts over the work and materials. When the rope is finished, stretch it thoroughly, and then grease it. To preserve its pliability, keep it continually greased.

CATGUT.—The catgut of commerce is never made from cats, any more than chamois skin is made from chamois; but it can be made from the intestines of almost any good-sized animal. Thoroughly cleanse the intestine from all impurities, inside and out; this is more easily done while the gut is still warm from the animal. Wash it and then scrape it with a blunt knife to remove slime and grease; then steep it in running water for a day or two, so as to loosen both the inner and outer membranes, which are then removed by scraping. To turn the gut inside out, double back a few inches of one end, invert this, take the bag thus formed between finger and thumb and dip water up into it till the double fold is nearly full, when the weight of the water will cause the gut to become inverted. The fibrous inner membrane is then soaked three or four hours in water to which wood ashes have been added. It is then washed free from lye and can either be split into thin fibers when it has dried or may be twisted into a bowstring or similar cord. To twist it, plant two stout stakes in the ground, a little wider apart than the length of the gut; make a saw-cut in the top of each stake; cut two narrow, flat pieces of wood into the shape of knife-blades, thin enough to enter the saw-cuts, and notch one end of each; firmly lash each end of the gut to one of these notched ends. By alternately twisting these and fixing them in the saw-cuts, to prevent their running back, the gut may be evenly and smoothly twisted like a single-strand cord. Let it dry and then rub it smooth with a woolen rag and a little grease.

MEMBRANES.—Bladders only need cleaning, inflation with air and drying to preserve them. They may then be made pliable by oiling. The paunches of animals, after cleaning, can be expanded with grass until dried. Such receptacles have many uses in wilderness camps, where bottles and cans are unobtainable; for example, to hold bear's oil, wild honey, and other fluid or semi-fluid substances.

SINEW.—A very strong, pliable and durable sewing thread is made from sinew. It splits into even threads, is easy to work with when damp, and, on drying, it shrinks tightly and becomes almost as hard as horn; hence it is better material than any vegetable fiber for certain kinds of sewing, particularly in sewing leather or buckskin, and for binding together any two parts, such as a tool and its handle, where the former has no eye. For bowstrings and heavy sewing, the Indians preferred the sinews of the buffalo or the moose, and then the elk, these being coarse in texture; for finer work they chose those of the deer, antelope, and bighorn. The sinew of the panther or mountain-lion was esteemed as the finest and most durable. The ligaments that extend from the head backwards along each side of the spinal process were preferred to those of the legs.

The aboriginal method of preparing and using sinew is thus described by Isham G. Allen: "The sinew is prepared for use by first removing all adhering flesh with the back of a knife; it is then stretched on a board or lodge-pole and left to dry for an hour or so, preparatory to the separation of the fibers or threads by twisting in the hands. By

PELTS, BUCKSKIN, RAWHIDE 319

the same or similar twisting motion, and by pulling, the fiber can be extended to a reasonable length. [Dried sinews may readily be shredded by wetting, and, if necessary, by gentle hammering.] Cords or small ropes are made by twisting many fibers together between two forked sticks fastened in the ground, and, during the process, rubbing with thin skins of the elk or deer to soften them; the largest cord I have seen made in this manner was one-fourth of an inch in diameter. To prepare it for sewing, the sinew is wet, and, at the needle end, rolled on the knee with the palm of the hand to a fine, hard point, like that of a shoemaker's bristle. As suggested, the sinews are made sufficiently fine for use in fixing the guiding feathers, and fastening the iron or flint heads of arrows, and in wrapping of clubs, etc. Formerly the awl used in sewing was of bone taken from the leg of the eagle; this has been displaced by the common sailor's needle; the overstitch is that most commonly employed in aboriginal sewing."

To join two slippery strands of sinew, lay their ends side by side, as in Fig. 108, and then with this double strand tie a figure-of-eight knot (Fig. 101).

PARCHMENT.—It may sometime happen that one wishes to prepare a sheet of parchment on which to write an important document; this can be done in the wilderness, if one can kill some animal that has a gall-bladder. Make the parchment like ordinary rawhide, from the thin skin of a medium-sized animal, say a fawn or a wildcat. Rub it down with a flat piece of sandstone or pumice-stone. Then get a smooth, water-worn pebble and with it rub every part of one surface. (hair side) of the skin, making it firm and smooth. Then give this a coat of gall diluted with water.

The old-fashioned way of making ox-gall was as follows: take the gall of a newly killed ox and after having allowed it to settle twelve or fifteen hours in a basin, pour the floating liquor off the sediment into a small pan or cup, put the latter in a larger vessel that has a little boiling water in the bottom, and keep up a boiling heat until the liquor is somewhat thick; then spread this substance on a dish and place it before a fire till it becomes nearly dry. In this state it can be kept for years in a pot covered with paper, without undergoing any alteration. To use it, dissolve a piece the size of a pea in a tablespoonful of water. It makes ink or watercolors spread evenly on parchment, paper, or ivory. A coating of it sets lead-pencil or crayon marks so that they cannot be removed. It is also used for taking out spots of grease or oil.

Translucent Parchment.—To make parchment translucent, as for a window: take a raw skin, curried, and dried on a stretcher without any preservative; steep it in an infusion of water, boiled honey, and the white of eggs.

Another method is to soak a thin skin of parchment in a strong lye of wood ashes, often wringing it out, until you find that it is partly transparent; then stretch it on a frame and let it dry. This will be improved and made rain-proof if, after it is dry, you coat it on both sides with a clear mastic varnish, made as directed below.

Unsized paper or a thin skin is made waterproof and translucent by applying lightly to both sides a varnish made by putting ¼ ounce gum mastic in 6 ounces best spirits of turpentine, and shaking it up thoroughly, day by day, until dissolved. The bottle should be kept in a warm place while contents are dissolving.

Or, use equal parts Canada balsam (fir balsam) and turpentine: this dries slowly, but is flexible like map varnish.

Or, dissolve ½ ounce beeswax in ½ pint turpentine.

CHAPTER XVIII

TANNING SKINS—OTHER ANIMAL PRODUCTS

The methods used by regular tanners in making leather are complicated and beyond the resources of men in the woods. Vegetable tanning, with extracts or infusions of bark, etc., requires weeks or even months to complete the process. However, this sort of tanning is adapted mainly to heavy hides. Light skins, such as woodsmen usually handle, are best made into buckskin or else tanned with mineral salts or acids, which are comparatively quick and simple processes.

I will describe a good way to tan a pelt with the fur on. It may also be used to tan naked leather, except that the skin, in that case, is first soaked until the hair will slip and then grained like buckskin, before tanning.

Since one seldom makes a good job of tanning at the first trial, it is best to begin with a skin of little value, and one that is not of a greasy nature— a cat skin, for example, either wild or domestic. The tanning of a furred pelt proceeds in five stages: soaking, fleshing, pickling, washing, and softening:

1. *Soaking.*—A skin fresh from the animal needs no soaking, but one that has been dried must be relaxed before anything further can be done with it. Immerse the skin in running water from one to six hours (depending upon temperature, and thickness of skin), or, if this is not convenient, soak it in salted water, using a good handful of salt to the pailful. Take it out as soon as it is pliable, for

further soaking would loosen the hair or fur. Then flesh and pickle it at once.

2. *Fleshing.*—Even if the inside of a pelt has been well fleshed immediately after skinning, still, after it has dried, it will have a tough, glazed surface that must be cut and scraped away, after soaking, to open the pores so that the tanning liquor can penetrate at every point. Do this on a beam, as directed under BUCKSKIN in Chapter XVII. Thick hides must be shaved down uniformly before tanning.

If the skin is greasy, it will not take the tan. To remove grease, rub hot corn meal or sawdust, over the flesh side, being particular not to get it on the fur, as it might be hard to remove; then scrape well. An easier way is to soak the skin for an hour in gasoline, then hang up and dry before pickling.

3. *Pickling.*—Dissolve one quart of salt in one gallon of hot water. Let this cool, and then slowly pour into it one fluid ounce of commercial sulphuric acid. Do not inhale the fumes. These are the *proportions*: the amount, of course, will depend upon the size of skin and vessel used. The latter must not be of metal, but glass or earthenware, or a wooden pail or tub. Soak the skin in this, turning and working it around, once in a while, to ensure that every part gets the benefit of the tanning liquor. A thin skin will be tanned in about two days; a heavy one may take a week. The lower the temperature the slower the action. It will not hurt the pelt to let it stay in the pickle for months: taxidermists use this formula for preserving skins to be mounted at any future time. No, it does not injure hair or fur, but sets it, and discourages attack by moths and other insects.

If you are in a hurry, a stronger solution can be used: water two quarts, salt one pound, sulphuric acid one ounce, which will tan a light skin in about twenty-four hours; but this is likely to "burn" the

TANNING SKINS

skin unless you soak it thoroughly in an alkaline solution after taking it from the pickle.

4. *Washing.*—In fact, any skin tanned with an acid should be neutralized with alkali so that no free acid is left in it to cause deterioration. First put the skin on a beam and go over the flesh side with a scraper to press out all the surplus liquid that you can. Then soak it an hour or so in a solution of common washing soda (about a handful to a pail of lukewarm water). Rinse in clear water. Many pelts have been spoiled by omitting this part of the program, and thus the acid tanning has gotten in some quarters, a bad name.

5. *Softening.*—After washing the skin, hang it spread out on a line or frame until half dry. Then work it back and forth (flesh side down, of course) over the edge of a plank or a square bar of iron, and pull and stretch it in every direction with the hands, until it is white, dry, and supple all over. The object is to loosen up the fibers everywhere so that they do not shrink, stick together, and dry hard and stiff. An amateur is more likely to fail here than in any other part of the tanning operation; for it is hard work, and he may not stick to it long enough to ensure a good job.

If still there are hard spots on the skin, moisten them with the pickling liquor and keep them so until softened. A good way is to cover such spots with sawdust wet with all the liquor it will take up.

A final finish can be put on by rubbing with sandpaper or pumice stone.

Then rub into the flesh side a mixture of equal parts of tallow and neat's foot oil, or some butter, or lard, or vaseline, or (sparingly) with plain oil or viscol. Do not use a vegetable oil. To remove any surplus, so that the skin may not be left greasy, rub hot corn meal or sawdust over it.

Finally, comb out the fur, and the pelt is ready for making up into a rug or garment.

There are many other ways of "mineral tanning"

but the one here given is less complicated than most of them, as satisfactory as any, and is adapted to any kind of skin, big or little, with or without the hair or fur. Tanning with alum I do not recommend: it shrinks and thickens the skin, hardens it, and makes the fur dull and harsh if any gets on it.

ROBES INDIAN-TANNED.—One may be so situated that he can get none of the ingredients required by the above process, and still he may want to make a robe with the fur on. In such case, do as the Indians did, who had not even salt. A pelt can be "Indian-tanned" as soft as by any chemical process, and will be even stronger and more durable. The only trouble is that it takes more elbow-grease.

The method is similar to that of making buckskin, already described, except that the hide is fleshed without soaking enough to make the fur slip. Then the skin is stretched, the brain water rubbed into the flesh side, this is repeated several times, and then the pelt is suppled by thorough hand work.

One of my earliest recollections is of the cosy warmth and peculiar but not unpleasant scent of buffalo robes, as I lay comfortably under them in the big sled and rode over the shimmering white prairie in a temperature of twenty or thirty below zero. The following description of how those robes were prepared is quoted from Colonel Dodge. We have no more buffaloes to hunt, but we have caribou and reindeer, and the same workmanship can be used on their hides, though a white man would use a beam and fleshing knife instead of the ground and a squaw's adze:

"The skin of even the youngest and fattest cow is, in its natural condition, much too thick for use, being unwieldy and lacking pliability. This thickness must be reduced at least one-half and the skin at the same time made soft and pliable. When the stretched skin has become dry and hard from the action of the sun, the woman goes to work with a small implement shaped somewhat like a carpenter's adze; it has a short handle of wood or elkhorn, tied on with rawhide, and is used with one hand. With this tool the woman chips at the hardened skin, cutting off a thin shaving at every blow. The skill in the whole process consists in so directing and tempering the blows as to cut the skin, yet not cut too deep, and in finally obtaining a uniform thickness and perfectly smooth and even inner surface. To render the skin soft and pliable the chipping is stopped every little while and the chipped surface smeared with brains of buffalo, which are thoroughly rubbed in with a smooth stone. When very great care and delicacy are required the skin is stretched vertically on a frame of poles. It is claimed that the chipping process can be much more perfectly performed on a skin stretched in this way than on one stretched on the uneven and unyielding ground, but the latter is used for all common robes, because it is the easiest. When the thinning and softening process is completed, the robe is taken out of its frame, trimmed, and sometimes smoked. It is now ready for use. This is a long and tedious process and no one but an Indian would go through it."

Sometimes, after the fleshing of the hide was completed, a mixture of boiled brains, marrow grease, and pounded roast liver was thickly spread on the flesh side and allowed to dry in; then the hide was rubbed with fat, dampened with warm water, rolled up and laid away for a day. After this the hide was slowly dried in the sun or very carefully before a fire, being frequently and thoroughly rubbed over a riata while drying.

SNAKE SKINS.—Slit the skin down the center of the under plates from head to tail. Work carefully with a rattlesnake's tail, as the skin from vent to rattle is thin and easily torn. If the skin cannot be tanned at once, rub fine salt into the flesh side, after scraping off foreign matter, roll it up and keep in a cool place. Otherwise apply the tanning pickle already mentioned, and tack the skin out on a board, in the shade, to dry. Afterward it can be softened with a little oil. For a short time after shedding, the skin is thin and tender.

To tan a snake's skin into flexible leather for a belt or similar article, the scales must first be scraped off; then tan, and polish the outer side with a smooth but not hot iron.

FISH SKINS.—If you merely skin a fish, salt the skin or put it up in brine and ship it to a taxidermist, you will finally get from him a mounted *thing*, but it will be a mighty poor reminder of the beauty that you caught. Whoever mounts a fish should have an exact replica of its body to use as a foundation. This can be made on the spot with plaster of Paris in a sand mold, as described in Pray's *Taxidermy* (Outing Handbooks), provided you have the plaster. Since very few anglers will be so equipped, it is best to preserve the fish itself, and ship it to a taxidermist as soon as practicable. Mr. Pray has told, in *Recreation,* how to do this with common preservatives that can be procured in any village:

"To prepare a fish to ship a distance for mounting, remove the entrails and red gills, slitting the belly open along the side to be against the panel when mounted. When the 'innards' are out, peel up the skin toward the back carefully and score the meat deeply lengthwise several times with a sharp knife, being careful not to cut through the skin on the opposite side.

Now rub plenty of borax (use no salt on a fish to be mounted) into the head and belly and the knife cuts in the meat of the back and tail.

Lastly, put a teaspoonful of carbolic acid (as you buy it in the drug store) into a pint of water and wring a cloth out of this solution. Wrap the fish in this, laid out full length. Have enough cloth so that several thicknesses of cloth cover the fish. (If two or more fish are shipped together, wrap each separately in the damp cloth.) Wrap the whole at full length in a piece of thin, cheap oil-cloth, pack carefully in a box and send by either parcel post or express. (Always lay the fish out in approximate pose in relation to each other that you would like in the mount, so that you will open them on opposite sides, that they may hang front to front on the panel.)

Always send fish for mounting in the meat, never skinned, as the *ideal* mounted fish is a cast portrait of itself with the skin skilfully applied over it."

TANNING SKINS

GLUE.—Hoofs and horns are boiled down in water for many hours, until the water thickens, and this is cooled until it sets solid into glue. The oil skimmed from the pot in making glue is known as neat's foot oil, valuable in dressing leather.

To use the glue put the pan containing it into a small pot or pan partly filled with water, and heat this until the glue melts.

1. *Waterproof Glue.*—Soak the glue in water until swollen; then dissolve it by heating in four-fifths its weight of linseed oil.

2. Add some rosin to hot glue, and afterward dilute with turpentine.

3. Dissolve one pound of glue in two quarts of skim milk, by heating.

4. Take a handful of well burned quicklime and mix with it four ounces of linseed oil, rub the ingredients thoroughly together, and then boil until of the consistency of ordinary paste. Spread it on tin plates until it becomes dry and very hard. When required for use, heat it as you would common glue. This is not only waterproof, but also resists heat, and can be used as a lute for vessels.

CEMENTS AND PASTES.— Although these are not all animal products, I insert recipes here while on the subject of adhesives.

5. *Cement for Broken Vessels.*—A powerful cement or lute is made by kneading newly slaked lime (use a paddle) into a dough-like mass with a strong solution of glue, or blood, or white of egg.

6. *Cement for Casks, etc.*—A good cement for stopping leaks in casks, boats, etc., is made of tallow 25 parts, lard 40 parts, sifted wood ashes 25 parts. Mix together by heating, and apply with a knife blade that has just been heated.

7. *Flour Paste that will Keep.*—Make a strong tea of the bark of sassafras root. Mix flour in cold water to a thick paste, and stir into this the hot tea, gradually, until the paste is thin as wanted.

8. *Mucilage Substitute.*—Put a teaspoonful of

sugar in barely enough water to dissolve it, and let it come just to a boil.

WORKING IN HORN.—Horn is easily manipulated after soaking it in boiling water. If time permits, it is best to soak it first for several days in cold water, then boil until soft enough to mold into the desired shape. The horn must be kept free from anything sweaty or oily while being treated.

The western Indians used to make superior bows of buffalo horns, and from those of the mountain sheep, by leaving the horns in hot springs until they were perfectly malleable, then straightening them and cutting them into strips of suitable width. Two buffalo horns were pieced in the center and riveted; then bound strongly at the splice with sinew.

Turtle or tortoise-shell can be worked up in a similar way.

Horn is useful for handles, spoons, cups, and various other items of backwoods equipment. When split, flattened, and scraped, it makes good window panes where glass is unobtainable.

A *Horn Cup* is better than any other for one to carry with him when campaigning. It is lighter

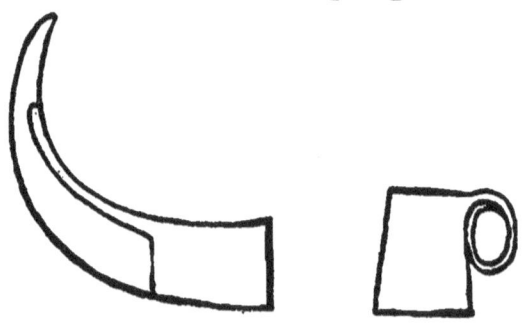

Fig. 186.—Horn cup

than a metal cup, does not dent nor break, and is pleasanter to drink tea or coffee from, as it is less conductive of heat.

To make it: Select the largest ox horn you can find that has a sharp bend in it. The broader

TANNING SKINS

the base the better, so that the cup will not be tall and "tippy." Trim the butt end smooth and even for the bottom of the cup; then, back from this, at a distance equal to the proposed height of the cup, saw through the greater part of the horn, as shown in Fig 186, but leave enough of the top for a handle, the latter strip being about 6 inches long and ¾-inch wide. Scrape the handle gradually down to ⅛-inch thickness at the end. Then soak the handle in a strong boiling solution of lime until it is soft, bend it backward around a stick and bind the end fast to base of handle at top, until it has cooled and hardened; then fit a wooden bottom in it, and tack and lute it in place. A good cement or lute for the purpose is either No. 4 or No. 5, among the recipes given above. Before putting in the bottom, scrape and sandpaper the cup inside and out. The cup can be ornamented with scrimshaw carvings, like some of the revolutionary powder horns you see in museums.

A HUNTSMAN'S HORN.—The following description of how to make a huntsman's horn is condensed from one given a good many years ago by D. M. Morris: Select a cow's horn 14 to 16 inches long, although 12 inches will do. With a limber stick determine how far the hollow extends and saw off the tip about an inch above that point. With a gimlet bore down to the hollow, taking care to hit it fairly. Ream out the hole from ¼ to 5-16-inch diameter. Dress the horn down with a half-round file but do not scrape it. Be careful to get a fair and even surface. To avoid working the horn too thin, press the thumb on doubtful places to see if there is any spring. Work down the neck as much as it will safely bear. A brass ferrule should now be fitted tightly around the neck to prevent the stem of the mouthpiece from splitting it. Now, to polish the horn: take a piece of sandpaper 2 or 3 inches square, and a little finer than the file, in the palm of the right hand; then, grasping the horn with the left hand, twist it around and around from end to end, occasionally rubbing it lengthwise. Continue this process with finer grades of sandpaper till the very finest has been used and complete the polishing with pumice or rotten stone and water. Then get from any dealer in musical instruments an E flat or cornet mouthpiece, fit it perfectly, drive it in tightly and your horn is complete. Or, take the small end of another horn, or the piece sawed off, and with a sharp and round-pointed pocket-knife work out a conical cavity at the large end, and make a hole through the small end for the stem. Work off the outside, shaping it in the form of a cone the sides of which are concaved near the base and convexed toward the stem. This shape will look well, and the top will be thick enough to rest easily against the lips. The hole should be about the size of a rye straw. The shape of the mouthpiece and the size of the hole—provided it be large enough—do not materially affect the horn. The stem of the mouthpiece should be $3/4$ to 1 inch long. If shorter, the sound will be too harsh; if longer, too soft and not far-sounding. Long horns produce flat sounds, shorter ones sharp sounds. A good horn may be heard three to three and a half miles. The best horns have a double curve (crooks in two directions), gradually tapering from butt to tip, highly colored, or with black or dark points. A part of the butt must always be removed, as it is thin and brittle.

Gun Oil.—It is easy to make excellent gun oil from the fat of almost any animal. Never use a vegetable oil on a firearm—it is sure to gum. Rattlesnake oil has more body than almost any other animal oil; but that of woodchucks, squirrels, 'coons, etc., is good. A fine oil can also be made from the fat of the ruffed grouse, or from the marrow of a deer's leg bones. Put the fat on a board and

TANNING SKINS 331

with a sharp knife cut it up fine; then put it out in the hot sunlight, or warm it gently (do not let it get hot) before the fire; now force the oil through a strong cloth bag by squeezing it. To clarify it so that it will never become viscid, put it in a bottle with a charge of shot, or some shavings of lead, and stand the bottle where the sun's rays will strike it. A heavy deposit will fall. Repeat, and you will then have an oil equal to that of watchmakers, but with enough body to stay where it is put, rather than running down into the chamber of the gun so as to leave unprotected spots in the barrel. A large squirrel will yield over an ounce of tried oil, a fat woodchuck nearly a pint, and a bear several gallons—eight gallons of grease have been procured from a big grizzly.

BEAR'S OIL.—Bear's oil, by the way, is better than lard for shortening biscuit and for frying, and, when mixed with sugar and spread on bread, is not a bad substitute for butter and sirup. It is rendered by cooking in a pot hung high over a slow fire, so as not to scorch the fat, which would give off an acrid smell and make the oil less bland. No salt is added; the oil will keep sweet without it, unless in very hot weather (when it should be kept in a cool room, or in a spring, or in a pot sunk in the earth). The Indians, who were very fond of bear's grease, used to preserve it so that it would not turn rancid even when they were traveling in summer, by adding the inner bark of the slippery elm (one drachm to a pound of grease), keeping them heated together for a few minutes, and then straining off. They also used sassafras bark and wild cinnamon for the same purpose. Bear's oil is superior to olive oil for the table, and can be used with impunity by people whose stomachs will not endure pork fat. I happened to be rendering some bear's grease at the time of this writing. The yield was a gallon of oil to ten pounds of fat.

RATTLESNAKE OIL.—Rattlesnake oil is solemnly

regarded by the old-fashioned Pennsylvania Dutch, and by many backwoods folk, as a specific for rheumatism, ringworm, sties, sore eyes generally, and even for hydrophobia! A large fat snake yields from two to two and a half ounces of oil. A piece of muslin is stretched over a glass jar, and the fat, which resembles that of a chicken, is spread on this. The hot summer sun renders it, and the muslin strains it. The Dutch are reported to have a curious way of telling whether the snake has bitten itself and thereby poisoned its fat. They drop a little of the oil into a glass of milk. If the oil floats as a film on top it is good; but if it separates into small beads and the milk gathers in thick white flakes, as though soured, it is a sign that the snake bit itself.

SLUSH LAMPS.—While I am on the subject of animal fats and oils, I may as well say something about extemporized lights for a fixed camp that is far in the wilderness. A slush-lamp is made by taking a tin can, half filling it with sand or earth, sticking in it a thin rod of pine or other inflammable wood, wrapping around this a strip of soft cotton cloth, and filling the can with melted fat which contains no salt. Grease can be freed from salt by boiling it in water. This is a much better arrangement than to use a shallow dish (as I have seen done) or a mussel shell, and letting the end of the immersed wick project over one side, where it will drip grease. But such a light, although it was the best that many of our pioneers had in the olden days, is at best a smoky and stinking affair. The estimation in which it is held by those who have had to use it may be judged from the fact that in English-speaking countries it has universally been known as a "slut," except in the Klondike, where they call it a "bitch."

If more light is wanted than one wick will afford, use a square vessel with a wick at each corner. Make snuffers or tweezers, by bending a

TANNING SKINS

piece of wire, with which to trim the wicks when they smoke.

A rush-light is made by soaking the pith of rushes in melted tallow. When dry, a length of the rush is then placed in a split stick, or any kind of clip, and lighted.

CANDLES.—Wherever deer, elk, or other animals whose fat is tallow, are procurable, there is no excuse but laziness for such vile illumination. Very satisfactory candles can be made by the following process, which is called "dipping." For wicking, use cotton cord loosely unwound, or dry shredded bark. Put your tallow in a kettle with some boiling water. One part of hog's lard to three of tallow may improve the product. A mixture of tallow and beeswax is still better. Scald and skim twice. Lay two poles sidewise and about a foot apart on supports, so that they shall be about as high from the ground as the top of an ordinary chair; cut some sticks about 15 or 18 inches long for candle rods; twist your wicking one way, then double it; slip the loop over the candle rod and twist the other way, making a firm wick; put about six wicks on each rod, a couple of inches apart. Dip a row of wicks into the melted tallow, place the rod across the two long poles, and thus dip each row of wicks in turn. Each will have time to cool and harden between the dips. If allowed to cool too fast they will crack: so work slowly. When the first dipping has hardened, repeat the process, and so on until the candles are of desired thickness. Replenish the tallow as needed, taking it off the fire, of course, for each dip. This is the way our foremothers made candles before they got candle molds.

For a candlestick, split the end of a stick for several inches, then again crosswise; open these segments by pushing a flat, thin stick down each; insert candle, and remove wedges; sharpen the other end of the stick, and jab it into the ground where-ever wanted. Or, put a loop of bark in the cleft end of a stick, the loop projecting at one side. Or, cut the end of a large potato square off, and gouge a hole for the candle in the opposite end. Other makeshifts are to mold clay around butt of candle, with flat base; bore a hole in a block of wood, or drive three nails in it; use a hollow bone; or, if you want a candlestick attached like a bracket to a vertical pole, take a pocket-knife with blade at each end, drive one blade into pole so that knife sticks out at right angle, open the other blade half way, on top, and stick candle on it.

CANDLE LANTERNS.—A very good lantern can be extemporized with a candle and a large tin can, or,

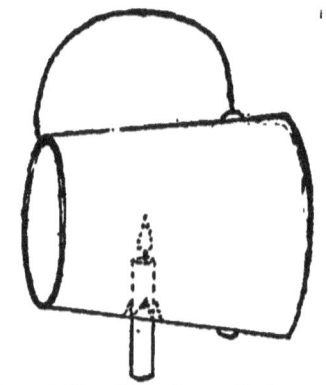

Fig. 187.—Lard pail lantern

better, a 5-lb. lard pail, the latter having the advantage that its flaring sides help to reflect the light. At a point a little beyond the middle of the can or pail make two cuts, crossing each other, through the tin, and bend the triangular points inward so as to grip the candle, when it is shoved up through the hole, and prevent it from slipping back. Then fix a wire bail on top. If a can is used, run the bail wire through a hole in the closed end, on through to the open end, and up into a loop for handle. If a pail, cut the candle hole directly in line with one of the bail ears, detach the bail from this ear, but leave it on the other, and run the free end around and hook it under flange of bottom (Fig. 187). The candle is shoved up only a little

TANNING SKINS. 335

inside the pail, at first, and shoved on farther as it burns down.

TORCHES.—If a dead pine tree can be found, chop off one of the old stubs of limbs, cutting deep into the trunk at the joint so as to get as much of the heavy resinous bulb as you can. Cut a few splinters on the big end of this pine knot, if need be, and light it.

A bark torch is made by peeling several strips of birch bark four or five inches wide, double or fold them several times if the strips are long, and place these bunches in the split end of a stick for handle. Or, take half-inch strips, two feet long or more, from the rough bark of a cedar, bind them together into a faggot with strings of the green inner bark, and set one end afire. It will not make much of a blaze, but will burn for several hours, giving at least enough light to read a compass by.

A good torch is made by winding cotton yarn or rags around a forked stick, in the form of a ball, and soaking in oil or melted tallow.

Southern Indians, when exploring caves, used joints of cane filled with deer's tallow and supplied with wicks.

SOAP MAKING.—Soap can be made wherever there is wood and grease. A rough-and-ready way is to boil wood ashes from the camp-fire in a little soft water (rainwater is best, hard water will not do) and allow them to settle, the clear liquid being decanted off; this can be done from day to day until the required quantity of weak lye has accumulated. Evaporate this by boiling until it is strong enough to float an egg. Then melt down any kind of animal fat (do not have the kettle more than half full), and while it is hot, add it to the boiling lye. Continue boiling and stirring until the mixture is of about the consistency of thick porridge; then pour it into any flat vessel and let it cool. The result is soft soap. To make hard soap, you have merely to stir into the above, as soon as it is poured out, some salt, in the proportion of two or three pints to five gallons of soap. A little powdered rosin added gradually to the melted tallow, before mixing with the lye, will make the soap firmer. Soap can be made without boiling, but it takes longer.

Lye-Running.—Only the ashes of hardwoods are good for lye; those of resinous woods will not mix with the fat in boiling. The woods richest in potash are hickory, sugar maple, ash, beech and buckeye. The poisonous kernels of buckeye are soapy and can be used to cleanse fine fabrics. As lye is often useful to a backwoods tanner, and for other purposes, it may be worth while to put up an ash-hopper at a permanent camp. Take a section of hollow tree, or a barrel with both heads knocked out, or with auger holes bored in bottom. Stand it on a wide board that is elevated high enough for a bucket to stand below it. Cut a Y-shaped groove in the board part way around the bottom of the barrel and out to front of board. Tilt the board a little and fasten it so that the liquor from the barrel will follow the grooved channel to the front of the board and thus trickle into a pail set below it. Now put two or three layers of small round sticks in the bottom of the barrel, laying each course crosswise of the one below, cob-house fashion, and on top of this lay a couple of inches of straw or coarse grass; then put your ashes in the barrel, tamping them down firmly as they are shoveled in; make a funnel-shaped depression in the top and pour a bucket of rainwater into it. It will be from half a day to a day before the leach will run. Thereafter keep some water standing in the depression, adding only when the other water has disappeared. If the ashes have been firmly tamped, the leach will only trickle through, and that is what you want. The first run will be strong enough to cut grease; later runs should be put through twice. Such lye needs no boiling down.

CHAPTER XIX

CAVE EXPLORATION

To those who love the tang of adventure in strange and untrodden places there is no experience, nowadays, that compares with opening up and exploring caverns. To find a mountain that has never been ascended, or a region on the earth's surface that has never been mapped, one must make long journeys and spend a fortune. Caves may be found wherever there are thick beds of permeable limestone with sink-holes on the surface, or other evidence of subterranean water-courses. The descent calls for no costly equipment. It may be made at any season of the year. The trip will take only a day or two. And cave exploration is a sport that yields quick results: the moment you get underground you are face to face with the unknown.

Yes, there may be nothing new under the sun, but under the earth nearly everything is new. It is safe to say that not one per cent of the subterranean passages in our limestone regions have been explored. In Kentucky alone, according to Professor Shaler, there are at least 100,000 miles of caverns that have not filled up. A similar honeycombed formation extends over large parts of Indiana, Illinois, Missouri, Arkansas, and Tennessee. Superb caverns have been found in the Shenandoah Valley of Virginia, in the Black Hills of South Dakota, and in other parts of our country. Very few, even of our best-known caves, have yet been completely explored. There are hundreds, and perhaps thousands, that no man ever has entered. They are sealed or masked from our observation, and yet have left marks by which their existence can be proved.

CAVE "SIGN."—The surface indications of a cavernous region are easy to read. Take the Ozark Plateau, for example. Anyone traveling cross-country from the Missouri River toward Arkansas will notice that the surface rock mostly is limestone and that it is commonly porous or fissured, being easily "eaten" by the elements. Often he will observe what geologists call vermicular limestone, full of little holes like those that earthworms bore in the soil, or like what "sawyers" bore in pine timber. He will cross some fine rivers, generally very clear, but will marvel at the almost total absence of brooks and spring branches; this even in a country that is distinctly mountainous.

In summer one may travel sometimes for a day in the Ozarks without finding running water. He may come to the perfectly dry bed of a water-course that evidently drains a considerable territory, and his driver will tell him that this "dry fork" carries surface water only for a short time after a heavy rainfall. The real drainage stream flows underground.

When a spring is met in this region it is likely to be a large one. A typical "big spring" boils out of a hillside and fills a crater-like basin sixty to a hundred feet in diameter. Its surface is blue as indigo. The water is so clear that, by immersing your face, you can see the white bottom forty or fifty feet below. The outlet is strong enough to turn a mill, and forms at once a creek navigable by canoes. Such are the St. James Spring on the Meramec, the Round or Blue Spring on the Current River, Bryce's Spring on the Niangua, and Mammoth Spring near the Missouri-Arkansas line.

On wide plateaus, where the drainage is not abrupt, our traveler will see numerous funnel-shaped depressions in the fields, into which sur-

CAVE EXPLORATION

face water either disappears quickly after a rain, or collects in ponds, according to whether the vent of the "sink-hole" is open or has been closed. Often one comes to a place where the fields are fairly pock-marked with such holes.

All this tells a plain story. There are few small springs and brooks because the surface rock is so porous or fissured that rain almost immediately seeps through it to underground channels. The sink-holes are simply old cavern chambers with the roofs fallen in. Generally there are deeper chambers or galleries below them, into which the drainage flows if the sieve or tube in the funnel's neck has not been closed by accident or design. The great springs are outlets of subterranean rivers.

Whenever the underground waters have eroded a channel at a lower level than that which drained the original gallery the latter is left dry and forms an extensive cavern that can be opened for exploration. This is provided that the old passages have not filled up again by a process that will be described hereafter.

CAVE DISTRICTS.—Some of the caverns already known in the Ozarks are of noble dimensions. The Marble Cave, forty miles from Marionville, Mo., has been traversed for many miles, and to a depth of 400 feet below the surface. One of its vaulted chambers is 350 feet long, 125 feet wide, and 195 feet high, by actual measurement. Three miles away is the exquisitely beautiful Fairy Cave, which is entered through a sink-hole 100 feet deep. There are said to be over a hundred known caves in Stone County alone.

Crossing the Mississippi into southern Illinois, we find a cavernous limestone belt in comparatively level country. Near Burksville is a cavern that is said to have been explored fourteen miles one way and six miles in the opposite direction, without finding either end. It has a lake, and a river in which there are blind fish.

Southern Indiana has scores of caves that contain eyeless fish and crustaceans, beds of niter, epsom salts, great deposits of alabaster, and Indian relics. In the Wyandot Cave is a domed chamber 1,000 feet in circumference and 185 feet high, from the floor of which rises a pyramid to within 50 feet of the roof. In another vast hall is a symmetrical pillar 40 feet high and 75 feet in periphery, rising from a base that is 300 feet around, the whole mass being solid, homogeneous alabaster as white as snow.

The finest cavern district in the world is about the head waters of the Green River, in Kentucky. Here the limestones have a depth of several hundred feet, and hence are peculiarly favorable for the formation of stupendous caverns. Edmonston County by itself has some five hundred caves, one of which, the Mammoth Cave, is certainly the largest that has yet been discovered on the globe. Within a section of about ten square miles, and a thickness of 300 feet, where this gigantic cavern is centered, there are probably more than 200 miles of galleries large enough to permit the passage of a man. The "Long Route" for visitors in the Mammoth Cave, which is mostly quite smooth and easy, takes eight or nine hours of steady walking at an average pace of two miles an hour. One of the domes is 300 feet high. The Mammoth Dome is about 400 feet in length, 150 feet in width, and from 80 to 250 feet high, according to position.

The cave district of the Shenandoah Valley, in Virginia, differs from those hitherto mentioned in that the rock, instead of lying in horizontal strata, is folded and uptilted. This peculiarity limits the Virginia caverns to moderate dimensions, but affords extraordinary bases for the growth of alabaster "cascades" and other fantastic formations of dripstone. Here are the far-famed Caves of Luray, which contain the most weird and beautiful grottoes in the known world.

How Caves are Formed.—No one should try

CAVE EXPLORATION 341

to explore a cavern until he has learned how these underground passages are formed. To go ignorantly into such places is to lose most of their interesting features and to court disaster.

It is a common error to imagine that our caverns have been caused by earthquakes or by volcanic forces. An earthquake may crack great crevices in the crust of the earth, as at New Madrid, in 1811, and at Charleston, in 1886, but these are very narrow in proportion to their length and depth. It never forms vaulted chambers or smoothly rounded passages.

More numerous are the rifts and chasms left by "faults" in the rock where strata have been folded in the slow shrinkage of mountain-building and then have been pulled apart by a subsidence. These, too, are only narrow fissures, and not caves at all.

A volcano may form a sort of cave with its lava when the fluid mass underneath flows away and leaves an arch of its hardened crust in place. Such action is never found save in volcanic countries.

Hot springs or geysers bore channels of escape from their deep reservoirs to the surface. Where the rock is soluable they may eat out large chambers, but they do not excavate lateral galleries.

There is a class of horizontal caves in the faces of cliffs, very common in the Appalachians and in the Southwest, that are called "rock houses." These always are shallow enough to admit daylight throughout their interiors, and they are dry. Their origin is evident. Where an exposed stratum of very soft rock underlies one of hard and impervious material, on the face of a cliff, the soft stone absorbs water, and when this freezes it is cracked off and disintegrated. The debris is whirled around by the winds and helps to grind out a "room" under the hard ledge that projects like a porch roof overhead. Such places often are used for shelter by man and beast. They are the "robber caves" and "bear dens" of song and story, but true caverns they are not.

Along the sea-coast are many interesting but shallow grottoes that have been pounded out by rocks hurled by the incoming waves, and worn into curious forms by the restless waters themselves. Neither these nor any of the preceding kinds of natural excavations or fissures are extensive enough to rank with the caverns that abound in limestone formations throughout the earth.

Vast subterranean passages and chambers are

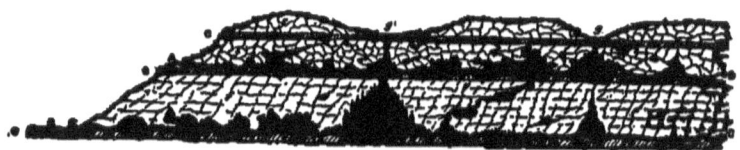

Fig. 188.—Cross section of cavern
A B, upper gallery (ancient); g g, sink-holes; C D, lower gallery (modern); h, stream; A, old mouth of cavern; f f f, limestone; C, present mouth of cavern; e e e, hard rock

formed in limestone by an agency far gentler than any of those mentioned above.

First, there must have been at some time a deciduous forest, shedding, each autumn, a thick layer of leaves. Upon these leaves the rains fall, and their waters absorb from the decaying vegetation charges of carbonic acid (the same gas that is used in soda fountains). This acidulated water, seeping into crevices in the limestone, dissolves out much of the lime and leaves only a shell of the original rock. Thus the cracks in the surface gradually widen and deepen.

When the rainwater reaches an underlying bed of sandstone, or of some other rock that is not easily dissolved by carbonic acid, its downward course is stayed. Then, under pressure from above, it begins eating and cutting a more or less horizontal course along the underground drainage plane. This mining process is hastened by erosion. Whenever there is a crack or fault large enough to admit a considerable rill of water, sand and gravel are car-

CAVE EXPLORATION 343

ried below, which, being whirled about in a vortex, rapidly cut the walls of the cave bed. Nodules of flint, washed out from the honeycombed rock above, lend powerful aid to this grinding and drilling process. Thus in time a large chamber is excavated below the main fissure and an underground river finds its channel to some exit which may be miles away.

When a cave chamber forms near the surface of the ground its arch or vault may gradually weaken until it can no longer sustain the weight overhead. It collapses, leaving a pit strewn with rubbish that was formerly the dome of the cave. Slowly some of this rubbish is pulverized and washed away. The edge of the pit wears smooth and sloping sides are formed, tapering downward to a common center. The result finally is a funnel-shaped cavity in the earth that we call a sink-hole.

ABYSSES.—In some districts, as in the cavernous region of Kentucky, these sink-holes, varying greatly in size, may average a hundred to the square mile. Occasionally one will be found that covers several acres and descends gradually to a hundred feet at its throat. The distance thence downward through a pit or dome to the floor below is usually not great, but in some instances exceeds a hundred, or even two hundred, feet. The Devil's Hole, near Fordland, Mo., is so deep that when large logs are tumbled into it they are never heard to strike bottom; but I have not learned of any trustworthy measuring having been done at this place. It is claimed that the famous Rowan Pit in Yorkshire, England, has been descended vertically six hundred feet without finding bottom. How true this may be I do not know. Strange errors have been made by earnest and sincere men in "measuring" pits and caverns. I will quote a remarkable example from Mr. Hovey:

"Eldon Hole . . . is a famous pit in the Peak of Derbyshire, about which Hobbes wrote in Latin and Cotton in English. The latter thus testifies in verse:

> "'I myself, with half the Peak surrounded,
> Eight hundred, four score and four yards have sounded;
> And though of these four score turned back wet,
> The plummet drew and found no bottom yet!'

"In other words, the poet's measurement found no bottom at the astonishing depth of 2,652 feet! Probably Mr. Cotton let the rope coil on the bottom, mistaking the weight of it for that of the plummet—a mistake actually made by a civil engineer in Kentucky, who reported a pit to be 300 feet deep, which afterward was proved to be but 90 feet. Concerning the Eldon Hole, it is further stated that the Earl of Leicester hired a man to descend, who, after going down 750 feet, was drawn up a raving maniac, and died in eight days. Very likely he imitated the Knight of La Mancha, when in the Spanish cave, who ensconced himself on a convenient shelf, and let the rope dangle as far as it might below, while he dreamed the rest of the adventure. At all events when Mr. Lloyd, a member of the Royal Society, took it in hand to sound the bottom of the Eldon Hole, he found it at the exact depth of 186 feet, and told the story in the Transactions of the Society."

When the roof at both ends of a cavern chamber drops in, leaving the central arch intact, the result is a "natural bridge," such as the noted one in Rockbridge County, Virginia, the lower face of which is 160 feet, and the upper surface 215 feet above the water of Cedar Creek. Larger ones are found in other localities.

When both ends of a cavern gallery or long corridor fall in, and the bridge thus formed is very wide, we have a "natural tunnel." I know of one on a fork of the Current River in Missouri, where the stream pierces a mountain ridge. Near the

CAVE EXPLORATION

Clinch River, in Virginia, a creek flows through a great arch for more than half a mile. In Mammoth Cave there is an arcade 4,000 feet long, 100 feet wide, and 45 feet high. If both ends of this hall should fall in there would be another of these natural tunnels.

Fig. 189.—Map of a part of the Mammoth Cave
(shaded parts are at low level)

At first sight it seems incredible that such vast excavations could be made by chemical action and erosion. And yet there have been greater ones in former caverns that kept on hollowing out the rock until their roofs could no longer stand the strain.

The debris then being disintegrated and washed away, there remain no traces of the old caverns except ravines or valleys that originally were arched over and were wholly underground. The part that minute agencies and gentle but persistent forces play in building up and reshaping the earth is illustrated by the fact that most of the limestone itself is derived from the remains of very small animals that covered the floors of the ancient seas.

STALACTITES AND STALAGMITES.—Caves are obliterated by other means than by collapse. Strangely enough, the very process that hollows out a cavern has a tendency to fill it up again. Everyone who has visited a limestone cave of any consequence has noticed the stalactites hanging from the ceiling and stalagmites rising from the floor directly beneath them. These are formed in the following manner:

The vault of a cave chamber is seldom dry. Water still seeps very slowly through it. Now, when acidulated water pours through a crevice in little rills it has a cutting and eating effect upon the rock. But where there is no perceptible crack, and it seeps through the room and falls drop by drop, each drop remains long enough upon the ceiling to deposit some of its dissolved lime upon the ceiling in the form of a ring. The next drop leaves another layer, and so on. Thus there is built, at first, a slender, delicate tube of soft lime resembling a pipestem. By and by this tube fills up, and it hardens through crystallization. Thereafter it grows thicker and longer from constant deposits by evaporation on the outside, and it forms what we call a stalactite.

Meantime all those drops that did not evaporate wholly on the ceiling leave the rest of their lime at the points where they strike the floor. Thus there grow upward a series of mamillary concretions or stalagmites rising higher and higher toward the long pendants overhead. In time a stalactite and

CAVE EXPLORATION 347

a stalagmite will join, forming a pillar. If the seepage from above exudes chiefly through a long fissure, the dripstone will join along this line into a solid partition. In this way small chambers are formed out of large ones, passages are obstructed, defiles are closed, ceilings and floors grow toward each other, until finally a whole cavern may be closed up by the same process that started its excavation.

Dripstone is the general name given to all deposits made by dripping water, regardless of their forms and composition. Originally it is nothing but soft sulphate or carbonate of lime, with perhaps a trace of iron or other metal soluble in carbonic acid. Gradually it hardens into gypsum or alabaster or calcite, as the case may be. Often its crystalline forms are of great beauty, both in structure and in coloration. The shapes that dripstone assumes in stalactites, in pillars, and on cavern walls, are as varied as those in a kaleidoscope, ranging from delicate filigree to baronial ruins, from boiling springs or cascades of water to imitations of animals or grotesque figures suggesting phantasms of mythology.

The thickness of dripstone is a very uncertain measure of the age of a deposit. Limestone rocks vary in composition and in the solubility of their lime. Underground waters vary in their percentage of carbonic acid, from weak solutions to those that effervesce and have an acid taste. The rate of seepage varies. So a stalagmite may grow at the rate of nearly an inch a year, for a time, and afterward less than that in ten or twenty or fifty years.

How to Explore.—Before trying to explore a cavern it is advisable to study the topography of the surrounding country. Note where the main stream of the district lies. Its level determines how deep the cave can possibly go. The thickness of the limestone bed above that level shows the maximum possible altitude of the cave chambers.

Most of the caves that have been explored are entered through a passage into a hillside. Such an opening usually indicates that this was once the drainage outlet of the cave. If no water be running out of it now, the underground stream must have worked a way down through the original cave bed and opened a new gallery below.

A novice should first gain some experience in company with a guide, in some cave that is easily entered. Everybody is nervous on his first expedition underground, unless the course is well known to companions who have been there before. A cavern is the worst of all places to get "rattled" in. When you do start exploring on your own account, take it gradually, until you can bore into the unknown as coolly as you would bite off the end of a cigar.

When a new cave is to be entered, do not go with a large party. They will confuse each other with their reverberating babble, discussions as to the best route will arise, and the larger the party the greater the chance that someone will flunk. Three is a good number: then there are two men to help one who may have got into difficulties.

OUTFIT.—The importance of thoroughly dependable lights is paramount. Big, clumsy lanterns should not be taken; they are always a nuisance when one is climbing or crawling. The best light for cave exploration that I know of is an acetylene lantern with small bail, shaped like a conductor's lantern, giving a 20-candle-power light for five to six hours on three ounces of carbide. It spreads light all around, instead of merely throwing a beam in one direction like a bull's-eye lantern. If one such light is in the party the others may be small acetylene bull's-eye lamps. The best of these has a sparking attachment that lights without matches (but don't leave out the matches), and is fitted with folding handles on the side. The hook and spring attachment used on miners' lamps may

CAVE EXPLORATION 349

be substituted, but personally I do not like it so well.

Spare carbide to last at least twelve hours should be carried by each man, in air-tight tins specially made for the purpose; and everybody should have a canteen of water, both for the lamp and for his own use, as there is no certainty of finding any in an unexplored cave.

See that the lanterns are in perfect working order. If previously used a good deal, they should be refitted with fresh felt packing, as the old packing may be clogged with carbide dust.

Besides his lantern, every member of the party should carry one or two good hard candles. There is no telling when an accident may happen to a lantern; it may balk, may be crushed, or may be dropped into a pit. The candle is also needed when recharging the lantern.

Matches should be waterproofed, either by dipping in melted paraffin, or in collodion, or in shellac varnish thinned with alcohol. An emergency supply of matches not to be used except when there are no others, should be carried in a waterproof box with cover fitted so it cannot drop off. This match-box ought to have a small swivel or eye attached so it can be fastened to one's belt by a key chain. Then it will stay with you to the death. Inside this box, with the matches, stow a little strip of emery cloth, folded, to strike a match on when you and all your surroundings are sopping wet.

A compass may be useful if the general course of the cave is fairly straight, but in the labyrinths that most caves are contorted into it is of little or no avail. Neither is a pedometer. A pocket aneroid may be useful to indicate one's depth from the surface, but it is by no means necessary.

Wear old clothes, of course. Everything should be of wool, except that the coat should be of conventional hunter's pattern, khaki or duxbak, with plenty of pockets. Such a coat carries all the impedimenta except the lantern, and keeps them stored away where they will not flop nor stick out to impede one's progress in climbing or in squeezing through narrows. Wear the flaps closed at all times.

The hat should be soft and with narrow brim. Gloves are useful to keep the hands from being lacerated. Shoes should be studded with cone-headed Hungarian nails (*not* calks nor broad hobnails) around the *edges* of heels and soles, including the arch of the foot. This makes them cling better to the rocks. Too many nails defeat the purpose, for they will not "bite" well. Hard steel calks are slippery on rocks.

Waterproofs are an utter nuisance in cave hunting. The wetting you may get will do you no harm at all in the cave air, which is always of uniform temperature. Do not wear a lot of bunchy clothing from dread of cold. You will be exercising all the time in the most exhilarating air you ever breathed. Go slow in entering and emerging from the cave; then there will be no risk of a chill.

Take for granted that the cave will prove to be a labyrinth of three dimensions, far more puzzling than anything you have ever encountered on earth. It may not be so; but most caverns are. There is only one absolutely safe way to explore an unknown cave, so far as not getting lost is concerned, and that is for each member of the party to carry plenty of common white twine, and take his turn as file closer in paying out this twine as he advances. In some places you can buy cord put up in tubes that unreels itself without danger of tangling. Where the going is good there may be no need for the twine; but don't neglect this simple precaution in all parts of the cave where there may be the least doubt of the route back again.

Someone should carry a strong cord for lowering a lantern into pits or gulfs.

In the game pocket of your coat stow a lunch and an emergency ration, along with the small canteen

CAVE EXPLORATION

of water. Somebody should carry a cup, as you may have to catch drip-water. Let another man bear a cold-chisel and a small hammer for collecting specimens, marking passages, and cutting nicks for handhold and foothold. If there is any likelihood of descending into a lower gallery, take about fifty feet of Alpine rope (to be had of some camp outfitters).

Large cavern chambers cannot be illuminated with lanterns. So go provided with strips of magnesium ribbon. Do not try to use this ribbon as a substitute for flash-powder in photographing: it will show the most freakish bolts of lightning in your pictures. Satisfactory interiors, in caves, can only be taken with a wide-angle lens, as the range is nearly always short.

CAVE MEASUREMENTS.—In estimating distances beware of "cave miles." It is almost impossible to keep from overestimating distances in labyrinths underground, unless one trails a cord behind him wherever he goes. A cave mile, when tried by tape-line, generally proves to be only a few hundred yards long. Heights, depths, and widths are also very deceptive by lantern light.

It may be asked, How are heights of cavern domes measured? They used to be "measured" by timing the flight of rockets made for the purpose, but such expedients were very inaccurate. The only easy and reliable way that I know of is by sending up toy balloons with cord attached. There are no draughts in the interior of caves, and this method can be depended on, no matter how high the vault may be.

DESCENDING INTO ABYSSES.—Do not be afraid of fire-damp, unless you are going down a sink-hole that may have been sealed at the bottom. The air of a true cave is purer and more invigorating than any to be breathed on earth. One can work with less fatigue in a cave than in the open air.

The chance of finding caverns that no one else has explored is now limited, in our country, mostly to those that can be entered by descending sink-holes. This is work that calls for deliberate preparation and cool heads. After effecting an opening in the bottom of the "sink," if it has been closed, erect a strong frame over the opening to hold a hoisting-tackle, and use a rope which has been stretched enough to insure that it will not spin round when a weight is suspended from it. This rig is better than a windlass, if for no other reason than that the explorer has more confidence that it will not let fly and drop him. For short descents it is sufficient to fasten the rope around the left ankle of the adventurer and then make a stirrup-loop for his foot. Generally it is better to rig a boatswain's chair to sit in (Fig. 149). This is simply a board seat with an auger-hole at each end·through which a slack rope is roved and the ends knotted, after which the hoisting rope is made fast to the middle of the slack at a convenient height.

Before a man starts down he fastens a signal cord to his waist, which is then passed to one side of the opening, where it cannot become entangled with the hoisting rope, and is managed there by somebody who has no other duty to distract him. One jerk on this cord means *stop,* two, *lower,* three *hoist.* Such an appliance is absolutely necessary in deep holes, unless some sort of telephone is substituted. There should be three trusty men for the main rope and one for the signal-cord. The explorer should have a staff to help him swing clear of impediments, and it must be tied to him by a lanyard.

Before the descent is made all loose stones should be removed from around the mouth of the pit, for a pebble falling from a considerable height may stun or kill a man. A ball of something like cotton waste, saturated with oil, should be ignited and dropped into the pit before descending, to guard against accident from fire-damp.

WHAT IS FOUND IN CAVES.—The chief commercial product of caves, up to date, is the so-called "Mexican Onyx," which is a fine-grained, translucent, and beautifully colored variety of dripstone. Occasionally the "cave pearls" found in shallow pools, where they have been polished by attrition, have been set as gems. In olden times nearly all the niter used by our forefathers in making gunpowder was procured from caverns. Guano, ochre, and the sulphates of soda and of magnesia are found in caves. The chance of discovering mineral veins is lessened by the incrustation of dripstone that coats the walls; there is no "bloom" to attract the eye.

The animal life of caverns is peculiar. It includes transparent fish, white crayfish, cave lizards, white mice and rats, cave crickets, and minor species —all blind, and some of them quite eyeless—besides the usual colonies of bats. Snakes are never met inside of caverns, but sometimes may be encountered in sink-holes, or in the "rock-houses" previously mentioned.

Digging in the floors of caves for relics of prehistoric man has long been a favorite branch of science in Europe, but comparatively little of this work has been done in America. Sometimes human skeletons of our own era are found encased in the dripstone, as at Luray, at Mammoth Cave, in the Adelsberg, and in the Cave of Melidoni, where the remains of three hundred Cretans, who were smoked to death by the Turks in 1822, are gradually disappearing in a stony shroud.

CHAPTER XX

BEE HUNTING

The craft of the bee hunter, although based upon some curious woods lore, is not hard to acquire under proper tutelage. The theory is simple enough. First capture a few wild bees and let them fill up on honey or other bait that has been brought along for the purpose; then liberate them, follow in the direction of their flight as far as you are sure of it, capture and send out more guides, and so on until the tree is reached. In practice, successful bee hunters resort to some shrewd arts unknown in any other branch of wildcraft.

A backwoodsman's way of "lining" bees, when he merely chances upon them, not prepared for regular bee hunting, is to capture one of the insects and fasten to it, or stick into it, a small, downy feather, a bit of straw or thistle-down, or some other light thing by which he can distinguish the insect in its flight; then he liberates it, and follows it as far as he can by sight. The bee, bothered by its strange incumbrance, and finding that it cannot rid itself of the thing by its own exertions, goes home for help. Then the hunter, having secured a few more bees, follows the line of flight as far as he can, sets free another marked bee, and thus proceeds until he either finds the hive or at least gets a clear notion of its whereabouts. Then he, too, goes home, and prepares for bee robbing in earnest.

That sort of thing is accidental. But a regular bee hunter does not depend upon luck at any stage of the game. He goes out looking for bees, and for bees only. He knows where to look, where not to

BEE HUNTING

look, and what to do when he finds the bees, all according to the season of the year and the lay of the land.

SPRING.—The easiest time to find a bee-tree is early in the spring, or late in the fall, because then there is no nectar for the bees and they will take kindly to bait; also, because then there are no leaves on the trees to interfere with the hunter's vision. Of course, it is poor policy to rob a beehive in spring, for what honey is left will be old, dark colored, and not so well flavored as new honey; but this is a good time to mark the bee-tree for future attack. The methods for spring and summer hunting are different; so I will describe them in sequence.

In the first warm days of spring, while there still is snow on the ground, a hive may sometimes be located by listening for the humming of the bees in their cleansing flight, and by looking for dead bees on the snow, under likely looking trees, where they have been dropped by workers in cleaning the hive. But, as a rule, it will be necessary to find where the bees are collecting early sweets, or, in default of this, to lure them to bait specially prepared for the purpose.

As soon as the sap of the sugar maple begins to rise, which may be as early as the middle of February if the season is forward, but commonly is later, the bee hunter goes among the maples and birches. Wherever a gash or bruise in the bark lets the sap ooze out, or "bleed," as he calls it, he may find bees at work. The sap flows best on a warm day following a freezing night. A regular bee hunter will purposely wound a number of trees in different localities, in anticipation of this.

Early in March he looks for skunk-cabbage, which, by the way, is not the only malodorous thing that bees frequent at this season. Toward the middle or end of March the willow catkins attract a buzzing throng. In April the beech and some of the maples are in bloom and fragrant with sweets.

Then come the columbine and dicentra (Dutchman's breeches), from which the honey bee gathers pollen only, for its tongue is too short to reach the nectar as the bumblebee's does.

BAITING.—If such scouting trips fail, the hunter will resort to lures. A backwoodsman who has neither honey, nor sirup, nor sugar, with which to prepare bee-bait, will steep corn-cobs for a couple of days in what, by way of euphemism, he calls "sour-bait," or in strong brine scented with anise or bergamot. These he places on stumps in his fields, where the bees are pretty sure to take them for treasure-trove. A surer way to attract them is by roasting honyecomb or beeswax. For this purpose a piece of tin or a flat stone is heated in the fire, and the comb or wax, moistened with water, is placed on it. The chief objection to this method is that it is bothersome to carry the hot rock or tin from place to place.

Bees are fond of certain essential oils, such as oil of anise and oil of bergamot, which, either singly or in combination, may be used as a lure by adding a few drops to a vial of sugar-water. This may be done at any season. Some bee men prefer to take flowers of the particular plant or tree that the bees are favoring at a given time, pack them well down in a wide-mouthed jar, add just enough diluted alcohol (25%) to cover, and let stand a few days. In this way you can make your own essences of buckwheat, goldenrod, clover, etc., with which to dope your sugar-water. The latter is a thin sirup made by dissolving granulated sugar in three times its bulk of water, or clear honey thinned with an equal bulk of warm water, or a mixture of sugar and honey in water. A 4-ounce vial of it is plenty.

The reason why ordinary thick honey will not do so well as the diluted mixture is this: You will wish to judge, from the time of the bees' flight, how far away the bee-tree is. Their time of absence when carrying nectar is pretty accurately

BEE HUNTING

known, for different distances. But honey is much thicker, heavier, and more sticky than the nectar that bees gather from flowers, the latter being little more than sweetened water plus aroma. Consequently it takes the bees longer to fill up on honey, they stagger with it in their flight, and it takes longer to discharge their cargo.

So the hunter will set out a bait of, say, diluted honey to which a drop of oil of anise has been added. Bees will smell such an enticing odor for a mile or more. In any case, the object is first to capture some wild bees as guides. The way to manage them after they are caught is to be described later.

NECTAR.—Early sweets are gathered by bees from the bloom of all kinds of fruit-bearing trees and plants, from violets, hepaticas, and other flowers. In May the busy insects forage on the clematis, dandelion, honey locust, tulip or "yellow poplar." The locust bears nectar only at intervals of several years, but the big blossoms of the tulip tree are commonly rich in it—so rich that sometimes the nectar can be dipped out with a spoon—as well as in pollen, which is a necessity to the bee. That unhappily imported weed among our trees, the ailanthus or "tree of heaven," is another favorite of the bees, despite its ill-smelling blossoms.

Through the summer months there is almost a surfeit of sweets for the honey-maker: boneset, borage, bugloss, white clover, coralberry, figwort, goldenrod, milkweed, motherwort, mustard, rape, sage, Spanish needle, spider-flower, sumac, sunflower, teasel, willow-herb—a legion of others—and, favored of all in forested regions, the cream-colored blossoms of the linden or basswood.

The West has a famous nectar-bearer called the Rocky Mountain bee-plant. In the South, the bees of the lowlands use the cotton plants; those of the mountains, where there is a bewildering variety of "honey-bloom," seek by preference the linden and the delightfully aromatic blossoms of the sourwood.

As summer wanes, the bees turn to the asters, catnip, fireweed, fleabane, heartsease, and other late-blooming plants. Wherever there is a buckwheat field they will be found in their glory. Later they work in the turnip patches. Some of the many species of goldenrod yield nectar until well on in October.

OUTFIT.—The equipment for bee hunting is very simple. You will need a small box or two, same thinned honey or sugar-water (scented or not as you choose), a few pinches of flour in a little box or bag (or, preferably, a small tube of artist's white paint and a camel's-hair brush). A watch, compass, and perhaps an opera glass, should be taken along, particularly if you are an amateur; and do not omit a lunch, for you are likely to be out all day.

As for boxes, a couple of half-pound candy boxes will do; but it is better to make a special one for the purpose. This is merely a light wooden box about four inches cube, without top or bottom, but with a glass slide at the top working in saw-cuts in the sides. About an inch below these saw-cuts, and parallel with them, are narrow strips to support a little feeding tray, which is about an inch and a half wide, just long enough to fit inside the box, and of such height that its top will come within a half inch of the glass slide. Do not use an old cigar box for material, since bees, like other insects, detest the odor of tobacco. Some boxes are made with sliding wooden bottoms, and others are double, hinged together, with a wooden slide between; but the simpler one here described will do very well.

BEE GUIDES.—Now, early in the morning of a warm, still day, go where there are nectar-bearing flowers. The place must be at least a mile, preferably two miles, away from any house where tame bees are kept, or you will be annoyed by them. Few bees go more than two miles from home in search of honey.

BEE HUNTING

Choose an open glade or hillside, or an old field, or a fire-burnt waste where weeds and vines have sprung up, but free from leafy trees and shrubs, so that you can see for a considerable distance all around.

If bees are working here, put a little of your honey bait in the feeding tray of your box, cautiously set the box over the first bee that you find on a flower, and close the bottom with your hand. The bee will buzz up against the glass, and then soon will seek the honey. Now set the box on a stump or other elevation in the midst of a clear space. As stumps are not always to be found where wanted, some bee hunters carry with them a staff pointed at one end and with a bit of shingle tacked to the other end to serve as a platform for the box.

As soon as the bee is hard at work on the honey, approach quickly and withdraw the glass slide. Dust him slightly with flour, or put a bit of paint on his back just large enough to be noticeable, so you can identify him when he returns. Then withdraw to one side, get into a comfortable reclining position, and, if you have an opera glass, get it ready for action.

When the bee has gorged himself he will rise from the bait in half-circles and sudden dodges, generally to one side of the bait, returning toward it, and oscillating back again. He is getting his bearings. Now he mounts higher and higher in an increasing spiral. Then, so suddenly that it takes good eyes or a glass to follow him, he darts off for home. Watch him as far as you can, and note the direction of his flight. He will not go through woods, but over them. If he flies toward a farmhouse, pay no further attention to him, for he is a tame bee. In that case, go somewhere else and begin anew. But if he goes to the big woods, look at your watch and time his absence. You will know him when he returns by the mark that you have put on him.

On an average, a bee flies a mile in five minutes, and he spends about two minutes in the hive, disgorging. Bees vary in their flight, but a good general rule is to subtract two from the number of minutes absent, and divide by ten; the quotient is the number of miles, or the fraction of a mile, from your stand to the bee-tree. The time of the bee's second flight will be a more reliable datum than that of the first, because by that time he will have established his bearings and will go straight to and fro.

The pioneer bee will probably come back alone from his first trip. Let him fill up and depart as before; but now watch the course of his flight very closely, for it will be a "bee-line" for home. His course will be slightly sinuous, but its general direction will be straight for the hive, unless the ground is so rough as to cause contrary air currents, in which case he will seek the lee of woods or the shelter of a ravine, or unless there is a lake or large pond in the way, which he probably will sway around—for some reason known only to themselves, bees dislike to pass over a body of water—so a bee-line is not necessarily a straight line. Pick out some tall or peculiarly topped tree, or other prominent object in line with his course, take its bearings by compass, and study it carefully, so that you may recognize this landmark thereafter.

After two or three trips, your first bee probably will bring some companions with him from the home hive. Capture several more bees, say half a dozen, mark them, and let them go as before. If they all go in the same direction they belong to the same hive. But you may get two or more lines working from the same bait, in which case select the more numerous one, as it is likely to be nearest.

CROSS-LINING.—When once you get a line of bees working back and forth it is time to bestir yourself. Now you can choose between two schools of bee hunters: those who cross-line from the start, and those who claim that this is a waste of time

BEE HUNTING

and that no cross-lining should be attempted until the hunter has passed beyond the treasure tree and finds the bees back-tracking. I incline to the latter school; but I will describe the working methods of both.

To cross-line at the start; leave some bait at your first stand, take your box, capture a number of bees, cover the top and bottom of the box, to exclude light and thus keep them quiet, and go away at a right angle to the bee-line, about 200 or 300 yards. Here set down your box, uncover, but do not open the top; leave the box alone for a minute or two until the bees recover from their surprise and begin feeding; then liberate them, and note their course as before. This gives you the base of a triangle, the apex of which, where the two lines of flight converge, is near the hollow tree that contains the wild bees' hoard. If you do not see where the lines meet, the hive is beyond your present range of vision.

Whether you do this or not, as soon as you can follow the line for a considerable distance, clean the feeding tray, capture a number of bees in the box, and take it with you as far as you are sure of the course. Then put a little more honey-water in the feeder, and start your bees again. Thus work progressively toward the goal.

HIVES.—Sometimes the kind of tree that the hive is in can be foretold from the color of the insects themselves, which is modified, after a few months' residence, by the nature of the timber: light colored bees in pine, poplar, chestnut; darker ones in oak, beech, maple. But it is not likely that you will find the hive by merely following the bee-line and examining such or such trees along the way. Look for an old squirrel hole or knot-hole where the bees fly in and out.

Not infrequently bee hives are in rock crevices. I remember a hive that was well known for years to nearly everybody in that part of the country, but which had never been disturbed, because it was deep in the cranny of a big rock ledge that overhung the public road.

Occasionally a hive is found in a fallen tree or in an old stump, but this is exceptional. Bees have trouble enough, as it is, from squirrels, 'coons, bears, and other climbing marauders, to say nothing of men.

In searching, it is well to remember that bee-trees seldom are found far from water.

BACK-TRACKING.—If the bees that you liberate finally turn back on the course, or if they do not return to the bait, it shows that you have passed the hive and must "back-track." Then make two stands close together, only 50 to 100 yards apart, lining them carefully. You may now have two squads of bees flying from opposite directions into the tree. If this fails, take a stand 50 yards off to one side (the distance depends upon how thick the woods are), and examine every tree in the neighborhood with keen scrutiny. Pour out a liberal amount of feed, so as to get a large number of bees at work. If still you do not find the bee-tree, try again in this place a day of two later, or whenever the weather is favorable.

MARKING THE TREE.—In settled regions, where statute-law prevails, a hive of bees in a tree belongs to the owner of the soil, unless a former owner proves and reclaims them. In the wilderness, by law of the woods, ownership is to the first comer who makes a blaze on the bark and cuts or pencils his initials on it. Anyone else meddling with the treasure, unless it be claimed in time by the owner of the land himself, is a trespasser, like the interloper who sets traps along another trapper's line.

Having found a bee-tree, and marked it, then, unless you are very well acquainted with the woods, mark your trail outward with bush-signs; otherwise you may easily miss it on your return.

ROBBING THE HIVE.—Now you are ready to declare war. Men who have had much experience with bees disdain to wear armor; but I would not advise a novice to emulate their boldness. Get a broad-brimmed hat, say a farmer's straw hat, and fasten to it a head-net of mosquito bar long enough to come well down over the shoulders. A pair of long gloves or gauntlets is needed. Cut two sticks five or six feet long, and bind to one end of each a ball of cotton about as large as a hen's egg. Soak these cotton balls in melted sulphur. Get a sharp axe, and some pails to receive the honey; also a lantern, for your burglarizing is to be done at night. If you are not a good axeman, take with you a man who is.

When you reach the tree, decide which way it should be thrown, and attack it on that side. The bees will not disturb a man while he is felling the tree, as they do not realize what is going on. When the tree is almost ready to fall, put on your mask and gloves. Button the former under your coat, or draw it under your suspenders. Tie your trousers round the ankles, and the gauntlets round your wrists.

A companion should light one of the sulphur balls and have it ready; if the tree is hollow at the butt, he should light both balls. When the tree falls he must quickly apply one of the burning sticks to the bees' doorway, and the other to the hole in the butt, if there is one. The fumes will stupify the now angry insects or at least enough of them to make the work easier.

Chop into the tree until you have located the honey. It is now that the fun begins, for the bees understand by this time that they are being robbed, and the able-bodied ones will pounce upon the offenders, perhaps rushing upon the axeman in a mass so thick that he cannot see through his veil and must brush the fierce little warriors away. On a cold night they will be less active than if the weather is warm.

Having found the honey, cut through the trunk both above and below it, split out the slab, and thus expose the hoard, being careful not to "bleed" the comb. The bees will now stop fighting and will bend every energy to the work of carrying away all of the honey that they can, storing it in some hastily chosen retreat. You now may help yourself without fear of renewed attack.

Backwoodsmen, when they have no sulphur, use a smudge of punky wood, the acrid smoke of which suffocates the bees or renders them helpless for the time. They take the punk from a log or stump that is rotten enough to break easily in the hands and dry it near the fire. It will not blaze, but neither will it go out. It burns slowly and will give out a dense smoke for several hours. Of course, it kills many bees, and such a method should never be employed except in the far-back wilderness when there is downright need of something to take the place of sugar. Woodsmen who have no mosquito netting sometimes smear themselves with tobacco juice, or with water in which tobacco stems have been steeped, to protect them against stings. In any case they take chances boldly. Bees respect courage, but are quick to detect a wincing timidity and give it its deserts.

If, in spite of precautions, you are stung, apply some honey to the spot. Wet clay, oil of sassafras, ammonia, or onion juice, will relieve the pain and swelling; but honey is at hand, and it is about as good a remedy as any.

If you wish to capture the bees themselves, fix the broodcombs (those containing pollen or "beebread") the right distance apart in a bucket or basket, and set this to one side. The bees will collect about them, after their panic is over, and the next evening, when darkness begins to fall, they may be carried home. There are better ways, described in bee-keeping books, but they call for special appliances.

HONEY.—The amount of honey in a tree may vary from almost nothing to 100 pounds or more. There is record of 264 pounds being taken from

BEE HUNTING

one tree. Bees work with great zeal where there is a good supply of nectar, and will fill a hive in a short time.

Basswood bloom may be placed at the head of honey-producing plants. The apiarist, Root, says that during a period of twenty-two years he never knew basswood to fail to yield nectar, the shortest season yielding for three days, and the longest twenty-nine. In one of his hives the bees stored 66 pounds of basswood honey in three days. Ten pounds a day was the best recorded from clover.

John Burroughs has stated that there is no difference in flavor between wild honey and tame. Of course there is no difference in regions where wild and tame bees gather nectar from the same sources; but in the wilderness, where bees can forage only on the blossoms of wild plants and trees, with no access to fields and orchards, the honey has a distinct flavor, or flavors, of its own, as different from that of commercial honey as the flavor of pure, old-fashioned maple sugar is from that of the modern adulterated or "refined" article. To my taste, the honey of the wilderness is as much to be preferred as is the honest, kettle-boiled sugar of "the bush."

The bouquet of honey varies, of course, according to the kind of nectar gathered by its makers. The minty flavor of the linden is quite distinct from sourwood. Anyone can tell buckwheat honey from that which comes from the clover field. As a rule, wild honey has a pungent taste, not so cloyingly sweet as tame honey, and nearly always it is darker colored, even if the hive is new.

Honey gathered from the bloom of rhododendron or mountain laurel, or from the catalpa or catawba trees, is more or less poisonous to human beings. Root says that it causes symptoms similar to those exhibited by men who are dead drunk; or, in less violent cases, a tingling all over, indistinct vision (caused by dilation of the pupils), an empty, dizzy feeling of the head ,and an intense nausea that is not relieved by vomiting. The effects may not wear off for two or three days. We recall that the Ten Thousand of Xenophon were made ill by laurel honey. However, I doubt if anywhere in the world there is a more luxuriant bloom of laurel and of rhododendron than where I live in the Great Smoky Mountains, and yet I have not heard of a single case of poisoned honey in this region. Doubtless this is due to the profusion of other nectar-bearing trees and plants. Bees will not work on laurel when there is plenty of basswood and tulip and sourwood, which bloom in the same months.

BEESWAX.—Wax is a valuable commodity in the backwoods. To prepare it, break up the honeycomb, press out the honey, then boil the comb until melted in a small quantity of water, squeeze it through coarsely woven cloth, and cool it in molds.

THE SPORT OF BEE HUNTING.—There is an element of luck in bee hunting, and a spice of small adventure, that entitle it to rank among field sports. One must match his wits against the superior agility of the game; he must keep his eyes skinned, follow a long chase, and risk the stings of conflict if he would enjoy the sweets of victory.

The most unlucky thing that can happen is to spend half a day pursuing bees and then line them up in some farmer's hives. As Robinson's "Uncle Jerry" said: "I've lined bees nigh onto three mile, an' when a feller 's done that, an' fetches up agin a tame swarm in someb'dy's do' yard, it makes him feel kinder wamble-cropped."

CHAPTER XXI
EDIBLE PLANTS OF THE WILDERNESS

There is a popular notion that our Indians in olden times varied their meat diet with nothing but wild roots and herbs. This, in fact, was the case only among those tribes that pursued a roving life and had no settled abodes, such as the "horse Indians" and "diggers" of the Far West—and not all of them. The "forest Indians" east of the Mississippi and south of the Great Lakes, particularly such nations as the Iroquois and Cherokees, lived in villages and cultivated corn, beans, squashes, pumpkins, and tobacco. Still, wild plants and roots often were used by these semi-agricultural peoples, in the same way that garden vegetables are used by us, and, in time of famine, or invasion, they were sometimes almost the sole means of sustenance.

To-day, although our wild lands, such as are left, produce all the native plants that were known to the redmen, there is probably not one white hunter or forester in a thousand who can pick out half of the edible plants of the wilderness, nor who would know how to cook them if such were given to him. Nor are many of our botanists better informed. Now it is quite as important, in many cases, to know how to cook a wild plant as it is to be able to find it, for, otherwise, one might make as serious a mistake as if he ate the vine of a potato instead of its tuber, or a tomato vine instead of the fruit.

Take, for example, the cassava or manioc, which is still the staple food of most of the inhabitants of tropical America and is largely used elsewhere. The root of the bitter manioc, which is used with the same impunity as other species, contains a milky sap that is charged with prussic acid and is one of the most virulent vegetable poisons known to science. The Indians somehow discovered that this sap is volatile and can be driven off by heat. The root is cleaned, sliced, dried on hot metal plates or stones, grated, powdered, the starch separated from the meal, and the result is the tapioca of commerce, or farina, or Brazilian arrowroot, as may be, which we ourselves eat, and feed to our children and invalids, not knowing, perchance, that if it had not been for the art of a red savage, the stuff taken into our stomachs would have caused sudden death.

Another example, not of a poisonous but of an extremely acrid root that the Indians used for bread, and which really is of delicious flavor when rightly prepared, in the common Indian turnip. Every country schoolboy thinks he knows all about this innocent looking bulb. He remembers when some older boy grudgingly allowed him the tiniest nibble of this sacred vegetable, and how he, the recipent of the favor, started to say "Huh! 'tain't bad"—and then concluded his remark with what we good, grown-up people utter when we jab the black-ink pen into the red-ink bottle!

However, not all of our wild food-plants are acrid or poisonous in a raw state, nor is it dangerous for any one with a rudimentary knowledge of botany to experiment with them. Many are easily identified by those who know nothing at all of botany. I cannot say that all of them are palatable; but most of them are, when properly prepared for the table. Their taste in a raw state, generally speaking, is no more a criterion than is that of raw beans or asparagus.

It goes without saying that this chapter and the one that follows are not written for average campers—townfolk mostly, who know almost nothing about our wild flora. They are for the more daring sort who go far from the beaten trail, fend for themselves, and owe it to themselves to study matters of this kind before venturing into inhospitable regions. I have in mind more than one example of extreme suffering, and even of tragedy, that might have been averted by such precaution. Besides, there is a great number of people on this continent who spend a good part of their lives far back in the woods, where cultivated vegetables are hard to get. Having myself "lived the life," I know how insistent grows the craving for green stuff to vary the monotonous diet, and how profitable as well as pleasant is a little amateur botanizing with a pocket guide, such as Schuyler Mathews's *Field Book of American Wild Flowers,* which suffices to identify most of the plants on the following lists.

I have been much amused, by way of variety, at the attitude of a few skeptics who seem to doubt that the writer knows what he is talking about. One of my correspondents even wrote to inquire whether I "had any personal experience in eating any of these plants!" I suppose he inferred from my citations of authorities here and there that the whole thing was cribbed. It is not fashionable nowadays, I know, for writers who seek popularity to quote directly from others, or even to acknowledge indebtedness for ideas that they appropriate through paraphrasis. However, I am old-fashioned enough to give credit where credit is due, whenever I can identify the one from whom I first got a fact or idea that to me was new. In the following catalogue my citation of an authority does not mean, then, that I have not tried the thing for myself, although in some cases that is so. During the years that I have lived in the woods I have tested a great variety of wild "roots and yarbs"—tried them in my own stomach; otherwise I would not have written a line on the subject. Here is a rather odd example, taken from my notebook under date of May 10, 1910, at which time I was boarding with a native family on upper Deep Creek, Swain County, North Carolina:

Mrs. Barnett to-day cooked us a mess of greens of her own picking. It was an *olla podrida* consisting of (1) lamb's quarters, (2) poke shoots, (3) sheep sorrel, (4) dock, (5) plantain, (6) young tops of "volunteer" potatoes, (7) wild mustard, (8) cow pepper. All of these ingredients were boiled together in the same pot, with a slice of pork, and the resulting "wild salat," as she called it, was good. This is the first time I ever heard of anyone eating potato tops; but a hearty trial of them has proved that the tops of young Irish potatoes, like the young shoots of poke, are wholesome and of good flavor, whereas it is well known that the mature tops of both plants are poisonous.

I am told that the young leaves of sweet potato vines "make an excellent spinach."

To give a detailed account of all the edible wild plants of the United States and Canada, with descriptions and illustrations sufficing to identify them, would require by itself a book as large as this. I have only space to give the names and edible properties of those that I know of which are native to, or, as wild plants, have become naturalized in the region north of the southern boundary of Virginia and east of the Rocky Mountains. Besides those mentioned below, there are others which grow only in the southern or western states, among the more important being the palmetto, palm, yam, cacti, Spanish bayonet, mesquite, wild sago or coontie, tule plant, western camass, kouse root, bread root, screw bean, pimple mallow, manzañita, piñons, jumper nuts, many pine seeds, squaw berry, lycium berry—but the list is long enough. Those who wish further details should examine the publications of the U. S. Department of Agriculture, and especially those of one of its officers, Mr. F. V. Coville, who has made special studies in this subject.

I have given the botanical name of every plant cited herein, because without it there would be no guarantee of identification. The nomenclature adopted is that of Britton and Brown in their *Illustrated Flora of the Northern States and Canada* (Scribner's Sons, New York), which, as it con-

EDIBLE PLANTS

tains an illustration of every plant, is of the first assistance to an amateur in identifying. Wherever Gray's nomenclature differs, it is added in parentheses.

The months named under each plant are those in which it flowers, the earlier month in each case being the flowering month in the plant's southernmost range, and the later one that of the northernmost. In the case of wild fruits, the months are those in which the fruit ripens.

It is necessary to remember that most of the edible plants become tough and bitter when they have reached full bloom.

SUBSTANTIAL FOODS

ACORNS.—The eastern oaks that yield sweet mast are the basket, black jack, bur, chestnut, overcup, post, rock chestnut, scrub chestnut, swamp white, and white oaks, the acorns of chestnut and post oaks being sweetest; those producing bitter mast are the black, pin, red, scarlet, shingle, Spanish, water, and willow oaks; of which the black and water oak acorns are most astringent.

None of these can be used raw, as human food, without more or less ill effect from the tannin contained. But there are tribes of western Indians who extract the tannin from even the most astringent acorns and make bread out of their flour. The process varies somewhat among different tribes, but essentially it as as follows:

The acorns are collected when ripe, spread out to dry in the sun, cracked, and stored until the kernels are dry, care being taken that they do not mold. The kernels are then pulverized in a mortar to a fine meal, with frequent siftings to remove the coarser particles, until the whole is ground to a fine flour, this being essential. The tannin is then dissolved out by placing the flour in a filter and letting water percolate through it for about two hours, or until the water ceases to have a yellowish tinge. One form of filter is contrived by laying a coarse, flat basket or strainer on a pile of gravel with a drain underneath. Rather fine gravel is now scattered thickly over the bottom and up the sides of the strainer, and the meal laid thickly over the gravel. Water is added, little by little, to set free the tannin. The meal is removed by hand as much as possible, then water is poured over the remainder to get it together, and thus little is wasted. The meal by this time has the consistency of ordinary dough.

The dough is cooked is two ways: first, by boiling it in water as we do corn-meal mush, the resulting porridge being not unlike yellow corn-meal mush in appearance and taste; it is sweet and wholesome, but rather insipid. The second mode is to make the dough into small balls, which are wrapped in green corn leaves. These balls are then placed in hot ashes, some green leaves of corn are laid over them, and hot ashes are placed on the top, and the cakes are thus baked.

(Coville,. *Contrib. to U. S. Herbarium,* VII. No. 3.—Palmer, in *Amer. Naturalist,* XII, 597. Another method, used by the Pomo Indians, who add 5 per cent. of red earth to the dough, is described by J. W. Hudson in the *Amer. Anthropologist,* 1900, pp. 775-6.)

NUTS.—Among the Cherokees, and also in Italy and in Tyrol, I have eaten bread made from chestnuts. The Cherokee method, when they have corn also, is to use the chestnuts whole, mixing them with enough corn-meal dough to hold them together, and then baking cakes of this material enclosed in corn husks, like tamales. The peasants of southern Europe make bread from the meal of chestnuts alone—the large European chestnut, of course, being used. Such bread is palatable and nutritious, but lies heavily on one's stomach until he becomes accustomed to it.

EDIBLE PLANTS

Our Indians also have made bread from the kernels of buckeyes. These, in a raw state, are poisonous, but when dried, powdered, and freed from their poison by filtration, like acorns, they yield an edible and nutritious flour. The method is first to roast the nuts, then hull and peel them, mash them in a basket with a billet, and then leach them. The resulting paste may be baked, or eaten cold.

Hazel nuts, beech nuts, pecans, and wankapins may be used like chestnuts. The oil expressed from beech nuts is little inferior to the best olive oil for table use, and will keep sweet for ten years. The oil from butternuts and black walnuts used to be highly esteemed by the eastern Indians either to mix with their food, or as a frying fat. They pounded the ripe kernels, boiled them in water, and skimmed off the oil using the remaining paste as bread. Hickory nut oil was easily obtained by crushing the whole nuts, precipitating the broken shells in water, and skimming off the oily "milk," which was used as we use cream or butter. The nut of the ironwood (blue beech) is edible.

The kernel of the long-leaved pine cone is edible and of an agreeable taste. Many western pines have edible "nuts." The acridity of pine seeds can be removed by roasting.

KIND	Protein per ct.	Fat per ct.	Carbohydrates per ct.	Ash per ct.	Fuel Value per lb. calories
Beechnut	21.8	49.9	18.0	3.7	2,740
Butternut	27.9	61.2	3.4	3.0	3,370
Chestnut, dry	10.7	7.8	73.0	1.4	1,840
Hickory nut	15.4	67.4	11.4	2.1	3,345
Peanut	29.8	43.5	17.1	2.2	2,610
Pecan	12.1	70.7	12.2	1.6	3,300
Pine nut, Piñon	14.6	61.9	17.3	2.8	3,205
Walnut	18.2	60.7	16.0	1.7	3,075
By comparison:					
Beef, r'd steak	19.8	13.6	0.0	1.1	950
White bread	9.2	1.3	53.1	1.1	1,215

All nuts are more digestible when roasted than when eaten raw.

ARROWHEAD, BROAD-LEAVED. Swan or Swamp Potato. *Sagittaria latifolia* (*S. variabilis*). In shallow water; ditches. Throughout North America, except extreme north, to Mexico. *July-Sep.*

Tuberous roots as large as hens' eggs, were an important article of food among Indians. Roots bitter when raw, but rendered sweet and palatable by boiling. Excellent when cooked with meat. Indians gather them by wading and loosening roots with their feet, when the tubers float up and are gathered. Leaves acrid.

ARUM, GREEN ARROW. *Peltandra Virginica* (*P. undulata, Arum Virginicum*). Swamp or shallow water. Me. and Ont. to Mich., south to Fla, and La. *May-June.*

Rootstock used by eastern Indians for food, under the name of *Taw-ho*. Roots very large; acrid when fresh. The method of cooking this root, and that of the Golden Club, is thus described by Captain John Smith in his *Historie of Virginia* (1624), p. 87: "The chiefe root they haue for food is called *Tockawhoughe*. It groweth like a flagge in Marishes. In one day a Salvage will gather sufficient for a week. These roots are much of the greatnesse and taste of Potatoes. They vse to cover a great many of them with Oke leaues and Ferne, and then cover all with earth in the manner of a Cole-pit [charcoal pit]; over it, on each side, they continue a great fire 24 houres before they dare eat it. Raw it is no better than poyson, and being roasted, except it be tender and the heat abated, or sliced and dryed in the Sunne, mixed with sorrell and meale or such like, it will prickle and torment the throat extreamely, and yet in sommer they vse this ordinarily for bread."

ARUM, WATER. WILD CALLA. *Calla pallustris.* Cold bogs. Nova Scotia to Minn., south to Va., Wis., Iowa. *May-June.*

"Missen bread is made in Lapland from roots

of this plant, which are acrid when raw. They are taken up in spring when the leaves come forth, are extremely well washed, and then dried. The fibrous parts are removed, and the remainder dried in an oven. This is then bruised and chopped into pieces as small as peas or oatmeal, and then ground. The meal is boiled slowly, and continually stirred like mush. It is then left standing for three or four days, when the acridity disappears." (Lankester.)

BROOM-RAPE, LOUISIANA. *Orobanche Ludoviciana* (*Aphyllon L.*). Sandy soil. Ill. to Manitoba, south to Texas, Ariz., Cal. *June-Aug.*

"All the plant except the bloom grows under ground, and consequently nearly all is very white and succulent. The Pah Utes consume great numbers of them in summer. . . .Being succulent they answer for food and drink on these sandy plains, and, indeed, are often called sand-food." (Palmer.)

BULRUSH, GREAT. Mat-rush. Tule-root. *Scirpus lacustris.* Ponds and swamps. Throughout North America: also in Old World. *June-Sep.*

Roots resemble artichokes, but are much larger. Eaten raw, they prevent thirst and afford nourishment. Flour made from the dried root is white, sweet and nutritious. A great favorite with the western Indians, who pound the roots and make bread of them. When the fresh roots are bruised, mixed with water, and boiled, they afford a good sirup.

CAMASS, EASTERN. Wild Hyacinth. *Quamasia hyacynthia* (*Camassia Fraseri*). In meadows and along streams. Pa. to Minn., south to Ala. and Texas. *Apr.-May.*

Root is very nutritious, with an agreeable mucilaginous taste.

GOLDEN CLUB. *Orontium aquaticum.* Swamps and ponds. Mass. to Pa., south to Fla. and La., mostly near coast. *Apr.-May.*

The *Taw-kee* of coast Indians who liked the dried seeds when cooked like peas. The raw root is acrid, but becomes edible when cooked like arrow-arum.

GRASS, DROP-SEED.   Sand Drop-seed.   *Sporobolus cryptandrus*.   Also Barnyard or Cockspur Grass (*Panicum Crusgalli*).

When the seeds, which are gathered in great quantities by western Indians, are parched, ground, mixed with water or milk and baked or made into mush, they are of good flavor and nutritious. Also eaten dry.

GRASS, PANIC.   *Panicum*, several species.

The ripe seeds are collected, like the above, cleaned by winnowing, ground into flour, water added and the mass is kneaded into hard cakes, which, when dried in the sun are ready for use. Also made into gruel and mush.

GRASS, FLOATING MANNA   *Panicularia fluitans* (*Glyceria fl.*).

The seeds are of agreeable flavor and highly nutritious material for soups and gruels.

GREENBRIER, BRISTLY.   Stretch-berry.   *Smilax Bona-nox*.   Thickets.   Mass. and Kansas, south to Fla. and Texas.   *Apr-July*.

The large, tuberous rootstocks are said to have been used by the Indians, who ground them into meal and made bread or gruel of it.

In the South a drink is made from them.

GREENBRIER, LONG-STALKED.   *Smilax Pseudo-China*.   Dry or sandy thickets.   Md. to Neb., south to Fla. and Texas.   *March-Aug*.

Bartram says that the Florida Indians prepared from this plant "a very agreeable, cooling sort of jelly, which they call *conte* [not to be confounded with coontie or wild sago]; this is prepared from the root of the China brier (*Smilax Pseudo-China*)

They chop the roots in pieces which are afterwards well pounded in a wooden mortar, then being mixed with clean water, in a tray or trough, they strain it through baskets. The sediment, which settles to the bottom of the second vessel, is afterwards dried in the open air, and is then a very fine reddish flour or meal. A small quantity of this, mixed with warm water and sweetened with honey,

EDIBLE PLANTS 377

when cool, becomes a beautiful, delicious jelly, very nourishing and wholesome. They also mix it with fine corn flour, which being fried in fresh bear's oil makes very good hot cakes or fritters."

GROUND-NUT. Wild Bean. Indian Potato. *Apios Apios* (*A. tuberosa*). Moist ground. New Bruns. to Fla., west to Minn. and Kan., south to La. *July-Sep.*

This is the famous *hopniss* of New Jersey Indians, the *saagaban* of the Micmacs, *openauk* of Virginia tribes, *scherzo* of the Carolinas, *taux* of the Osages, and *modo* of the Sioux, under one or other of which names it is frequently met by students of our early annals. "In 1654 the town laws of Southampton, Mass., ordained that if an Indian dug ground-nuts on land occupied by the English, he was to be set in the stocks, and for a second offence, to be whipped." The Pilgrims, during their first winter, lived on these roots.

The tubers vary from the size of cherries to that of a hen's egg, or larger. They grow in strings of perhaps 40 together, resembling common potatoes in shape, taste, and odor. When boiled they are quite palatable and wholesome. The seeds in the pod can be prepared like common peas.

INDIAN TURNIP. Jack-in-the-Pulpit. *Arisaema triphyllum* (*Arum triphyllum*). Moist woods and thickets. Nova Scotia to Florida, west to Minn., Kan., La. *April-June.* Fruit ripe, *June-July.*

The root of this plant is so acrid when raw that, if one but touch the tip of his tongue to it, in a few seconds that unlucky member will sting as if touched to a nettle. Yet it was a favorite bread-root of the Indians. I have found bulbs as much as 11 inches in circumference and weighing half a pound.

Some writers state that the acridity of the root is destroyed by boiling, while others recommend baking. Neither alone will do. The bulb may be boiled for two hours, or baked as long, and, while the outer portion will have a characteristically pleasant flavor, half potato, half chestnut, the inner part will still be as uneatable as a spoonful of red pepper. The root should either be roasted or boiled, then peeled, dried, and pounded in a mortar, or otherwise reduced to flour. Then if it is heated again, or let stand for a day or two, it becomes bland and wholesome, having been reduced to a starchy substance resembling arrowroot. Even if the fresh root is only grated finely and let stand exposed to air until it is thoroughly dry, the acridity will have evaporated with the juice.

The roots may be preserved for a year by storing in damp sand.

It is said that the Indians also cooked and ate the berries.

LILY, TURK'S-CAP. *Lilium superbum*. Meadows and marshes. Me. to Minn., south to N. C. and Tenn. *July-Aug*.

LILY, WILD YELLOW. Canada Lily. *Lilium Canadense*. Swamps, meadows and fields. Nova Scotia to Minn., south to Ga., Ala., Mo., *June-July*.

"Both of these lilies have fleshy, edible bulbs. When green they look and taste somewhat like raw green corn on the ear. The Indians use them, instead of flour, to thicken stews, etc." (Thoreau.)

LILY, YELLOW POND. Spatter-dock. *Nymphaea advena* (*Nuphar ad.*). Ponds and slow streams. Nova Scotia to Rocky Mts., south to Fla., Texas, Utah. *Apr.-Sep.*

The roots, which are one or two feet long, grow four or five feet under water, and Indian women dive for them. They are very porous, slightly sweet, and glutinous. Generally boiled with wild fowl, but often roasted separately. Muskrats store large quantities for winter use, and their houses are frequently robbed by the Indians. The pulverized seeds of the plant are made into bread or gruel, or parched and eaten like popcorn.

NELUMBO, AMERICAN. Wankapin or Yoncopin. Water Chinquapin. *Nelumbo lutea*. Ponds and

EDIBLE PLANTS 379

swamps. Locally east from Ontario to Fla., abundant west to Mich., Okla., La. *July-Aug.*

Tubers of root somewhat resemble sweet potatoes, and are little inferior to them when well boiled. A highly prized food of the Indians. The green and succulent half-ripe seed-pods are delicate and nutritious. From the sweet, mealy seeds, which resemble hazel nuts, the Indians made bread, soups, etc. The "nuts" were first steeped in water, and then parched in sand to easily extricate the kernels. These were mixed with fat and made into a palatable soup, or were ground into flour and baked. Frequently they were parched without steeping, and the kernels eaten thus.

ORCHIS, SHOWY. *Orchis spectabilis.* Rich woods. New Brunsw. to Minn., south to Ga., Ky., Neb. *Apr.-June.*

"One of the orchids that springs from a tuberous root, and as such finds favor with the country people [of the South] in the preparation of a highly nourishing food for children." (Lounsberry.)

PEANUT, HOG. Wild peanut. *Falcata comosa* (*Glycine comosa*). Moist thickets. New Brunsw. to Fla., west to Lake Superior, Neb., La. *Aug-Sep.*

"The underground pod has been cultivated as a vegetable." (Porcher.)

POTATO, PRAIRIE. Prairie turnip. Indian or Missouri Breadroot. The *pomme blanche* of the voyageurs. *Psoralea Esculenta.* Prairies. Manitoba and N. Dak. to Texas. *June.*

The farinaceous tuber, generally the size of a hen's egg, has a thick, leathery envelope, easily separable from the smooth internal parts, which become friable when dry and are readily pulverized, affording a light, starchy flour, with sweetish, turnip-like taste. Often sliced and dried by the Indians for winter use. Palatable in any form.

RICE, WILD. *Zizania aquatica.* Swamps. New Brunsw. to Manitoba, south to Fla., La., Texas. *June-Oct.*

The chief farinaceous food of probably 30,000 of

our northern Indians, and now on the market as a breakfast food. The harvesting is usually done by two persons working together, one propelling the canoe, and the one in the stern gently pulling the plants over the canoe and beating off the ripe seed with two sticks. The seed, when gathered, is spread out for a few hours to dry, and is then parched in a kettle over a slow fire for half an hour to an hour, meanwhile being evenly and constantly stirred. It is then spread out to cool. After this it is hulled by putting about a bushel of the seed into a hole in the ground, lined with staves or burnt clay, and beating or punching it with heavy sticks. The grains and hulls are separated by tossing the mixture into the wind from baskets. The grain will keep indefinitely.

Before cooking, it should have several washings in cold water to remove the smoky taste. It is cooked with game, or as gruel (boil 35 minutes), or made into bread, or merely eaten dry. Its food value is equal to that of our common cereals. "An acre of rice is nearly or quite equal to an acre of wheat in nutriment." (For details see *Bulletin No. 50* of the Bureau of Plant Industry, U. S. Dep't. of Agriculture.)

SILVERWEED. Wild or Goose Tansy. Goose-grass. *Potentilla Anserina*. Shores and salt meadows, marshes and river banks. Greenland to N. J., west to Neb.; Alaska, south along Rocky Mts. to N. Mex. and Cal. *May-Sep.*

Roots gathered in spring and eaten either raw or roasted. Starchy and wholesome. When roasted or boiled their taste resembles chestnuts.

SUNFLOWER. *Helianthus,* many species. Prairies. etc. *July-Sep.* "The seeds of these plants form one of the staple articles of food for many Indians, and they gather them in great quantities. The agreeable oily nature of the seeds renders them very palatable. When parched and ground they are highly prized, and are eaten on hunting excursions. The meal or flour is also made into thin cakes and

EDIBLE PLANTS

baked in hot ashes. These cakes are of a gray color, rather coarse looking, but palatable and very nutritious. Having eaten of the bread made from sunflowers, I must say that it is as good as much of the corn bread eaten by whites." (Palmer.)

The oil expressed from sunflower seeds is a good substitute for olive oil.

VALERIAN, EDIBLE. Tobacco-root. *Valeriana edulis.* Wet open places. Ontario to B. C., south to O., Wis., and in Rocky Mts. to N. Mex and Ariz. *May-Aug.*

"I ate here, for the first time, the *kooyah* or tobacco-root (*valeriana edulis*), the principal edible root among the Indians who inhabit the upper waters of the streams on the western side of the [Rocky] mountains. It has a very strong and remarkably peculiar taste and odor, which I can compare to no other vegetable that I am acquainted with, and which to some persons is extremely offensive. . . To others, however, the taste is rather an agreeable one, and I was afterwards always glad when it formed an addition to our scanty meals. It is full of nutriment. In its unprepared state it is said by the Indians to have very strong poisonous qualities, of which it is deprived by a peculiar process, being baked in the ground for about two days." (Fremont, *Exploring Expedition,* 1845, p. 135.)

POT-HERBS AND SALADS

All of the plants hitherto mentioned are native to the regions described. In the following list will be found many that are introduced weeds; but a considerable proportion of these foundlings may now be seen in clearings and old burnt tracts in the woods, far from regular settlements. Directions for cooking greens are given in Vol. I., pp. 369-371.

ADDER'S-TONGUE, YELLOW. Dog's-tooth Violet. *Erythronium Americanum.* Moist woods and thickets. Nova Scotia to Minn., south to Fla., Mo., Ark. *Mar.-May.*

Sometimes used for greens.

BEAN, WILD KIDNEY. *Phaseolus polystachyus*

(*P. perennis*). Thickets. Canada to Fla., west to Minn., Neb., La. *July-Sep.*
Was used as food by the Indians; the Apaches eat it either green or dried.

BELLWORT. *Uvularia perfoliata.* Moist woods and thickets. Quebec and Ont. to Fla. and Miss. *May-June.*

"The roots of this and other species of *Uvularia* are edible when cooked, and the young shoots are a good substitute for asparagus." (Porcher.)

BROOKLIME, AMERICAN. *Veronica Americana.* Brooks and swamps. Anticosti to Alaska, south to Pa., Neb., N. Mex., Cal. *Apr-Sep.*

"A salad plant equal to the watercress. Delightful in flavor, healthful, anti-scorbutic." (*Sci. Amer.*)

BURDOCK, GREAT. Cockle-bur. *Arctium Lappa.* Waste places. New Brunsw. to southern N. Y., and locally in the interior. Not nearly so widely distributed as the smaller common burdock (*A. minus*). *July-Oct.*

A naturalized weed, so rank in appearance and odor that nothing but stark necessity could have driven people to experiment with it as a vegetable. Yet, like the skunk cabbage, it is capable of being turned to good account. In spring, the tender shoots, when peeled, can be eaten raw like radishes, or, with vinegar, can be used as a salad. The stalks cut before the flowers open, and stripped of their rind, form a delicate vegetable when boiled, similar in flavor to asparagus. The raw root has medicinal properties, but the Japanese eat the cooked root, preparing it as follows: The skin is scraped or peeled off, and the roots sliced in long strips, or cut into pieces about two inches long, and boiled with salt and pepper, or with soy, to impart flavor; or the boiled root is mashed, made into cakes, and fried like oyster plant.

CHARLOCK. Wild Mustard. *Brassica arvensis* (*B. Sinapistrum*). Fields and waste places. Naturalized everywhere. *May-Nov.*

Extensively used as a pot-herb; aids digestion.

EDIBLE PLANTS 383

CHICKWEED. *Alsine media.* (*Stellaria m.*). Waste places, meadows, and woods. Naturalized; common everywhere. *Jan-Dec.*

Used like spinach, and quite as good.

CHICORY. Wild Succory. *Chichorium Intybus.* Roadsides, fields, and waste places. Nova Scotia to Minn., south to N. C. and Mo. *July-Oct.*

All parts of the plant are wholesome. The young leaves make a good salad, or may be cooked as a pot-herb like dandelion. The root, ground and roasted, is used as an adulterant of coffee.

CLOVER. *Trifolium,* many species.

The coast Indians of California use clover as a food. The fresh leaves and stems are used, before flowering. "Deserves test as a salad herb, with vinegar and salt."

COMFREY. *Symphytum officinale.* Waste places. Newf. to Minn., south to Md. Naturalized. *June-Aug.*

Makes good greens when gathered young.

COW PEA. China Bean. *Vigna Sinensis.* Escaped from cultivation. Mo. to Texas and Ga. *July-Sep.*

The seeds are edible.

COW PEPPER. A plant resembling toothwort (*Dentaria diphylla*) but bearing a yellow instead of a white flower, and developing a bur. Tops used in the southern Appalachians for salad, and the roots as a substitute for horseradish.

CRESS, ROCKET. Yellow Rocket. Bitter Cress. *Barbarea Barbarea* (*B. vulgaris*). Fields and waste places. Naturalized. Labrador to Va., and locally in interior; also on Pacific coast. *Apr.-June.*

The young, tender leaves make a fair salad, but inferior to the winter cress.

CRESS, WATER. *Roripa Nasturtium* (*Nasturtium officinale*). Brooks and other streams, Nova Scotia to Manitoba, south to Va. and Mo. Naturalized from Europe. *Apr.-Nov.*

A well-known salad herb. The leaves and stems are eaten raw with salt, as a relish, or mixed as a salad.

CRESS, WINTER. Scurvy Grass. *Barbarea praecox.* Waste places, naturalized. Southern N. Y., Pa., and southward. *Apr.-June.*

Highly esteemed as a winter salad and pot-herb; sometimes cultivated.

CRINKLE-ROOT. Two-leaved Toothwort. *Dentaria diphylla.* Rich woods and meadows. Nova Scotia to Minn., south to S. Car. and Ky. *May.*

The rootstocks are crisp and fleshy, with a spicy flavor like watercress. Eaten with salt, like celery.

CROWFOOT, CELERY-LEAVED OR DITCH. *Ranunculus sceleratus.* Swamps and wet ditches, New Brunsw. to Fla., abundant along the coast, and locally westward to Minn. *Apr.-Aug.*

Porcher cites this as a good example of the destruction of acrid and poisonous juices by heating. The fresh juice is so caustic that it will raise a blister, and two drops taken internally may excite fatal inflammation. Yet the boiled or baked root, he says, is edible. When cleansed, scraped and pounded, and the pulp soaked in a considerable quantity of water, a white sediment is deposited, which, when washed and dried, is a real starch.

CUCKOO-FLOWER. Meadow Bitter-cress. *Cardamine pratensis.* Wet meadows and swamps. Labrador to northern N. J., west to Minn. and B. C. *Apr.-May.*

Has a pungent savor and is used like water cress; occasionally cultivated as a salad plant.

DANDELION. *Taraxacum Taraxacum (T. Officinale).* Fields and waste places everywhere; naturalized. *Jan.-Dec.*

Common pot-herb; also blanched for salad. In boiling, change the water two or three times.

DOCK, CURLED. *Rumex Crispus.* Fields and waste places, everywhere; naturalized. *June-Aug.*

The young leaves make good pot-herbs. The plant produces an abundance of seeds, which Indians grind into flour for bread or mush.

FERNS. Many species.

The young stems of ferns, gathered before they

are covered with down, and before the leaves have uncurled, are tender, and when boiled like asparagus are delicious.

The rootstocks of ferns are starchy, and after being baked resemble the dough of wheat; their flavor is not very pleasant, but they are by no means to be despised by a hungry man.

FETTICUS. Corn Salad. *Valerianella Locusta.* Waste places. N. Y. to Va. and La. Naturalized. *Apr.-July.*

Cultivated for salad and as a pot-herb. The young leaves are very tender.

FLAG, CAT-TAIL. *Typha latifolia.* Marshes. Throughout North America except in extreme north. *June-July.*

The flowering ends are very tender in the spring, and are eaten raw, or when boiled in water make a good soup. The root is eaten as a salad. "The Cossacks of the Don peel off the outer cuticle of the stalk and eat raw the tender white part of the stem extending about 18 inches from the root. It has a somewhat insipid, but pleasant and cooling taste."

GARLIC, WILD OR MEADOW. *Allium Canadense.* Moist meadows and thickets. Me. to Minn., south to Fla., La., Ark. *May-June.*

A good substitute for garlic. "The top bulbs are superior to the common onion for pickling."

GINSENG, DWARF. Ground-nut. *Panax trifolium (Aralia trifolia).* Moist woods and thickets. Nova Scotia to Ga., west to Minn., Iowa, Ill. *Apr.-June.*

The tubers are edible and pungent.

HONEWORT. *Deringa Canadensis (Cryptotaenia C.).* Woods. New Brunsw. to Minn., south to Ga. and Texas. *June-July.*

In the spring this is a wholesome green, used in soups, etc., like chervil.

HOP. *Cannabis sativa.* Waste places. New Brunsw. to Minn., south 'to N. C., Tenn., Kansas. Naturalized. *July-Sep.*

Used for yeast. "In Belgium the young shoots

of the plant just as they emerge from the ground are used as asparagus."

INDIAN CUCUMBER. *Medeola Virginiana.* Rich, damp woods and thickets. Nova Scotia to Minn., south to Fla. and Tenn. *May-June.*

"The common name alludes to the succulent, horizontal, white tuberous root, which tastes like cucumber, and was in all probability relished by the Indians." (Matthews.)

JERUSALEM ARTICHOKE. Canada Potato. Girasole. Topinambour. *Helianthus tuberosus.* Moist soil. New Brunsw. to Manitoba, south to Ga. and Ark. "Often occurs along roadsides in the east, a relic of cultivation by the aborigines."

Now cultivated and for sale in our markets. The tubers are large, and edible either raw or cooked, tasting somewhat like celery root. They are eaten as vegetables, and are also pickled.

LADY'S THUMB. English Smartweed. *Polygonum Persicaria.* Waste places throughout the continent, except extreme north. Naturalized; often an abundant weed. *June-Sep.*

Used as an early salad plant in the southern mountains.

LAMB'S QUARTERS. White Pigweed. *Chenopodium album.* Waste places, range universal, like the above. Naturalized. *June-Sep.*

A fine summer green and pot-herb, tender and succulent. Should be boiled about 20 minutes, the first water being thrown away, owing to its bad taste. The small seeds, which are not unpleasant when eaten raw, may be dried, ground, and made into cakes or gruel. They resemble buckwheat in color and taste, and are equally nutritious.

LETTUCE, SPANISH. Indian or Miner's Lettuce *Claytonia perfoliata.* Native of Pacific coast, but spreading eastward. *Apr.-May.*

The whole plant is eaten by western Indians and by whites. In a raw state makes an excellent salad; also cooked with salt and pepper, as greens.

LUPINE, WILD. Wild Pea. *Lupinus perennis.*

EDIBLE PLANTS

Dry, sandy soil. Me. to Minn., south to Fla., Mo., La. *May-June.*
Edible; cooked like domestic peas.

MALLOW, MARSH. *Althaeea Officinalis.* Salt marshes. Mass. to N. J. *Summer.*
The thick, very mucilaginous root, has familiar use as a confection; also used in medicine as a demulcent. May be eaten raw.

MALLOW, WHORLED OR CURLED. *Malva verticillata (M. crispa).* Waste places. Nova Scotia to Minn., south to N. J. Naturalized. *Summer.*
A good pot-herb.

MARIGOLD, MARSH. Meadow-gowan. Cowslip. *Caltha palustris.* Swamps and meadows. Newfoundland to S. C., west through Canada to Rocky Mts., and south to Iowa. *Apr.-June.*
Used as a spring vegetable, the young plant being thoroughly boiled for greens. The flower buds are sometimes pickled as a substitute for capers.

Beware of mistaking for this plant the poisonous white hellebore (*Veratrum viride*).

MEADOW BEAUTY. Deer Grass. *Rhexia Virginica.* Sandy swamps. Me. to Fla., west to north N. Y., Ill., Mo., La. *July-Sep.*
The leaves have a sweetish, yet acidulous taste. Make a good addition to a salad, and may be eaten with impunity.

MILKWEED. *Asclepias Syriaca (A. Cornuti).* Fields and waste places generally. *June-Aug.* Also other species.

The young shoots, in spring, are a good substitute for asparagus. Kalm says that a good brown sugar has been made by gathering the flowers while the dew was on them, expressing the dew, and boiling it down.

MUSHROOMS. The number of edible species is legion. It is not difficult to distinguish the poisonous ones, when one has studied a good text-book; but no one should take chances with fungi until he has made such study, for a few of the common species are deadly, and for some of them no remedy is known. A beginner would do well, perhaps, to avoid all of the genus *Amanita*. All mushrooms on the following list are of delicious flavor.

Coprinus comatus
Hypholoma appendiculatum
Tricholoma personatum
Boletus subaureus.
Boletus bovinus
Boletus subsanguineous
Clavaria botrytes
Clavaria cinerea
Clavaria inaequalis
Clavaria vermicularis
Clavaria pistillaris
Lactarius volemus
Lactarius deliciosus
Russula alutacea
Russula virescens
Cantharelles cibarius
Marasmius oreades
Hydnum repandum
Hydnum caput-Medusae
Morchella esculenta
Morchella deliciosa

It would be well for every outer to learn the easily distinguishable beefsteak fungus (*Fistulina hepatica*) and sulphur mushroom (*Polyporus sulphureus*) that grow from the trunks of old trees and stumps, as they are very common, very large, and "filling."

MUSTARD. *Brassica,* several species. Fields and waste places. Naturalized.

The young leaves are used for greens.

NETTLE. *Urtica dioica,* and other species; also the Sow Thistle, *Sonchus oleraceus.* Fields and waste places.

Should be gathered, with gloves, when the leaves are quite young and tender. A pleasant, nourishing and mildly aperient pot-herb, used with soups,

EDIBLE PLANTS 389

salt meat, or as spinach; adds a piquant taste to other greens. Largely used for such purposes in Europe.

NIGHTSHADE, BLACK OR GARDEN. *Solanum nigrum.* Waste places, commonly in cultivated soil. Nova Scotia to Manitoba, south to Fla. and Texas. *July-Oct.*

This plant is reputed to be poisonous, though not to the same degree as its relative from Europe, the Woody Nightshade or Bittersweet (*S. Dulcamara*). It is, however, used as a pot-herb, like spinach, in some countries, and in China the young shoots and berries are eaten. Bessey reports that in the Mississippi Valley the little black berries are made into pies.

ONION, WILD. *Allium,* many species. Rich woods, moist meadows and thickets, banks and hillsides.

Used like domestic onions.

PARSNIP, COW. Masterwort. *Heracleum lanatum.* Moist ground. Labrador to N. C. and Mo., Alaska to Cal. *June-July.*

"The tender leaf and flower stalks are sweet and very agreeably aromatic, and are therefore much sought after [by coast Indians] for green food in spring and early summer, before the flowers have expanded. In eating these, the outer skin is rejected."

PEPPERGRASS, WILD. *Lepidium Virginicum.* Fields and along roadsides. Quebec to Minn., south to Fla. and Mexico. *May-Nov.*

Like the cultivated peppergrass, this is sometimes used as a winter or early salad, but it is much inferior to other cresses. The spicy pods are good seasoning for salads, soups, etc.

PIGWEED, ROUGH. Beet-root. *Amaranthus retroflexus.* Fields and waste places. Throughout the continent except extreme north. Naturalized. *Aug.-Oct.*

Related to the beet and spinach, and may be used for greens.

PIGWEED, SLENDER. Keerless. *Amaranthus hybridus* (*A. chlorostachys*). A weed of the same wide range as the preceding. Naturalized. *Aug.-Oct.*

Extensively used in the South, in early spring, as a salad plant, under the name of "keerless."

PLANTAIN, COMMON. *Plantago major*. A naturalized weed of general range like the preceding. *May-Sep.*

Used as early spring greens.

PLEURISY-ROOT. *Asclepias Tuberosa*. Dry fields. Me. to Minn., south to Fla., Texas, Ariz. *June-Sep.*

The tender young shoots may be used like asparagus. The raw tuber is medicinal; but when boiled or baked it is edible.

POKEWEED. *Phytolacca decandra*. A common weed east of the Mississippi and west of Texas. Now cultivated in France, and the wild shoots are sold in our eastern markets.

In early spring the young shoots and leaves make an excellent substitute for asparagus.

The root is poisonous (this is destroyed by heat), and the raw juice of the old plant is an acrid purgative. The berries are harmless.

PRICKLY PEAR. *Opuntia*. Several species. Dry, sandy soil. Along eastern coast, and on western prairies and plains.

The ripe fruit is eaten raw. The unripe fruit, if boiled ten or twelve hours, becomes soft and resembles apple-sauce. When the leaves are roasted in hot ashes, the outer skin, with its thorns, is easily removed, leaving a slimy but sweet and succulent pulp which sustains life. Should be gathered with tongs which can be extemporized by bending a green stick in the middle and beathing it over the fire.

PRIMROSE, EVENING. *Onagra biennis* (*Oenothera b.*). Usually in dry soil. Labrador to Fla., west to Rocky Mts. *June-Oct.*

Young sprigs are mucilaginous and can be eaten as salad. Roots have a nutty flavor, and are used in Europe either raw or stewed, like celery.

EDIBLE PLANTS 391

PURSLANE. Pussley. *Portulaca Oleracea.*
Fields and waste places. A weed of almost worldwide distribution. *Summer.*

This weed was used as a pot-herb by the Greeks and Romans, and is still so used in Europe. The young shoots should be gathered when from 2 to 5 inches long. May also be used as a salad, or pickled. Taste somewhat like string beans, with a slight acid flavor. The seeds, ground to flour, have been used by Indians in the form of mush.

RED-BUD. *Cercis Canadensis.*

French-Canadians use the acid flowers of this tree in salads. The buds and tender pods are pickled in vinegar. All may be fried in butter, or made into fritters.

SAXIFRAGE, LETTUCE. *Saxifraga micranthidifolia.* In cold brooks. Appalachian Mts. from Pa. to N. C. *May-June.*

Eaten by Carolina mountaineers as a salad under the name of "lettuce."

SHEPHERD'S PURSE. *Bursa Bursa-pastoris* (*Capsella B.*). Fields and waste places everywhere. Naturalized. *Jan.-Dec.*

A good substitute for spinach. Delicious when blanched and served as a salad. Tastes somewhat like cabbage, but is much more delicate.

SKUNK CABBAGE. *Spathyema foetida* (*Symplocarpus f.*). Swamps and wet soil. Throughout the east, and west to Minn. and Iowa. *Feb.-April.*

The root of this foul-smelling plant was baked or roasted by eastern Indians, to extract the juice, and used as a bread-root. Doubtless they got the hint from the bear, who is very fond of this, one of the first green things to appear in spring.

SOLOMON'S SEAL. *Polygonatum biflorum.* Woods and thickets. New Brunsw. to Mich., south to Fla. and W. Va. *April-July.*

Indians boiled the young shoots in spring and ate them; also dried the mature roots in fall, ground or pounded them, and baked them into bread. The raw plant is medicinal.

SORREL, MOUNTAIN. *Oxyria digyna.* Greenland to Alaska, south to White Mts. of N. H. and in Rocky Mts. to Colo. *July-Sep.*

A pleasant addition to salads.

SORREL, SHEEP. *Rumux Acetosella.* Dry fields and hillsides. Throughout the continent, except in extreme north. *May-Sep.*

The leaves are very acid. Young shoots may be eaten as a salad. Also used as a seasoning for soups, etc.

The European sorrels cultivated as salad plants are *R. Acetosa, R. scutatus,* and sometimes *R. Patientia.*

SORRELL, WHITE WOOD. *Oxalis Acetosella.* Cold, damp woods. Nova Scotia to Manitoba, mts. of N. C., and north shore of Lake Superior. *May-July.*

Not related to the above. "The pleasant acid taste of the leaves, when mixed with salads, imparts an agreeable, refreshing flavor." The fresh plant, or a "lemonade" made from it, is very useful in scurvy, and makes a cooling drink for fevers. Should be used in moderation, as it contains binoxalate of potash, which is poisonous. Yields the druggist's "salt of lemons."

STORKSBILL. Pin-clover. *Erodium cicutarium.* Waste places and fields. Locally in the east, abundant in the west. *April-Sep.* Naturalized.

The young plant is gathered by western Indians and eaten raw or cooked.

STRAWBERRY BLITE. *Blitum capitatum (Chenopodium c.).* Dry soil. Nova Scotia to Alaska, south to N. J., Ill., Colo., Utah, Nev. *June-Aug.*

Sometimes cultivated for greens. Used like spinach.

TRILLIUM. Wake-robin. Beth-root. *Trillium erectum;* also *T. undulatum* and *T. grandiflorum.* Woods. Nova Scotia to Minn., and south to Fla. *April-June.*

The popular notion that these plants are poisonous is incorrect. They make good greens when cooked. The root has medicinal qualities.

TUCKAHOE. *Pachyma cocos.* A subterranean fungus which grows on decaying vegetable matter, such as old roots. It is found in light, loamy soils and in dry waste places, but not in very old fields or in woodlands. Outwardly it is woody, resembling a cocoanut or the bark of a hickory tree. The inside is a compact, white, fleshy mass, moist and yielding when fresh, but in drying it becomes very hard, cracking from within. It contains no starch, but is composed largely of pectose. The Indians made bread of it, and it is sometimes called Indian Bread. (For details, see an article by Prof. J. H. Gore in *Smithsonian Report,* 1881, pp. 687-701.)

UNICORN PLANT. *Martynia Lousiana* (*M. proboscidea*). Waste places. Me. to N. J. and N. C. Native in Mississippi Valley from Iowa and Ill. southward. *July-Sep.*

Cultivated in some places. The seed-pods, while yet tender, make excellent pickles. The Apaches gather the half-ripe pods of a related species and use them for food.

VETCH, MILK. *Astragalus,* several species. Prairies. *May-Aug.*

Used as food by the Indians. The pea is hulled and boiled.

VIOLET, EARLY BLUE. *Viola palmata.* Dry soil, mostly in woods. Me. to Minn., south to Ga. and Ark. *April-May.*

"The plant is very mucilaginous, and is employed by negroes for thickenig soup, under the name of 'wild okra.'" (Porcher.)

WATERLEAF. *Hydrophyllum Virginicum.* Woods. Quebec to Alaska, south to S. C., Kan., Wash. *May-Aug.*

"Furnishes good greens. Reappears after being picked off, and does not become woody for a long time."

WILD FRUITS

It would extend this chapter beyond reasonable limits if I were to give details of all the wild fruits native to the region here considered. As fruits may be eaten raw, or require no special treatment in cooking, a mere list of them, with the time of ripening, must suffice:

Carolina Buckthorn. *Rhamnus Caroliniana. Sep.*
Woolly-leaved Buckthorn. *Bumelia languinosa. June-July.*
Buffalo-berry. *Lepargyraea argentea. July-Aug.*
American Barberry. *Berberis Canadensis. Aug.-Sep.*
Common Barberry. *Berberis vulgaris. Sep.* Naturalized.
Bailey's Blackberry. *Rubus Baileyanus.*
Bristly Blackberry. *R. setosus.*
Dewberry. *R. Canadensis. June-July.*
High Bush Blackberry. *R. villosus. July-Aug.*
Hispid Blackberry. *R. hispidus. Aug.*
Low Bush Blackberry. *R. trivialis.*
Millspaugh's Blackberry. *R. Millspaughii. Aug.-Sep.*
Mountain Blackberry. *R. Alleghaniensis. Aug.-Sep.*
Sand Blackberry. *R. Cuneifolius. July-Aug.*
Dwarf Bilberry. *Vaccinium caespitosum. Aug.*
Great Bilberry. *V. uliginosum. July-Aug.*
Oval-leaved Bilberry. *V. ovalifolium. July-Aug.*
Thin-leaved Bilberry. *V. membranaceum. July-Aug.*
Black Blueberry. *V. atrococcum. July-Aug.*
Canada Blueberry. *V Canadense. July-Aug.*
Dwarf Blueberry. *V. Pennyslvanicum. June-July.*
High Bush Blueberry. *V corymbosum. July-Aug.*
Low Blueberry. *V. vacillans. July-Aug.*
Low Black Blueberry. *V nigrum. July.*
Mountain Blueberry. *V. pallidum. July-Aug.*
Southern Black Huckleberry. *V. virgatum. July.*
Mountain Cranberry. Windberry. *V. Vitis-Idaea. Aug.-Sep.*
Black Huckleberry. *Gaylussacia resinosa. July-Aug.*

EDIBLE PLANTS

Box Huckleberry. *G. brachycera.*
Dwarf Huckleberry. *G. dumosa.* July-Aug.
Tangleberry. *G. frondosa.* July-Aug.
Appalachian Cherry. *Prunus cuneata.*
Choke Cherry. *P. Virginiana.* July-Aug.
(Edible later.)
Sand Cherry. *P. pumila.* Aug.
Sour Cherry. Egriot. *P. Cerasus.* June-July. Naturalized.
Western Wild Cherry. *P. demissa.* Aug.
Western Sand Cherry. *P. Besseyi.*
Wild Cherry. Crab Cherry. *P. Avium.* Naturalized.
Wild Black Cherry. *P. serotina.* Aug.-Sep.
Wild Red Cherry. *P. Pennsylvanica.* Aug.
American Crab-Apple. Sweet-scented C. *Malus coronaria.* Sep.-Oct.
Narrow-leaved Crab-Apple. *M. angustifolia.*
Soulard Crab-Apple. *M. Soulardi.*
Western Crab-Apple. *M. Ioensis.*
American Cranberry. *Oxycoccus macrocarpus.* Sep.-Oct.
Small Cranberry. Bog C. *O. Oxycoccus.* Aug.-Sep.
Southern Mountain Cranberry. *O. erythrocarpus* July-Sep.
Cranberry Tree. *Viburnum Opulus.* Aug.-Sep.
Crowberry. Curlew-berry. *Empetrum nigrum.* Summer.
Golden Current. Buffalo or Missouri C. *Ribes aureum.*
Northern Black Currant. *R. Hudsonianum.*
Red Currant. *R. rubrum.*
Wild Black Currant. *R. floridum.* July-Aug.
Elderberry. *Sambucus Canadensis.* Aug.
Wild Gooseberry. Dogberry. *Ribes Cynosbati.* Aug.
Missouri Gooseberry. *R. gracile.*
Northern Gooseberry. *R. oxyacanthoides.* July-Aug.
Round-leaved Gooseberry. *R. rotundifolium.* July-Aug.

Swamp Gooseberry. *R. lacustre.* July-Aug.
Bailey's Grape. *Vitis Baileyana.*
Blue Grape. Winter G. *V. bicolor.*
Downy Grape. *V. cinerea.*
Frost Grape. *V. cordifolia.* Oct.-Nov.
Missouri Grape. *V. palmata.* Oct.
Northern Fox Grape. *V. Labrusca.* Aug.-Sep.
Riverside Grape. Sweet-scented G. *V. vulpina.* July-Oct.
Sand Grape. Sugar G. *V. rupestris.* Aug.
Southern Fox Grape. *V. rotundifolia.* Aug.-Sep.
Summer Grape. *V. aestivalis.* Sep.-Oct:
Ground Cherry. *Physalis,* several species.
Hackberry. *Celtis occidentalis.* Sep.-Oct. Berries dry but edible.
Black Haw. *Viburnum prunifolium.* Sep.-Oct.
Scarlet Haw. Red H. *Crataegus mollis.* Sep.-Oct.
May Apple. Mandrake. *Podophyllum peltatum.* July.
Passion-flower. *Passiflora incarnata;* also *P. lutea.* Fruit known as Maypops.
Pawpaw. *Asimina triloba.* Fruit edible when frost-bitten.
Persimmon. *Diospyros Virginiana.* Fruit edible after frost.
Beach Plum. *Prunus martima.* Sep.-Oct.
Canada Plum. *P. nigra.* Aug.
Chickasaw Plum. *P. angustifolia.* May-July.
Low Plum. *P. gracilis.*
Porter's Plum. *P. Alleghaniensis.* Aug.
Watson's Plum. *P. Watsoni.*
Wild Goose Plum. *P. hortulana.* Sep.-Oct.
Wild Red Plum. Yellow P. *P. Americana.* Aug.-Oct.
Ground Plum. *Astragalus crassicarpus;* also *A. Mexicanus.* Unripe fruit resembles green plums, and is eaten raw or cooked.
Black Raspberry. Thimble-berry. *Rubus occidentalis.* July.
Cloudberry. *R. Chamaemorus.*

EDIBLE PLANTS

Dwarf Raspberry. *R. Americanus.* July-Aug.
Purple Wild Raspberry. *R. neglectus.* July-Aug.
Purple-flowering Raspberry. *R. odoratus.* July-Sep.
Salmon-berry. *R. parviflorus.* July-Sep.
Wild Red Raspberry. *R. strigosus.* July-Sep.
Service-berry. June-berry. *Amelanchier Canadensis.* June-July.
Low June-berry. *A. spicata.*
Northwestern June-berry. *A. alnifolia.*
Round-leaved June-berry. *A. rotundifolia.* Aug.
Shad-bush. *A. Botryapium.* June-July.
Silver Berry. *Elaeagnus argentea.* July-Aug.
Creeping Snowberry. *Chiogenes hispidula.* Aug.-Sep. Berries have flavor or sweet birch.
American Wood Strawberry. *Fragaria Americana.*
Northern Wild Strawberry. *F. Canadensis.*
Virginia Strawberry. Scarlet S. *F. Virginiana.*
Black Thorn. Pear Haw. *Crataegus tomentosa.* Oct.
Large-fruited Thorn. *C. punctata.* Sep.-Oct.
Scarlet Thorn. *C. coccinea.* Sep.-Oct.

MAPLE SUGAR AND SIRUP

Anyone who has access to maple trees in the spring of the year can make the best of sirup and sugar, without any special appliances, provided he takes some pains to keep the sap clean and unsoured.

The sap season generally begins about the middle of March and lasts until the third week in April, but varies with a late or an early spring. Sap may begin to flow in mid February, or may be held back until the first of April. It continues "good" from three to six weeks; that is, until the buds swell, after which the sap becomes strong and "buddy." It flows best on a warm day succeeding a freezing night. Trees with large crowns yield the most sap. Those standing in or near cold springs discharge the most and sweetest sap. An average tree may yield, in favorable weather, about two gallons of sap in 24 hours.

The Indians' and early frontiersmen's method of

tapping a tree was to "box" it by cutting a slanting notch in the trunk, about 8 inches long, two or three feet from the ground, and inserting an elder or sumac spout in the bark below the lower end of the notch, from which the sap was caught in a trough or pail; or, two gashes would be cut like a broad V, and a spout was put in at the bottom. Such notching yields a rapid flow, but spoils the tree.

A better way is to bore a hole through the outer bark and just into the sapwood (say from one to two inches depth) on the sunny side of the tree, and insert a spout. With wooden spouts the hole must be larger than when iron ones are used, but make it no larger than necessary (certainly not over one inch), or you will injure the tree. The hole should slope slightly upward.

Place a bucket under each spout. It may be necessary, in a wild region, to drive stout stakes around the buckets in such way that they cannot be robbed; for wild animals, as well as domestic ones, are inordinately fond of maple sap, which seems to exhilarate them when taken in large quantities.

Collect the sap every morning, before it can get warm from the heat of the sun, as it sours easily. Boil it in a kettle to the consistency of honey; then dip it out, pass through woolen strainers, and allow it to stand several hours until impurities have precipitated. It is then ready for use.

To make maple sugar, boil the sirup in a kettle deep enough to keep it from boiling over. Keep it simmering over a slow fire until a heavy scum rises to the surface. Skim this off, and continue the boiling until, when a little of the sirup is stirred in a saucer, it grains (granulates); or until, when spread on the snow, it candies on cooling. Then pour it off into molds. As a rule, it takes about four gallons of sap to make a pound of sugar, and 35 gallons to make a gallon of sirup, but there are wide variations, according to quality of sap.

Sap may be reduced to sugar by alternate freezing and thawing, the ice being thrown away each time it freezes.

Just as good sugar and sirup are made from the red maple and from the silver (white or soft) maple as from the sugar maple (rock maple or sugar tree), but the sap is not quite so rich in sugar, and the running season is shorter. Since these trees bud earlier than sugar maple, they should be tapped earlier. The sap of the ash-leaved maple (com-

EDIBLE PLANTS 399

monly called box elder) has similar qualities; also that of the striped maple (moosewood, striped or swamp dogwood), but this tree seldom grows large enough to be worth using.

There is a decided maple flavor in the sap of the shellbark hickory. A good sirup can be concocted by steeping a handful of the dried and crushed inner bark of this tree in hot water to a strong "tea" and adding sufficient brown sugar. An extract commercially made from the bark is used in making a spurious "maple sirup" out of cane or corn sirup. It is safe to say that not one-tenth of the alleged maple sugar and sirup now on the market is free from this or similar adulteration.

As a backwoods expedient, sirup may be made from the abundant and sugary sap of the black birch (sweet birch). In times of scarcity the pods of the honey locust have been utilized to the same end. They must be used within a month after maturity; later they become bitter.

BEVERAGES

None of our native plants contain principles that act upon the nerves like the caffein of coffee or the thein of tea; consequently all substitutes for coffee and tea are unsatisfying, except merely as hot drinks of agreeable taste. Millions of war-bound people are suffering this deprivation now.

In the South, during the Civil War, many pitiful expedients were tried, such as decoctions of parched meal, dried sweet potatoes, wheat, chicory, cottonseed, persimmon-seed, dandelion-seed, and the seeds of the Kentucky coffee-tree. Better substitutes for coffee were made from parched rye, from the seeds of the coffee senna (*Cassia occidentalis*) called "Magdad coffee," and from the parched and ground seeds of okra. Governor Brown of Georgia once said that the Confederates got more satisfaction out of the goldenrod flowers than out of any other makeshift for coffee. "Take the bloom," he directed, "dry it, and boil to an extract" (meaning tincture).

Teas, so-called, of very good flavor can be made from the dried root-bark of sassafras, or from its early buds, from the bark and leaves of spicewood, from the leaves of chicory, ginseng, dittany, the sweet goldenrod (*Solidago odora*), and cinquefoil. Other plants used for the purpose are Labrador tea, Oswego tea, and (inferior) New Jersey tea. Our pioneers also made decoctions of chips of the arbor-vitae (white cedar) and of sycamore, the dried leaves of black birch, and the tips of hemlock boughs, sweetening them with maple sugar; but here we approach the list of medicinal teas, which is well-nigh endless. The Indians made a really good "maple tea" by boiling sassafras-root bark for a short time in maple sap.

Agreeable summer drinks can be made by infusing the sour fruit of the mountain ash (*Pyrus Americana*), from sumac berries (dwarf and staghorn), and from the fruit of the red mulberry. The sweet sap of both hard and soft maples, box elder, and the birches (except red birch) is potable. Small beer can be made from the sap of black birch, from the pulp of honey locust pods, the fruit of the persimmon, shoots and root-bark of sassafras, and the twigs of black and red spruce. Cider has been made from the fruit of crab-apples and service-berries.

CONDIMENTS

Vinegar can be made from maple or birch sap, or from fruit juices, by diluting with water and adding a little yeast. The very sour berries of sumac turn cider into vinegar, or they may be used alone.

Our fields and forests afford many pleasant condiments for flavoring. Sassafras, oil of birch, wintergreen, peppermint and spearmint will occur to every one. Balm, sweet marjoram, summer savory and tansy are sometimes found in wild places, where they have escaped from cultivation. The rootstock of sweet cicely has a spicy taste, with a strong odor of anise, and is edible. Sweet gale gives a pleasant flavor to soups and dressings. The seeds of tansy mustard were used by the Indians in flavoring dishes. Wild garlic ("ramps"), wild onions, peppergrass, snowberry and spicewood may be used for similar purposes.

Perhaps the greatest privation that a civilized man suffers, next to having no meat, is to lack salt and

EDIBLE PLANTS

tobacco. In the old days they used to burn the outside of meat and sprinkle gunpowder on it in lieu of salt; but in this age of smokeless powder we are denied even that consolation. The ashes of plants rich in nitre, such as tobacco, Indian corn, sunflower, and the ashes of hickory bark, have been recommended. Coville says that the ash of the palmate-leaf sweet coltsfoot (*Petasites palmata*) was highly esteemed by western Indians as a substitute for salt. "To obtain the ash the stem and leaves were first rolled up into balls while still green, and after being carefully dried they were placed on top of a very small fire on a rock, and burned." Perhaps a better plan is to make lye by pouring boiling water on wood ashes, strain, and evaporate to a white crystalline alkali. Use sparingly.

Many Indians, even civilized ones like some of the eastern Cherokees, do not use salt to this day. Strange to say, the best substitute for salt is sugar, especially maple sugar or sirup. One soon can accustom himself to eat it even on meat. Among some of the northern tribes, maple sirup not only takes the place of salt in cooking, but is used for seasoning the food after it is served. Wild honey, boiled, and the wax skimmed off, has frequently served me in place of sugar in my tea, in army bread, etc.

KINNIKINICK

Men who use tobacco can go a good while hungry without much grumbling, so long as the weed holds out.

> Thou who, when cares attack,
> Bidd'st them avaunt! and Black
> Care, at the horseman's back
> Perching, unseatest!

But let tobacco play out, and they are in a bad way! Substitutes for it may be divided into those that are a bit better than nothing and those that are worse. Among the latter may be rated tea. Yes, tea is smoked by many a poor fellow in the far North! It is said to cause a most painful irritation in the throat, which is aggravated by the cold air of that region. Certainly it can have no such effect on the nerves as tobacco, for it is full of tannin, and tannin destroys nicotin.

Kinnikinick is usually made of poor tobacco mixed with the scrapings or shavings of other plants, although the latter are sometimes smoked alone. Chief of the substitutes is the red osier dogwood (*Cornus stolonifera*) or the related silky cornel (*C. sericea*) commonly miscalled red willow. These shrubs are very abundant in some parts of the North. The dried inner bark is aromatic and very pungent, highly narcotic, and produces in those unused to it a heaviness sometimes approaching stupefaction. Young shoots are chosen, or such of the older branches as still keep the thin, red outer skin. This skin is shaved off with a keen knife, and thrown away. Then the soft, brittle, green inner bark is scraped off with the back of the knife and put aside for use; or, if wanted immediately, it is left hanging to the stem in little frills and is crisped before the fire. It is then rubbed between the hands into a form resembling leaf tobacco, or is cut very fine with a knife and mixed with tobacco in the proportion of two of bark to one of the latter.

A more highly prized kinnikinick is made from the leaves of the bear-berry or uva-ursi (*Arctostaphylos-uva-ursi*), called *sacacoommis* by the Canadian traders, who sell it to the northern Indians for more than the price of the best tobacco. The leaves are gathered in the summer months, being then milder than in winter. Inferior substitutes are the crumbled dried leaves of the smooth sumac (*Rhus glabra*) and the fragrant sumac (*R. aromatica*), which, like tea, contain so much tannin that they generally produce bronchial irritation or sore throat.

CHAPTER XXII
LIVING OFF THE COUNTRY—
IN EXTREMIS

As I said at the beginning, the supreme test of woodcraft comes when the equipment has been destroyed by some disaster. Such misfortunes are not uncommon; if we seldom hear of them it is because they happen in far-away, isolated places, and the survivors are not interviewed by the press. A man gets lost and has to wander for a week, two weeks, or longer, before he meets a human being. A canoe is smashed to bits in a rapid, a hundred miles from the nearest outpost, and the men get ashore with nothing but the clothes they stand in and the contents of their pockets. And worse has happened. Robinson Crusoe had a prentice job compared to the actual experiences of hundreds of men and women whom fate has thrown, destitute of tools or weapons, far from the paths and courses of civilization.

The pity is that such disasters befall, in so many cases, people who have no knowledge of how to meet them. Helplessness breeds despair. One woodsman, at such a time, will rustle more food than a company of tenderfoots. At the worst he will find something to keep him going—something that the others, though starving, would pass by without knowing that it could give them energy.

In this sort of emergency, needless to say, there is but one law: self-preservation. Game laws and other rules of sportsmanship are, for the time, non-existent. The sufferer will kill anything that can be eaten, in any way that he can get it. If all game has migrated, and fish cannot be caught, he will eat anything that will give him strength, no matter how unpleasant it would be at other times.

A man without a gun will depend, for animal food, chiefly upon fish and upon such game as he can capture with snares. When one ventures into the wilderness he knows well enough that he may meet disaster at the most unexpected moment, and there is no excuse for him ever being caught without a jackknife, a waterproof box filled with matches, a compass, a good length of stout fish-line, and some hooks. (A woodsman sleeps in his trousers, and he will not even risk bathing where there is danger of losing them.) If he must spend all the daylight in traveling, he can at least set out a night-line for fish and snares for rabbits or other small mammals.

SNARING.—It is not worth while here to describe deadfalls, pitfalls, coop traps, and the like; for our adventurer probably has no tool to make them, nor anything to bait them with. Anyway, a snare will serve just as well, takes much less time and material to set up, and game can be caught in it without any bait at all.

Ground snares, which catch by the feet or legs, are not to be considered, as they are likely to be broken by the animal's frantic plunges, or may be chewed off, unless made of wire. The surest way is to fix a noose to a spring-pole, and set it with a trigger, so as to catch the animal round the neck and jerk it up into the air where its struggles are soon over.

Just how to set a snare depends upon what kind of animal you try for. Take, for example, rabbits (I use this word generically to include cottontails and hares of all degrees). They are the commonest of game everywhere, from far north to farthest south, in swamps, in woodlands, on the plains, and up the mountains to tree limit. Since they are fond of beaten paths, and are not of a suspicious nature, they can be caught without bait;

LIVING OFF THE COUNTRY 405

although their food is such that even a lost man can find it if he chooses to bait his snares. They do not hibernate, but are out all the year round. So the rabbit is a lost man's main chance in the meat line.

A good snare for setting in a runway is shown in Fig. 190. It catches "coming or going." A small, springy sapling (*A*), growing a few feet to

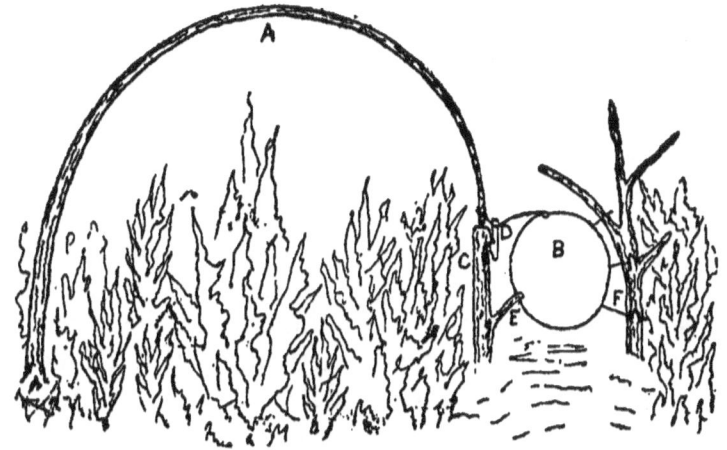

Fig. 190.—Runway snare

one side of the rabbit path, is trimmed, and will be bent over for setting. If none grows in the right place, cut one and drive it firmly into a hole made with a sharpened stick, or lash it to a tree or stub. The best place for a snare is in the bend of a runway with plenty of bushes on both sides. Drive a stout stake at *C,* and notch it for the trigger *D*. Plant opposite it, at *F,* a dead branch that forks over top of snare so the animal will run under, but not in such a way as to entangle the loop when sprung. Now take a length of soft brass or copper wire, or a strong cord (No. 1-0 braided linen fish-line is good), twist or tie it to the end of spring-pole and around the little wooden trigger, and form the long part into a noose. Bend the pole and set the trigger, as shown, extending loop over the runway, a couple of inches off the ground. The noose may be about six inches in diameter. If of wire, it can be held in place by drawing it lightly into the cleft end of a stub, as at *E,* or a split stick stuck in the ground for that purpose. If cord is used, hold it in place with little twigs or with blades of grass bent round it and drawn back into nicks made with a knife in the stakes at each side, as at *F.* No bait is needed.

This is also a good snare to set at the mouth of a den or burrow.

As for baited snares, there are many ingenious ways of rigging them. One example will suffice. The bait itself will depend, of course, upon the kind of animal to be caught. For rabbits it may be succulent roots or wild fruits. The 'coon, 'possum, and skunk have a varied diet: grasshoppers, crickets, beetles, grubs, mussels, fish, crayfish, frogs, snakes, lizards, birds, eggs, nuts, fruits, roots; and lots of other things. The wildcat and the lynx are lured by any kind of meat, particularly if it is bloody. If the bait is so small or so delicate that it cannot be tied to the bait-stick, make for it a little pan of bark fastened to the stick. All wild animals are passionately fond of salt, and, if you have any of it, a pinch of salt rubbed on the bait will make it all the more enticing.

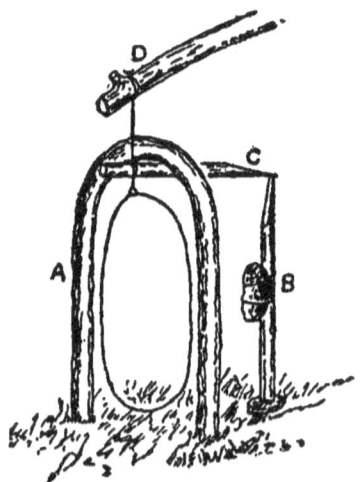

Fig. 191.—Baited snare

The snare shown in Fig. 191 is easy to rig, requires only a short length of wire or cord, and goes off like a hair trigger. Its dimensions will depend on the size of the animal it is set for. The idea is to have the loop only large enough for the prey to stick its head through without touching on more than one side, if any, and just high enough from the ground so as not to catch by a leg or foot. The bait sets back only far enough for the noose to catch around the throat and behind the ears—except in case of a 'coon, which always reaches in with its paw, so the bait-stick must be set far enough back to allow for this.

For rabbits, cut a limber stick about two feet long and as thick as your thumb; sharpen both ends, bend in the middle, and drive in the ground in the form of an arch (A). The end of the spring-pole, when bent over, comes just over the top of this arch (D). Now cut a stick (B) of length corresponding to height of arch, trim one end to a slightly wedge-shaped point, and tie the bait to the middle. A similar stick (C) is cut of such length that, when rigged as here shown, the bait will stand at the right distance back of the arch. The figure shows how the noose is attached. If the ground is soft, set the butt of the bait-stick on a flat stone or chip.

To make the animal stick his head in through the arch, instead of elsewhere, drive dead sticks in a semi-circle, with the arch for an entrance, leaving twigs on them to give a natural appearance to the little den.

Such a snare can be used with success on large animals, a stronger spring-pole and noose being required, of course, and the pen made larger, accordingly. Even such powerful beasts as the bear and the moose can be caught with snares of twisted rawhide or rope—but we are considering only small game.

When setting for animals that are wily and suspicious, use no green sticks, but sound dead ones, rub dirt over the cuts, drop no chips about the snare, leave the ground undisturbed, and handle things as little as possible, for your own scent is a "give-away."

It is of no use to set snares or other traps except where there is recent "sign," such as tracks, droppings, twigs and bark nibbled, feathers or hair of animals eaten, and so on. You must find where your quarry lives, or where it often goes in search of food.

If there is likelihood of a finely-set snare being sprung by birds or mice, make the ends of the trigger-sticks flat, with good bearing, and tie the bait on so firmly that it will take a smart tug to release the trigger.

A very simple and effective snare for birds, as well as for small mammals, is rigged by dropping a small evergreen or other bushy tree across a trail or runway, so that its stem is a foot or so above the ground (depending upon size of animal); then trim off enough under branches to leave an opening in the middle of the trail, and set a noose in it, attached to the tree. Two or three such openings may be made, with a noose in each. Scatter bait along the path on both sides of the tree. An animal finding a noose drawing about its neck will push onward, instead of backing out, and so choke itself to death.

If you have neither wire nor cord to make nooses with, use any of the strong, pliable rootlets, or bark cords, mentioned in Chapter XV. After one animal is captured, its skin and intestines can be made into strings or thongs for such purposes.

FISHING FOR THE POT.—Trout, perch, pickerel, and various other fishes, may be taken with hook and line any month in the year—when they are in the humor. In cold weather, fish the deep still water, through holes in the ice, if there is any.

Where suckers lie motionless, in plain view, they can be snared with a wire noose by dropping it gently in front and under one of them, and giving a jerk. Other fish sometimes may be taken in the same way. In hot weather, if you have no tackle at all, seek a small spring-hole, close its outlet with sticks and brush, build an artificial outlet, with rocks, etc., leading to a flat; then get into the spring-hole, thrash around with a stick, poke under the ledges, and scare the fish out to where they will be stranded, so you may catch them with your naked hands. Some spring-holes can be made into traps themselves by digging a deeper outlet and running the water off.

BAIT.—The commonest of all baits, earthworms, are *not* common in a wilderness. Generally they are creatures of the barnyard and garden. Out in the big woods they are too scarce to consider, except as accidental findings. If you chance upon an old lumber camp or saw-mill site, you may find worms in abundance by digging under piles of chips and sawdust. Sometimes, in a damp place in the forest, you can get active little red fellows (fine bait) under overturned rocks or logs, or under the moss on the banks of brooks. The largest worms I ever saw are found, after a warm shower, or just before nightfall, on the grassy summits of "balds" in the Great Smoky Mountains, nearly 6,000 feet above sea-level; some of them are full two feet long.

The best all-round bait is a lively minnow. You may catch minnows on a very small hook with most of the barb filed off, or even on a bent pin, baited with a tiny bit of meat, a maggot, a grub, or a small insect. In winter, try a spring-hole, or cut through the ice close to shore.

Three men working together can capture plenty of minnows in a few minutes, wherever there is a small stream, by using what we called in the Ozarks a "brush seine." Simply get a lot of willows or other pliable brush, lay the stuff overlapping to length desired, and twist a little until the branchlets interlock (like a farmer twisting a hay rope). Then, with a man at each end to haul, and another at the middle to hold the "seine" down in the water, drag the shallows and run the minnows ashore.

On dark days, or in rough or turbid water, the best baits are shiners, silversides (redfins), and other bright colored minnows; but they do not live long on the hook. In sunny weather, and for clear, still water, chubs and other tough species are preferred, being more active and enduring. Almost any small fish will do in a pinch. Young yellow perch make excellent bait if the dorsal spine is clipped off. On the Potomac and the Susquehanna rivers a favorite bass bait is what they call a madtom, which is nothing but a small yellow catfish (stone cat) with its spines cut off. To keep a tom from running under a rock and anchoring himself there, they peel a bit of skin off the back of his head: one bump on that tender spot cures him!

For bass, pickerel, and mascalonge (spell it to suit yourself—here in the Carolina mountains the natives call it the "jack fish"—yes, we have the real mascalonge) don't use minnows under three inches, if you can get better ones. A half-pound bass will get away with a five-inch minnow.

When fishing with a short line and no reel, hook your minnow through the back, instead of the mouth, just behind the dorsal fin, being careful not to injure the backbone. The reason is that you have no chance to let your bass run and turn the minnow for swallowing—you must strike quick, while he is holding it by the middle. (Now don't get your own back up, Mr. Angler, this whole chapter is for men in extremity, and sportsmanship has nothing to do with it.)

Frogs often are good bait in still fishing (the only method we are considering), although most favored by bait casters. Use none but small ones; the big fellows are of no account except for your own eating. The young of the common leopard frog is best. Hook him through both lips, from the bottom up, but to one side, so as to miss the artery in the center of the upper jaw. Let the hook come out near one eye; then the frog will wriggle around in trying to right himself. Keep him in motion a good deal, and bring him up now and then for a breathing-spell, or he will drown. Young frogs are to be found from June to August

LIVING OFF THE COUNTRY

along the grassy banks of creeks, muddy margins of ponds, around springs, and wet swales. To capture without a net, approach stealthily until within sure reach; then strike swiftly, with fingers outspread.

In May and June, tadpoles can be used with success. The little red newt (often called "spring lizard," although it is not a reptile but a batrachian) is greedily taken by trout and other fish. It abounds in the woods as early as April, under stones and decaying logs or stumps, and comes out in great numbers after warm rains.

Crayfish (generally called "crawfish," by some "crabs") are found under flat stones in shallow water. They shed their hard armor periodically, and are at their best as bait when in the "shedder" stage. In this condition they may be hooked through the body, avoiding the heart, which lies close to the back just forward of where the tail joins the body. When in the hard shell, pass the hook upward through the tail; or, if the hook is too small to project enough in this way, pass it into the shell and out again. Use a float on the line, so as to keep the crayfish a few inches off the bottom, or he will cling like grim death to the first thing he can get hold of. Bass are very fond of crayfish at times.

One of the best natural baits for bass, when the water is clear, is that fierce-looking creature called hellgrammite, dobson, or grampus. This is the larva of a large winged insect, the horned corydalis.

It is found under stones or other submerged objects in shallow, swift-running water. To catch it, turn the stone over, upstream; the hellgrammite then will curl up into a ball and float down into the net or hat held to receive it. Seize it by the sides of the neck, to avoid its sharp pincers, and, holding your hook sidewise so the barb will be horizontal, pass the point under and close up against the hard "collar" on the back of the neck, from behind forward, bringing the hook out just behind the thing's head. A hellgrammite is so tough and tenacious of life that two or more fish may be caught with one of them. Like the crayfish, it should be kept off the bottom by a float or by moving it frequently. The mature corydalis fly can be used as bait, after plucking off its wings, but it it much softer than the larva and does not live long on the hook.

From early spring until June, or even July, it is easy to get "stick bait" (the larva of the caddis fly) in almost any trout stream. This little white grub or creeper, with short black thorax and black head armed with nippers, makes for itself a cylindrical case out of tiny twigs, bits of leaf, sand, etc., stuck together with silk that it secretes, the whole being a good example of protective resemblance, for it looks just like a broken piece of dead twig. Caddis worms, hidden in these cases, strew the bottom of still shallows at the sides of streams, along with trash collected there by the eddies. Pinch off one end of the case, draw the worm out by its head, and impale it on a small trout hook. Fish take it very greedily.

Various other aquatic larvae, such as those of stone flies, drakes, and water beetles, will be found in spring and summer under stones and sticks, or attached to them, in shallow water with rocky or gravelly bottom. Almost any creeper that you find in such a place is good bait.

Throughout the hot summer months the best of all live baits for trout are certain species of grasshoppers. Some of these may be captured even as late as October. There is a little, hard-bodied, green grasshopper, active and hard to catch, that appears early in the season and is a good fish lure at that time; but the later green ones are too soft and pulpy to stay on a hook, and they seldom bring a strike, anyway. Then there are the large, slow-flying, dry-looking locusts that become so numerous late in summer—they are worthless. What the fish want, and will go after, are the medium-sized

LIVING OFF THE COUNTRY 413

'hoppers with darkish, well marked bodies, red or yellow under wings, and a *juicy* appearance. In the dog-days, when trout lie deep in the pools, sluggish and scornful of all other lures, it takes this sort of a grasshopper, kicking madly along the surface, to interest, excite, and compel your big old stager to an athletic contest.

The time to catch grasshoppers is in the early morning, when the grass is still heavy with dew, or after a shower, or by moonlight after the dew has fallen. They are cold and torpid then, and you can pick up a boxful in no time. Common ways of hooking are through the upper part of the thorax, or through the "breastplate" and upward out through the head. Either of these will do in rippling water, though the bait dies quickly; but to provoke a lazy trout from the bottom of a still pool you must give your 'hopper every chance and encouragement to play the gymnast, and keep it up. This he certainly cannot do if impaled through the vitals. Tie a loop of thread around his body, under the wings and just ahead of the hind legs. Then run a small hook, from behind and forward, through this loop, on the under side of the insect's body, so that the bend of the hook hangs straight down between the legs and pointing backward. Harnessed in this way, the grasshopper is uninjured, and he is naturally balanced on the water. Drop him in, as far above the pool as circumstances will permit, and let the current carry him along while he kicks like a fury to rid himself of his incumbrance. It is a lump and a sot of a trout who can stand such a performance over his very nose.

Crickets have the same "season" as grasshoppers, and are used in the same way. You will find them under rocks and logs, or they can be captured in the open after a shower. Bass are not so fond of grasshoppers and crickets as trout are; and yet, in the hot months, there are times when our notional small-mouth will take nothing else.

During the time of frost, bait may be hard to

get; but fish have less choice then, and, correspondingly, are not so fanciful about their diet, when they have any appetite at all. Grubs may be found in decaying tree trunks, down-logs and stumps, which you can kick open or knock to pieces. Many insects hibernate under logs and rocks, loose old bark, rotting leaves, etc., and so do snails and lizards. A warm, thawing day will bring many of them out.

If the wanderer has saved a bit of bacon, he has fish bait ready at hand. Having caught one fish, then he has bait for others by utilizing the "throat latch" (the V of tough skin and tendon directly under the tongue), or a strip of white, glistening fish belly, which he will skitter on the water to imitate the motions of a live minnow. If the skin of a small trout or perch is used, leave the belly fin on.

NIGHT LINES.—If one has enough stout line and hooks, he can set out a trot-line overnight, and stand good chance of fresh fish for breakfast. Methods vary, according to circumstances. Suppose you are on the bank of a river, and have no boat. To one end of your line tie a stone about the size of your fist. Three feet back of it tie on your first snood, and add others at similar intervals—two, three, or more of them. The snood is a bit of line, twelve to eighteen inches long, with a stout hook at the end of it. Coil the rest of the line neatly on the bank and tie its near end to a stake driven firmly into the ground. Bait the hooks, as directed below. Now get a forked stick as long as a broom-handle, poke its crotch under the stone, and heave the line into the stream. In this way there is no danger of hooking your hand when throwing. The stick gives extra leverage; so don't throw too hard, or you will outrun your line and break it. If there is slack line left, draw it in until you feel the tug of the stone anchor. Then drive a limber stick in front of your stake, split its top, and draw your line through the split to keep all taut. If a fish hooks itself while you are by, you will know it by the jerking of the trigger stick. Then haul in and bait afresh. In this way we used to catch barrels of catfish, redhorses, buffaloes, and white suckers, when I was a kid, out West. We would set out several trot-lines, put a ball of mud on each trigger stick, go off skylarking, come back, and—wherever a mud ball had tumbled off we knew we had a fish!

If minnows or crawfish or hellgrammites are used as bait, or if the bottom is rough, it is a good plan to float the hooks of a trot-line a few inches off the bottom. This also keeps the bait in sight of passing fish. A split cork, or a bit of light wood, about four inches back of each hook, will do the business.

For bait on a set-line you can use anything that fish will eat, and this is a broad order, since most of your catch will be ground-feeders who are not at all fastidious. For catfish one of the best baits is raw, red meat. Entrails and other offal of animals you may have snared will do very well. Soft or delicate bait, such as liver, should be threaded on the hooks, or inclosed in a bit of mosquito netting, if you should chance to have any. This hinders turtles and eels from stealing the bait.

Lacking a long line, you can tie short "bush lines," here and there along the bank at likely places, to limbs of projecting trees, or to poles securely planted in the bank. It pays to take up the outlines several times during the night, to rebait, and to get fish or turtles that might break away if left on too long.

FROGS.—Hitherto we have considered frogs only as bait. Let my revered and oft-quoted mentor "Nessmuk" tell how to get them for the pan. A man without equipment can easily extemporize all that is needed.

"And when fishing is very poor, try frogging. It is not sport of a high order, though it may be called angling—and it can be made amusing, with hook and line. . . . There are several modes of taking the festive batrachian. He is speared with a frog-spear; caught under the chin with snatch-hooks; taken with hook and line; or picked up from a canoe [or ashore] with the aid of a headlight, or jack-lamp. The two latter modes are best.

To take him with hook and line: a light rod, six to eight feet of line, a snell of single gut with a 1-0 Sproat or O'Shaughnessy hook, and a bit of bright scarlet flannel for bait; this is the rig. To use it, paddle up behind him silently, and drop the rag just in front of his nose. He is pretty certain to take it on the instant. Knock him on the head before cutting off his legs. . .

"By far the most effective manner of frogging is by the headlight on dark nights. To do this most successfully, one man in a light canoe, a good headlight, and a light, one-handed paddle, are the requirements. The frog is easily located, either by his croaking or by his peculiar shape. Paddle up to him silently and throw the light in his eyes; you may then pick him up as you would a potato. I have known a North Woods guide to pick up a five-quart pail of frogs in an hour, on a dark evening. On the table, frogs' legs are usually conceded first place for delicacy and flavor. . . . And, not many years ago, an old pork-gobbling backwoodsman threw his frying-pan into the river because I had cooked frogs' legs in it. While another, equally intelligent, refused to use my frying-pan because I had cooked eels in it; remarking sententiously, 'Eels is snakes, an' I know it.'"

"SMALL DEER."—It goes without saying that men traveling through a barren region cannot be fastidious in their definition of "game." All's meat that comes to a hungry man's pot. A few words here may not be amiss as to the edible qualities of certain animals that are not commonly regarded as game, but which merit an explorer's consideration from the start; also as to some that are not recommended.

Probably most sportsmen know that 'coon is not bad eating, especially when young, if it is properly prepared; but how many would think to remove the scent-glands before roasting a 'coon? These glands should be sought for and extracted from all

LIVING OFF THE COUNTRY

animals that have them, before the meat is put in the pot. Properly dressed, and, if necessary, parboiled in two or three waters, even muskrats, woodchucks, and fish-eating birds can be made palatable. (See Vol. I., pp. 281, 313, 316, 318.)

Prairie-dog is as good as squirrel. The flesh of the porcupine is good, and that of the skunk is equal to roast pig. Beaver meat is very rich and cloying, and in old animals is rank; but the boiled liver and tail are famous tid-bits wherever the beaver is found. A man would have to be hard pressed to tackle any of the other fur-bearers as food, excepting, of course, bear and 'possum.

The flesh of all members of the cat tribe, wildcats, lynxes, and panthers, is excellent. Doctor Hart Merriam declares that panther flesh is better than any other kind of meat. The Englishman Ruxton, who lived in the Far West in the time of Bridger and the Sublettes and Fitzpatrick, says: "Throwing aside all the qualms and conscientious scruples of a fastidious stomach, it must be confessed that dog meat takes a high rank in the wonderful variety of cuisine afforded to the gourmand and the gourmet by the prolific mountains. Now, when the bill of fare offers such tempting viands as buffalo beef, venison, mountain mutton, turkey, grouse, wildfowl, hares, rabbits, beaver-tails, etc., etc., the station assigned to dog as No. 2 in the list can be well appreciated—No. 1, in delicacy of flavor, richness of meat, and other good qualities, being the flesh of panthers, which surpasses every other, and all put together."

Lewis and Clark say of dog flesh: "The greater part of us have acquired a fondness for it. . . While we subsisted on that food we were fatter, stronger, and in general enjoyed better health than at any period since leaving the buffalo country." Again they say: "It is found to be a strong, healthy diet, preferable to lean deer or elk, and much superior to horse flesh in any state." Many other travelers and residents in the early West commended dog meat; but the animals that they speak of were such as had been specially fattened by the Indians for food, and not starved and hard-worked sledge animals.

One who was driven by starvation to eat wolf's flesh says that it "tastes exactly as a dirty, wet dog smells, and it is gummy and otherwise offensive." But it seems that tastes differ, or, more likely, that all wolves are not alike. Ivar Forsheim of Sverdrup's second Norwegian polar expedition says: "They were two she-wolves in very much better condition than beasts of prey usually are, with the exception of bears. The fat really looked so white and good that we felt inclined to taste it, and if we did that, we thought we might as well try the hearts at the same time. Although most people will consider this a dish more extraordinary than appetizing, I think prejudice plays a large part here; as, at any rate, we found the meat far better than we expected."

I am assured by more than one white man who has eaten them that the flesh of snakes and lizards is as good as chicken or frogs' legs. One of my friends, however, draws the line at the prairie rattler. Once when he was on the U. S. Geological Survey he came near starving in the desert, and had to swallow his scruples along with a snake diet. "Probably," he said, "a big, fat diamond rattler might be all right, but the little prairie rattler is too sweetish for my taste; it's no comparison to puff-adder; puff-adder, my boy, is out of sight!"

This much I can swallow, by proxy; but when Dan Beard speaks approvingly of hellbenders as a side dish, I must confess that I'm like Kipling's elephant when the alligator had him by the nose: "This is too buch for be!"

Another of my acquaintances assured me that the prejudice against crow (real *Corvus*) is not well founded, and I found by testing that he was in the right. The great gray owl is good roasted, despite what it may be when "biled." The flesh of the whippoorwill is excellent. Turtles' eggs are better than those of the domestic fowl (soft-shell turtles deposit their eggs on sandbars about the third week in June).

It is the testimony of gourmets who survived the siege of Paris that cats, rats, and mice are the most misprized of all animals, from a culinary point of view. "Stewed puss," says one of them, "is by far more delicious than stewed rabbit. Those who have not tasted *couscoussou* of cat have never tasted anything."

Anyway, who are we, to set up standards as to the fitness or unfitness of things to eat? We shudder with horror at the idea of eating dog or cat, but of such a downright filthy animal as the pig we eat ears, nose, feet, tail, and intestines. How about our moldy and putrid cheeses, our boiled cabbage and sauerkraut, raw Hamburgers and "high" game? The hardihood of him who first swallowed a raw oyster! And if snails are good, why not locusts, dragon flies, and the like? I tell you from experience that when you get to picking the skippers out of your pork, and begrudge them the holes they have made in it, you will agree that any kind of fresh, wild meat that is not carrion is clean and wholesome. Caspar Whitney, after describing his menu of frozen raw meat in the Barren Grounds, says: "I have no doubt some of my readers will be disgusted by this recital; and as I sit here at my desk writing, with but to reach out and press a button for dinner, luncheon—what I will—I can hardly realize that only a few months ago I choked an Indian until he gave up a piece of muskox intestine he had stolen from me. One must starve to know what one will eat."

I trust that none of my readers may be cast down by reading these somewhat lugubrious pages. After all, it is not so bad to learn new dishes; but think of the predicament of that poor wight—he was a missionary to the Eskimo, I believe—who, being cast adrift on an ice floe, and essaying to eat his boots, did incontinently sneeze his false teeth into the middle of Baffin's Bay!

IN EXTREMIS.—The Far North is Famine Land, the world over, and to it we must look for examples of what men can subsist on when driven to the last extremity.

In all northern countries, within the tree limit, it is customary, in starving times, to mix with the scanty hoard of flour the ground bark of trees. It is possible to support life even with bark alone. The Jesuit missionary Nicollet reported, more than two centuries ago, that an acquaintance of his, a French Indian-agent, lived seven weeks on bark alone, and the *Relations* of the order, in Canada, contain many instances of a like expedient. Those were hard times in New France! Such an experience as this was dismissed with a single sentence, quite as a matter of course: "An eelskin was deemed a sumptuous supper; I had used one for mending a robe, but hunger obliged me to unstitch and eat it." Another brother says: "The bark of the oak, birch, linden, and that of other trees, when well cooked and pounded, and then put into the water in which fish had been boiled, or else mixed with fish-oil, made some excellent stews." Again: "they [the Indians] dried by a fire the bark of green oak, then they pounded it and made it into a porridge." It seems that the human stomach can stand a lot of tannin, if it has to do so.

The young shoots of spruce and tamarack, the inner bark (in spring) of pine, spruce, and hemlock, young leaf-stems of beech, hickory and other trees, the buds of poplar, maple and wild rose, and the young leaves and flowers of basswood are nutritious; but these can be had only, of course, in spring. Far better than oak bark are the inner barks of alder, quaking aspen, basswood, birch, sweet bay, cottonwood, slippery elm (this especially is nutritious),

LIVING OFF THE COUNTRY 421

white elm, pignut hickory, yellow locust, striped maple, poplar, and sassafras. The Chippewas boil the thick, sweetish bark of the shrubby bittersweet or staff-tree (*Celastrus scandens*) and use it for food. Young saplings of white cedar have a sweet pith of pleasant flavor which the Ojibways used in making soup.

The following entry in the diary of Sir John Franklin sounds naive, when stripped of its context, but there is a world of grim pathos back of it: "There was no *tripe de roche,* so we drank tea and ate some of our shoes for supper." The rock tripe here referred to (*Umbilicaria arctica* or *Dillenii*) is one of several edible lichens that grow on rocks and are extensively used as human food in lands beyond the arctic tree limit. Reindeer moss (*Cladonia rangiferina*) and the well-known Iceland moss (*Cetraris Icelandica*) are other examples. These are starchy, and, after being boiled for two or three hours, form a gelatinous mass that is digestible, though repulsive in appearance, one of the early Jesuits likening it to the slime of snails, and another admitting that "it is necessary to close one's eyes to eat it."

CHAPTER XXIII

ACCIDENTS AND EMERGENCIES: THEIR BACKWOODS TREATMENT

The present chapter is boiled down for the use of men of little or no surgical experience, who may suddenly find themselves wounded, or with an injured companion on their hands, when far away from any physician.

In operating upon a comrade, the main things are to keep cool, act promptly, and make him feel that you have no doubt that you can pull him through all right. Place him in a comfortable position, and expose the wound. If you cannot otherwise remove the clothing quickly and without hurting him, rip it up the seam. First stop the bleeding, if there is any; then cleanse the wound of dirt (but do not wash it); then close it, if a cut or torn wound; then apply a *sterilized* dressing; then bandage it in place. Of course, if the injury is serious, you will immediately send a messenger hot-foot for a surgeon, provided there is any chance of getting one.

As for the patient himself, let him never say die. Pluck has carried many a man triumphantly through what seemed the forlornest hope. Let me take space for an example or two.

Kit Carson once helped to amputate a comrade's limb when the only instruments available were a razor, a handsaw, and the kingbolt of a wagon. Not a man in the party knew how to take up an artery. Fine teeth were filed in the back of the saw, the iron was made white-hot, the arm was removed, the stump seared so as to close the blood-

ACCIDENTS AND EMERGENCIES 423

vessels, and—the patient recovered.

Charles F. Lummis, having fractured his right arm so badly that the bone protruded, and being alone in the desert, gave his canteen strap two flat turns about the wrist, buckled it around a cedar tree, mounted a nearby rock, set his heels upon the edge, and threw himself backward. He fainted; but the bone was set. Then, having rigged splints to the injured member with his left hand and teeth, he walked fifty-two miles without resting, before he could get food, and finished the 700-mile tramp to Los Angeles with the broken arm slung in a bandanna.

Richardson tells of a Montana trapper who, having his leg shattered in an Indian fight, and finding that gangrene was setting in, whetted one edge of his big hunting knife, filed the other into a saw, and with his own hands cut the flesh, sawed the bone, and seared the arteries with a hot iron. He survived.

FIRST-AID MATERIALS.—Many of the operations hereinafter described can be performed with extemporized materials; but antiseptics and sterilized dressings, ready at all times for instant use, are so essential in the treatment of wounds and other injuries, that every wise traveler will carry on his person some sort of first-aid packet. Even if this be nothing more than one of the Red Cross dressings for small wounds and a few antiseptic tablets, sealed up in a waterproof and greaseproof envelope, which weighs practically nothing and takes up hardly any room, it may make all the difference between a quick cure and long suffering or death from blood-poisoning. The pocket emergency case that I mentioned on page 103, along with a soldier's first-aid packet for major injuries, are sufficient to give emergency treatment in any case, yet the two together weigh less than half a pound and can be carried in a coat pocket.

424 CAMPING AND WOODCRAFT

Dressings.—Roller bandages are not recommended, save to men already trained to use them properly. Anybody, on the other hand, can apply the small ready-to-use Red Cross dressings, and adhesive plaster for strapping them on where they cannot be tied. For large wounds, the triangular bandage in a soldier's packet is easy for anyone to use, as there are cuts and directions printed on it showing how to apply it to any part of the person.

A roll of adhesive plaster (zinc oxide plaster) is almost indispensable; but never apply it directly to a wound—first cover the hurt with a sterilized pad.

Court plaster, although the commonest of first-aid dressings, is the poorest. It is likely to be surgically unclean, and has no antiseptic properties, but, on the contrary, it seals up the wound so as to confine whatever germs may have invaded it—the very worst thing it could do, for it defeats Nature in her effort to get rid of the poison by suppuration. Flexible collodion ("new skin") is likely to do the same thing, unless the cut or abrasion is first sterilized with a strong antiseptic.

Never turn a compress (or other dressing) over and use the other side; it is infected.

Antiseptics.—Such dressings, however, are not enough in themselves to cleanse wounds and keep them free from infection. A supply of some good antiseptic is indispensable in the kit. Those commonly used in domestic practice are either bulky liquids, impracticable on a "go-light" trip, or ineffective powders, like boric acid, that are only soothing, not really germicidal.

Mercury bichloride (corrosive sublimate) is a powerful agent, but it is so corrosive that it does not make fit solutions in metal vessels, which are all that a woodsman or explorer has. Besides, it is a deadly poison. Carbolic acid in solution is too bulky, and the full-strength liquid is mean to carry on a rough trip.

ACCIDENTS AND EMERGENCIES 425

Hitherto I have recommended iodine; but a bottle of it will make a sad mess of things if it leaks or breaks; an ampule in the pocket case serves for but one treatment, and, being in a wooden tube, is bulky in proportion. Iodine is poisonous, corrosive, painful in use, and impossible on delicate tissues. It has the further disadvantage that it clots blood serum, and so cannot penetrate a punctured wound unless the hole is slit open with a knife.

Thanks to the discoveries of Dr. Carrel, with calcium hypochlorite, in the military hospitals of France, and of Dr. Dakin, who has produced a chlorine-carrier that does not deteriorate, we now have what seems to be the ideal antiseptic. I am at present using Dakin's antiseptic, as made here under the trade name of chlorazene. It is put up in tablet form. Chlorazene is neither poisonous nor corrosive in any marked degree. It can be employed, in proper solution, anywhere, even in the eye, as well as for sterilizing instruments and the hands of the operator. Yet it is one of the most powerful of all known antiseptics.

Stimulants.—In many accidents a stimulant is required. Don't carry whiskey—if you don't drink it up yourself the first time you feel bad, then someone will surely steal it. For the camp medical kit, get a bottle of pure grain alcohol. Put a fake label on it—"Antiseptic—Poison"—with a death's-head that even a savage will understand. For internal use, give a teaspoonful of it in three times the quantity of water. For dressing wounds, or giving an alcohol rub, use three parts alcohol to two of water; for a sprain, half-and-half.

Another good and quickly diffusible stimulant is aromatic spirits of ammonia, one teaspoonful in half a glass of water. It is useful for various other purposes that will be mentioned later.

No liquid can well be carried in a pocket emergency case; but there is room for a few strychnine sulphate tablets to be used as a heart tonic and nerve bracer in case of snake bite, shock, exhaustion, alcoholism, or as may otherwise be needed. The dose is 1-30 grain hypodermically or 1-20 grain by mouth.

Emetics.—To treat poisoning, and some other ailments, an emetic is required. A tablespoonful of salt, or of dry mustard, in half a pint of lukewarm water, will serve the purpose. Repeat if necessary.

Liniments and Lotions.—Most of the "patent" liniments are humbugs, considering the claims made for them. Treatment with heat or cold, as the case may be, is far more curative, nine times out of ten, and an alcohol rub will take good care of the other tenth.

An excellent astringent lotion for sprains and bruises can be prepared by dissolving in water one or more tablets of lead acetate and opium, which are small enough for the emergency kit.

Wherever witch hazel grows, one can make his own decoction (strong "tea") of the bark; it is also good as a poultice. The inner bark of kinnikinick, otherwise known as red willow or silky cornel, makes a good astringent poultice for sprains and bruises.

Ointments.—These seldom are good applications for wounds. Grease attracts and holds dirt; dirt breeds infection. But there is proper use for some zinc ointment, resinol, unguentine, or carbolized vaseline, in cases of skin affections, sunburn, ivy poisoning, erysipelas, blistered feet, and so on.

Extemporized Dressings.—In case no regular antiseptic is at hand, there are pretty good wound dressings to be found in the woods. Balsam obtained by pricking the little blisters on the bark of balsam firs is one of them. Others are the honeylike gum of the liquidambar or sweet gum tree, raw turpentine from any pine tree, and the resin procured by boxing (gashing) a cypress or hemlock

ACCIDENTS AND EMERGENCIES 427

tree, or by boiling a knot of the wood and skimming off the surface. All of these resins are antiseptic, and the first two are soothing.

Poultices may be needed to relieve the tension of an inflamed part and to hasten suppuration ("draw the pus to a head"). They have no other curative effect than hot-water compresses, but act more efficiently because they hold the heat better and do not require so frequent renewal. A poultice is easily made from cornmeal or oatmeal (flaxseed is not supposed to be in the kit). Mix by stirring a little at a time into boiling water, making a thick paste free from lumps; then spread on cloth to a thickness of ½-inch, leaving a 1½-inch margin all around for folding in. The poultice should be made thoroughly antiseptic by dissolving tablets in the water. To prevent it from sticking, grease the part or smear it with oil. Then put on the poultice and, if convenient, cover with a waterproof material. Remember that a cold poultice does no good whatever, and that an old one should not be reheated—make a new one. Renew a large poultice every four or five hours, a small one every one or two hours.

The woods themselves afford plenty of materials for good poultices. Chief of these is slippery elm, the mucilaginous inner bark of which, boiled in water and kneaded into a poultice, is soothing to inflammation and softens the tissues. Good poultices can also be made from the soft rind of tamarack, the root bark of basswood or cottonwood, and many other trees or plants. None of these should be spread more than ¼-inch thick. Our frontiersmen, like the Indians, often treated wounds by merely applying the chewed fresh leaves of alder, striped maple (moosewood), or sassafras. You may remember Leatherstocking (he was "Hawkeye" then) advising a wounded companion that "a little bruised alder will work like a charm." Saliva carries germs: so don't chew but bruise the leaves.

A poultice of the leaves of the common plantain weed is a first-rate application for burns, scalds, bruises, erysipelas, and ivy poisoning. The powdered leaf applied as a paste, or simply the dry leaf powdered, stops bleeding in a short time.

Mustard plasters are used as counter-irritants. A strong one is made of equal parts of dry mustard and flour; for gentler effect use less mustard in proportion. Make into a paste with lukewarm water, and spread between layers of thin cloth. Leave it on 15 to 20 minutes, or until the skin is well reddened.

Heat and Cold.—Direct application of heat is one of the prime resources of first-aid. A canteen will do instead of a hot-water bag, or a hot stone may be rolled in blanketing or other thick cloth; but a better expedient, because it shapes itself to whatever part it is applied to, is a bag partly filled with hot sand, salt, rice, or the like. The stuff may be heated quickly in a frying-pan. If the patient is unconscious, you must be careful not to burn him. Observe his skin, frequently, and feel the cover of the hot article, which should not rise above 115 deg.

To produce the most effect, heat should be applied between the thighs, between the arms and the body, and to the soles of the feet. Cloths wrung out in hot water, then inclosed in dry ones, are the best means to reduce swelling after an injury.

Cold is used also to reduce swelling, as well as to stimulate breathing, and to reduce temperature in sunstroke. Of course, ice cannot be obtained in the wilderness, save in winter, but, if the affected part cannot be soaked in a running stream, then cloths may be wrung out in water from a spring or cold brook, or an arrangement can be rigged to discharge a continuous stream of it upon the patient.

UNCONSCIOUSNESS.—If you should find a person lying in a stupor'or quite unconscious, seek the cause, before treating him, or you may do more

ACCIDENTS AND EMERGENCIES

harm than good. If it be a case of drowning or freezing, you will know at once. Sunstroke is marked by a hot, dry skin. Bleeding, bruises, and swelling speak for themselves. If, however, there are none of these symptoms, examine the patient with care.

Observe, first, whether the face is pale or flushed. If pale, and the pupils of the eyes are natural, it is a simple case of fainting; if the pupils are dilated, the face pale, with cold sweat, the pulse weak and quick, probably there has been concussion of the brain.

On the other hand, a flushed and turgid face, respiration snoring, a slow and full pulse, are symptoms common to apoplexy, drunkenness, and opium poisoning. It is very important to distinguish between these. Odor of liquor in the breath is not conclusive; for a person struck down by apoplexy may have been drinking. A drunken man may have fallen and suffered concussion of the brain, thus complicating the case.

In apoplexy due to hemorrhage in the brain, one side of the patient generally is paralyzed. He cannot be aroused, even with ammonia to the nose. His *eyeballs* are *not sensitive* to touch. A man drunk or "doped" generally can be aroused for a moment by dashing cold water in his face. A bottle of liquor, laudanum, or morphine, is likely to be found on or near him. In alcoholic poisoning the pupils are dilated and equal; in opium poisoning, they are extremely contracted.

DROWNING.—Clean any mud or water from the mouth with a handkerchief on the finger, loosen all tight clothing, and expose the chest and waist. Slip your hands under the man's waist and lift him high enough for his head to hang down and drain the water out of him. Give two or three quick, smarting slaps on his naked chest with the open hand. If this fails to restore breathing, then start at once to perform artificial respiration. The best way for an inexperienced person, or for one who has to work alone, is what is called the "prone-pressure method," as follows:

Turn the patient face downward on the ground, arms extended above the head, *face to one side.* If his tongue does not fall forward, grasp it with a handkerchief and pull it out, so that air may enter.

Kneel astride of him, and grasp him firmly on both sides of the chest, just above lower margin of ribs. Press steadily and *heavily* downward and forward, for three seconds, to expel the air from the lungs. Then, gradually (two seconds) release the pressure. The elasticity of the chest makes it expand and draw air into the lungs. Repeat this operation with a regular rhythm of 12 to 15 to the minute. You will conserve your own strength by swinging your body forward and backward so as to let your weight fall vertically upon the wrists and then be released.

While you are doing this, if there is an assistant, have him remove the patient's wet clothing, dry him *without* rubbing, and cover him with a dry blanket or articles of clothing; but do not let this interrupt your own work for a single moment. Do not rub nor apply heat to restore circulation until natural breathing has been established; to do so might be fatal.

Continue this treatment until the subject shows signs of life; then, with more gentle pressure, until the breath comes naturally. There must be no let up. Two or more helpers can work in relays, changing about without losing the "stroke." In most cases the patient revives within thirty minutes; but it may take an hour or two of continuous work to restore life. Do not be discouraged.

As soon as natural breathing has been restored, rub the person's limbs and body with firm pressure *toward the heart,* to bring back circulation. Now

ACCIDENTS AND EMERGENCIES

wrap him in warm blankets and apply hot stones or other dry heat, as described early in this chapter. When he can swallow, give him hot stimulants, a little at a time. Then let him sleep.

Rescue of the Drowning.—In case you must swim for the drowning person, then, if possible at the moment, take with you a float of some sort for him to cling to. It takes only a small buoyant object to support a man's head above water. Cast off at least your shoes before striking out.

When you get near, shout cheerily that you will get him out all right if he does not struggle. But a drowning person is likely to get frantic, as soon as water enters his lungs, and grasp desperately at a rescuer. So be cool and wary. You must manoeuvre for position, lest he drown you both. If he sinks once or twice, little harm will be done—it may even be for the best. The first two sinkings are very slow, and he does not go down deep.

Get at him *from behind,* if possible. If he turns on you and tries to seize you, reach your left arm forward and push him away with your hand against his lower jaw. He may succeed in gripping your arm: in that case, turn so as to get your foot under his chest, and push him away with a powerful kick. If he should be strong enough, however, to hold you in a grip that you cannot loosen, then take a good breath and sink with him. You can stand it longer than he can; his hold will relax before your own air gives out. The "death grip" that never loosens is common in fiction, but rarely, if ever, in fact. In the unlikely event that he should hold out longer than you consider safe, strike him in the face and break loose. This sounds brutal, but it may be the only way to save him, and yourself, too.

If the person is tractable, or has weakened until no longer dangerous, get him by the hair, or by an inside hold on the collar, and, swimming ahead of him on your back or side, tow him out. If he is naked and short-haired, then, if he is not insanely struggling, he can be rescued by approaching from behind, rolling him suddenly on his back, turning on your own back, partly under him, and drawing his head up on your chest. A child or woman, even though struggling, may be managed in this way if you seize one of the wrists and pull it behind the person's head. Then swim out on your back.

When a drowning man has sunk to the bottom, in smooth water, his exact position is shown by air bubbles that occasionally arise.

If some one has broken through the ice, and there is no plank nor rope to be had, lie down flat on your belly and crawl out near enough to reach him a stick or toss one end of your coat to him. Then back out, still lying flat, so as to distribute your weight over as much surface as possible, and pull while he helps himself as well as he can.

Cramp while Swimming.—This may result from going into the water too soon after eating, or when overheated, or from staying in so long as to become chilled. It is not serious for a swimmer who keeps his wits, but if he gets frightened it may cost his life. Turn on your back and keep your chest inflated. Float, and swim with the unaffected limbs. Even if you be far from shore, the cramped member may soon relax if you keep cool.

SUFFOCATION.—If a person has suffocated from inhaling gas or smoke, or from choking or hanging, get him into the fresh air as quickly as possible, loosen his clothing, sprinkle cold water on face and bare chest, and, if he still fails to breathe, perform artificial respiration as for drowning. Then apply heat and give a stimulant.

FAINTING.—If attacked with vertigo, bend your head down so it is between the knees, to help the blood into it; do not keep this up if not promptly effective. Cold air, and sprinkling with cold water, often prevents fainting.

ACCIDENTS AND EMERGENCIES 433

If one has fainted, take him into the fresh air and lay him on his back, with *feet higher than head* (unless the face is flushed or blue). Loosen the clothing. Spatter the face and chest with cold water. Rub limbs toward the heart. Apply ammonia to the nose. When consciousness has returned, give a stimulant, or put the patient to bed and apply heat.

Never raise a fainting person to a sitting posture.

SHOCK.—In case of collapse following an accident, operation, or fright: treat first as for fainting. Then wrap the person in blankets, apply heat, and rub his limbs toward the body, keeping him well wrapped up the while. If he is conscious, and *not bleeding* externally or internally, give him hot tea or coffee, or just one good drink of liquor, or ammonia. But if the shock is from an injury and attended by bleeding, the first thing to do is to check the flow of blood.

Stunning (Concussion of the Brain).—Lay the man on his back with head somewhat raised. Hot water poured on his head will help to arouse him. Apply heat as for shock, but keep the head cool with cold wet cloths. Rub his limbs. Ammonia may be held under the nose, but do not give any stimulant: that would drive the blood to the brain, where it is not wanted. Keep the patient quiet. Light diet and laxatives.

LIGHTNING STROKE.—If the heart has stopped, the case is fatal. If not, but breathing is suspended, practice artificial respiration for at least half an hour, and other treatment as for drowning. Electric burns are treated like any other.

SUNSTROKE.—Observe the difference between this and heat exhaustion (see below). In sunstroke proper the face is red, the skin very hot and dry, and the subject is quite unconscious. Lay him in a cool place; position same as for stunning. Remove as much of his clothing as practicable. Hold a vessel or hatful of cold water four or five feet above him, and pour a stream first on his head, then on his body, and last on his extremities. Continue until consciousness returns. If this cannot be done, then rub cold cloths over face, neck, chest, and armpits. Hold ammonia under the nose. When the patient becomes conscious, let him drink cold water freely, but no stimulants.

Heat Exhaustion.—Generally the person is conscious, but very depressed and weak. His face is pale and covered with clammy sweat. Do not apply cold externally, but let him sip cold water. Give a little strong black coffee, or a mild stimulant. Let him rest in bed.

APOPLEXY.—When a blood-vessel bursts in the brain, the subject falls unconscious. The face is flushed, lips blue, eyelids half open, eyes insensitive to touch, respirations snoring, pulse full and slow, skin usually cool. Generally one side of the body is paralyzed. The case may or may not be fatal.

Lay the patient in bed with head and shoulders propped up. Apply cold cloths to the head and heat to the limbs. No stimulants. Absolute quiet and rest.

ALCOHOLISM.—If you find a man lying apparently dead drunk, make sure, first, that it is not a case of apoplexy.

Usually a dash of cold water in the face will rouse a drunken man. Make him vomit. Then a cup of hot coffee will aid to settle the stomach and clear the mind. To sober quickly, and brace him up, administer a teaspoonful of aromatic spirits of ammonia in half a cup of water.

If the skin is cold and clammy, lay him in a comfortable position, apply dry heat, keep the man covered, and rub his limbs toward the body to increase circulation. Keep the bowels open. Feed first with concentrated broth or soup well seasoned with red pepper. Give him some liquor at judicious intervals, if it can be procured (to deny it is

ACCIDENTS AND EMERGENCIES 435

a brutality of ignorance) until he gets on his feet. But if there is none, give him red pepper tea (enough cayenne steeped in hot water to make the stomach tingle). This braces his nerves and helps to avert "the horrors."

If threatened with collapse, apply heat, and inject strychnine.

In delirium tremens, watch the patient carefully, that he may not injure himself or others, or commit suicide; but avoid physical restraint as far as possible. The serious symptoms are due chiefly to sleeplessness, which is to be combatted with such means as you have at hand. Try trional, veronal, or a bromide, if you can get them. An opiate is the last resort. If the heart weakens, give ammonia or strychnine.

FIT OR CONVULSION.—Kneel by the patient's head place one arm under it, and undo collar and belt. Insert in the mouth something that he cannot swallow, such as a stick, or a pocket-knife wrapped in handkerchief, to prevent the tongue from being bitten. Get him away from anything against which he might strike and injure himself, but do not try to open his hands or restrain his movements. When the attack has passed, do not rouse, but let him sleep, with warmth to the feet.

HYSTERIA.—Do nothing. Appear quite indifferent. A show of sympathy will only make matters worse.

PTOMAINE POISONING.—The exciting cause is eating certain varieties of food that have partly putrefied, such as meat, sausage, fish, shellfish, cheese, and especially, in the case of campers, canned meats, etc., that have spoiled.

It is distinguished from cholera morbus by marked nervous symptoms (twitching of facial muscles, tingling sensations, dilated pupils, breathlessness, dizziness, perhaps convulsions) and usually a low temperature.

Cause repeated vomiting by giving three or four glasses of warm water, each containing salt or mustard. Then give stimulants to support the heart and nerve force. Put the victim to bed, with head low, and apply dry heat. If a syringe can be procured, empty the lower bowel with an injection of soapsuds and water. After a thorough cleaning out, give an intestinal antiseptic.

POISONING FROM MUSHROOMS (or from unknown plants)—Treat as for ptomaine poisoning. In case of mushroom poisoning, if the patient can swallow, get some charcoal from the camp-fire, powder and administer it. This may absorb much of the poison. Castor oil is the best purgative, to be followed by a soapsuds enema. Atropine by injection, if you have it; otherwise, unless you can get a physician within two or three hours, the chance of recovery is slight; but do your best.

SNAKE BITE.—The only dangerous snakes in the United States are the rattlesnake, the copperhead, and the cottonmouth moccasin. The small coral snake (harlequin, bead snake) of the Gulf states, and the Sonoran coral snake of New Mexico and Arizona, are somewhat venomous, but their bite is not fatal to a healthy adult. The Gila monster of the Southwest is a dangerous lizard—the only one that is venomous—but can scarcely be provoked to bite.

All other snakes and lizards of our country and Canada are harmless—their bite is no more to be feared than that of a mouse. The notion that the bite of our so-called "puff-adder," "spreading adder," "blowing viper," must be dangerous, because the snake puffs up its neck and hisses like a goose, or that the common watersnake is a moccasin and consequently venomous, is all moonshine, like the story of the hoop-snake and the snake with a poisonous sting in its tail.

However, that other notion that a rattlesnake's bite is not a serious matter is moonshine, too. Men

ACCIDENTS AND EMERGENCIES 437

who know nothing about other rattlers than the little prairie rattlesnake are not competent to express an opinion on the subject.

A bite from any venomous snake is dangerous, *in proportion to the size of the snake,* and to the *amount of venom that enters the circulation.* A bite that does not pierce an important blood vessel is seldom fatal, even if no treatment is given, unless the snake be quite large.

The rattlesnake, copperhead, and cottonmouth are easily distinguished from all other snakes, as all

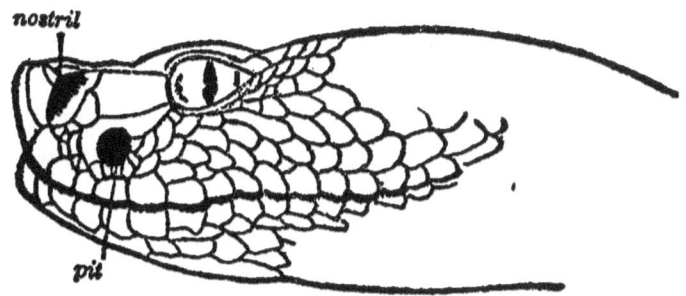

Fig. 192.—Head of rattlesnake (after Stejneger)

three of them bear a peculiar mark, or rather a pair of marks, that no other animal possesses. The mark is the *pit,* which is a deep cavity on each side of the face between the nostril and the eye, sinking into the upper jawbone. Its position is shown in the accompanying cut (Fig. 192). All of them have an upright elliptical, instead of round, pupil in the eye.

All venomous snakes have fangs, and no harmless ones have them. The fangs are in the upper jaw only. In the coral snakes they are permanently erect, but in the other venomous snakes here named they lie flat against the roof of the mouth, when not in use, pointing backward, and are erected by the reptile in striking. They are long, slender, sharply pointed, perforated like a hypodermic needle, and connected by a duct with the venom glands which lie behind the eyes. Auxiliary fangs lie in a sac underneath the regular fang on each side, and, in case the latter is broken off or extracted, a new fang will be ready for business within a few days.

Here are a few characteristics of the pit vipers, as our three deadly snakes collectively are called:

1. *Copperhead* (also called deaf adder, upland moccasin, pilot snake, chunk head).—A small snake, 2 to 3 feet long, with moderately thick body, broad and triangular head quite distinct from the neck, tail short, dark colored, and pointed. Color of back, a bronze hazel or light reddish brown; with 15 to 20 darker bands, which are narrow on the back and expand to wide blotches on the flanks, the shape being somewhat like that of a dumb-bell with very short handle. Head, a bright copper-red, with two small dark-brown spots close together on the forehead at upper part of head-shield, and with a cream-colored band around the mouth.

The copperhead inhabits the mountainous and hilly regions from Massachusetts southward to the Gulf, and westward (south of Michigan, Wisconsin, Iowa, and Nebraska) to Kansas, Oklahoma, and Texas.

Its venom is as deadly as that of the rattlesnake, but it is not secreted in as large quantity as that of the larger rattlers; consequently the wound is not likely to be so serious. Still, the copperhead is a particularly dangerous creature, because it gives no warning of its presence, nor, according to my observation, does it try to get out of the way, but holds its ground and springs at any intruder.

Only one species.

2. *Cottonmouth moccasin* (water moccasin).— A larger snake, ordinarily about 3 ft., sometimes 4 ft. long. Stout body, head shaped like that of the copperhead and similarly distinct from the neck. Back brown, reddish, or olive, with 11 to 15 rather inconspicuous bars, or pairs of bars, of dark brown, with light centers on each flank. Tail short, pointed, and dark brown or banded. Belly brownish-yellow mottled with dark blotches.

ACCIDENTS AND EMERGENCIES 439

Habitat, North Carolina southward to the Gulf, westward through Kentucky, southern Illinois, and Missouri, to Oklahoma and eastern Texas.

Not so poisonous as the larger kinds of rattlesnakes, but still dangerous to human life. Quite numerous in the southern states. More aggressive than the rattlesnake, striking at everything within reach; but usually rather deliberate about striking, first opening its mouth widely for some seconds, as if to intimidate, and showing the white interior (hence the name "cottonmouth"). Usually found near water, and often on low limbs overhanging the water.

Only one species. The other so-called "moccasins" are either the copperhead or harmless snakes.

3. *Rattlesnake.*—Of rattlers we have no less than sixteen species, but only two of them, the massasauga and the banded or timber rattlesnake, are found in the eastern and central states. The little prairie rattlesnake, which is not very dangerous, is abundant on the plains west of the Missouri River. The great diamond rattlesnake of the South, which sometimes grows to a length of nearly nine feet, is the most formidable member of this group. The small ground rattlesnake of the southern states is aggressive, and gives only a faint warning, and on this account is more dreaded by the negroes than the larger species; but its bite is seldom fatal to grown people. The other species are confined to the Southwest and the Pacific coast.

Rattlesnakes are easily identified by their rattles. These generally last only long enough to become 8 or 10 jointed. Rattles with as many as 15 to 18 joints are quite rare. The number of rattles does not indicate the snake's age. Their office is not clearly understand. Doctor Stejneger says: "They are a substitute for a voice."

When a rattlesnake sees a man approaching, it generally lies quiet to escape observation, so long as it thinks itself concealed. It seldom strikes unless provoked. If alarmed when it is wide-awake, it nearly always springs its rattle before striking, the sound being very similar to that made by our common "locust" or cicada. If the reptile is trodden on when asleep, it strikes like lightning, and does its rattling afterward. Unfortunately for us, the poisonous snakes do their sleeping in the day time and hunt at night. They are prone to seek the warmth of bed-clothes, and sometimes will coil up alongside of a sleeping man. Mosquito netting is an effective bar against snakes. Snakes despise musk, tobacco, and turpentine.

A snake is not obliged to coil before striking, but can strike from any position; it will coil first, however, unless attacked very suddenly or taken at a disadvantage. A snake does not intentionally throw its venom; but, if it misses its mark, the act of hissing may throw the poison several feet. The blow is delivered with lightning rapidity, and the fangs are instantly sunk into the victim. No snake can leap entirely from the ground, nor can it strike more than two-thirds its own length, unless it has the advantage of striking downhill or from some purchase on a rock or bush. A snake does not expend all its venom at one blow. It is not rendered permanently harmless by extracting its fangs, for auxiliary ones, in various stages of development, lie in a sac in the roof of the mouth, and the foremost of these soon will emerge and be ready for business.

The venoms of different species of snakes differ in composition and in action. That of the cobra, for example, attacks the nerve centers of the cerebrospinal system, causing paralysis that extends to the lungs and finally to the heart, but the local symptoms are not very severe. In marked contrast are the effects of rattlesnake bite, which spread very rapidly through the system, making the blood thin and destroying its power to clot. The wound is

ACCIDENTS AND EMERGENCIES 441

speedily discolored and swollen. Within about fifteen minutes, if no cautery or ligature or serum injection has been applied, the victim becomes dull and languid, breathing with difficulty. The venom first enfeebles the heart, then the lungs. Great swelling and discoloration extend up the limbs and trunk. The temperature rises, the victim staggers, becomes prostrated, is attacked with cold sweats and vomiting, may swoon repeatedly, and death may ensue within ten or twelve hours. If an important blood vessel has been pierced by a fang and considerable venom injected, the victim may die within twenty minutes.

Rattlesnake poison has a tendency to rot the blood-vessels, and may cause a general seepage of blood throughout the system. In some cases a whole limb is soaked to the bone with decomposed blood. Frequently there is suppuration, and gangrene may set in, from which a patient who had recovered from the constitutional symptoms may die a week or more after the injury was received.

Much depends upon the part struck, and the quantity of venom injected. Often it happens that only one fang penetrates, or only the surface of the skin may be scratched. Bites on the bare skin are more dangerous than those received through the clothing. In a large majority of cases the wound does not touch a blood-vessel directly, and the patient will recover with no other treatment than a ligature promptly applied, and a free cutting and kneading of the wound to expel as much as possible of the poison before it has had time to enter the circulation. Such measures, however, must be taken *at once,* as absorption works quickly.

REMEDIES.—The only positive antidote for snake poison, after it has entered the circulation, is anti-venom serum. This is prepared by injecting into a horse or mule a fractional dose of the venom of a snake, or a mixture of those of different species.

When the animal recovers from the effects of this preliminary dose, a slightly larger one is injected, and so on, every two or three weeks, for a year or two. Finally the serum of the animal's blood has developed an anti-toxin that makes him immune to snake venom. Some of his blood is then withdrawn, and the serum is separated, sterilized, and put up either in liquid or dried form in sealed tubes. These must be kept in a cool, dark place, to preserve the serum from deteriorating. A large hypodermic syringe is used to inject the serum into a patient. This treatment will cure the gravest cases of snake bite, if employed before the victim has collapsed. As it is not toxic, it is safe for even inexperienced people to use.

As I have said, there are marked differences in the nature and effects of venoms, according to the species of snake. Cobra venom, from which the Chalmette serum is principally derived, while effective in treating such bites as would be received in India, is not so sure a remedy in our country as an anti-venom developed by using the poison of rattlesnakes or other species of the *Crotalidae*. To cure bites inflicted by the deadly snakes of South Africa, Fitzsimons employs a mixture of venoms from various species in that region with which to immunize horses and develop a remedial serum. In South America, Dr. Vital Brazil, of the Institute of Serum-Therapy of Sao Paulo has made several types of serums that are specific for bites of the rattlesnake, the lance-head snake, the coral snakes, respectively, and one compounded from three venoms, to be used when the identity of the snake is unknown.

The chief disadvantage of anti-venom serum is that its kit is too bulky to be carried habitually on the person. If, however, it is kept in camp, and a first-aid remedy for snake bite is always in one's pocket during the snake season, the adventurer need fear no snakes whatever.

ACCIDENTS AND EMERGENCIES 443

The first-aid for snake bite is very simple and compact. It consists merely of a little permanganate of potash (potassium permanganate) and a lancet or a sharp penknife blade, with belt or other article of clothing that can be used like a tourniquet. The permanganate can be used either in crystals or in tablet form. It must be carried in a waterproof container of glass or rubber. A convenient arrangement is a hard rubber tube resembling a fountain pen, but only 2½ inches long and weighing less than an ounce, which is sold for a dollar by some outfitters. One of the capped ends contains some permanganate, and the other a small spear-shaped lancet (to be honed keen before it is fit to use).

Permanganate of potash merely neutralizes such venom as it comes in direct contact with; it does not follow up the poison and kill at a distance from the wound. Since snake venom diffuses rapidly through the system, it is absolutely necessary to use the permanganate quickly. If more than three minutes have elapsed before application, its value is doubtful; if more than five minutes or six minutes, it will do no good at all.

TREATMENT.—(1). When one has been struck by a venomous snake, he should waste no time chasing the creature to kill it. Within a minute, at most, he should have a ligature bound between the wound and his body to cut off the return flow of blood and lymph to the heart. (It is assumed that he has been struck in a limb, as generally happens.) The ligature may be a neckerchief, handkerchief, or a strip of cloth torn from the shirt, twisted, and tied as tightly as possible around the limb. A belt with tongueless buckle is excellent for the purpose. A stout cord will do. If the bite is anywhere below the knee, apply the ligature just above the knee; if below the elbow, then just above the elbow, because here there is only one bone and compression is more effective. Another may be tied closer to the wound if a foot or hand has been bitten.

Do not twist the ligature up so tightly with a stick as to bruise the flesh. Remember, its object is not to compress an artery, but only the veins, all of which lie near the surface.

(2). Make three parallel cuts, say an inch long and a quarter-inch deep, lengthwise of the limb and through the seat of the wound, then two crisscross through the fang punctures (unless the bite be on the wrist or top of foot, where you might sever sinews). This is better than a simple X-cut because it makes the wound bleed more freely and opens it more thoroughly to receive the permanganate. Plenteous bleeding carries out a good deal of the poison by itself. Assist it by squeezing or "milking" the wound. The poison of North American snakes (not of the cobra) is harmless to the stomach, and so it may be sucked out, *provided* that the operator has no hollow tooth, nor scratch or abrasion of the mouth, through which it might reach the circulation. It is useless to suck merely the tiny fang punctures—you must first cut them open.

(3). Moisten, with saliva, enough of the permanganate to fill the wound (if it is in tablets, crush two or three of them in the palm of the hand) and rub it thoroughly into the cuts. It is extremely caustic; but the emergency calls for heroic treatment.

(4). If you have a companion, send him at once for the anti-venom kit, or for a doctor. If you are alone, and far from help, stay where you are. Moving about would only force circulation and aggravate the case. The chances are fine for your recovery without any further treatment. If you have strychnine, swallow 1-20 grain to stimulate the heart and nerves, whenever you feel them "going back on you." Or, if you have it, use whiskey or ammonia.

Whiskey is not an antidote; it has no effect at all on the venom; its service is simply as a stimulant for the murderously attacked heart and lungs, and

ACCIDENTS AND EMERGENCIES 445

as a bracer to the victim's nerves, thus helping him over the crisis. For this purpose some pretty stiff drinks may be needed, if strychnine is not to be had; but don't guzzle inordinately; an excess, by its depressive reaction later, may weaken the system alarmingly after the venom itself has been conquered.

(5). In half an hour you should gradually loosen the ligature, permitting some blood to flow back from the injured limb and fresh blood to enter it. Then tighten again. This admits only a little of the poison at a time to the heart. Repeat the alternate tightening and loosening at intervals for a considerable time, until the danger is over. To leave the ligature unloosened for more than an hour, at the farthest, would put you in grave danger of gangrene.

HERBAL REMEDIES.—Many species of wild plants are supposed to have the property of counteracting the effects of the poison of serpents. In any backwoods community you may find some one who claims to know some sovereign herb that will do this. In the seventh edition of my *Book of Camping and Woodcraft* (1915) I named many of these plants and discussed them. This book is out of print, but may be consulted in public libraries by anyone curious in such matters. Scientists of to-day have no faith whatever in herbal "cures." There are plants that will assist Nature in the way of heart and nerve stimulants, or possibly by inducing copious sweating; but there is none that acts as a real antidote against snake poisoning. As for the backwoodsmen who use herbs as "snake-masters," it will be observed that they have firm faith in the efficacy of "lots o' whiskey" as an adjuvant, if not as a panacea *sine qua non*.

One time I asked an old moonshiner, "Quill" (that was his first name) "if a snake bit you, when you had no whiskey, what would you do?"

"And no liquor to be had?"

"Yes."

"Sir, if a snake tuk sich advantage of me, I'd throw him in the fire!"

BITES OF OTHER ANIMALS.—Ordinarily the bite of a non-venomous animal needs no other attention than cleansing and an antiseptic dressing, unless there is enough laceration to require surgical measures. Still, the bite of any animal, from mouse to man, may be dangerous. Germs from foul teeth may be carried into the wound. Vindictive and long-sustained anger sometimes seems to create a virus in the saliva, so that the bite of a teased and infuriated animal may act almost as a venom. If there be reasonable doubt, cauterize the wound as for snake bite, or with nitrate of silver, or with a nail brought to a *white* heat (not so painful as if only red-hot). This will not, in all likihood, prevent an attack of hydrophobia if the animal was rabid, but it will kill such other poison or germs as may have been introduced.

RABIES.—Hydrophobia (fear or aversion for water) is only a symptom, and is shown only by man, not, as is commonly believed, by dogs. Notwithstanding that there are cranks (even a few of them in the medical profession) who assert that there is no such disease as rabies, it is in fact the most terrible ailment that afflicts mankind. In a great majority of cases, unless the patient is given the Pasteur treatment in due time, he will suffer the most excruciating agony, and death is certain, since no known drug is of any avail. Faith in the curative powers of "the madstone" is nothing but a superstition: the compacted fiber from an animal's stomach, or calculus, or porous stone, which goes by that name merely clings if there happens to be a discharge of blood or pus from the wound, and draws out no virus whatever; for there is none in the circulation—the virus of rabies travels along the nerves.

Epidemics of rabies are by no means confined to domesticated animals. They occur among wolves, foxes, jackals, hyenas, bears, skunks, rats, and even

ACCIDENTS AND EMERGENCIES 447

among birds. It is likely that this disease accounts for the sudden disappearance of certain animals from a given locality, when other explanations fail, as was the case with wolves in the Alleghanies about the beginning of the 19th century.* In Arizona and other parts of the Southwest it is generally believed that the bite of the little spotted or rock skunk is more than likely to transmit rabies; so the animal often is called "hydrophobia skunk." I have already discussed this matter in Vol. I., p. 262.

As regards symptoms, there are two types of rabies:

(1). Furiant or irritable.—First the animal's disposition changes: if formerly playful, it becomes morose; if quiet and dignified, it now grows unusually affectionate, as if seeking sympathy. In the course of a day or two it becomes irritable, and may snap if startled. It begins to wander about, and disappears at intervals, hiding in corners or dark places, from which it resents being removed. Its bark is indiscribably changed. There is no appetite, and the animal has difficulty in swallowing. Saliva may dribble from the mouth, but it does not froth as in a fit. Restlessness and irritability increase until the beast becomes furious, biting at anything thrust toward him, and even at imaginary objects. The creature now begins to take long journeys, and will assault other animals, but never makes any outcry during these attacks. Then signs of paralysis appear. It overcomes first his hind legs, then the lower jaw, and ultimately becomes general. He dies in from five to eight days after the appearance of the symptoms.

(2). Dumb or paralytic.—This type is uncommon. There is no marked irritability. The animal lies stupidly in seclusion. Paralysis comes early and is quickly progressive. Death usually ensues in two or three days.

In man, the period between the bite and the appearance of the symptoms averages forty days. It

---

*See *Notes on the Settlement and Indian Wars of the Western Parts of Virginia and Pennsylvania, from 1763 to 1783*, by the Rev. Dr. Joseph Doddridge, a contemporary and excellent authority.

may be a year or more; it may be only two weeks, or even less if the bite was a bad, lacerating one affecting important nerves, or in the face. Consequently, when a man is bitten by an animal known to be rabid, or by one that develops rabies within less than forty days after it has inflicted the bite, he should be sent at once to a Pasteur institute. If he goes in time, he has ninety-nine chances in a hundred to recover. Otherwise, unless the wound was so superficial as to have done no injury under the skin, and it was promptly cauterized, his chance is scarce one in a hundred.

INSECT STINGS AND BITES.—These have already been discussed at some length in Vol. I., pp. 241-259. An application of honey, moistened salt, or of ammonia, or a cloth saturated in a solution of baking soda, or even wet earth, will suffice in all ordinary cases. Our most dangerous insect is the common housefly: "it does not wipe its feet."

WOUNDS.—There is no room in this chapter to describe and illustrate the structure and mechanics of the body, nor how to apply bandages and splints, nor to give any but general directions for the treatment of wounds, dislocations and fractures. If one is going far from medical help, I cannot too highly recommend that he should take some instruction in such matters, or at least carry with him the very clear and concise *American Red Cross Abridged Text-book on First Aid* (general edition), by Májor Charles Lynch, of the Medical Corps, U. S. A. This book, as well as a variety of first-aid packets and fitted boxes, is sold by the American Red Cross, Washington, D. C., from whom a catalogue may be procured on application.

Bleeding.—Rather free bleeding is good for a wound, because the blood washes out many, if not all, of the dangerous pus germs that may have entered at the time of the injury. Do not touch the wound with the fingers, nor with anything else than a surgically clean instrument and compress. Observe whether the bleeding is arterial or venous.

ACCIDENTS AND EMERGENCIES 449

If it comes from a *vein,* the blood will be *dark* red or purplish, and will flow in a steady stream. If an *artery* is cut or lacerated, the blood will be *bright* red, and it probably will spurt in jets. Bind the compress on firmly. Generally this will suffice to stop the bleeding.

In case of arterial bleeding, try to locate the artery *above* the wound (between it and the heart) by pressing very hard where you think the artery may pass close to a bone, and watch if this checks the flow. If so, then, if the vessel is only a small one, just continue the pressure: it is likely that a clot will form and the artery close itself. In extremity, the flow from even a large artery can be checked for a while by pressing very firmly with thumb and finger directly into the wound. There is record of an Austrian soldier who stopped bleeding from the great artery of the thigh for four hours by plugging the wound with his thumb; if he had let go for a minute he would have bled to death. But if the injury is so situated that a tourniquet can be applied (anywhere except in the neck, body, or very close to the body) one can readily be extemporized.

Tourniquet.—Tie a strong bandage (handkerchief, belt, suspender, rope, strip of clothing) around the wounded member, and between the wound and the heart. Under it, and directly over the artery, place a smooth pebble, a cartridge, piece of stick, or other hard lump. Then thrust a stout stick under the bandage, and twist until the wound stops bleeding. The lump serves two purposes: it brings the most pressure where it will do the most good, and it allows passage of enough blood on either side to keep the limb from being strangled to death. However, do not apply more pressure than is needed to stop the bleeding—excessive pressure of a hard lump may rupture the blood-vessel.

If the position of the artery above the wound cannot be determined, then, in case of a gaping wound that would be hard to plug, apply the tourniquet without any lump, and twist it very tight indeed. This can only be done for a short time, while you are preparing to ligate the artery; if prolonged, it will kill the limb, and gangrene will ensue. In case of a punctured wound, such as a bullet hole, it is better to push a plug of sterilized gauze hard down in the wound itself, leaving the outer end projecting so that a bandage will hold the plug firmly on the artery. This must be done, anyway, wherever a tourniquet cannot be used.

Ligating.—The above expedients are only temporary; for a cut artery, if of any considerable size, must be ligated—that is to say, permanently closed by tying one or both of the severed ends. To do this you must have at least a pair of sharp-pointed forceps or strong tweezers. Get hold of the end of the artery with this, draw it out, and have some one hold it. Then take a piece of strong thread that has been sterilized in boiling salt water (supposing you have no regular antiseptic) make a loop in it as for a reef knot, but pass the right hand end of the thread *twice* around the other, instead of once (Fig. 193—surgeon's knot—it will never slip). Slip this loop down over the forceps and around the end of the artery, and draw tight. If the vessel bleeds from both ends, ligate both. When an artery is merely ruptured, not severed, cut it clean in two before operating; it will close better.

Fig. 193.—Surgeon's knot

Nosebleed.—If the nose does not stop bleeding of itself, hold against the nape of the neck a cloth wrung out in cold water. Put a roll of paper between the upper lip and the gum. Do not blow the nose nor remove the clots. Holding the arms above the head will help. If the bleeding still continues, dissolve a teaspoonful of salt in a cup of water, and snuff some of this brine up the nose.

Should these measures fail, make a plug by rolling up part of a half-inch strip of gauze or soft cloth, push the plug gently up the nose with a pencil, pack the rest of the strip tightly into the nostril, and let the end protude. If there is leakage backward into the mouth, pack the lower part of plug still more tightly. Leave the plug in place several hours; then loosen with warm water or oil, and remove very gently.

Internal Bleeding.—This may be either from the stomach or from the lungs. In hemorrhage from the *stomach,* the blood is vomited. It is *brown* or "coffee-ground," and may be mixed with food. There is tenderness and pain in the region of the stomach.

Bleeding from the *lungs* is preceded by a saltish taste in the mouth. Blood rushes from the mouth and nose. It is bright *red* and *frothy.*

Although the disease producing one or other of these symptoms may be grave, yet the attack of bleeding itself is not likely to result seriously. In either case the first-aid treatment is absolute rest in bed, and cold cloths over the affected part. If the bleeding is from the stomach, the patient's head should be kept low; if from the lungs, the head and shoulders should be propped up, unless there be a tendency to faintness.

Cleansing Wounds.—All inflammation of wounds, suppuration, abscesses, erysipelas, "blood-poisoning," gangrene, and lockjaw, are due to *living germs* and nothing else. These germs are not born in the wound, but enter from the outside. We may as well say they are present everywhere, except in the air (pus germs do not float in air). To prevent their entrance is much easier than to kill them once they have gained foothold.

The only guarantee of a wound healing nicely is to make and keep it *surgically* clean. Sterilize everything that is to be used about a wound: hands, instruments, and the dressing. Do not trust anything to be germ-free merely because it *looks* clean. The micro-organisms that cause inflammation of a wound, fever, putrefaction, may lurk anywhere, even in spotless linen fresh from the laundry, unless killed by antiseptics.

Do not swab out a fresh wound, nor even wash it; that would only drive germs deeper in. Simply cover it with a sterilized dressing for the time being, and cleanse it later with an antiseptic wash, if need be. Plain water is likely to contain germs. If it is necessary first to pick out hard foreign matter that has been driven into the wound, do so with an instrument sterilized by heat or by antiseptics, or made from a freshly cut green stick.

Whenever practicable, shave off the hair for some distance around the wound. Hairs, no matter how small, are grease-coated and favor the lodgment and growth of germs. Shaving also scrapes off the surface dirt and dead scales of skin.

Closing Wounds.—Never cover a wound with court plaster. It prevents the free escape of suppuration, inflames the part, and makes the place difficult to cleanse thereafter. Collodion should be used only to cover small, clean abrasions of the skin, protecting the raw surface.

The only legitimate uses for adhesive plaster are to hold a compress in place where bandaging is difficult, and, in case of a cut, to keep the edges closed without sewing the skin. In the latter case, after placing a narrow compress over the cut, the wound may be drawn together by crossing it with narrow but long strips of plaster, leaving spaces between. A better way, by which I have nicely healed some rather bad gashes, is as follows:

Lay a broad strip of adhesive plaster on each side of the cut, half an inch apart, and extending beyond the wound at each end. Stick these strips firmly in place, except about a quarter of an inch of the inner margins, which are left loose for the present. With needle and thread lace the strips (deep stitches, so they'll not pull out) so as to draw the edges of the wound together, and then stick the inner margins down, not covering the wound.

Sewing a wound should be avoided by inexperienced persons, unless it really is necessary, as in the case of a foot partly severed by an axe-cut. If an ordinary needle and thread must be used (by no means an easy job) sterilize them by soaking in a boiling solution of salt and water. (It is here assumed that no better antiseptic agents are available. Sugar and water, or vinegar will do in a pinch.) Do not sew continuously over and over, but make a deep stitch and snip off the thread, leaving enough at each end to tie with by and by. Repeat this at proper intervals, until enough stitches have been taken; then, go back and tie them, one after another, with surgeon's knot (Fig. 193). Such sewing is easy to remove when the proper time comes, say within about six days.

Punctured Wounds.—To remove a splinter: slip the point of a small knife-blade under the protruding end and catch it with the thumb-nail; or, use a needle sterilized in flame, or tweezers. Bits of glass should be cut out, lest they break.

If a fish-hook is embedded in the flesh, never try to pull it out backward. Push it through until the barb appears, clip this off with nippers, and withdraw. If you have no nippers, cut the hook out—in fact this is good treatment, anyhow, for the wound then is open for antiseptic treatment, and will heal without danger of festering.

A puncture from a rusty nail, or the like, should be slit open so that your antiseptic is sure to reach the bottom. This hurts less than cauterizing, and is quite effective. If a small punctured wound is not cut open, soak it in sterilized hot water, and squeeze out as much as possible of the poisonous matter that may have been introduced. Never cover a punctured wound with plaster or collodion.

Gunshot Wounds.—If it is only a flesh wound from a rifle or pistol, simply apply a sterilized compress and bandage it in place, being careful not to touch the bullet hole with your fingers or anything else unclean. When a bone is broken, apply splints. If the bullet has not gone through, but is deeply embedded, let it alone; the chances are that it will do no serious harm. Never probe a bullet wound. Do not pick out pellets of shot unless they are just underneath the skin.

If bits of clothing have been driven into the wound, and they are not too deep to reach by a little cutting, remove them; the cloth is almost sure to be alive with germs.

When there is extensive laceration, as from an expanding bullet, or from a charge of shot fired at close quarters, check the bleeding, apply an antiseptic dressing, keep the patient still so as not to renew bleeding, and treat for shock. No stimulants, unless absolutely necessary to prevent collapse.

BRUISES.—Severe bruises should be treated promptly by applying very cold water to the part, if it can be obtained. A cloth wrung out in very hot water will accomplish the same purpose, which is to limit swelling, prevent discoloration, and reduce pain. "It always seems strange that the two opposites—cold and heat—should have the same effect on the blood-vessels, but this is actually the case. . . . Every one knows how shrunken the hands look after they have been in hot water for some time."

SPRAINS.—These, too, may be treated with either heat or cold. Perhaps the best way, before swelling has commenced, is to immerse the injured member in very cold running water, or let cold water drain on it from an elevated vessel. The joint itself, should be elevated, too, if possible. Keep this up as long as you can stand it. Then dissolve tablets of lead acetate and opium (directions on bottle) in water, soak a cloth in it, bind round the joint, and keep the cloth wet with the lotion.

If no treatment can be applied until the joint has already become swollen and painful, then immerse it in water as hot as can be borne, and raise the heat gradually thereafter to the limit of endurance (much hotter than you could stand at first). When the pain lulls, change to an application of cloth

ACCIDENTS AND EMERGENCIES 455

wrung out in very cold water, and keep pouring cold water on as this warms up. A little later, strap the joint with adhesive plaster.

According to Gibney, the following treatment for a sprained ankle "involves no loss of time, requires no crutches, and is not attended with any impairment of functions":

A number of strips of rubber adhesive plaster, about 9 to 12 inches in length and of appropriate width, are prepared. Beginning at the outer border of the foot, near the little toe, the first strip partially encircles the joint, and ends behind the foot. The second strip is begun on the inner side of the foot and is applied on the opposite side, nearly meeting the first strip behind. Other strips are applied in like manner, each one over-lapping the last and crossing its fellow of the opposite side in front, so that the ankle is snugly and smoothly encased, care being taken not to encircle completely the joint with any one strip. After having bound the foot firmly, it is well to add one broad strip, running around the foot from the internal side of the leg down the internal side of the foot, across the sole of the foot, and up the outside of the leg, "as much as possible to take the place of the middle fasciculus of the external lateral ligament, which is so often the one most injured." It is a good plan to place a pad of absorbent cotton over the external malleolus [outer knob of ankle] and in the depression below, to prevent undue pressure and chafing. Any one of the injured ligaments may receive a similar reinforcement from an extra strip. Then apply a roller bandage smoothly over the entire surface, allowing it to remain until the plaster takes firm hold.

The pain of a sprained joint may be alleviated by gently rubbing in a mixture of equal parts of alcohol and water, or arnica, or witch hazel. Rubbing should always be toward the body.

HERNIA (Rupture).—This may result from violent exertion, over-lifting, or other cause. Have the patient lie on his back, with a pillow or pad under his hips, and thigh drawn toward the body. Tell him to breathe evenly and naturally. Gently press the neck of the hernia back in line with the middle of the canal through which it has descended. If it does not return after a little manipulation, apply cold cloths for an hour, then try again. Do not persevere long enough to set up inflammation. If successful, cover with a pad tightly bandaged over the groin. If not, keep the patient on his back until medical help arrives.

DISLOCATIONS.—If a joint is dislocated, or a bone broken, don't grasp the limb at once and pull; but first consider the anatomy of the injured part. Rough and unskilled handling is likely to do more harm than good.

A dislocation means that the head of a bone has slipped out of its socket, probably tearing the ligaments, and has failed to slip back again as in a sprain. Some dislocations, particularly of the wrist or ankle, are hard to distinguish from fractures.

When you must operate on a comrade, go to work at once, before the muscles have become rigid and the joint badly swollen. Should much difficulty be experienced, do not persist in trying to get the joint into place, but surround it with flannel cloths wrung out in hot water, and support with soft pads, until a surgeon can be found.

After a dislocation has been reduced, the joint must be kept rigid with bandages or splints for a considerable time, as the ligaments are weak and a recurrence of the trouble is all too easy.

Three dislocations out of every four are in the shoulder, arm, or hand, and among these, dislocation of the shoulder is most frequent.

Fingers.—Pull straight out away from the hand. Generally the bone will slip into place. Dislocation of the thumb is more likely to be forward than backward. Press the thumb backward and at the same time try to lift the head of the bone into its socket. If you fail, after one or two trials, go for a surgeon.

Wrist.—Fracture is more common than dislocation of the wrist. If in doubt, treat as a fracture.

ACCIDENTS AND EMERGENCIES

When there is only a bone out of joint, it may be replaced by pulling strongly upon the hand.

Elbow.—Leave this dislocation for a surgeon, if practicable. Otherwise, have the patient sit on a chair or log, and plant your foot against it. Place your knee against the front of his upper arm just above the bend of the elbow. Then, grasping the bone of the upper arm with your right hand, and the wrist with your left, forcibly bend the forearm, using your knee as a fulcrum. If the dislocation is forward, however, pull upon the forearm while the upper arm is fixed. Your thumb can assist in pressing the head of the bone in the desired direction. Put the arm in a sling (hand higher than elbow) and bandage it in place to prevent movement.

Shoulder.—About one-half of all cases of dislocation are of the shoulder joint. Have the man lie down flat on his back, and seat yourself by his side, facing him. Remove your shoe, put your foot in his arm-pit, grasp the dislocated arm in both hands, push outward and upward with the heel, and at the same time pull the wrist downward and outward, then suddenly bring it against the patient's hip. When a snap is heard or felt, the joint is in place. Bandage the upper arm to the side, with a thick pad under the arm-pit, forearm carried across chest, and hand on opposite shoulder.

Lower Jaw.—This dislocation must be reduced immediately. It looks serious, and alarms the patient, but in reality is very simple to reduce. Wrap both of your thumbs in several thicknesses of cloth, to protect them. Place them upon the patient's lower back teeth, and press forcibly downward and backward, while the fingers force the chin upward. As soon as the jaw starts into place, slip your thumbs off the teeth into the cheeks, to avoid being severely bitten. Put a jaw bandage on the patient.

Hip.—To reduce this dislocation is a job for nobody but a good surgeon.

Knee.—Try a strong, steady pull. If successful apply a splint. There will be a great tendency to inflammation, which is to be combatted with cold applications, or lead and opium lotion.

Ankle.—The patient lies down and bends his leg to a right angle at the knee. Then he, or an assistant, grasps his hands around the thigh and pulls backward, while you pull the foot steadily toward you. When reduced, support the joint with a right-angled splint made by nailing two pieces of board together in that position, one for the foot and the other for the lower leg.

FRACTURES.—If a bone is broken, and a surgeon can be summoned within a couple of days, do not try to reduce the fracture. Place the man in a comfortable position, the injured part resting on a pad, and keep him perfectly quiet. In lifting the limb to slip the pad under, one hand should support the bone on each side of the break. Be very careful that the flesh and skin shall not be cut by the knife-like edges of broken bone, as such after-injury may have serious consequences.

It may be, however, that you must act as surgeon yourself. If the bone is broken in only one place, and it does not protrude, the injury is not serious. Get splints and bandages ready. Rip the clothing up the seam, and steadily pull the broken parts in opposite directions, without the slightest twisting. Begin gently, and gradually increase the strain. It may take a strong pull. When the two pieces are end to end, an assistant must gently work them till they fit. This will be announced by a slight thud. Then apply splints, and bandage them so as to hold the injured member immovable while the fracture heals.

Bark, when it can be peeled, makes the best splints for an arm or leg. Pick out a sapling (chestnut, basswood, elm, cedar, spruce) as near the size of the limb as possible. Remove the bark in two equal pieces by vertical slits. These should

ACCIDENTS AND EMERGENCIES 459

be longer than the bone that is broken, so as to clamp the connecting joints as well. Cover the concave insides with cloth, dry moss, crumpled grass, or other soft padding, to cushion the limb and prevent irritation. The edges of splints should not quite meet around the limb. Then get a long bandage, about two inches wide. Having set the bone, apply the splints on each side, and bandage them firmly enough to hold in place, but by no means so tightly as to impede circulation.

In default of bark, almost anything will do for splints that is stiff enough to hold the parts in place—barrel staves, thin boards, sticks, bundles of rushes, etc. Pad them well.

If a bone is broken in more than one place, or if it protrudes through the skin, and you cannot fetch a surgeon to the patient, then get him out of the woods at all hazards. The utmost pains must be taken in transporting him, lest the sharp edges of the bones saw off an artery or pierce an important organ.

TRANSPORTATION OF WOUNDED.—A two-horse litter is better than a travois; but if the latter must be used, then make one shaft a little shorter than the other, so that, in crossing uneven places, the shock will not all come at one jolt.

"A travois may be improvised by cutting poles about 16 feet long and 2 inches in diameter at the small end. These poles are laid parallel to each other, large ends to the front, and 2½ feet apart; the small ends about 3 feet apart, and one of them projecting about 8 or 10 inches beyond the other. The poles are connected by a crossbar about 6 feet from the front ends and another about 6 feet back of the first, each notched at its ends and securely lashed at the notches to the poles. Between the crosspieces the litter bed, 6 feet long, is filled in with canvas, blanket, etc., securely fastened to the poles and crossbars, or with rope, lariat, rawhide strips, etc., stretching obliquely from pole to pole in many turns, crossing each other to form the basis for a light mattress or an improvised bed; or a litter may be made fast between the poles to answer the same

460 CAMPING AND WOODCRAFT

purpose. The front ends of the poles are then securely fastened to the saddle of the animal. A breast strap and traces should, if possible, be improvised and fitted to the horse. On the march the bearers should be ready to lift the rear end of the travois when passing over obstacles, crossing streams, or going up-hill." (*U. S. A. Hospital Corps.*)

An emergency litter can be made of two coats and two strong poles. Turn the sleeves of the coats inside out. Place the coats on the ground, ends reversed, bottom edges touching each other. Run the poles through the sleeves on each side. Button up the coat, and turn the buttoned side down.

Another way is to spread a blanket on the ground with the two poles at the edges of its long sides. Then roll the edges on the poles till a width of about 20 inches is left between them. Turn stretcher over before using it.

An excellent litter is a big trough of heavy bark, padded or lined with browse, and attached to a frame swung between two poles.

Always test a stretcher before placing a patient upon it. Do not carry it upon the shoulders, except as the rear man does so in going up a steep place. Keep it level. Carry the occupant feet foremost, unless going up-hill. The bearers should walk out of step, to avoid a jolting motion.

Two men can carry one, if he is conscious, very comfortably by forming a "two-handed seat." Number 1 grasps with his right hand the left wrist, and with his left hand the right shoulder, of the other bearer. Number 2 grasps with his left hand the right wrist, and with his right hand the left shoulder, of No. 1. The injured person is seated on his comrades' crossed fore-arms, and throws his own arms over their shoulders.

One man can carry another across his back, even though the stricken one be insensible, and a heavy-weight at that. Turn the patient on his face. If he is conscious, tell him to relax (make himself limp). Step astride his body, facing toward his

ACCIDENTS AND EMERGENCIES 461

head. Lean forward and, with your hands under his arm-pits, lift him to his knees. Then, clasping your hands over his abdomen, lift him to his feet. Immediately grasp his right wrist with your left hand, draw the arm over your head and down upon your left shoulder. Then, shifting yourself in front, stoop and clasp the right thigh with your right arm passed between his legs, your right hand seizing the patient's right wrist. Finally grasp the patient's left hand with your left, steady it against your side, and rise.

BURNS AND SCALDS.—First exclude the air and apply cold. If you are near a running stream of water, plunge the burnt member in it. This is all that is needed in ordinary cases. A good emergency treatment is to make a thick lather of toilet soap, smear it over the burn, and apply a bandage.

A standard remedy is common baking soda (not washing soda*). Dissolve some in as little water as is required to take it up; saturate a cloth with this, and apply, covering the burned area closely, and keep the dressing wet with the solution. Carbolized vaseline, resinol, unguentine, plain vaseline, or almost any clean and unsalted grease or oil, are good applications. Or, make a thin paste of flour and water, smear it on the burned part, and on the cloth used for covering. In lack of anything else, moist clay or earth will do if the skin is unbroken.

If clothing sticks to the burn, do not try to remove it, but cut around and flood with oil or water. Prick blisters on two sides, with a needle sterilized in flame, and remove the water by gentle pressure.

In case of shock, give a stimulant and apply heat to the extremities. When the destroyed flesh of a deep burn softens and begins to slough, hasten its removal by hot applications and cutting the loose ends away with scissors.

*Baking soda is the bicarbonate; washing soda, or plain soda, is the carbonate; do not confuse them.